IN SPOTS

MW01118759

by
*Nancy and
Richard Woodworth*

& SPECIAL PLACES

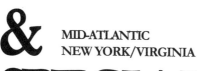

MID-ATLANTIC
NEW YORK/VIRGINIA

*A guide to
where to go,
stay, eat and
enjoy in 34
of the region's
choicest areas.*

Wood Pond Press
West Hartford, Conn.

The authors value their reputation for credibility and have personally evaluated the places included in this book. They have stayed at hundreds and toured countless more, which gives them a rare perspective in the field. Unlike others, they do not ask the owners to fill out information forms or to approve the final copy. Nor do they rely on researchers or field inspectors with varying perspectives and loyalties to do their leg work. They make their recommendations based on their experiences and findings. No fees are accepted or charged for inclusion.

Prices, hours and menu offerings at inns and restaurants change seasonally and with business conditions. Readers should call ahead to avoid disappointment. The prices and hours reported in this book were correct at presstime and are subject, of course, to change. They are offered as a relative guide to what to expect. Rates quoted are for bed and breakfast, unless otherwise specified (MAP, Modified American Plan, breakfast and dinner; EP, European Plan, no meals).

For updates between editions, check out the Wood Pond Press web site at www.getawayguides.com. Favorite inns, B&Bs, restaurants and attractions from this book and from others by the authors are detailed under Getaway Guides Online.

The authors welcome readers' reactions and suggestions.

Cover Photo: Breakfast table at The Inn at Perry Cabin, St. Michaels, MD.

Contents

Introduction

This is yet another inn book. But it's far more, too.

We enjoy reading others, but they rarely tell us what we *really* want to know – which inns and B&Bs are especially good and what they are like, where to get a good meal and what there is to do in the area. No inn is an island – they are part of their locale. With their neighbors, they share a sense of place.

These insights are what we now share with you. We start not with the inn but with the area (of course, the existence of inns or lack thereof determine the 34 special destination areas to be included). Then we tour each area, with the eyes and ears of the first-time visitor and the perspective of seasoned travelers and journalists. We visit the inns, the restaurants and the attractions. We *work* these areas as roving journalists, always seeking out the best and most interesting. We also *live* them – staying in, eating in, and experiencing as many places as time and budget allow.

The result is this book. It's a selective compendium of what we think are the best and most interesting places to stay, eat and enjoy in these 35 special destinations, some of them the Mid-Atlantic's best-known and some not widely known at all.

The book reflects our tastes. We want creature comforts like private bathrooms and comfortable reading areas in our rooms. We like to meet other inn guests, but we also cherish privacy. We seek interesing and creative food and pleasant settings for meals. We enjoy unusual, enlightening things to do and places to see. We expect to receive value for our time and money.

While researching this book as well as its companion editions for New England and the Southeast, we continue to be surprised by how many innkeepers say we are among the few guidebook writers who visit their facility and do not expect them merely to fill out a questionnaire and forward it with a considerable fee.

We also were struck by how many inns report a growing impact from the Internet. They say increasing numbers of travelers find places to stay and book via the Net. The prospective guest likes the immediacy, the ability to see pictures and get detailed descriptions, the instant gratification of a quick, visual reservation. And yet, the realists among both innkeepers and browsers worry that the Web traveler finds only what the Web site wants them to know. They miss the insights offered by well traveled observers who have been there.

The inn experience is highly personal, both for the innkeeper and the inn-goer. The listing services, the advertising and the Web site fluff do not have an objective perspective. Nor can they convey the personality of the place.

That's the role of experienced guidebook writers who make the rounds year after year and report things as they see them. Yes, the schedule is hectic and we do keep busy on these, our working trips that everyone thinks must be nothing but fun. One of us says she never again wants to get up in the middle of the night and cope with a strange bathroom. The other doesn't care if he never eats another bedside chocolate.

Nonetheless, it's rewarding to experience a great inn and to discover a promising B&B. We also enjoy savoring a good meal, touring a choice musuem, poking through an unusual store and meeting so many interesting people along the way.

And that's what this book is about. We hope that you enjoy its findings as much as we did the finding.

Nancy and Richard Woodworth

About the Authors

Nancy Webster Woodworth began her travel and dining experiences in her native Montreal and as a waitress in summer resorts across Canada during her McGill University years. She worked in London and hitchhiked through Europe on $3 a day before her marriage to Richard Woodworth, whom she met while skiing at Mont Tremblant. They lived for the first ten years of their marriage in upstate New York and became familiar with the Mid-Atlantic during trips to visit his brother in Baltimore and his parents in Lynchburg and Smith Mountain Lake, Va. She started writing her "Roaming the Restaurants" column for the West Hartford (Conn.) News in 1972. That led to half of the book, *Daytripping & Dining in Southern New England*, written in collaboration with Betsy Wittemann in 1978. She since has co-authored *Inn Spots & Special Places in New England, Inn Spots & Special Places in the Southeast, Getaways for Gourmets in the Northeast, Waterside Escapes in the Northeast, Weekending in New England* and *The Restaurants of New England*. She and her husband have two grown sons and live in West Hartford.

Richard Woodworth has been an inveterate traveler since his youth in suburban Syracuse, N.Y., where his birthday outings often involved train trips with friends for the day to nearby Utica or Rochester. After graduation from Middlebury College, he was a reporter for newspapers in Syracuse, Jamestown, Geneva and Rochester before moving to Connecticut to become editor of the West Hartford News and eventually executive editor of Imprint Newspapers. With his wife and their sons, he has traveled to the four corners of this country, Canada and portions of Europe, writing their findings for newspapers and magazines. With his wife, he has co-authored six editions *of Inn Spots & Special Places in New England* and *Getaways for Gourmets in the Northeast,* as well as *The Restaurants of New England* and their newest book, *Inn Spots & Special Places in the Southeast.* Between travels and duties as head of Wood Pond Press, he tries to find time to ski in the winter and weed the garden in summer.

Excerpts from the authors' books are on line at www.getawayguides.com.

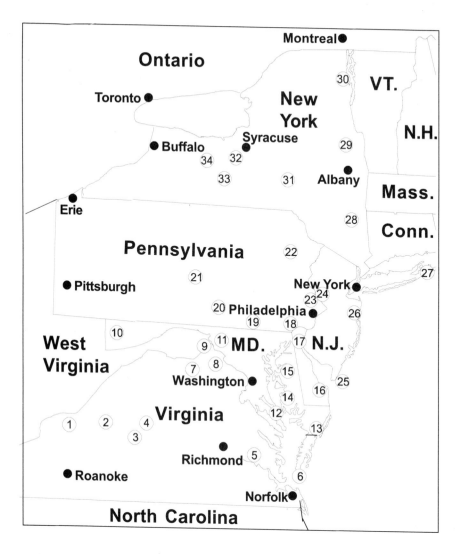

1. Hot Springs
2. Staunton
3. Charlottesville
4. Orange
5. James River
6. Cape Charles
7. Washington
8. Loudoun County
9. Harpers Ferry
10. Deep Creek Lake
11. Frederick
12. Solomons

13. Snow Hill/Berlin
14. St. Michaels
15. Chestertown
16. Lewes
17. New Castle
18. Chadds Ford
19. Lancaster County
20. Gettysburg
21. State College
22. Canadensis
23. Bucks County

24. Lambertville
25. Cape May
26. Spring Lake
27. East Hampton
28. Rhinebeck
29. Saratoga Springs
30. Westport/Essex
31. Cooperstown
32. Skaneateles
33. Ithaca
34. Canandaigua

Championship golf courses are among attractions at Hot Springs and The Homestead.

Hot Springs, Va.

The Lure of the Baths

Since the days of Washington and Jefferson, the warm medicinal springs that emanate from the valleys of the Allegheny Highlands have lured the nation's elite. Their curative powers and social importance are legendary, having spawned two of America's world-class resorts, The Homestead at Hot Springs and The Greenbrier in White Sulphur Springs, W.Va.

This remarkably scenic area tucked between mountain ridges along the Virginia-West Virginia border offers much for today's visitor. You can soak in the "baths" in the same structures that Thomas Jefferson and Mrs. Robert E. Lee did. You can enjoy contemporary spa treatments that would do California proud. You can play golf on some of the world's most challenging and scenic courses. You can partake of the good life at the Homestead and the Greenbrier.

You also can bask in one of the most picturesque, unspoiled regions we know. Verdant mountains, idyllic valleys, backroads hamlets, untrafficked byways and an exhilarating climate are the draws. Ninety percent of Bath County – so named because its warm waters reminded the settlers of those in Bath, England – is forested. And half of that is part of the George Washington National Forest. The entire county has neither an incorporated town nor a traffic light. About the only signs of commercialism – and they're a lovely, colorful touch – are the trademark wildlife mailboxes donated to every Bath County homeowner by the local Bacova Guild Factory.

What this area offers are endless tranquility and rural pleasures, from walks to waterfalls. Its mountain air yields cool, restorative summer days and nights, as well as long springtimes and spectacular autumns (the fall foliage outshines even the showy redbud and dogwood that light up the hillsides in spring). Small inns and B&Bs contrast nicely in scale and price with the grand resorts, and their guests can take advantage of Homestead and Greenbrier facilities.

Even those ensconced at one of the resorts (and paying dearly for the privilege) should get out and about to enjoy fully a region of uncommon beauty. If you're staying at the Homestead, visit the Greenbrier for lunch, or vice-versa. Stay at one of the smaller inns or B&Bs and the money you save will allow you to do both.

Some people do energetic things, like hiking, fishing and golfing. Others never get beyond the front veranda or backyard hammock.

Inn Spots

The Homestead, Hot Springs 24445.

The Homestead and Hot Springs have been synonymous, ever since the first hotel was built around the hot springs in 1766. In fact, The Homestead *is* Hot Springs, its presence dominating the small community in every respect. The hotel exudes tradition and grandeur, Southern style.

Becoming frayed at the edges and near bankruptcy in 1993, the oldest family-run resort in the world entered into a joint venture with the Dallas-based ClubCorp Resorts Inc., one of the nation's leading owner/operators of golf and conference resorts. More than $25 million was invested to "restore this grand dame of American resorts to the splendid glory it has boasted for more than 200 years," in the words of new president Gary K. Rosenberg.

The Homestead's setting is stupendous. The landmark hotel tower is the only real break in 15,000 privately owned acres of Allegheny Mountains and valleys. The 521 rooms and suites, most in low-rise wings, look out onto hillsides and golf fairways. Most are spacious and have all the amenities.

Our parlor suite at the far end of what the staff calls "the older and more elegant" West Wing had a kingsize bed, a loveseat and two side chairs, a writing desk, a console TV, no fewer than four telephones and a full-length, screened veranda big enough to seat a party of twenty. Extra touches included European percale sheets, good reading lights, maid service twice daily and a walk-in closet that lighted automatically.

Gone are such traditions as nightly turndown service (now available only on request), a holdover from the days when old-name families like the Vanderbilts arrived with their trunks for the summer. The new management concentrates on things it deems more important to today's visitor. Guests are still

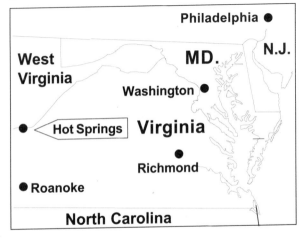

greeted in the majestic Great Hall, where afternoon tea is accompanied by live music and guests mingle at all hours in a grand living-room setting. They eat and drink in ten dining and entertainment venues (see Dining Spots). They play tennis on fifteen courts, swim in three pools, bowl on eight lanes, dance during dinner and take in a movie in the theater. In winter, they ski at the South's first ski area.

The original hot springs are incorporated into The Homestead's European-style spa, built in 1892 and recipient of a state-of-the-art renovation in 1996. Their 104-degree waters provide a variety of treatments from $25 for a mineral tub bath to $72 for "The Cure." The Homestead also operates the original baths at Warm Springs.

The new look at The Homestead blends seamlessly with the old. Landscapers have added thousands of flowers to the grounds. Brick pavers replaced asphalt in the porte-cochere entry. The entire East Wing with 86 guest rooms was refurbished, and 100 more in the West Wing were renovated in 1999. The vast dining room was reconfigured and acquired a spiffy new wine room. The Grille was beautifully renovated. The Tower Corridor of shops was transformed into a boutique setting opening one into the next like the rooms of a house. Archival photos line the refurbished corridors of the West Wing, and portraits of thirteen presidents who have visited the Homestead hang in the Presidents' Lounge. Murals tracing the history of Hot Springs enhance the Jefferson Parlor. The Casino, located between the spa building and hotel, was converted into a sports shop and a casual, indoor/outdoor grill. A formal Spa Garden was completed. A new Homestead Kids' Club program operates behind the casino, and a state-of-the-art Equestrian Center was opened. The old Tower Lounge was transformed into a richly paneled library, game room and historical museum.

The Homestead's warm and personal tradition, updated for the millennium, continues.

(540) 839-1766 or (800) 838-1766. Fax (540) 839-7670. 440 rooms and 81 suites with private baths. Rates, MAP. May-October: doubles, $460 to $522 weekends, $410 to $468 midweek; suites, $644 to $1,270 weekends, $562 to $1,126 midweek. Rest of year: doubles, $308 to $460 weekends, $264 to $424 midweek; suites, $512 to $1,108 weekends, $442 to $1,010 midweek.

The Greenbrier, 300 West Main St., White Sulphur Springs, W.Va. 24986.

If the Homestead is the grand dame of genteel Southern tradition, The Greenbrier just across the West Virginia border is the vivacious debutante – or maybe post-debutante, for surely this five-diamond resort has come of age.

Although both roughly of the same vintage, The Greenbrier is new money rather than old, corporate-owned rather than family-run (as The Homestead had been until lately), glittering and eye-popping. Where it lacks the scenic setting of The Homestead, it compensates with spectacular landscaping and flowers. Splashes

Horses await at The Greenbrier entrance.

of vivid colors and chintzes in the Dorothy Draper style make the interiors of its Virginia counterpart look a bit pale. Its three eighteen-hole golf courses are highly rated, and the new Spa, Mineral Baths and Salon building is state-of-the-art. In fact, everything at The Greenbrier is up to date and spiffy, and not in any understated way.

Here you'll ogle an indoor pool to end all pools with a billowing white sail-cloth above, peach-hued walls and wicker furniture all around. Pause at the bar for "healthy-living drinks" made of whole fruit. The black and white marble floors of the Georgian lobby reflect the sunlight from sixteen-foot windows and french doors dressed in the brilliant florals that made Draper and protégé Carleton Varney, who redecorated The Greenbrier, famous. The entry lobby gives way to a succession of smaller lobbies and living rooms, each a study in interior design. From wallpaper to china, Draper's signature rhododendrons accent the columned dining room (see Dining Spots). Crystal chandeliers contrast with pecky wood walls and are a sight to behold in the Old White Club, the deluxe lounge named for the former hotel on the site, called the Old White. Draper's Cafe serves informal meals of cutting-edge cuisine. Such grandeur prompted columnist Elsa Maxwell to write, upon the hotel's reopening after service as a military hospital in World War II: "The Greenbrier is perhaps the most beautiful hotel in the world."

The public spaces tend to overshadow the 637 guest rooms, which include 46 suites and 71 guest and estate houses, all decorated in the Dorothy Draper style and no two exactly alike. Draperies and wallpapers are color-coordinated and the refreshment center in each room matches the furniture. Our room, more spacious than many we saw, was most comfortable and provided every amenity but was not as superlative as the public facilities. We admit we did not visit the fourteen-room Presidential Suite that covers two floors.

Always upgrading, The Greenbrier now offers LaVarenne at The Greenbrier, supplementing the original resort cooking school founded in 1977 (Julia Child was among the guest chefs in 2000). It offers the Sam Snead Golf Academy and the Land Rover Driving School for guests. Other amenities range from falconry, trap shooting and horseback riding to afternoon tea with music and irst-run movies.

The adjacent Greenbrier Clinic performs complete health diagnostic evaluations. The Gallery of Shops on the lower level includes some of the fanciest we've seen, and makes you wonder how they manage to stay open with only a limited, though captive, audience.

A veteran staff of 1,600 (average tenure: thirteen years) caters to the needs of guests, who number no more than 1,400 at a time. The clientele here appears to be as rich as the facility, but as hotel historian Robert Conte pointed out during a tour, guests "stay as long as the money holds out – it used to be weeks, and now it's usually days."

(304) 536-1110 or (800) 624-6070. Fax (304) 536-7834. 520 rooms, 46 suites and 71 guest and estate houses with private baths. Rates, MAP. April-October: weekends, doubles $532 to $656, suites $694 to $832; midweek, doubles $486 to $596, suites $632 to $756. Rest of year: doubles $392 to $596, suites $476 to $654.

The Inn at Gristmill Square, Old Mill Road, Box 359, Warm Springs 24484.
This good-looking complex of guest rooms, recreation facilities, a shop and a restaurant resembles a small village and, indeed, is the biggest enterprise in the dear little hamlet of Warm Springs (population, 250, and every building redone in

Meadow Lane Lodge is centerpiece of a rural, sixteen-acre farm estate.

the last few years, according to innkeeper Janice McWilliams). Former owners of a ski lodge in Vermont, the McWilliams family took over this going concern in 1981 and have continued to expand.

Seventeen guest accommodations are scattered in four 19th-century buildings around an old gristmill that now houses a good restaurant (see Dining Spots). Rooms vary widely in size and decor. Each has antique furnishings, TVs, refrigerators, hair dryers and phones, and half have fireplaces. One is called the Silo for obvious reasons, and the two-bedroom Tower Apartment has a round living room and a fantastic tin chandelier. The Blacksmith Shop containing the inn's office has a Loft Room with kingsize bed and deck and the Spring Suite with a living room, a jacuzzi tub and a queensize bed in the bedroom, which opens to a private patio beside babbling Warm Spring Run. We enjoyed the Board Room, cozy and dark in barnwood with two double beds and a clawfoot tub. Others are partial to the extravagant Singapore Room and its two-part bathroom, one part being a tub in a niche behind a screen.

A country flavor prevails in the adjacent Miller's House, which offers two rooms and two suites. Four smaller rooms are across the street in the Steel House, close to the pool, a small sauna and three tennis courts.

In the morning, Mrs. McWilliams delivers a picnic basket to each room. It contains juice, coffee and breads, plus the day's Richmond Times-Dispatch.

(540) 839-2231. Fax (540) 839-5770. Twelve rooms and five suites with private baths. Doubles, $80 to $100 B&B, $155 to $170 MAP. Suites, $85 to $140 B&B, $160 to $210 MAP.

Meadow Lane Lodge, Star Route A, Box 110, Warm Springs 24484.

The rural tranquility that is this area's main allure is perhaps nowhere more alluring than at Meadow Lane Lodge. The tradition launched by the late gentleman-farmer, Philip Hirsh, is being continued by his widow Catherine and grandson, Carter Ancona, who offer a variety of rooms with private baths in their lodge and two cottages on a 1,600-acre estate complete with fishing streams, fields and woods. A big white barn is full of exotic animals, from peacocks to nubian goats.

Set well back from Route 39 at the end of a long driveway, the accommodations are spacious and luxurious in a country-manor kind of way. Fireplaces at either end, antiques, sofas and a big table full of magazines attract guests to the lodge's long common room. The lodge includes a kingsize suite, an upstairs suite with sitting area and a screened porch and, most in demand, a small room with a corner porch affording the best view. The Snuggery, with a loveseat and TV tucked beneath the eaves, attests to the late owner's knack for architectural design. Furnishings are a mix of items from the Hirshes' travels. Phil was the third generation of a thoroughbred horse-breeding family (his father was the author of Yale's "Boola Boola"), and Mrs. Hirsh still occupies the main house next to a swimming pool (available to guests by invitation).

Near the lodge, Craig's Cottage contains a suite with a small kitchen and living room, plus a fireplaced room with a kingsize bed and a bay window. The Car Barn has two more contemporary bedrooms sharing a living room.

The newest accommodations are in the Granary – three bedrooms, living room and kitchen in a converted 19th-century grain barn at the rear of the property.

Grandson Carter, now resident innkeeper with his wife Michelle, and a couple of longtime Hirsh assistants serve a full Southern breakfast. Expect things like curried scrambled eggs, sweet pea omelets, creamed turkey and chicken, batter bread and fried grits, many of the ingredients coming from the farm. The meal is taken in a sunny breakfast room at tables set with floral mats.

Outside are a tennis court, a croquet court, fifteen miles of walking trails and the Jackson River, two private miles of which pass through the property. You can swim there, fish or go canoeing. A favorite spot is a wooden deck, built atop a cliff overlooking a slough and the river bottom below. Guests take cocktails and even picnic suppers here to watch the beaver, deer, herons, ospreys and such. Few can resist stopping in the barn to check out Harvey the donkey, Mrs. Hirsh's favorite, who bunks with Nelson the horse. You'll hear guinea hens squawking and geese honking. Peacocks and Japanese silkies, a type of chicken with black skin and white feathers, parade about.

The Hirshes conceived, built and operated the Inn at Gristmill Square in Warm Springs before selling it in 1981 to concentrate on their home property. They retain the two-bedroom Francisco Cottage for guests in Warm Springs.

(540) 839-5959. Fax (540) 839-2135. Four rooms, three suites and three cottages with private baths. Doubles, $115 to $125. Suites $125. Cottages, $145 to $450. Two-night minimum on peak spring and fall weekends. Children in cottages.

King's Victorian Inn, Route 220, (Route 1, Box 622), Hot Springs 24445.

Atop a sloping lawn, this turreted Victorian house with a wraparound veranda overlooks the Homestead golf course. Inside, all is crisp and country elegant, with none of the clutter and darkness often associated with the period. "I like it light and airy," explains ex-Richmonder Liz King, innkeeper with her husband Richard, who is with the U.S. Postal Service in Staunton.

They have decorated six guest rooms, four with private baths, in traditional Williamsburg colors against a backdrop of reproduction antiques. A solid mahogany Charleston rice bed graces one room with two sitting areas, one in a sunny alcove over the living room, and a bath with a double vanity and colored

Guests at King's Victorian Inn enjoy turrets and wraparound porches.

soaps arrayed in a wicker basket. Another room, pretty in teal and rose, has a step-up bed and a wicker sitting area. The Victorian Room contains a porch-like nook, a fireplace and a sitting area with a double bed. Two bedrooms on the third floor share a bath and a sitting area beneath a colorful glass ceiling.

The Kings offer cottage accommodations in an adjacent former icehouse. It comes with a deck, an efficiency kitchen, a sofa and TV, plus an upstairs bedroom with a queen bed and a shower bath. Lately, they acquired and refurbished a duplex cottage next to the Homestead's Cascades Inn. Each side of the duplex contains two bedrooms, a kitchen and living area and a porch.

Public areas in the main inn include a second-floor garden room with wicker and TV, a smashing living room with a mauve carpet, two enormous sectional sofas dressed in a yellow floral print and a card table in a sunroom alcove, and an elegant parlor with a white sofa, two rose wing chairs and an oriental rug. A raised fireplace with three stained-glass windows above, silver service on the sideboard and an 18th-century reproduction Chippendale table and chairs enhance the dining room. A piano is tucked in a hallway alcove beneath the stairway.

A full breakfast might include sausage and eggs with homefries, fried apples and coffeecake. Tea, crackers and cheese are offered in the afternoon.

(540) 839-3134. Four rooms and three cottages with private baths, two rooms with shared bath. Doubles, $85 to $105. Cottage, $115. Two-bedroom cottages, $120 to $150. No young children. No smoking. No credit cards.

Vine Cottage Inn, Route 220, Box 918, Hot Springs 24445.

"We're the next best thing to the Homestead," say the owners of this B&B just a stone's throw away. Most of the resort facilities are available to guests on a fee basis, as they are to Homestead guests who are not on package plans. Here you can pay for golf, horseback riding, bowling, the spa and meals and enjoy the Homestead experience at a fraction of the price.

Upstate New Yorkers Sandy and Joel Reber and her sister, Jean Rapp, took over in 1997 what had been a lodging facility since 1905. Their predecessors had adapted the late Victorian theme to what they called "country comfortable." There's a big TV in the comfy living room full of books. At the other side of the entry is a large, fireplaced dining room in red and blue with bentwood chairs at tables topped with quilted mats.

Upstairs are eight guest rooms with private baths, four with shared baths and three former bunk rooms now billed as "family rooms" that accommodate three to five persons and share baths. Rooms come in quite a variety of configurations, but most of those with private baths have queen or kingsize beds. Biggest rooms are on the third floor, where the Presidents' Room with kingsize bed is decked out in red, white and blue and the Honeymoon/Anniversary Room on the end has a kingsize bed covered in lace, framed anniversary cards, wedding photos and a statue of a kissing couple.

The Rebers have enhanced the breakfast fare. They serve a fruit cobbler or apple crisp with homemade breads or sticky buns. These are preliminaries to a hot dish, perhaps stuffed french toast, blueberry pancakes or an egg casserole.

(540) 839-2422 or (800) 410-9755. Eight rooms with private baths, four double rooms and three family rooms with shared baths. Doubles, $70 to $75 shared bath, $80 to $90 private bath. Family rooms, $90 for three occupants to $120 for five. Children and pets welcome.

Hidden Valley Bed & Breakfast, Hidden Valley Road, Box 53, Warm Springs 24484.

Hidden in the back of beyond beside the Jackson River, three roundabout miles west of Warm Springs, is this many-dimensioned treasure that was the setting in 1992 for the movie "Sommersby." Hidden Valley is at once a small and historically true antebellum B&B, an ongoing archaeological dig, a teaching site, and a wilderness mecca for hikers and trout fishermen. It's also quite a story.

The story begins more than 9,000 years ago with the Indians; the resident archaeologist and college students have catalogued thousands of artifacts from the area. Fast forward to 1848 when Bath County Judge James Warwick began construction of Warwickton, one of the finest Greek Revival mansions in western Virginia. It eventually fell into disrepair and became in succession a hunt club, a school and a hay barn. Fast forward to 1965, when the George Washington National Forest acquired the 6,400-acre tract for recreational purposes but had no use for the mansion, which is listed on the National Register of Historical Places. Enter Pam and Ron Stidham from Ohio, who had fallen in love with the place in 1978. "I wanted a brick house with a babbling brook and Ron wanted a house in the mountains with solitude," recalls Pam. "We got the best of both worlds here."

They also got more than they bargained for. It took years of pleading and bureaucratic maneuvering for the Stidhams to persuade the U.S. Forest Service to lease them the house and issue a special-use permit to run a B&B. The unprecedented agreement allowed the Stidhams to operate a commercial venture for 30 years in return for restoring the structure and opening it to the public for tours. They moved in 1990 into a house "in dire need of massive restoration."

Hidden Valley Bed & Breakfast provides historic plantation experience.

Some of the restoration coincided with the filming of "Sommersby," which required an antebellum mansion and a 360-degree panorama without a sign of modern civilization. The moviemakers built a set of eighteen structures (only two of which are left), but also delayed the Stidhams' plans for opening. They could do no restoration work during the six months of production, and then spent months returning the mansion to the condition it was in before the film crews arrived. Meticulous to a fault, Pam stripped off nine coats of paint that a set artist had applied to one fireplace mantel for a faded marble look because it was not the color used when the house was built. Her work was continually interrupted by curious sightseers who stopped to visit the interpretive center in the new, film-built summer kitchen and to visit the mansion (tours by appointment, $4).

"People said we were crazy," Pam recalled, "but all this work was worth it. You just sit out on one of the porches and you'll realize it." Pam and Ron, who works full-time for the Virginia Department of Corrections, opened their B&B in 1993. They offer three spacious, antiques-filled bedrooms, served by three private baths in a special bath and laundry wing. They also offer fine formal furnishings and antiques collected over 25 years and displayed in "a house that tells a story as it unfolds," according to Pam. Guests enjoy a Music Room and a high Victorian parlor, which holds an 1844 square grand piano. A formal dining room is the setting for a full plantation breakfast, including fresh fruit, banana or zucchini bread and perhaps a five-cheese egg strata. There are a couple of porches and a gazebo for taking in the utter stillness and marvel of it all. "When you enter the valley," as Pam says, "you leave the world behind."

There's really no choice. Hidden Valley is not just a B&B. It's a way of life.

(540) 839-3178. Three rooms with private baths. Doubles, $99. Children over 6. Pets welcome. No smoking. No credit cards.

The Anderson Cottage, Old Germantown Road, Box 176, Warm Springs 24484.

A two-story-high, wraparound veranda distinguishes this rambling house whose original four rooms were an 18th-century tavern. It then was a girls' school and an inn, and now is a private home-turned-B&B with two houses joined together. Jean Randolph Bruns, whose family has owned it since the 1870s, has been known to open it for tours for Homestead guests.

She offers a first-floor suite with a queensize bed, well-worn oriental rugs, a huge fireplaced parlor and the only modern bath in the house. Upstairs is a second suite with a queen bed, a clawfoot tub, and a parlor with a twin bed and a wicker sitting area. After staying here, guests from Chicago told Jean they were through looking for real estate – "they wanted to buy their room!"

A bedroom with a queensize bed comes with private bath. A large end room with beamed ceilings, working fireplace and a double and a single bed has a shared bath. A fifth large bedroom is seldom rented – "it's my museum room and pulls everything together on my historical tours," says Jean. With exposed chestnut log walls, it contains a little desk from the time it was a school, old textbooks and a museum-quality quilt of homespun, hand-stitched French fabric on the double bed.

Out back is an 1820s brick kitchen cottage with two bedrooms and a fireplaced kitchen-dining room, available for families and long-term rentals.

Guests pick out a mug from a huge collection and help themselves to coffee in the country kitchen, the only room in the house without a fireplace because it started as a porch. Breakfast, taken at a long table in the dining room, might include sausage, cheese strata and apples baked with brown sugar. The guest parlor opens onto the veranda, where church pews and rockers overlook two pleasant acres. The stream in back flows from the warm springs pools and is so tepid that "my grandchildren think all mountain streams must be warm," Jean reports.

(540) 839-2975. One room, two suites and two-bedroom cottage with private baths; one room with shared bath. Doubles, $60 to $70. Suites, $80 to $100. Cottage, $125 for first night, $90 thereafter. Closed December to early March; cottage open year-round. Smoking restricted. No credit cards.

Three Hills Inn, Route 220, Box 9, Warm Springs 24484.

Built in 1913 as a residence by early feminist novelist Mary Johnston, this is a stunner – a large mansion occupying a hilltop site with a wondrous view of the Warm Springs Gap and the Alleghenies beyond. The novelist   and her sisters operated the mansion as an inn, and a subsequent owner turned it into apartments. In 1984, a German woman purchased it and spent millions restoring it to its former status as an inn, which never measured up to its potential. She finally sold it in 1994 to Charlene and Doug Fike from Indiana.

The Fikes moved to Three Hills and planned to build a home on the 38-acre property. They also built a fitness center with an outdoor hot tub and a small conference center. Charlene wanted to continue her career of leading training sessions for small businesses and Doug, as executive director of a Mennonite organization, planned retreats for clergymen of various faiths. "We were both on the road traveling in separate directions and decided it was time for a change," Charlene said. "We wanted to pick a beautiful spot where instead of us going out all the time, people would come to us."

A more beautiful spot is hard to imagine. The Fikes set to work renovating and redecorating the entire inn and plan to offer dinner to inn guests and the public. (A highly acclaimed restaurant operation, The Muse, did not renew its lease after the 1997 season).

The Fikes inherited most of the heavy, European-style furnishings in the rambling main house and four older cottages. They lightened up the decor and modernized some of the bathrooms. The twelve guest accommodations in the main house still show their apartment heritage. Five are "hotel rooms" with double, queen or king beds. Three are one-bedroom junior suites with separate living room or kitchen. Four are master suites with one or two bedrooms, living room with fireplace and a kitchen. All have private baths and TV. The second-floor Birch Suite in front includes a formal living room with fireplace, kingsize bed, a huge mirrored armoire and a private deck on the porch roof. The rear Dogwood junior suite, with a kingsize bed and twin sleeper sofas in the wicker-furnished living room, overlooks the English boxwood garden.

Two cottages ranging from two to four bedrooms are available near the main house.

Resident innkeepers serve a full breakfast in one of the chandeliered dining rooms. Fresh fruit and muffins precede a main courses of fruit crêpes, puffed apple pancakes, stuffed french toast or individual omelets. Tea is offered on weekend afternoons.

The inn's **Rendezvous Café,** billed as a European-style bistro, serves soups, salads, sandwiches and desserts daily from 11 to 8, year-round.

(540) 839-5381 or (888) 234-4557. Fax (540) 839-5199. Five rooms, seven suites and two cottages with private baths. Doubles, $59 to $99. Suites, $119 to $179. Cottages, $169 and $189, two-night minimum. Children and pets welcome. No smoking.

Dining Spots

The Greenbrier, White Sulphur Springs, W.Va.

The dining experience at The Greenbrier is as extravagant as everything else about this world-class resort.

Most guests take dinner in the handsome **Main Dining Room,** a long space notable for enormous artworks on its yellow walls, crystal chandeliers and arched windows onto the gardens. It's nicely broken up by columns, dividers and a center platform where a pianist and violinist entertain nightly. Vichyssoise and a famous dessert of peaches and cream are traditional favorites. Everything is prepared from scratch by the culinary staff of 135, many of whom received their training through The Greenbrier's Culinary Apprentice Program instituted in 1957 to ensure the resort an ample supply of quality chefs.

The short MAP menu changes daily and is contemporary as can be. Start perhaps with corn and oyster chowder or an appetizer of blackened quail with grilled marinated vegetables and orzo pesto, and a spinach and arugula salad with marinated tomatoes and black olives. Main courses range from smoked arctic char with saffron seafood risotto to grilled veal filet with crayfish and lentil chili to roast leg of lamb with roasted garlic spoonbread. We've enjoyed several dinners here and were impressed both by the food and the flawless service.

Five-course dinners arrive beneath silver domes in the dark and masculine **Tavern Room,** with new Wine Bar and Wine Cellar adjacent. Cooking is at open rotisseries and the cuisine is contemporary, as in an appetizer of honey-smoked breast of pheasant with marinated peppers and warm cilantro potato salad or an entrée of charbroiled veal T-bone steak with morel cream sauce and a roasted barley pilaf.

Colorful in rose, white wicker and chintz, **Draper's Cafe** serves à la carte breakfast and lunch. For a mid-day treat, one of us enjoyed black bean soup topped artistically with jalapeño pepper and sour cream and a cobb salad that was tossed instead of composed in the traditional style. The other had an excellent seared salmon steak with green and red tomato salsa, sweet California mustard and salad greens and the specialty dessert, a Greenbrier peach on rum-raisin ice cream topped with blackberry sauce.

Want a different experience? Head for the Greenbrier Golf Club, where the old dining room and veranda have been transformed into **Sam Snead's at the Golf Club** and **Slammin' Sammy's** sports bar. Here chefs employ a wood-burning oven in an open kitchen to prepare lunch and dinner in more casual surroundings. Seafood cappellini, roasted stuffed Maine lobster and hickory-flavored rotisserie chicken may be on the menu.

Food and drinks also are available in the **Old White Club** and the **Rhododendron Pool Lounge**.

(304) 536-1110 or (800) 624-6070. Dining hours vary by venue and season. Lunch, 11:30 to 2:30, to 5 in café. Dinner nightly by reservation, 6:30 to 8:30 or 9.

The Homestead, Hot Springs.

"You eat at The Greenbrier and you dine at The Homestead," we were advised by several of the latter's admirers – and they are legion. Legendary executive chef Albert Schnarwyler, who has been with the resort since 1964, wrote the book, *Dining At The Homestead.*

The Main Dining Room is an L-shaped, football field-size expanse of the old school (lately enhanced with french doors, columns and greenery to serve as room partitions). At dinner, a band was playing for dancing as we gazed out at a sea of white tables and hovering staff. The dinner menu, somewhat pedestrian and passé at our first visit, has been elevated with the elimination of such traditional fixtures as tomato juice, vichyssoise and omelets. Now, along with the tried and true, the night's menu (available prix-fixe to the public for $63) yields innovations. Among them might be an appetizer of carpaccio of pork with dill-mustard sauce, a salad of belgian endive on mesclun with herbed cheese and taro root chips, and a main course of grilled ginger-marinated sea scallops, shrimp and swordfish with Turkish saffron rice and wilted spinach.

At our visit, we were well satisfied with appetizers of country pâté with foie gras in the middle and a lump crab and shrimp cocktail with rémoulade sauce, plus a couple of exotic salads. One of us had roast prime tenderloin with armagnac sauce, green peppercorns and grapes, served with ratatouille and macaire potato. The other chose rack of lamb with carrots, snow peas and a timbale of polenta with spinach. Desserts were blackberry pie and hazelnut-coffee ice cream pie, followed by cappuccino and espresso.

A delicious breakfast buffet was served in the dining room the next day. From the table with a fantastic array of fresh fruits (including gigantic strawberries, mangoes and kumquats) to the hot dishes of creamed beef, broiled fish, eggs and grits, it was a Southern treat to be remembered.

The pride of The Homestead is **The 1776 Grille,** a handsome room with huge windows onto the golf course. We found its French/American dinner menu (prix-fixe, $63) more innovative than that of the dining room.

Light fare is available seasonally in the casual new indoor-outdoor 19th-hole grill at the Club Casino adjacent to the first tee of the Homestead Course. Golfers are partial to eating in the **Cascades Club Restaurant** or the **Lower Cascades Clubhouse Restaurant.** The Homestead also operates **Cafe Albert** and **Sam Snead's Tavern,** which are popular with the public as well.

The Homestead's new management has changed hours of operations of most of

Dramatic table presentations are featured in Homestead's refurbished Grille.

its restaurants, especially early in the week and in the off-season, according to the number of guests. Visitors are advised to call ahead for specific hours.

(540) 839-1766. Dinner nightly in dining room, from 6:30, jacket and tie required. Grille, nightly from 6:30, jacket required; closed some nights in off-season.

The Waterwheel Restaurant, The Inn at Gristmill Square, Warm Springs.

Fed by Warm Spring Run, the old waterwheel rotates constantly outside this 1900 gristmill, now transformed into an appealing restaurant with barnwood walls, beamed ceilings and ladderback chairs at tables on different levels. Gears and cogs of the gristmill are still in evidence, but free-standing candles, fresh flowers, linens and service plates emblazoned with a waterwheel logo create an elegant ambiance. Off to one side is a small, ten-seat tavern called the Simon Kenton Pub.

One unusual touch: there's no wine list. Instead, diners descend to a wine cellar to pick their choice from bins of bottles. The hazard is that in winter, the cellar occasionally gets so chilly that the red wines have to be warmed before serving.

Innkeeper Janice McWilliams's son Bruce oversees the dining operation, which is highly regarded. His wife Gloria is the chef. Among appetizers, we liked the mountain trout smoked over hickory chips and the country pâté of sausage, chicken livers and pork tenderloin blended with brandy and spices and served with the house chutney. Entrées range from baked stuffed trout and broiled swordfish to veal cordon bleu. Our choices were tenderloin en croûte and New York sirloin with horseradish butter, each accompanied by a sprig of plain steamed broccoli and nothing else. Profiteroles, cheesecake, zabaglione, bourbon pie and walnut torte were dessert choices.

(540) 839-2231. Entrées, $18.75 to $22.50. Dinner nightly, 6 to 9 or 10. Sunday brunch, 11 to 2. Closed Tuesdays, November-April.

Chef Ed's Community Market, 3 Main St., Hot Springs.

This began as a market, but chef-owner Ed McArdle quickly turned it into a full-scale – albeit small – gourmet restaurant open for two dinner seatings a night. Ed, a Culinary Institute of America graduate, had attracted a loyal following when he operated a restaurant known as The Muse at Three Hills Inn in Warm Springs.

Here he seats upwards of 36 people in a narrow space squeezed between a drug store and a liquor store. It's colorful, furnished in country style, and accented with homemade wood products and green plants. There's a small bar.

From the open kitchen comes an array of creative contemporary treats. The night's appetizers might be flatbreads with changing toppings, portobello mushroom croustade, a salmon and potato napoleon, and crab cakes with creole mustard and beurre blanc. Typical entrées are grilled salmon over gingered bok choy and soba noodles, pesto chicken with tomato cream sauce and roasted garlic risotto, and beef tournedos with basil-mashed potatoes and roasted tomato jus. Homemade desserts include banana cream pie with toasted peanut crust, lemon gratin with raspberry sauce and an apple-custard tart with cinnamon cream.

The lights are dimmed, candles glow and the food is first-rate. On warm days, the crowds spill onto a couple of tables outside.

(540) 839-3663. Entrées, $14 to $17. Lunch, Monday-Saturday 11 to 3. Dinner, Monday and Thursday-Sunday, seatings at 6:30 and 8:30.

Sam Snead's Tavern, Main Street, Hot Springs.

Located in an historic bank building in the center of town, this was renovated by golfer Sam Snead in 1980. Its symmetry and weathered gray barnwood exterior give it a distinct Wild West look. Golf memorabilia is at the entry, naturally, and wines are stored in the original bank vault. Staff clad in Sam Snead golf shirts serve patrons in a small, paneled dining room with green leather booths and chairs, known as the "lunch room," or the larger dining area in the tavern with a fireplace and a dance floor. A porch on the second story is favored for outdoor dining in season.

The menu takes a golf theme, from chip shots for starters to the 19th hole for beverages. Dinner items range from pecan-crusted mountain trout with pecan crust to T-bone steak. Start with Buffalo wings, crabmeat chimichanga or a Gulf Coast shrimp cocktail. Finish with berry shortcake, ice-cream pie or rainbow sherbet.

(540) 839-7666. Entrées, $12.50 to $21.95. Lunch, Thursday-Sunday 11 to 4. Dinner, Thursday-Sunday 5 to 10. Hours vary.

Cafe Albert, Cottage Row, The Homestead, Hot Springs.

Light, casual fare is offered inside and out at this appealing cafe in the Homestead's quaint Cottage Row of shops and services. Jaunty umbrellaed tables on an outdoor deck provided the setting for our lunch of cold Virginia apple soup, a delectable croissant of turkey and spinach leaves and a good potato salad, and a tropical chicken salad sandwich on rye. Excellent chocolates, honey cookies and bread fresh from the Homestead's 19th-century ovens can be purchased along with meats, cheeses and other specialty items. Desserts range from pastries to sundaes.

(540) 839-7777. Open daily in summer, 9 a.m. to 8 p.m. Hours vary.

Diversions

The Springs. As did their forefathers, today's visitors can take part in the ritual of the baths. The Homestead's **Warm Springs Pools** remain as they were upon opening, the men's pool in 1761 and the ladies' pool in 1836. Thomas Jefferson took the waters here for his health. He is credited with designing the octagonal bathhouse that surrounds the men's pool, which has been in continuous use longer than any of its kind in the country. The crude device that lowered the ailing widow of Robert E. Lee into the restorative waters is still on view in the circular women's bathhouse. The waters, a constant 98 degrees, contain a greater variety of minerals than others in the valley. Visitors pay $12 for a towel, a very basic changing room and an hour's communal soak (in the nude for men) in a six-foot-deep pool that's 40 feet across and so clear that you can distinguish the stones on the bottom. The water has a gentle fizz of tickling bubbles. Bathers lie back against steps or float along ropes, but "this is not for swimming, it's for bathing," Steve the attendant advised at the men's bath. Shirdell Pryor, the women's attendant, makes the brightly colored calico bathing shifts trimmed with rickrack rack during the winter when the pools are closed. Women can bring a bathing suit, wear one of the shifts or bathe as the men do. Springs open Tuesday-Saturday 10:30 to 5, Sunday 1 to 5, mid-April through October; $12 per session. The **Hot Springs** at The Homestead are warmer, averaging 104 degrees. Attendants in the bathhouse built in 1892 follow practices of traditional European spas in offering mineral baths, sauna, steam room, massages and hydrotherapies year-round.

The Spa. The Greenbrier's $7 million Spa, Mineral Baths and Salon occupies a full wing of the legendary resort begun 217 years ago because of its healing waters. This is another of the few American spas to follow the European treatment of using fresh, natural mineral waters. The spa's bath facilities include walk-in whirlpool baths, Swiss showers, Scotch spray, steam, sauna and therapy rooms for massage and body wraps. Nineteen treatments are available, varying from 25 to 80 minutes in length. We tried the basic Greenbrier treatment ($93). The hour-long assault and battery by showers and massages, combined with relaxing baths and body wraps, left one of us so relaxed he could not walk his normal double-time pace back to the hotel room. It took an hour's nap to revive him for dinner.

Golf. World-renowned for golf, the Homestead and the Greenbrier each boast three eighteen-hole championship courses, and the Homestead's new management is putting even greater emphasis on golf (a new teaching facility, putting green and driving range). Built in 1892, the first tee of the Homestead Golf Course is the oldest in continuous use in the country. The Homestead's Cascades course, known for its tight fairways and undulating greens, is considered the most testing mountain course in North America. The Greenbrier courses also are highly rated, particularly the Greenbrier (the only resort course to have hosted both the Ryder and Solheim Cups) and the Old White. The Lakeside Course is open year-round.

Garth Newel Music Center, Route 220, Hot Springs, (540) 839-5018. The hillside estate of a former dean of the Yale School of Fine Arts is a destination for chamber music lovers. It's been called the Marlboro of the South. Summer weekend concerts feature the Garth Newel Chamber Players and guest artists Saturday evenings and Sunday afternoons, early July through Labor Day. The architecture and acoustics of air-conditioned Herter Hall are perfect for chamber music, and the mountain setting is unsurpassed. In the spring and fall, center directors Arlene and Luca DiCecco, who double as violinist and cellist with the Chamber Players, offer special Garth Newel holiday weekends. Up to twenty guests enjoy overnight lodging and gourmet meals, wine and nightly concerts.

George Washington National Forest. About half of Bath County lies in the George Washington National Forest, which encompasses numerous recreation areas, trails and campgrounds. Surrounded by the national forest, **Lake Moomaw** extends twelve miles along the Jackson River and offers boating, swimming and fishing.

Shopping. The **Tower Corridor** shops on the main floor of The Homestead are elegant and pricey, as you'd expect. Particularly impressive is **Southern Taste,** a gourmet food and kitchen shop with an espresso bar. Outside in the **Cottage Row,** shopping is slightly more down to earth. We particularly liked the interesting jackets made of old quilts and the fabric plant sculptures at **Quilts Unlimited,** the toys at **Just for Fun** and the women's apparel at **Lemon Twist.** Hunting and fishing equipment is featured at **The Outpost. The Rocking Chair** is a good home and garden shop. The artworks, ceramics and kitchenware at the **Gallery of Hot Springs** and the variety of items at **The Gift Caboose** along the old railroad platform are highlights in the center of Hot Springs.

Warm Springs Gallery, at the foot of Courthouse Hill in Warm Springs, features original art and fine crafts by regional artists. South of Hot Springs is **Mustoe House Antiques,** specializing in fine English antiques.

The **Greenbrier Creative Arts Colony** is in a group of cottages known as Alabama Row at the Greenbrier. Craftsmen are among those who work and sell their wares here. The extravagant Gallery of Shops at The Greenbrier includes **The Candy Maker,** where the resort's famous chocolates are made by hand; the **Greenbrier Shop,** purveying Greenbrier signature merchandise, including the rhododendron-patterned china; the **Best of West Virginia Shop,** showcasing handiwork of local artisans; the **Carleton Varney Gift Gallery** and the **Greenbrier Gourmet,** one of the best kitchen shops we've seen. **Land Rover at The Greenbrier** and **La Cheval,** an equestrian shop, are also here.

Extra-Special

Bacova Gallery, Route 687, Bacova.

The charming company town of Bacova, a few miles west of Warm Springs, was the original headquarters of the Bacova Guild factory famed for making mailboxes with wildlife scenes. The Guild has been taken over by Burlington Industries, and the colorful company store in Hot Springs has closed. Bacova remains a destination for art-lovers, thanks to William Grove. In 1998, he bought the country-gothic Bacova Chapel, which had been built by hand in 1920, and artfully restored it to its former glory. In place of pulpit and pews, the sanctuary is filled with century-old oil paintings, antique prints and watercolors, bronzes, porcelain, 19th- and 20th- century antiques and a line of hardwood Mission furniture crafted in the Warm Springs Valley. Sunlight pouring through the arched windows illuminates a stunning gallery space.

(540) 839-2399. Open Thursday-Monday 10 to 5, April to mid-December; other times by appointment.

Dogwoods are in bloom along brick sidewalks in front of Woodrow Wilson Birthplace.

Staunton, Va.

A Frontier Town Grown Up

The first thing you should know about Staunton is that its name is pronounced STAN-ton. The second is that this is Virginia's oldest town west of the Blue Ridge Mountains and was part of America's first western frontier. The third is that it is the Queen City of the Shenandoah Valley, a showcase for architecture and the arts.

Founded in 1732, just a decade later than Richmond, Staunton was settled by the first wave of immigrants heading west from the thirteen original colonies into Appalachia and beyond. Its boom days lasted from the Civil War past the turn of the century. Lately, its downtown has been held up as an example of historic rejuvenation.

Staunton is what you might call a frontier town grown up.

Thanks to local architect T.J. Collins, who designed or remodeled more than 200 local buildings between 1891 and 1911, Staunton has an architectural importance far greater than its population of 25,000 would indicate. It contains no fewer than five historic districts. One is the wharf area – a wharf without water, incidentally – where the coming of the railroad produced the largest collection of Victorian warehouses still standing in Virginia. The wharf area is now the centerpiece of a downtown revitalization known for dining spots, shopping, lodging and two emerging Shakespeare theaters.

A city of hills that some think give it a European look, Staunton is wonderfully focused for the visitor. Most attractions are within walking distance of the tight little downtown, which, as local innkeeper Michael Organ likes to say, embraces "ten delicious dining experiences within ten blocks, all in historic buildings."

Old buildings thrive in new incarnations. The Belle Grae Inn, offering both guest rooms and dining, grew up around a Victorian mansion. The Frederick House harbors lodging in five restored townhouses and two older houses. An old grain mill is now the Mill Street Grill. Part of the train station houses The Pullman Cafe and a Victorian ice-cream parlor and another part the Depot Grille.

Staunton's best-known attraction is the Woodrow Wilson Birthplace, lately expanded with the addition of a full-fledged museum. Up and coming is the Frontier Culture Museum, a state-backed museum of living history showing early farm life. The Statler Brothers Complex is of interest to fans of the red-white-and-blue country singers who for 25 years favored their hometown with a Happy Birthday USA celebration every July 4. Some fine little shops and unusual garden enterprises are scattered around the countryside.

Staunton is surrounded by schools: Mary Baldwin College, Stuart Hall prep, the College of the Holy Child Jesus for students from Spain. And it is surrounded by scenery: the Blue Ridge Mountains, the Appalachian foothills and Shenandoah National Park. It makes a good base for exploring a compact area bounded by historic Lexington, Charlottesville, Hot Springs and the Skyline Drive.

This old frontier town has matured well, indeed.

Inn Spots

Sampson-Eagon Inn, 238 East Beverley St., Staunton 24401.

Some B&Bs seem to have everything going for them, and this is one. Restorationists Frank Mattingly and his wife Laura, business dropouts from the Washington area, renovated the 1840 house into a deluxe B&B that won the Historic Staunton Foundation's annual Preservation Award in 1992. A marker relates that the house is on the site of a blacksmith shop in which the first United Methodist Church was organized in 1797 and from which the fashionable Gospel Hill area derived its name. The house is "an absolute textbook of architectural styles," says Laura, including Empire, Greek Revival, Egyptian Revival, Colonial Revival and Victorian.

The main floor contains one guest room, a guest living room and a center dining room, plus a side porch with a two-seater swing overlooking the garden. They and the upstairs rooms showcase the couple's various collections. "We had a small antiques business and our dream was to have a place to show our collections," explains Laura. They range from antique delft to horse brasses.

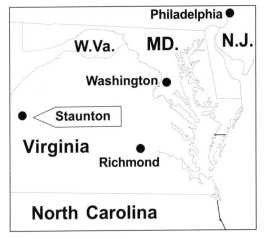

Each of the five guest accommodations is large enough for a queensize canopied bed with down pillows, reading chairs, a desk, TV/VCR, telephone and private bath. We liked the

Sampson-Eagon House won Historic Staunton's annual preservation award.

Eagon master suite with a sleeping porch outfitted in wicker and balloon curtains, and an immense T.J. Collins-designed bathroom. The designer sheets were neatly folded back on a diagonal atop the bed covers. Rooms are decorated to perfection and with great attention to detail – from flashlights to hand-held mirrors, from albums of local restaurant menus to bottles of mineral water in each room. A guest refrigerator hidden off the second-floor hallway holds juices, mixers, ice and wine glasses. A pail at the foot of the stairway is full of candies, and gourmet chocolates are put out at nightly turndown.

A full breakfast is served on Royal Doulton china in the formal dining room. Ours started with fresh raspberries and blueberries with lemon yogurt made by Frank, along with homemade breads, including cranberry, apple and Laura's favorite bourbon-pecan. The pièce de résistance was Laura's specialty grand marnier soufflé pancakes with ham and grand marnier-strawberry and orange syrups. Eggs benedict, pecan belgian waffles and Frank's sugar and spice-baked apples are other favorites.

After breakfast, Frank, an avid Staunton booster, will supply you with enough ideas to keep you busy around here for a week.

(540) 886-8200 or (800) 597-9722. Three rooms and two suites with private baths. Doubles, $96. Suites, $120. Two-night minimum weekends, May-October. Children over 12. No smoking.

Frederick House, 28 North New St., Staunton 24401.

Twenty rooms and suites varying in size from small to vast are offered in five side-by-side townhouses and two houses across the street. All have been grandly restored by Joe Harman, one of the few Staunton natives we encountered on our rounds here. The ex-Washington banker came home to purchase a jewelry store and to save from demolition a cluster of empty buildings. He and wife Evy turned them into a small hotel at the edge of downtown, a task that took ten years to complete and was continuing at our latest visit.

"We've taken this little corner and made it nice," says Joe in an understatement masking the massive effort and expense that have gone into the undertaking. Theirs is a comfortable refuge of uncommon appeal and value.

Because of the buildings' heritage and layout, rooms vary widely. The twelve in the original townhouses – all recently refurbished – range from a second-floor suite reached by a graceful, curved stairway and containing a large living room and two bedrooms to a walkout English basement bedroom with a queensize bed and a sitting area with floral sprigged wallpaper. Works of Virginia artists, American antiques, ceiling fans, good reading lamps, phones, TVs and terrycloth robes are in each room. All have modern baths.

Most rooms have private entrances, and guests are not likely to run into each other except on the nicely landscaped cobblestone terrace, an outdoor gathering spot, or in the spacious tearoom below, where breakfast is served by the hands-on innkeepers, who live upstairs. The edible landscaping produced a bounty of beets, peppers, onions, squash, zucchini, tomatoes, blueberries, raspberries, muskmelons and cherries as well as colorful flowers for the 1998 show and harvest.

Lately, the Harmans added more rooms, suites and common facilities in two substantial residences across the street, one dating to 1820 and the other to 1898. Decorated to the period, some have fireplaces and jacuzzis. We admired a new suite with twelve-foot-high ceilings, a solid walnut canopy bed and an armoire with TV/VCR – a considerable value for $125. The new properties include meeting and dining rooms for groups, and add to the Frederick House's billing as "a small hotel in the European tradition."

As classical music played, we enjoyed a breakfast of orange juice, grapefruit and a choice of ham and cheese quiche or egg casserole with whole-wheat toast. Upon request, Joe Harman played tapes of the Statler Brothers country singers, hometown boys who made good.

(540) 885-4220 or (800) 334-5575. Fax (540) 885-5180. www.frederickhouse.com. Twelve rooms and eleven suites with private baths. Doubles, $75 to $155. Suites, $115 to $170. Children accepted. No smoking.

The Belle Grae Inn, 515 West Frederick St., Staunton 24401.

The first of Staunton's innkeepers, Michael Organ started in 1983 with a rambling 1873 Victorian mansion. He now has nineteen rooms and suites in six restored houses encompassing nearly an entire block in a residential section just west of downtown. "You can tell our matriculations by our restorations – 1983, '85, '87, '89, '91 and '93," says he. "That also tells where our heads were." In more recent years, he has changed some of the smaller rooms into suites with bedrooms, sitting areas and fireplaces.

The main red brick house harbors a good restaurant (see Dining Spots), a parlor and a garden room with chess and backgammon games on the first floor, plus seven guest rooms of varying size with antique beds and private baths. A rocking horse is in one, a wicker seating area in another and armoires are in most. Choicer accommodations appealing to business types are found in four restored Victorian houses called the Townhouse, the Bungalow, the Bishop's House and the Jefferson House. The last is a two-story duplex, where four suites are outfitted with sitting areas, wet bars, TVs, phones, queensize four-poster beds and courtyard verandas. Gilchrist & Soames toiletries and decanters of sherry abound. Pathways and

Thornrose House at Gypsy Hill faces a 300-acre municipal park.

boardwalks join the various buildings and a conference center in a cottage across a pleasant garden terrace.

Rooms keep getting a new look because the contents are for sale. "If you like your bed," says Michael, "you can take it home with you."

Breakfast involves what he calls "innkeeper's fare," anything from french toast to steak and eggs and perhaps including roast pork with cheese soufflé.

The inn derives its name from two nearby mountains, Betsy Belle and Mary Grae, named by Scotch-Irish settlers for landmarks in Scotland.

(540) 886-5151 or (888) 541-5151. Fax (540) 886-6641. Seven rooms and seven suites with private baths. Doubles, $139 weekends, $99 midweek. Suites, $169 weekends, $139 midweek. Two-night minimum weekends in May and October. Children 12 and over. Smoking restricted.

Thornrose House at Gypsy Hill, 531 Thornrose Ave., Staunton 24401.

The previous owners got this "B&B in the English manner" off to a good start. But it has come of age with considerable sophistication under new owners Suzanne and Otis Huston, who were widely traveled during his career as an executive with du Pont.

They lightened up the decor with lace curtains and good-looking fabrics, added two bedrooms (with private baths), restored the masterful gardens surrounding a brick terrace and a couple of pergolas, and imbued the place with their enthusiasm and hospitality. Although some rooms are on the small side, not so is the master bedroom, with two twins joined together as a kingsize bed and windows on three sides. Suzanne's favorite is the smallest – the rear Yorkshire Room with a clawfoot tub, overlooking the gardens. A daughter's bedroom was converted into a cozy guest sitting room when she left the nest.

The Hustons continued the tradition of tea, served in season on the inviting veranda or beneath the pergolas by the gardens. On cooler days it's taken in the living room, where a gas fireplace, grand piano and a TV are among the amenities.

A heart-healthy breakfast is served in a cozy dining room. It might feature crêpes stuffed with strawberries or vanilla yogurt, mushroom and cheese omelets, banana-pecan pancakes or oat whole-grain waffles with apples along with choice of juices and, at our visit, cantaloupe with blueberries. Otis makes his own muesli, for which guests frequently request the recipe.

Besides enjoying the Hustons' gorgeous property, guests only have to cross the street for golf, tennis, swimming and walking in the 300-acre Gypsy Hill Park.

(540) 885-7026 or (800) 861-4338. Fax (540) 885-6458. Five rooms with private baths. Doubles, $69 to $89. Children over 4. No smoking.

The Iris Inn, 191 Chinquapin Drive, Waynesboro 22980.

Stands of iris line the wide, curving driveway leading up to this stunning structure on a forested, 21-acre hillside overlooking the western mountains. The irises reflect one of the themes that Iris Karl, innkeeper with her husband Wayne, have executed throughout their very personalized inn.

Be advised that this is very different from the "old" inns with which Virginia is well endowed. The Karls looked at scores of potential properties to restore as a B&B when Wayne retired from the Federal Aviation Agency. "He was an engineer and always saw the things that were falling down," says Iris. "One day he said, 'why don't we build?' We started looking for land and never looked back."

They found a secluded hilltop high above an I-64 interchange just southeast of Waynesboro, the sister city of Staunton in Augusta County. An architect designed a sprawling, two-story inn with seven guest rooms and suites off two 92-foot-long porches running the width of the structure, a lookout tower above a whirlpool spa and a soaring, 28-foot-high great room enhanced with a large and realistic wall mural of a woodland scene. They since have added two more deluxe suites with fireplaces, wet bars and what a fellow innkeeper calls "the world's only rolling bed," which slides in and out of a wall to be hidden away for meetings. "You don't have to be in an old, historic building to succeed in this business," Iris contends. Thanks to a receptive business clientele (one du Pont Co. physician books here every month, and two Texas businessmen stayed for six months), the inn enjoys unusually high occupancy year-round. "People like a place that's new, spacious and comfortable," says Iris.

Our quarters were in the Bird Room, the last available that evening. A kingsize bed, modern bathroom, refrigerator/wet bar and TV blended nicely with the bird theme, which included pictures of birds, birds on the wallpaper border, birds pictured along the tiled bath, a bird in a nest resting on the sink and a mélange of bird feeders outside. Other rooms are larger; some have day beds and jacuzzi tubs. Iris has decorated all to the nth degree in accordance with their names, from Deer to Hawk's Nest. The Woodland Forest even adds a Secret World for little children, an attic alcove with a single bed and a teddy bear's picnic.

The Garden Path suite with kingsize canopy bed has a vaulted ceiling, a corner fireplace and a wraparound deck overlooking the valley. Potman, a life-size figure made of different-size clay pots, occupies a niche overlooking the sitting area, and a squirrel is painted on a kitchen drawer with a hole for acorns. A spiral stair-case leads to a loft with treadmill, recumbent bicycle and day bed.

The rear Deep Woods suite, where pocket doors hide the movable bed, comes with a jacuzzi and fireplace. Paw prints painted on a wall were left by a koala bear

Breakfast is taken beside remarkable wall mural in Great Hall at The Iris Inn.

in a tree on the loft, and creatures of the woods are found inside a hanging lamp above the dining table.

Breakfast is an event in the Great Room, alongside the remarkable wall mural. At our visit, a plate of fresh fruit preceded a choice of light, heart-shaped belgian waffles or baked eggs with crabmeat. Banana bread, good bran muffins and bird-shaped rolls accompanied. The treats began with a glass of milk and homemade chocolate-chip cookies from a bottomless jar the evening before. They culminated with a loaf of "road bread," wrapped in saran with a plastic knife, and a hug from Iris upon departure.

(540) 943-1991. www.irisinn.com. Seven rooms and two suites with private baths. Doubles, $90 to $105 weekends, $85 to $100 midweek. Suites, $150 weekends, $140 midweek. Children by arrangement. Two-night minimum weekends. No smoking.

The Inn at Keezletown Road, 1224 Keezletown Road, Weyers Cave 24486.

Pastel pink with white gingerbread trim, this handsome B&B is located in a rural village with an odd name about ten miles north of Staunton. It's favored by those who want to be out in the countryside and near the new Shenandoah Valley regional airport (for quick hops to the big cities).

Sandy and Alan Inabinet from Northern Virginia chose this area for a B&B in 1994 because they were familiar with it from having a weekend ski home in Massanutten. They redid the 1896 valley Victorian farmhouse into a refuge of style and comfort.

The four guest rooms, all with private baths bearing the inn's own amenities, come with sitting areas and small TVs. They're furnished with Shenandoah Valley antiques, oriental rugs, ceiling fans and down comforters. The Rose Room with a gas fireplace and a high, step-up antique queen poster bed is on the ground floor. The others are upstairs. Beds vary from canopied queens to twins joined as kingsize.

White gingerbread trim graces pink facade of The Inn at Keezletown Road.

Besides enjoying a parlor with a fireplace, guests like to rock on the unusual, inverted-curved front porch or hang out at umbrella-shaded tables on the brick terrace situated between several rear outbuildings. One is the attached wash house in which the Inabinets reside; another is a small building in which Sandy was about to open a small antiques shop at our visit. The rear yard harbors a lily pond, an herb garden, a flower garden that provides bouquets for the rooms and edible garnishes, and the chicken house. The hosts' chickens lay unusual green, blue, brown and pink tinted eggs that turn up for breakfast in the morning.

The first wakeup call may be issued by Benny, the Aracuana rooster. Guests gather later for a hearty southern breakfast served in the dining room or in a delightful skylit garden porch overlooking the rear patio. Sandy's North Carolina upbringing stands her in good stead for the likes of country ham biscuits, pumpkin pancakes, grand marnier french toast, cheese grits, sausage and fruit compote.

(540) 234-0644 or (800) 465-0100. Four rooms with private baths. Doubles, $85 to $95. Children over 14. No smoking.

Dining Spots

Belle Grae Inn, 515 West Frederick St., Staunton.

Occupying the front portion of the main floor of this inn are three elegant Victorian dining rooms plus a veranda and a garden terrace, as well as an art deco bistro for lighter dining and entertainment.

We dined in front of a fireplace amidst tables dressed in white and pink with blue china and glassware and an assortment of family keepsakes and heirlooms. Tables are well spaced and some seating is on couches. The short, contemporary menu might list such entrées as pan-seared salmon with sweet pepper and lobster cream sauce, baked chicken breast with figs and pancetta, herb-rolled beef tenderloin with mushroom-thyme sauce, and Chincoteague crab cakes with puree of sweet red pepper and herb mayonnaise, a seasonal treat that we enjoyed here.

Tasty appetizers included a smoked chicken, fig and roast shallot tart, terrine of lobster and boursin with herb puree, and roast quail with leek stuffing and corn vinaigrette. The basket of "bubble bread," spicy with caraway, was so good we readily accepted a refill. That meant we had to forego such desserts as almond-amaretto torte, chocolate-mocha crêpe and chocolate mousse pie.

"Fun dining" is offered in the airy Garden Room bistro, billed as Staunton's only indoor-outdoor cafe, with lots of glass. The short menu ranges from a grilled prime rib sandwich with garden salad to a chicken and cheese quesadilla with Mexican salad.

(540) 886-5151 or (888) 541-5151. Entrées, $14.95 to $21.95; bistro, $8.95 to $11.95. Breakfast daily, 7 to 9. Dinner nightly, 6 to 9.

L'Italia Restaurant, 23 East Beverley St., Staunton.

Highly regarded is this branch of the well-established L'Italia Restaurant of Harrisonburg, which took over the site of the late, great 23 Beverley restaurant. Owner Emilio Amato retained the elegant decor and filled the recessed niches in the walls with paintings by art students from James Madison University.

The extensive dinner menu, more Sicilian than northern Italian, may suffer from the breadth of more than four dozen choices. They include fifteen pastas (from manicotti to fettuccine alfredo with shrimp). As Neapolitan love songs played during the dinner hour, we enjoyed the shrimp scampi with honey-mustard glaze over angel-hair pasta and a house salad with red wine vinaigrette. Less satisfactory was the veal saltimbocca, billed as a house specialty.

The appetizers are predictable, although the low prices may not be. How about antipasto salad for two for $6.90? Ditto for desserts, from spumoni and cannoli to grasshopper pie and tirami su. A few Virginia wines are on the mostly Italian wine list, priced primarily in the teens.

Many of the same dishes turn up at lunchtime, when you can order anything from an Italian hoagie to veal parmigiana.

(540) 885-0102. Entrées, $7.50 to $13.50. Lunch, Tuesday-Saturday 11 to 3:30. Dinner, Tuesday-Saturday from 3:30, Sunday noon to 10.

The Depot Grille, 42 Middlebrook Ave., Staunton.

Immensely popular is this steak and seafood house opened in part of the old C&0 facility, called Staunton Station. It's one of the few complete train complexes in the country and lately rejuvenated by developer Victor Meinert. By complete we mean an operating passenger terminal with a couple of new eateries. Also a stunning curved outdoor concourse that's the scene of a series of free outdoor Shakin' at the Station concerts in summer. Plus a free-standing signal tower, a freight depot, and three cabooses and three baggage cars that have been turned into antiques shops and boutiques.

The old terminal houses the **Whistlestop Soda Shop,** with an extraordinary 1880s ice-cream parlor and pharmacy interior for which Vic Meinert outbid the Smithsonian. Ice-cream treats are featured beneath four massive bronze and stained-glass chandeliers salvaged from the old Milwaukee train station. Occupying part of the station concourse is the **Pullman Restaurant,** where we admired the ornate bar with swinging doors as we lunched on a crab cake sandwich and the offerings from a help-yourself salad bar that was more interesting than most. A new chef from Duner's in Charlottesville has a great New Orleans flair.

The depot restaurant contains a 50-foot-long, 19th-century oak bar obtained from an old upstate New York hotel and believed to be the longest in the country. It also has a solarium with windows opening onto the outdoors and a vast dining room displaying railroad memorabilia and lit by oil lanterns even at noon. There's an old shoeshine chair at the door.

The all-day menu appeals to all tastes, and the seafood and nightly specials come highly recommended. We hear good things about the backfin crab cakes, the mesquite-grilled chicken, the slow-roasted prime rib and the grilled shrimp and feta pasta. The prices certainly are right, and salad and a choice of two sides (fries, applesauce, coleslaw, steamed vegetables, rice or new potatoes) come with. Heath Bar crunch is a favorite dessert.

(540) 885-7332. Entrées, $9.95 to $17.95. Open daily, 11 to 10:30.

Mill Street Grill, 1 Mill St., Staunton.
If this restaurant in the first Wharf Historic District building to be restored looks a bit like a gallery, thank the former owner whose wife also used to own the interesting art gallery upstairs (now a noisy sports bar).

Six panels of stained glass are a focal point of the decor of the old White Star Mills flour mill. Done by a local couple, they depict the journey of wheat from the harvesting to the baking of bread. There's much to look at on several levels with exposed beams and thick fieldstone walls: paintings and collages, old light fixtures, etched glass and copper rails.

Tablecloths and candlelight are the setting for dinner. The specialty here is ribs, slow-cooked baby back ribs and beef ribs in the Midwest style. A barbecue platter yields samples of both. One well-traveled innkeeper calls them the best ribs she's ever had. She says the rest of the food has zip as well. The menu ranges widely from raspberry chicken or curried pork tenderloin to filet mignon sautéed in peppercorn cream sauce. Grilled mahi-mahi, charbroiled yellowfin tuna, crab cakes and pastas are among the offerings.

Appetizers run to steamed spiced shrimp, Buffalo wings, potato skins and chicken nachos. Key lime, hazelnut-cappuccino and Reese's peanut butter pies are featured desserts.

(540) 886-0656. Entrées, $9.95 to $15.25. Dinner nightly, 4 to 10. Sunday brunch, 11:30 to 3.

Byers Street Bistro, 18 Byers St., Staunton.
Gourmet pizzas and pastas are the specialties at this informal downtown restaurant in a restored warehouse. Formerly known as J. Rugle's Warehouse, it offers a large bar, an upstairs dining room and, in season, a popular sidewalk cafe.

The specialty pizzas come in various sizes and with a variety of toppings, so in effect you create your own. Or you can choose one of the "history-making combinations:" spinach and artichoke hearts, cajun chicken or white cheese and pesto.

There's more. Entrées, served with house or caesar salad, include things like steamed crab legs, blackjack chicken (flamed with Jack Daniels), chicken pesto, steak kabobs and New York strip steak. There also are sandwiches and appetizers, from potato skins to nachos to mozzarella sticks.

Homemade desserts range from snicker bar pie and fried ice cream to tiramisu. Cappuccino, lattes and Italian wines also are featured.

(540) 886-4399. Entrées, $9.95 to $13.95. Dinner nightly, 5 to midnight.

The Heavenly Bake Shop, 101 West Beverley St., Staunton.

A wall mural of clouds painted by one of the owners enhances this downtown favorite. The baked goods and pastries are imported from Charlottesville, but the son of one of the owners prepares the sandwiches, salads and lunches, including a handful of vegetarian items.

Stop in for a breakfast snack of scones, muffins or sour cream coffeecake to go with a cappuccino or latte. For lunch, try a smoked turkey cobb sandwich or roast beef with watercress and alouette cheese on French bread. Or how about the California Dream salad – greens tossed with marinated chickpeas, avocado, steamed broccoli, mushrooms, tomato, red onion and sprouts, garnished with cilantro? Or a caesar chicken salad? Prices are in the $4 to $6 range.

Dinner with live music is offered weekends in a coffeehouse setting.

(540) 886-4455. Breakfast and lunch, Monday-Friday 7:30 to 3, Saturday brunch, 9 to 3. Dinner, Friday and Saturday 6:30 to 9:30.

The Pampered Palate, 26-28 East Beverley St., Staunton.

The old Atlantic Lunch hot-dog stand has been transformed into this sprightly deli and gourmet food and wine shop. Sandwiches with local names are "the Palate's pride." We liked the New Theater (vegetables, mushrooms and havarti) and the Statler (a quartet of meats and cheeses). Both were stuffed in pita bread. A few salads, quiche, pampered potatoes, cheese boards, bagels and sweets round out the fare. The menu is priced in the $3.50 to $5 range. There are tables in an ice-cream parlor setting and everything's available to take out.

All espresso drinks are a bargain $1 during "cappy hour" from 2:30 to 4:30.

(540) 886-9463. Open Monday-Saturday 9 to 5:30, Sunday 11 to 2:30.

Rowe's Family Restaurant, Route 250 at I-81, Staunton.

A local institution since 1947, this is an enormous red wood house conveniently situated beside the interchange of two interstate highways. It's a destination for travelers and national food writers.

Clippings about founder Mildred Craft Rowe are at the entry and her cookbook ($8.95), preserves, barbecue sauce and pastries are for sale at the counter. Son Michael says she still comes in four days a week "and quickly knows if anything is wrong."

More than 230 patrons can be seated in two large rooms. The basic menu is supplemented by white-card specials changing daily – minced pork barbecue dinner and golden fried wing dings at one visit. The other offerings include fried fillet of flounder, grilled liver, baked pork tenderloin with gravy and a hamburger that comes on a wooden plank, with a choice of vegetables and salad. All the homemade breads, biscuits, muffins, cookies and pies are baked daily to Mrs. Rowe's specifications. They are available for purchase from the cashier.

(540) 886-1833. Entrées, $6.25 to $8.95. Open daily, 7 a.m. to 9 p.m. in summer, to 8 in winter; Sundays, 7 to 7.

Diversions

Historic Walking Tours. The Historic Staunton Foundation, founded in 1971 to promote preservation over demolition, has concentrated its efforts in the downtown and adjacent residential areas. That makes it easy to view the results on foot.

Indeed, tourism promoters note that visitors can arrive at the restored railroad station by Amtrak, walk to lodging and restaurants, and never need a car – a rarity for a small town these days. The foundation's walking tour map and brochure focuses on 59 sites of outstanding architectural or historical merit in the Downtown, Wharf Area, Newtown, Gospel Hill and North End. Many sites were designed or remodeled around the turn of the century by local architect T.J. Collins, whose son continued the tradition. Visitors accustomed to Virginia's formal Jeffersonian brick styles will be struck by Staunton's exuberance, the result of one family having a major impact on the design of a community.

Woodrow Wilson Birthplace & Museum, 18-24 North Coalter St., Staunton.

The Presbyterian manse in which America's 28th president was born in 1856 is a registered National Historic Landmark. On guided tours every half hour, visitors see the room where he was born, the crib in which he slept and the chair in which his mother rocked him. The tour and furnishings emphasize the way of life of Stauntonians in the 1850s – "the way they would have lived as a Southern family," according to our guide. You see twelve rooms containing many items that belonged to the Wilson family. The rear balcony affords a view of the historic gardens restored by the Garden Club of Virginia, the cream-colored buildings of Mary Baldwin College and the downtown. "Now you're part of the family," says the guide at tour's end. "You get to leave by the back door."

Before the tour, browse through the only museum in the country spanning Wilson's entire life. Seven galleries cover everything from his parentage to his funeral. The re-creation of his Princeton University study contains his old Hammond typewriter. Other galleries trace his economic and social reforms, the tumultuous war years, and his search for peace and a new world order. The well-spaced displays are tasteful, significant and not at all overwhelming. A highlight is his beloved 1919 Pierce-Arrow White House limousine, donated by his widow to be shown in his hometown in a large garage beside the museum. An attractive gift shop adjoins the garden.

(540) 885-0897 or (888) 496-6376. Open daily 9 to 5, March-October; Monday-Saturday 10 to 4, Sunday noon to 4, rest of year. Adults, $6.50.

Shenandoah Shakespeare, 11 East Beverley St., Staunton, (540) 885-5588.

Staunton has been the home base for a globe-trotting traveling theater company called Shenandoah Shakespeare Express. In 2000, a non-profit corporation spearheaded by tireless innkeeper Joe Harman of the Frederick House was creating a replica of the Blackfriars Theater and, eventually, a replica of the Globe Theater. Downtown Staunton was being billed as "the only site in the world with two authentic replicas of Shakespeare theaters." The indoor Blackfriars Theater on South Market Street was scheduled to be up and running year-round in 2001. The outdoor Globe Theater was scheduled for opening in 2005 on North Louis Street. The existing traveling company will be joined by a resident company to stage Shakespeare plays in each theater. "We intend to present plays the way Shakespeare did, without lots of costumes and props," according to promoter Harman. An education component will offer school programs as well as a master's degree in Shakespeare studies.

Statler Brothers Complex, 501 Thornrose Ave., Staunton, (540) 885-7297.

Opposite Gypsy Hill Park is this renovated school building, now the corporate headquarters of the Statler Brothers country singers, all of whom reside in the

Rear of Woodrow Wilson Birthplace overlooks restored gardens.

area. Still on view is the gymnasium stage where the brothers won their first talent show in 1955. Hallway cases sparkle with Grammys and records. One tour a day is given Monday-Friday at 2. Gift shop hours are weekdays, 10:30 to 3:30.

André Viette Farm and Nursery, Long Meadow Road (Route 608), Fishersville, (540) 943-2315 or (800) 575-5538.

In early spring, the rolling countryside here is ablaze with tulips. These spectacular perennial gardens – said to be the largest in the eastern United States – continue with more than 3,000 varieties of poppies, peonies, iris and, their real claim to fame, lilies. André Viette's fame, spread through his national gardening radio program, draws people from afar to his garden center and flower clinics.

Shopping. As you walk around downtown, you'll surely be struck by the interesting plants and gardens that are the work of a fulltime city horticulturist. The area is also being spruced up with brick sidewalks and gas lamps. **The Emporium** at 101 East Beverley St. stocks nice pottery, baskets, windsocks, unusual birdhouses, silk flowers, stuffed animals and the like. Tommie Duke and Stephen Fitzpenn offer exceptional garden furniture, accessories and antiques with a New Orleans accent in The Garden Room at **Duke and Fitzpenn Ltd.** Among a spurt of emerging galleries is **Co-Art,** a cooperative of about 40 artists. It joins the established **White Swan Gallery** and the **Avery Studio Gallery** of contemporary art. **Turtle Lane** is filled to the brim with appealing gifts. We liked the jewelry from exotic places at **Silver Linings. Honeysuckle Hill** offers antiques and collectibles. If you're into oriental rugs, one of the best selections on the East Coast is opposite the train station at **Victorian Rug Co.,** 9 Middlebrook Ave. Quite a sight is the old automobile showroom now housing **Bruce Elder Antique and Classic Automobiles;** it has an elevator to transport cars to all three floors.

The Virginia Made Shop at Exit 222 from I-81 is full of local items. If you'd like a peanut basket – with peanut soup, peanut butter and an assortment of peanuts –

this is the place. The Staunton-Augusta **Farmers' Market** is a Saturday fixture; all participants produce what they sell.

Side Trips. Don't miss the jaunt about eighteen miles south of Staunton to the hilly, rural Raphine area. Here, almost side by side along Route 606 west from I-84 Exit 205, are two must stops:

Buffalo Springs Herb Farm, Raphine Road, Raphine

Former florists from northern Virginia restored a 1793 brick and stone homestead and a big red barn beside a rushing creek, a grand space that lent itself to workshops, drying and demonstration areas and an exceptional shop. Don Haynie and Tom Hamlin offer herbal products, dried flowers and designs, garden books, herb plants in season, nature trails, an arbor garden and herbal happenings, from workshops to picnics to herbal lunches by reservation. Their 170-acre educational farm is so scenic that it's been a setting for weddings.

(540) 348-1083. Open April through mid-December, Wednesday-Saturday 10 to 5, also Sunday 1 to 5 except June-August.

Wade's Mill, 55 Kennedy-Wade's Mill Loop, Raphine.

This neat place is one of the few operating gristmills actually producing flour as a business in this country. The miller and his wife are Jim and Georgie Young, ex-Washington bureaucrats who bought the circa 1750 mill in 1991. Now Jim grinds a couple of thousand pounds of flour exclusively on mill stones each week. They also sell fresh breads and muffins in the fall, run cooking classes and occasional brunches in their renovated farmhouse, published a cookbook now in its second edition, and give tours and demonstrations in their mill, which is powered by a 21-foot water wheel fed by the nearby stream. Georgie's shop features local pottery and baskets, buckwheat pancake mixes and apple syrup, and a cook's corner with everything you need to cook and bake with flour.

(540) 348-1400 or (800) 290-1400. Open same hours as Buffalo Springs Herb Farm.

Extra-Special

Frontier Culture Museum, Route 250 at I-81 Exit 222, Staunton.

Curiously juxtaposed next to the interchange of two interstate highways, this outdoor, living-history museum opened in 1990 to interpret the American frontier. This is not the frontier of the Wild West, but rather of America's first frontier – the Shenandoah Valley. The state-owned tract has four reconstructed farmsteads, three of which are from European nations (England, Northern Ireland and Germany) that the pioneers left behind. They are authentic reconstructions of historical working farms from each country, and costumed interpreters demonstrate daily life to visitors. The fourth and largest farm is the American synthesis, reflecting the melding of European influences. You might see a carpenter making pegs for the German barn, a pig-calling contest at the English farm, rare Kerry cattle, wonderful fencing in different styles and even stray farm cats. This is a special place for the young and the young at heart. The contemporary visitor center and the sounds of interstate traffic are in marked contrast to the farmsteads from the 18th and 19th centuries.

(540) 332-7850. Open daily, 9 to 5, mid-March through November; 10 to 4, rest of year. Adults, $8.

Thomas Jefferson's Monticello lures visitors to Charlottesville.

Charlottesville, Va.

Jefferson's Lively Mountain Eden

History. Mountain vistas. A lively university town. Vineyards and wineries.

These are among the assets that draw visitors to Charlottesville, the Piedmont area favored by Thomas Jefferson. He built Monticello, his "little mountain" home, in the rolling countryside he later described as "the Eden of America." It overlooks the Blue Ridge Mountains, the town and the University of Virginia, which he founded.

Jefferson also persuaded his friend and fellow president, James Monroe, to build a home nearby. Another colleague, James Madison, lived two dozen miles to the north in Orange.

Jefferson's influence is everywhere obvious in the Charlottesville area. The University of Virginia that he designed is the region's major presence. Thousands of tourists are directed to Monticello from a large visitor information center at the foot of its access road. A dozen or more small wineries fulfill the hopes of Jefferson, a wine connoisseur and would-be grape grower.

The Blue Ridge Mountains to the west are a spectacular backdrop for a prosperous university town tugged between tradition and change. The visitor to Charlottesville detects few Southern accents, testimony to the influx of outsiders and their amalgamation into a sophisticated, academic culture. The city is rife with dining, lodging, shopping and cultural opportunities. The new Charlottesville Ice Park and a six-screen movie theater thrive at the edge of downtown.

Traditionalists lament some of the changes. They contend that Charlottesville (with a metropolitan population of 125,000) isn't the place it used to be. Rush-hour gridlock stalls traffic on the expressways, and shopping malls have sprung up on farmlands. But this is urban sprawl with a difference: highways and commerce co-exist with antebellum plantations and an amazing number of palatial new homes, each with sizable property and a view of the surrounding Blue Ridge.

Sir Bernard Ashley chose the Charlottesville area as the site for his third and largest country-house hotel. He was struck by the beauty and heritage of the town and countryside. "It's not just a modern, thrown-up town," he said. "It has heart."

Inn Spots

Clifton – The Country Inn, 1296 Clifton Inn Drive, Charlottesville 22901.

Superlatives and Clifton go hand-in-hand. But for a gracious plantation built by Thomas Mann Randolph, who married Thomas Jefferson's daughter Martha and was an early governor of Virginia, this luxurious inn is surprisingly unpretentious. A hilltop away from Monticello on a cliff astride the Rivanna River, it has fourteen spacious rooms and suites, each with wood-burning fireplace and private bath. The 45 acres of verdant grounds off Route 729 in rural Shadwell harbor a sunken croquet pitch, a hard-surface tennis court, a neat swimming pool with terraced waterfall and lots of loungers amid the landscaping, an outdoor spa heated year-round, a 26-acre private lake, walking trails and wildlife, plus a couple of resident sheep.

"We want the atmosphere to be relaxed and casual, yet elegant," said a spokesman for owner T. Mitchell Willey, the Alexandria attorney who bought Clifton in 1984 and turned it into one of our favorite inns anywhere. "We don't want to lose the quaint, Jeffersonian feeling."

That is not to say rustic. Clifton is anything but. The six guest rooms in the main house offer lots of space and border on the majestic. Among their various accoutrements are antique beds with canopies built into the high ceilings and draped at the corners, cedar closets and comfortable sitting areas or rooms. Our most recent stay was in the refurbished Rivanna Suite, which has a huge bathroom with one of inn's five new walk-in spray showers, a clawfoot tub and a plump settee, not to mention a fireplace beside the queen bed in the bedroom and a sitting room with a sofabed and window seat. Evening turndown service provided ice, Perrier and fresh towels. A sampling of fruit, coffee and the morning paper were delivered the next morning.

At another visit, our quarters in the cathedral-ceilinged carriage house involved an expansive living room with a fireplace and french windows on both sides opening to let the breeze flow through, plus a kingsize bed in a loft and a private hot tub outside the door. Two guest rooms on the lower floor of the carriage house also have full-length windows across the back. They and two large rooms fashioned from Randolph's old law office share a garden courtyard and a number of historic fixtures from the recently dismantled Meriwether Lewis home in Charlottesville. We've also stayed in one of the three suites in the secluded

Clifton occupies mansion built by Thomas Jefferson's son-in-law.

Livery. It came with a queensize bedroom, full bath with separate shower and a sunken sun room with sofabed and fireplace, and opened onto a patio and garden sloping toward the lake, shielded from view in summer by the woods all around.

Guests enjoy the run of the inn's sumptuous main floor. Here are a formal living room, a country library, a paneled dining room, a garden room and a rear dining porch, created by enclosing the old veranda, overlooking a new rear patio. Afternoon tea is put out in the garden room. At our latest visit, the copious spread teamed hot tea, herbed cranberry punch and lemonade with scones, rich chocolate cake and luscious canapés of goat cheese.

Breakfast is served on white linens and Villeroy & Boch china at five tables in the dining room or, our choice on a lovely summer morning, at individual tables on the rear dining veranda. A fruit smoothie (orange, pineapple and banana juice) and apple-bran muffins began one repast; a platter of fresh fruit and apple coffeecake the next. The main dish at a recent visit was spectacular: poached eggs on a toasted croissant topped with a sauce of potage lyonnaise, tomatoes and chèvre. "I made it up in my head last night," the sous chef said when we asked the ingredients.

That didn't particularly surprise us, given the quality of dinner the preceding evening. It began with potage paysanne with chive oil and crème fraîche and a salad of greens, stilton and fresh apples with walnut focaccia. A tart passionfruit ice, served in a brandy snifter, cleared the palate an exceptional breast of duck with mulberry demi-glace, basmati rice and a julienne of carrots and haricots verts. Dessert following such a superb feast was hardly an anti-climax: dark chocolate cognac pots de crème with shaved chocolate, fresh berries and whipped cream.

The prix-fixe dinner, with a choice of two entrées, is five courses on weekdays and six courses on weekends, when there is live music by a pianist. Dinner is open to the public by reservation.

At a recent visit, the innkeeper showed the new 10,000-bottle wine cellar with an African mahogany ceiling. Clifton, like a fine wine, improves with age.

(804) 971-1800 or (888) 971-1800. Fax (804) 971-7098. Seven rooms and seven suites with private baths. April to mid-November: doubles, $175 to $325; suites, $295 to $475. Rest of year: doubles, $150 to $275; suites, $250 to $395. Two-night minimum weekends. Children over 12. No smoking.
Prix-fixe, $70 on weekends, $60 midweek. Dinner nightly by reservation, 7:30.

Keswick Hall at Monticello, 701 Country Club Dr., Keswick 22947.

This 48-room country-house hotel, developed by Sir Bernard Ashley of Laura Ashley fame, was acquired in 1999 by Orient-Express Hotels. It's adjoins a private golf club and residential development on 600 acres of rolling countryside east of Charlottesville next to Shadwell, first owned by Thomas Jefferson's father.

The Ashley interests added a 40-room wing to the Italianate-style Villa Crawford, built in 1912 as a private residence within sight of Monticello. It overlooks the eighteen-hole golf course designed by Arnold Palmer, which includes an indoor/outdoor pool and spa facilities for hotel guests.

Although Keswick Hall is imposing to the point of being intimidating, we found the service solicitous and the amenities first-rate. Our third-floor Regency Room with its kingsize pewter bed was spacious and quite comfortable. One of eleven "studios," it ranked in price behind four suites and ahead of twenty-one state rooms and twelve house rooms. All are furnished in a mix of European antiques and appointments from the Laura Ashley collection, and no two are alike. Every decision down to the selection of dessert spoons awaited Sir Bernard's final approval. Most accommodations have king or queen beds, but a few have twins or doubles. Each has a different armoire, a writing desk and an old reproduction radio. A handful of bathrooms possess oversize jetted tubs with separate showers.

More showy are the public rooms: the Great Hall in which arriving guests are greeted by a butler, the comfortable Morning Room (a study in off-white), the elegant main Drawing Room, the Snooker Room with a billiards table and a beautiful fireplace, and the large Crawford Lounge at the foot of a majestic staircase. Downstairs is a boardroom with state-of-the-art audio-visual equipment and antique trains perched on a high shelf.

After a tour, we toddled down the path to the Keswick Club Pavilion for a swim in the pool, surrounded by beautiful terraces. Overnight guests are granted access to the pool, tennis courts, spa, sauna and steam rooms. Golf costs extra.

Meals are served in three serene dining rooms, dressed in light pastels with white tablecloths and striped and patterned upholstered chairs. Chef Rick Small, who was raised on a Virginia farm, has cooked for James Beard Foundation dinners in New York.

Dinner in the Ashley Room is prix-fixe, $58 for four courses. (A six-course dégustation menu is available for $70, or $99 with wines.) One of us sampled the salmon argenteuil with asparagus and a sauce of roma tomatoes and basil, a foie gras terrine with black pepper brioche and artichoke salad, and grilled turbot on an exquisite sauce with broccoli. Dessert was pear sorbet served with wafer-thin crystallized slices of pear. The other enjoyed the bouillabaisse terrine in aspic, a potato and vegetable mille-feuille, braised monkfish and shrimp with salsa and baby bok choy, and a stellar iced lemon soufflé with berries. A pink champagne sorbet was served between courses. Coffee and mignardises followed.

Keswick Hall (left) overlooks Keswick Club and golf course.

Breakfast the next morning was another culinary treat. It began with unlimited fresh orange juice and an iced pineapple surprise that was like a sorbet. A basket of croissants, blueberry muffins and Virginia ham biscuits preceded the main dishes, a tomato and sausage frittata with hash browns and a platter of fresh fruits with fruit compotes. We'd return anytime to partake of the English mixed grill with eggs, tomatoes, blood sausage, mushrooms and the like.

The Palmer Room at the Keswick Club offers lunch and casual dining for hotel guests. Light meals are served seasonally outside the Pool Pavilion.

(804) 979-3440 or (800) 274-5391. Fax (804) 977-4171. Forty-four rooms and four suites. Doubles, $215 to $475. Suites, $375 to $575.

Prix-fixe, $58. Dinner nightly, 6:30 to 9:30. Sunday brunch, 11:30 to 2. No smoking.

The Inn at Monticello, 1188 Scottsville Road (Highway 20), Charlottesville 22902.

Nestled at the foot of Monticello Mountain on spacious dogwood-dotted lawns set back from quiet Route 20 is this small country manor house, ideally located near Charlottesville's main attractions. The house dates to 1850 but does not seem that old in its new incarnation. It was converted in 1989 into a comfortable, welcoming B&B and expanded in 1997 by new owners Norm and Becky Lindway, retired educators from Cleveland who were "not ready to retire."

The Lindways offer five air-conditioned guest rooms with private baths, each decorated in a different period with antiques and reproductions. Cotton sheets and down comforters are on every bed, now all king or queensize. Our quarters on the first floor, fashioned from the former dining room, had a high, step-up queensize bed and a private screened porch. Another favorite is the second-floor Victorian room with a carved walnut Eastlake bedstead and an antique mantel over the working fireplace. A loveseat slants across a corner. Guests in the other up-stairs front bedroom can look out to adjacent Willow Lake, a pond with catfish and snapping turtles, at the edge of the property. Another main-floor bedroom has an arched canopy queen bed.

Homemade chocolate-chip and oatmeal cookies, tea and other beverages are offered in the long, comfortable common room outfitted with Virginiana. Breakfast is served at a dining table beside the fireplace in the common room. The fare the day of our visit included orange juice, melon and strawberries, a frittata with peppers and mushroom, and diced potatoes flavored with rosemary. Praline french toast, Southwest chili cheese puff and a spinach and egg casserole are other offerings.

Unlike their predecessors, the Lindways are living on the property in an addition they built.

(804) 979-3593. Fax (804) 296-1344. Five rooms with private baths. Doubles, $110 to $145; 10 percent less in off-season. Two-night minimum weekends. Children over 12. No smoking.

200 South Street, 200 South St., Charlottesville 22901.

Two side-by-side houses at the edge of downtown were a shambles when a team of investors acquired them in 1986. After $1.5 million worth of renovations and at least that much in antique furnishings, they were opened as a suave in-town B&B in the Charleston and Savannah idiom. Most downtown restaurants are within walking distance.

Seventeen rooms and three suites are handsomely outfitted with 18th- and 19th-century antiques from England and Belgium. Most have queensize canopy or four-poster beds and sitting areas, and a few add fireplaces and whirlpool baths.

At our visit, a scrapbook in each room detailed the furnishings, most of which were for sale. In our first-floor front room, we were informed about the Georgian mahogany armoire circa 1800, the mahogany bow front chest of drawers (1815 and apparently having been sold, the more ornate replacement not being described), and eight other prized pieces, down to the Seljuk rug and brass candlesticks on the mantel. A clock radio and a telephone equipped with modem were concessions to the times, and a TV set was available beneath the eaves in a small third-floor lounge (more than half the rooms now have TVs). The room was extra-comfortable and, given its proximity to the street, surprisingly quiet.

Afternoon tea as well as wine and cheese are set out in the main inn's library, chock full of local reading material. The library also has three scrapbooks portraying the inn's restoration plus more descriptions of all the antiques in living color. A buffet breakfast is served here and on the side veranda and a tranquil terrace courtyard. On a warm morning on the veranda, we were blessed with a breeze along with fresh orange juice, cantaloupe and cut-up fruit, cereal, molasses muffins, scones and blueberry cake.

Brendan Clancy, one of the early investors, and his wife Jenny bought out their early partners to "run the inn the way we wanted it." They have upgraded the furnishings and switched four rooms with twin beds to kingsize. They converted part of a second-floor suite into an extra sitting room with a fireplace for guests. In 2000, they purchased the former Memory & Co./Corbett's Bistro restaurant building across the street and planned to convert it into their family's residence. They wanted to be closer to the inn and be more of a presence.

(804) 979-0200 or (800) 964-7008. Fax (804) 979-4403. Seventeen rooms and two suites with private baths. Doubles, $115 to $200. Suites, $210 and $220. No smoking.

The 1817 Historic Bed & Breakfast, 1211 West Main St., Charlottesville 22903.

Owner Candace DeLoach is an antiques dealer, and all the furnishings in the B&B beside her DeLoach Antiques Shop are for sale. The two adjoining townhouses were built by one of Thomas Jefferson's master craftsmen, an Irishman who was the principal carpenter for Monticello and for the Rotunda at the University of Virginia, a few blocks away.

A Georgian who formerly was an interior designer in New York, Candace has imbued her B&B with a spirit as eclectic as the decor. The living room is appointed with American Empire chests, Venetian tables, Biedermeier chairs, a large zebra-skin rug and a bowl of M&Ms.

Upstairs are four bedrooms with private baths. Rooms vary widely and décor changes as furnishings are sold. One room in the interior has no windows whatsoever (it's air-conditioned, our guide pointed out). Miss Olive's Room in the rear has a kingsize poster bed, a sitting area and a marble bathroom with shower. The Mattie Carrington Suite in front has a kingsize four-poster in the bedroom and a queensize mahogany bed in the purple parlor with French antiques and a glass chandelier. That room can be rented instead as part of the more formal James Dinsmore Suite in the adjacent townhouse, which comes with a study with a sofabed and a queensize pencil-post bed in the bedroom.

All quarters have TVs, and the three largest also have telephones. The other two have double beds, one an antique rope four-poster.

A continental breakfast includes fresh fruit, granola, and homemade muffins and breads. In the afternoon, tea is available to guests and the public on the sun porch. Half a dozen savories and sweets are offered from 1 to 4 for $12.

(804) 979-7353 or (800) 730-7443. Fax (804) 979-7209. Three rooms and two suites with private baths. Doubles, $89 to $159. Suites, $189 to $199. Children accepted.

The Inn at Court Square, 410 East Jefferson St., Charlottesville 22901.

After a year's renovations, the oldest house in downtown Charlottesville reopened in 2000 as the city's newest B&B. Candace DeLoach, an antiques dealer and interior designer who caught the innkeeping bug at her 1817 Historic Bed & Breakfast out West Main Street, offers five elegant guest rooms, a handsome living room and a dining room that's open to the public for upscale lunches.

The house, dating to 1785, had been converted to offices across Court Square from the Courthouse. Candace converted it back to its residential look and named the guest quarters for people associated with the house.

Overlooking the park in front are two beautiful second-story rooms with working fireplaces. The Stonewall Jackson facing its namesake's statue has a gilded ebony kingsize four-poster bed, sitting area and whirlpool tub. The Edward Butler, named for the original owner who built the house, has a kingsize mahogany four-poster bed and an enormous bathroom with an oval whirlpool tub for two, a separate glassed-in shower and an antique vanity with a marble sink. The beds in these and two other second-floor rooms have beds so high that steps are provided.

On the main floor is a guest room with a lower antique queensize French Empire bed and a bathroom with a two-person, hand-held shower. It adjoins a fireplaced library "that I painted myself to look like mahogany," Candace advised. It serves as an extra common room on weekdays and is rented with the bedroom as a suite ($219) on weekends. There's also a spacious living room for a common area.

Silver Thatch Inn is known for fine dining and lodging.

Besides her hands-on restoration work, Candace transported by rental truck a number of antiques and reproductions she acquired in Savannah, Ga., where she grew up. The furnishings here, as at the 1817 House, are for sale.

A continental-plus breakfast of homemade muffins and scones, muesli and yogurt is offered in the dining room. At midday, the twenty-seat dining room is open to the public for lunch with a beer and wine license. Candace's chef offers a seasonally changing menu of soups, fancy sandwiches (perhaps sliced pork loin or chicken and pesto) and salads (dilled shrimp was an early winner) in the $8 range. Based on her lunch experience, Candace planned to offer afternoon tea in the style of her 1817 B&B.

(804) 295-2800. Five rooms with private baths. Doubles, $149 to $259. Lunch, Monday-Friday 11 to 2.

Silver Thatch Inn, 3001 Hollymead Drive, Charlottesville 22911.

A New England look and air pervade this rambling white clapboard house, built by Hessian soldiers who were imprisoned on the site during the Revolutionary War. The original 1780 log house now is a small common room. Later owners expanded so that the inn backing up to a residential subdivision has seven guest rooms with private baths, a cozy bar and three dining rooms (see Dining Spots).

New innkeepers Terri and Jim Petrovits moved here from Southern California after a lengthy inn search. They added more queen and kingsize beds and totally redid a couple of rooms in the guest cottage. Watermelon stenciling, wooden slices of watermelon and a watermelon wreath grace the bright and airy James Madison Room, a Federal period room upstairs in the main house with pencil-post queensize canopy bed, working fireplace and square bathtub. A brick patio and a sitting area are available for guests who stay in the four rooms in the adjacent cottage. The burled wood armoire in the George Washington Room is so tall that the ceiling had to be cut back for it to fit. Less formal is the Tyler Room with country pine furniture, deep mulberry walls, an old quilt and a fireplace. The upstairs Harrison Room has been redone with new furnishings and a queen bed.

Coconut-granola-honey or chocolate-chip cookies are placed at bedside at night. Breakfast in a cheery sunroom is continental-plus, from melons, berries and home-made breads and muffins to cereals and what our informant described as the best granola ever.

Guests have access to a large pool at the adjacent Hollymead neighborhood association.

(804) 978-4686 or (800) 261-0720. Fax (804) 973-6156. Seven rooms with private baths. April-December: doubles, $140 to $175 weekends, $125 to $140 midweek. Rest of year: doubles, $130 to $160 weekends, $115 to $130 midweek. Two-night minimum weekends in spring and fall. Children over 8. No smoking.

The Foxfield Inn, 2280 Garth Road, Charlottesville 22901.

Built in 1951 as a single-story residence, this elegant country home set back on three acres of shaded lawns has been restored into a stylish B&B. it offers five modern, comfortable guest rooms and a quiet setting in the rolling and posh residential countryside northwest of Charlottesville.

Mary Pat and John Hulburt renovated the house, which had been empty for a dozen years, with the idea of opening a B&B, all air-conditioned and on one floor. They hired a contractor to build additions on both sides of the original house, one wing as guest quarters and the other as innkeeper quarters. Common rooms are in the middle. John, a woodworker, made most of the kitchen and bathroom cabinets as well as the four-poster beds, while Mary Pat painted every inch of the house.

The four premier rooms come with queensize poster or canopy beds, sofabeds, jacuzzi baths and separate showers, remote-control fireplaces and bay windows. They are crisply decorated in traditional Colonial style with painted walls and artworks. Most have hardwood floors with scatter rugs. Bay windows let in light, especially in the airy Garden Room, which has ready access to an outside porch. The Hunt Country Room takes on a foxhunting theme with deep green colors and a hooked rug. John Audubon prints accent the Audubon Room, whose guests watch bluebirds and yellow finches at feeders outside the windows. The Dogwood, the smallest room, has a queensize cherry bed and an original bathroom. Hair dryers and clothing irons are among the room amenities.

Guests enjoy the living room with piano, a sunroom with TV, porch, coffee bar and, outside, two patios, a lily pond with waterfall, and a new eight-person whirlpool spa. Gourmet coffee is prepared mornings in the coffee bar, where homemade cookies, fresh fruits, tea, hot chocolate and popcorn are available all day and the guest refrigerator is stocked with bottled water.

A full country breakfast is served by the fireplace in the dining room or on the patio. Eggs benedict, omelets, french toast and pecan pancakes are among the offerings.

(804) 923-8892. Fax (804) 923-0963. Five rooms with private baths. Doubles, $125 to $160. Children over 14. No smoking.

The Inn at Sugar Hollow Farm, Sugar Hollow Road, Box 5705, Charlottesville 22905.

Thirteen miles west of Charlottesville at the back of beyond is this sophisticated rural retreat. It's part of a 70-acre farm well past the hamlet of White Hall, at the edge of the Shenandoah National Park. Dick and Hayden Cabell built their hand-some, contemporary clapboard house with the idea of sharing it with B&B guests.

The Cabells provide a number of comfortable common areas. On the main floor are a family room with a stone fireplace, a library with TV set, a cheerful sunroom and a living room with a large palladian window. There's a reading nook off the upper foyer leading to the second-floor deck. Tea and other beverages from the butler's pantry may be taken to the nook or outside, where a passing stream is within earshot. Birds and butterflies thrive in the organic fruit, vegetable and flower gardens around the property.

A stairway with a teddybear on every step leads to five bedrooms with private baths, light-colored walls, plump beds, quilts and cheery fabrics. Handpainted wall designs add interest. The Wildflower master suite comes with a fireplace, a double jacuzzi and a kingsize four-poster bed with a canopy of white organdy. A window seat is in front of a bay window with panoramic views of the Blue Ridge Mountain. A kingsize rice poster bed, fireplace, double jacuzzi, a sofa and accents of Battenburg lace are attributes of the Country Manor Room. Barnwood paneled walls warm the Woodland Room, with queen bed, fireplace and handpainted flowers. The Hunt Country Room has a queen bed and fireplace, while the traditional Colonial Room furnished in cherry has extra-long twin beds.

Wild turkeys and deer may wander across the pasture during breakfast, served at a long table for eight beside a large bay window in the dining room. Egg dishes, cinnamon french toast or buttermilk pancakes may be the main dish. Fresh fruits, juices, homemade muffins and biscuits accompany.

"After searching for just the right setting for our inn," said Dick, "we finally found our corner of paradise in Sugar Hollow." Some might find it a mixed blessing, in that the nearest place for dinner is a dozen roundabout miles away. The Cabells compensate by offering family-style diners to guests by reservation ($25 per person) on Saturday nights.

(804) 823-7086. Fax (804) 823-2002. Five rooms with private baths. Doubles, $95 to $160. Two-night weekend minimum. Children over 12. No smoking.

Dining Spots

Metropolitain, 214 West Water St., Charlottesville.

Tops on most lists of local dining favorites is this establishment that moved in 1997 from its former downtown diner quarters into fancy mod digs in a onetime hardware store a couple of blocks away. The decor is minimalist in pale yellow and black, with high ceiling, well-spaced tables and black banquettes.

Great food emanates from the open grill and deep fryer installed owners Vincent Derquenne, a young Frenchman, and partner Tim Burgess. They have expanded their choice wine cellar, adding a reserve list. They also offer a six-course tasting menu, available for the entire table at $42 each.

Good sliced bread, a plain salad of Boston lettuce with a mustardy vinaigrette and a simple muscadet from a wide-ranging wine list were mere preambles to the triumphs that were ahead the night we dined. Among entrées, a paillard of plate-cooked (and barely cooked) salmon with basil puree, diced tomatoes and shoestring vegetables was a masterpiece, magnificently presented on an oversize plate speckled with parsley flakes. Equally presented was the grilled pork loin with spring onion puree, absolutely delicious fried cilantro wontons and cabbage slaw, the dish so ample that even two of us could not finish.

We had to save room for dessert. Good thing, because the champagne granité with fresh citrus and mint goes down as one of the most refreshing finales we've had. A close runner-up was the grilled banana bread with homemade honey vanilla ice cream and warm praline sauce. The descriptions hardly do justice to the presentations, again on oversize plates – one with a rainbow of strawberries, peaches and grapefruit; the other surrounded by squiggles of caramel and powdered sugar.

The two young innovators are equally at home with starters. How could one choose among wild mushroom bisque with fried leeks, seared venison carpaccio with red shiso and blackberry vinaigrette, duck quesadilla with adzuki bean salsa and chipotle cream, and gâteau of portobellos with grits and fried leeks?

Every menu gets more interesting, and dinner has become such a success that weekday lunches have been terminated.

Lunch and more casual dinners continue at **Bizou,** the owners' high-style diner restaurant in the deco space at 119 West Main St. where we first knew the Metropolitain.

(804) 977-1043. Entrées, $19.95 to $27.50. Dinner nightly, 5:30 to 9:30 or 10.

OXO Restaurant, 215 West Water St., Charlottesville.

A former chef from Keswick Hall, John Haywood from Great Britain, and his wife, Alice Kim, opened their own restaurant in 1999 in downtown Charlottesville. It's across the street from Metropolitain, with which it has been compared for fine dining.

The couple wanted a short name and christened it Oxo for a maker of bouillon cubes in England. Their renovated, 65-seat dining room is chic and contemporary, with plush couches and seating, oversize pillows – "like a sultan's den," in Alice's words. Lighting is by candles and a 300-pound crystal chandelier from Europe.

The contemporary menu is as exotic as can be. Consider a sweet potato and smoked bacon soup with sweet potato chips and a drizzle of blueberry coulis. Other winter starters range from spinach and gruyère cheese baked in puff pastry with pickled shiitake mushrooms and a truffle-brown butter vinaigrette to foie gras with yorkshire pudding, crispy sweetbreads, and sage and onion gravy.

A sorbet clears the palate for main courses, perhaps pan-seared grouper with shrimp-lemongrass emulsion and steamed bok choy or oven-roasted rockfish with lobster pommes puree, roasted salsify and truffled cabbage coulis. The grilled angus beef tenderloin comes with a mushroom duxelle and foie gras jus; the grilled veal loin with ratatouille marmalade and grain mustard jus.

(804) 977-8111. Entrées, $21 to $25. Dinner nightly, 5:30 to 9:30 or 10, Sunday to 9.

Ivy Inn, 2244 Old Ivy Road, Charlottesville.

A new chef-owner and his wife updated this landmark traditionally favored by sedate types on the outskirts of town. Angelo Vangelopoulos, an American whose father was born in Greece, and his wife Farrell brightened up the interior of the lovely old red brick dwelling built around 1800. In partnership with his parents, who were in the restaurant business in Washington, D.C., they added oriental carpets and more gold and ivory tones to the small and intimate dining rooms upstairs and down. They seat 90 diners on two floors, plus 30 more on a canopied patio.

Angelo's modern American fare appeals to the sophisticated tastes of a younger clientele. Trained in classical French style with northern Italian overtones, he features local product on a dinner menu that changes nightly.

A typical autumn night offered a dozen entrées. Among them were grilled local mountain trout with smoked bacon and pecans, grilled swordfish with rock shrimp and toasted pumpkin seed sauce, Virginia crab cake with red bell pepper sauce, local venison with dried cherry sauce, fricassee of rabbit with chanterelles in pommery cream, and a trio of local lamb.

Starters included a smoky three-bean soup with grilled rabbit sausage, marinated shrimp with cheese grits and creole tomato sauce, and a smoked salmon and potato napoleon with horseradish cream.

Among desserts were chocolate-macadamia decadence cake, warm apple crisp with homemade cinnamon ice cream, chocolate bourbon fudge cake with wild turkey crème anglaise, and profiteroles with cappuccino-kahlua ice cream.

The wine list is as select as the rest of the menu, with the preponderance of offerings priced in the high teens and twenties. Six local vineyards are included. *(804) 977-1222. Entrées, $16 to $24. Dinner nightly, 5 to 10. Sunday brunch, 11 to 2.*

Duner's, Route 250, Ivy.

From the outside it looks like a roadhouse, but locals as well as itinerant chefs on their nights off pack the place for some of the area's most inventive fare. Beyond a main room with booths and tables overshadowed by a brass canopy-topped bar lies a porch, dressed up with brick walls, patterned wallpaper above wainscoting and white-clothed tables with oil lamps and flowers in bud vases.

The water comes in beer mugs. The noise level is high, and so is the lighting. No matter. The food is good to excellent, especially the dozen or more nightly specials that supplement a fairly pedestrian menu. For starters, how about grilled duck and spinach salad tossed with pinenuts and a peach-cherry dressing or poached calamari in coconut milk and Moroccan spices? The latter dish came spiced with lots of coriander and a soupy broth that was great for dipping the accompanying monkey bread.

Among entrées, we felt the somewhat dry crab cakes cried out for a sauce. "No sauce," the waitress advised. "Needs sauce," we insisted. The kitchen obliged with an interesting chili tartar sauce. The veal sweetbreads with shiitake mushrooms and cream sauce were heavenly, though a minimal portion. A zesty salad with Greek olives and red onions accompanied. One of us wanted to splurge for the night's "entrée salad" of Louisiana oysters with greens tossed in caesar dressing for an extra $12.95. Ginger pound cake with local mulberries, strawberries and raspberries and a peach and pistachio crumb tart were satisfying endings.

A local Montdomaine chardonnay was a good choice from an extensive wine list, which contained a front page of specials under $20. A restaurant since the 1950s, Duner's was named for a former owner, a Turk whose wife bought it for him as a toy. It was about to close in the late 1980s, when manager Robert Caldwell took over and saved the day. "It's a crazy place," our waitress acknowledged, "but a lot of good chefs have come through here."

(804) 293-8352. Entrées, $13.95 to $19.95. Dinner nightly, 5 to 10. Sunday brunch, 10 to 3.

Silver Thatch Inn, 3001 Hollymead Drive, Charlottesville.

The inn's highly regarded restaurant has been enhanced under the auspices of new innkeepers Jim and Terri Petrovits. Jim, a former Los Angeles lawyer, went to culinary school and worked a year with celebrity chef Wolfgang Puck in preparation for a career change. Here, he oversees the menu and spends a little time as a line cook, but leaves the heavy-duty cooking to new chef Pierce McCleskey. Terri is the pastry chef, preparing the desserts as well as baking the inn's breads and muffins and making the chocolates that accompany the dinner checks. "Everything's now prepared on premises," Jim notes.

The two-level main dining room is pretty and pristine with huge spindle-back windsor chairs at well-spaced tables draped in white linens. A quilt spreads across one wall, baskets hang from an old ladder, and Villeroy & Boch china graces the tables. Windows look onto lawns and gardens. A smaller English dining room is pretty in green and rust, and diners in the lower sun room almost feel they're outside.

The complex dinner fare changes seasonally. Typical main courses are lacquered salmon with five-herb butter, a classic cioppino, free-range veal osso buco, and grilled rack of lamb with toasted pecan pesto and rosemary jus.

Appetizers intrigue, perhaps Thai steamed mussels, grilled quail with a white cheddar grit cake and oven-dried tomato compote, and grilled venison and blueberry sausage with a dried cherry-fig compote. Desserts follow suit: toasted coconut key lime tart in a macadamia nut crust, dark chocolate almond torte with raspberry sorbet, and a terrine of dense chocolate brownies and vanilla bean ice cream.

The wine list, honored by Wine Spectator magazine, features Virginia wines. Guests like to pause before or after dinner in the dark and comfy bar.

(804) 978-4686 or (800) 261-0720. Entrées, $18 to $28. Dinner, Tuesday-Saturday 5:30 to 9. No smoking.

C&O Restaurant, 515 East Water St., Charlottesville.

"The least prepossessing fine restaurant in America," the Washington Post calls it. A Travel-Holiday writer considers it the homeliest and "best restaurant in America." National food writers wax rhapsodic about the food, if not the atmosphere.

The local consensus seems to be that the C&O is resting on its laurels, however. Certainly our experience in the smoke-filled downstairs Bistro did not measure up, nor did that of fellow inn guests who termed their meal inedible. Another countered that her dinner was one of the best she'd had, a claim echoed by others at our most recent visit.

The contradictions emanate from a small brick building – identified by an old-fashioned Pepsi sign – across from the old Chesapeake & Ohio Railroad station. Upstairs is high-style, no-smoking dining area for 30 patrons in a simple room with high windows, pale yellow walls, high-back chairs and little to distract from the food. The traditional formal menu upstairs was discarded in 1997, and the bistro fare was upgraded and available upstairs and down.

Downstairs is a dark, noisy and claustrophobic little bistro with a long bar where smokers seem to gather. The bar is cheek to jowl with nine white-linened tables for two amid brick and barnwood walls, considerable bric-a-brac and illumination from three wagon-wheel chandeliers with every other light bulb off.

Our bistro dinner began with generous drinks and a decent artichoke pâté with good French bread. Disappointment set in with the wine list, an exorbitantly expensive affair starting in the high $20s and with many in the hundreds. We liked the steak chinois (flank steak) sliced with tamari and ginger cream sauce, but found the chicken breast with eggplant-avocado salsa bland beyond redemption. The small plates were overcrowded with new potatoes, tomatoes, carrots and onions. We passed up dessert, but heard that the crème caramel was perfect.

The offerings change nightly. Expect appetizers like Thai crab cake with peanut sauce and veal sweetbreads in marsala cream over sliced prosciutto. Main courses range widely from salmon fillet baked in a grape leaf with sundried tomato tapenade to flank steak chinois with tamari-ginger cream sauce. Desserts run to coupe maison, seasonal sorbets and baba au rhum.

(804) 971-7044. Entrées, $13.50 to $22. Lunch, Monday-Friday 11:30 to 3. Dinner nightly, 5:30 to 10 or 11.

Tastings, Market and Fifth Streets, Charlottesville.

This American grill and wine bar is an adjunct to a wine shop in the Downtown Parking Garage. It claims to be the first such combination of its kind on the East Coast, and boasts a wine list as big as its shop. The changing menu features items from a wood grill.

Dinner might include such treats as the chef's secret crabmeat casserole, available as an appetizer or as an entrée. Grilled salmon with béarnaise sauce, roasted tawny duck with spicy orange glaze and herb-crusted rack of lamb were among recent possibilities. Desserts could be caramel apple tart, Vermont maple cream flan and chocolate mousse with sundried cherries. Or you could order a late-harvest riesling or port for what Tastings calls "dessert in a glass."

Meals are taken in an informal room at tables made from the tops of wine crates, or at stools at a bar for six in the wine shop. A real plus is that the entire 1,000-bottle inventory is available for a $5 corkage fee, meaning splurgers can sample a $40 burgundy for a bargain $45. More than 100 wines are available by the glass or half-glass, some as part of a sampling of three.

(804) 293-3663. Entrées, $15.95 to $19.95. Lunch, Monday-Friday 11:30 to 2:30. Dinner, Tuesday-Saturday 6 to 10. No smoking.

Extra-Special

Historic Michie Tavern, Route 53, Charlottesville.

Southern cooking is featured in the 200-year-old converted log slave house called The Ordinary beneath one of Virginia's oldest homesteads.

And it's like no ordinary "Southern" cooking. That is, it's – dare we say? – tasty and not cooked to smithereens. Food with a bit of a kick is how we'd describe it. You stand in a cafeteria line, help yourself to the buffet, and sit at communal tables in the old log-walled tavern or at picnic tables in an enclosed garden courtyard. You may have a bigger meal than you want at midday, for a hefty price tag, plus $1 each for beverage and dessert.

Our fried chicken was moist and tender, the black-eyed peas and coleslaw fine, the stewed tomatoes interesting and the green beans had a nice herbed flavor. Good biscuits and cornbread came with, and the apple cobbler was far better than institutional fare. Ice water and a half bottle of Autumn Hill chardonnay were served in tin cups. Waitresses in Colonial costume refilled plates with items of the diner's choice.

Before or after, you can tour the tavern-museum, which has a large collection of pre-Revolutionary furniture and artifacts. The Meadow Run Grist Mill, a

Historic Michie Tavern houses a museum and a restaurant featuring Southern cooking.

separate building down a steep hill, contains the good **General Store** and the small **Virginia Wine Museum.**

(804) 977-1234. Buffet, $9.95. Lunch daily, 11:15 to 3:30, April-October, 11 to 3, rest of year. Museum and store, daily 9 to 5.

Diversions

The Monticello Visitors Center is located off I-64 at Exit 121 along Route 20 south, near the entry road to Monticello. It houses one of the larger local information centers we've seen, plus the Thomas Jefferson at Monticello Exhibition and a museum shop. The center offers a discounted combination ticket for tours of Monticello, Ash Lawn-Highland and Historic Michie Tavern Museum.

Monticello, Route 53, Charlottesville.

Starting in 1768, Thomas Jefferson designed and built his showplace hilltop home over 40 years, transforming his "essay on architecture" into an amalgam of Italian villas, Rome's Pantheon and a townhouse he observed in Paris while he was there as U.S. ambassador. Now as then, it is the area's chief attraction, having been saved by a private foundation in 1924. It draws more than 550,000 visitors a year who wait in line up to three hours for the privilege. Go early or late, and you may face only a twenty-minute wait, as we did, from the time you board a bus at the shuttle station until the lineup outside the rear of the house is shepherded inside, 25 at a time.

The 35-minute guided tour of the main floor is an unfolding revelation of Jefferson's inventive mind: a calendar clock in the entry "museum," automatic sliding doors, an upside-down mirror, a revolving bookstand, a contraption that made copies of everything he wrote, a rotating pole to hold clothes, and dumbwaiters for wine at either end of the fireplace in the dining room. Although ahead

Docent demonstrates spinning wheel at Ash Lawn-Highland.

of his time with skylights and such, his was a house better suited to a bachelor than a family, one of us thought. The tour ends somewhat abruptly outside. Visitors are left to troop on their own around lavish gardens and through the basement passageway past the kitchen to the household service dependencies built into the hillside.

We particularly liked the optional half-mile walk back down to the shuttle station, past flourishing vegetable gardens (said to include nineteen varieties of peas, Jefferson's favorite, all staked on branches and ready to pick at our mid-May visit). Pause at the family graveyard, where Jefferson's obelisk notes his fathering of the University of Virginia and his authorship of the Declaration of Independence and the Statute of Virginia for Religious Freedom, but makes no mention of his presidency. One family gravestone was as recent as 1988.

Back at the shuttle station, visit the **Thomas Jefferson Center for Historic Plants;** plants and seeds are available for purchase at a shop beneath a tent. The primitive **Little Mountain Luncheonette** serves a nice variety of sandwiches and salads. Top them off with Virginia apple cider.

(804) 984-9822. Open daily, March-October 8 to 5; rest of year, 9 to 4:30. Adults, $11.

Ash Lawn-Highland, 1000 James Monroe Parkway, Charlottesville.

The charming home of President James Monroe is dwarfed by its better-known neighbor, Monticello, whose gift shop is visible two miles away up a path from the front door. Thomas Jefferson persuaded Monroe to move to Highland to "create a society to our taste." Monroe's "cabin castle" is very different from Monticello, however. The squawks of resident peacocks could be heard (and their plumes seen) as our small group was led on a guided tour that was both more informative and more personal than the one at Monticello. This was a more lived-in and livable house than Jefferson's, and locals advise seeing it before Monticello, which they consider so novel and different. Monroe was forced to sell the house because of financial difficulties in 1826. It was bequeathed by one of its subsequent owners in 1974 to the College of William and Mary, which has just completed a major restoration. The tour ends when the guide turns you over to an "herb lady" for a five-minute talk on plants and herbs (we enjoyed her chat about nosegays). You can stay on to enjoy "lunch on the first lady's lawn." The **Kortright Cafe,** honoring Monroe's wife of 44 years, features foods from the Monroe table (from baked ham sandwich to a pâté plate), served with a cloth in a picnic basket to enjoy on the grounds.

(804) 293-9539. Open daily, March-October 9 to 6, rest of year 10 to 5. Adults, $8.

University of Virginia. Thomas Jefferson, who designed its buildings, planned the curriculum and was its guiding spirit as "a hobby of his old age," according to our guide, founded this prestigious university of 17,000 students in 1819. Its heart remains the "academical village" along the Lawn, focusing on the Rotunda – a design rated by the American Institute of Architects as the outstanding achievement in American architecture. Free hourly guided tours show visitors the finer points of the Rotunda, a masterpiece patterned after the Roman Pantheon. Our tour was led by a most informative graduate student in English. We peeked into some of the 52 rooms occupied by students as well as two-story faculty pavilions along the Lawn and overheard one guide telling prospective students that these fireplaced rooms are the most coveted housing for seniors who have distinguished themselves on campus, offering heat but no lavatories. Piped up one prospect's mother: It's an 'honor' to live in rooms without bathrooms?" Deadpanned the guide: "Yes, they have heat." Walk the magnificent campus, see Room 13 where Edgar Allan Poe resided (a raven is on his desk and there's a recorded commentary) and admire the gardens framed by serpentine walls throughout the academical village.

The Downtown Mall. Charlottesville's historic district, especially the Courthouse area and Market Street, surrounds its downtown pedestrian shopping mall. Main Street and its cross streets have been closed to vehicular traffic. The result is a pleasant, tree-shaded brick walkway interspersed with planters, benches, whimsical cutout figures, sidewalk cafes and frequent directory signs as in enclosed shopping malls. The downtown is struggling, having lost major stores to outlying malls. But specialty shops and restaurants have remained (or emerged), and this is one downtown that appears the place to be on a nice day. Good for browsing are such shops as **Palais Royal** (French linens for bed, bath and table), the outstanding **Signet Gallery, O'Suzannah** advertising "contemporary art and soul," and **The Cat House** boutique for cat lovers. Leather-maker **Charles Pinnell** produces alligator belts and English-style chaps for sale in his shop at 51 East Water St. At 218 West Water St., Ann Memory, who formerly ran the acclaimed Memory & Co. restaurant, makes new memories at her high-end kitchen shop called **The Seasonal Cook.**

More Shopping. College types gravitate to **The Corner,** an area of shops and restaurants centered along West Main Street between 14th Street and Elliewood Avenue. Upscale shops are concentrated at **Barracks Road Shopping Center,** where you'll find **Laura Ashley** and **Talbots** as well as such local prizes as the

Happy Cook kitchen shop, the extraordinary **Plow and Hearth** and **Nature by Design** stores, and the **Virginia Shop** with everything from Smithfield hams to Williamsburg candles. **HotCakes** is a nifty bakery, cafe and gourmet-to-go shop here.

If you love browsing through unusual grocery stores as much as one of us does, don't miss **Foods of all Nations** at 2121 Ivy Road. Everything Indian, Mexican and Indonesian, for example, is here. So is a huge selection of wines, takeout salads and sandwiches for picnics. If we lived in Charlottesville, we'd be here every week.

Wineries. Thomas Jefferson failed in his effort to cultivate grapes for wines at Monticello, but he would be proud of what has been accomplished in Virginia in recent years. Charlottesville bills itself as the winemaking capital of Virginia, claiming five wineries in Albemarle County and a dozen more in the surrounding area. The most picturesque is **Oakencroft Vineyard & Winery,** whose colorful red-barn winery occupies a stunning site between a farm pond and mountains in estate country just northwest of town. Owner Felicia Warburg Rogan started with a self-taught female winemaker, giving hers the distinction for nearly a decade as the only winery in America to be run by two women. Gabriele Rausse, described as "the sage of Virginia wines," is the legend behind **Jefferson Vineyards** (formerly Simeon Vineyards), just up the road from Monticello. You can sample quite a variety (from chardonnay to merlot to cabernet sauvignon, $16.95 to $26.95) in a tasting room with outdoor deck. Across the street is the affiliated **Brix Marketplace,** a country store where you can pick up sandwiches, salads, pastries and espresso for a picnic between Monticello and Ash Lawn.

Wines and view at Oakencroft Vineyard.

An unbelievably scenic, mountainous route leads to **Afton Mountain Vineyards** in nearby Afton. Former NBC News producer Tom Corpora and his Japanese wife, Shinko, produce stellar chardonnays, rieslings, cabernets and pinot noirs in the $10 to $17 range. Theirs is an unusual venture, combining state-of-the-art equipment with ancient technology – a gravity processing system and a unique, 100-foot-long wine storage cave. Their showroom offers wine tastings plus gourmet picnic foods that can be eaten in the second-floor luncheon room or on tables outside. We took home a $12 chardonnay to recapture the memories of a picturesque and true place.

Crowd gathers at Montpelier in Orange for annual Steeplechase races in November.

Orange County, Va.

On the Trail to Discovery

Few people outside central Virginia have heard of Orange County, much less been there.

Its county seat, Orange (population 2,700), is "still a sleepy little Southern town," in the words of a local restaurateur. Its landed gentry maintains a lower profile than that of its neighbors to the south in Albemarle County surrounding Charlottesville. "People come here from urban centers to escape to the country," says local booster Donna Bedwell. One writer even wrote a piece in a Charlottesville magazine about taking a country weekend respite from the stresses of Charlottesville in Orange, a mere twenty miles away.

But this dormant, unspoiled, scenic countryside that spawned presidents James Madison and Zachary Taylor is taking on a new role. A marketing effort has been launched to double the attendance at Montpelier, the lifelong home of James Madison, now undergoing a major restoration. With that increase will come an inevitable influx of tourism accompaniments along Route 20, the Constitution Trail (so named for the number of homes of presidents and governors along its path) that meanders through the heart of the county.

The horsey set of northern Virginia hunt country is moving toward Orange. The area is the center of the state's winemaking industry, Orange having more acres in grape production than any other Virginia county. B&Bs are emerging to supplement the more established inns. The area "is beginning to be discovered," says Suzie Blanchard, a former Chicagoan whose market research led her to this part of Virginia to establish the Inn at Meander Plantation.

Meanwhile, it retains the sense of history and unspoiled countryside of old Virginia, suspended in a time warp against the encroaching pincers of

Charlottesville to the south, Fredericksburg to the east and Washington to the north. The picturesque charms of the rolling Piedmont, the wineries, the emerging Montpelier, a couple of museums, the Civil War battlefields – all make an interesting destination for those who cherish peace and quiet.

Inn Spots

The Hidden Inn, 249 Caroline St., Orange 22960.

Hidden down a hillside beneath Route 15, this century-old Victorian inn offers tranquility on five wooded acres deeded from the forebears of Zachary Taylor. It also has some of the fanciest guest rooms around.

Ray Lonick, innkeeper with his wife Barbara and longtime mayor of Orange, greets guests with his own map and suggestions for touring and shows off his back yard containing "just about every tree that grows in Virginia."

The Lonicks – he an early-retired Xerox sales executive from New Jersey – acquired the inn in 1987 and totally redecorated, adding Barbara's samplers, her mother's quilts, family photos and their homemade bath salts and cinnamon soaps. They have added two deluxe suites in outbuildings and three guest rooms in an adjacent house.

Rooms now total ten, all with private baths and period furnishings and some with jacuzzi tubs and fireplaces.

Our expansive quarters in what was called the Verandah Room, upstairs and to the rear, included a queensize pencil-post bed with a fishnet canopy and ruffled pillows, a chaise lounge, an enormous bathroom with windows on two sides and, crowning touch, a private balcony with wicker furniture for viewing the back yard. Also special is the large upstairs room in the rear carriage house, dark and masculine with a rooftop balcony, jacuzzi, and paisley sheets and pillowcases matching the bathroom wallpaper.

A newer treat is the garden cottage, pink and flowery with a skylight in the ceiling, a queensize four-poster, TV, jacuzzi and rear deck.

The Lonicks offer candlelight picnics and bubble bath in the rooms of late-arriving guests on Fridays and for those on romantic getaway packages.

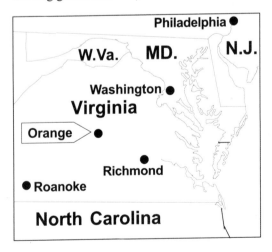

For breakfast, Ray handles the kitchen duties and Barbara serves. At our visit, he cooked french toast made with thick homemade bread and sausage following openers of peach-orange juice, cut-up grapefruit and carrot muffins. Orange-granola pancakes and cheese eggs with ham and biscuits are other favorites.

(540) 672-3625 or (800) 841-1253. Fax (540) 672-5029. Ten rooms with private baths. Doubles, $99 to $169. Two-night minimum on weekends. Children accepted. No smoking.

Dogwoods and azaleas provide springtime welcome to The Hidden Inn.

The Inn at Meander Plantation, James Madison Highway (Route 15), HCR 5, Box 460A, Locust Dale 22948.

"It's a real treat to be in a house where so many historical figures have tread the floors." So says Suzie Blanchard, co-innkeeper with her husband Bob of the Inn at Meander Plantation. They know. Their stately Colonial manor house with six pillars in front was built in 1766 by Henry Fry Sr., whose close friend, Thomas Jefferson, often stopped here on his way to and from Monticello. A print of the first official map of Virginia, as surveyed and drawn by the fathers of both Fry and Jefferson, hangs on their living room wall. And Robert E. Lee rested in the shade of a sycamore on Meander land while a blacksmith shod his horse and Confederate troops crossed the Robinson River en route to the Civil War Battle of Cedar Run.

Today, guests who stay at this inn can tread in the same footsteps. They are greeted in a reception room behind the pillared portico that's large enough to hold a grand piano. They gather in the sunken living room, long and comfortable, and on the rear porches of the L-shaped house. They stay in one of the four bedrooms, one of them a two-room suite. All have private baths and queensize four-poster beds and are elegantly furnished to the period with lacy pillows, down comforters, wing chairs, armoires and oriental rugs on the polished heart-pine floors.

The suite and a downstairs room both open onto the rear porches. The adjacent groom's cottage holds a sitting room with a sofabed, a queensize bed and a kitchenette. A former summer kitchen now holds a deluxe two-room suite with living room down and king bedroom above. Two dependencies with cathedral ceilings offer queensize beds and working fireplaces.

Guests also enjoy some fairly exotic meals whipped up by Suzie, a food writer for Pioneer Press newspapers in suburban Chicago. The former publisher there, Suzanne Thomas, shares innkeeping duties here with the Blanchards.

Breakfast, as delivered by these two articulate women, is a convivial affair in the formal dining room. You might start with fresh fruit (a seasonal favorite is sautéed orange slices and cranberries), a choice of juices and a spicy upside-down sausage cornbread. Next come scrambled eggs flavored with herbs from the garden and baked hash browns, Sour cream coffee cake, poppyseed bread or croissants might accompany. Others of Suzie's specialties include wild rice and walnut pancakes, spinach strata, crab or asparagus quiche and grits.

Dinner is offered by reservation for $37.50 a person. A typical meal might be spicy shrimp with homemade rémoulade sauce, crab bisque or cream of broccoli soup, a salad of baby greens with grilled portobello mushrooms, and a main course of grilled game hen with soy-pineapple marinade, accompanied by green beans with red pepper slices and garlic. Dessert could be a fresh strawberry tart. Virginia wines are available for purchase.

Adjourn to one of the white rockers on the expansive back porches to survey the scene. The 80-acre property contains formal boxwood gardens, a portion of the Robinson River and pastures for seventeen resident horses.

(540) 672-4912 or (800) 385-4936. Fax (540) 672-0405. Five rooms and three suites with private baths. Doubles, $115 to $140. Suites, $175 to $195. Children and pets accepted. No smoking.

Mayhurst Inn, off Route 15, Orange 22960.

This stunning white Italianate Victorian mansion built atop a hill in 1859 by Col. John Willis, great-nephew of President James Madison, looks like a wedding cake. The inside is tasty as well.

Undertaking two years of top-to-bottom renovations in 1996, new owners Peg and Bob Harmon from Colorado have endowed it with a true sense of style and seven comfortable guest accommodations with private baths. They also serve hearty breakfasts and Virginia wines and appetizers in the afternoon. Hundreds of visitors oohed and aahed over the Mayhurst restoration during the annual Orange County Holiday Tour in December 1997.

Former owners had abandoned the inn in the early 1990s. Part of a 1,700-acre plantation, it was the Northern Virginia army headquarters during the Civil War under Gen. A.P. Hill and was host to Stonewall Jackson and Robert E. Lee. "It's really something to think that three generals slept here," says vivacious Peg. The fanciful architecture includes a rare spiral staircase in an oval shape, ascending four stories to a rooftop gazebo.

The Harmons invested big bucks and employed Peg's eye for style in redoing the first five guest rooms and two suites, five with fireplaces and all with king or queen beds. She calls the prized Italian Suite "neo-Caesar in mode," decorated in black and cream with gold accents. It has a double jacuzzi of black granite in its sitting room, which also offers a fireplace and a rear balcony. The bright scarlet wallpaper in the king-bedded Madison Room wallpaper happens to be a reproduction of Dolley Madison's bed hangings. The rear Generals Room, furnished with antiques from the 1860s, is done in Confederate gray with gold touches. The ground level contains a Garden Room; done in a floral motif and with a bathroom that looks like a garden terrace with its slate floor, shower wall and vanity.

The Harmons offer a three-course breakfast in the 22-seat dining room on the ground level, handsome in blue and white with buff walls and antique German china. Bob's specialty is made-to-order omelets. Other favorites are creamy eggs with chives and apple-pecan french toast.

(540) 672-2243 or (888) 672-5597. Fax (540) 672-7447. Five rooms and two suites with private baths. Doubles, $130 to $169. Suites, $115 to $200. Two-night minimum peak weekends. No smoking.

White Italianate Victorian mansion housing Mayhurst Inn looks like a wedding cake.

Willow Grove Inn, 14079 Plantation Way, Orange 22960.

Perched on a hillside with 37 acres, this Federal and Classic Revival plantation home commands attention. You can see it as you approach along Route 15 from the south, and the number of cars in the parking lot attests to the popularity of its restaurant (see Dining Spots).

Like many houses of its size, Willow Grove had fallen on hard times when it was purchased in 1987 by Angela and Richard Mulloy to operate as a restaurant and inn. They're proud that the woodworking in the original 1778 portion was done by the artisans who crafted Montpelier, and that the brick portion was built in 1820 to Thomas Jefferson's design by workmen who had just finished his University of Virginia campus. The Mulloys are restoring the Victorian gardens and primping up the sloping lawns with their stately magnolias, English boxwood and the willows for which the place was named.

Three guest rooms and two suites on the second and third floors are named for Virginia presidents born along the Constitution Trail and decorated to the appropriate period. The corner Washington Room is an elegant space with six windows, double cherry poster bed with tester, sitting area and fireplace. It contrasts in style and price with the mid-18th-century Harrison Room tucked under the eaves. Here you'll find a double Jenny Lind bed, an antique washstand in the room and what Angela calls a sailboat's bathroom with a toilet beyond the step-through shower. The Taylor-Monroe Suite offers adjoining corner rooms, one with a 19th-century tiger maple poster bed and fireplace and a sitting room with a sofabed. The Wilson Suite has two bedrooms (one with a double brass and iron bed and the other with twin beds), a sitting room and a turn-of-the-century motif.

Five newer accommodations, all with whirlpool tubs and separate showers, are housed in antebellum outbuildings around the lovely property. The prized Weaver's Cottage offers a kingsize mahogany poster bed, a sitting room, fireplace and a private veranda. The Summer Kitchen, relocated from the Shenandoah Valley, has a kingsize brass and iron bed and a sitting area with antique wicker furniture. The

Butler's Quarters is an English country-style suite with kingsize mahogany sleigh bed and separate sitting room.

All rooms are handsomely furnished, contain beds with triple sheeting and down pillows, and possess such amenities as Saratoga water and a large basket of assorted toiletries, many of them Neutrogena.

A hearty breakfast of fresh fruit with scrambled eggs, frittatas or french toast is served in the front tavern room, full of hunting prints and atmosphere.

(540) 672-5982 or (800) 949-1778. Fax (540) 672-3674. Three rooms, two suites and five cottages with private baths. Doubles, $225 to $330 MAP. Cottages and suites, $275 to $330 MAP. Children welcome. Smoking restricted.

The Shadows, 14291 Constitution Hwy., Orange 22960.

"I target the child in every adult," says Barbara Loffredo, who goes so far as to put rubber duckies in the bathrooms so you can play in the tub. Ex-New Yorkers Barbara, a legal secretary, and husband Pat, once one of New York's Finest, fell in love with the area, bought the 1913 stone craftsman's cottage and opened in 1987 as a B&B. "Our debut was the Christmas tour," recalled Barbara, "and 320 people came through."

The house is up a long and winding drive through many trees (hence the name Shadows). The Loffredos have added lush cutting gardens of flowers and herbs to the side around a gazebo.

With Stickley furniture and a staircase that architects make a special trip to see, the downstairs common areas are charming. Lots of antiques and pieces the couple have collected decorate the four upstairs bedrooms, all with private baths. We like best the Rose Room, which has a huge private veranda overlooking the lawns and the Loffredos' goat, Nanny, grazing near the barn (guests feed her flowers and dog food to gain her affection). The Blue Room has a cedar-lined bathroom and a queensize walnut bed pre-dating the Civil War. The smaller Peach Room with a king bed of burled walnut is particularly pretty, and the Victoria Room is full of ruffles.

Also on the property are two outbuildings converted into sleeping quarters. The two-room Cottage has a separate sitting room with wicker furniture and its own deck. The Rocking Horse Cabin, also with two rooms and a porch, is all natural wood on the inside and decorated with country crafts. There's an array of rocking horses, and the horse motif extends from the cover on the kleenex box to the toilet lid. It has a queen bed and a new gas fireplace.

Pat is in charge of the wonderful breakfasts served on fine crystal and china: maybe a fruit course like poached pears in grand marnier cream or a big bowl of local strawberries. Stuffed french toast with cream cheese sauce and a dish of sautéed apples that comes out like a soufflé is a favorite. The ham, cheese and egg bake uses local eggs, their yolks so yellow they make the orange juice look pale, Pat says. Barbara calls his buttermilk biscuits the best around.

From refreshments like hot spiced cider or iced tea upon arrival to a homemade sachet when you leave, you'll be treated with TLC and a lot of mothering here.

(540) 672-5057. Four rooms and two cottages with private baths. Doubles, $80 to $95. Cottages, $100 and $110. Children over 10. No smoking.

Sleepy Hollow Farm, 16280 Blue Ridge Tpke. (Route 231), Gordonsville 22942.

Nestled in a hollow off Route 231, Orange County's prettiest byway, Sleepy

Main house at Sleepy Hollow Farm is surrounded by lawns, woods and pastures.

Hollow is a paradise of sorts. Beverley Allison, innkeeper with her daughter Dorsey Comer, moved to the house as a bride in 1950 and calls it "a poor man's Montpelier, a humble little frontier house in the midst of all the estates." Expanded over the years, the house is beautifully but comfortably furnished and has a lived-in feeling. It is surrounded by lawns, woods and pastures. In front is a farm pond beside a gazebo, a dock that says "swim at your own risk" and, at our visit, a bunch of ducklings scurrying after their mother.

Beverley, an ABC News journalist turned Episcopal missionary, calls hers an organic house that's still growing and evolving. The process continued with the conversion of a TV room into a sixth guest room with a queen bed, fireplace and jacuzzi and the enclosing of the adjoining terrace for a new TV room. The jacuzzi is "bowing to the trend," Beverley acknowledges, "even though this is a place for people not to lie in a bathtub but to go birding, to discover the wildlife, to smell the flowers."

Guests have plenty of space to spread out in a cozy living room, a beamed dining room and what used to be a country porch, now expanded into an enormous sun room with a showpiece dollhouse (Beverley provides a less precious one for the kiddies to play with). This is the setting for a breakfast of fruit compote, farm-fresh eggs (from Dorsey's chickens) or pancakes, and extra-good coffee because the water comes from a deep spring on the property.

Accommodations include a main-floor master bedroom with a queensize canopy four-poster, dressing room, full bath and a stunning handpainted chest from the Orient. Others are the downstairs Squire Room with a queen bed and a large bathroom with whirlpool tub overlooking the pond. Upstairs is a small bedroom known as the Ghost Room, though the ghost has not been seen since the house was blessed. What's called the children's suite has two bedrooms connected by a bath. Just outside is the Chestnut Wood Cottage made up of two suites: the kitchen house, which obviously has a kitchen, and the older and smaller slave house. Each has a deck, a fireplaced sitting room with a pullout sofa and a bedroom and bath upstairs. A recent two-story addition to the kitchen house made room for a larger bedroom upstairs and a whirlpool tub room below.

Baskets of fruit and Virginia peanuts are in the rooms. Beverley and Dorsey serve refreshments, from tea to local wine, upon guests' arrival.

(540) 832-5555 or (800) 215-4804. Fax (540) 832-2515. Three rooms and three suites with private baths. Doubles, $65 to $95. Suites, $105 to $150. Children welcome.

The Holladay House, 155 West Main St., Orange 22960.

This in-town, Federal-style brick house dating to 1830 offers six guest accommodations with private baths and, a treat for some, breakfast in your room. "My grandfather bought this place in 1899," says genial host Pete Holladay, "and some of the family have been here ever since." His father was raised in the house and, though Pete and wife Phebe had long talked of doing a B&B, it wasn't until 1989 when their kids were through college that they opened. He'd been in charge of food and housing services at private schools for 30 years, so considered this a logical move.

Pete prepares a full breakfast, heavy on fruits, fresh breads, perhaps scones with eggs or baked eggs with tomatoes and popovers, biscuits, peach puffs or apple muffins that were voted the best in Virginia by the state B&B association. He serves the meal in guests' rooms, anytime between 6 and noon, saying that's the way people want it. A lovely formal dining room is put into use if groups want to eat together.

Each bedroom is furnished with family pieces, including armoires, sleigh beds and four-posters, as well as a table and chairs for breakfast service. A ground-level suite contains a small sitting room, a large bedroom and a bath with a whirlpool tub and walk-in shower. It can be rented in conjunction with an existing ground-floor bedroom with kitchenette and bath.

The Holladays offer a recreation/game room on the ground floor. Guests also enjoy a side porch and two outdoor decks.

(540) 672-4893 or (800) 358-4422. Fax (540) 672-3028. Four rooms and two suites. Doubles, $95 to $135. Suites, $175 to $205. Children accepted. No smoking.

Rabbit Run B&B, 305 North High St., Box 535, Gordonsville 22942.

"We saw rabbits running around outside the house when we were looking to buy," said Virginia Hulvey. So Rabbit Run became the name of the B&B she operates with her daughter, Elizabeth Hupp. "We love rabbits. They're a sign of goodness and innocence."

Those traits also characterize this homey B&B in a 1880s farmhouse in a shady residential section at the edge of Gordonsville. "We don't have fancy antiques," advises Virginia. "Just family pieces."

They added private baths and closets for the three guest rooms, but otherwise a visit here is like coming home to a favorite aunt. The bedrooms are snug and warm, with quilts and country accessories. The nicest is a queen-bedded room in the rear. There's also a small single that shares a bath.

Guests enjoy a cozy TV/library and a larger living room on the main floor, as well as more than two acres of grounds.

A typical breakfast includes juices and fresh fruit, homemade bread and muffins, and eggs any way. "I make a mean omelet," says Virginia. Tea is offered in the afternoon.

(540) 832-2892 or (800) 791-9204. Fax (540) 832-0801. Three rooms with private baths. Doubles, $80. Children over 5. No smoking.

Pathways lead from main house to dependencies at Prospect Hill Plantation.

Prospect Hill Plantation Inn, 2887 Poindexter Road, Trevilians 23093.

Although often thought of in connection with Charlottesville, which is fifteen miles to the west, this renowned inn is closer to Orange, and is recommended by Orange innkeepers for its dining.

Out in the middle of nowhere, the place is idyllic: a thirteen-room country inn and restaurant (see Dining Spots) on a 40-acre wheat plantation dating to 1732. A stunning boxwood hedge lines the driveway leading to the handsome, pale yellow main house, the oldest continually occupied frame plantation manor in Virginia. Boxwoods also frame paths to the original dependencies, all transformed into deluxe lodgings tucked away in the trees. All but one room have fireplaces and eight have double jacuzzis. Afternoon tea, a fixed-price candlelight dinner and breakfast in bed are included in the tariff. A basket of fresh fruit, a box of raisins, homemade cookies and a half bottle of red wine are in each room.

The five guest rooms in the manor house vary in size from servant quarters to the Overton. The latter is dark, quiet and rich in blue with a high queensize four-poster bed, sitting area and a balcony overlooking the back lawn.

Most coveted are the eight suites in dependencies on either side of the manor house. They are cherished for their privacy as well as their comforts. The original summer kitchen is dark and historic and offers a double jacuzzi. The carriage house contains two expansive suites with sitting areas. The walls of the boys' cabin, oldest on the property (1699), are exposed logs, reminding one of us of summer camp long ago. Overlooking the inn's swimming pool, it has a large cedar bathroom (nothing like the shower houses of summer camp) and a double jacuzzi.

Twittering birds, bees and butterflies kept us amused on the afternoon deck of the Overseer's Cottage, which came with a sun porch/sitting room outfitted with wicker and an oriental carpet, a queen poster bed near the fireplace in the bed-room and a covered morning porch. It was here we learned that Prospect Hill is part of the Green Springs National Historic District, a pristine area of thirteen plantations, stores, chapel and other historic houses preserved as "a gently civilized countryside" – of which we felt a part, if only for an evening.

The next morning, our sun porch proved a delightful setting for a breakfast of exotic fruit, orange juice and french toast, strewn with raspberries and blueberries and garnished with pansies.

Founding innkeepers Bill and Mireille Sheehan, who converted the plantation into an inn in 1977, have turned day-to-day operations over to their son Michael, his wife Laura and caring managers.

(540) 967-0844 or (800) 277-0844. Fax (540) 967-0102. Five rooms and eight cottage suites. Doubles, $285 to $325, MAP. Suites, $330 to $365, MAP.

Dining Spots

Willow Grove Inn, 14079 Plantation Hwy., Orange.

The rural setting is tough to beat and the dining rooms are as luxurious as can be. The dining experience has its ups and downs, according to local reports, at what most concede is Orange's most ambitious food and lodging undertaking.

Dining is in three interior venues, plus a garden veranda in season. The Jefferson Library is a comfortable room dressed in white with different floral china at each table (as is the case throughout the inn). The larger and more formal Dolley Madison Room has a crystal chandelier, Queen Anne chairs and deep rose swags over the windows. The casual, ground-floor Clark's Tavern sports a bar of heartpine, hand-hewn beams and assorted antique china on the tables. Service was leisurely at lunch (no longer served), when we sampled a mesquite chicken salad and poached salmon with a cucumber salad. We also enjoyed the inn's specialty, Willow pie, a decadent concoction with chocolate chips, walnuts and bourbon in a puff pastry shell topped with real whipped cream.

The cuisine is regional American, and four-course meals upstairs are prix-fixe. Typical main courses are seared diver scallops with ratatouille, pan-seared duck breast with blackberry gastrique, and rack of lamb crusted with peanuts and pecans and served with fortified lamb jus.

Starters could be shrimp and corn chowder, oyster fritters with caviar, and crab étouffée with smoked tomato sauce and corn fritters. For dessert, how about orange-white chocolate mousse, dark chocolate cake with raspberries and chocolate ganache, or sweet almond and hazelnut crisp with vanilla ice cream?

Virtually the same menu is offered à la carte downstairs in the tavern. Dinner is available to house guests on weeknights. A vocalist and pianist entertain on weekend evenings. Live jazz is played at brunch.

(540) 832-2892 or (800) 949-1778. Prix-fixe, $48; tavern entrées, $17 to $26. Dinner, Thursday-Saturday from 6, Sunday from 4. Sunday brunch, 11 to 3.

Prospect Hill Plantation Inn, 2887 Poindexter Road, Trevilians.

Dining is an event at this plantation inn, so secluded that it feels it must offer dinner to house guests who have nowhere else to eat, but so special that it draws outsiders from Orange, Charlottesville and beyond.

Executive chef Michael Sheehan changes the menu for the set (no choice), five-course meal nightly. Guests are invited into the manor house half an hour before the appointed dinner hour to help themselves to complimentary wine and cider in the entry hall, relax by a fireplace in the parlor or stroll the grounds.

When the innkeeper rings the dinner bell, everyone is seated at a private table – in the front dining room, the Rose Room or the Conservatory. The innkeepers introduce themselves to the diners in each room, describe what they are about to be served, offer a grace and the meal begins.

Although we're partial to the Conservatory with its summery wrought-iron chairs and view onto the back lawns, we think each room is pretty as a picture. Tables are set with cut glass, fine china, heavy silver (including four forks) and a vase of alstroemeria. Michael has added contemporary and international accents to the inn's traditional French cooking that reflected his mother's background in Provence.

Our dinner began with an ethereal strudel of rabbit mousse with Asian pear slices over alfalfa sprouts, a warm hazelnut vinaigrette and beet relish. Watercress soup and a salad of baby greens with shaved red onions came next. The main course was seared veal tenderloin medallions with shiitake mushrooms, accompanied by a yucca root puree with smoked tomatillo and haricots verts. A lemon cloud mousse, presented in pastry cups with chilled blueberry coulis and fresh berries, was a refreshing ending to a memorable meal.

There's an excellent wine list. A nightly special offered at $20 a bottle, in our case a Côtes du Rhone, is perfectly adequate.

(540) 967-0844 or (800) 277-0844. Prix-fixe, $50. Dinner by reservation, Sunday-Thursday at 7, Friday and Saturday at 8.

Palladio Restaurant, Barboursville Vineyards, 17655 Winery Road, Barboursville.

Winemaker-manager Luca Paschina is a food and wine connoisseur, so you'd expect his dramatic new restaurant at the vineyard to be great. And it is, according to all reports – "world-class," exclaimed one innkeeper after her first dinner there. Advised Luca: "Palladio fulfills our dream of offering food and wine pairings on a permanent basis."

Ensconced in a brick building between his office and the Tuscan tasting room, the rustic yet elegant, 38-seat dining room is likened to being in a private country villa. Native Virginia chef John Marshall's fare is contemporary northern Italian. Meals are prix-fixe for both lunch and dinner, with suggested wines paired to go with. The menu changes weekly.

A typical weekend dinner menu ($48 for five courses, or $69 with wines) offers an exotic antipasti of prosciutto-wrapped grilled shrimp with gorgonzola, followed by a primo course of chilled sorrel soup or risotto with asparagus and mushrooms. The main course involves a choice among poached halibut in saffron broth, roasted quail stuffed with pancetta or an herb-crusted lamb chop with sausage-wrapped lamb loin. Dessert could be chocolate amaretto custard and panna cotta served with vanilla-scented berries. Espresso or cappuccino follow. The meal, served at a single seating, typically takes three hours.

Similarly extravagant lunches are available in three or four courses ($28 or $38), again paired with recommended wines.

(540) 832-7848. Prix-fixe, $48. Lunch, Wednesday-Sunday noon to 3. Dinner by reservation, Friday and Saturday at 7:30.

Toliver House Restaurant, 209 North Main St., Gordonsville.

This Victorian house converted into a restaurant has undergone major changes and expansion lately. Owner Mike DeCanio brought in two friends from the Midwest as partners, chef Gary Johnson and manager Jim Reber. They added a screened dining porch, a new kitchen and a new lounge, and redecorated existing dining areas in the front parlor, dining room and paneled library. The result is a spiffy, white and green decor that varies from room to room, with more seating for dining on the porch and in the lounge.

White tablecloths, colored overcloths and candlelight are the backdrop for an extensive menu with an emphasis on fresh seafood and down-home Southern cooking. Dinner entrées ranges from chicken breast in a lemon and parsley cream sauce to filet mignon and porterhouse steak. The specialty is crab cakes, available as an appetizer or a main course. Other favorites are broiled jumbo shrimp stuffed with sherried lobster filling, grilled swordfish or salmon, and charbroiled pork chops topped with fried apples. A fried oyster sandwich is a luncheon standout. Popular starters include Brunswick stew, french onion soup with madeira and gruyère, smoked salmon and shrimp cocktail. The dessert tray might hold pumpkin or brandy alexander cheesecake, coconut-carrot cake and sweet potato-pecan pie.

Chef Johnson added ethnic fare on Thursday nights, the themes changing monthly and planned a year in advance. An all-you-can-eat fried chicken dinner is offered every Sunday night in honor of Gordonville's onetime claim to being the "fried chicken capital of the world – if not the universe," according to Mike.

Tinted photos of Gordonsville and area are displayed in the new Nathaniel Gordon lounge, named for the town's founder and featuring an oak bar custom-made by a cabinetmaker from Charlottesville. The restaurant serves wines from Virginia exclusively.

(540) 832-3485. Entrées, $13.95 to $22.95. Lunch, Tuesday-Saturday 11:30 to 2:30. Dinner, Thursday-Sunday 5:30 to 9. Sunday brunch, 11:30 to 2:30.

Firehouse Cafe & Market, 137 West Main St., Orange.

The old firehouse with its high ceilings, tall front windows and abundant greenery provides lots of atmosphere for this cafe and market, which features gourmet foods and Virginia wines. Partners Dornin Formwalt and Marty Van Santvoord started with breakfast and lunch seven days a week, but tired of the pace. They now offer lunch, deli takeout fare and dinner late in the week, plus a house band on Friday nights, when we're told that local yuppies have made it the place to be and people often end up dancing in the streets.

Things were quieter at our lunchtime visits. We enjoyed a cup of gazpacho, a pasta salad, and a vidalia onion quiche with house salad on one occasion, and a turkey quesadilla, a cup of sweet onion soup and half a pastrami sandwich the next. Specials included cold curried broccoli and cold zucchini soups, minted fruit salad and chocolate-almond torte. The menu is limited, but you'll find nachos, a burrito plate, deli sandwiches and desserts, and everything is in the $2.75 to $5.95 range.

The dinner menu reflects higher aspirations. Typical main courses range from pan-fried catfish with fresh tomato salsa and broiled salmon with Mediterranean orange and olive compote to roasted pork tenderloin with blackberry sauce and grilled New York strip steak topped with button mushrooms. The signature dish is filet mignon, topped with béarnaise sauce.

(540) 672-9001. Entrées, $11 to $22. Lunch, Thursday-Saturday 11:30 to 3. Dinner, Thursday-Sunday 5:30 to 10. Sunday brunch, 11 to 3.

Happy Garden, 130 East Main St., Orange.

There don't seem to be many takers for Chinese food in downtown Orange. But city folks from Washington rate this place highly, and we certainly liked our chicken with garlic sauce, hot and spicy, and a dish called "mish mosh" that brought roast pork, chicken and shrimp stir-fried with vegetables on a nest of pan-fried egg noodles. The crispy wide noodles with two sauces that preceded were extra good; the tea that followed, rather strange. We passed on the honey-banana ice cream in favor of rainbow sherbet.

A sea of white-linened booths and tables with accents of pink and black and small globes on the walls, the place is fairly large and brightly illuminated. "Sizzling Triple Delight," sliced beef, chicken and shrimp sautéed with Chinese greens on a sizzling hot platter, is a recent specialty.

(540) 672-1044. Entrées, $8 to $12.95. Lunch daily, 11 to 3; dinner, 3 to 10 or 11.

Diversions

Montpelier, 11407 Constitution Hwy. (Route 20), Montpelier Station.

A Johnny-come-lately as tourist attractions go, the home of President James Madison was opened for public tours in 1987 by the National Trust for Historic Preservation. It's very much a restoration in progress, so don't expect to find a furnished home as at nearby Monticello or Ash Lawn. Do expect to see what was – and will be again when finished – a showplace renowned for entertaining. Started as an eight-room house, it was expanded over the years to the point that when the National Trust inherited it from Marion du Pont Scott, it was a 55-room mansion that the du Pont heiress had made into a hunt-country mecca. Since 1984, it's been the site of the Montpelier Steeplechase races, staged annually the first Saturday in November. The trust is restoring the house to show both the Madison and du Pont influences. A bus shuttles visitors from the excellent gift shop called the **Montpelier Store** up a pretty hillside drive to the imposing home, somewhat the worse for years of neglect. Interior highlights include the Corning Glass fireplace with enormous mirror above in "La Modern" Red Room, all Art-Decoed up by Marion du Pont, the horsewoman. She was also responsible for the Adams Room, the most "furnished" room with a rare Persian carpet, reproduction Steinway piano and gilt ceiling. Visitors can amble through the restored double-tiered gardens, quite a sight against a forested hillside backdrop, and follow a tree walk brochure that points out 40 trees from across the world. The shuttle bus traverses a portion of the 2,700-acre estate, which has 100 other structures including houses, a bowling alley and stables, plus race courses, thoroughbred horses and working farmlands leased to tenants. On the way out, notice the Montpelier station the owner built in 1910 at the entrance to the estate. Although the train no longer stops, the station lives on as a post office. And Montpelier lives on as a social center for the county, hosting wine festivals, the county fair and such – preserving not only the architecture but also the cultural heritage of the area.

(540) 672-2728. Open daily 9:30 to 4:30, April-November; 9:30 to 3, rest of year. Adults, $7.50.

Exchange Hotel Civil War Historic Museum, 400 South Main St., Gordonsville.

Built as a railroad hotel in 1860, this handsome Greek Revival was transformed into a military hospital during the Civil War and later abandoned. A forward-looking

Barboursville Ruins area is backdrop for winery and, in summer, Shakespeare plays.

group of women formed an historical society to buy it in the 1970s for $14,000; it was recently appraised at $340,000. It's furnished to illustrate both its hotel and hospital functions and has quite a collection of Civil War memorabilia, from weapons and uniforms to medical artifacts and surgeons' implements used in the very room in which they are displayed.

(540) 832-2944. Open mid-March to mid-December, Tuesday-Saturday 10 to 4; also Sundays in summer, 1 to 4. Adults, $4.

Barboursville Vineyards and Ruins, 17655 Winery Road, Barboursville.
Virginia winemaking started here in 1976, nearly two centuries after pioneering vintner Thomas Jefferson's vineyards of European stock were blighted. The Zonin family from Italy were the first in the state to plant viniferas successfully and have many awards to show for them. Barboursville won the 1999 Virginia Wine Competition Governor's Cup for its cabernet franc, and its ten awards covered the broadest spectrum of wines in the state. Specializing in premium viniferas, winemaker-manager Luca Paschina offers a crisp chardonnay for $11.99, along with riesling, pinot grigio and sauvignon blanc and some mighty fine merlots, pinot noirs and cabernet sauvignons ($14.99 to $24.99) in an impressive tasting room with a Mediterranean facade. Visitors get to sample at least four of the more than twenty wines, some of which are fairly unusual. Seventy-five scenic acres are under grape cultivation and more than 10,000 cases are produced annually. Next to the recently expanded tasting room is an acclaimed new restaurant, **Palladio** (see Dining Spots). Nearby on the property are the **Barboursville Ruins,** the Jefferson-designed home of Gov. James Barbour, which was destroyed by fire in 1884. Open to public view behind dense shrubbery, the shell of the mansion is remarkably close to two handsome outbuildings, joined into one and lived in today as the primary residence of the estate.

(540) 832-3824. Ruins on view, Monday-Saturday 10 to 5, check in at winery office. Winery: tastings, Monday-Saturday 10 to 5, Sunday 11 to 5.

Shakespeare at the Ruins, Barboursville, (540) 832-5355. The Barboursville Ruins are a spectacular backdrop for the annual Shakespeare at the Ruins in late July and early August. The Four County Players, Central Virginia's longest-running community theater, stages one of its year's five productions under the stars, combining Renaissance costumes and music with a Shakespearean play on three weekends. Dinner and wines are available from the winery before the show.

Shopping. Downtown Orange got a shot in the arm with the conversion of its old railroad depot into a transportation center and visitor center with a park beside. New businesses opened, among them **Not the Same Old Grind** at 113 East Church St. Jim and Nancy Bosket offer specialty coffees and teas, New York-style bagels, sandwiches, baked goods and chocolates, plus a sofa and a few tables for partaking. Pick up some reading material from **Bookends,** a new and used bookstore also in the building.

We liked the wares at **The Country Mouse,** 143 East Church St., an herb cottage where several rooms are filled with baskets, baby and bath things, hats, herbs, spices, organic foods, garden items and great jewelry, especially that depicting animals. The relocated **Somerset Shop,** part of a larger store at 110 East Main St., has every kind of country gift, handcrafted item and accessory you could imagine. Back near its old home in Somerset is the **Old Somerset Print Shop & Fine Art Gallery,** an excellent gallery specializing in upscale watercolors, mostly pastoral scenes from the English countryside. We love the paintings of the Blue Ridge Mountains by Frederick D. Nichols, but they are out of our price range. See them at **Beth Gallery,** Route 678 in Barboursville.

Extra-Special

Ed Jaffe Gallery, 108 West Main St., Orange.

This 5,000-square-foot studio and gallery – "unlike any other north or south of Manhattan," according to its creator – opened in a former five-and-dime store in downtown Orange in 1994. Sculptor Jaffe had tired of the way traditional galleries showed his sculptures for twenty years on the East and West coasts. As the middleman, "the gallery tends to put up a wall between the artist and the collector," Ed said. He liked having collectors visit his farmhouse-studio in southern Vermont, discovering "a bond that comes from direct contact." He also didn't care for the way the galleries handled pieces that were as dear to him as family members, so he "pulled all my babies home" and decided to open his own gallery. The question was where. He didn't want to return to New York City, where he'd worked as a professional photographer, and a Vermont mountaintop was not the place to reach a broad market. His search took five years; the change took five months. The center of his universe is now downtown Orange, which he calls the heart of the nation's North-South corridor. He converted part of the store into a studio and his living quarters, and the rest is like a museum in need of a few more exhibits. The entire space is devoted to the works of one man, mostly sculptures but some paintings. They carry price tags from $300 to $15,000.

(540) 672-2400 or (800) 672-8588. Open most Saturdays 10 to 4, and by appointment.

James River Plantation Country
Where Time Is On Hold

Plantation Country. The name evokes images of early aristocracy, vast tracts of farmlands, lazing riverboats, manor homes, belles in hoop skirts and gentlemen attired for the hunt.

What could be more Southern? And where – with the possible exception of Natchez – is that Southern lifestyle more in evidence today than along the James River in Virginia's Tidewater? Its way of life has been established since the area was settled during the first westward expansion of English-speaking America in the early 1600s and the James became the highway to inland commerce.

Close to Virginia's busy Historic Triangle (Williamsburg, Jamestown and Yorktown), plantation country goes its own way just inland along the James. Time has been put on hold in this rare Southern oasis where American history officially began.

About a dozen plantations of note still thrive, and half are open to the public. Miles of fields, farmlands and forests give way to the occasional river vista in this far-flung, sparsely populated stretch along both sides of the river.

There are no cities. Indeed, Charles City County, home of most of the great plantations on the river's sylvan north side, is really a county without a city. Charles City, a one-horse hamlet with little more than a courthouse and a school, stands in stark contrast to its neighbor to the east, touristy Williamsburg. The main route along the north bank, Route 5 (also called the John Tyler Highway), is America's oldest highway and appears nearly deserted.

Upriver and across the James is industrial Hopewell, America's busiest port during the War Between the States.

Across and down the river on the south side are two relatively undiscovered prizes. Surry, population 300, is the center of peanut country and a lazy Southern hamlet, if ever there was one. Smithfield, population 4,700, is a 1750s river town that produces the world's most famous ham. It's the epitome of Tidewater and the center of the aptly named Isle of Wight County.

Only at the far ends of Plantation Country does one sense a few urban encroachments from Williamsburg, Norfolk and Richmond.

Otherwise, all is peaceful and quiet at the plantations as the Harrisons, the Tylers, the Carters and the rest go about their business.

They reflect to this day the web of kinship that has linked Virginia aristocracy from the beginning.

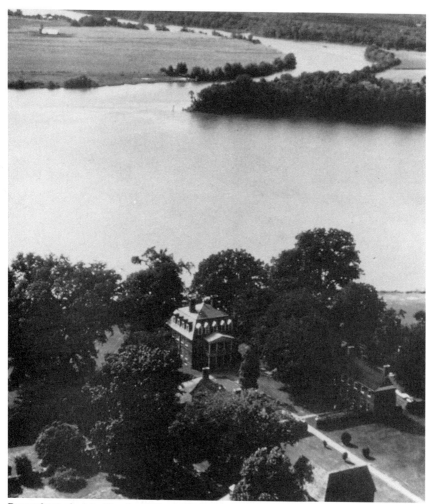

Descendants of original family still live in Shirley Plantation complex beside the James River.

Inn Spots

Several plantations take in overnight guests, and a few B&Bs have sprung up on both sides of the river. More traditional and more numerous accommodations are available in Williamsburg and Hopewell.

Edgewood Plantation, 4800 John Tyler Memorial Hwy., Charles City 23030.

When in Plantation Country, why not stay in a plantation, even if it is not a typical manor house and is relatively small in comparison? Don't stay here, mind you, if you want to be in the thick of Williamsburg activities, don't care for antiques, dislike clutter and want a large bathroom.

Prepare to be overwhelmed. Dot and Julian Boulware have assembled a collection to end all collections at their home and B&B. They created it in 1984 from an ugly duckling of an 1849 Gothic Revival that no one else wanted across

Bedroom at Edgewood Plantation holds canopied bed, loveseat and perambulator.

from, and once part of, the Berkeley Plantation. Dot, a Richmonder who has an eye for displaying things stylishly, has furnished the place with "a little bit of everything" – and lots of it. She must have thousands of dolls, books, buggies, dollhouses, hatboxes, hats and antiques and they are everywhere. At our first July visit, she still had some of her eighteen Christmas trees up and lit.

A gorgeous spiral staircase, its banister draped in lace, pink satin, baby's breath and evergreen branches, winds to the second floor. Here off a central hall are four bedrooms, all with private baths, fireplaces and at least fourteen pillows on each bed.

"Each room is a fascination," says Dot. She's tried to hide the TV/VCRs that she recently installed in each room, "because I hate them, and you have plenty of entertainment anyway." Roses abound, for Edgewood caters to romance. "This is a lady's house," explains Dot. "The men ask, 'where do we sleep?'" That's no idle question. Although the beds are high and comfy, Dot must remove all those pillows and layers of antique coverings at night. Empty your pockets before retiring and you could lose their contents in all the collections, for there's not an uncovered space to be found. If you head for the bathroom in the dark of night, you might mistake a headless mannequin costumed in white for the resident ghost and land, as one of us nearly did, in a waiting perambulator. Showering the next morning in what must be the world's smallest bathroom was a feat. The bathrooms aren't big, Dot concedes, but contain "everything you need to have."

On the third floor is a sitting area, set with a teddy bears' tea party and a TV ensconced in a dollhouse, between two bedrooms that share a bath.

Upstairs in the old slave quarters behind the house are two more rooms, one a honeymoon suite called Prissy's Quarters. Grapevines strung with dried flowers festoon the pencil-post queen bed and the quilt is patched with hearts. The country decor is simpler than in the main house, and amenities include a small kitchen and a sitting area with TV.

What next? "I'm not finished yet," said Dot as she talked of more rooms in a 1725 grist mill built by Benjamin Harrison at the side of the property. Julian has planted a large, symmetrical boxwood garden with gravel walks lined in brick, a trickling fountain and a tiered terrace descending to a pond.

Already, Edgewood offers a swimming pool and hot tub, a side patio, two gazebos, a front veranda overlooking colorful landscaping, a 38-foot-long living room full of Victoriana, a formal dining room and a country kitchen so cluttered it's a wonder that breakfast can be prepared. But prepared it is, and served by candlelight at a long, lace-covered table in the dining room. At our visit, orange juice in a pewter cup and fresh berries and other fruit in a pewter dish preceded delicious thick french toast with cinnamon and powdered sugar. The hostess sits with her guests and keeps up a running commentary on all the fascinations of her place.

The house is open daily except Monday for tours ($8, including second-floor bedrooms), led by Dot in Victorian costume. She also serves lunch and tea by appointment ($20 to $30) in the downstairs tavern and tearoom, as chock full as the rest of the house.

(804) 829-2962 or (800) 269-3343. Five rooms and one suite with private baths; two rooms with shared bath. Doubles, $158 to $188 with private bath, $125 with shared bath. Suite, $188.

North Bend Plantation B&B, 12200 Weyanoke Road, Charles City 23030. This unpretentious, 1819 Greek Revival house at the end of a long road harbors a lot of history. Owner George Copland is a great-great grandson of Edmund Ruffin, the Southerner who fired the first shot of the Civil War. Union General Sheridan used the house as his headquarters. And the owner still farms the plantation, when he's not busy with his four-room B&B.

George and his wife, Ridgley, a family nurse practitioner, offer four large guest rooms, all with private baths. Each is furnished with family antiques and collectibles in the spare Federal style. The rear Magnolia Room overlooking the swimming pool has a canopied queensize rice bed and a connecting bedroom in the maid's quarters. The Sheridan Room features a canopied step-up queen tester bed bearing a gunshot wound from the Civil War and covered by a floral comforter. Also here are a velvet settee, a rocker and the general's Civil War desk containing special orders from New York. The Rose Room, also with a queen canopy bed and a chaise lounge, has a more feminine look with dolls and pillows. The Federal Room contains an 1850 sleigh bed, a rich patterned gold loveseat and a cast-iron bath.

Guests watch passing deer in the fields and listen to chattering birds from an enclosed upstairs sun porch outfitted in wicker. Downstairs are a double parlor, a dining room with an old billiards table with a marble base at one end and a homey kitchen where most guests prefer to eat as George whips up his specialty waffles. Eggs with sausages and biscuits are another breakfast favorite.

(804) 829-5176. Fax (804) 829-6828, Four rooms with private baths. Doubles, $120 to 135. Children over 6. Smoking restricted.

Jasmine Plantation B&B, 4500 North Courthouse Road, Providence Forge 23140

Candles are lit in every window of this handsome, gabled white and green 1750s farmhouse on 47 rural acres. Chickens and roosters are on display in back, and walking trails wind through the woods past tranquil sitting areas.

A country store off the front foyer, where guests check in, is stocked with antiques for sale. Owners Joyce and Howard Vogt, who live next door on the property, offer six guest rooms, four with private baths and working fireplaces. The two oldest rooms in the 1700s section share a bath and are furnished with antiques dating to the 1600s. The George Morris Room, the most spacious, is furnished in Empire style and has a fireplace, sitting area, TV/VCR and private bath with clawfoot tub and separate shower. Period antiques also prevail in the other rooms. Two are Victorian and the Rose Room has a 1930s theme.

Three working fireplaces are evident on the main floor, all of which is devoted to common areas. Among them are a formal parlor, a rear den with TV and a couple of dining areas. The Vogts serve a country breakfast of fresh fruit, bacon and Surry ham, and an entrée of perhaps omelet, waffles or french toast.

(804) 966-9836 or (800) 639-5368. Fax (804) 966-5679. Four rooms with private baths and two rooms with shared bath. Doubles, $85 to $125. Children over 12. No smoking.

Piney Grove at Southall's Plantation, 16920 Southall Plantation Lane, Box 1359, Charles City 23030.

Out in the middle of nowhere is this delightful restoration, not really a plantation home of the dimensions considered hereabouts but a remarkably historic and appealing place nonetheless. Restorationists Joan and Joseph Gordineer of Williamsburg first purchased a general store and residence that had begun life in 1800 as a log corn-crib.

With son Brian, whose graduate thesis focused on tourism in the James River Plantation Country, they opened a B&B with one room in the National Register-listed main house that's as atmospheric as can be. In 1989, they moved a modest Greek Revival plantation house from Ladysmith to a site behind the main house. It backs up to woods and a farm corral, and faces gardens and loblolly pines and an open shed housing Joseph's collection of old cars. At its side is a gazebo next to an idyllic, hidden swimming pool surrounded by lounge chairs. The Gordiners now offer three guest rooms and a suite with private baths and considerable comfort.

Brian and his father did the restoration of the Ladysmith house themselves. The son's artistry is evident in the stenciling and in the ongoing mural of Greek buildings working its way around the walls of both floors of the center hall. The four rooms on either side of the hall, upstairs and down, have been granted extra space, thanks to a rear addition that holds the bathrooms. Each high-ceilinged room has a fireplace and comes with a double bed (two also have a twin), loveseats, wing chairs and/or rockers, mini-refrigerator and coffeemaker. One is a two-bedroom suite suitable for three people.

A decanter of apple brandy is in the hall, and mint juleps or hot toddies are served upon arrival. A farm bell is rung ten minutes before breakfast is ready in the main house. It's served at three tables in the parlor/library of the oldest, log-walled section. The fare includes juice, fruit, Virginia ham or sausage, homemade breads and one of six casseroles made from fresh eggs. Afterward, adjourn to the neatest little screened porch, snug with two wicker chairs facing a wicker loveseat and screened from the odd passing vehicle by a boxwood hedge, or linger by the fire in the formal parlor with its rich blue walls, wood moldings and stenciling.

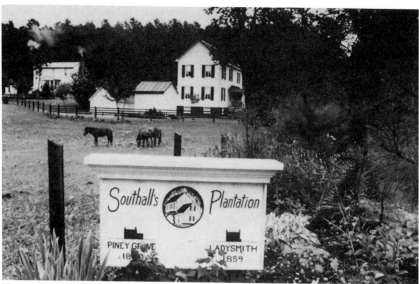

Horses graze outside Piney Grove at Southall's Plantation.

Rows of rose of sharon trees, hibiscus gardens, pear and plum trees, trellised grapes and raspberries, a corral holding ducks, geese, sheep and a goat, and the swimming pool offer plenty of diversion. A nature trail leads through the woods to a ravine with springs and a swimming hole.

(804) 829-2480. Fax (804) 829-6888. Three rooms and one suite with private baths. Doubles, $130 to $145. Suite, $170. Children accepted. No smoking.

Seward House Inn, 193 Colonial Trail East (Route 10), Box 352, Surry 23883.
British-born Cynthia Erskine was picking pole beans and cucumbers in her backyard garden at our first visit. She led us in the back way past the kitchen, the dining room and the living room, where a TV shared space at the time with a sewing machine "because we're still making curtains."

The B&B was opened in 1990 by Cynthia and a Norfolk friend, Jacqueline Bayer. It is homey and welcoming, from the pictures of Jackie's children in the front hall to the jars of basil jelly that Cynthia makes and gives to guests. The sewing machine is long gone, but there's now a piano in the hall.

The four guest quarters are furnished with mementos of three generations of their families, including handcarved beds, old toys, bits of needlework, a handcarved trunk, and prints of Andrew Wyeth and Maxfield Parrish. The front corner downstairs room has a private bath. A bathroom with a clawfoot tub serves two upstairs bedrooms, one with a queensize bed. The other has twin beds, a teddybear on a trunk and a fireplace mantel bearing a miniature sewing machine and toy soldiers. We stayed in a small guest cottage at the side is called the Surgery; this is the office in which Jackie's great uncle used to practice medicine. It now offers a full bath, a queensize bedroom and a living room with a rattan loveseat and chair.

Although almost in the center of town (what there is of it), the inn is surrounded by fields of soybeans and corn. Guests enjoy a front veranda and a trellised side deck overlooking the tranquil scene, including a small fishpond. A jigsaw puzzle is at the ready in the living room of what Cynthia calls "a family-friendly house." For breakfast, "we do things family style, and lots of it." Ours was an omelet with shiitake mushrooms, parsley and parmigiano-reggiano cheese, with a side of country ham from the nearby Edwards Virginia Ham Shoppe. Or the main course could be waffles containing pecans picked from trees outside. Spicy sausage gravy over biscuits has been a hit lately. Overnight guests may use the hosts' barbecue grills for dining al fresco on the trellised deck or have dinner prepared by reservation. The tab averages $30 for something like organically grown salad with homemade dressing, biscuits, French bread, pasta with garden vegetables, fruit and cheeses. In winter, Cynthia might do a roast or chicken.

Besides the basil jelly, Cynthia puts up wild blackberry jam and sent us on our way with a small jar. It sure did liven up our toast while it lasted.

(757) 294-3810. One room and one suite with private baths; two rooms with shared bath. Doubles, $65 to $70. Cottage, $80. Children accepted. Smoking restricted.

Porches on the James, 6347 Old Stage Hwy. (Route 10), Smithfield 23430.

A "modern B&B," this was built for the purpose in 1998 on a bluff 60 feet above the James River. It's set well back from the road and identified only by a small green sign.

After years of looking, Jane and Greg Kilduff never found the right old house in the right location for a B&B. They did come across the right location, however. So they built from scratch what Greg called "a more or less old-fashioned design: central hall, high ceilings and wraparound porches." They called it modern to convey its conveniences. Yet the place looks and feels old enough that "even friends who should know better ask about the remodeling," Greg reported.

Aptly named, it has porches on three sides for panoramic river views through a grove of tall bald cypress trees growing at river level and extending as high as the house. A beach and a boat dock are available for guests. Greg claims their bird feeders attract the best-fed flock of goldfinches in Virginia. Osprey, bald eagles and occasionally deer and foxes also visit the property.

The Kilduffs offer two handsome bedrooms with queen beds and a third with twins. A fourth bedroom was awaiting county approval. Generally, the house is furnished in traditional furniture, some made by a local craftsman. He made walnut furniture for one bedroom with boards all from the same tree.

The innkeepers join guests for a wine and cheese get-together in the late afternoon. They serve a full breakfast at a common table in the dining room or on the porch. Seasonal fruit, homemade breads and Smithfield ham or hickory-smoked bacon accompany the main dish, which could be a grits casserole, quiche, eggs, waffles or french toast.

(757) 356-0602. Three rooms with private baths. Doubles, $95 weekends, $85 midweek.

Smithfield Station, 415 South Church St., Smithfield 23430.

Built in 1986 and with water on three sides, this was designed by a local businessman/sailor to look like a Victorian Coast Guard station. Its busy marina and restaurant (see Dining Spots) draw crowds, but overnight guests can be above the hubbub in fifteen guest rooms on the second and third floors, or away from the fray in two suites in a lighthouse.

Seward House Inn and small adjacent cottage offer four guest accommodations.

In contemporary motel style, the upstairs rooms are attractive with pine furnishings, kingsize or two double beds, TV, phone, a table with two chairs and waterfowl pictures on the walls. By far the most appealing are those overlooking the Pagan River and Cypress Creek across deep rear balconies running the length of the building. Our balcony would have gotten a workout except that we were there during weather so torrid that we couldn't venture outside our air-conditioned room even after the sun had gone down.

A continental breakfast is served buffet-style on weekdays in one of the dining rooms. Fruit, danish and homemade rolls filled with Smithfield ham are the fare.

Lately, owners Ronald and Christina Pack added a boardwalk with gazebos, a swimming pool and an outdoor bar and grill. They offer three Boardwalk rooms with queen beds, two of them with gas fireplaces, and decorated them variously in golf, fly-fishing and nautical motifs. They built a lighthouse for use as two deluxe suites and a conference center, surrounded by water. The Captain Sinclair features a king bed, gas fireplace, microwave and wet bar, double whirlpool tub, steam shower and a spiral staircase to the cupola of the lighthouse for the best view in Smithfield. The Captain Todd offers a kingsize murphy bed, fireplace, kitchenette and dining area as well as a site for small business meetings.

(757) 357-7700. Fax (757) 357-7638. Eighteen rooms and two suites. Doubles, $79 to $150. Suites, $175 and $225.

Four Square Plantation, 13357 Four Square Road, Smithfield 23430.

Amelia and Roger Healey moved in 1994 from a small B&B in Wrightsville, Pa., to a larger and older home built in 1807 as the centerpiece of a 23-acre plantation. Here, in a house listed on the National Register and declared a Virginia Landmark Property, they offer three large bedrooms with fireplaces and private baths.

A Pennsylvania quilt graces the kingsize poster bed in the Thomas Room, comfortable with thick carpeting and two armchairs. A secluded bedroom in the rear of the house is nineteen feet square and furnished in the Empire style with a queen bed and large walnut armoire.

European and American antiques enhance the public rooms. A Spanish portable writing desk dating to the 1600s takes center stage in the parlor. The dining room holds a French trestle table from a monastery, dating to the 1500s and the oldest piece in the house. Quite a collection of French tinkers' miniatures (copper pots and pans) adorns one wall.

Amelia serves a full breakfast – a Southwest omelet with Virginia ham and banana bread the day of our visit. Fruit compote, lemon-poppyseed muffins and blueberry pancakes were on the docket the next day.

(757) 365-0749. Three rooms with private baths. Doubles, $75 to $85. Smoking restricted.

Dining Spots

Indian Fields Tavern, 9220 John Tyler Hwy., Charles City.

In an area of few people (other than plantation-goers, many of whom don't spend the night), a young man who grew up on one of the biggest plantations is making a go of it with a most appealing restaurant. In 1988, Archer H. Ruffin Jr., a relative of the family that owns nearby Evelynton Plantation, turned a ramshackle, century-old farmhouse into a bustling eatery accommodating 90 patrons in four dining rooms upstairs and down, plus 30 more on screened porches. The name derives from the surrounding fields, which natives were farming when the first English settlers arrived in Virginia.

Archer's mother and his sister-in-law helped with the decor. They went with an early tavern look and a burgundy, green and beige color scheme. Bare hardwood floors, windsor chairs and well-spaced tables topped with burgundy cloths, votive candles and bud vases bearing large lilies set the stage for an ambitious dinner menu of contemporary Southern specialties, which change frequently.

For starters, we sampled the night's gazpacho and the huge Indian Fields garden salad with dijon vinaigrette as we munched on homemade sweet Sally Lunn bread. Other possibilities were grilled wild mushrooms with red wine and stilton cheese and pan-seared oysters over grilled sweet corn bruschetta and red pepper rouille. Among entrées, we liked the soft-shell crabs served with a spicy pecan butter, carrots and yellow squash. Also excellent was the mixed grill of lamb, quail and Surry sausage with a brandied pear demi-glace, accompanied by broiled potatoes and haricots verts. We hear great things about the oysters or crab cakes harrison, new signature dishes served with hollandaise sauce over Smithfield ham and toasted Sally Lunn bread

The wine list is quite select and reasonably priced. Desserts are to groan over, particularly if you're into cakes or bourbon-chocolate-pecan pie. The raspberry cheesecake was extra-good.

Indian Fields also serves interesting fare for lunch and Sunday brunch. The throngs pouring in for weekday lunch at our latest visit attested to the success and drawing power of a restaurant way off the beaten path.

(804) 829-5004. Entrées, $15.95 to $24.95. Lunch daily, 11 to 3:30. Dinner nightly, 5 to 9 or 10. Sunday brunch, 11 to 3:30.

Archer H. Ruffin Jr. turned ramshackle farmhouse into Indian Fields Tavern.

Coach House Tavern, 12602 Harrison Landing Road, Charles City.

Once the place where Benjamin Harrison garaged his coaches, this small out-building at Berkeley Plantation has been transformed into a thing of beauty for special-occasion dining. With blue over white cloths and fanned napkins, large tables on two levels look through french doors onto an expanse of lovely gardens.

Votive candles flicker on wall sconces among dark beams and posts at night, when the room is positively magical. Dinner is leisurely and the table is yours for the evening. The concise menu offered by Sandra Capps changes often. Entrées might include pan-seared salmon with herbed butter sauce, quail with apple-walnut stuffing, veal marsala and loin lamb chops with rosemary wine glaze. Start with a signature french onion soup "served en boule," oyster stew or baked mushrooms stuffed with crab imperial.

At lunch, waitresses in Colonial dresses pour non-stop iced tea. Between plantation tours we enjoyed a crab cake sandwich and a seafood salad in a halved avocado. Pretty as a picture, the latter was garnished with an abundance of fresh fruit, from strawberries to kiwi to honeydew. It came with potato salad and cold roasted peppers. The crab sandwich arrived on thick toasted bread described as "baked bass." Was it Sally Lunn bread? "No, suh, it's fresh baked bah-us." For dessert, the famous Berkeley rum cake lived up to its billing. Surrounded by blueberries, raspberries and strawberries and resting on crème anglaise, it was one of the best cakes we've tasted.

(804) 829-6003. Entrées, $21.95 to $26.95. Lunch daily, 11 to 4. Dinner, Wednesday-Saturday 6 to 9, Sunday 11 to 5.

David's White House Restaurant, 3560 Courthouse Road, Providence Forge.

The original chef and partner from Indian Fields, David Napier, opened his own restaurant to equally good reviews. The setting is a turn-of-the-century house built by the town miller in the center of historic Providence Forge. Well-spaced tables in four dining rooms are dressed with white cloths and fresh flowers. David set out to offer "fine dining in plantation style" with an added embellishment: the food at this White House "could easily by served at any state dinner held at the one in Washington."

The regional food press agreed. David earned considerable acclaim for dinner appetizers like sherried crab, grilled oysters on corncakes topped with chipped Smithfield ham, and homemade hunter's sausage, patties of venison, lamb and tenderloin seasoned with sage and fennel seed and topped with berry glaze. His Big Daddy seafood gumbo blends shrimp, okra and garlic with French bread croutons.

Main courses range from baked Virginia ham with bourbon-glazed apples to grilled quail stuffed with hunter's sausage. A sampler plate teams three house favorites: sautéed oysters topped with Smithfield ham, filet mignon with a red wine and roquefort glaze, and slow-roasted baby pork ribs. Crab cakes with caper mayonnaise and grilled duck breast with fried grits are other favorites.

(804) 966-9700. Entrées, $13.50 to $20. Lunch, Tuesday-Saturday 11 to 4. Dinner, Tuesday-Saturday 5 to 10. Sunday, brunch 11 to 3, dinner, 4 to 10.

The Smithfield Inn, 112 Main St., Smithfield.

The stylish restaurant at this newly restored and reopened inn – built in 1752 and one of the oldest buildings in town – receives high marks from locals.

Beyond a front veranda with a lineup of rocking chairs are two dining rooms, elegant and formal in Victoriana. Fringed lamps and serrated glassware are on each large, well spaced table. More dining is available in the English-style William Rand Tavern and on a side brick patio outfitted with white wrought-iron furniture.

The fare is contemporary American with a Southern accent. Expect dinner entrées like pecan-crusted rainbow trout on a sauté of Smithfield ham and granny smith apples, lump crab cakes over Smithfield ham, game stew, brochette of pork, venison chops with a currant compote and medallions of lamb with a rosemary concasse. Appetizers could be oysters fontina, tempura shrimp and grilled quail. Other favorites are crab and spinach soup, brunswick stew and oyster stew.

Appetizers, soups, stews and sandwiches are available for supper in the tavern. Similar fare is offered on the lunch menu. We'd like to try the oyster fritter and the open-face lump crab cake sandwich.

After a million-dollar plus restoration, the inn – now owned by meat packer Joseph Luter III of Smithfield Foods – offers five upstairs suites for overnight guests. They're said to be elegant and pricey. We were unable to verify because when we tried, the manager relayed a curt message that the inn was not interested.

(757) 357-1752. Suites, $125. Entrées, $14.95 to $22.95. Lunch, Tuesday-Sunday 11:30 to 3. Dinner, Wednesday-Saturday 5:30 to 9 or 10. Tavern, Tuesday-Saturday 4 to 10. No smoking.

Smithfield Station, 415 South Church St., Smithfield.

Nicely nautical to go with its setting, the main floor of this contemporary hotel-marina-restaurant has four dining areas including a lounge, plus a solarium and a waterside deck, and seats up to 150. Burgundy napkins and votive candles top formica tables edged in wood.

The extensive menu has something for everyone, from baked chicken stuffed with Smithfield ham, swiss cheese and roasted peanuts to pork oscar and T-bone steak. Seafood is king here, along with ham. It comes as nautical pasta, blackened catfish, crab norfolk, seafood rockefeller, surf and turf (crab cakes and Smithfield ham), and what have you. We can vouch for the sampler of Smithfield ham, the Station pasta combining shrimp, smoked salmon and Smithfield ham chunks over spinach fettuccine, and seafood norfolk, accompanied by yellow squash parmesan. A peach-berry sundae, the fruit marinated in triple sec and served over vanilla ice cream, made a refreshing ending. Other favorites are peanut pie and bread pudding with bourbon sauce.

A Smithfield ham platter, served with fried apples and vegetable of the day, is a favorite at lunch.

Outside on a boardwalk along the Pagan River bridge, the **Boardwalk Raw Bar & Grill** serves Wednesday-Saturday from 4 to 10 or 11, Sunday from 1 to 10.

(757) 357-7700. Entrées, $14.95 to $22.95. Lunch daily, 11 to 4. Dinner nightly, 4 to 10.

Surrey House Restaurant, Routes 10 and 31, Surry.

Predictable Southern cooking is served up with lots of local color at this oldtimer in the heart of peanut country. New owner Michael Stevens expanded the menu, but retained the old favorites rendered by longtime owner Helen Gwaltney Lenox. Even though it now serves Williamsburg wines, iced tea with frequent refills remains the beverage of choice at noon or night.

At lunchtime, one of us sampled a cup of peanut soup, a creamy chicken broth with spices and crunchy peanuts, and a club sandwich like those we remember from thirty years ago, overflowing with Edwards ham, bacon, turkey, cheese, lettuce and tomato. The other went for the surf and turf ($12.99), a midday whopper of Edwards ham with a crab cake, plus a trip to the salad bar, an apple fritter, hushpuppies and rolls. Four kinds of sauces in a pewter relish tray accompanied.

Those in the mood can sample the famous Surrey House peanut butter board ($4.99). This do-it-yourself affair involves slices of white and brown bread, a jar of peanut butter, down-home honey, a rasher of bacon, raisins, jelly, a whole ripe banana, apple wedges and cheese, served up on a Surry County pine cutting board.

Ham comes any number of ways, from eggs benedict at breakfast to a dinner special with fried oysters. The all-day menu also offers local seafood, fried chicken, delmonico steak and roast turkey.

The paneled dining room is down-home homey, with booths, banquettes and a hodgepodge of art on the walls. Waitresses in vaguely Colonial ankle-length dresses with puffed sleeves provide quick service. The Carriage Room is more formal with white and blue tablecloths.

(757) 294-3389 or (800) 200-4977. Entrées, $5.25 to $15.99. Breakfast on weekends from 7:30. Lunch and dinner, 11 to 9.

Smithfield Gourmet Bakery and Café, 218 Main St., Smithfield.

Bon Appétit magazine requested the recipe for the orange muffins at this prized little bakery and homey café seating 40 diners.

Owner Carolyn Burke is best known for her cheesecakes. Patrons wax enthusiastic over her sandwiches, including one called the Windsor Castle stuffed with roast turkey, cheddar, grilled onions, honey mustard, lettuce and tomato on grilled tomato-basil bread, a steal for $4.19 – the top price, except for a hamburger or a grilled chicken sandwich. The breads are fresh baked, the ham is Smithfield, and the sides of potato, garden or pasta salads first-rate. For dessert, the coconut cake comes highly recommended.

(757) 357-0045. Open Monday-Saturday 9 to 6, Sunday 11 to 5.

Diversions

Most visitors come here to see the plantations (only a few of which are open to the public). Be advised that there also are a couple of historic towns, a marvelous state park with a model farm, peanut farms, purveyors of Smithfield hams, and more peanut, tobacco, soybean and cotton fields than we ever thought we'd see.

Plantations. Of the dozen or so landmark plantations, some like **Brandon** and **Westover** are open to the public only by appointment and during Historic Garden Week. Others like **Weston** and **Appomattox Plantation** are off the beaten path in Hopewell. Still others like **Bacon's Castle** and **Smith's Fort** are undergoing restoration, and **Chippokes** was inexplicably closed when we were there. Those plantations that are open help support their upkeep by charging for tours. Our favorites:

Shirley Plantation, 501 Shirley Plantation Road, Charles City.

Started in 1613, the home of ten generations of Hills and Carters (and the mother of Robert E. Lee) is perfectly poised with a long view up the James River. Its dependencies form the only Queen Anne forecourt in America, and here you may encounter the Carter pets at play. We found this to be the most personal of plantations, the only one in its original condition and the only one with direct descendants of the original family still in residence. Charles Hill Carter Jr., the county supervisor and handyman about Shirley, lives upstairs with his wife, who runs the gift shop, and two sons who eventually will take over Shirley but who had just opened a clay shooting course at our visit. Guided tours run continuously and there are no roped-off areas. You'll learn the intriguing story behind the family portraits done by an itinerant painter, see dates etched in the dining-room window by ladies testing the quality of their diamond rings, spot two spigots beside the dining-room fireplace for cleaning dishes, and marvel at a unique free-standing square staircase with no visible support in the foyer. The family's silver, coats of arms and other heirlooms are out for all to see.

(804) 829-5121 or (800) 232-1613. Open daily, 9 to 5. Adults, $8.50.

Evelynton Plantation, 6701 John Tyler Hwy., Charles City.

An air of modern luxury pervades Evelynton, to our minds the most appealing and livable of plantations. It's on a shady, tiered lawn overlooking Herring Creek. The impressive Georgian Revival manor house was built in 1936 on property purchased in 1847 by Edmund Ruffin Jr., the states' rights activist and agricultural reformer who fired the first shot in the Civil War at Fort Sumter. The war came to Evelynton when Union General George McClellan occupied the area, burning the original house belonging to the Southern martyr. Today, rope hammocks and two Adirondack chairs flank a cannon and a plaque commemorating the Battle of Evelynton Heights. Ruffin's great-grandson built the showplace home that stands today as testimony to the good life. A guide points out the Chippendale necessary chair in the front bedroom, a sunken family garden room glamorous in brick and chintz, the carved moldings along the ceilings, the formal dining room with an

18th-century Heppelwhite curved buffet, and recent portraits of the four offspring of Saunders Ruffin, current occupant. Portions of three movies were filmed here. The canopied rear terrace was added lately as a setting for weddings and corporate parties.

(804) 829-5075 or (800) 473-5075. Open daily, 9 to 5, March-December; Friday-Monday, rest of year. Adults, $7.50.

Berkeley Plantation, 12602 Harrison Landing Road, Charles City.

The most obviously commercial of the plantations, this is known for its firsts. It was the site of the first official Thanksgiving in 1619. It was the birthplace of Benjamin Harrison (signer of the Declaration of Independence) and of William Henry Harrison, ninth U.S. president, and the ancestral home of 23rd president Benjamin Harrison. And "Taps" was composed here in 1862. Following a slide show, costumed guides shepherd visitors through the main floor of the 1726 house, admonishing them not to touch or lean on the furniture. Exceptional Heppelwhite, Chippendale and Louis pieces abound. The late octogenarian owner, Mac Jamieson, often was mistaken for a groundskeeper as he rode around on a golf cart to oversee the magnificent gardens. His grandson has assumed his role.

(804) 829-6018. Open daily, 8 to 5. Adults, $9.

Bacon's Castle, Route 617, Surry.

The oldest documented brick house in English North America (1665) holds particular fascination. The high Jacobean-style structure is in the process of restoration, which gives insights into construction techniques as well as history spanning three centuries. A ten-minute audio-visual presentation precedes an informative 45-minute guided tour. Visitors see graffiti on a wall (one child's scrawl dated 1886 says "this day I am sick"), a love letter written in glass, a 1710 one-hand clock and a room full of artifacts acquired in archaeological digs on the property, from clay marbles to egg shells. Outside, what was thought to be a 19th-century garden turned out to be a Renaissance-style English garden from the 17th century. Uncovered in 1985, it prompted the New York Times to declare it the "earliest, largest, best-preserved and most sophisticated garden that has come to light in North America." The resident gardener likes to show off its prizes.

(757) 357-5976. Open Tuesday-Saturday 10 to 4, Sunday noon to 4, April-October, also weekends in March and November. Adults, $6.

Smithfield. Known for its hams, the hog capital of the world also is a case study of an early river port. Some say Smithfield's collection of 60-plus historic houses represents the best selection in Tidewater because it spans both 18th and 19th centuries. The Chamber of Commerce's walking-tour map notes a blend of more than 60 Colonial, Federal, Georgian and Victorian structures side by side – including Victorian Row, which would do Cape May proud. We chanced upon Hayden's Lane, a brick walkway beneath a canopy of flowering crape myrtle trees leading to Hayden Hall. Check out the old-time country store complete with early postal boxes, pot-bellied stove and revolving stools in the Barlow Gallery at the **Isle of Wight County Museum,** housed in two bank buildings.

Smithfield's is the kind of downtown where the Lord's Vineyard (cards, gifts and Bibles) occupies space next to Hamtown Barber & Styling. **Ashton Galleries** stocks fine gifts and accessories. At **Joyner of Smithfield's** downtown retail shop, you can sample and purchase a variety of Smithfield hams, their pungently salty and smoky taste distinctive partly because the hogs are raised on local peanuts. The shop also features peanuts. **Basse's Choice Ham Shop** features Gwaltney's hams. Also a specialty foods store, it stocks a variety of mostly Virginia-made products, from dips and hot pepper jelly to chocolates and wines. For deli sandwiches or desserts, check out the **Smithfield Confectionery and Ice Cream Parlour.** Art and handcrafts are offered at the interesting **Collage Art Gallery,** ensconced in one of the five Victorian Row houses. Twenty-three dealers show their wares in the **Smithfield Antiques Center** co-op.

Surry. Named for the English county of Surrey, this was the home of some of the first black settlers in America. Today, peanuts rule (the little Smithfield-Surry phone book carries two pages of listings for peanut products in its yellow pages). The annual Pork, Peanut & Pine Festival draws thousands on a mid-July weekend to **Chippokes Plantation State Park,** the oldest continuously farmed property in the country. Besides swimming, picnicking and hiking, the park offers an 1854 mansion with formal gardens, a visitor center with windows onto the James River, and a model farm and forestry museum illustrating agricultural life as it was in Colonial times. The farm tour alone is worth the trip. The **Surry-Jamestown Ferry,** one of Virginia's last, links the two sides of Plantation Country. In town, tours of the smokehouse are offered hourly on the half hour at **Edwards Virginia Ham Shoppe,** where you can snack on such local specialties as ham rolls, sausage sandwiches, peanut soup and Brunswick stew. **Farmer Joe's** gift shop sells flowery items and plants.

Extra-Special

St. Luke's Church, 14477 Benns Church Blvd., off Route 10, Smithfield.

Hidden English-style in the middle of a forested cemetery beside a creek, this is America's only original brick Gothic church and its oldest English-speaking church (1632). Its original traceried windows, stepped gables and buttresses are unique in American architecture. A guide points out the stained-glass window commemorating Pocohontas, the first convert in Virginia to the gospel. The pews were put together with wooden pegs on a raised platform to keep the feet warm. The triple-decker pulpit bearing the rector's hour glass is topped by a sounding board that served as an amplifier. A spectacular 1665 English organ has wood pipes in the shape of a three-dimensional hallway. The church's construction at a time when the Indians were still hostile explains the recessed doorway; "they would trip or hit their heads if they ran too fast, giving time for the men in the back of the church to get their guns," the guide said. Today the Anglican church is used once a year for a non-denominational service. Outside the Old Brick, as this precious church is called, the setting is shady and tranquil, like that of an English churchyard. There are benches, a bowl and a sundial, and graves of the locally ubiquitous Jordan family.

(757) 357-3367. Open daily except Monday, 9:30 to 5; donation.

Historic county seat at Eastville stores oldest court records in America.

Cape Charles, Va.

The Town that Time Forgot

Founded in 1884 as a planned community by railroad/ferry interests, this johnny-come-lately settlement at the southwestern tip of Virginia's historic Eastern Shore grew rapidly to become its largest and busiest town.

Railroad magnates William H. Scott and Alexander Cassatt laid out Cape Charles in perfect square blocks stretching back from the Chesapeake Bay. The seven avenues were named for famed Virginians and the six cross streets for fruits and trees. Substantial homes were built to house railroad executives and entrepreneurs attracted by climate, harbor and prosperity. The town thrived for more than half a century because anyone who traveled up and down the Eastern Shore had to pass through it. Up to two million people arrived annually by train or car to catch the steamer or ferry to or from Norfolk.

After World War II, however, the ferry terminal relocated south of town and the trains stopped carrying passengers. The Chesapeake Bay Bridge-Tunnel, which opened in 1964, provided access to the mainland and a new highway bypassed the town.

Time virtually stopped in Cape Charles after the last steamer left in 1953. Fewer than 40 buildings have been erected in the post-war era. Most of its 568 original structures were built between 1885 and 1920, producing one of the largest concentrations of turn-of-the-century buildings on the East Coast. In 1991, the historic district was placed on the National Register.

Today, the bayside town is undergoing a renaissance. New enterprises are reviving a downtown that had been eerily abandoned. Newcomers are restoring aging houses as vacation or permanent homes. B&Bs and restaurants have emerged to promote Cape Charles as a destination area for tourists. "This is a town on the way up" and "you won't recognize the place in five years" are themes heard time and again from the most diverse of sources.

In 1996, ground was broken for the nation's first eco-industrial initiative, the Port of Cape Charles Sustainable Technology Industrial Park along the sleepy harbor. The first two enterprises got started quickly, a museum of local African American history was emerging in the old black high school, and a technical center was planned to attract visitors.

In 1997, a Virginia Beach developer won approval for a luxury retirement community called Bay Creek. It will encircle the town with up to 3,000 residential units and two eighteen-hole golf courses designed by Arnold Palmer and Jack Nicklaus.

Intriguing contrasts abound. Neighboring Eastville has a courthouse where visitors can inspect the oldest court records in America, dating to 1632. The national wildlife refuge has a state-of-the-art visitor center that the ranger on duty believed to be the most advanced in the country. A longtime merchant has furnished a turn-of-the-century general store as a museum. A block away a Library of Congress staffer has created a gift shop that would be at home in Georgetown. A food retailer has turned a truck stop into something of a gourmet restaurant. A Washington chef has opened a true gourmet restaurant in a Victorian mansion.

Excitement is in the air, but don't be surprised to find half-blocks of abandoned stores between the rising stars or ramshackle eyesores amid the residential restorations.

"I tell prospective visitors that if they're looking for fun and cha-cha, don't come here," says Chris Bannon, dean of local innkeepers. "But if they want the beach, birding, friendly people, rural Americana and history, we've got them all."

Inn Spots

Cape Charles House, 645 Tazewell Ave., Cape Charles 23310.
Looking for a lifestyle change, Bruce and Carol Evans stayed at the Sea Gate B&B (see below) with innkeeper Chris Bannon and put in a bid for this Colonial Revival frame house built in 1912 the same week. They started renovating and upgrading the house, turning it into one of the grandest on the Eastern Shore. Bruce became chairman of the town planning commission and the county's industrial development authority. Carol serves on the zoning board and is president of the chamber of commerce. They opened their B&B in

Carol and Bruce Evans, in front of Cape Charles House, are among the town's guiding spirits.

1994, and have been entertaining guests in a house party atmosphere and touting the charms of Cape Charles to one and all ever since. Their energy was recognized in 2000 when they received the governor's award for tourism and hospitality.

The pair come with credentials as well as enthusiasm. Bruce retired as a store manager for Sears. His wife, who trained in fashion design, was teaching microwave cooking for Sears and writing for a national cooking magazine. All these talents are manifest in their B&B.

Their two parlors offer plush seating, oriental rugs and some of Carol's collections: an old silk spool cabinet, paperweights and her grandmother's samplers. The chandeliered dining room, transformed from a library, is snazzy in hunter green and burgundy with a Schumacher print wallpaper border, roman blinds and matching antique glass on the fireplace mantel.

Corinthian columns frame the staircase to the second floor, which harbors five spacious guest rooms with king or queen beds and private baths. Each is identified with someone important in Cape Charles history. We were comfortable in a side room named for William Scott, the multi-millionaire who tried to get the Pennsylvania Railroad to come to town and finally put up the money himself. Five antique rug beaters were fanned on the wall above the queensize bed. A sofa and writing desk were situated against the bay windows, and a couple of old trunks held a decoy collection as well as our luggage. The large bathroom contained a clawfoot tub and shower.

The most coveted room is named for the original occupant, Julia Wilkins. It's a beauty in blue and white, with a kingsize bed, a border of Royal Copenhagen plates beneath the ceiling, a settee, a wicker loveseat, a private balcony and a bathroom with a jacuzzi. The rear B.F. Kellogg Room is cheery in yellow, while the front Alexander Cassatt Room in apricot colors is hung with Carol's prints.

Breakfast was a gourmet treat, quite amazing given that the Evanses were hosting a reunion of old friends and his fellow barbershop quartet singers and their wives for the weekend, making a total of sixteen hungry people at two seatings. Orange juice and cut-up mixed fruit preceded a work-of-art baked stuffed croissant bearing cream cheese, peaches and cinnamon, garnished with bacon and grapes and served with plain and hazelnut-flavored maple syrups. Other specialties include creamed eggs and mushrooms in dill sauce over homemade dill bread, an egg and cheese quesadilla with herbs and bell peppers, grits and cheese soufflé and banana-stuffed french toast. Carol was preparing a cookbook of favorite recipes, and offers five-course dinners for groups of guests by reservation.

Wine, cheese and hors d'oeuvres are offered in the early evening. Chocolate mints are bedside treats.

(757) 331-4920. www.capecharleshouse.com. Five rooms with private baths. Doubles, $85 to $120. No smoking.

Wilson-Lee House, 403 Tazewell Ave., Cape Charles 23310.

David Phillips is a stage designer and Leon Parham an architect, so they knew what they were doing when they started restoring this 1906 Colonial Revival four-square house, built for the owner of the old Wilson's Department Store and one of the finest residences in town. "This house spoke to us," David said as he recalled the purchase and subsequent weekends of commuting from New Jersey during nine months of renovations. The partners ran a two-bedroom townhouse B&B in Jersey City to try their hand at innkeeping before deciding to transplant their success to their native South.

They opened in late 1996 with six up-to-date rooms with tiled baths and pedestal sinks, queensize beds, dramatic decor, clock radio/CD players, hair dryers and terrycloth robes. Rooms come with the inn's own toiletries and chocolate mints on the pillows.

Named for members of the original family, the bedrooms are striking for their theatrics, especially the artworks and the bed covers and window treatments fashioned by a friend. They are furnished with a mix of contemporary accessories and period heirlooms from David's family.

The Alyce Wilson Room has an imported French iron canopy bed whose lines convey a stark simplicity. The James Wilson Room is Victorian in hunter green and red, with a stately carved walnut bed and bureau and thick carpeting. The bed and the bureau are art deco pieces in the Georgia Wilson Room. The third-floor Anna's Room has a walnut spool bed and an antique platform rocker. The premier James W. Lee Room, named for the Norfolk architect who designed the house, is designed in architectural and post modern style with contemporary waffle steel chairs. A glass block wall conceals a jacuzzi tub in the bath area and a double vanity.

David, an accomplished cook, prepares a Southern breakfast featuring biscuits and country ham, as well as a main dish like cheese grits soufflé, eggs florentine, oven-baked pancake with apples or a hash brown and sausage frittata. Coffee-walnut-chocolate chip muffins might accompany. The meal is served in a dining room appointed in black and burgundy or on a screened-in section of the wrap-around veranda.

Consummate hosts, the partners have succeeded in restoring the house to what they said was its original purpose: "fun and entertainment." They stock a butler's pantry for "guests to make themselves at home." By reservation, they will arrange for sunset sails with cocktails followed by a cookout on their deck.

(757) 331-1954. Six rooms with private baths. Doubles, $85 to $120. Two-night minimum weekends. No smoking.

Dogwoods and azaleas brighten grounds of Nottingham Ridge manor house in spring.

Nottingham Ridge, 28184 Nottingham Ridge Lane, Cape Charles 23310. A beautiful brick manor house built in 1975. A sandy beach alongside the Chesapeake Bay. A secluded, hundred-acre property two miles off the main road.

These are among the attributes of Bonnie Nottingham's home, which she shares with guests in four B&B rooms. "The sun sets in our back yard," says Bonnie. "We take it for granted, but guests are so awed by it."

She and her sister-in-law, Sara Nottingham Goffigon, who runs the Pickett's Harbor B&B, are the original B&B hostesses in this section of Virginia's Eastern Shore. Their substantial houses also are the only ones along a half-mile stretch of dirt road called Nottingham Ridge Lane, nestled between woods and farmland on one side and the bay on the other.

Guests enjoy nettle-free swimming from a sandy beach that stretches as far as the eye can see in either direction. They also enjoy the showy azaleas and rhododendrons in the backyard and the view over the dunes from the screened porch across the rear of the house.

Inside are a fireplaced family room in which a wide cabinet displays Bonnie's collection of blue and white china, an elegant front living room with a fireplace, and a formal dining room where breakfast is served when it's too cool to be outside on the porch.

A main-floor guest room, pretty in pale yellow with green trim, comes with a queensize iron bed and a full bathroom with a view of the bay.

Upstairs are three more bedrooms, all quite spacious and with private baths. One in the rear with bay views has a double mahogany sleigh bed, a writing desk and two chairs. A front bedroom offers a queen poster bed, floral fabrics, two rattan chairs and a bathroom with a sit-down shower. At the far end of the house is a suite with a queensize spool bed, Duncan Phyfe sofa, antique cedar chest, oriental rugs and a TV/VCR. An anteroom with a twin bed turns it into a family suite.

Bonnie serves a full breakfast. The day of our visit she chose grapefruit, muffins, scrambled eggs with bacon and fried apples. Other main courses include sweetpotato biscuits with Smithfield ham, egg casserole, quiche and french toast. Wine and cheese are offered in the afternoon.

(757) 331-1010. Three rooms and one suite with private baths. Doubles, $90 to $100; suite, $100 to $130. Two-night minimum weekends, April-October. Children over 8. No smoking. No credit cards.

Pickett's Harbor B&B, 28288 Nottingham Ridge Lane, Cape Charles 23310. Sara Goffigon gets up at 4 a.m. some days to prepare breakfast for guests before leaving for her job as a teacher of advanced placement courses at a private school up the shore. How can she maintain the pace? She and her husband Cooke raised five children, "so everything has been easy ever since."

Part of the Nottingham family that has farmed 100 secluded areas along the Chesapeake Bay since the 1600s, Sara started taking in B&B guests in 1982 in a handsome brick and gray clapboard house the couple built to look old in 1976. The rambling house is nestled in a forest of oaks and loblolly pines, with landscaped grounds leading toward the sand dunes along the bay.

The Goffigons offer six guest rooms in a variety of configurations. Three have private baths and the others share two baths. Three have queen beds, two are doubles and one is a three-quarter bed. We looked into a couple of rooms with country antique furnishings and handsome wood floorboards obtained from a tobacco warehouse in Richmond.

Guests take breakfast in a stunningly handsome formal 18th-century dining room with oriental rug and fireplace or on the back porch looking toward the bay. The fare includes fresh fruit, sourdough bread or muffins, Virginia ham and a main dish such as asparagus quiche or cheese, sausage and egg casserole.

(757) 331-2212. Three rooms with private baths and three rooms sharing two baths. Doubles, $85 to $135. No smoking.

Sea Gate B&B, 9 Tazewell Ave., Cape Charles 23310.

A tropical look prevails at this delightful B&B. Chris Bannon, a hospitality professional who had run the Holy Family Monastery's retreat weekends in Connecticut, tired of wintry weather and decided to return to his native Norfolk area. He settled on Cape Charles and opened the first B&B in town in 1988.

"I always wanted a palm tree and now I have three," he says by way of explanation for the swamp palms beside the front door of a house painted a summery peach color. The screened porches full of plants add to a tropical look that Chris likes to call eclectic.

The main floor is a happy mélange of side dining porch at one end, a large foyer, a country kitchen and a formal living room, both opening onto a solarium porch furnished in rattan. A spiral staircase wends its way through the solarium greenery to a second porch overhead.

Upstairs are four spacious corner bedrooms. Two in back have queen beds, one with a stunning blue and yellow quilt, and private baths. A front room has a king bed with half-bath in the closet, while the other also has a lavatory and opens onto the upstairs porch above the solarium. These two share a full bath.

Chris puts his hotel-restaurant background to the test, preparing and serving a hearty breakfast of juice, fresh fruit, two or three breakfast meats and a main dish, perhaps french toast, omelets or a Mediterranean egg dish with cheese and tomatoes. It's taken at individual tables on the dining porch between 8 and 10.

The personable host occupies "the Cloister" on the third floor when he's not entertaining guests, serving on the Town Council, ecumenicizing the local Catholic church into a community center or drumming up enthusiasm for Cape Charles. This one-man band lends to civic duties the same passion he extends to innkeeping. *(757) 331-2206. Two rooms with private baths and two rooms with private lavatories and shared bath. Doubles, $80 to $90. Children over 7. Smoking restricted.*

Chesapeake Charm B&B, 202 Madison Ave., Cape Charles 23310.

Pale yellow with green trim, this square house built in 1921 is furnished with 1930s family heirlooms. Barry and Phyllis Tyndall from North Carolina moved here in 1995 to open this as a B&B. He commutes to work in Virginia Beach, while she runs the house and takes care of their toddler.

The Tyndalls did all the renovation work themselves. The second floor holds three guest rooms with private baths. Granny's Treasures is furnished with items made by or given to them by their four grandmothers, including a double bed with a hand-carved headboard. The Eastern Shore Room has a rolled oak queensize bed, pictures by Eastern Shore artists and a jacuzzi tub in the bathroom, the ceiling and walls of which talented Phyllis wallpapered and painted to resemble pressed tin. The Queen Anne's Lace Room has an Eastlake queen bed with a lace crocheted cover and pillows, two upholstered chairs and a vintage pedestal tub in the bath.

Downstairs is a pump organ in the vestibule. Beyond the living room is a dining room where breakfast is served. Barry cooks on weekends and Phyllis on weekdays. Expect fresh fruit, homemade muffins and perhaps Barry's apple pancakes or Phyllis's unique strawberry omelets. Afternoon refreshments include many of their grandmothers' Southern treats, including homemade cookies and pound cake. *(757) 331-2676 or (800) 546-9215. Three rooms with private baths. Doubles, $75 to $90. Children over 2. Smoking restricted.*

Trekernow, 117 Randolph Ave., Cape Charles 23310.

British-born diplomat/writer Tim Trevan was preparing to return to his homeland following his New York posting when he took a parting trip down the East Coast. His second stop was Cape Charles. "I immediately fell in love with the place," he said. So he looked at properties for sale, saw this rundown house the next morning and put in an offer from London.

He gutted the interior to open it as an upscale B&B in June 2000. He shares his home with guests in four corner bedrooms on the second floor, each with a modern bath, TV and telephone. He described their decor as eclectic – English and Edwardian, primarily (the B&B's name is Cornish for home). Three bedrooms have queensize beds. One can connect through double doors to an adjoining room with twin beds that can be joined as a king.

The main floor has a living room, a dining room and a large kitchen, from which Tim serves a gourmet breakfast from a repertoire of about two dozen recipes. Scrambled eggs with chives is one of his favorites. *(757) 331-2516. Four rooms with private baths. Doubles, $90 to $120.*

Sterling House, 9 Randolph Ave., Cape Charles 23310.

Edward Brinkley, a world-renowned birder, and local carpet merchant Steve Hairfield acquired a landmark Victorian bungalow and were renovating it to open as a B&B in 2001. It takes its name from an early mayor, who built the house in

1888 and with his brothers founded Cape Charles's first industry, the Sterling seafood plant on the harbor. Steve said the house, which needed work, would have four bedrooms with private baths, two on the main floor and two on the second. They planned to furnish it in Craftsman-style furniture.

Ned Brinkley, who writes birding books and takes birders on tours across the country for Field Guides, will store his birding library in the house and lead birding tours for guests. Steve, who discovered Cape Charles during a sailing excursion on the Chesapeake Bay, plans to give kayak and canoe trips as well as sunset cruises on his sailboat. Their house is one of the closest to the beach and pavilion.

Both men cook, and plan to serve their guests gourmet breakfasts.

(757) 331-2483. Four rooms with private baths. Doubles, $80 to $115.

Dining Spots

Eastville Manor, 6058 Willow Oak Road (Route 631), Eastville.

Since this restaurant's opening in 1996, there's no doubt among Eastern Shore gourmands that they have a treasure in their midst. William Scalley, a chef who had cooked at the Mayflower and Four Seasons hotels in Washington, D.C., and his New Orleans-born wife Melody bought an 1886 Victorian mansion on the outskirts of Eastville and opened a restaurant of distinction. They did so with trepidation because, Melody said, "we're offering the only fine dining in the county and the locals find us expensive."

Doing much of the renovation work himself, Bill – whom his wife describes as a Renaissance man – created three small dining rooms with well-spaced tables dressed with votive candles and fresh flowers. He made the stained glass for the front door and crafted the corner shelf for a collection of show plates. Doorways with wrought-iron overhead trim separate two rooms done in pale yellow atop blue patterned wainscoting. Masses of colorful zinnias – grown by a waitress and still blooming at our mid-November visit – decorated the foyer. Melody planted 5,000 bulbs amid the majestic boxwoods and gardenia plants "taller than I am" on the showy grounds outside.

Flowers turned up as garnishes on our dinners, starting with an appetizer of a delicious crab cake decorated with a baby mum, carrot curls, an onion blossom and coriander. Basil butter accompanied a basket of sensational breads, among them corn and sourdough. The short menu bore prices that would have been expected at lunch in many a city restaurant. Main-course choices ranged from grilled tuna with roasted red peppers, jicama, peanuts and sesame seeds in curry butter to roasted chicken breast stuffed with spinach, Smithfield ham and sundried tomatoes with cheddar grits in a grainy mustard sauce. We were impressed with our selections: medallions of duck with fried plantains in a ginger-orange sauce and sliced beef tenderloin in a cabernet-tarragon sauce. Each was abundantly presented in something of a hodgepodge atop a couple of dozen fresh vegetables and sides. Eight fantastic-sounding desserts included a quartet of exotic, homemade sorbets that were a refreshing ending to a memorable meal.

Working with local farmers and fishermen, the Scalleys caught the attention of the James Beard Foundation in 1999, culminating in an invitation to cook at a fund-raising dinner for 75 in New York. That prompted its listing among only eleven Virginia restaurants in the James Beard worldwide directory for 2000.

Chef Bill, who mans the kitchen from 9 a.m. to midnight, offers five-course

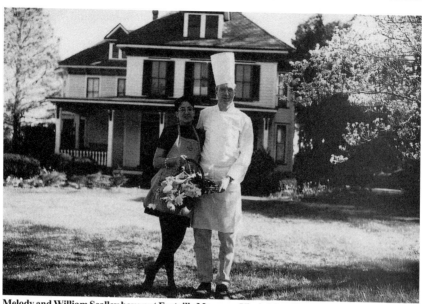

Melody and William Scalley have put Eastville Manor on Virginia's culinary map.

wine-tasting dinners monthly. He serves lunch in season, and cooks a full breakfast for overnight guests who book the manor's two upstairs rooms, each with queensize bed and double whirlpool tub, for $160 a night.

(757) 678-7378. Entrées, $10.95 to $14.95. Lunch, Wednesday-Friday 11:30 to 2, spring and summer. Dinner, Wednesday-Saturday 5:30 to 9. Closed in January.

Sting-Ray's Restaurant, 26507 Lankford Hwy. (Route 13), Capeville.

They dub it "Chez Exxon," this semi-gourmet restaurant that Ray Haynie built from a twenty-seat truck stop he bought in 1985. With a background in food retailing, he expanded the rear restaurant with an open kitchen into more than 100 seats in three usually packed dining areas.

"I'm Sting-Ray," he said when introduced, having taken the name when he entered chili cook-offs in which his version was honored for its deep, smoky flavor that stings on the palate. "We make everything from scratch," said Ray, who now has an enormous kitchen staff and spends most of his time greeting customers out front. He features fresh seafood and angus beef, plus Southern side vegetables and inspired homemade desserts that keep regulars coming back.

The fare is truck stop by day, upscale at night. Decor is basic: bright lighting and bare booths and tables, each dressed with a ketchup bottle, salt and pepper shakers, an ashtray and packages of artificial sweeteners. You order from a blackboard menu at the counter, and waitresses bring the meal.

At our visit, the menu offered a staggering 22 entrees (after a couple had been erased because they'd sold out by 5:30). They ranged in price from fried oysters or pan-fried pork chops to shrimp or flounder stuffed with crab imperial. The salmon is to die for, according to one fan. So is the Smithfield crab imperial, layered with Smithfield ham and topped with cheese. It's almost everybody's favorite, except for old-timers who disdain the fancy choices and opt for pork ribs, delmonico steak or the dinner platter of roast beef with gravy. Creamy crab soup is the starter of choice. Sweet-potato pie and Tennessee bread pudding are among the desserts.

An extensive selection of wine is displayed on racks as you enter the restaurant area from the service station/convenience store. Customers so inclined pick out their choices, pay the retail price and there's no corkage fee. But wine imbibers might feel conspicuous among all the beer-guzzling and iced-tea sipping locals.

(757) 331-2505. Entrées, $8.95 to $17.95. Open daily from 5:30 a.m. Dinner, 4:30 to 9 or 9:30.

The Watch House, 7 Strawberry St., Cape Charles.

Home cooking of the greasy spoon school is the strength of this establishment likened to a Southern hometown cafe of 50 years ago.

At our initial Cape Charles visit it was the only place in town open for lunch, other than the soda fountain at Rayfield's Pharmacy. So we settled in for a crab cake sandwich and a fried oyster dinner with coleslaw and french fries, tasty and filling. The menu reads like the 1950s, with things like a BLT and fried chicken featured at lunch. The dinner menu yields liver and onions, steamed shrimp, soft-shell crab, crab imperial and fried or broiled seafood platter, with a choice of ten side vegetables.

Homemade cobblers, pies (pecan and white chocolate/banana cream) and bread pudding are among the desserts. Beer and wine are available.

Decor is plain: a pine-paneled room with basic booths, tables and chairs. As elsewhere in town, everyone seems to know each other.

(757) 331-3879. Entrées, $4.75 to $13.95. Open daily except Tuesday, 11 to 9.

Diversions

Nature, history and old-time Americana are the draws here.

The area has one of the highest Christmas bird counts (more than 150 species) north of Florida. The October birding festival attracts thousands, and more species are sighted here than in better-known Cape May, N.J. Monarch butterflies migrate through. Birders band everything from hummingbirds to bald eagles.

Eastern Shore of Virginia National Wildlife Refuge, 5003 Hallett Circle. This 750-acre wildlife refuge at the northern end of the Chesapeake Bay Bridge-Tunnel was established in 1984 to manage and protect habitats for migrating birds along the Atlantic Coast flyway. Audio-visual displays in the state-of-the-art visitor center detail everything one could want to know about shore wildlife. Two stationary telescopes and two sets of binoculars in an observation room with large glass windows yield close-up views across the salt marshes toward the barrier islands. Pictures identify birds frequently sighted. Young and old enjoy what a ranger called the "think tank," a touch-and-feel display of exotic shells and skeletons. Twenty-seven videos lasting from four minutes to an hour are available for showing in the auditorium. In front of the replica of a waterman's shack, we listened to a recording of Cigar Daisey of Chincoteague talking about decoy carving. Outside, a half-mile interpretive trail loops past an old graveyard to a World War II bunker, where a 60-foot-high observation platform overlooks marshes, islands, inlets and ocean. Offshore beneath the bridge is the Fisherman Island wildlife refuge, a special haunt for birders.

(757) 331-2760. Open daily, 9 to 4. Free.

Kiptopeke State Park, 3540 Kiptopeke Drive, (757) 331-2267. Situated along the Chesapeake Bay three miles north of the bridge-tunnel is Virginia's newest state park, established in 1992 and under development as a mecca for nature lovers. Near the boat ramp is the old terminal building for the ferry service that moved here from Cape Charles in 1950. The 375-acre park has a swimming beach, picnic areas, camping facilities, a hiking trail, a fishing pier, a hawk observatory and a bird banding station. Visitors join volunteers to participate in bird banding on fall weekends. Parking, $4 weekends, $3 midweek.

Touring Cape Charles. Points of interest are detailed in a brochure and map published by the town's B&B association. Sights vary from several Sears, Roebuck mail-order houses to two houses that have settled toward each other to the point where their roofs overlap. The landmark water tower visible as you approach town turns out to have been designed in 1992 and patterned after the old Cape Charles Lighthouse. Nearby, the old Delmarva Power Plant was converted into the **Cape Charles Museum and Welcome Center,** open weekend afternoons. Two railroad cars were being restored behind the museum for excursions to neighboring towns. Virginia's first memorial library is housed in an old Presbyterian church at Tazewell and Plum. Visit the gazebo at the foot of Randolph Street, where a dolphin sculpture is beside the path to the public beach. A narrow boardwalk parallels the beach along Bay Avenue. There's a new jetty pier at the harbor, where Applaud the Sunset parties are staged in the Key West idiom. A parade is the highlight of the annual Cape Charles Day celebration in September. The Pride of Baltimore showed up in 1997 at the annual Schooner Feast, part of the Great Chesapeake Bay Schooner Race from Norfolk to Baltimore. The Fourth of July fireworks here are considered the best on the Eastern Shore.

Look across the harbor for the pioneering **Port of Cape Charles Sustainable Technologies Industrial Park,** the first of four in the nation. It is designed for companies that do not generate waste or that use as a resource the discharge of those that do. A technical center is expected to be of interest to visitors.

Arts Enter Cape Charles, 17 Mason Ave., Cape Charles, (757) 331-2787. This multi-disciplined arts venture symbolizes the rebirth of Cape Charles. "We started in 1996 with nothing – just a group of people who wanted to talk about the arts," said Clelia Sheppard, founder and now executive director. From a room in the old high school, where art classes are taught, the community-based enterprise expanded into the old Palace movie theater. It added a **Stage Door Art Gallery** around the corner at 10 Strawberry St. Movies are shown twice monthly, visiting musicians perform, the Virginia Symphony of Norfolk scheduled a summer pops concert and Arts Enter thespians produce several shows a year. The 500-seat theater, undergoing restoration, is a marvel of Art Deco style with tapestry murals, terrazzo floors and a walnut foyer. Local artists show in the Stage Door gallery, which is open Tuesday-Sunday.

Eyre Hall, Route 636, one of the best preserved 18th-century houses in Virginia, is a state historical landmark down a shady lane off Route 13. The 1735 home is open during Garden Week in April, but the rare boxwood and perennial gardens may be visited year-round. The family graveyard is walled in brick delivered from England as ballast in sailing ships.

Eastville. Compared with nouveau Cape Charles (founded 1884), the somnolent Northampton County seat about six miles north appears positively historic. It was settled shortly after Captain John Smith explored the peninsula in 1608 on his way to establishing the first permanent English colony in Jamestown. The Colonial Courthouse, built about 1731, contains the oldest continuous court records in the nation, dating from 1632. They can be examined at the court clerk's office on the first floor. Outside on the tiny Courthouse Green are a confederate monument, a debtor's prison, an ancient whipping post, and a couple of ancillary buildings that now are attorneys' offices.

Shopping. Abandoned storefronts, indeed blocks, strike visitors along Mason Avenue, the once thriving main street. Between them, however, are some promising newcomers, as many as ten in one year alone. The standout is **Cape Charles Trading Co.**, which started as an antiques shop but evolved into an eclectic gift shop. Owner Paul Dwyer commutes weekends from his work at the Library of Congress to oversee a veritable bazaar of one-of-a-kind gifts and collectibles that you don't expect to find in Cape Charles. Nearby is the small retail showroom of **Delisheries, Ltd.**, wholesaler of gourmet baking mixes. Patterned after his mother's Sugar Plum Bakery in Virginia Beach, the enterprise is overseen by Chris Marshall and his wife, Meg, who were preparing "easy, one-bowl mixes" for cookies and muffins in the back production area at our visit. One of the first participants in the new Sustainable Technologies Industrial Park, the pair plan to train handicapped workers to help with production.

A special place up the shore at Onley is **Turner Sculpture,** the foundry and gallery where world-renowned artists David and William Turner produce remarkable bronze sculptures of wildlife in action. One of their pieces, two Canada geese about to land, is on display outside the entrance to the visitor center at the Eastern Shore of Virginia National Wildlife Refuge.

Extra-Special

Charmar's Old Country Store Museum, 213 Mason Ave., Cape Charles.

This is a turn-of-the-century country store like no other – partly because it's a museum and nothing's for sale, partly because it's one man's labor of love, and partly because everything is authentic (the soap boxes and containers are full, not cardboard or metal showpieces). Antiques dealers Charles and Margaret Carlson opened the museum by happenstance in 1979 in a storefront next to their **Charmar's Antiques** shop. Why? "It's a long story," says Charlie, holding forth in his museum. "My wife says I'm a sucker for buying anything." It seems a friend called one day to offer a 21-foot store counter and cajoled the dealer into accepting it if it was delivered. "We stuck it in here and I started filling it up with all the boxes of stuff I had collected." Soon he had a full-fledged country store, with a post office in the back, a potbelly stove, shelves of merchandise (from cow tonic to lice killer to Blossom Bloomers to a can of Caster Oil axle grease). We could relate to all the old soap detergents of our youth, if not to the strange wire contraption he called a chicken catcher. "See my customer," he pointed to a mannequin. "And my butcher." Quite the character, Charlie has great fun showing one and all the intricacies of his special collection. School groups visit to observe and hear his tales of life in the past.

(757) 331-1488. Open by appointment or by chance via the antiques shop, Monday-Saturday 10 to 5. Donation.

Washington, Va.

The Place That an Inn Built

After seventeen-year-old surveyor George Washington laid out its streets in 1749, this was to become the first of 28 towns named for the father of our country and the only one so designated before he became president. Not until rather lately had it been lifted from obscurity by an unlikely catalyst, a restaurant and inn playfully called The Inn at Little Washington.

This was "almost a ghost town," in the words of Patrick O'Connell. He teamed with Reinhardt Lynch to convert what once was a garage at the main crossroads into a restaurant in 1978. Rave reviews quickly attracted the movers and shakers from big Washington, along with food and lodging cognoscenti from around the world. Because their clientele complained of the late-night drive back to the other Washington, the partners eventually added bedrooms and suites to become a full-service inn. Not an ordinary inn, mind you, but a pricey paragon that has been exalted to incredible heights. It is the only establishment ever to capture five-star awards for both dining and lodging from the Mobil Travel Guide and the first inn to receive five-diamond awards for both food and accommodations from the American Automobile Association.

Its accolades – and the adulation of the nation's elite – have put on the map, for better or worse, the two-bit hamlet in which it resides. But, its press to the contrary, this is no one-inn nor one-restaurant town. Others have popped up in the inn's footsteps.

Happily, success has not spoiled little Washington. The entire village is designated an historic district and remains unscathed by development.

Washington is the county seat of Rappahannock County, though you'd scarcely know it from the unassuming government buildings a block off Main Street. With 6,000 people, Rappahannock is the second smallest of Virginia's counties. It's a relic of the past, situated between prosperous hunt country to the east and the bucolic Blue Ridge Mountains to the west. It's a detour off the main road and not really on the way to anywhere else. At the dawn of the new millenium, local people conceded the village was in transition, poised – in one innkeeper's words – to become "the next Middleburg."

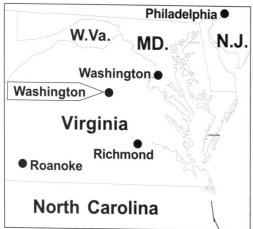

The village's estimated population of 232 ranks it as the county's largest, ahead of Sperryville and Flint Hill. The mountainous county has more cows than people and more apple trees than cows. There are no traffic lights (only a couple of flashers), no supermarkets or chain stores. It is a spectacularly scenic mountain area, yet tranquil and gentle. A few good shops, wineries and outdoor activities, plus the area's cachet, make it a destination for weekenders (almost everything is closed early in the week).

It's a diverse area because it is home to the poorest of the poor as well as the richest of the rich. Sometimes it's hard to tell which is which because almost everybody drives a pickup truck – except for those visitors, most in luxury cars or limousines, whose destination is the Inn at Little Washington.

Inn Spots

The Inn at Little Washington paved the way, but others have followed – and are much in demand as lodging alternatives for visitors who don't wish to pay top dollar. Like the inn, some of the B&Bs carry surcharges for weekends and the month of October. Although 75 percent of their business at certain times comes as a result of overflow from the inn, each is increasingly able to stand on its own.

The Inn at Little Washington, Middle and Main Streets, Washington 22747.

There's no sign to detract from its aura of exclusivity. Only by the process of elimination does the visitor determine that the unremarkable, three-story white building festooned with flags at what passes for the village crossroads is, indeed, the celebrated Inn at Little Washington. Depending on the time of day, the handful of fancy cars parked in pickup territory might give it away. But lace curtains on the windows and a closed entry thwart the gaze of curious passersby.

This is an inn turned inward unto itself, as one might find in a large city. From the inn's perspective, the village is not particularly compelling, and those with the wherewithal to spend a night or two here seem to want to screen themselves from the outside. Owners Patrick O'Connell and Reinhardt Lynch provide a cocoon of luxury patterned after an English manor home. Everything has been draped, flounced and swagged by a London stage-set designer who, curiously, never saw the place until she attended the grand-opening party. Her elaborate conceptual drawings of each room hang in the hallways.

The restoration of the two-story lobby alone cost more than the original building. Its gilt ceiling is decorated with a collage of 500 hand-drawn blocks that resemble stained glass. Surely the inn's reported $2 million renovation tab does not include the furnishings. Otherwise, the reports of bedspreads costing $10,000 are apocryphal.

The banister leading upstairs to a second-floor lobby favored by overnight guests for tea or cocktails is wrapped in velvet. The twelve accommodations here range from standard (one) to intermediate (three) and superior (four) to suites (four). An additional intermediate room and suite in the inn's guest house above the Rare Finds gift shop down the street are described by its proprietor as "just as nice if not nicer" in comparison with the main accommodations. The latest in a 1997 addition behind the inn are the ultimate. Called junior suites, they are side by side on the second floor atop a new kitchen and share a wide rear balcony. Larger than the original rooms, one has a fireplace and a bathroom that's as big as the inn's smallest room.

The inn's recent expansion also produced a new library, a bar and lounge area, and a small private dining room in space freed up by vacating the old kitchen.

Each accommodation is "utterly decadent in detail," in the words of the inn's

Exotic plants are featured in inner courtyard at The Inn at Little Washington.

extravagant, sixteen-page brochure. All are decorated to the nth, up to the wallpapered ceilings and down to the oriental rugs on the floors. Each has a bathroom with countertops of Greek marble, heated towel racks, a shoe polisher and Gilbert & Soames toiletries. There are terrycloth robes, padded and removable coat hangers, a telephone but no TV or radio, lush beds draped within an inch of their lives, and double doors at the entry to eliminate hallway noise. All have a cozy chair with a hassock and a throw on top. Some have window seats and others have private balconies. Those looking onto the garden courtyard appeal more than those facing the street. Each is furnished with antiques and custom-made contemporary pieces, and "Mr. O'Connell is always on the lookout for new things," our guide offered. Clad in black and white, a staff of more than 60 attends to every detail and are quite a presence in the center of town as they move between buildings.

Two duplex suites, furnished and decorated similarly except for their color schemes, crown the inn's third floor. In the more striking of the two, an arched doorway leads to a sitting area with a velour sofa/banquette a dozen feet long, all draped in mulberry and awash with pillows. Walls are a soft sponged peach and oriental throw rugs cover the oatmeal-colored carpeting. A side balcony overlooks the garden. A wet bar and a stereo system separate the sitting room from the bathroom. The latter contains a jacuzzi in a window alcove, a double sink, a dressing area with a built-in seat, a w.c. and bidet behind one door and, behind another door, a shower stall for two with English hinged glass doors. One entire wall is mirrored. Upstairs in a loft is the bedroom with another balcony, from which you can see most of the village. Layered fabrics like those used in the sitting area decorate the kingsize bed. A stunning canopy is painted on the ceiling that slopes to the floor below.

Fresh flowers furnished by the inn's full-time gardener (often supplemented by orchids grown for the inn by a nearby purveyor) greet guests. Bottles of mineral water await. Tea and a fruit and cookie tray are served in the room at check-in.

The patio beside an exotic garden incorporating oriental and native Virginia plants is a favorite spot for breakfast. Fresh fruits, juices and homemade breads and pastries like applesauce-walnut croissants are included in the rates. A hot breakfast that brings the acclaimed pan-fried rainbow trout or eggs scrambled with Scottish smoked salmon and cream cheese costs extra.

Is a stay here worth the expense? Yes, for those who aspire to the ultimate in decor and service, though some might find the cocoon claustrophobic. The cache of glowing press reprints in the lobby and the flyer headlined "Avalanche of Awards Hits Inn at Little Washington" surely must dispel any doubts.

(540) 675-3800. Fax (540) 675-3100. Nine rooms and five suites with private baths. Doubles, $340 to $495. Suites, $550 to $640. Add $225 for all Saturdays and some holidays, add $125 for all Fridays and other holidays, add $50 for all Sundays. Add an additional $100 for October. No smoking.

The Middleton Inn, 176 Main St., Box 254, Washington 22747.

Uncommonly sumptuous for a B&B and one of the few with a four-diamond AAA rating, this hilltop brick manor house was opened to guests in 1995 after eight months of top-to-bottom renovations. Mary Ann Kuhn, a former Washington Post reporter and CBS News producer, found a new calling as a restorer of old buildings and as a hostess par excellence.

Sparing no expense, vivacious Mary Ann produced plush common rooms and four deluxe guest rooms in the main Federal house built in 1850 by Middleton Miller, who manufactured Confederate uniforms during the Civil War. She turned the former slave's quarters behind into a romantic little cottage and boarded her horses in a rear barn on the six-acre hunt-country estate.

The bedrooms are sights to behold. Each comes with a marble bath and a working fireplace. Fine linens dress the queen or king beds. Bottles of spring water are at the ready, and chocolates are placed at bedside during turndown service.

The queensize wicker Chartwell sleigh bed in the front-corner Ivy Room is a reproduction of one from Winston Churchill's family home in England. A leather loveseat and a wing chair take advantage of the mountain view from the other front-corner Hunt Country Room. An antique bookshelf becomes a closet in the rear Morning Room, pretty in yellow with floral fabrics. A large 1830s vanity

Mary Ann Kuhn renovated her brick manor house into The Middleton Inn.

topped by a mirror in the bedroom is the focal point in the Man's Vanity Room. Bath facilities are enclosed on either side.

The most sought-after quarters are in the rear cottage. It has a small living room with TV, a little refrigerator and stove, and a bathroom with a jacuzzi tub from which you can look out the window at the mountains. Upstairs is a bedroom with beamed cathedral ceiling and a queensize sleigh bed.

Guests enjoy afternoon tea and wine in the formal drawing room. A focal point is an 1830s grand piano upon which rests a striking bronze sculpture of George Bush pitching a horseshoe, the work of syndicated cartoonist Patrick Oliphant, Mary Ann's ex-husband.

The most visually striking space is the dining room, where five round tables are dressed in long white linens, sterling flatware and Herrend china for breakfast amidst museum-quality hunting prints and an extravagant floral display. Every course arrives on a silver platter. Fresh orange juice, fruit and homemade muffins are preliminaries to such treats as raspberry pancakes with country sausage or eggs benedict with smoked trout and asparagus. Linger over coffee on the front porch and enjoy the view of the mountains.

(540) 675-2020 or (800) 816-8157. Fax (540) 675-1050. www.middleton-inn.com. Four rooms and one cottage with private baths. Doubles, $260 to $325 weekends, $195 to $225 midweek. Cottage, $425 weekends, $275 midweek. Two-night minimum for October and holidays. Children over 12. No smoking.

Bleu Rock Inn, 12567 Lee Hwy. (Route 211), Washington 22747.

Morning may be the best part of the experience here, say staff and guests at this deluxe inn, which began as a pretender to the Inn at Little Washington's throne. That's because of the lavish breakfasts served in a matchless setting: in a dining room beside the garden or on a rear terrace overlooking a Napa Valley-ish vista toward a pond, vineyards and the Blue Ridge Mountains.

The dominant inn cannot match the newcomer's complimentary breakfast, scenery or value. Consider the morning repast, which changes daily: perhaps grand marnier french toast, shrimp and tomato omelet, poached eggs with smoked salmon or omelets with shiitake mushrooms, chives and local goat cheese. Little drop biscuits, carrot and poppyseed muffins and blueberry and cinnamon rolls with three homemade preserves might accompany. "We try to do something extra," says co-chef Lynn Mahan in a reference to the lack of a full breakfast included in the rates at the other inn.

The Bleu Rock, which has been known to serve mighty good meals (see Dining Spots), also offers a spectacular, rural setting on 80 acres. It was opened in a converted farmhouse a few miles southwest of the village in 1990 by brothers Bernard and Jean Campagne, who operate La Bergerie Restaurant in Alexandria. They were tinkering with this as a place to which they would retire, until early 2000 when they sold it to Harry Carlip and Josephine Mariea, new owners of the Heritage House B&B in the village.

The five unpretentious guest rooms with private baths are pristinely elegant (but why the small, stand-up balconies without chairs)? The four upstairs rooms have queensize beds. The largest is outfitted in peach and moss green colors with draped lace curtains. A nearby room, much smaller, is done in blues and yellows. Another room in deep blue has a dark blue comforter adorned with tulips. The shower curtains in most bathrooms match the bed covers. Fresh flowers, a hair dryer and fancy Kingsbridge toiletries, pretty dried wreaths and potpourri are hallmarks. Fruit baskets and candies are placed in each room. A downstairs room in blue-green and deep rose offers two double iron and brass beds and a large bath tiled in pink.

An attractive and spacious sitting room, quite elaborately furnished, harbors books and games and a fireplace. Out in front of the restored white stucco farmhouse with a tin roof and blue accents are colorful gardens and a trickling fountain. And in back, well away from Route 211, are the pond, vineyards and mountains, with plenty of seating to take them all in.

(540) 987-3190 or (800) 537-3652. Fax (540) 987-3193. Five rooms with private baths. Doubles, $195 weekends and October, $125 midweek. Children over 10. Smoking restricted.

Sycamore Hill House & Gardens, 110 Menefee Mountain Lane, Washington 22747.

Off by itself on 52 acres at the end of a mile-long driveway up Menefee Mountain, this is one of the few contemporary B&Bs in all Virginia. "No dolls, ducks or bunnies here," says Kerri Wagner, innkeeper with her husband Stephen. Just tasteful furnishings, exquisite flowers and plants, original artworks, three comfortable rooms with queen beds and private baths, gourmet food and a view that won't quit.

Kerri, a former lobbyist in the other Washington, and Steve, a well-known illustrator, spotted a for-sale sign on a Sunday drive in 1987. "We came back as a lark, saw the house and had to have it," says Kerri. "Steve's job was portable and mine was not, so that was the impetus for the B&B." They opened on New Year's Day in 1988, having decided the house was so big and the location so special that they ought to share it.

And share they do. Kerri greets summertime guests with iced tea and homemade cookies on the 65-foot, semi-circular veranda, where Amish bentwood rockers take in a 180-degree panorama of the Blue Ridge Mountains across Kerri's prized gardens. The originals of Steve's illustrations for Time-Life Books (and others)

Sycamore Hill House & Gardens, as portrayed by illustrator-innkeeper Stephen Wagner.

enhance each room. His illustration of the inn on a winter night with deer in the snow and a zillion stars is magical. It hangs in the master bedroom, where we awoke in a waist-high four-poster bed to a mist-shrouded vista that looked like an oriental landscape. No fewer than four arrangements of garden flowers decorated our bedroom, dressing room and the bathroom with its double sinks. A decanter of brandy had provided a nightcap beneath the stars on the veranda the night before.

Though the master bedroom is the biggest and has the best view, the other choices are no slouches. A closet that once blocked the view in the Peach Room has been opened up; wicker chairs and built-in shelves full of books and lush African violets have been added on either side of the new window. White wicker furniture gives the smaller Wicker Room its name; its bath across the hall was Kerri's rejuvenation project one winter.

All three rooms have sitting/reading areas. But most guests prefer to relax in the airy living room with its circular wall of glass and accents of plants or on the veranda beyond. That is, when they're not enjoying the grounds. The massed floral plantings are spectacular, and wildlife and birds are abundant. Kerri no longer grows the vegetables and herbs that were in such demand at local restaurants. Instead she has taken up running, finishing second among women over age 50 in the annual local Fodderstock marathon.

The glass table in the open dining room is covered with a pink cloth for breakfast at 9 o'clock. Classical music played as we enjoyed orange-pineapple juice, slices of melon and strawberries with ham, and Kerri's special apple puff, almost like a soufflé and served in a quiche dish. Other entrées could be steak and eggs, light-as-a-feather angel pancakes and sometimes a shrimp soufflé.

Good as they are, the breakfasts here necessarily play second fiddle to the setting. Not to mention the views.

(540) 675-3046. Three rooms with private baths. Doubles, $100 to $200. Two-night minimum spring weekends, fall and holidays. No smoking. Closed Tuesday.

Sunset Hills Farm, 105 Christmas Tree Lane, Washington 22747.
The front doorbell chimes out a ragtime melody in this architect-designed, stone house in the Frank Lloyd Wright tradition high up Jenkins Mountain. Betty and Leon Hutcheson moved here in 1978 from Alexandria after their four offspring had left for college. They were responsible for bringing the principals of Bleu Rock Inn to a site below theirs along Route 211. In 1993, they started taking in overnight guests in their showplace of a house.

For starters, the Hutchesons offer three bedrooms, each with marble bath and TV and furnished in traditional style. Two in the rear come with queensize beds and fieldstone walls made of stones from the property. The extra-large Gazebo Room has a kingsize poster bed, a sitting area with TV and a bath with jacuzzi tub, twin vanities and a wall mural of belgian horses painted by Betty and a friend. It has direct access to a large side deck, full of heavy Adirondack-style chairs and tables and prolific flowers, leading to a screened gazebo. Both are great spots for enjoying the farm gardens, the horses grazing near the sunken pond in front, and the Blue Ridge vistas.

Guests also enjoy a huge, circular, open living/dining room with a table for six looking somewhat lonely in the center. Here or in the gazebo is where Betty serves a full breakfast. Expect fresh fruit (the couple pick their own berries and peaches), juice, and perhaps pancakes or an egg casserole with blueberry muffins. Beverages come from an espresso-cappuccino machine. Afternoon treats include lemonade, iced tea and cakes. Bedrooms are stocked with soft drinks and fruit.

The Hutchesons, who live in a separate section of the house, have plans for three more guest rooms and a library. Meanwhile, they oversee production of brandied peaches, fruit butters, other fruit products and gift baskets at their mountaintop Sunset Hills farm store and Christmas shop in a barn near their house. *(540) 987-8804 or (800) 980-2580. Fax (540) 987-9742. Three rooms with private baths. Doubles, $150 and $195. No children. No smoking.*

Fairlea Farm Bed & Breakfast, 636 Mount Salem Ave., Box 124, Washington 22747.
For an edge-of-town residence, this fieldstone manor house has a remarkable setting. It's surrounded by a working 40-acre sheep and cattle farm and yields 180-degree vistas. "You really feel like you're in the country," says Susan Longyear, who with husband Walter moved here from Falls Church and opened their home as a B&B after raising a family. The property was the old county fairgrounds, and a shed near the backyard gazebo and shady flagstone terrace was once a concession stand.

Few would guess its background, for today all is quite elegant and comfortable, from the lovely living room with fireplace and oriental rugs to the four guest quarters with queensize beds and private baths. The Magnolia Room, so named because it looks onto a couple of magnolia trees, is the main-floor master bedroom with a sofa, bathroom with double vanity, and a collection of miniature mirrors (53 at last count) on one wall. Upstairs, the Meadow Room has a brass bed, while the Rose Room overlooking the rose garden contains a canopy bed. A suite in the walkout basement is fashioned from a paneled family room. It has a four-poster bed, a sofabed, a stone fireplace, TV and kitchenette.

Fresh fruit and flowers are in each room, and ice water accompanies nightly turndown. A sumptuous breakfast is served at guests' convenience. Expect things like strawberry-rhubarb compote, apple puff, egg casserole, crêpes with local fruit, homemade breads and muffins.

(540) 675-3679. Fax (540) 675-1064. Three rooms and one suite with private baths. Doubles, $85 to $115. Suite, $135. Children accepted in suite. No smoking.

Caledonia Farm - 1812, 47 Dearing Hill Road, Flint Hill 22627.

"I've been to 262 B&Bs in North America and we do it differently from any other," says broadcaster-turned-innkeeper Phil Irwin. And loquacious Phil, who was the Breakfast Show host on the Voice of America, is quick to tell you how he does it.

"We produce a custom breakfast on demand," says he. That means a choice of menu, from smoked salmon on a bagel with neufchatel cheese to eggs benedict, following Eastern Shore melon, juices and cereal. Aspenglow sparkling cider in a champagne glass opens the presentation; a hot apple strudel concludes. Breakfast is served at hourly intervals "because of our shared-bath situation." Which is fine if you get your hour of choice, but it's first come, first served, and no deviations are tolerated. You arrive late for breakfast and you may go hungry; you arrive late at night and your reservation may not be honored. Phil does things his way.

He really gets going as he leads guests on a tour of part of the 183-year-old stone house after sharing a glass of wine or beer in the late afternoon in a gorgeous front gathering room. Here you'll find exposed beams, a great stone fireplace, paneled window wells and cross-and-bible doors – some are "architectural impurities," Phil points out. Up a very steep staircase is a landing with seating to enjoy the mountain view and two guest rooms sharing a bath (lately, Phil has been trying to rent them as a suite). One has a double bed with old pine furniture and a fireplace; the other a single and a double. Both have oriental scatter rugs on wood floors, electric candles in the windows and "the thirstiest towels and the best foam mattresses money can buy." Phil assures, "you will have the best sleep you ever had." An oversize lantern, robes, a lighted makeup mirror and extra pillows and blankets in the closets are extra touches of hospitality that, Phil says, make his B&B unique.

Beyond a winter kitchen with a cooking fireplace is the Summer Cottage, billed as a honeymoon suite. It's connected to the main house by a breezeway with garden chairs. A huge spinning wheel rests in front of an enormous stone fireplace. A kitchenette offers a wet bar, mini-refrigerator and a microwave. Upstairs is a pretty bedroom with four-poster double bed, two armchairs and a full bath. "People often check in here and we never see them again," says Phil.

Those who are seen may enjoy three porches, stroll around the 52-acre working cattle farm crisscrossed by nearly a mile of stone fences, borrow bicycles, play badminton or climb the 3,000-foot mountain upon which the Skyline Drive passes behind the house.

(540) 675-3693 or (800) 262-1812. Two rooms with shared bath and cottage suite with private bath. Doubles, $80. Suite, $140. Fifty percent surcharge if only staying Saturday. Two-night minimum for holidays and October. Children over 12. No smoking.

The Foster-Harris House, 189 Main St., Washington 22747.

The area's first B&B to emerge in 1984 in the shadow of the Inn at Little Washington, this 1900s-vintage frame farmhouse was acquired in 1997 by John and Libby Byam from Morgantown, W.Va.

They purchased it from a former caterer from big Washington who was known for her sumptuous breakfasts, and they "built on her reputation." The meal is served at 9 or 9:30 in a small dining room furnished with country antiques. Juice, fruit, muffins and tea breads precede such treats as egg, spinach and mushroom strata; a potato, cheese and egg casserole, or Southwest-style poached eggs with breakfast meats. In the afternoon, tea or lemonade and cookies may be taken in the parlor, on the front porch or beneath an old plum tree.

Between meals, the Byams tend the country-style perennial gardens that border the turn-of-the-century house. They also have improved the room configuration and formalized the Victorian farm-style decor with some of their own furnishings.

All five guest quarters offer private baths and all but one of the beds is queensize. John's favorite is the Mountain View Suite with a wood stove, a bathroom with a whirlpool tub for two and a sun room with wicker chairs for taking in the scene. Another favorite is the side Garden Room, cool and serene and reminiscent of spring year-round. A mini sunroom with a table for two adjoins the rear Meadow View Room, where a duvet covers the step-up Eastlake bed. Folk art is the theme in the cozy Americana Room, which has a queen bed and excellent examples of faux painting in the full bathroom. The new Teal Room has a double bed.

(540) 675-3757 or (800) 666-0153. Fax (540) 675-1615. Four rooms and one suite with private baths. Doubles, $95 to $140. Suite, $160. Children over 12. No smoking.

Dining Spots

The Inn at Little Washington, Middle and Main Streets, Washington.

The restaurant here preceded the inn, Patrick O'Connell and Reinhardt Lynch having decided to settle down in one spot rather than expand the thriving catering business they had started in Virginia hunt country. With a teenaged kitchen helper as the only staff, they opened their dining room in a former garage on a January weekend in 1978. Seventy patrons showed up and the next weekend, a Washington Star reviewer visited and proclaimed it the best eatery within 150 miles of D.C. Since then, gourmands from across the world have joined the powers-that-be from that other Washington in seeking one of the 75 seats in culinary euphoria.

Today, they may snag one of the two chef's tables in the new, state-of-the-art European-style kitchen – said to be the first of its kind in the United States – and watch the behind-the-scenes proceedings. Here you can dine by the fire and watch "a great artist in a grand new studio," in the words of the inn's publicist.

Few are disappointed, but count us among them. We were unfortunate enough to encounter five-star lapses and gaffes in service along with five-star triumphs in food and surroundings.

First it should be noted what the inn is not. It is not particularly intimidating nor pretentious, unless you balk at a waiter refolding your napkin when you leave the table for the restroom. It is not unpopular; witness the need for reservations weeks in advance for weekends and the denial of up to 3,000 requests for dinner on a Saturday night. It is not inexpensive; meals are prix-fixe, $98 to $128, depending on the day). A seven-course tasting menu for the entire table is extra. A four-course vegetarian menu is available as well.

The main dining room and the smaller Terrace Room and Garden Room, both facing the inner courtyard, are as elegant as the rest of the inn. Peach-colored taffeta lampshades hanging over most tables in the main room are the decorative hallmark; the lamps cast a glamorous glow over patrons and more light over-all than one would expect. A ceramic swan holds a mass of flowers in the center of the rich but subdued room. More splashy is the Terrace Room, where a wall of banquettes faces the garden beneath fans whirring and fabric billowing from the ceiling.

Chef Patrick's menu blends classic French and new American creativity into what he calls "cuisine of the territory." The menu is relatively simple and straightforward, eschewing European terminology to the point that grilled poussin is described parenthetically as "young succulent chicken."

The food is anything but simple, however. Dinner begins with a couple of items not on the menu – in our case, a delicate puff pastry of leeks and a canapé with foie gras, one for each person, plus a demitasse of chilled vichyssoise accented with sorrel. A basket of rolls and breads accompanied. We gladly would have tried any of the ten first-course selections. Eventually we settled on a stupendous (and famous) sauté of New York State foie gras with smoked goose breast and local ham on a vinaigrette of black-eyed peas and a dish called salmon four ways, which turned up in three rosettes and three puffs with a superb dill-mustard sauce.

A half-hour delay between appetizers and our between-course selections of a mixed green salad and a grapefruit-tarragon sorbet signaled that something was amiss. Another half hour ensued before the arrival of our main courses, grilled rack of lamb and a sauté of veal sweetbreads. "Here's your lobster," the waitress said to the lamb-orderer, who was nursing a $40 bottle of Stag's Leap merlot, one of the least expensive wines from an extraordinary 14,000-bottle cellar. Informed that we had not ordered lobster, she whisked both dinners back to the kitchen. The original waiter in the team that served many tables returned five minutes later and asked how the lamb was to have been cooked. Five or so minutes later the waitress arrived with another salad and another sorbet without explanation; when asked what was going on, she replied "we thought you might be hungry." Fifteen minutes later the ordered main courses came with a perfunctory apology. Elapsed time between appetizer and entrée: more than an hour.

Only as he later cleared the main courses did the waiter offer to make amends: a complimentary after-dinner drink to follow dessert. Besides the chosen seven deadly sins (a sampler of the inn's remarkable offerings on a plate painted with strokes of chocolate and fruit sauces) and a trio of nut tarts with caramel ice cream, he also presented a complimentary "white chocolate mousse in bed between dark silky sheets." The house chardonnay that began our meal more than three hours earlier turned out to be on the house.

(540) 675-3800. Prix-fixe, $98 weekdays, $108 Friday and Sunday, $128 Saturday. Dinner by reservation, 6 to 9:30, Saturday 5:30 to 10:30, Sunday 4 to 9:30. Closed Tuesday except in May and October.

Four & Twenty Blackbirds, 650 Zachary Taylor Hwy. (Route 522), Flint Hill. Two alumni of the Inn at Little Washington run this urbane little place in an old general store. Chef Heidi Morf, who was dessert chef at the inn, and Vinnie DeLuise, a former waiter there, have an avid following who appreciate the creativity, the informality and the prices. It's the place to which local gourmands return time and again.

The main-floor dining room is colorful yet glamorous. The chintz draped around the windows matches the chair seats, walls are pale peach above the chair rail and deep green below, and the woodwork is deep purple. A downstairs room with a stone bar and red trim is more rustic.

We enjoyed a sensational lunch here (since discontinued), but a subsequent dinner by candlelight with live guitar music proved even more memorable. Unusual hot bread sticks, curled up at the end like a fiddlehead fern, tasted of fennel and hot chiles. Among appetizers were a great California sushi roll with crabmeat and avocado and an assertive tart bearing smoked peppers, caramelized vidalia onions and maytag blue cheese. A small salad of assorted greens with a lovely dijon vinaigrette prepared the palate for the main courses. One of us had sautéed soft-shell crabs atop a shrimp jambalaya with hush puppies. The other tried the grilled rockfish with the best sundried tomato aioli ever and orange couscous, garnished with tiny johnny jump-ups. Sweet endings were strawberry shortcake on heart-shaped biscuits with homemade lemon ice cream and a fresh plum, nectarine and almond tart with Rappahannock raspberry sauce.

This is the stuff of which culinary dreams are made, at prices that won't break the bank. A good wine list is priced in the teens and twenties.

(540) 675-1111. Entrées, $17.50 to $20.95. Dinner, Wednesday-Saturday 5:30 to 9. Sunday brunch, 10 to 2.

The Flint Hill Public House, 675 Zachary Taylor Hwy. (Route 522,) Flint Hill.

High atop a broad lawn, this majestic old structure built in 1899 served as a grade school for most of its years. Lately it has been a restaurant with a variety of dining options, including a great outdoor deck lined with impatiens and overlooking prolific gardens.

Owners John and Denise Pearson, young and energetic, have given it its most successful incarnation yet. John, the chef, employs Virginia products whenever possible in a straightforward manner that contrasts nicely with the more eclectic fare of Four & Twenty Blackbirds down the street. "It makes for good neighbors," John says, and his admiring competitors agree.

Dining is in the paneled Public Room, with a bar in the corner, floral placemats on old English pub tables and oriental runners on the floor. Beyond is a wicker parlor with dining tables opening onto the aforementioned deck, a great place for a summer meal.

All is quite stylish for contemporary fare that earns good reviews. Dinner might start with a choice of filé gumbo, polenta cakes with wild morels, fried Asian vegetable rolls and a salad of grilled cucumbers, vidalia onions and goat cheese. Expect main dishes like seared yellowfin tuna with pineapple-ginger glaze, monkfish with Israeli couscous, spicy soft-shell crabs with corn relish, roasted chicken with flageolets and seared beef tenderloin with roasted garlic mashed potatoes.

John has added thousands of bottles to his wine cellar, which he considers the area's best after the Inn at Little Washington. He also presents quarterly vintner's dinners and a variety of food events "designed to be a celebration of food in America today."

The Pearsons also have refurbished two spacious, high-ceilinged upstairs guest rooms with queensize beds and private baths, renting for $95.

(540) 675-1700. Entrées, $15.95 to $18.95. Lunch, 11:30 to 2:30; dinner, 5:30 to 8:30 or 9:30; Sunday, brunch 11 to 3, dinner 5 to 8. Closed Wednesday.

Blue Ridge Mountains are backdrop for dining terrace at Bleu Rock Inn.

Bleu Rock Inn, Route 211, Washington.

This newcomer with a misleadingly pretentious name (why not just "Blue?") aspired to the heights set by the Inn at Little Washington. Early on, it succeeded in food and service – at about a third of the cost – and its location is certainly unsurpassed. Set against a backdrop of vineyards and mountains, it looks like an inn out of California wine country, with a French provincial accent.

Dining is in two simple but elegant fireplaced rooms seating a total of 75, plus a spectacular rear terrace. One small room is striking for elaborately painted wall panels that remind one of Versailles. In the main dining room, tapestry chairs, white cloths over burgundy and pink, fanned napkins standing tall in wine glasses, white china, heavy cutlery, little lalique-style lamps and fresh flowers create an elegant backdrop for the food.

The longtime owners, who also run La Bergerie Restaurant in Alexandria, sold in 2000 to Harry Carlip and Josephine Mariea, who had only recently bought the nearby Heritage House B&B. They introduced a new pub, converted from the former Vineyard dining room. It features lighter fare. Chefs Richard and Lynn Mahan continued on the job, changing the menu seasonally.

Our earlier dinner here was a triumph, from appetizers of confit of duckling with grilled radicchio and an eggplant and goat cheese terrine to a peach shortbread tart with cassis sauce and a terrine of three sorbets.

Main courses range from Alsatian choucroute with champagne-apple sauerkraut to grilled local free-range lamb loin in a bacon-red wine broth. The chicken fricassee with glazed apples, shiitake mushrooms and spaetzle we tried here was one of the best chicken dishes we've had.

Reports were that the food and service had been inconsistent lately. The setting remains delightful as ever.

(540) 987-3190 or (800) 537-3652. Entrées, $17.95 to $28.50. Dinner, Wednesday-Saturday 5:30 to 9:30. Sunday, brunch 11 to 2, dinner 5:30 to 9. Pub open daily, 4 to midnight.

The Appetite Repair Shop, 20 Main St., Sperryville.

The young waitresses wear T-shirts labeled "service technician" and there's much memorabilia from auto repair shops and gasoline stations all around. Owners Cindy and Gregg Gillies have spent a lot of time around auto shops, so the theme seemed a natural.

Their vast space is mainly kitchen fronted by a counter, where you place your order for burgers, sandwiches, "fluids" and accompaniments from the "parts department." But there are unexpected surprises like fresh flowers atop some of the bare wood tables and a pastry case that includes blackberry cobbler and red raspberry pie. There's even a summer music series with live entertainment here on Sunday evenings.

We did a test drive on a couple of sandwiches, the grilled chicken with lettuce and tomato and the pulled pork barbecue topped with cheese and bacon. Served with coleslaw and great fried potato wedges, both proved quite satisfactory for a bit more than $4 each. Other sandwiches were priced from $1.50 for grilled cheese or a hot dog to $4.90 for the "luxury model" Italian chicken fillet with provolone, sautéed onions and peppers. Dinner specials add things like pizzas, liver and onions, baked chicken, deep-fried catfish and steak.

Noticing the slogan "appetite repair at a price that's fair," we had to ask the owner if this was a takeoff on a famous nearby restaurant that was born in a garage. "No, I didn't know that," came the laconic answer. "We started in Madison County."

(540) 987-9533. Entrées, $4.50 to $8.50 Open Monday-Thursday 8 to 3; Friday-Sunday 8 to 8.

Diversions

The Blue Ridge Mountains, Skyline Drive and Shenandoah National Park bestow on this area a spectacular backdrop, plus scenic drives and hiking trails. Old Rag Mountain is a hiking favorite. Drive the Skyline Drive for awesome scenery – and perhaps lunch on top of the world at Skyland Lodge.

Walking Tour of Washington. The Rappahannock Historical Society sells a pamphlet-size treatise billed as a walking tour along the quiet, tree-shaded streets of "the first Washington of them all." There's no map, and the text is for the truly interested. The Washington Business Council provides a more readily available free map, geared to commercial interests. Others will be satisfied with a leisurely stroll along Main and Gay and their connecting side streets, stopping to see whatever charms them. This really is a small rural village; that's the beauty of it. There are a few county and municipal buildings, a couple of churches and three log houses. Note the neat old printing press outside the door of the Rappahannock News building. **First Washington's Museum,** run privately and commercially by its creator, Ruby Jenkins, is an 18th-century tavern and schoolhouse all aclutter with historic and local memorabilia. **The Theatre at Washington** stages movies, recitals and other events, usually one night a weekend. It is known for its professional musical performances, including the noted Smithsonian at Little Washington chamber music series.

Driving Tours. The most rewarding way to sense the area's tranquility and beauty is to drive along any of the back roads (obtain a county map to avoid getting lost). You can bicycle if you bring your own, but this is winding, hilly territory, not for the faint of heart. Some of our favorite rural byways are Route 628 between Washington and Flint Hill, Route 729 between Flint Hill and Ben Venue and beyond to Laurel Mills or Viewtown (really!), and Routes 635, 688 and 726 in the winery country around Hume, Linden and Markham. You'll stumble onto surprises like the 1842 Leeds Church and its big parish house, manse and graveyard out in the countryside south of Markham. In foliage season, these are the best ways to beat the bumper-to-bumper traffic of leaf-peepers along main Route 211.

Horseback Riding. This is the western edge of Virginia hunt country, so why not do as the Virginians do? Rent horses at Marriott Ranches, Route 726, in Hume. Guided 90-minute trail rides are offered by reservation daily except Monday.

Wineries. Three nearby wineries are blessed with gorgeous locations like those of the Napa Valley. They are destinations for those who enjoy scenery as well as good wines.

Oasis Vineyard, 14141 Hume Road (Route 635), Hume.

This is one of Virginia's oldest and largest wineries. "We learned as we went and made every mistake," said Corinne Salahi, a Belgian married to an American, of the vineyard she and husband Dirgham established in 1975. They're best known for sparkling wines, produced by the traditional méthode champenoise, and representing about one-third of their extensive annual production. They tout the Oasis brut sparkling wine as one of the ten best in the world. Their chardonnay and cabernet sauvignon ($15.50) are also prize-winners. Visitors tour a large downstairs facility boasting oak barrels for chardonnay and concrete holding tanks from Italy. They sample wines upstairs on wine-barrel seats around tables facing the Blue Ridge. Lunch is available from the Oasis Café and Trellis Patio. Oasis also offers a cigar and wine menu on its new Cigar Patio.

(540) 635-7627 or (800) 304-7656. Open daily, 10 to 5.

Linden Vineyards, 3708 Harrels Corner Rd. (Route 638), Linden.

On a hilltop facing east, this versatile winery yields quite a view and makes the most of it with an outdoor deck. All the better to enjoy a snack of Virginia cheeses with a good bottle of chardonnay or a dry seyval – although the winery has dropped its earlier gourmet lunches, because visitors "started seeing us a restaurant rather than a winery," according to owner Jim Law. Along with chardonnauy, sauvignon blanc, riesling and cabernet sauvignon ($12 to $24), Linden produced a late-harvest vidal dessert wine that won a Virginia Governor's Cup as the best in Virginia. Jim also stages vintner dinners, winemaking seminars and barrel tastings.

(540) 364-1997. Open Wednesday-Sunday and some Monday holidays, 11 to 5, April-November; weekends only, rest of year.

Naked Mountain Vineyard & Winery, 2747 Leeds Manor Road (Route 688), Markham.

Up a mountain and down a hairpin driveway lies this prize, nestled between hills and producing Virginia's most-honored chardonnay. Sold here for a bargain $16, it's so esteemed that it's one of only two East Coast wines served at Domaine Chandon's restaurant in California wine country. Not bad for what had been a hobby for amateur winemakers Bob and Phoebe Harper. Most of their 3,000 cases a year are chardonnay. A few rieslings, sauvignons and clarets also are produced. The cathedral-ceilinged tasting room overlooks a close-in vista that has been described as the most picturesque of any East Coast winery.

(540) 364-1609. Open Wednesday-Sunday 11 to 5, March-December; weekends only, rest of year.

Shopping. Washington has a few excellent galleries, gift and antiques shops, many open only weekends or by appointment. Our favorite is Elaine Kramer's **Talk of the Town,** a wonderful shop with suave cards, jewelry, T-shirts, accessories, garden implements and such. She recently opened a downstairs gallery. She also connected her store to the showroom of her husband, master cabinetmaker Peter Kramer, "so now we're a mall!" His stunning furniture is much prized locally, and customers like to watch the cabinetmakers at work. A 200-year-old building is home to **Gay Street Mercantile Art and Antiques,** which offers antique furniture and accessories as well as the country paintings of local artist Geneva Welch. **Rare Finds** is an antiques, gift and accessory shop, every bit as eclectic as the guest room and suite offered upstairs by the expanding Inn at Little Washington. The inn, incidentally, has an ultra-suave gift shop of inn-related items across Main Street from the main building.

Sperryville harbors good shops, among them the **Old Sperryville Bookstore** in a converted country church. The wondrous **Faith Mountain Company** kept expanding its farmhouse, a ramble of rooms full of dolls, prints, country clothing, kitchenware, specialty foods and garden accessories, until there was no room left to expand. In 1998 it moved to larger quarters in a renovated building that was the old Sperryville School House. Out Route 211 west is the Mountainside Market Shopping Center, which includes the **Odyssey Collection,** with an exceptional array of jewelry, pottery, paintings and clothing, with a focus on native American and Indonesian art. **Mountainside Market** is a terrific gourmet, whole-foods emporium with a small deli section of prepared sandwiches and pastries. With tables out front, it's something of a community hangout – "the No. 1 pit stop for local yokels, bikers and hikers," according to its web site. A sign on the door as you leave warns, "Beware of hitchhiking cats." Also here is the **Blue Moon Café,** a casual family place serving dinner Wednesday-Sunday and offering up live music late into the evening.

Extra-Special ⸻

Laurel Mills Store, 461 Laurel Mills Road (Route 618), Castleton.

The one-horse hamlet of Laurel Mills, population 15 (as tabulated on her fingers by Mary Frances Fannon, one of the fifteen), is the unlikely home of a general store, gallery and antiques shop. And Mrs. Fannon, whose husband is a prosperous oil dealer in big Washington, is the unlikely proprietress. When the store, dating to 1877, was about to be converted into apartments, she bought the place and "thought I'd have all this time to sit behind the counter and read books, as the former employees did." Not at all. She stocked the shelves, made sandwiches, lent books, manned the cash register and pumped gasoline, all the while chatting amiably with farmers, truckers and politicians who make the front porch their own and fill their coolers with water from the spring at the side. Mrs. Fannon has since branched out, restoring the stone cellar into an antiques shop and gallery called Down Under Laurel Mills Store. Here she showcases country antiques and one-of-a-kind pieces from area artisans and furniture-makers – an upscale adjunct to a down-home country store.

(540) 937-3015. Open Monday-Saturday 7 a.m. to 7:30 or 8 p.m., Sunday, 8 to 6.

Hounds lead foxhunters in front of Morven Park mansion in Leesburg.

Loudoun County, Va.
Heart of Hunt Country

Less than 40 miles from the Washington Monument and the halls of Congress lies hunt country and some of America's most hallowed ground. The transition from the nation's capital to the horse and hunt capital to the west occurs rather suddenly around Leesburg in eastern Loudoun County. Left behind are Interstate 66, Washington Dulles International Airport and all the trappings of galloping suburbia. Ahead, the farms and pastures of horse country undulate toward the Blue Ridge Mountains.

It's a curious juxtaposition, this feeling of being so near, yet so far – so close to Washington, yet so far removed in body and spirit. The juxtaposition is most striking in Leesburg, the commercial seat of Loudoun County. Docents in Colonial costume spin tales and yarn beside the timbered cottage holding the Loudoun Museum's gift shop as shoppers converge on the municipal ramp parking garage in the center of town. On the outskirts, the congestion of residential subdivisions, highways and strip shopping centers yields abruptly to the tranquility of plantation estates, dirt roads and country stores.

If bustling Leesburg reflects Loudoun's commercial and historic interests, tony Middleburg represents the equine theme so imbued in the fabric of the region. In prime horse and foxhunt country, some of the horses live better than ordinary Americans, as the well-heeled farms around Upperville and Waterford attest. The retailing emphasis (Dominion Saddlery, the Sporting Gallery and The Tack Box Saddlery) and shop names (The Finicky Filly, the Upper Crust) tell the story. The Middleburg Police Department sports a red fox on its insignia. The paintings hung in homes, restaurants, inns and banks adhere to the theme.

Middleburg is the home of The Chronicle of the Horse, the weekly hunt newsmagazine. Leesburg is headquarters of the Masters of Foxhounds Association, the Morven Park Equine Medical Center and the U.S. Combined Training Association. The fact that one of the nation's richest counties declines to pave many of its roads is not a sign of impoverishment – it's better for the horses that way.

Horses and horse people are everywhere. That does not mean the casual visitor is likely to see a foxhunt, however. The hundred or so members of each of the dozen hunt clubs in the area usually ride with the hounds three times a week from fall through spring, but their territories are out of the public eye. More visible are the point-to-point races, steeplechase meets and polo games staged weekends in spring and fall.

Its proximity to Washington and its affluent lifestyle draw the rich and famous. The Roman Catholic church in Middleburg was built in 1963 for President John F. Kennedy; his family rented the Glen Ora estate locally and Jacqueline Onassis rode with the Piedmont Fox Hounds and Orange County hunts until just months before her death in 1994. Writer Russell Baker, actor Robert Duvall, philanthropist Paul Mellon, the Smothers Brothers and Washington business magnates like Donald Graham have homes here.

Spectacularly scenic is this rolling, manicured and serenely undeveloped landscape, crisscrossed with the pristine fences and corrals of horse country. It seems more English than England, in the words of one resident Brit, and not just in terms of topography. Loudoun retains its early hamlets, settled variously by Quakers, Scots and Germans. There's no more picturesque a Cotswolds hamlet than tiny Waterford, the entire village a designated National Historic Landmark and preserved as a community of a century ago.

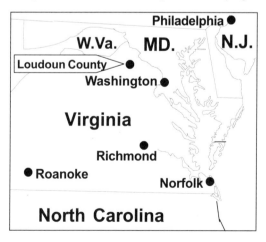

Waterford, Lincoln, Aldie, Philomont, Lucketts, Upperville – these are the quiet places that add dimension to the Loudoun sheen forged by Leesburg and Middleburg. Some of the historic inns that housed the Lees and Washingtons have been upstaged by a flurry of small and promising newcomers. One plantation owned by descendants of America's first organized hunt takes in overnight guests.

The aura of history and the

The Ashby Inn & Restaurant are headquartered in this white brick house built in 1829.

mystique of foxhunting are palpable here. Plantation houses and museums, good restaurants, wineries, shops and recreation facilities help make Loudoun County uncommonly popular with visitors, especially on weekends. This is, after all, a place for escape. And Washington, eminently escapable, is so near yet so far.

Inn Spots

Ashby Inn, 692 Federal St., Paris 20130.

When John and Roma Sherman purchased in 1984 the property that started this fine inn, it was an old farmhouse with one bathroom. They now have an acclaimed restaurant, six guest rooms with private baths in the inn and four deluxe suites in a building nearby. Theirs is a class act all the way.

The tiny town of Paris and its quiet main street, fortuitously bypassed by busy Route 50, are the setting for the whitewashed brick main inn, built in 1829. Its restaurant draws folks from Washington and beyond, and its four newer suites in the old schoolhouse – 60 paces, as the inn brochure says, down the street – draw from everywhere.

Two upstairs and two down, the suites are of the same configuration but each is painted in a different glowing color, one a dazzling pumpkin gold and ours a restful deep red. The upper rooms come with a cathedral ceiling and a high round window over the door to their own porch, through which we found it entrancing to watch the passing clouds. They could not be more comfortable with queensize canopy bed, fireplace, small TV, telephone, a cushioned window seat, a two-part bathroom with steeping tub and many amenities, including coffee service, and two wing chairs placed strategically in front of the fireplace. We even found a copy of "Middlemarch" in the bookshelf. Biggest treat of all is the covered porch, where we lounged in Adirondack chairs and watched black angus cows roam up and down the hill in back – a truly pastoral scene.

The six rooms the Shermans started with are upstairs in the main inn. All are handsomely furnished with antiques, oriental rugs and hunting prints. The grand

Fan Room, with palladian window in back and a fan bed handmade by a friend, has its own entrance and balcony.

A small front common room in the inn is available to overnight guests and to those coming in for dinner. Adirondack chairs dot the spacious lawns behind the inn, and the lavish gardens are a joy to behold.

Breakfast involves a choice of juices, muffins, eggs any style, pancakes, homefries, breakfast meats and grilled tomatoes. We particularly enjoyed the tomatoes alongside fat, juicy sausages.

British-born Roma, who hunts with the Blue Ridge Hunt and can tell the guest all about foxhunting, handles the breakfast detail. Husband John, an ex-journalist and Congressional speechwriter, is ever present at dinnertime, keeping the four dining rooms running smoothly. He became enamored with food and restaurants during his Army days in France and, despite a high-profile Washington career that caused him to commute until lately, "always knew I eventually wanted to do this." He and Roma do it very well indeed.

(540) 592-3900. Fax (540) 592-3781. Six rooms and four suites with private baths. Doubles, $145 to $180. Suites, $250. Deduct 15 percent midweek. Children over 12. No smoking.

Poor House Farm, 35304 Poor House Lane (Route 756), Round Hill 20141.
"If you have to end up in the Poor House, this is the one." So reads one of the adulatory notes in the guest book in the Cook House Cottage, a deluxe retreat fashioned from the cookhouse at what was first a plantation and later served as the Loudoun County home for the indigent.

Dottie and Fred Mace, transplants from Machias in the easternmost reaches of Down East Maine, bought the circa 1814 property in 1987, spent four years renovating the cottage and main house, and produced some of the most appealing and comfortable B&B accommodations in Loudoun County.

This really is out in the country, an utterly quiet twelve acres reached by dirt roads. About the only "traffic" comes from the horses and hounds of the prestigious Piedmont Fox Hounds hunt club, which passes out front in its thrice-weekly rituals with occasional guests like the late Jacqueline Onassis.

The Maces started with a guest room and a small suite in the main house, both stylishly decorated and designed for comfort, and the romantic brick Cook House Cottage. The latter has an open living room with sofabed and armchair facing a small TV and a huge fireplace, a kitchen and dining area, and a second floor with a queensize pencil-post bed and a clawfoot tub in the bath.

Following Fred's untimely death, Dottie put major expansion plans on hold and enhanced three guest rooms in the main house. The Unison Room, a cozy Victorian affair, has a queen canopied poster bed, working fireplace, TV, and a new bath with a footed slipper tub and European hand-held shower. The larger Airmont Room with working fireplace comes with a queen feather poster bed, a couple of comfy lounge chairs and a similarly equipped bathroom. The third-floor suite offers a white wicker queen feather bed, extra day bed, TV, phone and private bath with shower.

A full breakfast is served in the dining area or, our choice, on the wicker-filled side veranda overlooking the plantation outbuildings, rolling farmlands and a farm pond. Amid an abundance of flowering plants, Villeroy & Boch china and fine crystal, we feasted on bowls of perfect fresh fruit (raspberries, blueberries, grapes

Veranda overlooks lawn at Norris House.   **Breakfast on veranda at Poor House Farm.**

and sliced peaches), homemade scones and a feather-light quiche with ham, onions, vegetables and cheese. Another of Dottie's breakfast favorites is stuffed french toast with cream cheese.

Birds twittered and flitted in and out of a birdhouse dubbed "Nest and Breakfast" as we took in the tranquil scene from a chintz-covered wicker swing. Who wouldn't think, this is the life?

(540) 554-2511. www.poorhousefarm.com. Three rooms and one cottage with private baths. Doubles, $125 to $135 weekends, $115 to $125 midweek. Cottage, $155 weekends, $130 midweek. Two-night minimum weekends in May and October. Children over 12. No smoking.

The Norris House Inn, 108 Loudoun St. S.W., Leesburg 20175.

Elegant common rooms, a long side veranda, award-winning gardens and grounds, and an adjacent tearoom are among the attributes of this handsome, three-story brick Federal residence built in 1806 at the edge of downtown Leesburg. Californians Pam and Don McMurray, former traveling business executives, searched the country before settling on Leesburg and the house owned by the Norris family, builders responsible for many of Loudoun County's better houses.

With painstaking renovation and attention to detail, they have imbued the property with taste and charm. Guests enjoy a main-floor library with built-in cherry woodwork, a formal living room with windows onto the side veranda (a particularly photogenic scene), and a formal dining room graced with sterling silver, crystal and antique Royal Doulton china. Especially enjoyable in the urban Leesburg setting is the spacious side yard with prolific gardens, an old magnolia tree and a 65-foot-tall black walnut tree, the biggest in Loudoun County. Take it all in from the wicker furniture on the side veranda, screened from the street by shrubbery and the living-room wing, where afternoon libations include wine from nearby Tarara Vineyard.

When it's time to retire, settle into one of six upstairs guest rooms, three with working fireplaces. We enjoyed the Norris Room, "which fulfills most guests' fantasies," in Pam's words. It's pretty in pink, blue and white, with a lacy canopy queensize bed, a plethora of pillows, beautiful sheets and towels, and a Victorian settee. It comes with a fireplace and a refrigerator stocked with Evian water and soft drinks outside the door. The second floor also contains three other bedrooms, one done with a hunt country look and another in English garden decor. The four share two commodious bathrooms. Two smaller rooms on the third floor also share a bath. Potpourri is in all the rooms, and you're apt to find handmade and handpainted chocolates on your pillow when the beds are turned down at night.

Pam serves a breakfast to remember. We liked the oven-baked pancakes, really more like crêpes, filled with fresh berries and served with Smithfield ham sausage patties. A frittata with red, yellow and green peppers, zucchini and roma tomatoes was on tap the next day. These are accompanied by fresh fruit and a special blend of coffee.

The McMurrays acquired the oldest stone building in Leesburg next door. Their daughter, Shannon, operates it as **The Stone House Tea Room.** Here you can order specialty teas with an appropriate menu ($15). The goodies are served at calico-clothed tables in two atmospheric rooms, one in which Henry Clay inscribed his name on the wall for posterity.

You just know the energetic McMurrays aren't finished with the Norris House complex. They already manage and lease out four nearby rooms on weekends. The finicky guest hardly minds the absence of private baths or the lack of a parking area. You simply stash your vehicle a block away in the municipal parking garage and, trite as the saying is, step back in time, elegantly and with style.

(703) 777-1806 or (800) 644-1806. Fax (703) 771-8051. Six rooms with shared baths. Doubles, $105 to $150 weekends, $85 to $125 midweek. Two-night minimum weekends except in winter. No smoking. Tearoom by reservation, weekends noon to 5.

The Goodstone Inn, 36205 Snake Hill Road, Middleburg 20117.

If you want to partake of the good life in the middle of hunt country, this deluxe new B&B may fit the bill – if your pocketbook can afford it.

The inn, part of the 265-acre former Goodstone Dairy farm dating to the mid-18th century, was purchased by Frederick Warburg of the New York banking family in 1937. It became synonymous with foxhunting in Middleburg and continues to serve as the starting point for foxhunts. The original mansion burned early in the century, but the Warburgs converted its ruins into a vine-covered backdrop for a swimming pool still in use today. The farm remained in the family until 1996, when the new owner from the Washington area undertook a multi-million-dollar renovation to provide elegant lodging and a retreat for equestrians and businesspeople.

The first of a planned complex of twenty guest rooms are situated in the carriage house and two nearby residences called cottages. Room decor varies from early American to English country but is invariably sumptuous.

The focal point is the carriage house, which holds a rich, lodge-like great room with a huge stone fireplace, plus six luxurious guest quarters converted from former stables. The original antique wood stable doors and palladian windows are complimented by heart-pine floors and oriental rugs. English country antiques and fine artworks are everywhere evident. Guest quarters here include a bedroom and four suites (one with two bedrooms), each with a queensize poster bed and a jacuzzi tub. Sitting rooms add sofabeds, TV/VCRs and stereo CD players.

The Dutch Stone Cottage offers two bedrooms, one with a clawfoot soaking tub and the other with a jacuzzi, as well as a common living room and eat-in kitchen. The Springhouse Cottage is a three-story, double-porch stone house with a large living room, kitchen and dining area. It contains three bedrooms with jacuzzi tubs, one with a separate steam shower, plus a suite. One of the bedrooms and the suite open through french doors onto the second-floor porch. Three more rooms were to open here in the summer of 2000.

Tea is offered in the lodge in the late afternoon. A full bar is available in the living room of each residence. In the morning, wake-up beverages are set out in the living rooms. Breakfast is offered later in the lodge's great room, on a deck overlooking Goose Creek or in the cottages. Fresh fruits, breads, omelets and belgian waffles are typical fare. Box lunches are available for foxhunters, hikers, canoeists or swimmers who lounge around the pool and hot tub.

The original innkeepers who helped develop the property departed in 2000. The management was in transition as this edition went to press.

(540) 687-4645. Fax (540) 687-6115. Nine rooms and five suites with private baths. Summer and fall: doubles, $295 to $375 weekends, $195 to $275 midweek; suites, $395 to $475 weekends, $295 to $375 midweek. Rest of year: doubles, $275 to $310 weekends, $175 to $210 midweek; suites, $325 to $375 weekends, $225 to $275 midweek. Two-night minimum weekends.

The Longbarn, 37129 Adams Green Lane, Middleburg 20118.
A renovated century-old barn imparts Italian country-style elegance, thanks to Chiara Langley from Bologna, whose sister runs an inn in Italy. Chiara decided to do the same in Hunt Country in 1994 after moving from San Francisco with her American husband Roland, a high-powered Washington business executive. "I fell in love with this house," she explains. "You can see why."

Hidden back in woods and gardens behind a farm pond, The Longbarn is the epitome of a country-elegant retreat. It takes a good imagination to visualize this architect-designed restoration as a barn, despite the abundant barn wood and a loft above the glamorous, soaring living room, with two separate sitting areas below. "This house just keeps going on and on," says Chiara as she shows the "dinette" used for breakfast beside her large kitchen at one end of the structure and the Garden Room guest quarters at the other end. Here, with a view of the garden, you'll find a queensize bed dressed with a floral quilt and a down comforter, with matching pillows and fabric draped behind the bed.

Head upstairs to a loft dining area so big that the Langleys can entertain 40 for a Thanksgiving buffet dinner. It's warmed by a museum-quality art collection and terra cotta sculptures by Italian sculptor Don Gianni Gilli. Chiara enticed him to Middleburg to create similar works for St. Stephen the Martyr Church, built three decades earlier for the Kennedys. Off the loft is an expansive deck facing gardens, gazebo and pond. Beyond is the Blue Room, named for its blue metal queen bed, again with private bath. Adjacent is a third, twin-bedded guest room that's often pressed into use, when it's not serving as the hostess's laboratory (she used to work as a scientist). You get the idea that Chiara will do more with the house, which has five bedrooms and five bathrooms. At our visit, she was hosting special events, "but I'm going to move slowly."

That's the way to go, given the serene setting and the classical music that plays throughout the house. Chiara serves a lavish continental breakfast – from cereal to croissants, "everything but eggs." She has been known to give complimentary facials to guests, and sometimes a friend presents piano concerts in the great room. "We do enjoy this house," she says. "It's like living inside a violin, with all this wood paneling. It's such a joy to be here."

(540) 687-4137. Fax (540) 687-4044. http://members.aol.com/thlongbarn. Three rooms with private baths. Doubles, $115 to $130. Children over 12. No smoking.

Welbourne, Welbourne Road, Middleburg 20117.

No inn property in the area better reflects the past than Welbourne, a time warp and truly a special place. It's not for everyone, but comes highly recommended by authorities ranging from Gourmet magazine to innkeeper John Sherman of the Ashby Inn, who advised that if he had to choose one place to spend an evening, it would be here.

Welbourne, a circa-1775 working plantation, is hardly your typical inn. It's a living museum, occupied by the seventh generation of the family of Col. Richard Dulany. He was the Civil War general who in 1840 founded the country's first horse show and hunt club, the Piedmont Fox Hounds. His great-great-grandson, Nathaniel Morison, a Piedmont board member, lives here today with his wife and children.

"I'm the host, not the innkeeper," advises Nat, who is proud that Welbourne has no brochure. To keep the place going, the family started taking in paying guests "by introduction" in the 1930s; the Morisons continue by word of mouth. "I call the experience faded elegance," says Nat, who fortuitously happened to arrive home in his pickup truck as we stopped by. "If you want interesting history and something real, it's here. If you want TVs and jacuzzis, it's not for you."

"Something real" pervades the entire 550-acre plantation in the heart of prime Middleburg hunt country, reached by the dirt road named Welbourne, County Route 743. The front foyer opens on one side into two living rooms, placed end to end and flanked by a great back porch. The other side opens into the library, where you can spot the date 1862 inscribed in a window and where some of the family's vast collection of miniature giraffes is housed along with such treasures as a sword from the Civil War and Stonewall Jackson's gloves. The library opens into a bedroom of majestic proportions, outfitted in vaguely oriental style with a canopy bed, clawfoot tub, a Tiffany set on the desk and a tray of bottled waters and mixers on a sideboard. F. Scott Fitzgerald and Thomas Wolfe stayed here, and you can, too, for $80 a night. A friend made a plaque to designate this as the Jeb Stuart Room, Nat says in his typical droll style, "but we never used it." So what do they call it? "The End Room."

Upstairs is the Over the Parlor Room, with two twin beds, and another room with two twins joined as a king. In back is the Over the Gun Room, Sherry Morison's favorite, because it gets lots of light. A settee and a window seat take advantage of the view through the vine-covered windows.

The five main guest rooms in the house plus two cottages have private baths. Four smaller bedrooms share baths and are used for overflow. All come with family memorabilia reflecting a way of life. "I tell people it's like visiting Grandma's house as a child," says Nat. Most reply that theirs didn't have a house like this.

Welbourne is a living museum of antebellum plantation life.

The household staff, who are like family, help oversee the place while Sherry is at work as a real-estate agent and while Nat is taking care of the 65 "retired" horses he boards here for owners who want them to live out their days with grace. The Morisons and staff serve a grand southern breakfast amid much silver and china in the dining room, where the table is set for ten to fourteen. Bacon, eggs, sausage, grits and fried tomatoes are the usual fare, with pancakes reserved for Sundays.

When we arrived, Nat said he has five friendly hound dogs that "you have to climb over to get inside," which we did. As we eventually drove away, we happened to look in the back seat of our car. There was Danny the hound, who had jumped in an open window, settled down for a nap and refused to budge. Nat's teenaged son Joshua had to be summoned to get Danny out.

(540) 687-3201. Five rooms and two cottages with private baths; four small rooms with shared baths. Doubles, $80. Cottages, $90. Small rooms, $60. Two-night minimum weekends in spring and fall. Children welcome.

Tarara Winery Bed & Breakfast, 13648 Tarara Lane, Leesburg 22075.

This happening place is the "retirement project" of Margaret and Whitie Hubert, she now an innkeeper and he a developer and contractor in Gaithersburg, Md.

They bought a 475-acre corn and soybean farm atop the palisades of the Potomac River near Lucketts in 1985 and planted more than a hundred acres of grapes, fruit trees and nursery stock. They named it Tarara, Margaret explains, after the river flooded the year they bought the place. "We felt we'd landed and come to rest like Noah's Ark at Ararat up here on this cliff – but we didn't like the rat at the end of Ararat, so we spelled it backward."

Although the winery is the focal point for visitors, the Huberts now share half their spectacular contemporary house with overnight guests. "We have five grown children and built this with five extra bedrooms and baths," Margaret said. But with their offspring scattered across the country, they found the space under-used. "And besides, I missed the company," said Margaret, who was "retired – or fired" from her hostessing and merchandising role in the downstairs winery. "People said we ought to open a B&B, and it's the best thing I ever did." Three elegant bedrooms, one on the main floor and the rest upstairs, and a suite are available. Beds range from double to kingsize. The Chardonnay Suite with a queensize bed includes a sitting room and kitchenette. It connects with the king-bedded Terra Rouge Room to form an even larger suite for two couples.

The common area has a stone fireplace, a baby grand piano, oriental rugs on granite floors, and sliding glass doors onto a stone terrace overlooking an apple orchard, a ten-acre stocked lake and a lighted tennis court.

Guests are greeted with lemonade, tea or wine. They find a bottle of Tarara wine and two complimentary etched wine glasses in their rooms. In the morning, Margaret serves an expanded continental breakfast of fresh fruit, cereal, yogurt and homemade breads and muffins.

(703) 771-7100. Fax (703) 771-8443. Three rooms and one suite with private baths. Doubles, $120. Suite, $135.

Little River Inn, 39307 John S. Mosby Hwy. (Route 50), Box 116, Aldie 20105.

One of the area's earlier B&Bs, this was established by antiques dealer Tucker Withers, who had moved his shop here from Bethesda, Md. He bought his great-uncle's house for the first six rooms of his B&B in 1982. He later added the 1790 patent house and 1810 log cabin across the driveway and the newer Hill House across the road, and now offers an historic complex with ten guest quarters, six with private baths.

Aldie is built around a restored grist mill on the Little River. With his antiques shop and other interests in the hamlet, Tucker seems to be Aldie's chief landholder as well as its main persona. Breakfasts here are legendary as he spins tall tales and local recollections while a varied repast is served. The fare includes juices and fruit, homemade poppyseed muffins or banana bread, cereals, and main dishes like dutch apple baby, local sausages with eggs, baked french toast and pancakes. The meal is taken in a dining area beside the kitchen in the main house, at tables scattered through two atmospheric main-floor common rooms, out back at wrought-iron tables on the flagstone patio or in guest quarters in the outbuildings.

The bedrooms are furnished authentically and rather sparsely with double or twin beds, antique chests and bureaus, quilts, and hooked or braided rugs. One coveted room has a loveseat and a working fireplace. It shares a bath with another bedroom on the second floor, while a third room with double bed has a new private bath. Other chairs in the bedrooms we saw were wood and not the kind you'd feel comfortable sitting in for long. Traffic lumbers along busy U.S. Route 50 just outside. Quieter and more spacious are some rooms in the outbuildings. The Hill House has a fireplaced living room, dining room, kitchen and two bedrooms with private baths, plus a library with a sofabed and half bath. The terraced, two-acre yard contains towering boxwoods, an herb garden and a 50-foot pergola.

(703) 327-6742. Six rooms and cottages with private baths, four rooms with shared baths. Doubles, $95 to $115. Cottages, $175 and $195. House, $240 for two, $30 each additional.

Stonegate Bed & Breakfast, 225 West Colonial Hwy., Box 100, Hamilton 20159.

Civil War memorabilia plays a role in this B&B run by retired Navy submariner

Bill Gallant and his wife Vicki. They share their fieldstone Georgian home with guests in two bedrooms named for opposing Civil War generals.

The Grant Room has a double poster bed, private bath and quite a collection of hats. "Grant gets the smaller room in Virginia," quips Bill, who leads the way to the Lee Room, with a queensize bed, day bed, sitting area and a large bathroom with a whirlpool tub in what had been a pine-paneled play room. An antique crib holds two dolls in a corner.

A hat stand in the front foyer holds another array of hats. Guests enjoy a formal parlor and a side screened veranda where breakfast is often served, with music provided by chirping birds outside. Typical fare are belgian waffles or cheese strata with grits and ham cornbread.

Two acres of grounds offer lawn and trees, including a rare cucumber magnolia tree that Bill says is ranked No. 1 in Loudoun County and No. 2 in the state. Cajole him into telling tales of his role as a navigation expert on the first patrol of the nuclear submarine USS Lee.

(540) 338-9519. Two rooms with private baths. Doubles, $90 and $110. Closed December-March.

The Red Fox Inn, 2 East Washington St., Box 385, Middleburg 20118.

A handsome four-story stone structure dating to 1728, this represents many people's vision of a large but quaint old inn from days of yore. Billed as America's oldest original inn, it's cloaked in all the appropriate honors, from sometime AAA four-diamond ratings to Travel/Holiday dining awards. Lately it seems to be resting on its laurels – or is it simply too big for its breeches? We found the welcome to be lacking, service indifferent, management not on hand and the guest rooms lackluster and pricey.

The Red Fox advertises 23 "romantic accommodations" with private baths in the original inn and three nearby buildings. We were given keys to view two "typical" rooms up steep stairs on the third floor. The spacious Bridal Suite had the requisite kingsize canopy bed, a parlor with a sofa, two wing chairs and a huge built-in armoire, hooked rugs on wide-board floors, two TV sets and two telephones. Another kingsize bed graced the corner Martha Washington Room. Its two wing chairs were spaced twelve feet apart on either side of a bureau, facing the bed and not the TV set. The beds were covered with white chenille spreads that looked like Bates, the bathtubs were equipped with hand-held showers, the toiletries consisted of a Gilbert & Soames shoeshine cloth and sewing kit and a plain bar of Camay soap, and the welcoming touch was two bottles of local Meredyth wines in each room, "available for consumption or to take home, $16." An order form outlined fairly basic choices for a continental breakfast, to be delivered to the room at a specified time in the morning for $1 service charge per person. The front desk, which gave our queries short shrift, assured that what we saw was representative of the inn. We would hope that the newer rooms in the Stray Fox Inn annex on a side street behind the inn might be more inviting.

Tourists and big spenders gravitate to the downstairs dining rooms, full of atmosphere, in the main inn. Singles and families like **Mosby's Tavern,** the inn's barn of a pub nearby at 2 West Marshall St. Lunch and dinner are served daily in both venues.

(540) 687-6301 or (800) 223-1728. Fax (540) 687-6053. Fourteen rooms and nine suites with private baths. Doubles, $140 to $160. Suites, $150 to $250.

Dining Spots

The Ashby Inn & Restaurant, 692 Federal St., Paris.

If the name Paris brings culinary thoughts to mind, the Ashby Inn at the crossroads of this rural town obliges. Innkeepers John and Roma Sherman have created a restaurant of distinction with an unpretentious atmosphere and friendly, flawless service.

About 80 diners are accommodated in four small rooms, ranging from a cozy tavern to a room with high booths and small engraved plaques bearing names of friends and regulars, of which the Ashby seems to have many. A thunderstorm had rendered the handsome, wisteria-covered side courtyard out of commission the night we dined, but the sun porch dressed in white (the Ashby's favorite "color") proved as radiant as a bride. Rotating artworks by a Leesburg artist who paints in Provençe provide color throughout and sell briskly.

The waitress fulfilled a complicated dinner order without taking notes, as did innkeeper John Sherman at breakfast the next day. Great starters on the menu that changes nightly were a chilled carrot puree soup, artistically decorated with citrus crème fraîche, and a caesar salad with grated parmigiano-reggiano and unusual polenta croutons. Chef David Gedney's eight main dishes typically range from pan-roasted halibut with walnut-parsley pesto to grilled quail with roasted red pepper sauce or grilled New York strip steak with Jack Daniels sauce. We liked the Atlantic tuna sautéed with extra-virgin olive oil and white beans and the crab cakes (an Ashby Inn classic of 100 percent pure lump crabmeat with a bit of tarragon, moist and tasty as could be), accompanied by sides of potato ribbons and fresh spinach. Zesty grapefruit sorbet was a refreshing dessert from a choice that included crème brûlée, strawberry shortcake with biscuits and bittersweet chocolate torte with chocolate ganache and crème anglaise.

John has lovingly prepared a select wine list, whose spirit and underlying philosophy as described in the introduction are to be applauded. Though there are plenty of choices for a splurge, we felt quite comfortable ordering one of his recommended specials, a Honig sauvignon blanc for $16.50.

The Shermans are a major presence at Sunday brunch (a local institution), cooking omelets and carving ham at the buffet table set up in the sun porch.

(540) 592-3900. Entrées, $17.50 to $24.50. Dinner, Wednesday-Saturday 6 to 9. Sunday brunch, noon to 2:30.

Lightfoot, 11 North King St., Leesburg.

This with-it establishment of recent vintage is billed as a progressive American bistro in the heart of old-town Leesburg. It takes its name from Francis Lightfoot Lee, a signer of the Declaration of Independence and a member of the Virginia family for which the town was named. Sisters Carrie and Ingrid Gustavson feature food that is "gently prepared, graciously served and sensibly priced."

They moved from their original cafe in 1998 into an ornate 1888 bank building designed by the architect for Washington's Union Station. The two-story high interior with arched windows and marble pillars holds about 200 seats for dining. The concept remained the same – "this simply gave us room to expand," Carrie explained.

Ingrid, the chef who trained at the Culinary Institute of America, categorizes her dinner fare under starters, soups and salads, main plates and sides – a perfect setup for grazers.

One of us made a satisfying meal out of light offerings. The Lightfoot plate yielded a standout herbed feta cheese dip plus hummus and a tuna and kalamata olive spread, served with herbed pita chips and toasted baguette slices. The salad of cafe greens was tossed with soybean sprouts and oven-roasted walnuts. A couple of mini shrimp and crab cakes were fired by a Thai red curry sauce. Entrées range from orange-marinated seared salmon on a bed of cilantro couscous with snow pea shoots to grilled lamb on a bed of spring greens tossed with everything from asparagus and roasted cumin potatoes to anchovies, wild mushrooms and garlic aioli. The pasta de la casa, also an innovative mélange, was hearty and tasty: chipotle fettuccine with shrimp, swiss chard, oyster mushrooms, tomatoes and prosciutto tossed with roasted garlic, extra-virgin olive oil and romano cheese.

Desserts ranged from fresh berries to bread pudding, mocha ya-ya and shoofly pie.

(703) 771-2233. Entrées, $19 to $28. Lunch, Tuesday-Saturday 11:30 to 2:30. Dinner, Tuesday-Saturday 5:30 to 9:30, Sunday 11 to 9.

Tuscarora Mill, 203 Harrison St., Leesburg.

Popularly dubbed Tuskie's but far more sophisticated than that sounds, this was a working grain mill until 1985. Then it was moved a couple of blocks to form part of the restored Market Station shopping and business complex, which also includes a freight depot and station master's house, an 18th-century mill from Pennsylvania and a log cabin from West Virginia. The second-floor restaurant still holds many mill artifacts and equipment. Built into the floor is an old-fashioned scale that used to weigh bags of grain and now is occasionally tested by curious diners. Quilted wall hangings are spotlit on the soaring barnwood walls, and purple lacquered chairs and colorful patterned tablecloths provide plenty of color in the main bar and restaurant. Hanging plants and Victorian street lamp standards make the adjacent garden room, with walls of windows bridging the shopping complex below, a pleasant setting.

The menu covers are as artistic as the presentation of the fare described inside. At lunch, we were impressed by the gazpacho filled with crisp vegetables and topped with a bit of salmon and crabmeat, and a Thai chicken salad. Not so impressive was the wonderful sounding asparagus and crab salad marinated in tequila, lime and cilantro – great tasting but a niggardly portion for $8.95. Only a second helping of crispy rolls with herb butter and an order of frozen lemon mousse with strawberries and golden raspberries separated one of us from starvation.

The dinner menu incorporates many of the lunchtime appetizers and entrées, nearly half of which are available as small plates. Expect things like grilled swordfish with smoked pepper sauce, sesame-roasted salmon with ginger relish, beer-battered soft-shell crabs, grilled pork chops with bourbon-molasses glaze, and dijon-crusted rack of lamb with garlic-rosemary sauce.

Tuskie's wine selections earned the Wine Spectator award of excellence. Interesting imported beers are on tap, available by the pint or glass.

(703) 771-9300. Entrées, $16.60 to $25. Lunch and dinner daily, 11:30 to 9:30 or 10, Sunday 11:30 to 9.

Main dining room at The Eiffel Tower Cafe is modern and elegant.

The Eiffel Tower Cafe, 107 Loudoun St. S.W., Leesburg.

A bit of France in Loudoun County is the billing for this distinctive newcomer. Thirty years after they left Paris, Madeleine and Pierre Sonitsky settled here in 1998 following long restaurant runs in the Washington area at Sans Souci and at Pierre and Madeleine's in suburban Vienna, Va.

Leesburg reminded them of the South of France, so they renovated and expanded a 200-year-old building and opened an old-world, Parisian-style restaurant. They seat up to 180 people in two main-floor dining rooms, two upstairs rooms, a front terrace and an upstairs deck. The main dining room is modern and elegant in mellow pink, with sleek black pink-cushioned chairs, subdued lighting and French plates on shelves in a recessed ceiling. Some of the artworks were painted by Madeleine's father, a French artist.

Although both the owners are chefs, they assign kitchen duties here to Gregory Canizzaro, also from Paris, where he worked for La Tour D'Argent and the Guy Savoy restaurants. Their long-time service staff is European as well.

The understated menu is classic French, from the opening homemade pâté and escargots provençal to desserts like crème brûlée with fresh vanilla and financier au chocolat.

Typical of main courses are roasted salmon fillet with fava beans, roasted sea bass with green cabbage and bacon, spiced magret of duck, beef medallions with bordelaise sauce and rack of lamb with flageolets. The short menu is supplemented by daily specials.

Similar offerings are available for lunch.

(703) 777-5142. Entrées, $15.95 to $22.95. Lunch, Tuesday-Sunday 11:30 to 2:30. Dinner, Tuesday-Sunday 5:30 to 10.

Black Coffee Bistro, 101 South Madison St., Middleburg.

The 1790 Wright House, the second oldest residence in Middleburg, has been the home of many a restaurant. New owners Bryan and Annie Kimmett seem to have found a winning and lasting formula.

Bryan, a well-traveled chef, and his wife met when both were at Washington's

L'Enfant Plaza Hotel. Both keen gardeners, they moved to the country and when this space became available, he said, "it was a dream come true." They moved in upstairs and refurbished three downstairs dining areas. Bryan turned the old bar into a dining area, where an antique pastry case displays the wines. He installed a window of pressed herbs between that room and the main dining room, whose walls have been softened in beige and hung with local art. Antiques and family heirlooms, from a wood potty to a desk that belonged to Bryan's great-great-grandfather, are evident here and there.

Outside are a pleasant terrace and Bryan's gardens, "mostly organic and heirloom stuff." It turns up in most of his food, which he likes to describe as "comfort food with a twist." Some twist. It's some of the most innovative and beguiling of our travels.

Consider spring appetizers of pan-fried shad roe with crayfish spoonbread, lacquered quail with turnip mash and barley salad or – the original comfort food for some – grilled calves liver with welsh rarebit and applewood-smoked bacon. Or you could begin with Shaker herb soup with deviled biscuit dumplings, seafood gumbo with prawns and andouille, or a strawberry and goat cheese salad with field greens, roma tomato and benne seed crackers

Dinner entrées range from grilled catfish with okra, leek cloves and roasted fennel and a smoked tomato broth to spring leg of lamb steak with braised red cabbage, English peas and pearl onions, and yukon mashed potatoes. Others include roast chicken with beans, smoked chicken and sweet potato hash and field pea relish, and grilled veal loin with lavender bean minestrone, gremolata and pesto.

Similar innovation pervades the lunch menu, from a smoked salmon BLT on black olive bread to a hot steak salad with coriander, allspice vegetables, chickpeas and cilantro vinaigrette. The lamb steak turns up in a grilled tortilla wrap with cucumber dipping sauce. The burger is grilled antelope on a kaiser bun with sweet potato gaufrettes and savory onion jam. Even your basic hot pastrami and Swiss comes with lovage slaw and hot mustard on grilled rye.

Desserts include Meyers's dark chocolate pâté, riesling fruit terrine and pumpkin brûlée.

As for the name, it refers to a blues song from the 1920s in which people drowned their sorrows in black coffee. "It fit the atmosphere we were trying to create," Bryan said – an upbeat gathering spot with a sense of community.

(540) 687-3632. Entrées, $14.25 to $21. Lunch, Tuesday-Saturday 11:30 to 2:30. Dinner, Tuesday-Sunday 6 to 9 or 10. Sunday brunch, 11:30 to 2:30.

Back Street Cafe, 4 East Federal St., Middleburg.
Some locals rate this small Italian-American restaurant and catering establishment of more than a dozen years' vintage their favorite place to eat in town. Certainly its front patio is one of the more jaunty settings, and its salad bar is one of the better we've seen.

It's so good, in fact, that one of us decided to go with the consensus and made a fine lunch of the all-you-can-eat salad bar for $4.95. He got two hefty platefuls of mesclun, spinach and radicchio with a variety of accompaniments, plus such extras as tuna, curried chicken, three-bean and pasta salads. The other was satisfied with a cup of chilled cucumber soup and a toasted BLT with cheese.

Proprietress Tutti Perricone touts creative "pastas" on the dinner menu, ranging from chèvre cappellini and spinach pie to seafood cioppino over linguini and roasted pork chops topped with fontina cheese and served over polenta. The night's specials could be chicken al forno, grilled swordfish with a salsa of sweet bell pepper, avocado, tomato and mango, and strip steak with wild mushroom sauce. Steamed mussels, pizzas and crostini with crab and artichoke are among appetizers and light fare.

All this is served in a simple setting of close-together tables covered with green cloths or print mats, bentwood chairs and lots of ivy painted on the walls.

(540) 687-3122. Entrées, $10.95 to $17.95. Lunch, Monday-Saturday noon to 3. Dinner, 5 to 9 or 10. Closed Sunday. No smoking.

La Fleur de Lis, 2 Church St., Lovettsville.

Chef-owner William J. Walden returned to his roots in Lovettsville to open Billy Joe's Restaurant in the former Lovettsville Village Inn, where he had worked as a teenager making salads and waiting tables. For nearly a decade he had been sous chef at the famed L'Auberge Chez Francois in Great Falls, whose owner he considers his mentor.

He upgraded the interior of the unassuming-looking building to offer upscale French-American cuisine to wide acclaim. In 2000, he changed the name to project a different image. "Everybody knew me by my nickname, Billy Joe," he said. "I have a sense of humor." Some potential customers apparently didn't, however, so Billy Joe's as a formal identifier soon became history.

Focusing on country French cuisine, he offers appetizers like dilled salmon, crab-stuffed mushroom caps, pâtés and bouchée of lobster. Maine lobster bisque is a signature soup. Main courses could be fillet of rare tuna, pan-roasted fillet of Atlantic salmon, trout stuffed with crabmeat, a sauté of quail, venison and roast pheasant, twin lobsters and rack of spring lamb in a garlic parsley crust.

Desserts range from lemon torte to triple chocolate cake.

Crisp white linens and fresh flowers dress the tables, and good art works hang on the pale pink walls accented with wood trim. Downstairs is BJ's Pub, which has a full bar and offers dinner as well.

(540) 822-4700. Entrées, $15.95 to $36. Lunch, Monday and Wednesday-Friday 11:30 to 2:30. Dinner nightly except Tuesday, 5:30 to 10:30.

Candelora's at the Purcellville Inn, 36855 West Main St., Purcellville.

We first met chef-owner Frederick Petrello and Candelora's when they were ensconced in Lovettsville in the old Village Inn. Candelora's moved recently to larger and more elegant quarters in the century-old Purcellville Inn. The dining rooms are stylish with high beamed ceilings, fireplaces, beige walls and mauve-linened tables that match the color of the window treatments. Outside is a large outdoor patio with a bar.

"A taste of Italy in the country" is how Frederick billed his first Candelora's. Opera music played as we lunched on a crock of gazpacho, the assorted antipasti (the house specialty) and a chicken parmesan sandwich with pomodoro sauce and homemade mozzarella cheese in a Tuscan roll, followed by a dish of lemon sorbet and homemade spumoni with fresh berries.

Lunch has been discontinued at the new Candelora's, where the chef concentrates on dinner and his growing deli and catering operation. There's a full deli of imported meats and cheeses, breads, wines and Italian speciality items.

Reasonably priced pastas and a short list of entrées comprise the dinner menu.

Look for such specialties as shrimp adriana with sundried tomatoes and artichoke hearts in a cream sauce over pasta, sausage and ziti al forno, lamb sausage over polenta, veal saltimbocca and veal Candelora (sautéed with sundried tomatoes and served on a bed of greens). Because we had a long drive ahead of us, we picked up some goodies from the deli. The shrimp tagliatelle and the fusilli topped with grilled chicken, pinenuts and goat cheese made a delicious dinner that evening. *(540) 338-2075. Entrées, $10.95 to $18.95. Dinner nightly except Tuesday, 5 to 10 or 11.*

Diversions

Horses and foxhunting are the chief draws in this area. Unless you have local connections or book with knowledgeable (and well located) innkeepers, you're not likely to see – let alone participate in – a foxhunt, which is a private affair for members and invited (paying) guests. But you may hear or catch a glimpse of one of the area's dozen hunts in pursuit of their quarry, generally three days a week from September to March. You're more apt to catch the equine flavor at one of the horse shows, polo matches or the point-to-point or steeplechase events, usually scheduled for weekends in spring and fall.

Quaint Hamlets and Scenic Drives. From uppercrust and horsey Upperville to antiquey Millbrook to the German enclave of Lovettsville, quaint hamlets abound. Perhaps the quaintest is Waterford (see Extra-Special). To best appreciate the area, shun the main highways and get off the beaten path, which is done easily only if you have a good county road map. Having toured most of the area, we're partial to Routes 662 and 665 out of Waterford, Route 734 (the Snickersville Turnpike) from Aldie to Bluemont, Route 709 (the Zulla Road past huge horse estates south of Middleburg), Route 626 (the Halfway Road) south of Middleburg, and particularly Route 626 (the Pot House Road) north of Middleburg past the Glenwood Racetrack, through forested hill and dale to the fabled and surprisingly remote Foxcroft School for young ladies.

Morven Park, 17263 Southern Planter Road, Leesburg.

Turkey buzzards haunt the fences and two black lion sculptures guard the pillared portico of Morven Park, the stately home of Virginia reform governor Westmoreland Davis, whose widow gave the entire 1,500-acre estate in trust to the public in his memory. The Greek Revival mansion, left as it was and decorated to the hilt in a Renaissance theme, is truly a museum. Four Brabant tapestries – said to be in better condition than those in the Vatican – hang in the front foyer, vying for attention with graceful cherubs over the doorway. Those into showy European decor will enjoy the guided, hour-long tour of the mansion's sixteen restored rooms, rich with Tiffany silver in the formal Jacobean dining room, Hudson River School paintings in the informal dining room, and a Hapsbourg crown mirror in the ladies' drawing room. Those into foxhunting will enjoy the twenty-minute film and the memorabilia in the **Museum of Hounds and Hunting,** which occupies the north wing of the mansion (the fabulously wealthy Governor Davis was master of the Loudoun Hunt). Others like the **Carriage Museum,** built around the 100-vehicle collection donated by a Warrenton horsewoman and on rotating display in the old coach house. It includes everything from a charcoal-burning fire pumper and a ladies' phaeton to surreys and a funeral hearse. The magnificent grounds are known for rare specimen trees, including the oldest small-leaf linden on the East Coast, and the **Marguerite Davis Boxwood Gardens.** The Morven Park Steeplechase Races are held here in mid-October. Nearby is the **Morven Park Equestrian Center.**

(703) 777-2414. Open Tuesday-Friday noon to 5, Saturday 10 to 5, Sunday 1 to 5, April-October, also weekends in November. Adults, $6.

Oatlands, Route 15, Leesburg.

The 1813 plantation house built by a descendant of Virginia's famed Robert "King" Carter is better known and has a higher profile than Morven Park, thanks to its operation by the National Trust for Historic Preservation. It was purchased in 1903 by William Corcoran Eustis (of the Washington banking and Corcoran Gallery family), and Mrs. Eustis used it as her English-style country house during the summer and foxhunting seasons until her death in 1964. Their daughters, who live nearby at Little Oatlands and Oatlands Hamlet, left the house and the 261-acre estate to the National Trust. Unlike Morven Park, this is a livable house rather than a museum, and visitors feel as if "the family has just stepped out for a spell," in the words of our tour guide. You'll see George Washington's dessert service displayed in the formal dining room and William Eustis's foxhunting garb in his dressing room. Four acres of formal, terraced gardens are open to visitors, as is the carriage house visitor center and gift shop.

(703) 777-3174. Open Monday-Saturday 10 to 4:30, Sunday 1 to 4:30, late March to late December. Adults, $8.

Tarara Vineyard & Winery, 13648 Tarara Lane, Leesburg.

The centerpiece of this 475-acre vineyard and orchard is the 6,000-square-foot winery and wine cave blasted out of a rocky cliff 30 feet deep, beneath owners Margaret and Whitie Hubert's showplace of a house. The spacious tasting and sales rooms are full of interesting touches, among them the acrylic jewelry and baskets of artist-daughter Karen Hubert and the mixed-media artworks of daughter Martha Hubert, whose designs adorn the winery labels. Tarara sells its fruits to the public (we sampled a couple of delicious blackberries prior to the official pick-your-own weekend following our visit) and sponsors special events from wine dinners to grapevine decorating workshops to pig roasts to picnics to pony rides – all designed to bring people to the winery. Its barrel-fermented chardonnay ($12.99) and reserve cabernet ($15.99) are highly rated, but we and others are partial to the unique non-vintage charval ($7.99), a sprightly blend of chardonnay and seyval blanc. Tarara plans to triple the winery's output. Look for it to become one of the largest and best in Virginia.

(703) 771-7100. Open daily, 11 to 5; weekends only in January and February.

Piedmont Vineyards & Winery, Route 626, Middleburg.

Virginia's first commercial vinifera vineyard was established by Mrs. Thomas Furness in 1973 on 37 acres of a pre-Revolutionary farm called Waverly. Her daughter, Elizabeth Worrall, has made a name among connoisseurs for the boutique winery, producing 5,500 cases a year of some of the best white wines in Virginia. The small flagstone-floored tasting room, quite appealing with wicker furniture, is rather like a Southern veranda, and the picnic grounds among the trees beside a pond are enchanting.

(540) 687-5528. Open daily, 10 to 5.

Shopping. Leesburg is the commercial hub of Loudoun County, although most of its major and basic businesses have moved to strip plazas south and east of town. The Old Town downtown section has attracted antique dealers, some of whom show at the **Leesburg Downtown Antiques Center** at 27 South King St. and the **Leesburg Antique Gallery of Shoppes** in an old church at 7 Wirt St. Also of interest are **Leesburg Vintner,** which serves up great deli sandwiches along with wines and beverages; the **Kitchen Shop,** and **Yesterday's Memories** (with a native American and New Age theme). The feline-lover among us had a field day at **Classy Cat Gifts,** while the other checked out the Civil War titles at **Clio's History Bookshop.** Stores seem to come and go in Leesburg's restored **Market Station** at the edge of downtown.

Tiny Middleburg is perhaps of more appeal to visiting shoppers. Its quaint, tree-lined downtown is chock-a-block full of stylish stores, many with an equine theme, and we were impressed with the showy potted hibiscus trees placed on the four corners at Washington and Madison streets. Established in 1956, **The Fun Shop** with the curious name is a mini-department store in a warren of rooms, stocking everything from table linens and clothing to toys, books, lamp shades and notions (it even offers a toll-free 800 phone number for customers from afar). Also quite big and au courant is **Gourmet Kitchen Plus,** a dream store for those interested in culinary matters. The **Irish Crystal Company** is the first store in Virginia to carry the fine Tyrone Crystal and, unlike most shops of its ilk, the owner urges visitors to touch the merchandise. **The Finicky Filly** offers wonderful women's wear; it's the female counterpart to venerable horseman Tully Rector's men's store. He also offers a "painting of your horse" as one of the services of **The Shaggy Ram,** specialist in country antiques, hunt items and English imports. **A Little Something from Middleburg** offers home furnishings and accessories. English and European garden antiques and furniture are offered at **Wickets Garden Style.** Equestrian books are a feature of **The Book Chase.** Pick up a croissant or a sandwich at **The Upper Crust,** an excellent bakery.

Extra-Special

Waterford. Every state should have a Waterford, but precious few do. Reminiscent of the British Cotswolds, this treasured community of a few hundred souls is no longer an endangered species, having been saved by the Waterford Foundation, established in 1948. The must-see town, settled by Quakers in 1733, is one of the few communities totally encompassed on the National Register of Historic Places. Waterford's Quakers and thriving free black community supported the Union in the Civil War, when it was harassed both by Union forces because of its location and by Confederate forces because of its beliefs. Today, Waterford's buildings and rolling fields, wedged into a fold between hills, look much as they did a century ago. As you drive through on High Street (Route 662 northwest of Leesburg), don't make the mistake of thinking the town consists only of a few nice houses, the Catoctin Presbyterian and Waterford Baptist churches and the red-brick Loudoun Mutual Insurance Co. Instead, head west down one of the side streets to Second and Main streets. Here you'll find a remarkable variety of log, stone and brick houses, the Peaceable Kingdom gift shop, the Waterford Forge, the mapmaker-historian and who knows what all. On a weekday you're likely to have the place to yourself. But come the first weekend of October, thousands are drawn here for the Waterford Foundation's annual house tour and crafts exhibit, one of the nation's best juried shows.

Potomac and Shenandoah rivers converge at Harpers Ferry, as viewed from Overlook Cliffs.

Harpers Ferry, W.Va.
Worth the Voyage

The view of the convergence of the Potomac and Shenandoah rivers here is "one of the most stupendous scenes in nature – worth a voyage across the Atlantic."

So said Thomas Jefferson back in 1783. The view of Harpers Ferry continues to astound travelers, especially those emerging from the Baltimore-Washington megalopolis and suddenly confronting a different vista: one of rivers slicing between mountains, endless greenery and a rugged aspect all around.

Harpers Ferry, a boomtown that died after the Civil War, remains much the way it was during the days of John Brown's infamous raid. An old, hilly, European-looking town that never ceases to amaze, it's the start and the heart of this area known locally as West Virginia's Eastern Panhandle.

Beyond lies busy Charles Town, the Jefferson County seat where John Brown was tried and hanged. Young surveyor George Washington purchased his first land and settled members of his family here in 1748. More Washingtons lived here and more are buried in the Zion Episcopal Church graveyard here than anywhere in the country. Today, it's also distinguished by more traffic lights per capita than any small town we know of.

Make a triangle – that's the route the roads seem to take – from Harpers Ferry to Charles Town around to Shepherdstown, West Virginia's oldest town. A quaint college town, Shepherdstown has retained the charm that bustling Charles Town seems to have lost.

This area is paradise for mountain climbers, hikers along the old Chesapeake & Ohio Canal towpath, Civil War buffs and the rest of us. Country inns and B&Bs arrived here late (about 1985), but seem to be making up for lost time. Zoning limits their presence in most of Harpers Ferry, the soul of the area.

The National Park Service has restored Harpers Ferry's lower town, which draws more than a million visitors annually. Despite all the people, the view and the surroundings are just as Thomas Jefferson said they were.

Inn Spots

Except for the ancient Hilltop House, something of a time capsule that is appropriate for Harpers Ferry, accommodations here are generally limited to B&Bs of no more than two guest rooms. There is a new Comfort Inn, but that's uptown in Bolivar. Country inns and B&Bs prevail in Charles Town and Shepherdstown, each about six miles away as the crow flies. Some inns add surcharges for use of credit cards.

Briscoe House, 828 Washington St., Box 1024, Harpers Ferry 25425.

The "Brit B&B" license plate on their van tells where Jean Hale's loyalties lie. She and her American husband Lin traveled around the world during his Army career, which is "why we needed a twenty-room house" for all their furnishings. In 1995, they bought the substantial 1880s residence known locally as the old Briscoe house, once the home of two black professors at the local college, and turned it into one of the area's more comfortable B&Bs.

The Hales put up guests in two front suites on the second floor, both with private baths and TV. The Ivy Room has a sitting room in front, an ivy-patterned comforter on the queen bed and sprightly décor. The Rose Room is named for the flowers on its comforter and pillows, has a sitting area and a mirrored jacuzzi tub in the bathroom.

The front parlor/dining room are outfitted in Victoriana. In her enormous kitchen, Jean prepares a four-course English breakfast: fresh fruit, scones, coffeecake, cereal and, often, ham and eggs with fried potatoes. Guests "rave about her breakfasts," her husband advises.

(304) 535-2416. Two suites with private baths. Doubles, $95 weekends, $85 midweek. No credit cards.

Harpers Ferry Guest House, 800 Washington St., Box 1079, Harpers Ferry 25425.

This B&B looks and smells new. And it is. Al and Allison Alsdorf obtained photos of the original Victorian house on the property, which had burned ten years earlier, and rebuilt it to look much the same.

They offer three sprightly bedrooms with private baths and TV sets, two with queensize beds. One on the main floor is designed for the handicapped and has twin beds that can be joined as a king.

Quilts top the poster reproduction beds that were made in nearby Berkeley County. Alison is particularly proud of her West Virginia kitchen, built by a retired industrial-arts teacher and his wife.

The adjacent dining room is the setting for some grand breakfasts at a large table. Al cooks omelets and Allison prepares cornmeal or blueberry waffles to accompany juice, fruit and banana or lemon-poppyseed muffins.

Because of its newness, rooms in this house seem bigger than in the average Victorian. There's a large living room with TV. "Guests can be as private or as much a part of the house as they wish," says Alison.

The Alsdorfs moved from New Paltz, N.Y., when Al was transferred to Gaithersburg, Md. He likes trains and, when he came across the railroad bridge, Harpers Ferry reminded him of home.

(304) 535-6955. Three rooms with private baths. Doubles, $95 weekends, $65 mid-week. Children over 12. No smoking. No credit cards.

The Jackson Rose Bed & Breakfast, 1141 Washington St., Box 641, Harpers Ferry 25425.

Opened in 1990, this is the most historic of Harpers Ferry's B&Bs. The Georgian-Federal brick structure dates to 1795 and is on the National Register.

It takes its name from a climbing rose that reached the second-story of the house at the time Stonewall Jackson stayed here at the beginning of the Civil War. He wrote to his wife that he could not close the window for the rose that was so beautiful peeking in – the bush and the rose became known locally as the Jackson Rose. "The rose bush still exists and we liked the story," said new owner Deb Hale, innkeeper with her husband Phillip. They returned to his hometown from northern California and bought the house. She runs the B&B while he commutes to work in northern Virginia.

Taking over the former Lee-Stonewall Inn, they have upgraded and expanded – a measure allowed because they are located just across the town line in Bolivar and are not subject to Harpers Ferry's zoning regulations.

On the second floor are the Linden Room, named for a majestic weeping linden tree outside its window and decorated in deep colors for a European feeling, as well as the namesake Jackson Rose Room, outfitted in pink and rose. Both with high ceilings and tall windows, they come with private baths and share a common TV/game room.

On the third floor are the dormered Garret room with double bed, private bath and an Americana look. It becomes a family suite when rented with a small adjoining room with twin beds.

Guests relax on the back porch or on lawn chairs in the back yard beneath the linden tree as old as the house. They also enjoy the fireplace in the parlor.

A hearty breakfast, served fireside in the dining room, begins with fresh fruit, cereal and a sweet bread or coffeecake. The main course could be mushroom omelet with sides of ham and homefries, french toast or banana pancakes with sausage, or potato frittata with ham and fried tomatoes.

(304) 535-1528. Two rooms and one suite with private baths. Doubles, $95 weekends, $85 midweek. Family suite, $150.

Hillbrook Inn on Bullskin Run, Summit Point Road, Route 2, Box 152, Charles Town 25414.

This beauty of a Tudor mansion on fifteen levels and seventeen rural acres is an

Tudor-style Hillbrook Inn on Bullskin Run offers lodging and fine dining.

anomaly. It has earned national awards and magazine coverage, and yet is little known within the area and its brochures are not often available through visitor centers. Perhaps that's because innkeeper Gretchen Carroll is out to attract an upscale clientele that appreciates a richly furnished house in the English country style and gourmet dinners and is willing to pay for the privilege.

Only one room wide and in places only one room high, the stuccoed house of thirteen gables, timbered walls, windows with more than 2,000 panes of glass and an unmistakable English look tiptoes up a hillside. That makes things mighty interesting, inside and out.

Start in the living room, twenty feet high, with tall mullioned windows on two sides. It contains a battery of art objects, elegant furnishings and oriental rugs characteristic of the entire manor. Fireplaces on either end of the room add warmth in winter. Up one level from the living room is the large Bamford room with fireplace and porch, a queen bed in the corner and an old Vuitton steamer trunk for a luggage rack. The Bamford and the Cottage, reached by a private entrance and known as the room of the nine oriental rugs, command top dollar. The Cottage offers a queen bed, a glass-front wood stove, a red velvet chair and two side chairs, a balcony, and a deep red and blue paisley decor.

Also top-priced are four deluxe rooms in a new stuccoed building that resembles a half-timbered barn behind the main inn. Two rooms here have kingsize beds and two have queens. Each comes with a corner fireplace, whirlpool tub and separate shower. Gretchen decorated each differently according to "one of the four seasons of life."

Other rooms back in the main house include Locke's Nest, entered high above the living room and harboring two beds with thick brass headboards that are polished every other week. The tub and the toilet retain the colors of what had been an all-purple bathroom. Two smaller rooms, the queen-bedded Lookout and the Point with antique double bed, are tucked into the eaves. Sloping walls create odd angles and spaces in the former, windows look out in three directions, and a Thai spirit house intricately carved in teak sits atop an ancient English oak table. A six-foot-long tunnel leads to the Point, which reflects the innkeeper's passion for oriental rugs, rich but dark fabrics and upholstery, and rare paintings from Europe and Asia.

The public spaces are sights to behold, especially the dining room that is higher than it is wide, where a seven-course dinner is served at 8 o'clock (see Dining Spots). There's a library full of interesting books. A smashing tavern with a box-beam ceiling, a grand piano and lots of wing chairs looks like an English gentleman's club. The dining porch used for breakfast overlooks gorgeous back lawns, an old boxwood grove, a tall willow tree and a duck pond. A full country breakfast features pecan pancakes with ginger butter, and french toast tatiana, served with warm cranberry-orange syrup and sour cream. The inn serves lunch by reservation, and English teas are offered Sunday afternoons from November to April at $20 a head.

Fresh flowers and a small box of Lake Champlain Chocolates from Vermont are in each room. The guest book is full of raves, the theme being "a special, magical place."

(304) 725-4223 or (800) 304-4223. Fax (304) 725-4455. Eleven rooms with private baths. Doubles, $225 to $325 weekends, $150 to $250 midweek.

The Carriage Inn, 417 East Washington St., Charles Town 25414.

New owners have added a personal welcome and creature comforts to this B&B in need of the caring touch of innkeeper/owners in residence. Al and Kay Standish from northern Virginia bought the establishment in 1996, did some refurbishing, added personal possessions and turned a rear carriage house into a suite. He also became a board member of the state B&B association.

Built in the early 1800s, the corner house hides behind huge shade trees on the town's main street. The former owner, a contractor, is credited with devising the sunken private baths found in former stairwells to the rear of the house. He also made the beds by hand. Named for the color of their wallpaper, the four guest accommodations in the main house come with full baths and queen four-poster beds. Four have gas fireplaces. Some have day beds or a velvet loveseat with two side chairs, and a suite has its own enclosed porch with TV and refrigerator. The Blue Room has one of the highest step-up beds we've seen. You'd never know the Lavender Room on the third floor was once the attic; it has a four-poster bed, a sitting room with a daybed and a settee, and a franklin stove.

The Standishes converted the carriage-house apartment in which previous managers resided into a three-room suite. The main floor has a living room with a sofabed and a dining area, while the pine-paneled upstairs bedroom contains a queensize bed.

Guests enjoy a heavily shaded front veranda with a swing and a deep back yard. Breakfast with china and crystal is served at one large and two small tables in the dining room. It includes tropical fruit juice, sliced fruit, and perhaps German baked eggs and sausage plus double chocolate-banana muffins.

Afternoon tea is available in the drawing room, which has twelve-foot-high ceilings, a piano and TV.

The new George Washington Heritage Trail, a 135-mile travel route tracing the Washington family heritage, passes in front of The Carriage Inn.

(304) 728-8003 or (800) 867-9830. Fax (304) 728-2976. Four rooms and two suites

with private baths. Doubles, $119 weekends, $75 midweek. Suites, $129 and $135 weekends, $85 and $95 midweek. Children in carriage house suite only. No smoking.

Washington House Inn, 216 South George St., Charles Town 25414.
Built at the turn of the century by Samuel Washington, grandnephew of the first president, this fine example of late Victorian architecture offers six rooms with private baths, a turret and a wraparound veranda dressed in wicker. Owners Mel and Nina Vogel, who moved with two teenagers from suburban Washington, have added fine antiques, family heirlooms and handmade quilts crafted by a distant relative from Charleston.

Unusual corner fireplaces – two of seven in the three-story house – back up to each other in the pink and maroon parlor and the pink lace-clothed dining room, which is set with Limoges china. Ensconced in the turret, the parlor is the place for games like backgammon and cribbage.

The dining room, with regal oxblood-colored walls, is the setting for Nina's breakfasts. Her cooking interests were inspired by her parents' restaurant in Ohio. Expect juice, fresh fruit, gourmet coffees and a main dish like caramelized french toast, sausage and eggs or cinnamon raisin french toast stuffed with cream cheese.

A prized original lithograph of Abraham Lincoln graces the downstairs foyer near the carved oak staircase. The Lavender Room in the turret and the Rose Room next door are decorated in pale colors, as is the third-floor Turret Room. More vivid is the Green Room, done in hunter green with a four-poster bed, desk and two side chairs. The walnut sleigh bed in the Dormer Room is topped by a faux canopy of hunter green moiré and covered with an embroidered coverlet accented with a hand-crocheted throw made by Nina's mother. Some rooms have fireplaces and casablanca paddle fans. The modern baths have pedestal sinks and showers. Except for prized personal possessions, most of the furnishings are for sale.

Fresh fruit, homemade cookies and tea or coffee are offered in the afternoon.
(304) 725-7923 or (800) 297-6957. Fax (304) 728-5150. Six rooms with private baths. Doubles, $125 on weekends, $75 midweek. Children over 10. No smoking.

The Cottonwood Inn, Route 2, Box 61-S, Charles Town 25414.
Black and white cows from the farm up the road were lying in the shade beside Bull Skin Run as we approached this nearly 200-year-old farmhouse out in the countryside about five miles east of town. Joe and Barbara Sobol left his oil and gas business in the Texas-Louisiana area in 1995 to launch a new business here – the production of European video travelogues in a studio at the rear of an existing B&B. Cottonwood also is host to ItalySource, an Internet store arranging travel to Italy as well as selling Italian crafts and decorative accessories.

The six-acre property beside a stream, graced with prolific flowers, is quiet as can be. The seven guest rooms with private baths vary widely. Some, up an original staircase, are cozy and historic with clawfoot tubs, old beds and fireplaces. Others up narrow stairs in an older section are carpeted. One with a kingsize bed, a day bed and a full bath is cheery with white walls. A 1988 addition holds modern rooms that are quite inviting in their newness. All rooms have television, queen or king beds, sitting areas and air-conditioning.

Both the guest rooms and common rooms are designed for comfort. There's a large, beautiful living room with a grand piano in a corner and a well-stocked

New and old merge nicely at rural Cottonwood Inn.

library at the far end. Its floral blue carpet picks up the pale yellow and apricot colors on the walls. Windsor chairs are at tables in the beamed dining room, site of a huge brick fireplace with a raised hearth and butter molds hanging along a beam.

Breakfast consists of juice, fresh fruit and an entrée such as puff pastry with smoked turkey and cheese or an egg, onion and cheese casserole, plus orange-blueberry muffins or apple-cherry coffeecake. Afternoon refreshments are taken on Adirondack chairs on the front lawn, looking toward those cows lazing beside the creek.

(304) 725-3371 or (800) 868-1188. Fax (304) 728-4763. Seven rooms with private baths. Doubles, $75 to $120. Two-night minimum in October and holiday weekends. No smoking.

Thomas Shepherd Inn, German and Duke Streets, Box 3634, Shepherdstown 25443.

An early American but comfortable feeling pervades this cream-colored brick Federal house at the main intersection in Shepherdstown, West Virginia's oldest town. The warmth comes from Lori Capettini, a former high-tech marketing director from Baltimore, who bought the inn from its original owner in 1999.

The B&B, opened in 1985, has a rich, formal living room furnished with wing chairs, oriental scatter rugs and decanters of sherry at the ready. There are two dining rooms where a gourmet breakfast is served each morning. Another favorite gathering space is the library, with a TV/VCR, guest refrigerator, games and a stash of material on the area. Off this room is a tree-top balcony with rockers and lots of plants overlooking the rear garden.

Of the six guest rooms, we're partial to Room 6 in back looking out over the garden. It comes with a canopied bed, a full bath and a large sitting area. Other rooms vary: one is rather small with a double bed, another has a double and a twin, and still another a sleigh bed. A front corner room offers a partially canopied bed, two upholstered chairs and a large full bath with big, thirsty towels.

Breakfasts here are special. A typical day begins with chilled raspberry soup with a dollop of crème fraîche, followed by morning glory muffins. The main course could be dilled scrambled eggs with cream cheese baked in puff pastry. The next day might yield peaches and cream waffles with praline sauce. Garnishes like nasturtiums, pansies and calendulas from the side gardens accompany.

Sherry is offered in the late afternoon. And Lori will fix dinner for groups by prior arrangement.

(304) 876-3715 or (888) 889-8952. Fax (304) 876-3313. Six rooms with private baths. Doubles, $115 to $135 weekends, $85 to $105 midweek. Two-night minimum on weekends. Children over 8. No smoking.

Bavarian Inn & Lodge, Route 480 (Postal Route 1, Box 30), Shepherdstown 25443.

This was the area's first, starting as a restaurant in 1962 and adding lodging in chalet-style buildings overlooking the Potomac River in 1981 and a conference center in 1994.

Though the restaurant (see Dining Spots) remains the priority of Munich-born owner Erwin Asam and his English wife Carol, their overnight accommodations are attractive as well. Four Bavarian-style, beamed chalets bear exterior murals of mountains and castles. They contain 39 well-appointed rooms with queensize four-poster beds (mostly canopied), sitting areas with TV, many with sleep sofas, and private balconies high above the Potomac. Twenty-six have gas fireplaces and eighteen offer jacuzzi baths.

From our balcony we could watch canoeists below on the river and rabbits scurrying along the hillside and hear lovely birdcalls at both dusk and sunrise. Only the noise of traffic from the nearby highway bridge pierced the tranquility. Inside our spacious, stucco-walled room in white and light brown were a couple of welcoming apples, two wing chairs and an archway to the entry and the bath, which included a dressing room with extra vanity and an assortment of Lord & Mayfair toiletries.

Thirty more rooms, nine with fireplaces and jacuzzis, plus a conference and exercise facility, are located in a newer building between the chalets and Route 480.

There also are three guest rooms and suites in the main greystone inn and restaurant, uphill from the chalets. Twelve acres of nicely landscaped grounds include a secluded swimming pool. Breakfast is available at hotel prices in the restaurant.

(304) 876-2551. Fax (304) 876-9355. Seventy rooms and two suites with private baths. Doubles, $95 to $165 EP; suites, $195 to $275.

Dining Spots

Hillbrook Inn on Bullskin Run, Summit Point Road (Route 13), Charles Town.

We don't know whether the setting or the food is more the attraction here. It could be both, but who knows? Only the flush tend to eat here because of the pricing structure, which commands a hefty $70 for a prix-fixe dinner (the price includes table wines poured throughout the meal). Innkeeper Gretchen Carroll says the experience is designed to be relaxed and unpretentious, rather like a dinner party in a private home.

The dining room in this stunning Tudor mansion is taller than it is wide or long, which makes for an interesting sense of space. A brass chandelier comprised of old oil lamps casts soft shadows over a handful of tables showing the patina of old wood and set with brass service plates. Flickering candles in hurricane chimneys are reflected in the silver and crystal and in a brass teapot collection on the buffet, and the gold print on the wallpaper shimmers by candlelight. The adjacent breakfast porch, used for dinner overflow, overlooks the rear lawns and gardens that are spotlit at night.

Executive chef Christine Hale, a Pittsburgh Culinary Institute graduate who trained in France, oversees the single-choice menu. The seven-course dinner is served at individual tables at 8 o'clock. It might start with white button mushrooms in a garden herb marinade, curried onion soup and penne with a tomato-caper sauce. The main event could be grilled marlin with tarragon butter, teamed with jasmine rice, sautéed squash with thyme, pernod cucumbers and oil-roasted green beans. A salad of red leaf lettuce with avocado and mango follows. The meal concludes with smoked havarti cheese with bremner wafers, honeydew melon and red grapes, and a dessert like poached pears with caramelized pecans, chocolate ganache and strawberry coulis.

A prix-fixe lunch ($30) offering a sampling of the inn's specialties is served by reservation on the enclosed dining porch or on the garden terrace.

(304) 725-4223 or (800) 304-4223. Prix-fixe, $70. By reservation only. Lunch available daily, noon to 2. Dinner, Thursday-Sunday at 8. No smoking.

Yellow Brick Bank, 201 West German St., Shepherdstown.
Bright red apples hang from ficus trees in this colorful – make that flamboyant – restaurant inside an old yellow brick bank. In the main dining room, huge old posters decorate the pink walls, the chairs are pink and mauve, and the high coffered ceiling is edged in handpainted blue clouds. A casual dining room and bar, done up in white wicker, has tall windows onto a side patio.

At lunch, one of us enjoyed a bowl of sweet corn and jalapeño chowder, loaded with chopped ham and tomatoes and packing a spicy wallop, and an appetizer of shiitake mushrooms on lemon thyme toast. The other chose pesto pasta with chopped tomatoes, served in a big bowl with French bread alongside. We had no room left for desserts, among them lemon cheesecake with caramelized mascarpone, coffee ice cream with kahlua and coconut, and Mexican chocolate bread pudding with crème fraîche. On weekends, there are two sampler plates of four desserts each.

The dinner menu offers stellar pastas as well as entrées ranging from grilled salmon with dijon-balsamic glazed to grilled rack of lamb with curried mango chutney and creamed cucumbers. Bluefin tuna grilled with tamari and freshly grated horseradish, grilled trout with mango relish and grilled hanger steak are some choices. The cooking here is assertive, to go along with the eclectic atmosphere.

A wood-burning oven and an applewood grill have been installed in a large kitchen addition to add even more contemporary flair to the menu.

(304) 876-2208. Entrées, $15 to $23. Lunch, Monday-Saturday 11:30 to 4:30. Dinner from 5. Sunday brunch, 11 to 4.

Bavarian Inn, Route 480, Shepherdstown.
This well-known dining room attracts diners from near and far. It's not the kind

of place to which we were attracted for a Saturday lunch – we stopped, looked at the menu, saw all the staff and customers in dressy attire and decided to go on to a more casual place where we could eat outside. But it fit the bill perfectly for dinner at another visit.

The main dining room in the living room of the original greystone mansion resembles the interior of a Bavarian lodge with paneled walls, beamed ceiling, deer-antler chandeliers, a deer head over the huge stone fireplace and racks with displays of Bavarian china and beer steins. We preferred the pleasant, glassed-in terrace dining area with windows onto the gardens.

The extensive dinner menu covers all the bases, including Bavarian, continental, American, cold platters and "lean and healthy." When in Bavaria, do as...and one of us did. Wiener schnitzel with red cabbage and pan-fried potatoes with caraway seeds was the real thing. The other sampled the grilled medallions of pork tenderloin with red cabbage and green beans, which was unmemorable. Good German bread arrived as we sat down. A small slab of the chef's mellow veal, liver and duck pâté with all the trimmings and house salads tided us over until the entrées came. A Bavarian nut ball – vanilla ice cream rolled in peanuts and topped with chocolate sauce and coconut flakes – was not cold enough but quite good.

There are interesting, reasonably priced international coffees and after-dinner drinks. You might want to adjourn downstairs to the **Rathskellar,** a very alpine place that wraps around the bar and offers weekend entertainment.

(304) 876-2551. Entrées, $12.75 to $21.95. Lunch, Monday-Saturday 11:30 to 2:30. Dinner, 5 to 10, Sunday noon to 9.

Charles Washington Inn, 210 West Liberty St., Charles Town.

The oldest home in Charles Town on property purchased from Charles Washington (for whom the town was named), this was known as the Tiffin House for most of its 203 years. New owners gave it a facelift and a new name, and expanded the dining capacity. Meals are served in three small fireplaced rooms, a casual one on the main floor and two fancier rooms upstairs, decorated in what the owners call "Colonial romantic" style. There are also a bar and a new garden dining room.

Crab cakes and veal dishes are the specialties, but the menu changes seasonally. For dinner, you might find cajun scallops, broiled salmon with lemon-dill beurre blanc, chicken sautéed with artichoke hearts and sundried tomatoes, veal saltimbocca, prime rib or filet mignon béarnaise sauce.

Start with stuffed mushroom caps or smoked trout. Finish with coconut cake, fresh strawberries or chocolate pâté with raspberry sauce.

(304) 725-4020. Entrées, $13.95 to $17.95. Lunch, 11:30 to 4. Dinner nightly, 5 to 9 or 10.

The Anvil Restaurant, 1270 Washington St., Harpers Ferry.

This oldtimer in the uptown Bolivar section packs in the tourists in a pub out front, a big early American dining room to the rear and an outdoor patio beyond. Although the dining room and patio were empty at our visit, there was a waiting line for lunch in the crowded pub and we couldn't wait.

Too bad, for this is considered the best place to eat in town. The menu is traditional continental-American. Seafood linguini en papillote is the house specialty. Blackboard specials at our visit were baked potato soup, chicken roulade and blackened grouper. Other entrées could be crab cakes, broiled salmon, grilled swordfish, chicken piccata, veal marsala and filet mignon.

Starters include french onion soup, crab balls, baked brie and steamed mussels. Among desserts are cheesecake, Kentucky derby pie and tortilla ice cream. *(304) 535-2582. Entrées, $12.95 to $22. Lunch, 11 to 4:30. Dinner, 5 to 9 or 10. Closed Monday.*

Diversions

Harpers Ferry National Historic Park, Harpers Ferry.

The immensely picturesque area that Thomas Jefferson said was "worth a voyage across the Atlantic" to see remains little changed from the 19th century. From an information center west of town, buses shuttle visitors into the historic lower town, which is blissfully tranquil because vehicular traffic is light.

The town of Harpers Ferry boomed after it was designated a federal armory and arsenal, manufacturing many of the munitions used in the War of 1812 and the Civil War. The buildings were the targets of abolitionist John Brown's raid, aimed at arming the slaves for insurrection. The town of 3,000 declined rapidly because of destruction wrought by the Civil War and repeated flooding. It was a sleepy little hamlet when taken over by the National Park Service in 1944 and restored in what has since become a national model for historic park preservation. The park's four themes are industry, John Brown's raid on the arsenal, the Civil War and black history. The last is represented by Storer College, a normal school for the education of freed blacks that started in an abandoned armory dwelling in the upper town. Park employees in period clothing present living-history programs and guided tours in the streets and restored buildings during summer.

Most of the sites are clustered along Shenandoah Street in **Lower Town.** The old Stage Coach Inn is now the Harpers Ferry Historical Association's excellent bookstore and an information center. The Master Armorer's House is a museum on gunmaking. Stop at the old dry goods store, where the 1850s price list puts neckties at 35 cents each. John Brown's Fort is the old armory firehouse where he and his followers were captured. Other attractions include the Blacksmith Shop, Provost Office, John Brown Museum, Whitehall Tavern and a confectionery.

From the lower town, the town marches in European fashion up a steep hill without a 20th-century intrusion. The **Stone Steps** – we counted 56 of them – begin a trail to the upper town. A sign says the trail takes 45 minutes and is steep at the start, but the views of rivers, bridges, lower town and surrounding heights "are well worth it." First comes the 1775 **Harper House,** built by the town's founder, now restored as an 1850s tenant house to represent the crowded conditions and lack of housing in the town's industrial heyday. Opposite are springhouses and root cellars, small caves carved into the shale cliffs. Next is St. Peter's Roman Catholic Church, an 1833 stone church and a commanding presence, but difficult to reach by car for Sunday Masses. Beyond are the ruins of St. John's Episcopal Church and **Jefferson Rock,** vantage point for the "stupendous" view. *(304) 535-6223. Visitor Center open daily, 8 to 5. Parking, $5.*

Other Towns. Charles Town, the busy county seat, does not have much to commend it to visitors unless they are Washington family buffs or racetrack fans. A Washington descendant still lives in Harewood, the 1770 home of Samuel Washington, but all six Washington family homes are privately owned and not opened to the public. A brochure illustrates a walking tour of historic points so spread out that most prefer to drive. More to our liking is quaint **Shepherdstown,**

endowed with street after street of historic homes, good shopping and the campus of Shepherd College. Current and foreign films are shown in the Old Opera House, and the Contemporary American Theater Festival presents four new plays each July at Shepherd College.

Hiking. The **Appalachian Trail** crosses the Potomac on the same railroad-pedestrian bridge that tourists use to get near the railroad tunnel and onto the Chesapeake & Ohio Canal towpath. Favorite hikes are to Maryland Heights and Overlook Cliffs, a four-mile round trip that rewards the hardy with the view of Harpers Ferry that is the trademark of the area.

Shopping. We aren't particularly impressed with a lot of the shops in Harpers Ferry, most of them geared to tourists and the better ones tucked away out of sight. But there are exceptions: the handcrafted stoneware and porcelain at **Westwinds Potters** and the original folk art collectibles and handmade crafts in an 1829 dwelling called **Marmion House Gifts. Grape Expectations** offers "something grape for everyone," especially West Virginia wines, picnic baskets, glassware and ceramics. We like the handicrafts at **Sleepy Hollow Creations** and the collectibles at **Stone House Antiques.** Almost every other building along High Street seems to be a snacky café, ice cream or coffee shop. Their names (The Garden of Food, Hot Dog Haven, Old-Fashioned Cookies and Peanuts) indicate what they are about.

In Shepherdstown, **Dickinson & W**ait is an exceptional pottery studio and craft gallery. **Village Green** is a trove of gifts and decorative accessories, with **Village Finery** for women's apparel upstairs. **Cocoa** stocks accessories and gifts, and **O'Hurley's General Store** is a must stop. **Maggie's Marketplace** specializes in natural foods. For a snack there's **Ye Olde Sweet Shoppe,** a bakery that makes everything it sells, specializes in whole-grain European breads with no sugar or additives, and the coffee is 35 cents if you bring your own cup (otherwise, 45 and 80 cents). Wonderful artworks share the stage with coffee and espresso at **Lost Dog Coffee. The Old Pharmacy Café & Soda Fountain** is recommended for lunch and light supper. Besides coffee and candles, the **German Street Coffee & Candlery** offers oil lamps, glassware and garden accents.

Extra-Special

The Chesapeake & Ohio Canal National Historic Park.
With 74 lift locks and designation as a national historic park, the C&O Canal stretches 185 miles from the heights of Cumberland, Md., to Rock Creek in Georgetown. The towpath along the Maryland side is immensely popular with joggers, walkers and bicyclists because it's so level, and nowhere more so than in the Sharpsburg-Harpers Ferry area, where it incorporates six miles of the Appalachian Trail. Here a stone and dirt path follows the Potomac beneath a canopy of trees. Particularly interesting is the 3.5-mile stretch south of Shepherdstown to Antietam Creek, where you'll see the Antietam Viaduct, Lock No. 38 and the sites of two bloody Civil War battles along Antietam Creek. Park rangers lead periodic tours to various locks, aqueducts and even caves. Information is available at park headquarters in the impressive **Ferry Hill Place,** an 1813 plantation manor above the Potomac off Route 34 in Sharpsburg, Md.

(301) 739-4200. Visitor center open daily, 8 to 4:30.

Deep Creek Lake, Md.
Mountain-Top Playground

A variety of both mountain and lake activities in one compact area draws those in the know to an area that many Americans have never heard of. Hiking, whitewater rafting, boating, swimming, skiing – all are available in westernmost Maryland's rural Garrett County, home of Deep Creek Lake.

Maryland's highest mountains first drew visitors as the frontier developed in the 19th century. The Baltimore & Ohio Railroad opened up the area, building summer resorts in Oakland and Deer Park. Presidents Grant, Harrison and Cleveland vacationed here and attended services in the old Garrett Memorial Church in Oakland, now called the Church of the Presidents. Henry Ford, Thomas Edison and Harvey Firestone camped at the foot of Maryland's highest waterfall in 1918, a visit commemorated in Swallow Falls State Park.

The area's popularity ebbed until manmade Deep Creek Lake was created in 1925 and Wisp Ski Resort rose above its shore. Originally a "cabin lake" favored by people from Pittsburgh less than two hours away, Maryland's largest freshwater lake has gone upscale in the last decade or so. A building boom has created large homes and condominiums along much of its meandering, 65-mile shoreline.

"We've changed from honky-tonk cabins to B&Bs and from spaghetti to French restaurants," notes Mary Bender, who opened the Carmel Cove Inn in 1994. A Pittsburgh resident, she credits the upscaling of Deep Creek Lake from its early Steel Town image over the last decade to an influx of people and money from Baltimore and Washington, D.C.

With an uncharacteristically wimpy name for a ski area, Wisp has the only downhill slopes in Maryland. Located astride Marsh Mountain, part of the Allegheny Range, it rises 610 feet from the lakeshore to an elevation of 3,080 feet. Wisp also has a golf course and a resort hotel that looks like a hospital.

The area's beguiling charms remain relatively undiscovered (the AAA Mid-Atlantic Tour Book barely mentions the area). Never mind. Those in the know enjoy swimming and boating in a mountain lake that looks as if it's been relocated from the Adirondacks (a 30-foot power company easement along the shore ensures a natural, forested setting). Wilderness lovers enjoy the county's 70,000 acres of mountainous state park and forest lands, which offer everything from waterfalls to whitewater boating to cross-country skiing.

Photo by Carol McNiece

Refreshments await visitors on stone porch overlooking Deep Creek Lake at Lake Pointe Inn.

The lake area is blessedly free of mosquitoes, and, in summer, is ten degrees cooler than nearby cities. Fall foliage colors rival those of New England and average yearly snowfalls of 100 inches create a winter wonderland.

Arts festivals and a few good restaurants and shops add to the mix. The only town is Oakland, the county seat with a population of 1,700.

Little changed is the unspoiled nature of an area populated partly by Amish and Mennonites and a Bible-belt mentality that bars the sale of alcoholic beverages on Sunday. "We're behind the times," says Ken Bock of the Savage River Inn. "We haven't had to lock our doors in the 25 years we've lived here."

Inn Spots

Lake Pointe Inn, 174 Lake Pointe Drive, McHenry 21541.

Put aside any skepticism when you proceed through an emerging development of rather pretentious residences at the foot of Wisp Ski Area and face a trailer park across the lake. Ahead lies an 1890 farmhouse, partly hidden in pines at lake's edge, right beside the water and in a world unto itself.

The oldest house along Deep Creek Lake shore was built long before the lake was created, but was in such disrepair that the Lake Pointe developer planned to raze it. George and Linda Pettie, longtime lake vacationers from northern Virginia, saw its potential and stepped in to save it. A scrapbook details its extensive restoration in 1995 into a luxurious B&B in the style of an Adirondack lodge.

The stone house has an idyllic stone and pillared porch wrapping around the side and back. Here you can sit in wicker rockers and watch boats come and go on a cove with the main lake in the distance. Water's edge is a mere thirteen feet away. Power company easements require any structures dating after 1925 to be set back at least 30 feet from shore, but this property was grandfathered.

The lodge feeling continues inside, where the original wormy chestnut wood panels the walls and ceiling of the great room – dark and cool in summer, and warmed by a soaring stone hearth in the winter. The main floor also holds a couple of sunny breakfast rooms, a guest kitchen and pantry, and the living quarters for well-traveled innkeeper Carol McNiece, whose previous career was in corporate travel planning.

On the second floor are six small but comfortable guest rooms with private baths, queensize beds with down comforters and pillows, small TV/VCRs and telephones. Each is named for a local personage, whose life detailed in the room's scrapbook. Furnishings throughout are in the Arts and Crafts tradition. We enjoyed the Browning Room with windows onto both lake and ski mountain. Its full bath with shiny brass fixtures was equipped with all kinds of luxuries, from huge Egyptian cotton bath towels to terrycloth robes to Neutrogena toiletries. The larger McHenry Room adds a double whirlpool tub. A shelf in the hallway was stocked with complimentary beverages and a video library, and coffee was ready here the next morning.

Originally planned as dormitory bunkrooms, two large rooms on the third-floor loft now have queen beds with daybeds as adjuncts. Each has a private hall bath.

Substantial hors d'oeuvres are offered upon arrival. Carol will prepare special dinners for inn guests by reservation on certain holiday weekends.

The breakfast menu is posted daily. Ours included choice of juice, a delectable half grapefruit flavored with ginger sauce and vanilla beans, nutmeg-cinnamon muffins made with Vietnamese nutmeg, and creamy pesto eggs in puff pastry with ricotta cheese and asparagus, hash browns and maple-link sausage. Between courses, Carol took part in her morning ritual: feeding cashews to a cheeky chipmunk and getting a duck to eat out of her hand. She pointed out resident loons on the lake. Later she took us for a ride around the lake on the inn's speedy pontoon boat. We never did have time to try out the hot tub overlooking the cove.

(301) 387-0111 or (800) 523-5253. Fax (301) 387-0190. Nine rooms with private baths. Summer and winter: doubles $148 to $189 weekends, $133 to $174 midweek. Rest of year, $133 to $174 weekends, $118 to $159 midweek. Two-night minimum on weekends. Children over 16. No smoking.

Carmel Cove Inn, Box 644, Oakland 21550.

A former monastery has been transformed into the area's largest upscale B&B. Mary and Peter Bender from Pittsburgh acquired the Carmelite Fathers monastery in 1994 from a Carmel Cove developer who was superstitious about tearing it down. With their young children, they had been scouring the East to search for a B&B site and found it here.

The monks' "cells" were gutted to produce ten guest rooms, all with private baths and most with queensize beds. Two in the middle of the rambling, T-shaped house are decidedly small, five deluxe are slightly bigger and three premier rooms come with whirlpool baths and separate showers. One of the last opens onto an expansive deck along the side of the building; the others on the lower floor have fireplaces or franklin stoves. All are bright and cheery, furnished simply but stylishly with matching bed covers and window treatments, herb wreaths on the doors and family antiques. Complimentary half-bottles of the local Deep Creek Cellars wine with a private Carmel Cove Inn label await in each room.

Our deluxe room with queen bed opened onto the deck, and the only sounds to be heard were birds twittering at daybreak. The quarters were tight and the bath-room big enough only for a shower, but all the requisite amenities were at hand

Former monastery is now home of Carmel Cove Inn.

(or in a chest in the hall, for those who forgot). Breakfast was served on the deck outside our room the next morning.

And what a breakfast it was! Beforehand, we helped ourselves to juice, fresh fruit, coffee date-raisin scones and croissants in the airy, cathedral-ceilinged dining room. At the appointed hour, the table on our deck was dressed with linens and set with a fruit platter. Each of us was given an oversize plate laden with a shiitake mushroom omelet (the mushrooms grown by the waitress), the best-ever blueberry-raspberry pancake of the melt-in-the-mouth variety with local syrup, a mound of hash-brown new potatoes accented with yellow and red peppers and lots of herbs, plus a plump local Mennonite sausage. We couldn't possibly finish, and couldn't face lunch until mid-afternoon.

The culinary treats began the day before when Mary and her resident innkeeper, Ed Spak, once a chef in California, put out wine and exotic goodies for guests in the afternoon, followed by sherry and chocolate-covered strawberries in the evening. These were served in the monks' former chapel, now an English-style great room. It has a billiards table at one end, a large TV/VCR at the other, and comfortable seating amidst an array of food and travel magazines plus four metropolitan Sunday newspapers in the middle.

The location off the beaten path in an area of substantial second homes means the inn will always be secluded. The cove is a five-minute walk through woods for swimming. Two tennis courts are available, and a hot tub is just off the deck.

The innkeepers go the extra mile for their guests. They even provided a bottle of wine and picked up a carryout dinner from Uno's Restaurant for us to enjoy on our deck because it was Sunday and restaurants either were closed or were not serving wine because of the county's blue laws. Such service prompted more than one couple to write in the guest book, "we felt like visiting royalty."

(301) 387-0067. Fax (301) 387-2394. Ten rooms with private baths. Doubles, $120 to $160 weekends, $100 to $140 midweek. Children over 12. No smoking.

Savage River Inn, Dry Run Road, Box 147, McHenry, 21541.

A successful building contractor who later manufactured pushcarts for hot dog vendors, Ken Bock took on a new project in 1993. He added a floor to his hilltop farmhouse at the edge of the Savage River State Forest, installed new bedrooms

Contemporary residence on four levels has been converted into Savage River Inn.

and baths, spiffed up the common areas and opened a B&B. "I used to be Mr. Hot Dog," says Ken, who's too active to think of retirement. "Now I'm Mr. Innkeeper."

His B&B hideaway – secluded amidst 53 acres surrounded by state forest – is heaven on earth for hikers, cross-country skiers, nature lovers and others who prefer mountain solitude to the hustle and bustle of Deep Creek Lake eight miles to the west. Here, near the crest of the Eastern Continental Divide, is a panorama of mountains and valleys populated by deer, wild turkeys, grouse and bears.

The four-level structure, which bears few traces of its farmhouse past, is an architectural showplace. The ground floor contains a country kitchen and a two-story great room with vaulted ceiling and massive fieldstone hearth, large-screen TV, comfortable seating, a dining area and french doors onto expansive decks on two sides. The loft holds a library and leads to the kitchen and main entrance on the second level. Here also is an expansive suite with queensize bed, a bathroom hidden behind a mirror and a cozy sitting area with a franklin stove on a sun porch, where we would gladly have spent the evening had we not been lured outside by Ken onto the front deck for drinks and conversation. "Our guests need a little wine and cheese after driving three or four hours from Down East," he says, employing the local geographical reference to the Baltimore-Washington metro area.

On the third floor are two smaller guest rooms with queen beds and the country-pretty décor evident throughout the house. Sue Bock, who works as a nurse, designed the splashy window treatments, but her husband takes credit for the little flower-basket wreaths on the doors: "I made them myself."

The owners' former quarters on the fourth floor are now a penthouse suite, accessed by an elevator. The Bocks moved into a nearby barn, freeing space for guests in a side-by-side sitting room and bedroom with 24 feet of windows onto the mountains, not to mention a TV and fireplace and a full-width balcony.

They also installed a kidney-shaped pool to supplement the outdoor hot tub.

Lately, they have been converting the barn into a lodge. They plan five suites, each with whirlpool tubs, fireplaces and walls of windows facing the mountains.

Breakfast is taken at an Amish-crafted table for ten in the great room, or outside on a nicely landscaped, tiered patio-deck beside an ornamental lily pond. After serving orange juice and a fruit plate, Ken, who loves to chat, whipped up an admirable vegetable omelet with hash browns and toast with homemade raspberry jelly between conversational asides.

"I've never stayed overnight in an inn," says Ken. He's having too much fun with his own.

(301) 245-4440. Two rooms and two suites with private baths. Doubles, $110. Suites, $130 and $150. No smoking.

Haley Farm B&B, 16766 Garrett Hwy., Oakland 21550.

Hidden down a steep hill off the main highway between Deep Creek Lake and Oakland is this farmhouse B&B at the heart of a 65-acre working farm.

The exterior of the house and grounds can best be described as family farm, the front porch and yard cluttered with lawn chairs, swings and a trampoline. The inside is a beauty. The main portion, attached to the front of a 70-year-old brick house, was built in 1991 as a B&B by a previous owner. Wayne Gillespie, an Army retiree, and his wife Kam, who was with the World Bank, took over in 1993. They offer five spacious guest rooms and a two-room family suite in the main house, all with full baths and queensize four-poster beds. Each has different stenciling, eclectic art, Amish quilts and thick carpeting. Amenities include hair dryers, robes and – a different twist – slippers, for trips to the outdoor hot tub.

The newest accommodations are in a rear carriage house and a barn. In the carriage house, a honeymoon suite on the second floor offers a kingsize brass bed, a bathroom with shower and heart-shaped jacuzzi, a kitchenette to make one's own breakfast and a living room with gas fireplace and TV. The concept proved so successful that the Gillespies replicated the suite on the floor below and added another luxury suite and a mini-suite – each with sitting room, fireplace and jacuzzi – in the barn in 1999.

A hearty farm breakfast is served at a table for ten beside the fireplace in the dining room. Eggs benedict and homemade nut breads were the fare at our visit, but the possibilities range from blueberry soufflés to belgian waffles. Kam's signature frittatas are a Sunday morning treat.

Guests spread out in an expansive great room, full of objects from the owners' world travels, and a side TV room. Youngsters head outside to play on the lawn, fish in a stocked farm pond or watch horses grazing in three fields. As they depart, Ken is apt to load guests down with vegetables from his garden.

Haley Farm also operates as a retreat center for fitness and spirituality programs.

(301) 387-9050 or (888) 231-3276. Five rooms and five suites with private baths. Doubles $130, suites $170 to $195, $10 surcharge for holidays and foliage. Two-night minimum stay most weekends. Children over 12. No smoking.

Elliott House Victorian Inn, 146 Casselman Road, Grantsville 21536.

Located just off the first national road built in America and backing up to the Casselman River, this inn on seven acres is part of a complex containing the Penn Alps crafts store and restaurant and the Spruce Forest Artisan Village.

While a dozen nearby log structures date to the Revolution, the Elliott House is a prim and proper Victorian. The house was owned by the last millers on the adjacent 1797 Stanton's Mill property. Canadian-born Jack Dueck, administrator of Penn Alps and a Mennonite storyteller and motivational management consultant, and his wife Eleanor bought the rundown house and property to save it from unwanted development. They commenced a no-expense-spared, two-year rehab that produced four elegant accommodations in the main house plus three in out-buildings. All accommodations have TV/VCRs and telephones, and CD players are added in the cottages.

The stained-glass front door of the beautifully restored house opens into a foyer and a living room and a library-parlor. One guest room on the main floor and three upstairs are done in Victorian florals and dark woodwork. Most of the original furnishings were purchased from the estate. The queen or twin beds are topped with Amish quilts. Pedestal sinks, Neutrogena toiletries, robes and hair dryers are in the updated bathrooms. A small coffee bar with a stocked refrigerator for guests is located outside the Stanton Room, which faces the old mill, and the Louisa May Alcott Room, named for Eleanor's favorite Victorian author.

Out back on the carefully landscaped property are larger guest accommodations. A walk made of old millstones leads to a restored tool house, now the Audubon House, with a beamed ceiling, queensize bed, a sofabed and a river-view deck. The Drover's House, once a two-story wash house, features a living room with a sofabed and a kitchenette plus a queen bedroom upstairs with vaulted ceiling, loveseat and big windows onto the Casselman River across the meadow. The Amish built the benches and other elements of what Eleanor calls the Mission-style, "early settler" décor.

The Duecks' Canadian heritage shows up in the loony and toony coins embedded in a bullseye on the patio walk leading to the River View Room, part of a large new structure built as the innkeepers' cottage. An intricate and colorful quilt tops the room's queen bed. The rear deck juts out over the meadow toward the river.

Two porches and a rear patio with a hot tub are available for inn guests.

Rates include breakfast and lunch or dinner (Monday-Saturday 4 to 7 or 8) at the rustic Penn Alps restaurant across from the inn. The artisan village is close by, and across the meadow is the Casselman River, famed for its fly fishing.

(301) 895-4250 or (800) 272-4090. Four rooms and three cottages with private baths. Doubles, $115 to $140 weekends, $98 to $119 midweek. Cottages, $140 to $160 weekends, $119 to $136 midweek. Two-night minimum weekends. No smoking.

The Deer Park Inn, 65 Hotel Road, Deer Park 21550.

Three large guest rooms are available above the restaurant in the Pennington Cottage, a 110-year-old Victorian mansion listed on the National Register.

Baltimore architect Josiah Pennington designed the shingled, seventeen-room house with wraparound porch as a summer home for his family on the grounds of the famed Deer Park Hotel, since demolished. The rooms are furnished with prized Victorian antiques, many of them original to the cottage or the old hotel.

Guests enter a foyer with fireplace, rich woodwork, stained glass, antique furnishings and a majestic staircase. Two candlelit dining rooms draw knowledgeable diners from near and far (see Dining Spots).

Sandy Fontaine, innkeeper with her husband Pascal, the chef from France, decorated the high-ceilinged guest rooms with Victorian flair. The bathrooms are private, although one is in the hall. Two rooms have decorative fireplaces. Sandy's artistic sideline – she became a potter and a teacher of stained-glass production when they moved to this country from Paris in 1979 – is evident throughout.

Fine dining and lodging are offered in The Deer Park Inn.

Pascal prepares a full breakfast for overnight guests. A fruit plate and cereal precede the main dish, perhaps fruit pancakes, frittata or ham and cheese omelets. *(301) 334-2308. Three rooms with private baths. Doubles, $98 to $110.*

The Oak & Apple, 208 North Second St., Oakland.

One of the handsomest houses in the Oakland historic district, this Colonial Revival Victorian built about 1915 commands a large lawn with mature fruit and shade trees in a prime residential area. Jana Brown and her ex-husband rescued it after it had been abandoned for two years, and burned out two power mowers just getting the lawn in shape.

A columned front porch and an enclosed sunporch surround the formal Victorian living room and a dining room with ten-foot ceilings.

The second floor holds a comfortable front sitting room with TV as well as two side queen bedrooms with private baths, one with a jetted tub. On the third floor are three bedrooms, one in front with a double and twin bed and a private bath. Two others with queen beds and in-room pedestal sinks share a hall bath.

Jana, who works during the day as an audiologist, offers a continental-plus breakfast. Her fruit medley might be strawberries, bananas and blueberries from her back yard, topped with grand marnier cream sauce. Her granola is homemade. Pastries include scones, cranberry-orange muffins and macadamia nut bread.

(301) 334-9265. Three rooms with private baths and two with shared baths. Doubles, $85 to $105 private, $75 shared. Children over 12. No smoking.

Dining Spots

The Deer Park Inn, 65 Hotel Road, Deer Park.

Located off the beaten path in a summer colony that has seen better days between Deep Creek Lake and Oakland, this Victorian mansion is everyone's favorite locally for what one innkeeper calls "world-class dining."

Chef-owner Pascal Fontaine, who trained in Paris, struck out on his own after ten years as executive chef at the luxury ANA Hotel in Washington, D.C. His international travels influenced a cooking style that he describes as being "French with an American influence." Diners find the food and presentation exquisite, but the portions small.

Typical starters are cumin black bean soup with sour cream, sweet corn chowder with crabmeat, grilled portobello mushroom with goat cheese and pan-roasted scallops with asiago cheese and greens. Among the exotic salads is one with a terrine of layered yellow and red beets, greens and saffron oil.

The dozen main courses range from sautéed skate wing with lemon and capers to filet of beef with burgundy onion marmalade. Poached fillet of salmon scented with ginger, local rabbit with mushroom sauce and grilled veal chop with roquefort sauce are among the choices.

Desserts include a fragrant European-style plum tart, orange crème caramel with fruit garnish and, the chef's specialty, crêpes with ice cream and chocolate sauce.

In the French tradition, Pascal leaves the kitchen after dinner to make the rounds through two small, intimate dining rooms as candles glow and classical music plays.

(301) 334-2308. Entrées, $14 to $19.95. Dinner nightly in season, 5:30 to 9:30. Closed Monday-Wednesday in winter.

McClive's, Deep Creek Drive, McHenry.

Seldom is a waterfront restaurant and lounge known for its food, but McClive's is a happy exception. For ten years, it has been packing in customers to the point it does not take reservations, and the seats begin filling up at 5.

Big windows look out onto the lake from the main dining areas, dressed with linens and candles. Downstairs is a courtyard lounge with a lakeside patio that inexplicably was not open the night we dined. We lucked out by asking to be seated on the upstairs lakefront balcony, starting something of a trend until an intermittent shower intervened (the braver souls among us simply put up the umbrellas and stuck it out).

McClive's is known for its specialty prime rib, mesquite-grilled steaks and fresh seafood. Two in our party tried the special "double dinner deal," $19.95 for two Sunday-Tuesday. It provided salads plus a good chicken dish and a highly recommended shrimp and garlic pasta that turned out to be mostly angel hair. Another diner made a meal of two appetizers, mushroom caps stuffed with crabmeat and baked scallops in garlic butter. A $14.95 bottle of Geyser Peak sauvignon blanc accompanied. Tuxedoed waiters provided assured, smooth service that belied the bargain tab.

(301) 387-6172. Entrées, $10.95 to $16.95. Dinner nightly, 5 to 10 or 11.

Cornish Manor, Memorial Drive, Oakland.

Surrounded by tall trees on seven acres, this showy manor house at the edge of Oakland seats 100 in a couple of formal dining rooms and more on a delightful side patio. White lace runners accent tables dressed in pink or green, and French pans hang from a ladder suspended beneath the ceiling. A pianist entertains in the lounge on weekends.

French owner Christiane Bergheim and her husband Fred gave up their popular

French Café Bakery and restaurant alongside Deer Creek Lake to concentrate on this 50-year-old venture, of which they were only the third owners. Her son, Fabrice Du Four, manages the kitchen.

The extensive continental-American menu puts a highly rated appetizer of crab balls in spicy horseradish sauce amid such French standbys as country pâté, escargots and garlicky frog's legs. Main courses vary from salmon in parchment and broiled orange roughy with a pecan-frangelico sauce to chicken stuffed with crabmeat and French-cut lamb chops. Dessert could be crêpes suzette, bananas flambé or cherries jubilee.

(301) 334-6499. Entrées, $10.50 to $21.50. Lunch daily, 11 to 3. Dinner, Tuesday-Saturday from 5.

Canoe on the Run, 2266 Deep Creek Drive, McHenry.
Wedged in the woods off Route 219 near the turn-off to Wisp ski resort is this new cafe, bright and airy with warm woods and lots of windows. One chef likens its healthy, super-fresh food to the California nuevo style, employing lots of roasted red peppers, herbs and Italian cheeses.

Consider one spring day's soups: Southwestern roasted red pepper bisque and potato-corn chowder. Canoe salads include white albacore tuna on a mix of spring greens, walnuts and blue cheese with spinach, and roasted portobello mushroom strips tossed with the house caesar salad. Among panini are turkey and smoked gouda on pumpernickel and roast beef and baby swiss on a French batard. The grilled cheese deluxe combines cheddar, havarti and swiss with roasted peppers, red onions, spinach and tomato slices on vienna bread for a bargain $3.95.

Stop in the morning for oatmeal or granola or a breakfast burrito. Come later for mini-bundt cakes, cheesecake, biscotti and other sweets. Occasionally there are light dinner specials like lasagna or enchiladas. Beer and wine are available.

(301) 387-5933. Sandwiches and salads, $3.25 to $6.25. Breakfast, lunch and dinner daily, from 8 a.m. to 8 p.m., to 9 or 10 on weekends and in summer.

Uno's Restaurant, Route 219, Deep Creek Lake.
If you're feeding a family or simply want to take out on a Sunday night when no liquor can be served in most of Garrett County, consider this stylish lakefront eatery and pizzeria with a deck overlooking the water. Awarded the Chicago-based Pizzeria Uno franchise's pacesetter award, the local establishment goes its own way with an extensive menu from salads to pastas to baby back ribs and steaks. Deep-dish pizzas and California-style thin-crisp pizzas are featured.

We were quite happy with the house salads and a couple of pasta dishes – chicken pesto fettuccine and margarita chicken pasta. It being Sunday night, they were enjoyed with a bottle of wine on our own private patio back at our inn.

(301) 387-4866. Entrées, $10.95 to $17.50. Open daily, 11 a.m. to midnight or 1.

Diversions

One-fifth of Garrett County's land area is devoted to state parks, forests and lakes. Visitors tend to be active, self-reliant souls who follow their own pursuits.

Deep Creek Lake, the center of recreational activity, was created in 1925 as a hydroelectric project by the Pennsylvania Electric Co. Twelve miles long, it meanders every which way, creating 65 miles of shoreline with no particularly long and broad stretch other than the busy section along Highway 219 between the Deep Creek and Glendale bridges. The water is deep and quite clear, providing good swimming and fishing. Power boats, especially pontoon boats for fishing, abound. Sailboats are few. Visitors get their best views of the lake along Highway 219 in the vicinity of McHenry and Glendale. Otherwise, trees and large homes (many available for rental through realtors) block views and access to the lake.

The mile-long shoreline at **Deep Creek Lake State Park** includes a 700-foot sandy beach, with grills and picnic tables and a nifty playground beneath nearby shade trees. Hiking trails and campsites are available. A new concert amphitheater was readied for **Garrett Lakes Arts Festival** events; the Tommy Dorsey Orchestra was a series highlight one year.

Swallow Falls State Park. About ten miles west of Deep Creek Lake near the West Virginia state line, the heart of this 300-acre mountain park contains tall hemlocks and white pines estimated to be 300 years old, the last stand of its kind in Maryland. From the parking lot, well-maintained gravel trails lead through the stand to four waterfalls, including **Muddy Creek Falls**, at 52 feet Maryland's tallest. A sign notes that Mud Creek originates in the brackish waters of Cranesville Swamp. The site where Henry Ford, Thomas Edison, Harvey Firestone and naturalist John Burroughs camped beside the falls is marked. The roughly mile-long trail on to Lower and Upper Shadow Falls and Tolivar Falls takes about twenty minutes. You may pass sunbathers on the rocks and kayakers in the water. The cliffs covered with thick rhododendron and the sounds of various waterfalls and rapids are very cooling on a warm day.

Savage River State Forest. About a dozen miles east of Deep Creek Lake River site is Maryland's largest state forest, with 53,000 acres of forestland, wildlife habitat, a reservoir and two state parks. The aptly named Savage River is a narrow and harrowing stretch of whitewater for more than five miles. It was the site of the 1989 Whitewater World Championship races and the 1992 U.S. Canoe and Kayak Team Olympic Trials. A rugged hiking trail extends seventeen miles along the crest of Big Savage Mountain. A three-hour-long trail leads hikers through the gorge.

Whitewater Boating. Along with the Savage River, the upper Youghiogheny is one of the prime whitewater rivers in East. About twenty Class IV and V rapids challenge the experienced rafter and kayaker. Commercial outfitters run thousands of whitewater enthusiasts down the steep gorge each year. A scenic highway along the river leads to Ohiopyle Falls, just north of the Garrett County line in Pennsylvania. We've never seen so many rafters and whitewater-related activities in one place.

The Cranesville Sub-Arctic Swamp, near Cranesville. The most obscure of the area's natural phenomena is this 500-acre remnant of boreal forest producing growth normally associated with arctic regions. Famed naturalist John Burroughs led the Henry Ford camping party from nearby Swallows Falls into the swamp in 1918 to examine the plant life. Even with a good map, we got hopelessly lost for more than an hour trying to find Cranesville, let alone the swamp. Then we traipsed for half an hour looking for the bog. We turned back when we found ourselves reaching a forest, having seen only two deer and hearing several bullfrogs. Other visitors told us the forest trail actually was the entrance to the bog and we had not gone far enough. The Nature Conservancy has expanded the trails and boardwalk lately. Regulars say you can spend all day out there and never see the same trail twice.

The **Deep Creek Brewing Co.**, overlooking the lake and ski area behind the new visitor center at 318 Spring Glade Road, offers eight handcrafted beers. It's huge place with a brew pub and, one resident connoisseur reports, some of the best beer he has ever tasted.

Deep Creek Cellars, Frazee Ridge Road, Friendsville, is a fledgling winery near the Pennsylvania state line. It offers summer weekend tours and produces white, red and blush table wines, priced from $8 to $10.

Penn Alps, Route 40 East, Grantsville.

This rustic restaurant and crafts store is housed in the last surviving log tavern on the first National Road. It's near the famed Casselman River Bridge, the largest single-span stone arch bridge of its kind when it was built in 1813. Now the tavern is a restaurant with five charming dining rooms and a crafts shop featuring the largest display of indigenous handicrafts in the Alleghenies, made in the homes and studios of tri-state residents. A stunning collection of Amish quilts, hickory rockers and hand-thrown pottery are featured. Nearby, other log cabins and rustic structures comprise the quaint **Spruce Forest Artisan Village,** where craftsmen work and show their wares. The annual **Music at Penn Alps** series offers classical and folk concerts Saturday evenings in summer in the Great Hall at Penn Alps. *(301) 895-5985. Restaurant open daily from 7 a.m.; Crafts Shop from 9 a.m. Artisan Village open Monday-Saturday 1 to 5, Memorial Day through October.*

Shopping. Arrowhead Market, an upscale market and deli open 24 hours along Route 219 at Deep Creek Lake, carries everything a vacationing visitor needs, from full takeout meals to gasoline to camera supplies. Across the street is **The Tourist Trap,** a fairly stylish haven of local souvenirs. Its sweatshirts, coffee mugs, piggy banks and door mats all bear a Deep Creek Lake logo. Collectibles, crafts and country stuff are shown in three buildings at **Schoolhouse Earth**, where New Age music plays and a petting zoo in a rear barn keeps 0youngsters amused.

In Oakland, a hodgepodge of eight shops operates in one big red barn of building called **Grand Central Station.** The willow rockers and a line of yellow and black bumblebee kitchenware were nearly upstaged by all the beds in the sleep shop in the far corner at our visit. Oakland's old-fashioned main street is enhanced by the good little **Book Mark'et** and the **Book Mark'et Mezzanine** with antiques and collectibles.

Outside Oakland in Mountain Lake Park is a new **Simon Pearce** manufacturing facility, opened by the famed Vermont glassblower. Visitors can observe glassblowers at work from a catwalk above the factory floor. A retail store offers Simon Pearce glass and pottery as well as seconds.

Extra-Special _____

Fallingwater, Mill Run, Pa.

One of the surprises for many visitors to Deep Creek Lake is finding they are so close to architect Frank Lloyd Wright's most famous private home.

Fallingwater, built atop a waterfall, is less than an hour's drive across the state line. The weekend home was designed in 1936 for the family of Pittsburgh department store owner Edgar J. Kaufmann. They had indicated the area around a waterfall as the location, but were unprepared for Wright's suggestion that it rise over the waterfall, rather than face it. The house is open for hour-long guided tours, which reveal countless facets of the intriguing cantilevered structure

(including, at our visit, the revelation that one of the unsupported concrete decks had just been given a support). The place is bigger than one expects and, from every angle inside and out, you can hear the waterfall, even if you can't see it. Of all the rooms, we inn-goers liked best the top-level guest house nestled in the rhododendron beside a stream-fed pool. At tour's end, visitors

Fallingwater takes advantage of waterfall location.

gasped when told the entire house with all the built-ins cost only $155,000. That was triple the Kaufmanns' budget, so Wright lowered his fee to $8,000. The place would cost millions today. During the close-up tour, you never really get to see the overall house the way it looks in pictures and postcards. That view is offered from the lookout at the end of the path below. A well thought-out visitor center contains a gift shop and restaurant.

(724) 329-8501. Tours by reservation, Tuesday-Sunday 10 to 4, mid-March through November (also December weekends); $8 on weekdays, $12 weekends and holidays.

For more of a Frank Lloyd Wright day, stop at his 1953 house, **Kentuck Knob,** tucked into the side of a mountain near Ohiopyle, Pa. Built of tidewater red cypress and native fieldstone on a hexagonal grid, it's now owned by Lord and Lady Palumbo of London, England, patrons of the arts. Its hours and procedures are similar to Fallingwater's; reservations (724) 329-1901.

The drive to and from Fallingwater is particularly scenic, especially along the Youghiogheny River in the vicinity of Ohiopyle Falls in Pennsylvania. Also scenic is rural Route 1012 over Sugarloaf Mt. to the little town of Confluence, where the **River's Edge Café and B&B** at 203 Yough Street makes a good stop for lunch or dinner. The property slopes down to the Yough River, and butterflies flitted in the pretty gardens as we paused at midday on the porch for chicken salad and portobello mushroom sandwiches, accompanied by a couple of the chef's zesty soups. Open seasonally, Tuesday-Sunday 11 to 9; closed in winter.

Frederick, Md.

'So Proudly We Hail'

"Our town has been here since 1745 and is still thriving on the same streets," said the woman at Frederick's visitor center. You can feel its longevity as you view the 18th- and 19th-century structures throughout the city's 33-block historic district. You can sense its prosperity in its downtown, enlivened by restaurants, boutiques and galleries.

And you can empathize with its new slogan, "So Proudly We Hail," borrowed quite appropriately from the anthem written by native son Francis Scott Key. Here's a town that possesses a strong sense of identity, as reflected in its slick monthly city magazine called, simply, Frederick.

This area is "heaven in Maryland for yuppies," extolled a state tourism promoter. They come here to go antiquing, tour the battlefields, enjoy the restaurants and walk the sidewalks tread earlier by George Washington, Abraham Lincoln, the Marquis de Lafayette, Stonewall Jackson and Barbara Fritchie.

Barbara Fritchie? She's the Civil War heroine who challenged rebel troops to target her rather than the Union flag she was waving as they marched the city's streets. "Shoot if you must this old gray head, but spare this country's flag," she pleaded, her defiance immortalized by poet John Greenleaf Whittier.

Whittier's tale of "the clustered spires of Frederick" comes alive as the visitor explores the sights, an experience made much more worthwhile by the guided walking tours offered weekends and holidays. Court House Square was the scene of the first official repudiation of the British Stamp Act in 1765, ten years before the Boston Tea Party. A century later, Frederick was a town divided by the War Between the States, its sympathies lying both north and south. Churches and public buildings became hospitals for the wounded from nearby Antietam, site of the bloodiest battle on American soil.

The local battle of Monocacy is credited with saving Washington, D.C., from destruction. Frederick itself was spared, after Confederate General Jubal Early

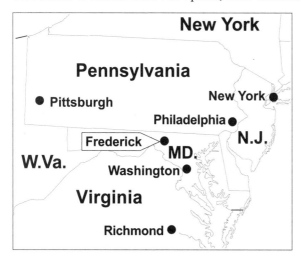

occupied the town briefly and levied a $200,000 ransom for its salvation – an amount borrowed from local banks and finally repaid in 1951. Thus the city is a model of original architecture – "almost as fine as Williamsburg and not reconstructed," in the words of our tour guide. Even the new downtown parking garages blend into the historic scene.

Steeped though it is

in the past, Frederick wears well its latter-day theme as "Cinderella City." Its proximity to the Baltimore-Washington megalopolis has turned it into the fastest growing city in Maryland, an up-to-date community of 40,000 with a vision and a sense of place tied to its past.

Tourism is said to be the area's second largest industry. Many are attracted by Newmarket, a one-street town called the antiques capital of Maryland, just east of the city. Others head west to Antietam, the graveyard of the Civil War. At the center of it all is Frederick, a delightful blend of old and new.

Inn Spots

Tyler-Spite House, 112-114 West Church St., Frederick 21701.

History was made here in 1814 when Dr. John Tyler, who performed the nation's first cataract surgery, built this classic three-story Federal mansion to prevent the city from extending Record Street through to the National Pike. The foundation was constructed literally overnight out of spite: hence the name.

Owners Bill and Andrea Myer worked quickly, too, opening Frederick's first downtown B&B in 1990 and adding the adjacent Nelson House a year later.

Theirs is a beauty of a place, boasting thirteen-foot-high ceilings and full of priceless antiques. It's blessed with a lush rear garden courtyard and the only swimming pool in downtown Frederick. The Philippine mahogany desk upon which guests register in the main hall was used by Gen. Douglas MacArthur to sign the peace treaty in Manila. The mirror in the hall is tall enough that Abe Lincoln is believed to have used it to adjust his hat during his Frederick visit. The chandeliers are reproductions from the Tryon Palace in New Bern, N.C. The stunning oriental screen in the library is a reproduction of the 14th-century "The Last Emperor." The Music Room harbors a Packard Victorian pump organ, a 1914 Ludwig grand piano and a victrola. Most of the eight working fireplaces sport imported carved marble mantels. Next door in the Lane House are crystal doorknobs, Chinese Chippendale beds and an 1820 chandelier of Waterford glass.

The inn has ten guest rooms, five with private baths and five that share – they generally are rented in pairs as suites so each has a private bath. "Once guests get here, a private bath is not an issue," Bill advises. Two of the "suites" are comprised of two bedrooms and three are "honeymoon" with bedroom and sitting room.

Guest rooms are commodious, most with queensize canopy beds and too many prized furnishings to enumerate. We were assigned originally to Bill's favorite Parsons Room, third-floor front. It shares with the Barbara Fritchie Room a large carpeted hall bath, big enough to include a sitting area. The room comes with a queensize sleigh bed and a cane and rattan side chair made in the Philippines. The dresser was made of shipping cartons, the lamps are old sake bottles and a Japanese chest serves as a coffee table. We decided to settle in what is now the Mosby Suite with a quieter, rear location overlooking the garden. It has a living room with queensize sofa bed and a bath with a whirlpool tub and a "rainforest" shower.

The 1820 Nelson House next door has three honeymoon suites and two other fireplaced guest rooms that share a bath. It has a parlor and dining room with fourteen-foot ceilings, matching fireplaces and a bible door unique to the area in between. Guests here also enjoy an enclosed rear porch with a tin roof, sofas and a TV, a sleek black and white kitchen, and an outside deck on two levels surrounding a giant swamp magnolia tree.

Tyler-Spite House backs up to garden courtyard and swimming pool.

Champagne is in the suites and decanters of cream sherry are in every room, supplementing the exceptional teatime spread –at our visit, lemonade, tea, wine, watermelon slices, cookies, an extravagant strawberry cake, cheese and crackers. Sometimes there are tea sandwiches. Breakfast is a gustatory treat as well, served on the patio or, with some pomp and circumstance, in the large and formal dining room graced by fancy wallpaper and a Chippendale screen in the corner. Juice and fresh fruits precede such main dishes as Roosevelt eggs scrambled with cream cheese, baked apple dumplings, creamed chipped beef or, at our visit, airy belgian waffles topped with fresh peaches and whipped cream.

An evening horse-drawn carriage ride through the historic district to a downtown restaurant of the guest's choice is available on weekends.

(301) 831-4455. Fax (301) 662-4185. Five suites with private baths and five rooms with shared baths. Weekends: doubles, $200 to $250; suites, $300. Midweek: doubles $150; suites, $175. Children over 6. No smoking.

McCleery's Flat, 121 East Patrick St., Frederick 21701.
They call it a flat, this 1876 Second Empire-style town house located on the "Street of Antiques" near the center of the historic district. The builder's family came from Ireland, where in Victorian times the term was used to describe a city row house as opposed to a country house, according to new owners Jetta and George Terrell. They acquired the elegant house and renovated for two years before opening it in 1998 as a B&B with three spacious rooms and two suites.

Decor is elegant yet casual with period antiques and reproductions and accents of whimsy. A queensize mahogany sleigh bed and an antique wardrobe dominate the second-floor General Lafayette Room. Spiderback chairs form a sitting area in a bay window, and both the room and the bath open onto a balcony overlooking the courtyard. Also looking onto the courtyard is the Cottage Garden Suite, furnished in wicker and cheery in yellow. It has hand-stenciled walls of brick, topiaries and ivy, plus English garden prints. Colorful Ralph Lauren linens adorn the queensize bed. The suite opens onto a semi-private, covered alcove on a balcony overlooking the garden. The haute-Victorian Caroline McCleery Suite, named after a former owner of the house, has a kingsize poster bed, a walk-out jib window and a little balcony. Its sitting room is dramatic in burgundy and plum. A chandelier lights the bath with whirlpool tub and separate shower.

The third-floor Benjamin Franklin Room offers a canopied queensize rice poster bed, toile fabrics, a wall of bookshelves, an extensive blue and white porcelain collection, and a bath with soaking tub and double vanity. An expanded Secret Chamber with big windows in the attic contains two double cast-iron beds dressed in Egyptian cotton damask and a sitting area surrounded by Mediterranean art and European pottery.

Jetta, whose father was a restaurateur in Germany, went to cooking school and loves to entertain. Employing a large collection of recipes from around the world, she offers a fancy breakfast in the dining room or outdoors beside a fountain on the courtyard. A fresh fruit parfait usually precedes the main course. The latter ranges from a California croissant to Irish cakes with apples to Southwest breakfast pie to "any number of frittatas," in George's words.

(301) 620-2433 or (800) 774-7926. Three rooms and two suites with private baths. Doubles, $110 to $115 weekends, $100 to $105 midweek. Suites, $130 to $135 weekends, $115 to $120 midweek. Children over 15. No smoking.

Turning Point Inn, 3406 Urbana Pike, Frederick 21701.

Set well back from the road on five nicely landscaped acres in the center of rapidly growing suburban Urbana, this Edwardian estate home with Georgian features is a full-service country inn known for its dining (see Dining Spots).

A gracious parlor is pretty in rose, pink and teal. It offers striped sofas, antique furniture, built-in bookshelves and a table with family pictures of innkeeper Charlie Seymour and his young son Tom as well as his mother and stepfather, Ellie and Bernie Droneburg, who founded the inn in 1985. The parlor separates the main dining rooms from the entry hall and a couple of small dining rooms on the other side.

Upstairs are five spacious guest rooms "out of the pages of House Beautiful," according to Charlie. All have private baths, TVs and telephones. The six-windowed Green Room contains two four-poster double beds and two upholstered chairs in a moss green decor. Steps are provided to climb into the queensize four-poster in the Blue Room. Fan windows overlook the countryside from two dormer rooms on the third floor, furnished in country style. The king-bedded Country Room here has a whirlpool tub.

Extremely popular are newer suites in outbuildings behind the inn. The three-level Carriage House cottage contains a living room with wet bar and small refrigerator, a bathtub with jets on the mid level, and a kingsize bed and formal country decor upstairs. Furnished in what the staff calls "country quaint" style is the spacious Dairy House room with kingsize bed and two reclining chairs.

A basket of fruit and a full country breakfast are included in the rates. The latter starts with assorted fresh fruit, juice and Swiss breakfast cereal. Then comes a choice of entrées, from eggs creole or benedict to corned beef hash with eggs.

(301) 874-8232. Five rooms and two suites with private baths. Doubles, $125 weekends, $80 midweek. Suites, $150 and $175 weekends, $100 and $125 midweek.

Impressive fieldstone structure is home to Stone Manor, country inn and restaurant.

Stone Manor, 5820 Carroll Boyer Road, Middletown 21769.

Elegant suites of uncommon spaciousness, a fine dining experience and a rural location as part of a 114-acre working farm. These are among the attributes that distinguish this country inn in the rolling hills southwest of Frederick.

The majestic, eighteen-room farmhouse dates to the late 1700s, with additions built in 1830 and the 1970s. "It was always a private residence and we want to keep that feeling," said Judith Harne, general manager and one of the five local business investors who bought it in 1991 to run as a B&B and restaurant (see Dining Spots).

They maintain the feeling of a country home – albeit one of considerable means – very nicely. The six suites are spaced well apart throughout the structure. Each is stylishly furnished with antiques and comes with extravagant bath facilities and tables for "in-suite dining" (used for breakfast and special-occasion dinners). Four have private porches and two have working fireplaces.

Largest and most formal is the second-floor Gardenia Suite with working fireplaces in both the living room and bedroom, a queensize rice-carved four-poster bed, crown molding around the ceiling, and unusual window treatments in which swags and sheers are pulled to one side. The canopied queen bed in the main-floor Hibiscus Suite is draped entirely in white. Vintage clothing and toys, including a pair of old figure skates, are hung instead of artworks in the main-floor Trillium Suite, charming for its Shaker-style poster bed and colorful antique quilt and quilted pillows.

But it is the bath facilities that command most attention. The Gardenia comes with a whirlpool bath for two, a separate shower, a double vanity and the thickest carpet imaginable. The Thistle, the smallest, has a double whirlpool bath in a corner of the bedroom, opposite the poster bed and not far from the dining table. And the Laurel Suite in the oldest section of the original farmhouse masks well its antiquity with a jetted shower spraying from six directions, a room with pedestal sink, w.c.

and bidet, and another vanity beside the oversize whirlpool, in which the waters are illuminated from below like a swimming pool.

Guests are welcomed with a plate of fruits and cheeses, delivered to the sitting areas of their rooms. In the morning, continental breakfast is served on the formal dining table in the room. The fare consists of juice, fruit, yogurt and breads.

There are lots of good magazines for perusing in the library at the top of the stairway. Outside are gardens, a pond, a stream and working farmlands and forests, from which deer might emerge to feed at the pear trees or drink from the fountain.

(301) 473-5454. Fax (301) 371-5622. Six rooms and suites with private baths. Doubles, $125 to $250. No smoking.

Hill House, 12 West Third St., Box 4124, Frederick 21705.

A three-story Victorian townhouse embellished with Eastlake detailing on the street façade at the edge of downtown was converted into an elegant B&B in 1996. Damian and Taylor Branson moved from southern Maryland to convert the structure's three apartments into a suite and three fancy B&B rooms.

The downstairs common rooms – a living room, sunroom and dining room with their well-worn orientals on parquet floors – set the stage.

Upstairs at the rear is the Mexican Room, a showplace from south of the border with twin beds, handpainted furniture and sponge-painted walls in yellows and burnt orange and reds. The enormous bathroom holds a stunning vanity washbowl that the Bransons "carted back" from one of their frequent trips to Mexico as well as a luxurious chaise lounge in a corner. It opens onto a second-floor)gallery/ porch overlooking the side garden, as does the Chesapeake Room, outfitted in floral chintz and tiger maple furniture, with an antique shaving mirror on the chest. Original oils and watercolors by Chesapeake artists are featured here. The front Victorian Room has a high step-up queen canopy bed and a deco-style bathroom in black and white.

The third floor holds the Steeple Suite, so called because "you can see a lot of the steeples of Frederick" from the rear windows, says Damian. Furnished in Colonial style, it has a living room with TV, a full kitchen and a queen canopy bed.

Original drawings, paintings and crafts are evident throughout this much-decorated house.

Damian offers a full breakfast, from fried tomatoes to french toast. It's served at a table for eight in the formal dining room or outside in the garden.

(301) 682-4111. Fax (301) 695-7802. Three rooms and one suite with private bath. Doubles, $105 to $125. Suite, $150. Children over 12. No smoking. Open Wednesday-Sunday by reservation only.

Middle Plantation Inn, 9549 Liberty Road, Frederick 21701.

The "rustic bed and breakfast" description on its brochure best describes this place ten minutes east of town in the village of Mount Pleasant. Or does it? Fronting on a suburban highway amid tract homes, it's really much more.

Shirley and Dwight Mullican tore down his grandfather's farmhouse on 26 acres and rebuilt in 1989 from the ground up, using logs, beams and floors from the original house. "It looks old," says Shirley, "but has all the modern conveniences."

Guests enter through a rear keeping room, cozy with a tall corner stone fireplace, a skylight and built-in stained-glass windows separating it from the Mullicans' quarters on the main floor. Upstairs are three guest rooms with private baths, each bearing novel touches but contemporary amenities like plush carpeting and hidden TVs. Dwight's elaborate hand stenciling graces the Victorian Room, which contains a carved walnut bed, a Victorian loveseat and side chair. There's a modern shower stall beside the clawfoot tub. Old hunting prints and white pine country furniture are in the Hunt Room, where the TV is hidden in the corner washstand and an old icebox with a shelf is for storing clothes. The rear Plantation Room has more stenciling, a tester canopy bed and the original poplar floor.

The most private lodging is in the Log Room with its own entrance at one side of the house, finished inside and out with logs. A colorful quilt brightens the blue iron bed, the TV is found in a dry sink, a harness holds the mirror and a pottery bowl serves as the washstand. Mints and vases of dried flowers are in each room.

Breakfast in the keeping room is continental-plus, involving juice, fresh fruit, cheese, cereal, granola, and homemade breads and muffins.

(301) 898-7128. www.MPInn.com. Four rooms with private baths. Doubles, $110 weekends, $90 weekdays. Children over 15. No smoking.

Strawberry Inn, 17 Main St., Box 237, New Market 21774.

Innkeepers Jane and Ed Rossig used to go antiquing in New Market and then have dinner at the famed Mealey's restaurant, like thousands before and after them. They bought their 1837 farmhouse in the center of town in 1973 for retirement from New Jersey. "We started restoring it and the mayor said, 'why don't you open a place to stay in this little town?'" recalls Jane. They gutted the building and reopened as a guesthouse, which took off immediately. "We didn't feel right sending people off without even a cup of coffee," says Jane. But four years passed before they added the breakfast part of their B&B.

The oldest B&B in Frederick County weathered well as the Rossigs moved into semi-retirement. After Ed's death in 1996, Jane continued with the assistance of son Bud and his wife Sonya. They offer four guest rooms, all furnished in Victoriana. One on the first floor with twin beds has its own side porch. The large upstairs rooms contain queen or two double beds, and one has a sitting room with a Victorian loveseat overlooking the rear garden. Common areas include a living room, a small front porch with rockers up against the sidewalk, a formal dining room with individual tables and a lovely grapevine-covered back porch. A continental-plus breakfast of fruit, cereal and homemade muffins, banana bread or soda bread is served in the dining room or on the porch.

Wild strawberries still grow along Strawberry Alley beside the house, from which the inn derives its name. The long back yard includes a gazebo, a distant patio where tomatoes grow beside park benches and a log house containing Rossig's Art & Framing gallery and the owner's quarters.

(301) 865-3318. Four rooms with private baths. Doubles, $95 to $125. Two-night minimum on weekends in season. No credit cards.

Inn at Antietam, 220 East Main St., Box 119, Sharpsburg 21782.

A sign over the clawfoot tub in the rustic Smoke House suite here says "showers are for the strivers of the world." When guests see that, advised one of the innkeepers, "they're content with the tub." And why not? The suite has a fireplace, a loft bed, a wet bar, barnwood walls, oriental rugs on the floors and a sofabed in the sitting room.

It is one of four suites in a B&B acquired in 1999 by Charles Van Metre and

Robert Leblanc, longtime singers and actors. They decided they did not like retirement so purchased the old 1908 farmhouse-turned-B&B as a turnkey operation. The former innkeepers had furnished the bedrooms and sitting rooms in country and Victorian styles with goods acquired from area estate sales. Each is decorated gracefully and without clutter.

The new owners added a third-floor Penthouse Suite in unfinished attic space. It's a large and modern room with skylights, queen bed, sitting area, wet bar, TV/VCR and an enclosed balcony overlooking the Blue Ridge Mountains. Guests here have only to descend a spiral staircase to the new second-floor library to pick out one of the 400 videos stored there. The library, also accessible from the second floor, has a TV/VCR for guests in other rooms.

Guests also enjoy a slate-floor solarium at the entry, a formal parlor and a front veranda that wraps around the house to an attractive rear patio. They may be entertained around the grand piano by the owners, who performed in summer musical theaters and sang on cruise ships.

Breakfast is served at three tables in the formal dining room. The fare might be baked swiss eggs, eggs benedict, blueberry pancakes or belgian waffles. Afternoon refreshments are offered on the patio with its view of the Blue Ridge Mountains.

(301) 432-6601 or (877) 835-6011. Fax (301) 432-5981. Five suites with private baths. Doubles, $135 to $175 weekends, $110 to $150 midweek. Children over 6. No smoking.

Antietam Overlook Farm, Porterstown Road, Keedysville 21756.

From the large rear porch, guests can see the Antietam National Battlefield, the town of Sharpsburg and mountains in four states. The view isn't all they get at one of the more comfortably elegant new B&Bs we've seen. They get five queen-bedded suites, each with gas-burning fireplace, its own screened porch and a bathtub surrounded by plants; a plush common room that's made for conversation in front of a huge fireplace; a table of cordials from which to help themselves after dinner, and a "groaning plate" of a country breakfast.

"I didn't think I was the only person in the world who likes a porch and a bubble bath," Barbara Dreisch said after opening her B&B with husband John. They added a contemporary wing to their existing 19th-century-style farmhouse on 95 acres and let the fun begin.

"Country but state of the art" is how Barbara describes it. The suites are carpeted, the fireplaces are operated by remote-control from the beds, the individual porches have two comfy chairs, the open steeping tubs fairly cry out for a bubble bath and there are sit-down showers in the bathrooms, where a basket of extras includes shaving cream, hair dryer and curling iron.

If you can tear yourself away from your own little heaven, you'll find a small kitchen area with welcoming wine or lemonade and an instant hot water tap for tea or hot chocolate. Beyond is the Country Room, a vast sitting room with dining area paneled, like the rest of the house, in rough barnwood. Off this is the big rear porch with four-state view. The dining area is where John provides the "groaning plate" in the morning, perhaps pancakes with honey, muesli, hot homemade applesauce, bacon and homemade sausage balls, pitchers of orange juice and carafes of coffee. The day before our visit he served English broil with mushrooms and tomatoes and french toast made with thick raisin bread and amaretto.

The house sits by itself atop a ridge in the middle of nowhere. The Dreisches

Private porches are among amenities at stylish Antietam Overlook Farm.

give directions via a roundabout route so guests don't pass the shanties of hillbilly country that lie close to this fantasyland. The direct route from Sharpsburg is much shorter.

(301) 432-4200 or (800) 878-4241. Fax (301) 432-5230. Five suites with private baths. Doubles, $125 to $165 weekends, $115 to $145 midweek. Two-night minimum weekends. Children over 12. No smoking.

Piper House B&B, Route 65, Sharpsburg 21782.

Most people who stay here are serious Civil War buffs, say innkeepers Regina and Lou Clark. That's understandable, for this is the mid-19th-century log and frame farmhouse that Confederate General James Longstreet claimed as his headquarters during the bloodiest single day of the Civil War. The house evokes haunting memories, situated as it is, surrounded by the Antietam National Battlefield and just down the road from the park entrance.

The Clarks saved the B&B in 1994. Its former principals, Hagerstown residents whose occupation is restoring old buildings, had decided to give up their long-term lease from the National Park Service. When word got out among Civil War buffs regarding the planned closing of the house, protests came from all over the country. The Clarks learned about it, visited the property and quickly negotiated a new long-term lease. Of the potential lessees, "we were the only married couple who wanted to live on-site," Regina said. They moved in and found it "simply wonderful to live in an historic home on federal property."

They share their small treasure with overnight guests in three bedrooms with private baths. Each is simply but attractively furnished to the Civil War period. The Clarks have tried to make the rooms more comfortable, and their live-in presence adds a dimension heretofore lacking. There are a couple of small downstairs parlors and an upstairs sitting room and rear screened porch. Regina serves guests a continental-plus breakfast of juice, fruit compote, cereals, muffins, breads and pastries at a long table in the kitchen.

The old slave house, smoke house and stone root cellar out front add to the Civil War ambiance here.

The Clarks were proud that the Piper House was honored as one of the 50 best-kept travel secrets in the world in 1998 by Travel-Holiday magazine.

(301) 797-1862. Three rooms with private baths. Doubles, $95 weekends, $85 midweek. Children over 10. No smoking.

Dining Spots

Turning Point Inn, 3406 Urbana Pike, Frederick.

For a special-occasion meal out in the country, this glamorous and expanding spot is where many locals go. The view of the surrounding landscape from the large garden-style dining room through floor-to-ceiling windows is lovely. Rose tablecloths, rattan chairs and vases of alstroemeria add to the setting. Two small, formal dining rooms are located on the other side of the entry.

Executive chef Dean Winning, who helped Mark Miller open the trendy Red Sage in Washington, D.C., helped advance inn owner Charlie Seymour's plans to take the dining operation to a higher level. There are a tavern and wine cellar in the basement. The former was designed as a rustic English pub serving casual fare, while the latter is the venue for ultra-fine dining.

The chef, known for unusual combinations and arresting presentations, tempts adventuresome palates with appetizers like carpaccio of tuna with a shiitake mushroom salad and wild morels with a garlic custard flan. Another dinner starter, a spinach-crabmeat tart with marinated tomatoes and cucumbers, turns up as a main course on the lunch and brunch menus as well. For main dinner dishes, he employs a spicy tropical fruit sauce and baby bok choy with his pan-seared rare tuna, and adds a bell pepper-crab relish and roasted onion sauce to his rainbow trout crusted with potato and garlic. A porcini mushroom crème fraîche dresses the pan-seared veal scaloppine.

Fresh strawberries and blueberries garnish the dark chocolate tower dessert, an ethereal stack of flourless chocolate cake rounds layered with pistachio cream.

(301) 831-8232. Entrées, $16.95 to $24.95. Lunch, Tuesday-Friday 11:30 to 2. Dinner, Tuesday-Thursday 5:30 to 9, Friday and Saturday 5 to 9:30. Sunday, brunch 11:30 to 2, dinner 4 to 8:30. No smoking.

Stone Manor, 5820 Carroll Boyer Road, Middletown.

For some of the most pure, exciting food in the area, drive fifteen minutes or so into the countryside southwest of town to this restored country inn and restaurant. It's in an impressive fieldstone manor house, and the experience is likened to that of dining in a private home – which it was, for its first 200 years.

Five local business investors have turned it into a refined restaurant of distinction. Dining is in the main beamed and stone dining room with an enormous fieldstone fireplace and damask-covered tables seating a total of 25 to 30 or in the gracious living room, where lace mats top the fine polished tables.

Periodic cooking demonstrations, a remarkably extensive wine cellar and special wine dinners attest to the fact that this is a restaurant that takes food and drink seriously. Chefs Charles Ceran and Chris Grossnickle grow many of their own vegetables and herbs and acquire others from nearby purveyors.

The menu is prix-fixe, $69 for a pre-selected five-course dinner. A typical meal might start with an amuse-gueule, followed by a grilled vegetable terrine with pan-fried goat cheese and basil vinaigrette, pan-seared loin of rabbit with sautéed rhubarb and wild berries, or a lobster couscous salad. An intermezzo sorbet (and perhaps an adjournment for a short walk in the gardens) precedes the main course, which could be pan-seared emu with haricots verts, artichokes and roasted garlic and cambozola-stuffed new potatoes. For the grand finale, you might find lemon-ginger cheesecake with mango, papaya and nectarines.

Other main courses in this talented kitchen's repertoire could be pan-seared sesame tuna with a bok choy-jicama-cucumber slaw, spicy yam fries and coconut relish; grilled breast of duck with orange-cumin oil and yogurt and a salad of amaranth, walnuts and citrus, and pan-seared medallions of beef with coriander corn pudding and black bean salsa.

Lunch is offered in three courses for $36. Expect treats like a gratin of blue crab with creamed corn and crispy leeks, a frittata of curried sea scallops and sweet peppers, and black raspberry ice cream with a pineapple compote.

Because this is a favorite place for private functions and because of its out-of-the-way location, meals are served by reservation only and the schedule may vary.
(301) 473-5454. Prix-fixe, $45 to $55. Lunch, Tuesday-Saturday 11 to 2. Dinner, Tuesday-Saturday 6 to 9. Sunday, brunch 11 to 2, dinner 4 to 7.

Tauraso's, 6 East St. at Everedy Square, Frederick.
This is quite an establishment, from the old Jaguar sometimes parked in front of the entry to a sleek dining room to the enormous, high-ceilinged **Victor's Saloon & Raw Bar** in the original Victor's Home Remedies patent medicine business that paved the way for the old Everedy factory. The Jaguar is "our mascot – I drive it every day," said Dr. Nicola Tauraso, a physician who opened the restaurant in 1987 for his son Michael, a talented chef not long out of Rhode Island's Johnson & Wales culinary program. "This is the toughest business I've been in," says Nick, who's been involved in his share. The place seats 300 and is open every day.

Although there's considerable show, the food is taken seriously here. We've seldom been served a better pasta dish than the luncheon special of linguini with seared grouper fillet, marinated green olives, roasted garlic and white wine, accompanied by a dish of grated parmesan cheese. We also liked the homemade seafood sausage with pepper and olive compote and the focaccia seasoned with sage, oregano and garlic. The cappuccino, dusted with fresh nutmeg and served like most drinks here in glass mugs, arrived with an amaretto cookie. All this was delivered by a tuxedoed staff at white wrought-iron tables on a large outdoor courtyard under a red, black and white canopy, beside a trickling fountain.

The soaring interior dining room is just as dramatic. Its high black ceiling contrasts with exposed ducts painted pinkish-mauve. The black marbled tables bear huge white service plates emblazoned with the Tauraso logo. An extensive list of daily specials supplements an ambitious menu categorized as pizzas, pastas and specialties ranging from chicken cutlets milanese to filet mignon with béarnaise sauce. Your only difficulty may be settling on a choice between gourmet pizzas from the wood-fired oven and specials like peppered tuna with braised vegetable ragoût and sundried tomatoes or grilled rockfish with tomato-basil vinaigrette.

Bananas foster, chocolate mousse, warm peach cobbler, cannoli and Italian ice creams are possible dessert selections. A staggering wine list has great range in both price and origin and is computerized for changes every week.
(301) 663-6600. Entrées, $12.95 to $19.95. Open daily, 11 to 11.

The Province Restaurant, 131 North Market St., Frederick.
Billed as a bistro-style restaurant, this is not French as its name might suggest, but creative American and international, in the words of co-owner Nancy Floria. It takes its name from the 1767 deed to the property, when the area was known as the Province of Maryland. The brick walls of the first building on the site form

the central part of the restaurant, which is cozy and historic in the front and middle, and opens onto an airy garden room addition in back.

The last is a stunning space for lunch, overlooking a flower and herb garden eked out between downtown buildings. New Age music plays against a backdrop of brick floors, comfortable snowshoe chairs and handmade quilts on the walls. Here we enjoyed chilled peach soup, a seafood pasta salad, a brie and almond pâté and a Greek salad. An orange mousse cake from a dessert tray bearing at least nine yummy desserts was a light and refreshing ending.

At night, the menu ranges widely from shrimp provençal and Asian glazed salmon to Parisian poulet, prime rib and veal piccata. Soft-shell crab with honey mustard-pinenut sauce and roast pork loin with fettuccine ragu were specials at a recent visit. The hummus and pita, antipasto plate, spanakopita and crab imperial in potato shells lend an international flavor to the appetizers.

Desserts vary from hazelnut cream cake to derby pie to Washington apple cake. They are made daily at the Bake Shop at **Province Two,** a caterer, baker and sandwich maker at 12 East Patrick St.

(301) 663-1441. Entrées, $12.95 to $18.95. Lunch, Monday-Friday 11:30 to 3. Dinner, Tuesday-Saturday 5:30 to 9 or 10. Saturday brunch, 11:30 to 3. Sunday, brunch 11 to 3:30, dinner 4 to 8.

The Brown Pelican, 5 East Church St., Frederick.

Pelicans are the theme of this elegant restaurant in the basement of a former downtown bank. They appear on drawings and paintings on the walls, in an etched-glass partition separating the bar from the dining room, and atop the oversize parchment menu that arrives rolled up like a scroll and refuses to lie flat. The atmosphere is serene: white-linened tables, captain's chairs, fieldstone walls and beamed ceilings.

Scallops scampi and crab norfolk might supplement the nearly two dozen entrées on the continental dinner menu, which seldom changes and appeals to traditionalists. It includes walnut bourbon chicken, shrimp czarina, lobster savannah, roast duckling with orange or green peppercorn sauce, mixed grill (filet, pork chop and German sausage) and New York strip steak. Appetizers cover all the bases from marinated herring and shrimp cocktail to baked brie and escargots. Six pasta dishes and caesar salad are listed under appetizers for two or more.

(301) 695-5833. Entrées, $12.95 to $27.95. Lunch, Monday-Friday 11:30 to 3. Dinner, Monday-Saturday 5 to 9:30 or 10.

DiFrancesco's, 26 North Market St., Frederick.

A beamed ceiling, arches, niches decorated with potter and hanging brass lamps lend a country Italian look to this local favorite.

Paul DiFrancesco's highly regarded homemade pastas are featured. Fettuccine with prosciutto and peas, fettuccine with smoked salmon, linguini calabrese, lasagna and cannelloni are a few of the choices. Entrées range from chicken cacciatore to surf and turf. Several veal dishes are offered, as are mixed grills and filet mignon from the wood grill. Some regulars say they've never ordered anything but the manicotti, the real thing and the best around.

Among appetizers are fried mozzarella and fried calamari. Assorted pastries make up the dessert tray. The wine list is short but serviceable.

(301) 695-5499. Entrées, $11.50 to $18.95. Lunch, Tuesday-Friday 11:30 to 3. Dinner nightly, 5 to 9:30 or 10. Sunday, brunch 11:30 to 3, dinner 3 to 9.

Cafe Kyoko, 10 East Patrick St., Frederick.
Upstairs over Province Too is this intriguing Japanese-Thai combination, a branch of Restaurant Kyoko in Washington, D.C. The high-ceilinged room could be any restaurant in Frederick, except for a couple of fancy chandeliers and some hanging lanterns on the landing and, of course, an authentic sushi bar. The third floor has a dining room with cushions on the floor.

The menu pairs Japanese tempura, teriyaki, sukiyaki and such side by side with Thai standards like goong-pad and seafood pattaya. The sushi choices are extensive, and Japanese and Indian beers are on tap.

(301) 695-9656. Entrées, $8.95 to $13.95. Lunch, Monday-Friday 11:30 to 2. Dinner, Monday-Saturday 5:30 to 9 or 10.

Mealey's Restaurant, 8 West Main St., New Market.
Dating to 1793, this old hotel turned into a dining institution is, as its name might imply, a place for a good meal. After a kitchen fire, owners Jose and Pat Salaverri rebuilt, to the approval of their large and loyal following. The main beamed dining room is dark, authentic and almost too atmospheric for words. Check out the vintage Wurlitzer jukebox near the entry in the bar.

The menu stresses seafood, from fried shrimp to crab imperial. Three cuts of prime rib, three steaks and three chicken dishes are alternatives. Crab bisque and smoked baby trout are among appetizers. Favored desserts are homemade cheesecake with raspberry sauce and bread pudding with bourbon sauce. Maryland selections are featured on the wine list.

(301) 865-5488. Entrées, $11.50 to $22.95. Lunch, Friday and Saturday 11:30 to 2:30. Dinner, Tuesday-Saturday 5 to 9, Sunday noon to 8. No smoking.

Diversions

Historic Frederick. The historic district embraces 33 blocks of central Frederick, but the important structures are concentrated along eight short blocks of downtown. The downtown Visitor Center offers a map for a short walking tour, but its 90-minute guided walking tour given weekends and holidays at 1:30 is well worth the $4.50 tab. Many of the fascinating sights (and insights) we were told about aren't detailed in the written tour. Among these are the unique top hats atop dormer windows, the cast-iron dog stolen by Confederate soldiers desperate for bullets and later returned and resting today in front of Dr. John Tyler's Home and the unbelievably realistic murals painted on downtown store walls under the city's Angels in the Architecture program. You see the law offices of Roger Brooke Taney and Francis Scott Key (famous brothers-in-law, one a Supreme Court justice known for the Dred Scott Decision and the other the author of the National Anthem) opposite City Hall and Court House Square. Other tour highlights: the oldest consecrated Catholic church in the country, the oldest ginkgo tree in the country across from the synagogue, the Barbara Fritchie House and Museum (open Thursday-Monday or by appointment, $2), the home of the first president of the Continental Congress, the Historical Society of Frederick County (same hours and price as Fritchie House, but free to walking-tour participants) and stately townhouses, mansions and public buildings shaded by trees and parks. Of particular interest are the stained-glass windows in All Saints Episcopal Church, one side of which is original Tiffany glass, beneath a ceiling that is a replica of Noah's Ark.

Antietam was scene of bloodiest one-day battle of Civil War.

Carroll Creek Park. A new promenade and linear corridor – the result of a flood-control project – stretch nearly a mile and a half through the city's heart. Benches, fountains, plantings, wood sculptures and a bridge with trompe-l'oeil stone walls are among diversions for passersby. The annual **Frederick Festival of the Arts** is staged here, and more activities and commercial and office developments were planned along the creek banks. Already, an old mill has been turned into the **Delaplaine Visual Arts Center** at 40 South Carroll St. and the **Frederick Brewing Company** brews Blue Ridge beers and ales and gives weekend tastings and tours at its microbrewery at 103 South Carroll St.

War Memorabilia. Frederick, a city where families and friends were divided by the War Between the States, is a center for devotees of the Civil War. It's centrally located between Gettysburg, Antietam and Harpers Ferry, among the more significant sites. More than 500 Confederate soldiers are buried in the city's vast **Mount Olivet Cemetery.** The Revolutionary War **Hessian Barracks,** the only surviving structures of the Civil War hospital complex here, are nearby. The **National Museum of Civil War Medicine,** 48 East Patrick St., details the story of care and healing amidst all the death and destruction. A new visitor center serves visitors at **Monocacy National Battlefield,** where Confederate General Jubal Early's advance on Washington was delayed long enough to allow Union reinforcements to enter and save the city.

Antietam National Battlefield. This battlefield is another story. One of America's best preserved (and least crowded) battlefields, it was the site of the bloodiest battle in U.S. history. More than 23,000 men on both sides were killed or wounded on Robert E. Lee's first invasion of the north on Sept. 17, 1862. Antietam Creek "actually ran red that day," we were told by our Frederick walking-tour guide. Pause at the visitor center to view the award-winning, 26-minute movie, "Antietam Visit." It's gripping, grisly and melancholy. An eight-mile-long tour road allows visitors to drive past important sites and more than 350 monuments, tablets, markers and cannons. Open daily, 8:30 to 6, to 5 in winter. Adults, $2.

Antiquing in New Market. Just off the interstate, this little one-street town crossed by alleys is heaven for antiquers. The village that originally served as a stopover for travelers on the National Pike between Baltimore and Frederick has staked its reputation on being a destination for those with a serious interest in antiques. More than 30 shops are tucked in and behind houses in a half-mile stretch. There's not a souvenir shop or boutique in sight. Most shops are open only the latter half of the week or on weekends. You can stop for lunch or dessert at the cozy **Village Tea Room & Antique Shop,** 81 West Main St., where the owner-baker makes 22 kinds of pies and offers sandwiches and vegetarian fare in the $5 to $7 range. Breakfast and lunch also are available in a cafe section of the atmospheric **New Market General Store,** which looks much as it did when it was built in 1881.

Shopping. Frederick's downtown has never been lost, and even retained a local department store into the early 1990s. Although boutiques and crafts shops have sprouted up, it still has a barbershop located on the main street, where the window was filled with old glass milk bottles and seven men were waiting on a Tuesday morning for the three chairs. And people are apt to say hello; even the policeman bade us good morning and the meter maid awarded us a reprieve with a courtesy parking ticket. The owners of the **Museum Shop Ltd.,** well-known for restoring museum paintings, moved from Washington to Frederick to open a gallery of exotic works, including a line of cards and plates with animal prints. **The Country Way** and **Options of Frederick** are among the gift shops. The **Candy Kitchen** has dispensed candy made the old-fashioned way for more than 50 years.

There's another concentration of shops, some of them hard to find or get to, at the restored **Everedy Square & Shab Row** east of downtown. **Flights of Fancy** is a colorful place on several levels with a New Age atmosphere, handmade items, educational toys and our favorite Salt Marsh Pottery from Massachusetts. Wonderful specialty foods, chocolates, Maryland wines and gift baskets are among the offerings at **The Frederick Basket Company.** In between is the local branch of **Talbots.** Across the street from each other are the **Calico Fudge & Creamery** and the **Frederick Coffee Company & Cafe.**

Extra-Special

Lilypons Water Gardens, 6800 Lilypons Road, Buckeystown.

If you've ever been interested in water gardening, and even if you haven't, you should drive out to this fascinating aquatic farm and shop (incidentally named for Lily Pons, the opera star) eight miles south of Frederick. Here are 300 acres of tranquility, with pond after pond containing lilies and lotus with names like queen of whites, glorisa, rosy morn, floating heart and pink sensation. Holding tanks in back of the shop contain koi, the colorful Japanese carp (some as expensive as $250), comets, calico fantails and the like. The shop carries everything one needs to start a water garden, from books to filters, pumps and pool de-icers. Lectures and demonstrations are offered from spring to fall. The annual Lotus Blossom Festival occurs around the middle of July when the lotus begin to bloom, and the Koi Festival takes place in early September. Any time, you can take a picnic, stroll around the ponds, and dream of your own lagoon-shaped pool with the underground lights, the fan fountain and the black Japanese snails, tadpoles and clams to help keep it all clean.

(301) 874-5133 or (800) 723-7667. Open daily 9:30 to 5:30, March-October.

Solomons, Md.

The Ultimate Watering Place

Barely a mile long, this strip of watery real estate conjures up many an image in the minds of Marylanders. They think of the shore, boating, bugeyes, crabbing, watermen, the Patuxent River and the Chesapeake Bay.

They also think of a village bustling with belated tourism development – a far cry from its earlier description as a typical coastal fishing village.

Typical it is not, this narrow peninsula jutting from the foot of the graceful Governor Thomas Johnson bridge that arches over the Patuxent widewaters as they empty into the bay. Airplanes soar overhead from the Patuxent Naval Air Station across the river. More boats seem to jockey for position in Solomons' deep-water harbor than in Annapolis. And more visitors from nearby cities descend during a summer weekend on what one booster calls "this sleepy little town" than it can possibly absorb.

Think of Ocean City – without the beaches and the high-rises – and you may get the picture. Life, though hectic on weekends, is quieter here along the bay and Maryland's western shore.

Solomons Island was named in 1870 for Isaac Solomon, who established the area's first oyster-packing facilities. The island part of the name was quickly dropped by the post office and Solomons really looks more like a peninsula than an island. It grew as a waterfront community, with a fishing fleet of more than 500 vessels, most built locally. More bugeyes – large, decked-over sailing canoes – were built here than in any bay community. Solomons gave birth to racing yachts of international fame. The maritime tradition continues today at the Calvert Marine Museum and the Chesapeake Biological Laboratory.

As with other resort communities of its ilk, this one is ever-changing. There were virtually no places to stay until a Holiday Inn opened in the mid-1980s. Today, Solomons has five bed-and-breakfast facilities offering a total of two dozen rooms. There are at least a hundred times that many restaurant seats. Singles jam the open-air Tiki Bar and whatever new restaurant and bar is au courant. "I've been here since 1977 and have seen a lot of coming and going," says shopkeeper Joann Kersey of all the changes.

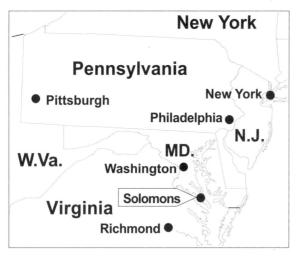

What doesn't change is the inherent Solomons appeal – its watery aspects, the sailing, the charter fishing and the natural attractions of a special place.

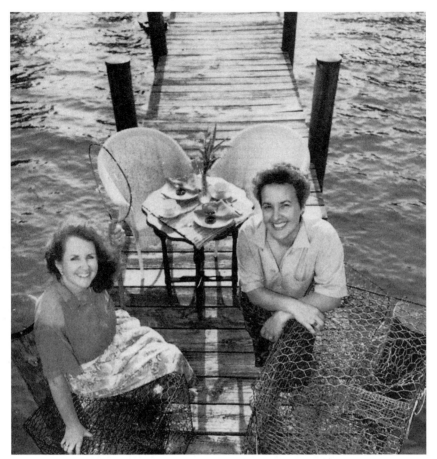

Innkeepers Lin Cochran and Carol Pennock are ready for breakfast at Back Creek Inn.

Inn Spots

Back Creek Inn, Calvert and A Streets, Box 520, Solomons 20688.

Location, location, location. The Back Creek Inn has that, plus tranquility, beauty, artistry and sophistication. Artist Carol Pennock and gardener Lin Cochran offer seven elegant guest accommodations in a century-old waterman's house, a newer addition and a great little cottage.

The pair were living in the area while their husbands were on military duty at Patuxent when the fledgling inn property became available. "It was love at first sight," Carol recalls.

The house is a couple of blocks off the island's main street in a residential section along the waterfront. Thick foliage blocks the front entrance; a gnarled paper mulberry tree along the side path makes you duck or go around. The verdant side lawn slopes gently to the deep waters of wide Back Creek. In the midst of lavish English-style gardens is a hot tub with a patio beside and a view of all the waterway goings-on.

Guests are welcomed with iced tea in big blue glasses bearing the inn's logo. It's served in a comfy, contemporary, brick-floored common room with floor-to-ceiling windows on two sides to bring the outdoor garden in. Beyond are an open kitchen and a stenciled dining room where four tables are set for breakfast. Lyn's beautiful herbal wreaths and Carol's paintings enhance both common and guest rooms. The art of the latter, who works in a variety of media, is so striking that we had to buy a couple of her small renderings of oysters and clams.

Off the dining room on the main floor is a room with a brass double bed and private bath. Upstairs are three rooms, two with queen beds and one with a double. All have private baths. They are nicely decorated with frilly curtains, an abundance of pillows and quilts made by Carol's sister-in-law.

Two suites are in the addition that also serves as a studio and living quarters for the innkeepers. Both suites have sitting areas, TV sets and oversize beds. One faces the vegetable-herb garden and the other the hot tub. But we'd splurge again to stay in the cozy, peaked-ceilinged cottage, with a queensize bed, a bathroom in shades of mauve, TV, fireplace and an idyllic screened porch from which to view the water and gardens.

Breakfast was a treat, even though an overnight rain had made things too wet for the usual service outside on the patio when we were there. Juice, coffee and fancy breads awaited on side tables in the dining room as Carol took orders for her "Back Creek Bennies Our Way," superb eggs benedict with a sweet tang (ask her what the mystery ingredient is). These came garnished with fresh fruit, including kiwis and figs. Other choices might be a ham and cheese omelet, waffles topped with warm fruit compote or crab quiche – "when we have time to pick our own crabs off the pier," Carol advises. Sunday often brings a buffet with two different casseroles.

(410) 326-2022. Fax (410) 326-2946. Four rooms, two suites and one cottage with private baths. Doubles, $95. Suites, $125. Cottage, $145. Two-night minimum weekends. Children over 12. No smoking.

Solomons Victorian Inn, 125 Charles St., Box 759, Solomons 20688.

New owners have upgraded this turn-of-the-century Victorian house on a rise overlooking water on three sides. Helen and Richard Bauer, sailing enthusiasts from Frederick, poured considerable resources and energy into the old Davis House, whose owners retired.

Originally the family home of Clarence Davis, renowned builder of early 20th century sailboats, the main floor holds a cozy sitting room outfitted in wicker and a more formal front living room.

Five second-floor guest rooms are named for Davis yachts, each bearing the appropriate picture. Furnishings vary from Victorian to casual white wicker. The front Orithia Room has a kingsize mahogany four-poster bed and a bay window yielding harbor views. The other rooms have queensize beds and three have water views.

The ultimate for views, however, is the huge third-floor Solomons Sunset suite, segmented into separate areas by sloping ceilings with skylights. Big windows front and side frame water scenes, enjoyed from two sitting areas. A double jacuzzi lies beneath another sloping window. The iron and wicker bed is kingsize. The suite comes with a fireplace, TV, a kitchenette and a dining area.

There's no need to cook, however, for the Bauers offer a hearty breakfast on a

Solomons waterfront is on view from third-floor suite at Solomons Victorian Inn.

breakfast porch they refinished after "stripping about 25 coats of paint." The fare the day of our visit featured summer melon grown by the Amish near Annapolis and a shrimp puff incorporating eggs, mushrooms, cheeses and shrimp, followed by sour cream coffee cake and blueberry muffins. Stuffed french toast with peach preserves, blueberry bread and currant muffins were on the next morning's docket.

Lately, the Bauers added two luxurious suites in a carriage house behind the main house. Both have double jacuzzi tubs and gas fireplaces. The upstairs kingsize suite is decorated in gold and white for romance. The downstairs suite with queensize iron bed was appointed in florals in shades of mauve and green.

(410) 326-4811. Fax (410) 326-0133. www.chesapeake.net/solomonsvictorianinn. Five rooms and three suites with private baths. Doubles, $90 to $110. Suites, $135 to $175. Lower rates in winter. Two-night minimum stay weekends April to mid-November; three-night minimum on holiday and special weekends. Children over 13. No smoking.

By-the-Bay Bed & Breakfast, 14374 Calvert St., Box 504, Solomons 20688.

Owners Joan and Tom Hogenson spent six years renovating their Victorian house beside Back Creek before opening as a B&B in 1988. They stripped and refinished all the stained-pine woodwork. They painted the exterior a striking mulberry rose color with pink trim. She did the stenciling and he the stained glass in the front door and living room. Victoriana is the rule here – fairly dark in the living room and quite light and airy in the guest rooms.

The three bedrooms possess what Joan calls "an old-time flavor with modern comforts," such as private baths, queensize beds and cable TV. A main-floor bedroom off the dining room has a private entrance, a potbelly stove and a small refrigerator. It opens to an adjacent sitting room for optional use as a suite. Upstairs is a rear room with a step-up iron bed and plants in the windows. The front room has a recliner chair and a rocker. You'll find decorative touches like two old irons, but little of the clutter that fussies-up some Victorian inns.

A full breakfast is served at a lace-draped table beneath an elaborate old chandelier in the dining room. Fresh fruit or baked apples, Tom's muffins, hot or cold cereal and omelets, french toast or strata could be the fare. The Hogensons offer a deep-water dock, a swing on the wraparound veranda, a rear patio, lovely rear gardens with statue and fountain, and a screened-in sitting room and terrace down by the water.

(410) 326-3428. Fax (410) 394-0930. Two rooms and one suite with private baths. Doubles, $75 and $80. Suite, $95. Two-night minimum weekends in season. Children over 12. No credit cards. No smoking.

Webster House, 14364 Sedwick Ave., Box 1607, Solomons 20688.

Running a B&B was "an afterthought" for Peter and Barbara Prentice, who had envisioned opening a place for retreats for clergymen. "We were riding our bicycles and wondering where we'd live when we saw the old Webster house," reports Barbara. They demolished and rebuilt the house, designing it to look old in front. "We felt we were giving a new house a history."

For six years they offered two rooms with shared bath in the main house. The prime accommodations have always been out back in The Haven, upstairs over a detached garage, where a private deck overlooks the long back yard and catches a glimpse of the broad waters in Back Creek. Here you'll find a queensize bed, private bath, a little kitchen with a dining table and cable TV.

Lately, the Prentices have stopped operating the Webster House but retained the name. The Haven remains available to guests under auspices of the nearby Back Creek Inn. Its occupants enjoy breakfast and the facilities of the Back Creek Inn.

(410) 326-0454. One room with private bath. Double, $135. Two-night minimum on weekends.

Adina's Guest House, 14236 South Solomons Island Road, Solomons 20688.

A wide front porch with comfortable lounge chairs faces the Patuxent River and the soaring Governor Thomas Johnson Bridge across a cornfield at this B&B, which opened in 1993.

Inside are a large living room with dining area, four bedrooms and the quarters of owners Adelaida and Glen Papure, who have done considerable renovations to the house.

The expense was such that both had to resume full-time jobs and, while officially open year-round, they tend to concentrate on weekends in season.

The guest rooms come with queensize beds and cable TV. Two on the main floor have private baths, while two upstairs share a bath. The rooms have a variety of beds from sleigh to four-poster and are furnished with a few antique pieces in country style.

On weekends, the Papures prepare a hearty breakfast of the guest's choice, including scrambled eggs with bacon, omelets or french toast, with fresh fruits and homemade muffins. Guests can make requests and "if I have it in my kitchen, I'll make it," says Adelaida.

The couple commute 90 minutes each way to their weekday jobs in Washington, D.C. Who said running a B&B in your spare time is easy?

(410) 326-4895. Two rooms with private baths and two rooms with shared baths. Doubles, $65 to $80. Children over 13. No smoking.

Diners at window tables at Dry Dock Restaurant enjoy view of harbor scene.

Dining Spots

Dry Dock Restaurant, C Street at Back Creek, Solomons.

Part of the impressive Zahniser's Sailing Center, Dry Dock is upstairs over a small bathhouse with great views of the harbor. Innovative fresh seasonal cuisine is featured on the blackboard menu, which changes daily, and the food is considered the best in Solomons.

Decor is simple and nautical, with eight bare wood tables bearing paper napkins, pepper grinders and candles in globes. A lineup of signal flags frames large windows overlooking the busy waterfront. We watched with fascination the parade of boats finishing the weekly Wednesday night race. Racers accounted for much of the activity in the noisy bar, which is cheek to jowl with the tables in the small, L-shaped room.

Dinner began with a complimentary wooden board bearing Wispride cheese spread and assorted crackers. We liked the oyster stew better than the highly touted spinach salad with fruit and nuts.

Good main courses were lightly breaded pan-fried oysters with herbs de provence and grilled tuna with tomato-basil salsa. They came with rice, broccoli and an abundance of non-edible garnishes. Other possibilities included grilled mahi-mahi with sweet and sour sauce, grilled rockfish with Southwestern mushroom fricassee, and shrimp and scallops sauté with sundried tomatoes and pinenuts. Prime rib and sautéed chicken with curried carrots and tart cherries were the only non-seafood items at a recent visit. Desserts included key lime pie, bourbon pecan pie and a number of chocolate extravagances.

Light dining is available in summer at the Dry Dock's jaunty outdoor **Pool Bar Cafe** beside the sailing center's pool. The menu includes salads, sandwiches and a few grilled items and specials.

(410) 326-4817. Entrées, $15.95 to $21.95. Dinner nightly, 6 to 9. Sunday brunch, 10 to 1.

Soaring windows overlook harbor from dining rooms at Lighthouse Inn.

Lighthouse Inn, Patuxent Avenue, Solomons.

The bar here is in a skipjack, the Spirit of Solomons, custom-built in the restaurant. It's a conversation piece at a contemporary, high-ceilinged establishment with huge windows onto the harbor and an outdoor deck that takes full advantage of its waterside location.

The chef's cuisine has won awards for the restaurant, which was built in 1986. Seafood takes precedence on the menu, which ranges from a vegetarian platter to surf and turf. Scallops with mushrooms and cheddar cheese, crab in the usual guises, baked stuffed shrimp, seafood platters and filet mignon are favorites; flounder renaissance and snapper royale could be specials. Start with clams casino, stuffed mushrooms or escargots. Among desserts are apple and key lime pies.

Interior dining is on two levels on the main floor and on a spacious mezzanine. Oil lamps cast shadows on each shiny wood table. Sandwiches, light fare and a half a dozen entrées are served outside at the **Quarter Deck,** a separate entity run by the same enterprise and open weekends seasonally for lunch.

(410) 326-2444. Entrées, $14.95 to $28.95. Dinner nightly, 5 to 9 or 10, Sunday 4 to 9. Quarter Deck: May-September, Monday-Friday 5 to 9, weekends noon to 9.

The C.D. Cafe, 14350 Solomons Island Road, Solomons.

Chef-owners Catherine File and Deborah Witmer used to cook at the Dry Dock Restaurant, so you'd expect the fare at their new cafe to be a cut above. Theirs is the full-service successor to a gourmet bakery and deli in the Avondale Center, a good-looking, contemporary retail complex built by Skip and Ellen Zahniser of the marina family. The Zahnisers thought the town needed another decent, casual restaurant serving dinner, and this is the happy result.

The sleek gray decor is minimal. Cane chairs are at butcherblock tables topped with gray inlays. The dinner menu is eclectic, to say the least. Under appetizers and light fare are things like caesar salad with grilled salmon, a hummus and couscous sampler, creole andouille sausage and Catherine's savory cheesecake, a walnut-crusted blend of herbs, goat cheese and cream cheese. For entrées, Deb's favorite is pan-seared chicken with pecans, apples and onions, deglazed with apple schnapps and topped with crumbled feta. Other possibilities are smoked salmon cakes, scallops with sundried tomatoes and blue cheese over orzo, Mediterranean pasta and cajun shepherd's pie. No heavy dishes here – the meatiest is steak au poivre, unless you include a bistro burger.

Catherine's desserts are special: crème brûlée, bourbon-pecan pie, chocolate mousse cake, amaretto pound cake and decadent brownies. We got a taste of the last after a quick lunch of a curried chicken salad sandwich and potato salad that really hit the spot..

The espresso-cappuccino machine is the only one on Solomons, which makes this a good place for continental breakfast and coffee in the morning. There's a full bar for drinks later on.

(410) 326-3877. Entrées, $8.25 to $17.95. Continental breakfast from 9. Lunch daily, 11:30 to 2:30. Dinner, 5:30 to 9.

Captain's Table, 275 Lore Road, Solomons.

Good food at affordable prices is the hallmark of this hidden waterfront restaurant run by Jim & Sherin Hise. You have to know about it and then find it, but the search pays off.

The setting is super: two nautical rooms, a bar and a waterside deck right beside Back Creek. The huge, eight-page menu is traditional plus: orange roughy parmesan, Chesapeake Bay rockfish, baked chicken cheddar. The specialty is baked stuffed shrimp with crab imperial, and the crab cakes were voted the best in Southern Maryland. The desserts are said to be some of the finest in town.

The deck is a great place for lunch, perhaps the specialty seafood quiche, a croissant stuffed with ham salad or a fried steak sandwich. An all-you-can eat breakfast bar is offered weekends for $5.99.

(410) 326-2772. Entrées, $12.95 to $19.95. Breakfast from 7. Lunch from 11. Dinner from 4.

The Naughty Gull, Lore Road, Spring Cove Marina, Solomons.

The view is everything from this nautical restaurant and pub, centered by a large bar in the middle, with tables on several levels. Alas, there's no deck for outdoor dining beside the water, but we lucked into the next best thing, one of the few window tables. The lunch menu yielded a soft-shell crab sandwich and an enormous, gloppy platter of aztec nachos, accompanied by plenty of guacamole, sour cream and hot salsa on the side.

Come nightfall, a varied menu ranges from fish and chips to filet mignon. Crab imperial, a crab cake platter, three shrimp dishes and prime rib are among the possibilities. Dessert could be carrot cake, cheesecake or chocolate cake.

(410) 326-4855. Entrées, $11.95 to $19.95. Open daily from 11. Sunday brunch, 9 to 2.

Bowen's Inn, 14630 Solomons Island Road, Solomons.

Full of local color, Bowen's has been serving watermen since 1918 and looks it. Behind a three-story shingled building angled to the street lie an atmospheric bar and the newish Captain Mortimer Room, where a handful of small windows offer glimpses of the water. Problem is, the windows are too high for patrons seated at most tables to see out.

Locals laud Bowen's for what it is – a family-owned operation run by Captain Mortimer's granddaughter – and care not a whit that some tables sport lacy white cloths and others paper mats, all with fake flowers to brighten things up. Some protest the loud music and the emphasis on beer and taco nights, however.

The menu is a typewritten sheet of mimeograph vintage. It ranges from spaghetti with meatballs through soft-shell crab and veal parmesan to New York strip steak and crab imperial. Salad and rolls come with. Those with hearty appetites can start with potato skins, Buffalo wings or nachos. Cheesecake and pies are favored desserts.

(410) 326-9814. Entrées, $6.95 to $14.95. Lunch and dinner, Tuesday-Sunday 11 to 9 or 10. Closed January to St. Patrick's Day.

Diversions

Solomons boasts an impressive **Riverwalk,** a sixteen-foot-wide boardwalk stretching a third of a mile along the bulkhead of the Patuxent River. There are benches as well as a pavilion and an amphitheater. A 46-seat water taxi known as the Stars & Stripes shuttles passengers around the island on weekends in summer.

Sailing, boating and charter fishing are the big attractions. They are available through various marinas, which seem to be the second most prevalent business activity here after restaurants. Hour-long cruises around Solomons Inner Harbor are offered by the 1899 log-built bugeye William B. Tennison, the oldest passenger-carrying vessel on the Chesapeake Bay. They're scheduled to leave at 2 p.m. Wednesday-Sunday, May-October, from the Calvert Marine Museum, but may depart early, as we found to our dismay upon arrival one afternoon at 1:56. Additional cruises are offered Saturdays and Sundays at 12:30 in July and August.

Calvert Marine Museum, 14200 Solomons Island Road, Solomons.

Started in the old school building, this growing museum specializes in local maritime history, the marine paleontology of the nearby Calvert Cliffs and the estuarine life of the tidal Patuxent River and adjacent waters. Its impressive exhibition building has extensive exhibits on the Patuxent, including 500 photographs, scale models and artifacts. Among them are a 28-foot-long, three-log canoe and an underwater mine and torpedo from World War II testing in the river. A permanent exhibit on the river and its life features seventeen aquariums, live otters and a discovery room with "please touch" area for children. A hall of fossils from the Calvert Cliffs traces ancient inhabitants of the region, including the enormous jaws and teeth of the extinct great white shark. Fascinating to visit is the Drum Point Lighthouse, which dominates the waterfront and is one of

View from Calvert Marine Museum store.

three remaining cottage-type lights from the bay. Fifteen visitors may go inside hourly on guided tours. Varied watercraft are on display in the small craft building or are afloat in the boat basin. Half a mile south of the main museum complex is the J.C. Lore Oyster House, which traces the region's commercial seafood industry and portrays the area's traditions of boatbuilding. Nautical and local items of interest are sold in the excellent Museum Store.

(410) 326-2042. Open daily, 10 to 5. Adults, $5.

Annmarie Garden, Dowell Road, Solomons.
Accented with contemporary sculptures, 30 acres of forests and gardens along St. John Creek are being developed into a world-class sculpture garden. Walkways in the woods take visitors past juried sculptures set in garden "rooms" cut out of the forest. A sculpture of an oyster tonger was a focal point at an early visit, followed by talking benches, a council ring and a surveyor's map. One local artist predicted the sculpture garden would ultimately rival the famous Brookgreen Gardens of South Carolina. The late Francis Koenig, who had donated the land and named it for his ailing wife, envisioned it as "a contemplative and creative place" for the public to commune amid floral and fauna. All kinds of visual and performing artists make the garden rooms come alive at the annual September Artsfest, which attracts 15,000 visitors and was named Calvert County's best event of the year in 1996. Gardenfest is a plant sale and exhibition staged annually in late April.

(410) 326-4640. Open daily, 10 to 4. Free.

Calvert Cliffs State Park, Route 765, Lusby.
Nearly 30 miles of cliffs along the Chesapeake Bay's western shore north of Solomons hold one of the world's richest concentrations of fossil whales among more than 600 species of fossils up to seventeen million years old. A two-mile hike through the 1,460-acre wooded park takes visitors to the cliffs. The area under the cliffs is closed due to landslide activity, but fossils can be collected along the open beach where there are no cliffs.

(410) 872-5688. Open daily, sunrise to sunset. Donation, $3.

Jefferson Patterson Park and Museum, 10515 Mackall Road, St. Leonard.
Pre-historic and Colonial sites, nature and archaeology trails, farm exhibits and a visitor center with exhibits on history and nature are featured in this 544-acre preserve along the banks of the Patuxent River. Tractor-pulled wagon tours are offered weekends in summer.

(410) 586-0050. Open Wednesday-Sunday 10 to 5, mid-April to mid-October. Free.

Point Lookout State Park, Route 5, Scotland, St. Mary's County.
The southernmost point in Maryland is at the tip of a 1,037-acre peninsula at the confluence of the Potomac River and the Chesapeake Bay. The park is so large and so far from the mainstream that it's almost always uncrowded. Attractions include miles of beaches on both river and bay, a fishing pier jutting 700 feet into the bay, a lighthouse, a swimming beach, a Civil War museum, an earthen fort built by Confederate prisoners and a Confederate cemetery. The Confederate Monument here is the only federal monument dedicated to those who died for the rebel cause. We liked the park's seclusion and the broad view across to the Northern Neck of Virginia.

(301) 872-5688. Open daily, 8 a.m. to sunset.

Shopping. Ensconced in a structure built right over the water along the boardwalk is **The Sandpiper,** a gift shop adjacent to the town dock, which also rents bicycles and sells ice cream. We picked up some clever Christmas cards from owner Joann Kersey's excellent selection at her other shop at the Holiday Inn Select. Handpainted clothing, T-shirts, jewelry, resort wear and gifts are featured at **Caren's Solomons Style.** Thousands of used and rare books are available at **Lazy Moon Book Shop,** where the owner is as interesting as his stock. The increasingly well-known **Carmen's Gallery** displays appealing artworks. Hoping to set a standard for future commercial development of Solomons, Ellen and Skip Zahniser of sailing-center fame erected Avondale Center, a retail and professional complex along the main street. Among its treasures are **Fine Things,** whimsically stocked with one-of-a-kind shell items, pottery, cut crystal, accessories and such, in exquisite taste. If we'd had a spare $155 we might have emerged with a gold-shell wreath. But it was on to **Solomons Mines,** where we ogled all the gems and jewelry.

Extra-Special

Historic St. Mary's City, Route 5, St. Mary's City.

Founded in 1634 by Catholic pilgrims, this National Historic Landmark was the fourth permanent settlement in British North America and served as the Colonial capital of Maryland until 1695. The abandonment of the town and the

subsequent shift to agriculture was an archaeological blessing, for most of the 17th-century town was preserved under the plowed soils, awaiting excavation. A low-key, outdoor living-history museum opened on the 800-acre site in 1984, and work continues to uncover and restore the nation's only Colonial capital still undisturbed by development or erosion. Four main exhibit areas include the Visitor Center with an archaeology exhibit hall, a tobacco plantation, the Chancellor's Point Natural History Area (site of a Chesapeake Indian Lifeways Center) and the Governor's Field. We found the last to be

State House at Historic St. Mary's City.

of most interest. You can walk out on a dock in the St. Mary's River to board the square-rigged replica of a ship that brought the first settlers from England, hear your footsteps echo as you explore the reconstructed State House of 1676 and stop for a lunch featuring traditional Colonial dishes and regional seafood specialties in the $5 to $10 range at Farthing's Ordinary. The remains of St. Mary's Chapel, whose excavation is in progress, marks the birthplace of the Roman Catholic church in America. The old town – what little there is – blends nicely into the waterfront campus of St. Mary's College, a liberal arts college of 1,500 students.

(301) 862-0990 o)r (800) 762-1634. Open Wednesday-Sunday 10 to 5, late March through late November. Adults, $7.50.

Tillie the Tug takes passengers for leisurely cruise along Pocomoke River.

Snow Hill/Berlin, Md.

300 Years Along the River

Like a waterway in the bayous of Louisiana, the Pocomoke River lazes through the flatlands and forests of Maryland's Lower Eastern Shore. Stands of bald cypress trees define its path. Bald eagles, osprey, egrets and other wildlife populate its shores. The river – deep, languorous, mysterious and hauntingly beautiful – was Maryland's first to be designated "wild and scenic."

Such is the watery backdrop for little-known Snow Hill, founded by English colonists in 1642 and billed today as "the undiscovered treasure of the Eastern Shore." The county-seat town of 2,200 is not really on the way to anywhere. It claims more than 100 homes that are at least 100 years old, a way of life that's 40 years behind the times and almost no downtown at all (other than a few refurbished antiques shops, local boosters were looking forward to the opening of an old-fashioned ice-cream parlor in 2000). The big social events are church suppers and monthly dances in summer under the stars beside the river.

Snow Hill's counterpoint in the path of non-discovery is Berlin, a town of 2,600 about fifteen miles to the northeast. The old houses here are not as compelling as the rejuvenated Victorian storefronts up against brick sidewalks on a maze of downtown streets. Berlin languished in the shadow of Ocean City until the late 1980s, when ten hometown boosters bought and renovated the Atlantic Hotel to wide acclaim. Now Berlin, pronounced BUR-lin by most natives, has a first-class restaurant, a restored theater, a working downtown, countless antiques shops and enough gawkers on weekends to qualify as the newly minted "jewel of the Eastern Shore."

The attractions of Snow Hill, Berlin and environs are diverse: the Assateague Island National Seashore, canoeing on the Pocomoke, riverside parks, the site of a vanished 19th-century industrial village called Furnace Town. The coastal habitat and temperate climate produce the best bird-watching opportunities in Maryland.

Three centuries of history converge in Snow Hill. Its Presbyterian church is the first of the American denomination. All Hallows Episcopal Church, a brick antique surrounded by gravestones in the center of town, displays a bible and bell presented to the community by Queen Anne. Chain stores and fast-food outlets are noticeably missing here and in Berlin. The two small towns live up to their theme, "where the good life still lives on."

Inn Spots

The River House Inn, 201 East Market St., Snow Hill 21863.

A two-acre, 700-foot-deep lawn slopes down to the Pocomoke River behind this 1850 Victorian beauty, blessed with a wraparound veranda in front and screened porches upstairs and down in the rear. Larry and Susanne Knudsen from Ohio turned the residence into an elegant B&B with an expanding guest complex.

Besides the porches, they offer a bevy of attractive, comfortable public rooms on two sides of a green center hallway: a parlor with TV, a rosy red sitting and game room, a formal dining room and a breakfast room with draperies puddled on the floor. The breakfast room, which would be a fairly formal dining room in anyone else's lexicon, was the site for an impressive feast of orange juice, cantaloupe, blueberry muffins and a cheese omelet with bacon or sausage at our first stay. A recent visited yielded a choice of huevos rancheros and shirred River House eggs, both sensational.

Chocolates are at bedside at night. In the morning the Baltimore Sun was at our door outside the East Room, outfitted in Sheraton furniture with plush carpeting, fancy floral wallpaper coordinated with the curtains, and a high-ceilinged bathroom with windows. Three of the four guest rooms in the main house have fireplaces. All have queensize beds and private baths. The decor is French in the rear River Room and American Chippendale in the West Room. A third-floor suite with a wicker sitting area is done up in pastel pink and green in American country style.

Guests like to gather on the upstairs back porch full of wicker or its downstairs companion, smashingly appointed in tropical colors with bamboo-rattan furniture. The black decorative wrought iron on the front veranda could be straight out of New Orleans. Matching the wrought iron are the Knudsens' two friendly big black poodles, Bonnie and Winner, who love to go for romps down by the river.

Out back is the deluxe

River House Inn occupies ornate 1850 Victorian on two-acre lawn.

River Cottage, fashioned from an 1890s carriage barn. It has an antique king bed, mini-refrigerator, entertainment center with radio and TV, and a neat wicker porch looking onto the lovely lawn with its Adirondack chairs and hammocks.

The most deluxe accommodations are called the Riverview Hideaways, a new building with two substantial rooms offering queen beds, whirlpool tubs, gas fireplaces, thick carpeting and TV/VCRs, and each with a private 28-foot porch overlooking the Pocomoke River. The upstairs hideaway has a corner jacuzzi right in the room. The canopy bed in the downstairs unit is draped with ivy.

The newest accommodations are the Little House suites. Billed as cozy and historic, each occupies one floor of an 1834 cottage. The Lilac Suite has a kitchen and a sitting room with fireplace, while the Dover Suite has a microwave and mini-fridge plus a fireplace in the bedroom. Each comes with a TV/VCR.

Dinner for house guests is available occasionally by reservation for $30, including wine. The meal might start with scallops seviche or crabmeat gratin and a salad. Barbecued steaks or salmon could be followed by frozen yogurt with fresh berries and homemade chocolate sauce.

The Knudsens have put in water gardens, lily ponds, fountains and walkways to supplement the lavish landscaping behind the main house. "Our objective is to make a home where guests feel comfortable," said Larry. It is a goal they quickly realized.

(410) 632-2722. Fax (410) 632-2866. www.riverhouseinn.com. Six rooms, three suites and one cottage with private baths. Doubles, $100 to $140. Suites, $130 to $150. Cottage $180. Riverview, $195. Deduct $20 December-February. Two-night minimum summer weekends and holidays. Children and pets accepted. No smoking.

Chanceford Hall, 209 West Federal St., Snow Hill 21863.

Museum-quality furnishings – some of them crafted by the previous owner, a furniture maker – are among the hallmarks of this refined B&B on an acre of landscaped grounds at the edge of Snow Hill. Randy Ifft, an architect, and his wife, Alice Kesterson, who is in publishing, relocated from Chicago to the Eastern Shore to acquire the property in 1999. They added more fine antiques and oriental rugs to a house that shows them to great advantage.

The narrow, deep brick Greek Revival mansion dating to 1759 was built by Robert Morris, financier of the Revolution. It combines both Georgian and Federal details to create a rich ambiance. Elaborate crown moldings, chair rails, fireplace mantels, paneled doors with original hardware and wide-plank floors enhance the high-ceilinged rooms.

With more than 6,000 square feet of finished space, the manor house comes in three sections: the original house, a ballroom that's now the kitchen and a middle section joining the two. Beyond the kitchen is a stunning five-sided, high-ceilinged solarium shaded by the second oldest black walnut tree in Maryland. Soft drinks or wine, cocktails and hors d'oeuvres are offered here in the late afternoon, overlooking a brick patio with a 32-foot-long lap pool beneath a trellis twined with wisteria. Beyond, a terrace sides up to a little pond and flower gardens.

Guest rooms bear English names starting with the letter "C." Three have working fireplaces (the house has a total of ten), private baths, wing chairs, oriental rugs and queensize four-poster beds, two with testers. Quality 230-count sheets, Egyptian cotton towels and terrycloth robes are standard. All have full private baths, one across the hall. The Conway and Chadwick are similar in size and can be opened to make a private, two-room suite. The largest is the Cliveden, above the dining room, with a spacious sitting area. The Chanceford Room on the main floor is notable for a highboy, dark wainscoting and molding and a fancy medallion in the ceiling. All guest rooms have quilt racks bearing antique quilts and bookcases full of books. Randy reports that guests are quite impressed by the eighteen-inch-thick interior and exterior walls that ensure privacy and soundproofing.

The public rooms also have bookcases and are full of treasured books – Alice's mostly fiction and Randy's tending to architecture and non-fiction. Guests may take a self-addressed mailer in which to return a book they have not finished.

Breakfast is served beside a fireplace in an impressive dining room. The period cherry table can seat twelve. Its matching buffet and china cabinet are filled with Stratfordshire china in a strawberry pattern. The repast begins with fruit smoothies and individual fruit crisps. The main course could be omelets, Italian strata, multi-grain pancakes or baked french toast.

Besides three black walnut trees, the grounds hold mature gardens, two large weeping cherry trees, majestic magnolias, English boxwood and holly trees. Randy, an avid gardener, planned to start a hedgerow maze in the side garden.

(410) 632-2900. Fax (410) 632-2479. Four rooms with private baths. Doubles, $130; add $20 for weekends June-September.

Merry Sherwood Plantation, 8909 Worcester Hwy., Berlin 21811.

Is this a museum or a B&B? The painstaking restoration and the priceless furnishings that owner Kirk Burbage lavished on his grandmother's grand ante-bellum beauty hint of the former, as does the sign "no guided tours today." But the run-of-the-house welcome for overnight guests and the energy of the staff attest to the latter.

Listed on the National Register, the Victorian showcase is a place where architectural historians, antiques enthusiasts and those into Victoriana are in their

Major restoration preceded opening of Merry Sherwood Plantation as a B&B.

element. True, the place has its incongruities. Built in classic Italianate style, it also has Greek Revival and Gothic influences. The long main parlor (once a ballroom) holds both a grand piano and a square Victorian piano, while a pipe organ awaits in the front sitting room. The honeymoon suite comes with a marble bath and jacuzzi, yet the sunken bedroom with carved Victorian walnut double bed is the smallest in the house, and as for "suite," there's a little sitting room with uncomfortable chairs made for viewing rather than sitting. The other seven corner bedrooms on the second and third floors, all but two with private baths, seem quite spacious, particularly those with high ceilings on the second floor. The bathrooms are wallpapered and have marble floors and showers. The bedrooms are painted in lighter colors to set off the dark wood flooring. Most beds are dwarfed by heavy, ornate headboards and footers of solid walnut; "these beds need a lot of dusting," the chambermaid volunteered. On the nightstands are mints and Bibles. Fine oriental runners lead to the fourth-floor widow's walk, all windows with another Bible under the only seat.

Extravagant oriental rugs and carpets are particularly notable in the main ballroom/parlor, full of burgundy velvet sofas and settees. In the center of this expanse is a marble table topped by an enormous artificial floral arrangement in a three-foot-tall sterling silver vase imported from Germany, one of three in existence (and the owner claims two). The main-floor rooms are lit by no fewer than five huge brass chandeliers; a particularly striking one hangs over the table in the dining room. The house was in restoration for two years to the tune of $1½ million prior to its opening in 1992. The plaster walls, the loblolly pine flooring and a few of the furnishings are original. Kirk brought in the rest of the furniture, some of which had been in storage at his family's funeral home, oldest in Maryland, and had come from the area's finest estates.

"This is not a museum," Kirk stresses. "We want guests to play the pianos and read the books in the library." Tea and cookies are served in the afternoon. In the great, dark dining room, guests sit down to a breakfast of apple pancakes, belgian waffles or egg casserole, served on fine china.

Although Kirk has no plans for expansion, he has enhanced the eighteen-acre property with seven formal Victorian gardens, a pagoda and a stocked pond, which make the place good for weddings and charity events. "We're doing our best to build the business to maintain this property the way my grandmother wished," says Kirk. "It's the most expensive hobby anyone could have, but she would be pleased."

(410) 641-2112 or (800) 660-0358. www.merrysherwood.com. Five rooms and one suite with private baths; two rooms with shared bath. Mid-May to mid-October: doubles $150, suite $175. Rest of year: doubles $125, suite $150.

Waterloo Country Inn, 28822 Mount Vernon Road, Princess Anne 21853.

A bit west of the area but an early restaurant destination for visitors to Snow Hill, this is one of the more sophisticated small inns to open in the Mid-Atlantic region lately.

Therese and Erwin Kraemer from Switzerland came across the riverfront property while visiting friends in the area. They decided that very week to buy the three-story brick Georgian plantation house built in 1755 to run as a full-service inn and restaurant. She was a banker and he an electric company manager in Zurich. "We'd done a lot of entertaining and thought this would be easier," Therese said.

Many hours and more than $1 million in renovations later, they opened in 1996 with five elegant guest quarters and a 36-seat restaurant. A year later they closed the restaurant to the public, finding it "too much work" and the hours too long. "That was not what we came here for," Therese advised.

We were quite struck by two bedrooms in a main-floor wing. The Wicomico has a kingsize bed whose tapestry-look feather duvet matches the curtains, a fireplace that appears to be tiled in Delft, a handsome armoire, an antique sewing machine resting on a bureau, a sitting area and a full bath. The Manokin Room offers many of the same features. A new room, the Tangier with queensize bed and fireplace, is attached to an outside building.

The prime accommodations are upstairs in the main house. The Monie Room has a fishnet canopy king bed with fishnet quilt and pillows, two wing chairs, fireplace and a large bath. The Somerset is a two-room suite with queen bed, a fireplaced sitting room with a sofa and two chairs on beautiful hardwood floors, plus a bath with jacuzzi tub/shower and a double vanity. The third-floor harbors the Chesapeake Suite with a kingsize bed and an enormous bathroom with a double jacuzzi, separate shower and double vanity. The sitting room with sofabed and a stunning antique Swiss buffet chest looks out onto a pond.

Each room is outfitted with TV, telephone, a closet with automatic lights and exotic fresh flowers. The decorative accessories, a mix of family Swiss pieces and American acquisitions, add personality and style. The stairway landing outside the Chesapeake Suite, for instance, harbors a huge fur-lined cowbell, a washtub with artwork that Therese hand painted and an old butter urn.

The main floor contains two parlors with fireplaces and a dining room, plus a large commercial kitchen. Therese cooks dinner for house guests by reservation, $30 for four courses. Zurich geschnetzeltes, a veal dish, is her specialty. She's also known for salmon, lamb cutlets and apple pie with almonds in puff pastry.

Erwin prepares a full breakfast of the guest's choice, which Therese serves

Waterloo Country Inn complex is reflected in placid waters of pond.

elegantly on Rosenthal china in the fireplaced dining room. She also runs a little gift shop in the doctor's house outside, selling her artificial flower arrangements and hand-painted accessories.

The Kraemers, who live in another house on the property, offer an angular swimming pool, a sizable pond, bicycles and canoes for paddling along the Monie Creek across the road.

(410) 651-0883. Fax (410) 651-5592. www.waterloocountryinn.com Four rooms and two suites with private baths. May-October: doubles $125 to $175, suites $205 to $245. Rest of year, doubles $105 to $155, suites $185 to $225. Two-night minimum on weekends. No smoking.

The Garden and the Sea Inn, Route 710, Box 275, New Church, Va. 23415.

For some time a restaurant of distinction (see Dining Spots), this out-of-the-way prize near the Maryland-Virginia line is now an overnight destination as well. Sara and Tom Baker from the Shenandoah Valley inherited a going concern when they bought the property in 1994. They offer four bedrooms in the showy Victorian restaurant building and three rooms in the oldest house in New Church, which was moved to the rear of the property in 1992. A handsome brick patio and rose garden with fountain and walkways connect the two. Their latest addition is a sumptuous suite on the second floor of a house they built as family quarters in back.

Our quarters in the Vaucluse Room at the rear of the new Garden House could not have been nicer. The kingsize bed, loveseat, chair and desk were pretty in French wicker. The green wood floor was partly covered by a large oriental rug, while the pale green walls were accented by green floral print wallpaper trim along the ceiling. The floral print theme extended to the wallpaper and the cover of the Kleenex box in the bathroom, which was equipped with twin wash basins and a jacuzzi tub beneath a skylight. We shared a screened side porch outfitted in green wicker with occupants of the adjacent room, and never did see the honeymooners in the Champagne Room upstairs. The Garden House offered plenty of common space: a living room formal in swags and florals, a dining area and kitchenette with a refrigerator in which to stash your own goodies, and a front porch. Sherry, chocolate and fruit were at the ready.

Three more guest rooms of French country sophistication are upstairs above the restaurant. You might find a dressing table draped in paisley fabric, lace and ribbons, rugs patterned with flowers, painted furniture, porcelain doorknobs painted with flowers, and squares of colored glass around the windows. The Chantilly Room has a wicker queensize sleigh bed and the Giverny Room a headboard draped in lace. The updated bathrooms here include bidets. The new Merlot Room adds a whirlpool tub. Lately, the Bakers converted a private dining room on the main floor into the deluxe Chardonnay with kingsize bed, loveseat sitting area, TV, outside deck, a skylit double jacuzzi and a separate shower.

Above the family quarters in back is the Chablis Suite, a 600-square-foot space with kingsize bed, sitting area, double whirlpool tub and a private deck.

A continental-plus breakfast is served in the sunporch section of the dining room. Ours included mixed berries and fruit, choice of cereals and granola, and melt-in-the-mouth croissants and blueberry muffins. The Bakers' restaurant background still shows, but their priority is now their accommodations.

(804) 824-0672 or (800) 824-0672. Seven rooms and one suite with private baths. Mid-June to mid-October: doubles, $125 to $185 weekends, $85 to $145 midweek. Rest of year: $125 to $165 weekends, $75 to $145 midweek. Two-night minimum on weekends. No smoking.

The Mansion House, 4436 Bayside Road, Public Landing, Snow Hill 21863.

This restored 1835 planters' mansion that once was an inn reopened in 1999 as a B&B after more than two years of renovations. It's handsomely furnished and nicely situated along the waterfront in the hamlet of Public Landing, about six miles east of Snow Hill.

The property overlooks a broad expanse of Chincoteague Bay with Assateague Island about six miles in the distance. The four-part stepped house, with a two-story, center-hall addition and a pillared, two-story veranda is listed on the National Register of Historic Places.

George Hogeboom and members of his family purchased the house some years ago. He and his wife, Carol Pauley, decided to turn it into a B&B when she retired from her job in Washington, D.C. She runs the B&B weekdays, but he's on hand weekends while commuting from Washington.

The couple offer four upstairs guest rooms, each with a fireplace, queensize bed with Swedish pressure-relieving mattress and private bath. Three yield water views, including one that overlooks the bay from all five windows, including the bathroom. Guests in the fourth room feel "nestled" in the boughs of a large hemlock tree, according to Carol. They can see the bay from the south-facing window, but she doesn't count that as a water view.

Guests mingle in the great room, curl up with a book in the parlor, or relax on one of the spacious porches at the front or side.

A four-course breakfast includes fresh orange juice, a fruit dish with homemade yogurt and typically an egg dish with bread or baked goods.

(410) 632-3189. Four rooms with private baths. Doubles, $140 to $150, June-September; $110 to $120, rest of year. Children accepted. No smoking.

Atlantic Hotel, 2 North Main St., Berlin 21811.

Built in 1894 and once the pride of what was the commercial capital of the Eastern Shore, this had seen better days before ten local partners got together to

Pier stretches into Chincoteague Bay from The Mansion House.

buy the building. Each put up $150,000 for its painstaking restoration in 1988. The hotel is now best known for its restaurant (see Dining Spots), but the upstairs lodging facility is no slouch.

The sixteen guest rooms on the second and third floors are the height of colorful Victoriana. Some are quite small, while others are large enough for two beds. All have private baths with clawfoot tubs and Gilbert & Soames toiletries. Beds come with dark and heavy wood headboards. The rooms we saw possessed wild floral carpets, Victorian lamps, mirrored armoires, fringed curtains and fishnet canopies. Decorated by one investor's wife who is an art teacher at Salisbury State College, each is distinctive for its antique furniture, window treatment and artworks. Telephones and clock radios are contemporary conveniences, and TV is available on request.

On the second floor is a small lounge for guests. A table contains a bowl of fruit, a scrapbook of area attractions and a photo album tracing the hotel's two years of restoration. A stark rear porch with a not particularly appealing view offers a couple of wicker chairs and rockers. More to guests' liking are the new sidewalk cafe and the lineup of rockers on the wide front veranda facing the goings-on in the heart of the rejuvenated downtown. Ditto for the Drummer's Café on the main floor, where the prevailing sedateness is enlivened by weekend singalongs. Rates include breakfast in the Drummer's Café.

(410) 641-3589 or (800) 814-7672. Fax (410) 641-4928. Sixteen rooms with private baths. July-August: doubles, $110 to $175 weekends, $95 to $115 midweek. November-March: $75 to $120 weekends, $65 to $85 midweek. Rest of year: $85 to $135 weekends, $75 to $95 midweek. Two-night minimum weekends in summer. No smoking.

Holland House, 5 Bay St., Berlin 21811.
A turn-of-the-century physician's residence at the edge of downtown was turned into the area's first B&B in 1986 by Jim and Jan Quick, he a chef at the Dunes Manor Hotel in Ocean City and she a dental hygienist. In 1997, they reconfigured some of the guest rooms and put on a rear addition. They now offer seven guest rooms, all with private baths and five with queensize beds. They are decorated

simply with early American furnishings. Three are on the main floor, where a plaque designates the site of the former doctor's office and maternity ward.

One room favored by families has two double beds and an adjoining sitting/dressing room. In their renovations, the Quicks converted an old upstairs bedroom into an extra sitting and reading room and put a queen bedroom with private bath in the rear addition.

Breakfast is served on pink violet china in a pink dining room, decorated to match Jan's collection of pink depression glassware on the side shelves. The fare could be whatever Jim feels like preparing: perhaps blueberry pancakes, french toast or crêpes accompanied by fresh fruit and muffins.

Guests enjoy a comfortable living room, a paneled TV room, a wicker-filled front porch and a rear patio. They also have access to a picnic table.

(410) 641-1956. Seven rooms with private baths. May to mid-October: doubles, $80 to $90. Rest of year: $55 to $65. Children accepted. No smoking.

Inn on Market Square, 112 North Church St., Snow Hill 21863.

Built in 1904 by a prominent banker, this imposing neoclassic, white stucco structure is being converted into a B&B by Paul Stark, who was in hotel management for twenty years and finally decided that if he had to work 24 hours a day, "I'm going to do it for myself." He became the fourth owner of the house, opened in 1996 with three rooms and, at our visit, offered six rooms. He was doing most of the painstaking renovations and meticulous decorating himself.

The main floor is a beauty. There's a huge foyer with a sitting area and one of two antique organs in the house. On one side is a square living room with windows on three sides, where classical music emanates from an elaborate stereo system. On the other side is a dining room bearing a striking mural of a Colonial scene. This is where Paul serves a full breakfast, typically juice, fruit and an egg dish (from scrambled to florentine), or perhaps pancakes or waffles. Refreshments are offered in the afternoon.

The upstairs foyer includes a TV and sitting area. All the bedrooms have queen beds and private baths. Two come with fireplaces. After completing the second-floor rooms, Paul envisioned three more rooms and suites on the third floor.

Architectural features include original brass and leaded glass light fixtures, beveled mirrors and maple floors.

(410) 632-0881. Six rooms with private baths. Doubles, $99 to $169. Two-night minimum weekends in peak season. Children accepted. No smoking.

Dining Spots

The Atlantic Hotel, 2 North Main St., Berlin.

The local investors who renovated this "jewel of the Eastern Shore" knew what they wanted: a fine, special-occasion dining room. They searched the nation for their first chef, who rewarded their trust with culinary honors (the Atlantic quickly became one of six four-star restaurants in Maryland as determined by the Baltimore Sun).

The 60-seat dining room is pretty in a hotel kind of way. Balloon curtains around tall etched-glass windows match the walls papered in deep rose, teal and dark blue. High-back upholstered chairs are at well-spaced tables topped with white linens.

The short, changing dinner menu ranges from scallion-crusted tuna with gingered

Victorian downtown Berlin is on view from veranda of Atlantic Hotel.

bok choy, herbed mashed potatoes and bouillabaisse sauce to roasted rack of lamb with montrachet goat cheese, the last a house specialty. Salmon stuffed with spinach and oysters in puff pastry, grilled veal chop puttanesca and tournedos au poivre might be other choices. Crabmeat prevails among starters – crab stew with Smithfield ham, a crab cake on a blood orange coulis, crab phyllo plus curried quail at our latest visit. Finish with a selection from the dessert tray: perhaps Bailey's Irish Cream cheesecake, lemon-lime curd cheesecake, chocolate-raspberry ganache cake or homemade ice cream. The Wine Spectator award-winning wine list is on the expensive side.

At a Sunday jazz brunch in the dining room, we sampled shrimp Americaine and tomato concasse in an herbed crêpe as well as poached eggs Chesapeake, served on an artichoke bottom, surrounded by lump crab and topped with a delicate hollandaise sauce. A more traditional breakfast is now offered Sunday in the **Drummer's Café,** the Victorian lounge with a new sidewalk cafe that's stylish with wicker furniture and petunias in planters. Interesting, less pricey fare is offered here day and night.

(410) 641-3589 or (800) 814-7672. Entrées, $21 to $29. Dinner nightly, 6 to 9 or 10. Cafe, all-day menu from 11:30 to 9 or 10. Sunday breakfast, 8 to 2.

Snow Hill Inn, 104 East Market St., Snow Hill.

When Jim and Kathy Washington took over this restaurant in 1991, it had nowhere to go but up. And up it went, to the point where we heard nothing but raves. Until lately, Jim manned the kitchen, while Kathy presided over the front of the house. The arrival of Harry Anderson as manager and chef has relieved them of some of their duties.

The main floor includes an airy dining room in the rear and a more intimate front room colorful with stained glass and a decor of hunter green with red accents. There are also a new lounge and a shady rear patio for dining al fresco.

Dinner selections include choice of tossed or spinach salad and homemade herbed bread or muffins, served with butter wrapped in aluminum foil – who said this was sophisticated dining? But it sure is affordable. At our first visit, we ordered a carafe of the house Sebastiani chardonnay. The waitress filled our glasses to the brim as we dug into tasty salads dressed with parmesan pepper and honey dijon. Main courses were the locally ubiquitous crab imperial and crab cakes, accompanied by red potatoes and mixed squash. We had no room for dessert, a choice of carrot cake, cheesecake or key lime pie. Entrée range from chicken marsala to a dish called Snow on the Hills, twin petite filets topped with imperial crab. Prime rib is far and away the most requested choice, according to Jim, and after sampling it at our latest visit, we understood why. The thick slab was succulent and sensational. Also good was the black and blue filet mignon

The restaurant is highly popular for lunch. Among the options are crab quiche, chicken caesar salad, sandwiches, pasta and shrimp scampi, with most items priced below $5. The lounge opens at 4 with a light menu.

The establishment also has three rooms with private baths (doubles, $75 to $100).

(410) 632-2102. Entrées, $9.95 to $16.95. Lunch, Monday-Friday 11 to 2. Dinner nightly, 5:30 to 9, Sunday 4 to 8.

The Garden and the Sea Inn, Route 710, New Church, Va.

The polished restaurant here made quite a name for itself under the previous innkeepers, she in the kitchen and he out front. The roles were reversed when it was purchased in 1994 by Tom and Sara Baker. Tom, a Culinary Institute-trained chef, is in the kitchen and Sara oversees the front of the house.

The sophisticated dining room is pretty with pale peach walls, dusky pink pillars and trim, and remarkable window treatments. China in the delicate "Plantation Blossom" pattern, pink-stemmed glassware and shell-patterned silver are as refined as the service.

Dinner is prix-fixe, the price varying by the choice of entrée, and available by reservation only at limited seatings. "We consider the restaurant mostly an amenity for inn guests now," says Sara. The offerings range from a signature seafood casserole of shrimp, scallops and oysters sautéed with mushrooms and tomatoes in white wine, served over rice or spinach or sometimes pasta, to filet mignon.

When we were there, a thick and tasty corn and crab chowder plus a good salad of romaine lettuce with caesar dressing preceded the main courses. One was a superior breast of chicken dressed with pecans and dijon cream, served with slivered carrots and wild rice. The other was sliced pork loin sautéed with backfin crabmeat and served with béarnaise sauce. Good rolls with two kinds of butter (one of them herbed) and a $20 bottle of our favorite Sanford sauvignon blanc from California (rarely seen on the East Coast) accompanied. Peach melba and crème brûlée were worthy endings to a memorable meal.

(804) 824-0672 or (800) 824-0672. Prix-fixe, $28 to $37. Dinner by reservation, Sunday-Friday 7 to 8, Saturday 6:30 to 8:30. Closed Thanksgiving to mid-March.

Globe Cafe & Deli, 12 Broad St., Berlin.

Just what the visiting lunch-goer ordered is served up at the deli counter adjacent to the Duck Soup Bookstore. Large, healthful sandwiches, bagels, soups, salads and quiche are ordered at the counter and delivered to tables scattered around the main-floor corridor outside the entry to the little Globe Theater. We liked the Globe sandwich (combining havarti, tomato, avocado, sprouts, cucumber and mayo on seven-grain bread for $3.25) and the chunky chicken salad sandwich called a chico ($3.50). Those and a couple of cafe lattes sent us happily on our way. *(410) 641-0784. Open Monday-Saturday 10 to 6, Sunday 11 to 5.*

Diversions

The **Pocomoke River** is the area's principal attraction and defines its character. You can view it from two riverside parks, Byrd and Sturgis, in Snow Hill and from Milburn and Shad landings in Pocomoke River State Park. Otherwise, it's pretty much hidden from public view as it winds like a tropical jungle stream past thick forests and an occasional farm. The tidal river is the deepest (up to 45 feet) for its width in the United States.

The best way to experience the river is by canoe. The **Pocomoke River Canoe Co.** at the Route 12 drawbridge in Snow Hill rents canoes and kayaks by the hour, day or weekend. The less adventurous can settle for a tour on **Tillie the Tug,** an open tugboat that carries 22 passengers downriver from Snow Hill to Shad Landing and back. We saw lots of lily pads, duck blinds and stumps of bald cypress trees, but found the boat too low to see much – not that there was all that much to see. The odd bird and passing speedboat helped while the hour away. We got the distinct impression that life in the Snow Hill area moves just as slowly as Tillie the Tug and the Pocomoke River. Cruises are available mid-June through Labor Day and fall weekends. Adults, $6.

Birdwatching. More than 350 species have been sighted in Worcester County from the Assateague coastline across the Pocomoke Forest and down the Pocomoke River. They are detailed in two lengthy brochures furnished by the country tourism office at 105 Pearl St., Snow Hill.

Historic Walking Tours. Maps for self-guided walking tours are available both for Berlin and Snow Hill. We like the shops and harmonious row of brick Victorian storefronts along Main Street in Berlin. The houses and the mix are more illustrious in Snow Hill, where most of the sights are concentrated along Market and Federal streets. Especially noteworthy are All Hallows Episcopal Church, established in 1692 and occupying its present structure since 1756, and nearby Makemie United Presbyterian Church, whose Gothic Revival facade hides the fact it was established in 1683 and is considered the birthplace of American Presbyterianism. The town's first three inns were among the houses opened for tours on Snow Hill's annual Heritage Weekend when we were there.

Viewtrail 100. About 100 miles of contiguous scenic bicycle trails along secondary roads are marked by Viewtrail logos and outlined on a map available through the County Extension Service.

Julia A. Purnell Museum, 208 West Market St., Snow Hill.

A former Catholic church houses local memorabilia involving Julia Purnell, a seamstress and storekeeper who lived here 100 years and took up folk art after breaking her hip at age 85. Because of her age and her penchant for relating stories of Snow Hill, her son opened a museum in her honor in 1942 and people flocked to see her and her creations before her death a year later. A few of her hundreds of needlework pictures are on display, but most of the space now operated by the town is devoted to a step-in boardwalk, a Colonial cupboard, the Purnell general store, a toy shop and Mrs. Purnell's sewing room. *(410) 632-0515. Open April-October, weekdays 10 to 4, weekends 1 to 4. Adults, $1.50.*

Globe Theatre, 12 Broad St., Berlin, (410) 641-0784. The old theater in the center of Berlin has been restored and revived, encompassing a cafe, a book and gift shop and an art gallery. At the rear is a small theater of about four dozen seats, which started showing movies in 1989 "after a twenty-year intermission." It now schedules live musical entertainment of increasing distinction on many weekends. A wildfowl carving display and an exhibit of heritage boats occupied part of the old stage of this eclectic building at one of our visits. The Balcony Gallery shows interesting works of more than a dozen artists.

Shopping. Most of the area's shopping opportunities are in Berlin, and those primarily involve antiques. They have names like **Victorian Charm,** the **Brass Box,** which had quite a collection of brass candlesticks, and **The Last Straw,** with lots of wicker things. The pharmacy was converted into **Town Center Antiques,** a co-op of antique dealers. **Findings** is known for antiques, architectural details and glassware. We liked the handpainted designs on wine glasses, dishes, vases and such at **Ta-Da** among its eclectic gifts

Until lately, the best part of Snow Hill's downtown has been the little triangular park, lushly dotted with flowers, at Green and Washington streets. **The Green Street Shop** offers antiques and collectibles. **Pusey's Country Store** is a relic stocking gifts and practical stuff from boots to birdseed. A display counter featured 36 microbrews at one visit. The old Cannery beside the river houses additional antiques and craft shops and a restaurant was in the plans.

Extra-Special _____

Furnace Town, Old Furnace Road, Snow Hill.

Rarely can you see the remains of a 19th-century industrial village, least of all one that rose like a phoenix and thrived briefly on the gathering and smelting of bog iron ore. A short-lived boomtown of 300 people produced iron here in the 1830s, floating it on barges down Nassawango Creek to the Pocomoke River and the Chesapeake Bay. Almost as rapidly as it emerged it failed and became a ghost town. The Furnace Town museum shows the gathering of bog ore, archeological relics, a model of the mansion house and a loom, plus Snow Hill newspaper pages of the time. Visitors can tour an old print shop, peer into the Old Nazareth Church, inspect the crumbling Nassawango Iron Furnace, watch a craftsman making brooms in the broom house and a smithy at work in the blacksmith shop, and ascend the reproduction charging ramp for a four-story-high view of the countryside. Markers show foundations of long-lost buildings. We enjoyed the mile-long Nature Conservancy trail along a curved boardwalk through the adjacent, bayou-like swamp forest. We passed the stumps and "knees" of one of the northernmost bands of bald cypress trees, whose needles hang like grass clippings on trees below, and saw what remained of the twenty-foot-wide shipping canal. At appropriate times of the year you may see American holly and sweet gum trees, muscadet grape vines and fifteen varieties of orchids. *(410) 632-2032. Open April-October, daily 11 to 5. Adults, $3.*

Lawn of The Inn at Perry Cabin faces Fogg Cove and St. Michaels waterfront.

St. Michaels, Md.

Waterfront Living in Style

Along the languorous shores of the Miles River, not far off the Chesapeake Bay, the historic town of St. Michaels has turned waterfront living into high style. The Eastern Shore's most upscale address is a mecca for visitors and second-home owners, some of whom eventually become year-round residents.

Tucked off the beaten path down a peninsula heading toward the bay, St. Michaels has long been known by yachtsmen and by affluent retirees who settled here for watery pleasures and a slower pace not far from the big cities. But it has been really discovered in the last decade. Large new inns have emerged (four B&Bs in 1997 alone), trendy restaurants and shops have opened, and waterfront properties sell at a premium.

Today's St. Michaels, though still small and rather self-consciously quaint, is a far cry from that of a generation ago – before the Bay Bridge opened up the Eastern Shore to outlanders, before James Michener wrote *Chesapeake* in a rented house along the Miles River, and before the Chesapeake Bay Maritime Museum evolved into a major tourist attraction.

The first settlers in 1632 called its landlocked harbor "Shipping Creek," an apt reference for a place that would become a busy trading and shipbuilding center. Around the first Episcopal Church, named for St. Michael the Archangel, developed the town that took its name.

During the War of 1812, St. Michaels staged the first blackout in recorded history. British warships gathered on the Miles River to shell this coveted target. Townspeople darkened their homes and hung lanterns in the treetops to trick the invaders into aiming high. When the shelling ceased, the ploy had worked; only the now-famous Cannonball House was hit. St. Michaels had earned a place in history as the town that fooled the British.

Now the year-round population of 1,500 is easily matched by visiting yachtsmen and landlubbers on summer weekends, and by even more decoy collectors and duck hunters in fall. A few skeptics pass off St. Michaels as something of a stage set – mainly fronts and no backs, at least along Talbot Street, the only thoroughfare. They obviously have missed the side streets, the boatyards, the undulating waterfront and the surrounding countryside that reflect the old St. Michaels, one of America's earliest port towns.

Inn Spots

The Inn at Perry Cabin, 308 Watkins Lane, St. Michaels 21663.

The first American innkeeping venture of Sir Bernard Ashley, widower of Laura Ashley, and lately acquired by Orient-Express Hotels, this is like no other inn on the Mid-Atlantic coast. With an idyllic waterfront location, beautiful grounds, sumptuous accommodations and a first-class restaurant (see Dining Spots), it's luxury to the max.

Many millions were spent redoing it for a 1990 reopening, even after multi-million-dollar refurbishings by previous owners of what started as a cabin for Commodore Oliver Perry ("we have met the enemy and they are ours") following the War of 1812. Still more millions went into a wing that more than doubled the inn's size in 1991. About the only change that accompanied the Orient-Express takeover in 1999 was a new logo reflecting the skipjack, a St. Michaels icon. The Laura Ashley theme remained.

Touring the inn on two occasions and staying on a third, we were stunned by the stripes, flowers, flounces, ruffles, fancy window treatments, beautiful colors, wallpaper, borders and painted furniture. Here is decoration to the nth degree. From the dining room to the lounges to the bedrooms, all is plush, plush, plush.

Each of the 41 rooms and suites is elegantly furnished in antiques, offset by what the promotion material calls "understated, classic Laura Ashley fabrics and wallpapers." Understated? Laura Ashley – in more guises than we'd ever hoped to see – is splashed everywhere. On our tour of all the rooms, we got Laura Ashleyed out.

Admittedly, if you were staying in only

one room, you would not find it overkill. You would likely find a four-poster bed topped by a draped corona, a wicker sitting area in a corner sun porch, a huge armoire imported from England, splashy colors, and a spacious bathroom with a striped ceiling and that most British of luxuries, a heated towel rack. Plus, of course, television, telephones, coffee-table books and magazines, terrycloth robes, fresh fruit and mineral water. In Room 5, you would sleep in Sir Bernard's unique kingsize four-poster from his home in Bermuda. In Room 16, you would raise the curtains by remote control onto soaring windows yielding the inn's best water view. A couple of prized two-story suites have living rooms on one floor, bedrooms on the next and jacuzzi bathtubs. They share a balcony overlooking the river and harbor. Evening turndown produces fresh towels, a refilled ice bucket and a couple of oatmeal-raisin cookies.

Breakfast is extra. Served in the dining room, ours was an unusual chargrilled "salmon ham" with scrambled eggs and scallions and a classic English mixed grill, from grilled tomato to kidneys to blood pudding, with a poached egg in the middle.

Three plush living rooms are filled with lovely antiques and spectacular flower arrangements. French doors lead to a brick terrace, where comfortable chairs invite sitting and looking at the water. House guests may take tea here or in the living rooms – a proper British one with little sweets and scones upon which to spread lemon curd and whipped cream. The newer wing adds an hibiscus-filled conservatory, where two model planes are suspended under the skylight, and a billiards room described as "a meeting room in disguise." An indoor swimming pool that we found rather tepid and an exercise facility with sauna and steam room are the latest attractions.

There's not even a check-in counter in the understated little reception area, where one of the friendly staff spots visitors through one-way glass doors and asks them to have a seat to check in.

The guest book at the concierge's desk is filled with superlatives, most relating to special occasions. "Perfection personified," one guest summed up.

(410) 745-2200 or (800) 722-2949. Fax (410) 745-3348. Thirty-five rooms and six suites with private baths. Rates, EP. April-October: weekends, doubles $245 to $525, suites, $695; midweek, doubles $215 to $395, suites $445. Rest of year: weekends, doubles $215 to $395, suites $445; midweek, doubles $195 to $295, suites $395.

St. Michaels Harbour Inn & Marina, 101 North Harbor Road, St. Michaels 21663.

Opened in 1986 and lately refurbished from top to bottom, this contemporary structure commands a prime location at the head of the busy St. Michaels harbor.

The L-shaped, three-story structure has 46 guest accommodations, 23 of them two-room suites facing the water. Each has a living room with a sofabed, desk, television and kitchenette with a sink and refrigerator, and a bedroom with one or two queensize beds, remote-control TV and a large bathroom with double vanities and thick towels. French doors lead from each room onto a private terrace or balcony with good-looking chairs and a table overlooking the harbor. One of us thought it quite a luxury to be able to watch her show of choice on the bedroom TV while her spouse was glued to a baseball game (this was playoff time) in the living room. Smaller quarters on the third floor have rooms with one queen bed, a refrigerator and a private balcony.

Knight in armor keeps watch over occupants of Guinevere Room at The Old Brick Inn.

During the recent refurbishing, bathrooms were updated throughout. Several now have double jacuzzi tubs with separate showers. Four suites on the third floor got expanded balconies.

The pleasant **Harbour Lights** restaurant serves three meals a day (see Dining Spots). At breakfast, we enjoyed a stack of apple-pecan pancakes while watching the harbor activity.

A small outdoor pool beside the harbor is flanked by a jacuzzi and a bar for beverages and snacks. Overnight docking slips are available for 60 boats. There's a **Ship's Store,** and an aqua center offers canoes and aquabikes for adventuring around the harbor.

(410) 745-9001 or (800) 332-8994. Fax (410) 745-9150. Eight rooms and 38 suites with private baths. Memorial Day through October: doubles, $209 to $465 weekends, $169 to $375 midweek. Spring and late fall: $179 to $369 weekends, $149 to $289 midweek. Thanksgiving to March: $125 to $269 weekends, $105 to $219 midweek. Two-night minimum on weekends, May-October.

The Old Brick Inn, 401 South Talbot St., Box 987, St. Michaels 21663.

The largest B&B in St. Michaels was opened in 1998 in a couple of brick structures and a new addition.

Martha Strickland, who had been general manager of the old Pasadena and Kent Manor inns, and partner George Wilson purchased the property in 1997 and readied the first four guest rooms within two weeks in what had been the Antiques & Such store in a carriage house along Mulberry Street. Five more bedrooms and suites were fashioned in the handsome brick structure designated as the Old Inn on the St. Michaels walking tour. The building, listed on the National Register, once housed the St. Michaels Bank and lately Nina's Antiques. Five rooms occupy a third-floor addition above and outward from the old inn.

The complex includes a small pool in a New Orleans-style, brick-walled garden courtyard, where tables are set for continental breakfast in season. The main inn contains a dining room.

The first four rooms with queensize beds in the old Antiques & Such store are eye-poppers – not the least of which are two high-ceilinged theme rooms on the ground floor with full-length windows up against the street. The Guinevere Room has a wrought-iron bed with a cathedral-style swagged tulle canopy against a brick wall, a brick floor and a life-size King Arthur suit of armor at the entrance to the full bath. Across the reception area is Annie Oakley's Room with a deer head overlooking the bed which is dressed in bright flannels, a holster and a cowboy hat on the wall and a sofa for seating. "I had a good time furnishing this room and found enough stuff to fill four more," said Martha, though she varied the themes elsewhere. The second floor contains a small common sitting area in the hall, plus two carpeted bedrooms – one furnished in wicker and the other in "traditional" with a floral-quilted poster bed and two wing chairs. Each comes with a small balcony front and back.

Five rooms in the main house and addition have fireplaces. One is a two-room corner suite with an existing marble jacuzzi tub and a handpainted sink. Another is a many-angled garret room on the third floor.

(410) 745-3323. Fax (410) 745-3320. Eleven rooms and one suite with private baths. April to mid-November: doubles $175 to $250 weekends, $95 to $125 midweek. Rest of year: $125 to $175 weekends, $95 to $125 midweek. Suite, $250 weekends, $175 midweek. Two-night minimum weekends in season. Children over 12. No smoking.

Black Walnut Point Inn, Box 308, Tilghman Island 21671.

This 57-acre portion of paradise at the end of Tilghman Island is surrounded by water on three sides. A gate blocks the entrance to the dirt road leading past a wildlife preserve and landscaped lawns to the secluded complex on a point between the widewaters of the Choptank River and the Chesapeake Bay. Once here, you're rather isolated, so it's understandable that this once was the summer retreat for the Soviet embassy. The state acquired the property in 1986 and ultimately leased it to Tom and Brenda Ward to run as a B&B.

Black Walnut Point Inn complex spreads over 557 acres on point at end of Tilghman Island.

In the charming main house, part of which predates the Civil War, they offer four guest rooms with private baths, each with a queen or a double bed as well as a twin bed. The Bay Room, with double poster bed, has a beamed ceiling and windows on three sides. Overlooking the pool is the refurbished Tilghman Room with a queensize bed. We stayed in the Choptank Cottage South, which has a spacious bedroom, small sitting room and a screened porch. With waves lapping at the rocky shore outside, it's just like the summer cottage of our dreams. Other cottage units raise the total number of bedrooms to seven.

The main house has a parlor with TV, VCR, games and grand piano, a chandeliered dining room and a summery sun porch with rattan furniture. Wine glasses and an ice machine are available in a room off the kitchen, where guests may help themselves to lemonade, iced tea, soft drinks or wine from the refrigerator. In the morning, Brenda serves a continental-plus breakfast with choice of juice, fresh fruit, cereal and homemade muffins.

Outside are a jacuzzi beside a delightful freeform swimming pool, with roses blooming all around, plus a lighted tennis court, a swing, rope hammocks and seemingly endless lawns. Once you stretch out in a hammock by the bay, perhaps watching one of the resident great blue herons, you won't want to get up. Tom may be persuaded to pilot guests around the island on a champagne tour in his speedy commercial fishing boat.

The Wards are outgoing hosts and energetic innkeepers. Their very special place has a casual, laid-back feeling in keeping with the St. Michaels of yesteryear.

(410) 886-2452. Fax (410) 886-2053. www.tilghmanisland.com/blackwalnut. Four rooms and three cottage suites with private baths. Doubles, $120 to $135. Cottages, $135 to $150. Two-night minimum weekends, three nights on holiday weekends. No children. Smoking restricted. Open weekends only in January and February.

Bay Cottage, 24640 Yacht Club Road, St. Michaels 21663.

A long tree-lined drive ends at a large gray house on a tranquil point stretching a quiet harbor cove, one of the prime waterfront properties in St. Michaels. It was built in the early 1900s by a man who ran the area's largest hunting and fishing guide business and was a leading benefactor of the Chesapeake Bay Maritime Museum nearby.

Bob and Jackie Fletcher, retirees from Valley Forge, bought the property as a summer place. They spent five years renovating for a B&B before opening to a full house in October 1999. "We wanted to share this unique place with other people," said Jackie. Her husband once owned the Humphrey-Hughes House, a B&B in Cape May, N.J. "He has the experience," she said. "I just clean and cook."

The Fletchers share their home with overnight guests in five air-conditioned bedrooms, furnished in the manner of an early Chesapeake cottage – that is to say, cottagey and masculine. Bedrooms have queensize beds, private baths and original pine floors. Each is a corner room with a water view. The best views are offered from the deck of the newest accommodation, the second floor of a cottage along the shore.

On the main floor are a living room with a stone fireplace, pine-paneled walls and homey furnishings. The enclosed sun porch is the favorite inside space for its wide water views as well as for catching the breeze and the morning sun. It is here that on good days, Jackie serves a full breakfast of fresh fruits, homemade muffins and croissants, cereals, yogurt, granola and perhaps eggs flavored with herbs from

Newly renovated and expanded Hambleton Inn overlooks St. Michaels harbor.

her garden. Breakfast also can be taken beneath an antler chandelier at an antique ten-seat harvest table in the dining room, where the works of Bay artists adorn the walls.

The grounds, enhanced by flowers and herbs in season, are surrounded by 500 feet of shoreline from which guests enjoy the water birds, fish or crab from the pier, launch a kayak or just savor the scene along Long Haul Creek, where James Michener wrote *Chesapeake*. A pleasant swimming pool by the shore is a bonus.

(410) 745-9368 or (888) 558-8008. Fax (410) 745-9369. Five rooms and one cottage with private baths. Doubles, $155 to $245. Closed mid-December to mid-April..

The Hambleton Inn, 202 Cherry St., Box 1007, St. Michaels 21663.

New owners have upgraded and revitalized this established B&B in an 1860 house that occupies a prime harborfront site in the heart of St. Michaels.

Real-estate broker Steve Furman bought the B&B in 1995 and ran it himself for two weeks until a North Carolinian named Kimberly checked in with her younger sister. "I never checked out," Kimberly recalls. "Steve discovered I could cook." Soon married, they found the common space lacking and the guest quarters dark and dreary. So the Furmans closed for three months in 1997 to build a new wing for themselves. That freed up space for a handsome fireplaced dining room in which they now serve a full breakfast at a table for ten. The fare could be vegetable quiche, orange french toast or belgian waffles.

All five guest rooms, each with at least a partial water view, were refurbished and lightened up in decor. A bedroom in the original living room has a fireplace, kingsize poster bed, plump chair, sage green walls and fancy window treatments characteristic of the rest of the house. Another king-bedded room, this with a crown canopy, is pretty in mauve colors, with upholstered chairs and fine furniture on a refinished floor. Queen poster beds are in two second-floor rooms, one with windows on three sides but the smallest bath in the house and the other with a large full bath and appointed in taupe and mint green. The old Crow's Nest on the third floor, where tall guests are warned not to bump their heads on the ceiling, is pretty in pale yellow. Chocolates are at bedside in each room.

The second-floor front porch serves as the common room here. Outfitted in wicker, Kimberly says it's "the best spot in the house." It certainly offers a great view of the harbor goings-on.

The Furmans installed a new dock, landscaped the entrance and grounds, and provide bicycles for guests.

(410) 745-3350. Fax (410) 745-5709. Five rooms with private baths. April to mid-November: doubles, $195 to $275 weekends, $145 to $195 midweek. Rest of year: $135 to $195 weekends, $115 to $155 midweek. Children over 13. No smoking.

Chesapeake Wood Duck Inn, Gibsontown Road, Box 202, Tilghman Island 21671.

Stephanie Feith was feeding ducks at the back door as we arrived. "We started with two and now have twelve," she said of the flock that has made the grounds of the inn their second home since she and husband David opened in 1993. "Now all we need is a pond for the ducks and a gazebo for watching them," she said.

The pond and the gazebo were in the planning stage for the long back yard leading to Dogwood Harbor, home of the last remaining working skipjack fleet in the country. You get the idea that they will soon be reality, given the speed with which the couple turned the 1890 boarding house and sometime bordello into an elegant seven-room B&B. Corporate dropouts from Atlanta, the Feiths scoured the country for the perfect B&B site and a simpler lifestyle. They found it on Tilghman Island.

Now David is a part-time working waterman, picking up substantial pin money to support the couple's penchant for dining out several nights a week. Cooking gourmet breakfasts, he goes all-out – arising at 5 a.m. to start prepping and baking fresh muffins from scratch, and you can taste the difference.

We started with a dish of cantaloupe, blueberries and kiwi and a glass of orange juice before digging in to some melt-in-your-mouth lemon-poppyseed muffins. The best was yet to come: an original that Dave calls a Tilghman omelet puff. Filled with cheddar and mozzarella cheeses, capers, tarragon and sundried tomatoes, it's wrapped in smoked ham and puff-pastry dough, then baked and topped with key lime-mustard sauce and raspberry puree, and served with fresh asparagus spears. Unforgettable! Sherried crab quiche, a crab pie that could well be a luncheon dish, and banana-stuffed french toast topped with cinnamon and roasted pecans are other specialties. Lately, Dave has added such side dishes as Spanish mackerel and crostini wrapped in bacon with caramelized brown sugar and mild chile pepper. Refreshments later in the day include 24-hour coffee and tea service, wine, soft drinks and sherry.

Stephanie has furnished the house in what she calls a "traditional/eclectic" style that's most comfortable except, perhaps, for the small antique double beds that she was gradually replacing with queensize beds. Each air-conditioned bedroom comes with private bath, assorted comforters, good artworks, savvy window treatments and antique furnishings. There are unexpected touches like a foxhunter's hat on the dresser in the Rutledge Room, which is handsome in deep blues and reds and paisleys, and a stunning Victorian stained-glass piece hanging in the window of the Magnolia Room, which is light and airy in shades of peach and green.

Lately, the Feiths have added a large suite with its own entrance and deck overlooking the harbor. French doors open into a living room with a sofabed and overstuffed chair, remote-control TV, CD player and stereo. Another set of french doors leads to a bedroom with queensize four-poster bed and a full bath with double vanity.

Porches of Kemp Building yield views of main house and bay at Wades Point Inn.

Interesting artworks – including a display of oyster plates – grace the walls of the kitchen, living room, dining room and sun room. Over the dining table is an antique chandelier that has followed the Feiths around from its original home in Charleston. There's plenty of space to spread out on the screened porch, the rear patio and soon, no doubt, in the gazebo beside the pond-to-be. *(410) 886-2070 or (800) 956-2070. Fax (410) 886-2070. Six rooms and one suite with private baths. Doubles, $135 to $165. Suite, $175 to $215. Children over 14. No smoking.*

Wades Point Inn on the Bay, Wades Point Road, Box 7, St. Michaels 21663. Very Southern looking, this imposing white brick plantation-style home at the end of a long lane is surrounded by unusually attractive grounds and backs up to the Chesapeake Bay about five miles west of St. Michaels on the way to Tilghman Island. The original house was built in 1819 by Baltimore shipwright Thomas Kemp. A summer wing was added in 1890 and it has operated as a guest house in the old Bay tradition ever since.

"We've been updating but want it to stay comfy and homey," said innkeeper Betsy Feiler, who's owned the inn with husband John since 1984. Their prime accommodations are in the newer Mildred T. Kemp Building, which has twelve hotel-style rooms with modern baths, some with kitchenette facilities to encourage families and all but two with waterfront balconies that you may never want to leave. Each is furnished traditionally and individually with down comforters, plush carpeting and interesting window treatments, with Bibles on the night stands, and TVs noticeably missing.

The main house has fourteen guest rooms, two with private baths and several more with wash basin in the rooms. Most rooms here are interestingly if sparely furnished, and the annex that Betsy once candidly described as a "sophisticated Girl Scout house" is now called "a country farmhouse." The summer wing is what you'd expect to find around the Tidewater area: rooms with high ceilings (and windows) open off the long corridor, the entrance to each containing a screen door inside the regular door, which guests tend to leave open for cross-ventilation on summer nights.

Guests enter a reception area in the original summer kitchen. The main parlor is furnished with two sofas, a piano, a tapestry over the fireplace and more books than a Southern gentleman could possibly have read. These rooms give little inkling of the astonishing Bay Room in back – a huge sun room that's a veritable sea of white wicker furniture with columns and arches, a fireplace, bleached floors topped with colorful patterned rugs and windows on all sides onto the water. Here is where guests linger over a continental breakfast of fruit salad, juice, cereal, muffins and french rolls or relax with a book and watch the boats go by. If you can stir yourself from the Bay Room or one of the hammocks and chairs spread out on the shady grounds beside the water, saunter along the special nature trail that curves along the shoreline and traverses the interior of the property. Be on the lookout for deer, rabbits, red foxes, terrapins, bald eagles, great blue herons, osprey and more. The prolific flower gardens in front of the Kemp House are worth a close look, too.

(410) 745-2500 or (888) 923-3466. Fourteen rooms with private baths and twelve rooms with shared baths. Doubles, $130 to $165 with private bath, $110 to $125 with shared bath, $175 to $230 in Kemp Building. Suite, $250. Two-night minimum weekends and holidays. Children welcome. No smoking. Closed January and February.

The Lazyjack Inn on Dogwood Harbor, 5907 Tilghman Island Road, Tilghman Island 21671.

Sailing enthusiasts Mike and Carol Richards from Reston, Va., converted this 160-year-old house backing up to Dogwood Harbor into a charming B&B. The outbuildings serve as a base for their charter boat business.

All four accommodations come with modern baths, interesting decorative touches and heirloom quilts. A Victorian settee and a chair with ottoman face the water in the spacious, high-ceilinged Nellie Byrd Suite, which offers a kingsize brass bed, a built-in vanity in the bureau, a double jacuzzi tub and a shower with three sides of glass. Like the Nellie Byrd, the Garden Suite contains a jacuzzi tub and one of the inn's three in-room fireplaces. A good water view is afforded from the East Room, with exposed beam ceiling, heart of pine floors and Waterfall series furniture bearing shell hardware.

Mike, whose background is in residential construction, enclosed the big side porch to serve as a breakfast room. That and the rear deck with water view are the sites for the morning repast, which included a fresh fruit cup in a phyllo flower and baked stuffed french toast with cottage cheese and apricot glaze at our visit. Folded crab omelets, banana rum cake and sticky buns are other specialties. Sherry and chocolates are put out when the beds are turned down.

Mike can take up to sixteen passengers daily onto the Chesapeake Bay on the Lady Patty, his 45-foot classic ketch built in 1935. Two-hour, half-day and full-day sails can be arranged.

(410) 886-2215 or (800) 690-5080. Fax (410) 886-2635. www.lazyjackinn.com. Two rooms and two suites with private baths. Doubles, $155 to $175 weekends, $140 to $160 midweek. Suites, $210 to $230 weekends, $195 to $210 midweek. Two-night minimum at peak periods. Children over 12. No smoking.

Old Pasadena Inn has been grandly refurbished into The Oaks.

The Oaks, Route 329 at Acorn Lane, Box 187, Royal Oak 21662.

The former Pasadena Inn gave way in 1997 to this handsome yellow and green structure on seventeen waterfront acres along Oak Creek southeast of town. Paul Milne and Candace Chiaruttini, who own the acclaimed 208 Talbot restaurant in St. Michaels, gutted the manor house erected in 1748 as a private residence but retained the antebellum facade. They reconfigured the interior layout and reduced the number of rooms to produce fifteen guest rooms with king or queen beds opening off a maze of hallways. Eleven have jacuzzi tubs, eight have gas fireplaces and some contain TVs. Twelve yield water views and all are furnished, in Candace's words, with "antiques that came with the place."

The premier accommodation is a large waterfront room on the third floor with a king bed, a double jacuzzi at the edge of the room, a two-person shower in the bathroom and a private balcony overlooking the water. A floral comforter, floral carpeting and interesting window treatments add color here and throughout most guest rooms.

The pastry chef for 208 Talbot provides the baked goods for a continental-plus breakfast that includes cereals, breads, quiches and, when we were there, delectable blueberry muffins. It's served in a large dining room with the original center fireplace in the middle. The vast main floor holds banquet space, a common room with TV in the original section and a screened side porch furnished in wicker and overlooking a watery scene. More seating is on decks all around overlooking grounds where shuffleboard, horseshoes, badminton and such facilities are available. Canoes and bicycles are complimentary for guests. There's a swimming pool, and a putting green was added in 2000. Eight basic rooms are available in an annex ($65 to $85). More guest rooms were envisioned in other outbuildings.

(410) 745-5053. Fifteen rooms with private baths. Doubles, $150 to $225 weekends, $100 to $190 midweek. Two-night minimum weekends.

The Inn at Christmas Farm, 8873 Tilghman Island Road, Wittman 21676.

For a change of pace, stay overnight in a church. Not any church, mind you, but a little dollhouse of a chapel that David and Beatrice Lee moved to the side of their circa-1800 farmhouse about seven miles southwest of St. Michaels. The 1893 Methodist church belonged to their housekeeper's congregation down the road, but was available when it merged with another.

"We moved it, rebuilt it and renovated it to the Victorian period," said David. They converted the interior into two bright and airy, high-ceilinged suites. Each has a wet bar and refrigerator, a kingsize black iron canopy bed topped with frilly coverings, and double sinks in the bathrooms. The front Bell Tower Suite, entered through the double doors of the belfry, enjoys a brick patio running the width of the building. At the other end of the structure is the Gabriel Suite, where a hand-carved angel with trumpet presides over pieces from the owners' collection of farm furniture. Its french doors open onto a large, raised deck. Relax on the wrought-iron furniture on patio or deck, watch the goats, hear the farm sounds and look across the fields to the spring-fed farm pond with a dock for swimming and sunning and the distant waters of Cummings Creek. Here's contentment.

There's more. The Lees offer a suite with a kingsize bed, sitting room and a wood stove on the first floor of their main house, plus a new kingsize Riverview Suite on the second floor with a two-person jacuzzi. Another suite called Christmas Cottage was transformed from a little waterman's house they moved to the property and attached to the side of their house. It comes with a private entrance, a sitting room with a two-person jacuzzi at the far end and, upstairs, a kingsize bedroom and bathroom. The private courtyard here looks onto a cove where peacocks seem to spend a lot of time.

The Lees serve a full breakfast, featuring perhaps poached pears and crab quiche or blueberry pancakes.

(410) 745-5312 or (800) 987-8436. Fax (410) 745-5618. Five suites with private baths. Weekends, $155 to $175. Midweek, $135. Two-night minimum weekends. Children over 13. No smoking.

Victoriana Inn, 205 Cherry St., Box 449, St. Michaels 21663.

A former private residence built in 1883 and facing the harbor, this elegant gem was opened as a B&B in 1988 by a perfectionist who was into Victoriana. She sold it in 1997 to a bachelor who let the place slide. To the rescue in 2000 came Charles and Maria McDonald of Alexandria, Va., who imparted much-needed T.L.C., repainted and refurbished, added a suite and finished an attractive water-view deck. They converted a garage into family quarters so they could be on the scene full-time.

The McDonalds offer a mix of period and traditional furniture in six guest rooms, all with private baths – lack of which had been a shortcoming in the past. The new junior suite off one side of the main floor has a queensize pencil-post bed, sitting area with loveseat, full bath and the only in-room TV. Sliding glass doors open onto a cedar deck facing the harbor.

In the center of the main floor are a fireplaced parlor and a dining room. On the other side of the same floor are two guest rooms, each with a fireplace and one with a canopy bed and water view. Two larger rooms upstairs also face the water.

A small sunroom overlooking the lawn and waterfront contains a TV/VCR. A front porch looks onto lovely flower gardens, one of the biggest magnolia trees we ever saw, a little fish pond and, of course, the boats in the harbor. Lounge chairs are scattered about, and the setting is quite idyllic.

Breakfast is sumptuous: fresh fruit and juice, cereals and perhaps pancakes, french toast or eggs benedict.

(410) 745-3368 or (888) 316-1282. Five rooms and one suite with private baths. Mid-April through October: doubles, $159 to $209; suite, $275. Rest of year: doubles, $139 to $189; suite, $249. Two-night minimum weekends. Children over 13. No smoking.

The Parsonage Inn, 210 North Talbot St., St. Michaels 21663.

Its entry tower topped by a steeple and flanked by two-story octagonal sections with paneled chimneys, this is one of the more architecturally striking structures along the main street. Check the unusual brick facade with its many inlay patterns and the Victorian gingerbread trim over the porches.

The house, built in 1883, was extensively renovated from a Methodist church parsonage in 1985. Five bedrooms were fashioned from the parsonage and three with separate entrances were added motel-style at the rear. All have private baths with Victorian pedestal wash basins and brass fixtures. Seven have king or queensize beds, plush carpeting and thick towels, Queen Anne-style furniture and Laura Ashley linens and accessories. Three possess working fireplaces. The two most appealing open onto an upstairs deck and two have television. A family suite contains a room with two double beds, a sitting room with TV and a bunk room with two twins.

Oriental rugs and fine Victorian furniture enhance the cozy fireplaced parlor and a large formal dining room, where a full breakfast is served by a resident manager for owner Willard Workman. The fare at our latest visit was waffles with sausage and peach crisp for dessert one day, and tomato strata and apple cake the next. Outdoors is a nicely landscaped patio with wicker furniture.

(410) 745-5519 or (800) 394-5519. Seven rooms and one suite with private baths. April-November: doubles, $145 to $185 weekends, $120 to $160 midweek. Rest of year: doubles, $125 to $175 weekends, $100 to $150 midweek. Two-night minimum weekends in season. No smoking.

Dining Spots

208 Talbot, 208 North Talbot St., St. Michaels.

Since its opening in 1990 in a mid-19th-century house, this has become the best-regarded restaurant in an area of many. A delightful lounge with a marble bar leads into a serene main dining room and three smaller rooms, one a garden room with floral paintings on the white brick walls. Decor is crisp in teal green and white, and the staff is informed and suave.

Culinary Institute-trained chef Paul Milne was featured on the public television series, Great Chefs of the East. He and partner Candace Chiaruttini present here what they call casual gourmet dining. Others call it quite sophisticated. Dinner is prix-fixe four courses on Saturdays and à la carte the rest of the week. Among dinner entrées might be pan-seared rockfish with wild mushrooms, peppered tuna with burgundy-butter sauce, grilled ribeye steak with homemade worcestershire sauce and a signature New Zealand rack of lamb with roasted garlic and rosemary sauce.

Start with a napoleon of smoked salmon with crispy wontons and wasabi sauce, fried Ipswich clams with oven-dried tomatoes and a brandy-tarragon mayonnaise or baked oysters with prosciutto, pistachio nuts and champagne cream sauce.

Brick walls and sconces create sohisticated setting for dining at 208 Talbot.

Candace makes the delectable desserts, perhaps lemon tart, apple spice cake with warm caramel sauce, tirami su and assorted ice creams. *(410) 745-3838. Entrées, $23 to $28. Prix-fixe Saturday, $48. Dinner, Wednesday-Sunday 5 to 9 or 10.*

Bistro St. Michaels, 403 South Talbot St., St. Michaels.

This urbane new bistro was opened by chef David Stein and his parents from Washington, D.C. They converted a 125-year-old clapboard house into an intimate, 75-seat restaurant. The ambiance is authentic French bistro on the main floor with a zinc bar, banquettes and marble-top tables, with a semi-enclosed porch alongside. Upstairs is a more formal dining room with close-together white-clothed tables. Prized century-old French posters and artworks enhance the walls.

David and a couple of assistants do all the cooking, favoring local farmers and fishermen for indigenous products. The dinner menu is short but sweet. At our autumn visit it started with a white bean and ham soup, Wellfleet oysters with a shallot-sherry vinaigrette and an exotic salad of frisée, duck confit, goat cheese and beets with crispy onion rings and roasted garlic vinaigrette.

Main courses included pan-fried salmon with mustard-tarragon vinaigrette, sautéed jumbo shrimp with lobster butter sauce over spinach linguini, braised lamb shank with an apricot-mustard glaze, and grilled ribeye steak with crushed garlic potatoes, sautéed mushrooms and oven-dried tomatoes. Desserts were a classic crème brûlée, chocolate mousse with strawberries and streusel-topped apple pie with whipped cream and vanilla sauce.

(410) 745-9111. Entrées, $17 to $23. Lunch, 11:30 to 2 or 2:30. Dinner from 5:30. Closed Wednesday and month of February.

The Inn at Perry Cabin, Watkins Lane, St. Michaels.

The dining room setting is as perfect as the rest of the first Ashley House venture in the United States. And executive chef Mark Salter's food measures up, although at prices that mere mortals find staggering.

The peak-ceilinged dining room is a panoply of rose, green and white chintz. Tables, skirted to the floor and dressed to the hilt, are flanked by chairs upholstered in a burgundy fabric. Expansive windows and french doors look out onto a terrace and treed lawns leading to Fogg Cove.

The complex, four-course dinner menu is prix-fixe, with a tasting menu available for the entire table at $125 each. Having over-indulged at afternoon tea, we asked if it were possible to eat lighter and were informed that we could order from the prix-fixe menu and be charged à la carte.

Three kinds of complimentary canapés – one with boursin cheese and another of salmon – whetted the tastebuds for treats to come. So did wonderful cheese-herb and sourdough rolls. Proper fish service was provided for our main courses, fillet of grouper with a pineapple and mint quinoa cake, mango chutney and pappadams for one, John Dory with wild rice, shiitake mushrooms and bok choy for the other. Options ranged from tuna with seared foie gras and port/red wine jus to the chef's signature tarragon-glazed lamb shank with sundried tomato sauce. Presentation was in the architectural style, beautiful and small portions. An obscure (and perfect) Oregon pinot gris for $28 accompanied. A selection of four sorbets (mango, pineapple, apricot and espresso, topped with chocolate curls in a silver bowl) was a refreshing ending to a memorable meal.

(410) 745-2200. Prix-fixe, $69.50. Lunch daily, 12:30 to 2:30. Dinner nightly, 6 to 10, jackets preferred.

Town Dock Restaurant, 125 Mulberry St., St. Michaels.
The waterfront setting at this huge establishment is one of the town's best. The food was elevated by chef-owner Michael Rork, who had made a name as executive chef at Baltimore's fancy Harbor Court Hotel. With his wife and three children, he sought a more rural location in which to run his own business. Although reviews were mixed, most locals felt he had succeeded in converting a touristy, 400-seat restaurant into his goal of "an upscale but casual dining destination."

The short daily specials menu is where the action is. Typical are grilled salmon topped with roasted leeks and peppers, soft-shell crabs with a tomato-herb cream sauce, grilled shrimp served over saffron orzo, and grilled duck breast with dried cherries and fresh currants. These are standouts on a seafood-oriented menu ranging from fried shrimp and oysters to lump crab cakes and arctic char. Brazilian lobster tail stuffed with crab imperial.

We were impressed with the change at a summer lunch, served outside on the waterfront terrace. Cups of crab bisque and saffron bouillabaisse preceded the main events, crab monterey and a fried oyster sandwich with brabant potatoes and homemade coleslaw. All proved exceptional, brimming with assertive tastes. Two big chocolate-covered strawberries came with the bill, making dessert redundant.

Still in the planning stage was an elegant upstairs dining room with an open grill kitchen. That would be the showcase for the grilled specialties of Michael's contemporary regional cuisine. Meanwhile, there's **Jon and Mike's on the Miles,** a piano-bar lounge where Michael teams with Jon Mason to feature light fare, live entertainment and cigars for the "over 30" crowd Thursday-Saturday from 5.

(410) 745-5577 or (800) 884-0103. Entrées, $15.95 to $24.95. Lunch daily, 11 to 4. Dinner, 4 to 10. Closed Monday and Tuesday in winter.

Harbour Lights, 101 North Harbor Road, St. Michaels.

The redecorated restaurant at the St. Michaels Harbour Inn and Marina was renamed and the food upgraded. The contemporary, nicely angled dining room here is decked out in cream tablecloths and blond wood chairs. Part is beneath billowing fabric and part beneath a pressed tin ceiling, but both areas command a great view across the harbor.

The chef was earning accolades for such entrées as cashew-crusted red snapper topped with a roasted corn salsa, shrimp and calamari scampi over angel-hair pasta, chicken imperial, and grilled bison steak topped with a worcestershire-glazed portobello mushroom. Grilled quail and a garlicky cheese and artichoke crab dip with focaccia were favorite starters. Desserts included strawberry tartlets with crème anglaise and bourbon pecan pie.

A good wine list offers many by the glass as well as pre-selected small samplings called flights, or you can create your own flights. Also available are specialty martinis, microbrews and espresso.

(410) 745-5102. Entrées, $21.95 to $29.95. Lunch daily, 11 to 5. Dinner 5 to 9 or 10. Closed Monday and Tuesday in winter.

Diversions

Chesapeake Bay Maritime Museum, Mill Street, Navy Point.

Built on mounds of crushed oyster shells, this growing museum founded in 1965 is the town's major tourist attraction. Its focal point is the 1879 Hooper Strait Lighthouse, one of only three cottage-type lighthouses remaining on the bay. You learn what a lightkeeper's life was like and pass some interesting exhibits of fog signals, lamps and lenses as you climb to the top level for a bird's-eye view of the St. Michaels harbor. The Waterfowling Building contains an extensive collection of decoys and guns. The museum has the largest floating fleet of historic Chesapeake Bay boats in existence, including a skipjack, log canoe, oyster boat and crab dredger. They're maintained in a traditional working boat yard, where you get to see craftsmen at work and view a small display of primitive boat-building tools. Other attractions include the Small Boat Shed, a bell tower, a Victorian bandstand where concerts are staged in summer and a good museum shop.

(410) 745-2916. Open daily, 9 to 7 in summer, to 5 in spring and fall, to 4 in winter. Adults, $7.50.

St. Michaels Walking Tour. A self-guided walking tour with a map is provided by the St. Mary's Square Museum. It covers the meandering waterfront, including the footbridge from Cherry Street to Navy Point (one wishes there were more footbridges to get from point to point), the Talbot Street business section and St. Mary's Square, an unusual town green laid out away from the main street and apt to be missed unless you seek it out. The map identifies 31 historic houses (none open to the public), churches and sites. We found equally interesting things along the way.

The St. Mary's Square Museum, On the Green, (410) 745-9561. One of the town's oldest Colonial houses was moved to this site, restored and furnished. It is joined to the 1860 Teetotum Building, so named because it resembles an old-fashioned top. The display areas of local memorabilia and history are open weekends and holidays from 10 to 4, May-October. Donation.

Shopping. Shopping is a big draw along narrow Talbot Street in St. Michaels. **Chesapeake Trading Company,** a bookstore and gift shop, is where you stop for espresso or great cold drinks as you browse among the wonderful collection of hats, apparel, jewelry, cards, music and paperbacks. Owner Linda Boatner stocks all the right things and displays them right. Those of us who like food spicy enough to bring tears to the eyes are in seventh heaven at **Flamingo Flats.** This shop must have every hot, spicy sauce or relish ever bottled, as well as numerous mustards and oils – more than 2,600, including many from the Caribbean. Now expanded into the former Celebrate Maryland space, it has a tasting bar, gifts and cards, cookbooks and entertainment. On Saturdays in season the staff barbecue out front on grills, and offer treats like smoked gouda with a cabernet, rosemary and thyme sauce. **Bags Aloft** stocks all kinds of bags from laundry to lunch. **Sailor of St. Michaels** offers sportswear and accessories of interest to the legions of sailing types that frequent this area. **Keepers-Orvis** appeals to the fly fisherman and carries clothing, equipment and decoys. Resort-type clothes are found at **Shaw Bay Classics, Chesapeake Bay Outfitters** and **Bleachers** (which also has some fun stuffed things like flamingos), while the **Broken Rudder** carries nice sportswear with a Chesapeake accent. A resident decoy carver works at **The Calico Gallery,** which has a large selection of local art posters. **The Mind's Eye Gallery** stocks unusual American crafts (check out the painted stools) and at the **Blue Swan,** we liked the nautical Christmas ornaments. **Canton Row Antiques** bills itself as an upscale antique mall, or at least a mews, with eighteen dealers. **The Cultural Art Gallery** has lovely things, including stained glass. We also liked the mobiles of stained glass at **Artiste Locale,** a showplace of local art. Among the newcomers is **Audrey Julian & Co.,** an offshoot of her venerable Dilworthtown Country Store in Chester County, Pa. It's full of the wonderful gifts, home furnishings and decorative accessories for which she is known. A new hot spot is the **Blue Crab Coffee Co.,** with a wide selection of coffees, teas, baked goods and desserts.

Extra-Special _____

Patriot Cruise, Navy Point, St. Michaels.
Since most of its meandering shoreline is very private and far from view, the best way to see and savor this part of the Eastern Shore is by boat. David Etzel provides a leisurely hour-long cruise up the Miles River on a two-deck boat carrying 180 passengers. He advised beforehand that he points out "birds, houses, duck blinds, whatever I see." We saw the Mystic Clipper in the distance, various kinds of bulkheading to prevent shore erosion, several osprey nests on channel markers, the ruins of St. John's Chapel, and some mighty impressive plantations and contemporary homes. We learned that James Michener wrote *Chesapeake* in a rented house along the river. Our only regret was that the boat didn't go closer to the sights the guide or the taped narration were pointing out on the eleven-mile round trip. (Smaller vessels like the workboat of **St. Michaels Lady Cruises,** 305 Mulberry St., can get closer and the waterman-captain tailors some excursions to special interests.)
(410) 745-3100. Cruises April-October, daily at 11, 12:30, 2:30 and 4 (weather permitting, minimum fifteen persons). Adults, $9.50.

Stately homes along Chestertown's Water Street back up to Chester River.

Chestertown, Md.

A Town that Has It All

The impression one gets upon entering Chestertown over the U.S. Route 213 bridge is unforgettable. Across the wide Chester River are grand brick mansions along the shore. In the center of town are great churches, squares and parks with monuments, the county courthouse, a couple of inns and suave stores. The streets in the nicely symmetrical downtown grid are lined with historic homes and townhouses, many dating to the 18th century.

Here's the perfect small town, you think – close to the water, with ties to the past, obviously prosperous, a manageable size, good quality of life. The first impression is not erroneous. Subsequent forays in and around the Eastern Shore town of 4,000 and conversations with its residents confirm that this is one great place to live, as well as to visit.

Local boosters are proud that Chestertown was rated in a national survey as the tenth favorite historic place in America. The lure is more than the fact that this small town claims the second largest district of restored 18th-century homes in Maryland, however.

Life is slower here, Chestertown lying well off the beaten path. As the county seat of Kent County, Maryland's smallest, it exudes an air of self-sufficiency and a sense of place that evades towns twice its size. The park fountain works, the clock tower is illuminated at night, tiny white lights twinkle in a downtown alleyway. Galleries, boutiques and shops, all owner-operated, purvey wares normally associated with metropolitan areas. Creative chefs have settled here to instill their culinary marks.

The good life is enhanced by the cultural offerings of Washington College, the nation's tenth oldest and the only one that George Washington allowed to use his name (he served as a trustee and received an honorary degree).

Not far away are attractions as diverse as the oldest Episcopal church in Maryland, the best bathing beach on the Chesapeake Bay at Betterton, a hokey but bustling auction house and Rock Hall, a once-sleepy fishing community that's become a happening place lately.

Who would challenge the claim that here is a small town that has it all?

Inn Spots

Brampton, 25227 Chestertown Road (Route 20), Chestertown 21620.

The thoughtful comments in the guest books in each room testify glowingly that innkeepers Michael and Danielle Hanscom do things right. Theirs is one of the more comfortable and elegant B&Bs in which we've stayed.

On 35 acres of plantation-like property about a mile out High Street (Route 20) south of town, the imposing three-story brick Italianate Greek Revival commands a hilltop set back from the road. Two gliders swing toward each other and an array of wicker chairs from either end of the pillared front veranda.

Inside the 1860 house, listed on the National Register, are a majestic living room with twelve-foot ceilings, high bookshelves and gray leather couches facing each other across an oriental rug next to the fireplace; a brick and paneled guest parlor and TV room (TVs also are available in guest rooms); a fireplaced dining room with peach draperies matching the wallpaper and four tables beneath a crystal chandelier, and solid walnut baseboards and doors that never suffered the humiliation of paint. What restoration needed to be done was ably handled during the six months prior to their 1987 opening by Mike, who had restored Victorian homes in San Francisco.

Danielle, a former flight attendant with Swissair, oversaw the decorating. Lately she has refurnished the living room with various Sheraton armchairs and an upholstered settee, all specially commissioned and then handcarved by a noted local cabinetmaker. There's also an exquisite 1860 Swiss secretary made for her great-great grandparents.

The ten air-conditioned guest rooms and suites are classics. Each has a private bath and a queen or twin beds that can be put together as a king, and eight have fireplaces or Franklin stoves. They are tastefully decorated with period and reproduction antiques, many of them from Switzerland. Rooms are perfect down to the smallest details: plump pillows, duvet comforters, thick towels, night lights in the bathrooms, and brass shoe horns on the closet doors. The bowl on our dresser in the Blue Room matched the blue and white wallpaper; a bird and butterfly from the stunning wallpaper pattern in the bathroom had been painstakingly cut out and pasted on the

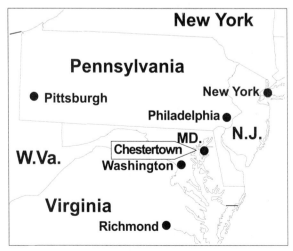

vanity. Most of the paintings in the house were done by Danielle's grandfather, an artist in Switzerland.

All rooms, with the exception of the Mezzanine Suite that is cozier, are unusually airy and spacious. Even the two guest rooms on the third floor are high ceilinged and big for their location, each measuring twenty by twenty feet. Choice

Italianate Greek Revival house is now Brampton, an elegant B&B.

new accommodations include the Fairy Hill Suite with a ground-floor sitting room and an upstairs bedroom notable for a Swiss cherry armoire and an antique chimney cupboard, and the renovated 19th-century Smoke House, now a high-ceilinged, beamed bedroom with couch, fireplace and an 1860 walnut armoire.

The premier lodgings were fashioned in 1995 from an old horse barn out back. Now known as the Garden Cottage, it has two extra-large rooms, each with sitting area, fireplace, TV, private patio and double whirlpool tub with separate shower. Oriental rugs cover the shiny, random-width cherry floors. The East Room, furnished in Victorian style, has a king bed, while the West Room has a queen canopy bed and Colonial décor.

The Hanscoms, who live with their young daughters in an outbuilding on the property, offer afternoon refreshments and wine or sherry in the evening. Breakfast in their beautiful dining room starts with orange juice, fresh fruit and sticky buns. Our entrée was a delicate puffed pancake with a fresh plum sauce. Others could be french toast, blueberry pancakes, waffles or sausage, and cheese and green pepper quiche.

(410) 778-1860. Fax (410) 778-1805. www.bramptoninn.com. Eight rooms and two suites with private baths. Doubles, $125 to $195. Suites, $135 to $165. Two-night minimum on weekends. No smoking.

The Imperial Hotel, 208 High St., Chestertown 21620.

Built as a hotel in 1903, the Imperial had been converted to apartments and shops before it was grandly restored into a small, urbane lodging establishment and restaurant in the mid-1980s.

Jan Macdonald, an Englishwoman, and her husband, Dick O'Neill, retired from the corporate world in New Canaan, Conn., and acquired the hotel in 1999. They reopened the restaurant, renovated the kitchen and redecorated the dining rooms.

The hotel's eleven guest rooms on the second and third floors are decorated to the Victorian hilt with original art and period furnishings. All have private baths with heated towel racks and Gilchrist & Soames toiletries. Five have kingsize beds, five have twins and one has a queen. Armoires conceal TV sets and antique potty cupboards hide the telephones. Bold wallpapers, wild borders, ornate lamps, floral carpeting, coordinated fabrics, lace curtains and heavy draperies are the rule. Rooms vary widely in size. Some are rather small, but we found the third-floor suite big enough for a cocktail party, what with a living room that is total Victoriana, a bedroom with kingsize bed, a mini-kitchen and a porch the size of a volleyball court across the front of the hotel.

The best room in the house may be No. 206 midweek, when rates are discounted. It's located in the front corner across from the guest parlor and beside the common second-floor porch, neither of which gets much use during the week. Two more accommodations are in the rear carriage house. A favorite is the spacious, country-style suite, a welcome break from the pervading high Victorian decor and good for families. It has a beamed cathedral ceiling, a skylit bathroom and a full kitchen.

Besides the award-winning restaurant (see Dining Spots), the Imperial has a handsome little cocktail lounge with a fireplace. Lunch, lounging and, occasionally, musical entertainment are offered on the landscaped rear courtyard.

A complimentary continental breakfast of juice and large, flaky croissants and other pastries is served in the dining room.

(410) 778-5000 or (800) 295-0014. Fax (410) 778-9662. Eleven rooms and two suites with private baths. Doubles, $100 to $135 weekends, $95 midweek. Suites, $200 weekends, $150 midweek.

Great Oak Manor, 10568 Cliff Road, Chestertown 21620.
Majestic. How better to describe this red-brick Georgian manor house grandly situated on twelve acres overlooking the Chesapeake Bay? Written descriptions, even photos, fail to convey fully the understated elegance and the alluring appeal of this winning B&B, as transformed by energetic owners Don and Dianne Cantor from California.

"What really attracted us was the large common rooms," said Don. "Our guests don't feel like they're intruding on the owners' quarters." The 25-room mansion, built in 1938 by an heir to the W.R. Grace shipping fortune, has regal public rooms, eleven guest rooms and plenty of space left over for the Cantor family at one end.

Guests enter a great hall worthy of the name, with a graceful spiral staircase on one side. Intricate carvings over the doorways announce each room's use (a rising sun over the entrance, a crab over the dining rooms). On the left are a formal living room, a rich-looking library with shelves of books, hunting prints and a huge oriental rug, and a side porch full of wicker and wisteria stenciling. On the right are the dining room and the Gun Room, dark and masculine with guns behind leaded glass doors, plush leather sofas and chairs, a TV/VCR and a small help-yourself bar hidden in a space beneath the spiral staircase. One of Dianne's stained-glass creations, a colorful parrot, stands sentry in a window.

The bedrooms vary in size and décor, but all are plush in an understated way. Each comes with full tiled bath, kingsize bed, a sitting area with comfortable chairs, and bottles of Perrier water. Five have working fireplaces and seven yield bay views. An artist hand-painted whimsical touches here and there: a squirrel on

Handsome brick Georgian house known as Great Oak Manor backs up to Chesapeake Bay.

a desk in one room, an extra window on the wall of another. Even the third-floor rooms convey an unusual sense of space with their high vaulted ceilings. The Cantors provide TVs in one room that lacks a view as well as in the largest Russell Room, which has a sofa in the sitting area.

A full breakfast is served at individual tables amid lots of silver and china in the dining room. The fare includes fresh fruit, cereals, bagels, Dianne's special peach-pecan muffins, and a hot entrée. The last is chef's choice: perhaps scrambled eggs, french toast or blueberry pancakes. We took ours on trays to the back terrace to enjoy the broad expanse of tree-shaded lawn. A screened gazebo and a deck with rocking chairs await on a bluff above the bay.

The Cantors are hands-on innkeepers whose innkeeping savvy shows.

(410) 778-5943 or (800) 504-3098. www.greatoak.com. Eleven rooms with private baths. April-November: doubles, $135 to $175 weekends, $122 to $158 midweek. Rest of year: $122 to $158 weekends, $108 to $140 midweek. No children. Smoking restricted.

Moonlight Bay Inn, 6002 Lawton Ave., Rock Hall 21661.

Guests at this B&B in a residential section along the Chesapeake Bay enjoy one of the more appealing water settings of any inn anywhere. A screened gazebo, garden chairs scattered about the large lawn and a wicker-filled porch take full advantage, as do the balconies of five deluxe rooms in a new structure opened in 1997 right along the shore.

As the sun sets over little Swan Island, yellow lights outline docks in the foreground, white lights twinkle on the Bay Bridge in the distance and the glow of Baltimore to the west lights up the evening sky. The feeling is nothing short of magical.

So it may be difficult to comprehend why innkeeper Dorothy Santangelo "cried for two weeks" after her husband Bob bought the place in 1992. "I thought I'd be at Great Oak Manor or Tara," said she. "I wanted a B&B and he wanted a marina." What they got initially was a fantastic marina location and an abandoned house that had successively been a post office, a restaurant and a boarding house. They razed all but the front of the house and, after fifteen months of rebuilding and renovations, opened in 1993 with five handsome bedrooms, all with private baths and caring touches, from clock radios to diaries for guest comments.

The largest Magic Moon suite is on the main floor off a spacious guest living room. It comes with a sitting room, canopy queensize bed and windows onto the water. Even more windows onto the water were evident in our upstairs corner room, the Harvest Moon, comfortable with kingsize bed, a large and elegant bathroom, and an antique rocker beside a chair with a rush seat. If you're so inclined, says Dorothy, you can lie in bed here or in the adjacent room and "watch the boats pass outside." The adjacent room is large and lovely in white and blue, the patterned fabrics here matching some of the miniature vases displayed on a shelf on the wall. The cozy side Crescent Moon room that's summery in white lace and wicker, with accents of pink, "is every woman's dream." Each room contains a decanter of sherry, fancy window treatments and a framed wall hanging called "Inn Reminders," in which the usual guest instructions are rendered in poetry.

We'd happily stay in any of the five rooms in the new West Wing, a two-story structure at bay's edge. Each has a kingsize bed (one can be separated into twins), private bath with whirlpool tub and a private balcony with a wooden chair and lounge overlooking the water. Four balconies face the bay head-on. Moon Struck, upstairs in the rear, has a side balcony with views of both bay and an inlet known as the haven. It's dressed in striking black and white florals, and both the room and balcony are larger than the others. Beneath it on the main floor is a parlor for guests.

The entire inn has been lovingly furnished by Dorothy. The decorating is quite remarkable, given that she did it herself and is legally blind.

She's also quite the cook, as evidenced at breakfast in the dining room and enclosed atrium porch overlooking a showy English garden. Waffles in many forms are her specialty. We enjoyed belgian waffles after preliminaries of orange juice, a fruit cup with bananas and strawberries, and two kinds of muffins. English tea is served in the late afternoon.

(410) 639-2660. Fax (410) 639-7739. Ten rooms with private baths. Doubles, $116 to $152. Two-night minimum weekends. No smoking.

The Inn at Osprey Point, 20786 Rock Hall Ave., Rock Hall 21661.

Philadelphia Main Line investors who like to sail built this yacht club, marina, inn, restaurant and bar from scratch in 1993 along a section of Swan Creek known as "The Haven," an inlet from the nearby Chesapeake Bay. The place looks and feels new, although it was scrupulously designed with the Williamsburg look and patterned after the Coke-Garrett House, the mayor's house in Williamsburg, Va. It's all rather slick for Rock Hall.

On a still rather barren landscape that first strikes visitors as mainly sailing masts and parking areas, the endeavor suffers from a split personality. Overnight guests "register" at a second-story office that also serves the marina or, after hours, in the main-floor restaurant. The seven bedrooms are on the second and third floors of the main house. All equipped with modern baths and TVs, they are true to the Williamsburg look, from paint colors to wide-plank floors, and feature "showcase furnishings and gallery art throughout," according to the slick inn brochure. Amenities are "the finest that can be found, from our 250-count pima cotton sheets to our authentic oriental rugs," added one of the inn managers. We found the Windigo room fairly spacious but rather spartan, with queensize poster bed, a windsor chair at a writing desk, nautical and bird prints on the white walls, swagged curtains matching the pillows and the skirt on the night stand, and a couple of oriental scatter rugs on the floors. Coat hooks along one wall are pressed into service in lieu of a closet. Less chilly and more comfortable is the Carina room, equipped with two twin beds and a small TV between the sofabed and a wing chair. Prim but pleasant is the Cotton Blossom, with a queen poster bed, a wing chair and two window seats. The two-room Escapade suite with a jacuzzi in the marble bathroom and the Bolero room with a gas fireplace and queen poster bed have the best water views, but the jacuzzi room "can be noisy due to the restaurant" below, the inn literature advises. A third-floor landing area, described as a common room, holds two wing chairs and some reading materials.

A complimentary continental breakfast is offered in the restaurant's Hunt Room. There's a nature trail along the woods in back of the inn, but the chief amenity here may be the large, club-like swimming pool and deck area with bathhouse.

(410) 639-2194. Fax (410) 639-7716. Six rooms and one suite with private baths. May-November: doubles $125 to $140, suite $160. December-April: doubles $105 to $120, suite $135. Children welcome. No smoking.

The Inn at Mitchell House, 8796 Maryland Pkwy., Chestertown 21620.

A long driveway leads, plantation-like, to this lovely old manor house seven miles west of Chestertown in the Tolchester section near Chesapeake Bay. The ten-acre property beside Stoneybrook Pond was part of a 1,000-acre working plantation. The manor, built in 1743 and expanded in 1825, is still fit for the landed gentry.

Jim Stone, a Washington native who summered here, and his wife Tracy share the expansive house with guests in six rooms, all with private baths. They serve sumptuous breakfasts and offer weekend dinners to guests and the public.

Theirs is very much a family home, reflecting heirlooms and mementos from both sides of the family. Jim acquired the eagle over the entrance from the cornerstone of a building in Baltimore. In one of the two parlors on the left is a portrait of Sir Peter Parker, a British commander who was wounded near here in the War of 1812 and was brought to the Mitchell House for aid; the portrait was found by coincidence many years later by Tracy's father. A signed Tiffany lamp graces the square baby piano converted into a desk. Family portraits cover a square grand piano, and a watercolor of Tracy and their children hangs on one wall. Who can help but be fascinated by the lineup of framed White House Christmas cards dating from Tracy's years at the White House when she handled President Reagan's mail? The side-by-side parlors are attractive in pale yellow and deep green decor.

Artworks from Jim's grandmother, who started painting oils at age 60, enhance the Joseph Mitchell Room, the largest bedroom with a queensize canopy bed, a fireplace and a sitting area with queen sofabed. The large Dr. William Ringgold Room has a queensize bed, a twin sofabed and a fireplace. On their way to other bedrooms, guests pass a refrigerator stocked with complimentary sodas and beer and a hallway decorated with flapper dresses and hats that belonged to Jim's great aunt. A king-bedded hideaway with private bath is up steep stairs in the beamed, low-ceilinged attic.

A country breakfast is served at five tables in the high-ceilinged dining room,

The Inn at Mitchell House is situated beside Stoneybrook Pond.

where the floor is brick and plates and artifacts dot the walls. The main course might be french toast, omelets, featherbed eggs, peach-raspberry coffee cake – "everything you can think of that's bad for you I do," says Tracy.

The Stones also offer dinners on Friday and Saturday nights by reservation, a single seating for up to sixteen people at 7 o'clock. A classical guitarist plays as guests sip a complimentary cocktail. The $26 to $30 tab includes hors d'oeuvres and wine with the meal. You might start with steamed shrimp or cold soup and salad, move on to grilled tuna with mustard sauce or pork tenderloin with blackberry sauce, and finish with homemade apple pie (with apples from the couple's orchard), chocolate mousse or ice cream pecan ball with homemade hot fudge.

Outside, guests enjoy a screened porch containing a 1956 jukebox with old records that belonged to Tracy's father. The porch overlooks the pond, which you can traverse by means of two bridges. Jim put in the raised herb and flower garden, terraced gardens and a fishpond beside the old smokehouse.

(410) 778-6500. Fax (410) 778-2861. Six rooms with private baths. Doubles, $95 to $120.

The White Swan Tavern, 231 High St., Chestertown 21620.

Stay here if you're into history. The White Swan, dating to 1733, is full of it. Its restoration began in 1978 with an archeological dig and produced a "museum" room of the old bar, showing artifacts in a lighted display window.

Despite its lavish refurbishing, the place conveys a rather impersonal and commercial feeling. The hired innkeepers, who live off-premises, may or may not answer the locked front door. Afternoon tea is served by the fireplace in a chandeliered tearoom for $2, with a plate of sweets available for $1.50. An article on the tavern's restoration is sold for $1. Occupants of the Sterling Suite find the bow window like that of a storefront, which it once was; though it's partially screened, one nevertheless feels on view to the street here.

Eighteenth-century period furnishings dignify the main-floor common rooms. An austere front parlor is set up as a game room. A more welcoming rear parlor, dressed in yellow floral chintz, contains a TV. All six guest rooms have private baths and at least an extra twin bed for additional guests. Various passages lead to the rooms, which range from the small Thomas Peacock with a lace canopy double bed and a twin under the eaves to the large T.W. Eliason Suite, with a twin bed in the entry, a kingsize bed with imposing wood headboard in the main room and a Victorian sitting room beyond. A favorite is the John Lovegrove Kitchen, a one-room dwelling that was the first building on the lot. It has a brick floor, dark beamed ceiling, twin beds and an old dining-room table in front of the enormous cooking fireplace. The room exudes atmosphere, but the fireplace (like those in other bedrooms) is not functional and the chairs aren't comfortable for sitting.

Guests are served a continental breakfast at the time specified on a "breakfast preference card." The fare is "changing," but the innkeeper on duty at our visit would not be specific. It comes with a fruit basket and the morning paper.

(410) 778-2300. Four rooms and two suites with private baths. Doubles, $120 to $160. Suites, $180 and $200.

The Parker House, 108 Spring Ave., Chestertown 21620.

Personality pervades this B&B lovingly run by John and Marcy Parker, veterans of the New York publishing trade, who returned in 1994 to settle in the town he first knew as a student at Washington College. The personality comes from the outgoing innkeepers, he the author of three books and she a former director of administration for Time-Life, and from a 19th-century farmhouse that oozes history, including the first indoor bathroom in Chestertown, circa 1876. Not to mention their cocker spaniel Half Pint, who barks a greeting and kisses the feet of new arrivals.

The pale yellow house with black and white trim occupies a shady property at the edge of downtown Chestertown. From the wonderful rear screened porch overlooking a landscaped lawn with statuary, a barn and an old privy, you forget that you're in the heart of town. Guests also spread out near the fireplace in a large side parlor that had been two rooms and in a long dining room that had served as the original kitchen. From her new kitchen on the other side of this house that seems to stretch forever, Marcy prepares a continental breakfast that, their brochure advises, will have you "rise from the table with a spring in your step and a song in your heart."

All three guest rooms are spacious and equipped with private baths. One is ensconced in the original summer kitchen at the rear of the main floor. It's bright and cheery with a floral quilt on the kingsize bed.

Upstairs, beneath a 10½-foot ceiling, is the Queen's Room, with a loveseat at the foot of the queen bed. An adjoining single room can turn it into a suite. Occupants use the first indoor bathroom in Chestertown, obviously updated but still with the original marble sink and etched glass in the door. The front Lincoln Room is so named for its carved antique double bed, similar to one belonging to Abe Lincoln. Bathrobes and bottled water are among the room amenities.

A stack of Time magazines from 1946 makes fascinating reading in the upstairs hall sitting area.

(410) 778-9401. Fax (410) 778-7318. Doubles, $110 to $125. Children welcome. No smoking. No credit cards.

Swan Haven Bed & Breakfast, 10950 Rock Hall Ave., Rock Hall 21661.

This B&B in an 1898 Victorian cottage started operating weekends only with four bedrooms as owners Diane and Harry Oliver commuted from weekday jobs

Porches mark facade of Imperial Hotel.

Elegant dining room at Imperial Hotel.

in Washington, D.C. An addition in 1997 produced three more guest rooms and meant Diane could be on hand fulltime.

The waterside location, with a pier on "The Haven" and a huge deck nearby, is a key asset. The new addition takes full advantage. The side Heron Room with cathedral ceiling and kingsize iron bed has a private balcony overlooking Swan Creek and marinas, although the room itself has no chairs. The rear Cygnet Room has a kingsize bed, a jacuzzi tub for two and an antique wooden glider chair in the room, plus a balcony facing the Haven.

Other rooms in the original cottage have a distinctly older feel. All have private baths, central air conditioning and TVs. Two on the second floor, one with a queensize bed, open onto an old-fashioned screened front porch. Two more are up steep stairs in the attic. One here has a double and twin bed in the garrets; the other has a double bed beneath a skylight.

The main floor holds a living room with a fireplace plus a breakfast room notable for a wooden bar. A continental breakfast is put out on the bar.

(410) 639-2527. Seven rooms with private baths. Doubles, $98 to $138. Children over 10.

Dining Spots

The Imperial Hotel, 208 High St., Chestertown.

Two opulent, intimate dining rooms, one on either side of the main corridor, are the setting for some of the area's better meals. The dining rooms have been refurbished in favor of a lighter, sophisticated look. "Victorian had its time," said co-owner Dick O'Neill, "but it was time to lighten up."

The Zagat survey of Washington-Baltimore restaurants rated the Imperial among the tops in the region for food. New chef Michael Martir took over in 2000, accompanied by his wife Elizabeth, the pastry chef. His opening menu ranged widely from pan-seared rockfish niçoise over arugula to sliced grilled lamb loin finished with lemon-basil oil.

Our dinner began with a complimentary cheese straw. Starters were a rich cream of wild mushroom soup with port and chives and a wondrous plate of smoked shrimp, mussels and bay scallops with a cucumber and dill cream. Next time we'd like to try the beef carpaccio with a roasted beet and goat cheese tart and truffle sherry vinaigrette or the wild rice crêpe filled with duck confit and julienned vegetables.

Among entrées, our party sampled the sautéed lump crab cakes with a tomato-lemon-caper sauce, grilled fillet of snapper with sundried tomatoes, grilled scallops with fresh tarragon and fennel, and New Zealand rack of lamb with artichokes, kalamata olives and pinenuts, all superb. The pan-seared Atlantic salmon with a tropical fruit relish over wilted greens and the filet mignon with a vidalia onion compound butter and cabernet-tarragon sauce were winners at another visit.

Desserts here earn much acclaim. Our chocolate praline triangle with grand mariner sauce was heavenly. We've heard good things about the frozen lemon mousse with cherry sorbet and the cranberry apple cake with green apple sorbet and caramel sauce.

The wine list earns an Award of Excellence from Wine Spectator.

(410) 778-5000. Entrées, $15.50 to $28. Lunch, Friday-Saturday noon to 2, also Wednesday-Thursday seasonally. Dinner, Wednesday-Saturday from 5:30. Sunday brunch, from noon.

Blue Heron Cafe, 236 Cannon St., Chestertown.

The old Ironstone Café gave way in late 1997 to this newcomer run by Paul Hanley, former general manager and partner in the highly rated Bayard House Restaurant in Chesapeake City. Previous owners Barbara Silcox and Kevin McKinney decided to concentrate fulltime on their newer restaurant, the Kennedyville Inn, eight miles north of Chestertown in Kennedyville.

The atmospheric, L-shaped dining room occupies an old carriage shop and glass company, which accounts for the garage door at the rear. The shelves that contained ironstone china now display Delmarva porcelain and stoneware commissioned by the Blue Heron for the restaurant. A local artisan obliged with a blue heron, skipjacks, chickens, Chesapeake workboats, redwing blackbirds and the like. An antique quilt from the 1920s hangs in the back dining room.

Paul says his team of chefs call their cuisine "traditional and innovative regional American." Typical main courses range from grilled swordfish with citrus-cilantro salsa to grilled veal chop with roasted garlic demi-glace. Pan-seared Atlantic salmon with oyster cream sauce, pasta Delmarva (with grilled chicken, fresh oysters, Smithfield ham, spinach and wild mushrooms in a romano cheese sauce over linguini) and honey-basted roast duckling in a grilled pineapple and shallot sauce were early favorites.

Among appetizers are oyster fritters in lemon-butter sauce – "to die for," as rated by a national magazine – barbecued shrimp cocktail on a bed of baby greens and red cabbage. Homemade desserts include crème brûlée, hot milk cake with mandarin orange glaze, chocolate bourbon cake with white chocolate and raspberry sauces, pecan pie and assorted ice creams.

Some appetizers turn up on the lunch menu, which featured a delectable-sounding lump crab frittata at our visit.

(410) 778-0188. Entrées, $15 to $24. Lunch, Monday-Saturday 11:30 to 2:30. Dinner, Monday-Saturday 5 to 8:30 or 9:30.

The Black Eyed Susan, 601 Washington Ave., Chestertown.

After training with leading chefs and the Marriott Hotel group restaurants, Steven Townsend returned to his hometown. He purchased the old Buzz's Steak House across from Washington College, renamed it for the state flower and turned it into a restaurant of distinction. The Annapolis newspaper rated it "worth the trip to the Eastern Shore," praising it as a "serious food kind of place" where imagination is at work.

The menu is extensive and the prices affordable, which guarantees a strong local following.

For dinner, you might start with local snapper (turtle) soup, blue crab bisque or a sampler of three. Or how about Florida stone crab claws, honey-touched alligator medallions or a Kennett Square mushroom quesadilla?

Main courses vary from the traditional (Maryland fried chicken, mile-high meatloaf and calves liver with onions) to local crab cakes, scalloped oysters roasted in an earthenware dish, grilled chicken with blackberry sauce, and Carolina peanut-crusted loin lamb chops, served with a sweet and spicy Asian sauce. Can't decide? Pick any two designated items from the menu and they will be presented together for $19.95.

Sandwiches and a children's menu also are available.

(410) 778-1214. Entrees, $8.95 to $19.95. Lunch, Monday-Saturday 11 to 3. Dinner nightly, from 4:30. Sunday brunch, from 9.

The Inn at Osprey Point, 20786 Rock Hall Ave., Rock Hall.

The food at the handsome restaurant in this waterside inn receives high marks. White linens cover the well-spaced tables in the L-shaped dining room, which wraps around a small, historic-looking bar. A formal Colonial Williamsburg look is conveyed by french doors and tall, many-paned windows, a large fireplace, and white walls with Williamsburg blue trim.

The short dinner menu bears a contemporary touch. Among starters, we heard raves for the sherried cream of crab soup. The braised calamari with spinach and tomato basil ravioli was a recent winner.

Main courses include sautéed shrimp and sea scallops with black bean cassoulet and bourbon barbecue sauce, pork rib chop on a bed of wilted spinach with a cranberry-balsamic vinaigrette and pan-seared duck breast with an amaretto-fig demi-glace.

The wine list spotlights boutique California wineries.

(410) 639-2194. Entrées, $13 to $19.95. Dinner, Thursday-Monday 5 to 9, Sunday 3 to 7.

Bay Wolf, Rock Hall Avenue (Route 20), Rock Hall.

A sidewalk patio is a welcome seasonal addition to this well regarded restaurant, housed in a former funeral home and notable for church-like stained-glass windows. Owners Larry and Hildegard Sunkler (he of the Schaefer's Canal House family from Chesapeake City) mix a heavy dose of Austrian fare with an Eastern Shore accent in three pleasant dining rooms. They bill their bar as "the most convivial – and certainly the longest – in town."

A different theme is featured daily. Monday is German Wurst Night; Wednesday is Oyster Night. Otherwise, the dinner menu features such choices as Austrian pork roast with sauerkraut and dumpling, chicken hubertus with an Austrian mushroom sauce, duck à l'orange, wiener schnitzel and pepper steak nesselrotte with brandy sauce. Baked flounder stuffed with crab imperial, crab cakes and shrimp scampi appease seafood lovers.

Start with camembert fritters, fried mushrooms or a specialty chilled crab dip for two. Finish with apple strudel, black forest cake, key lime pie or "spumoni ice cream."

(410) 639-2000. Entrées, $14.95 to $23.95. Open daily, noon to 10.

The Feast of Reason, 203 High St., Chestertown.

This is a simple place across the street from the Imperial Hotel with eight round tables, bentwood chairs and a few posters on the wall. Geoffrey Riefe and his wife Kathleen, who previously were innkeepers in the Berkshires, are in charge, he doing the cooking and she the baking.

To eat in or take out, they offer things like buttermilk-oatmeal muffins, spinach and corn quiche, flatbread pizza with shrimp or spinach and shrimp salad on a croissant. At our visit the soups were squash-honey and potato-scallion, and apple scrunch and butterscotch brownies were desserts of the day. We made a good picnic lunch of a roast beef sandwich with tomato-horseradish mayonnaise and a smoked salmon sandwich with dill and onion on pumpernickel. Dinner entrées to go ($8 to $10) included chicken breast with pesto sauce and flounder with tomato-shrimp sauce. Beer and wine are available.

(410) 778-3828. Open Monday-Friday 10 to 6, Saturday, 10 to 4.

Andy's, 337½ High St., Chestertown.

For a change of pace, come here for a drink and a snack at the extra-long stand-up bar with high stools opposite or, better yet, in the rear "living room" with a fireplace, piano and numerous conversation corners with easy chairs, sofas and coffee tables.

Guest entertainers perform here on weekends and on some Thursday nights. The varied menu offers such things as a tomato-basil tart, salads, wrap du jour, stuffed potatoes, burgers, quiche and gourmet pizzas, in the $5 to $8 range.

(410) 778-6779. Light fare, Monday-Saturday 4 to 11, to midnight on weekends.

Diversions

Historic Chestertown. The orderly grid of streets leading from the riverfront is a living museum of homes that stood in Colonial times. The sights along Water, Queen, High and Cross streets are best appreciated on foot, guided by annotations on a walking tour brochure published by the Kent County Chamber of Commerce. More details are available in a booklet, "Chestertown: An Architectural Guide." A Kent County map outlines a 110-mile driving tour of this picturesque county, which includes the old-line waterman's community of Rock Hall and the beach at Betterton, considered the best swimming beach on the Chesapeake. Maps for nine bicycle tours are included in a Kent County Bicycle Tour brochure.

Chester River Craft and Art Schools, 105 South Cross St., Chestertown, (410) 778-5954. Local civic leaders and artists formed this venture in 1997 to foster the arts in the Chestertown area and give it a national identity. "We hope to become similar to Haystack," said catalyst Carla Massoni in a reference to Maine's famed Haystack Mountain School of Crafts. The project has an office, gallery and gift shop. As its first major venture, it was building a replica of the 18th-century schooner **Sultana,** to be launched in 2002 and berthed on the Chester River as a floating exhibit and historical attraction (its construction progress quickly became a tourist attraction in itself). The project's ambitious, four-p. approach will involve crafts, visual arts, performing arts and a culinary art sch. and café.

Dixon's Auction Barn, Routes 544 and 290 off 301, Crumpton. Every Wednesday is auction day at Dixon's, when you might find seven or eight pianos in a field, a tractor-trailer full of plants, a small Amish farm market and a warehouse stuffed with concession stands, furniture and antiques. Buyers and sellers of used and antique furniture come from across the country to deal here in something of a circus atmosphere. Auctioneer Norman Dixon takes no more than fifteen seconds to sell any item on his lot; if it's not sold, he gives it to anyone willing to take it. Table after table full of bric-a-brac leave some cold, but if you spot something you want, you have to wait until the auctioneer reaches that table and bid fast. When he and the crowd move in, things happen so fast the unwary bidder scarcely has time to think. As the typewritten handout says, "the auctioneer does not miss you, you miss him. So if you want something, holler out before he sells it, not afterwards."
(410) 928-3006. Open Wednesdays from 7 a.m.

Waterman's Museum, 20880 Rock Hall Ave., Rock Hall. This little museum, nicely renovated from an abandoned house, preserves the history and lore of the watermen of Rock Hall. Three display rooms show exhibits on oystering and crabbing, plus fishing gear, local photographs, carvings and boats. "If it's been used on the water, we've probably got it," advised the curator. One of the more interesting exhibits involves a replica of a waterman's ark, a one-room shanty of a house on the scow of a boat. A pier was planned to accommodate several workboats, including a skipjack, for visitors to board.
(410) 778-6697. Open daily, 10 to 5. Free.

St. Paul's Episcopal Church, 7579 Sandy Bottom Road, Chestertown. Actress Tallulah Bankhead, whose family lives nearby, is among the notables buried in the cemetery outside this historic church, built in 1713 and the oldest in Maryland. Giant oak trees, some more than 300 years old, rise among the boxwoods in the churchyard. The interior is notable for embroidered kneelers and a beautiful stained-glass side window. A poster at our first visit piqued interest with word of an oyster roast celebrating the parish's 300th year.

Shopping. The shopping opportunities are myriad in Chestertown. Start at the **Kerns Collection,** Susan Kerns's dramatic two-story showplace at 210 High St. next to the Imperial Hotel. The deep blue pottery by a local teacher intrigued us and now a lovely shallow bowl sits on our coffee table. Sensational stoles woven by the wife of the college president, art clothing, hand-blown glass, bonsai, jewelry made of Japanese rice paper, unique cards, colorful tiles and much more catch the eye. The **Carla Massoni Gallery** that originally occupied the Kerns space has moved to a loft across the street, where the former owner of the Imperial Hotel displays the works of nationally known artists as well as the finest regional artists.

Rhodes at 241 High St. is a mecca of the impeccable taste of Holly and Frank Rhodes, he a cabinet maker who will custom-make any furniture, for instance an exquisite Queen Anne lowboy for $4,800. Pretty china, linens, fire screens, decoys, oriental rugs and estate jewelry are some of the other traditional wares.

Dockside Emporium has everything nautical, from cookbooks for the boat to sweaters with crabs thereon, and has expanded its clothing line. **A.H. Kepner Design Studio** is the place for fine decorative accessories and antiques. We admired an oyster plate in the window of **Bittersweet**, a consignment shop specializing in American country antique furniture. **The Finishing Touch**, which specializes in framing, offers nice prints. Unusual gifts are found at **Cornucopia of Treasures Ltd.** Everything from gifts to cards to linens to books is available at **Twigs and Teacups**. We loved the birdhouses and things for the garden among the gifts and antiques at **The Village House**. You'll find great sweaters at **Chester River Knitting Co.**, which moved and restored an entire building at its new location. The hub for coffee and local gossip is **Play It Again, Sam.**

In the heart of Rock Hall, you can visit a restored corner drugstore, 1930s style, at **Durding's Store.** Ice-cream sodas made with real vanilla beans are served at the original marble soda fountain amidst a selection of cards, gifts and sundries. Fine furnishings for the home and yacht, Chesapeake memorabilia and clothing are carried at **The Cat's Paw**, a gift shop at The Sailing Emporium. Clothing of interest to boaters and nice gifts are carried at **The Ditty Bag**, the marine store at Haven Harbor Marina.

The Shops at Oyster Court, 5761 Main St., Rock Hall. This started in 1996 as a homey bookstore and gathering spot called the **America's Cup Café** at Rock Hall's main corner. Arlene Douglas manages the café, which specializes in coffee ("America's favorite beverage") and light meals day and night. Her husband Tom Sabol, a real estate lawyer, buys up old fishing shacks and outbuildings to move to the property and lease to merchants and craftspeople. The result is a charming alleyway lined with colorful enterprises, among them **Sweet Annie's** herbs and everlastings, **Smilin' Jakes** casual apparel, **Gepetto's Toy Store, One Nightstand** (for handpainted furniture and glassware) and **CoCoNuts** for the Banjo Man's folk art and pottery. Already, the second-hand bookstore has spilled into an annex called **The Cup Runneth Over.** Tom planned to have twenty shops along the alley behind his café that began not with sailing races but a cup of coffee.

Extra-Special

Chesapeake Farms Wildlife Habitat, 7319 Remington Drive (off Route 20), Chestertown.

A driving tour leads through the 3,000-acre wildlife management demonstration area formerly known as Remington Farms, operated by the du Pont company in conjunction with Remington, the arms manufacturer. An informative brochure points out wildlife management practices being applied here. The self-guided tour takes one past ponds, swamps, woods and fields and involves fifteen marked – and some unmarked – stops for wildlife and plants. The leisurely drive is the closest thing we've found so far north to the famed J.N. "Ding" Darling National Wildlife Preserve on Florida's Sanibel Island, although the finds are neither so prolific nor so exotic. The quantity and variety of waterfowl you'll see depends on the season and the time of day. The habitat tour can take an hour or more, depending on stops. Other attractions of interest to nature lovers are the Eastern Neck National Wildlife Refuge in Rock Hall and the Millington Wildlife Management Area in Massey.

(410) 778-1565. Open daily from February to Oct. 10. Free.

Wide Lewes-Rehoboth Canal is on view from downtown Lewes.

Lewes, Del.

The First Town in the First State

Whoever thought up the "first town" slogan for Lewes was on the mark. The reference, of course, was to Lewes's founding by Dutch explorers in 1631, long before Delaware was to become the first state in the union. But age alone does not account for the popularity of this riverfront town that's pronounced "loo-iss" and takes its name from a town in Sussex County, England. As far as many are concerned, Lewes is first in charm and first in all-around appeal. For visitors, it's Delaware's most "visitable" – as opposed to its most visited – town.

Off the beaten path, Lewes is located on the lee side of Cape Henlopen, the strategic point where the Delaware Bay meets the Atlantic Ocean. It's long been home to skilled riverboat pilots who shepherd hundreds of cargo ships up the Delaware Bay to Wilmington and Philadelphia.

"This is a town with a beach – not a beach town," stresses the Lewes Chamber of Commerce. The distinction sets Lewes apart from its better-known neighbor to the south, Rehoboth Beach, with its glitzy sprawl of boardwalks and ballyhoo. This is a genuine town with a small but devoted year-round population (2,300), a working seaport town as opposed to a sailing or beachy town, a town that most folks would bypass on their way to or from the Cape May-Lewes Ferry.

No more. Now, restaurant waiters in Rehoboth are apt to steer their lunch patrons to Lewes for a rainy afternoon and innkeepers from across the bay in Cape May, N.J., come here for restorative day trips and overnights. In the last decade, Lewes has attracted good inns and B&Bs, satisfying restaurants and an uncommon array of small, sophisticated shops situated along Second Street beneath a canopy of unusual Bradford pear trees. It's now the side-by-side home of riverboat pilots, Delaware's first winery, the nation's first public park, an herb farm, some of

Delaware's oldest homes, World War II bunkers, "walking" sand dunes, a working blacksmith shop and a fascinating new residential development in which every structure is at least a hundred years old.

All are true, small-scale, understated places, as the town fathers have strived successfully to control development to avoid the all-too-evident fate of encroaching Rehoboth.

Once people discover the charms of Lewes, it seems, they become regular visitors or even residents. They like what one new innkeeper calls "a town of busy days and quiet nights."

Inn Spots

Blue Water House, 407 East Market St., Lewes 19958.

There are times when we veteran inn-goers don't even want to look at another Victorian sofa or chair, much less sit on one. That's why we heaved sighs of relief when we checked into our room at the comfortably but minimally furnished Blue Water House. The bed didn't have a headboard, much less a canopy (sacrilege!). The seats were deck chairs, the lamps weren't tasseled, the walls were white, the carpet was a dark industrial gray and the only amenity was a TV set. How refreshing! The air-conditioned room was large, the art was fascinating, the bathroom modern, and the french doors opened onto a wraparound deck from which we watched an incredible sunset.

Little more was needed, although that all changed in 1999 when the Blue Water was acquired by Rick Quill, a property owner and manager from Wilmington, who "fell in love with its unique design and secluded setting." Like his predecessors, he had no B&B training, but thought the place needed upgrading. He undertook a total refurbishing "from to bottom," adding headboards to the beds, comfortable chairs, large TV/VCRs, new artworks and lots of bright colors for a tropical look. "Everything is color-coordinated Martha Stewart style," he said. "Bold, bright, eclectic."

Six ample bedrooms with private baths, four on the corners and all open to the wraparound porch, ring the third floor and are spaced for maximum privacy. There

are ingenious touches: the railing of the porch is a white picket fence. On the fourth floor is a large quasi-widow's walk with good views of Lewes and the bay. Its big TV set and wicker furniture make this a gathering spot.

Rick added three more guest rooms on the second floor in space vacated by the former innkeepers and their children, who had built the inn as a family

Blue Water House rises above wetlands in Lewes.

project in 1993. The original owner, a fun-loving architect, designed it to be wonderfully whimsical, with little touches of the tropics all around – it reminded us of places we've seen in Key West. The ground floor, nicely landscaped, is open because the inn sits on wetlands. It includes a patio, picnic table, grill, hammock, bicycles and refrigerator for guests. We enjoyed taking out dinner from a local restaurant and enjoying it by candlelight here. Rick added landscaping, as well as statues and fountains, for a more finished look.

Guests congregate around the long dining room table for a hefty continental breakfast. Rick puts out cereal, pastries and homemade breads, among them coconut-pineapple and apricot-almond.

(302) 645-7832 or (800) 493-2080. Eight rooms with private baths. Mid-May to mid-September: doubles, $150 weekends, $125 midweek. Mid-November through March: $85. Rest of year: $100. Two-night minimum in season and spring and fall weekends. Children welcome. No smoking.

The Inn at Canal Square, 122 Market St., Lewes 19958.

This, the first and best-known new inn in Lewis, opened in 1988 and faces the wide Lewes-Rehoboth Canal. The brown-shingled facade of the four-story complex looks like a contemporary Cape Cod condominium.

Hidden from street view are nineteen guest rooms on the three upper floors, most with large balconies facing the water (though the views from some are screened by the adjacent lighthouse-turned-conference center). Rooms ascend in size and price by the floor. Ours on the top floor was quiet and comfortable and unusually spacious with 18th-century reproduction furniture including a kingsize bed, a sitting area with a loveseat and side chair, a dining table with two chairs and a TV hidden in the highboy. The two-part bathroom came with a separate vanity area and all kinds of toiletries. The balcony yielded a fine view over the lighthouse onto the busy canal.

The next morning, we were impressed with the continental breakfast spread set out in the ground-floor library/lobby. Four kinds of juices, three sliced fruits (kiwi, watermelon and pineapple), yogurt and a choice of a dozen assorted breakfast pastries put us in good shape for the ferry crossing to New Jersey. *(302) 644-3377 or (888) 644-1911. Fax (302) 644-3565. Nineteen rooms with private baths. Mid-June to Labor Day: doubles, $155 to $185 weekends, $125 to $160 midweek. Spring and early fall, $90 to $130 weekends, $70 to $110 midweek. December-February: $60 to $109 weekends, $45 to $89 midweek.*

The New Devon Inn, 142 Second St., Box 516, Lewes 19958.

Built in 1926, the former Valley of the Swans Hotel had deteriorated into a seedy boarding house. The "Ugly Swan" is how one newspaper described it. And when Rehoboth Beach realtor Dale Jenkins showed it to her investor-partner, Washington attorney Bernard Nash, they were met at the front door by a boarder emerging on a motorcycle.

Dale envisioned the possibilities, however. Acting as her own contractor and decorator, she gutted the building except for the main staircase, the pine floors in the bedrooms and a rickety elevator, barely big enough for two people with any luggage. She removed the kitchenettes and added baths for each of 24 bedrooms and two suites. Part of the lobby became a fashionable sitting area, with plush sofas and a couple of elephant chairs carved from solid teakwood in Thailand. A grand piano, a glass chandelier and a ficus tree lit by tiny white lights add elegance. The pool hall in the basement was converted into a breakfast area and a TV room.

The result is a small downtown hotel of considerable sophistication, one that wears its National Historic Register listing with pride. The rooms, though small, are squeaky clean and modern but for their original floors and antique beds. Lately, six rooms have been reconfigured to make three suites, each with a queensize bedroom, two baths and a sofabed in a sitting room. Two earlier suites have queensize beds. Four other adjoining rooms have been given twin beds.

Our room, the largest of the standard rooms, looked from its fourth-floor corner roost onto the cemetery beside St. Peter's Episcopal Church. The bed was small enough that one's extremities had to be draped over the edges. But there were thoughtful touches: in-room telephones, floral sheets, good prints on the walls, nightly turndown with a couple of small cordials, crystal glasses on a silver tray and windows that open.

Coffee, orange juice and pastries are put out for contintental breakfast. *(302) 645-6466 or (800) 824-8754. Fax (302) 645-7196. Eighteen rooms and five suites with private baths. Early June through Labor Day: doubles, $130 weekends, $95 midweek; suites, $170 weekends, $135 midweek. November-April: doubles, $65 weekends, $50 midweek; suites, $110 weekends, $90 midweek. Rest of year: doubles, $85 to $120 weekends, $50 to $65 midweek; suites, $130 to $155 weekends, $90 to $110 midweek. Two-night minimum weekends in season. Children over 16.*

Wild Swan Inn, 525 Kings Highway, Lewes 19958.

Pink with white gingerbread trim, this Queen Anne Victorian is long on personality and turn-of-the-century charm. Owners Mike and Hope Tyler moved here from suburban Wilmington to open a B&B with three bedrooms and private baths.

The breezy wraparound porch is notable for a corner gazebo, as well as a small refrigerator for guests' use hidden away at the far side. Also hidden from the street is a nice swimming pool flanked by a patio and another gazebo. Inside, a small front parlor is notable for a flock of five swans on a crystal chandelier. The

Wraparound porch at Wild Swan Inn features a corner gazebo.

parlor opens into a larger dining room, where one of the inn's antique brass chandeliers presides over the dining table and a number of the couple's collections, from a glass cabinet bearing old miniature liqueur bottles to a 1940 Zenith radio.

The stairway to the second floor is lined with colorful doorstops, all fruits and flowers except for swans, exceptions that are repeated throughout. Hope named the front bedroom Nan's Room because it holds her grandmother's furniture. A queen bed is angled toward the center of the room from the far corner; its headboard matches the bureau. The bathroom is decked out in lace. The Delaware Room, overlooking the pool, features a wall quilt symbolic of Delaware as well as other local artworks. One prized work is an Andrew Wyeth print of a barn, framed in wood from the subject barn when it was razed. The side Rose Room takes its name from the wallpaper. A plate of cookies is put out at night on the outstretched hands of the wooden butler beside the bed.

The dining room is the setting for some fairly fancy breakfasts cooked up by Mike, whose recipes have been included in three cookbooks. Besides a fruit dish like poached pears and fresh breads and muffins, expect such main courses as pumpkin waffles, asparagus pie or breakfast burritos, served with salsa made with ingredients from the Tylers' garden.

(302) 645-8550. Three rooms with private baths. July and August: doubles, $150 weekends, $135 midweek. Spring and fall: $120. November to mid-May: $85. Two-night minimum weekends. No children. No smoking. Closed in winter.

The Bay Moon, 128 Kings Highway, Lewes 19958.
Eclectic decor, modern conveniences and a casual ambiance are hallmarks of this B&B that opened in 1996 in a rustic-looking, brown clapboard Victorian house a long block south of downtown. The restoration made good use of the original oak woodwork, from a massive mantelpiece and shelves surrounding the

fireplace that separates the open living room and dining room to the wainscoting and even a bed headboard in the upstairs bedrooms.

"Amenities are our claim to fame," says innkeeper Pamela Rizzo, who took over in 1998 from the original owner. Down comforters adorn the queen beds, each designed by Laura and built by her husband. All with private baths, the three second-floor rooms are bright and cheery, painted in pastel colors with bold accents. Each has a small TV/VCR atop a tall, slender mod chest of drawers. The top-of-the-line Silver Moon Suite comes with a draped kingsize bed, a sitting room with a day bed and a private rear balcony. A fourth queen-bedded room with private bath is on the third floor.

Guests enjoy a happy hour with local wines and hors d'oeuvres, perhaps bean dips and quesadillas, in the side library and entertainment center. Equipped with books and videos, it adjoins a handsome bar room. The treats continue the next morning at breakfast, served at a table for ten in the dining room. The fare includes homemade breads and biscuits and perhaps a quiche, soufflé or artichoke strata.

Guests enjoy use of an outdoor hot tub and a barbecue grill.

(302) 644-1802 or (800) 917-2307. Three rooms and one suite with private bath. May-October: doubles $135, suite $150. Rest of year: doubles $95, suite $120. Two-night minimum stay in season. Children accepted. No smoking.

The Manor at Cool Spring/Lavender Farm Bed & Breakfast, County Road 290, RD 2, Box 238, Milton 19968.

Named for a hamlet about four miles west of Lewes, this farmhouse was converted into a small B&B by new owners Joe and Pauline Palenik. "We wanted to run a B&B and this house was a perfect fit," Joe explained.

The heart of the house is a sunken sun porch at the side. It holds a large jacuzzi tub, a wood stove and a glass table flanked by rattan chairs, where breakfast may be served. Also available to guests are a formal dining room, a living room containing a lineup of Pauline's Toby jugs from England as well as a display cabinet showcasing her collections of owls and glassware, and a big, turreted corner library with a fireplace, gaming table and chess board ready for action.

Upstairs are two guest rooms with private baths, one with a whirlpool tub. They're furnished with what Joe calls 1920s and 1930s vintage furniture, enhanced by floral curtains that match the covers and pillows on the queensize beds.

Pauline offers afternoon tea, as well as a five-course breakfast reflects her British background and her cooking studies at the Sorbonne. A typical meal includes fruit, eggs any style, and sausage and Canadian bacon. Special treats could be fruit crêpes or eggs benedict. Among the ingredients are herbs and vegetables the Paleniks grow on their rural four-acre property they now call Lavender Farm. Their lavender bath and massage oils and soaps proved so popular with guests that they have planted most of their acreage in lavender and now offer more than ten lavender products. Their seven cats also roam around the house and grounds.

(302) 684-8325. Fax (302) 684-8326. Two rooms with private baths. Doubles, $130 to $150.

Dining Spots

The Buttery Restaurant, Second and Savannah Streets, Lewes.

This chic yet casual bistro started in leased space at the side of the New Devon Inn. It proved so popular that it expanded into a back room, and eventually relocated in 1999 to the restored Trader Mansion at Second and Savannah streets. Now it's widely considered the top restaurant in town.

Owner John Donato added an enclosed porch with a gazebo and a patio for outdoor dining. Two interior dining rooms are candlelit and elegant, and the ambiance is romantic.

Service was solicitous and highly professional as we enjoyed zesty house salads sprinkled with gouda cheese and dressed with fresh garlic and a basket full of crusty sliced French sourdough bread, more than we could eat. Chef Gary Papp's innovative main courses range from seared red snapper with papaya salad, coconut-peanut sauce and Asian ginger-lime sauce to grilled veal chop with a smoked portobello mushroom sauce and filet mignon au poivre with brandied cream sauce. We settled for the Maryland crab cakes (very tasty with a rémoulade sauce), red bliss potatoes and an interesting dish of sautéed kale, and a rather strange bouillabaisse with a thick tomato sauce that masked the advertised "fennel-flavored tomato-saffron broth" and gave priority to the mundane fish fillet rather than the expected shellfish.

Appetizers were a house specialty seafood chowder, a selection of house pâtés, poached oysters in a pernod-laced champagne-shallot cream sauce over pastry, and a smoked fish sampler with herbed croustades.

Lorraine Papp, the chef's wife and pastry chef, is known for her desserts.

(302) 645-7755. Entrées, $19 to $26.95. Lunch, Tuesday-Saturday 11 to 2:30. Dinner, Tuesday-Sunday from 5. Sunday brunch, 10:30 to 2:30.

Kupchick's Restaurant, 3 East Bay Ave., Lewes.

Some of the area's finest and fanciest food is served in this unlikely looking building alongside the Delaware Bay beach. You'd expect burgers and frozen custard, perhaps. What you get is sophisticated continental and regional American fare, including some of the best crab dishes we've ever had.

Behind its undistinguished facade lie two dark, romantic dining rooms and a lively bar and grill. Traditionalists are partial to the formal restaurant, sedate with banquettes and windsor chairs at white-linened tables. Pink lalique-style shades over the candles and wall sconces and a few paintings provide accents of color.

The fare produced by chef-owner David Krasnoff is worthy of the setting. David is the grandson of Romanian immigrants who operated Kupchick's Restaurants in Toronto and Montreal in the first half of the 20th century. His fairly lengthy menu features "Delmarva Rim Cuisine," which translates to such entrées as flounder imperial, grilled veal chop with a shiitake mushroom sauté, sirloin steak "au poivre congolese" and a handful of "vegetarian vagaries." with tri-colored peppercorn sauce. Blackened tuna, seared duck breast with port wine glaze and steak diane could be the night's specials.

Among starters are the family's special mushroom and barley soup, chiffonade salad, carpaccio, smoked bluefish and baked brie. Desserts could be Bailey's Irish cream cheesecake, grand marnier strawberry shortcake, chocolate-walnut pie and crème caramel.

An extensive grill menu featuring pastas and light entrées is offered in the bar, which was obviously popular the weeknight we were there. The staff could barely keep up with the demand, although the food proved to be well worth the wait. One of us enjoyed pastry chef Daria Horn's favorite salad with assorted lettuces, bacon, egg, onion and mushrooms and the crab platter, a succulent crab cake served with roasted potatoes. The other liked the zesty caesar salad and the lump crab linguini, tossed with sherry and mushrooms and simply sensational. The heavy, coarse bread was served with real butter (as opposed to the ubiquitous foil-wrapped slices) and a $14 bottle of Chilean sauvignon blanc accompanied.

(302) 645-0420. Entrées, $14.95 to $23.95. Lunch, Monday-Friday 11 to 2:30, October to April. Dinner nightly, 5 to 9 or 10. Closed Jan. 1 to Valentine's Day.

Second Street Grille, 115 Second St., Lewes.
This trendy newcomer was opened by Ray Richardson, a chef from the Fenwick area, in quarters occupied by the old Jerry's American Café. One of his first special events was a week of French dinners in honor of the release of the year's beaujolais nouveau, an example of his priorities. He also upscaled the décor with white tablecloths, candles and framed French posters on the walls.

The contemporary fare ranges from oven-roasted pecan chicken to barbecued shrimp on a poblano quesadilla with tomato salsa or crab cakes with mustard slaw and hush puppies. Other main dishes could be sesame yellowfin tuna with cucumber salad and a spring roll, pork chops with bourbon sauce and apple fritters, and filet mignon with crispy onions and rosemary broth.

Starters could be Maryland crab soup, portobellos and brie in puff pastry, oysters rockefeller and coconut shrimp with pineapple chutney. Homemade desserts include raspberry cheesecake, chocolate mousse and lemon crème brûlée. There's an extensive wine list.

(302) 644-4121. Entrées, $12 to $23. Lunch, Monday and Wednesday-Saturday, 11:30 to 3. Dinner nightly except Tuesday, 5:30 to 9. Sunday brunch, 11 to 2.

Gilligan's Harborside Restaurant & Bar, Front and Market Streets, Lewes.
The kitchen is in a dry-docked boat, and the tropical bar, the side patio and the rooftop deck offer the best waterfront views of any local restaurant. New owner Patrick Shehan has upgraded the decor of this Canal Square standby.

The contemporary international fare is highly regarded, particularly the crab cakes served with varied sauces and baby greens, available as an appetizer or a main course. The with-it dinner menu starts with appetizers like a lobster tamale with a roasted tomato and chipotle pepper sauce. Main courses could be honey-pecan crusted red snapper with black-eyed pea relish, chile-rubbed chicken breast with tomatillo-mango salsa, and rack of lamb with warm citrus couscous. Hoisin-glazed swordfish on Asian ratatouille was to be a special the night we booked here, but a tropical storm cut the power and the restaurant closed for the evening.

Tarry with an after-dinner drink in the outdoor bar, with your back to a mural of a tropical island. Facing the boats passing by on the Lewes-Rehoboth Canal, you might think you were along the Intra-Coastal Waterway. Actually, you are.

(302) 645-7866. Entrées, $15 to $21. Lunch daily, 11 to 4. Dinner, from 5. Closed in winter, and Monday and Tuesday in off-season.

La Rosa Negra, 128 Second St., Lewes.
This long and narrow Italian downtown storefront restaurant is much loved by the locals, who rate the pastas the best around. The decor, a mix of black and white with red accents, is made more gala by tiny white lights at night. The food arrives on black octagonal plates.

Good starters are seafood focaccia, steamed New Zealand mussels and marinated blue crab claws. Pasta dishes are fairly standard, from spaghetti with meatballs marinara to fettuccine alfredo or puttanesca. More interesting were two specials of the day, red snapper with lump crabmeat topped with sundried tomato butter, and sautéed scallops with artichokes, prosciutto, parmesan and white wine over linguini. We also liked the chicken florentine gorgonzola, topped with sweet and sour bacon sauce and served with linguini. Other main courses run from chicken cacciatore to filet mignon and four veal dishes.

One couple we met, who were visiting Lewes for a week and had tried all the restaurants, liked this best and dined here twice.

(302) 645-1980. Entrées, $12.95 to $19.95. Lunch, Monday-Saturday 11:30 to 2:30. Dinner nightly, 5 to 9:30.

Rose & Crown, 108 Second St., Lewes.

The restaurant and pub here appear to be mostly bar, given the latter's position front and center and wrapping around the side. But appearances deceive. Beyond the bar, way out back, the place opens up into a two-story dining room with skylights in the ceiling, flags hanging from the brick walls and a mix of booths and tables.

The dinner fare is rather British with a local accent. Expect main courses like fish and chips, diced chicken and mushrooms in puff pastry, stuffed flounder, pork tenderloin and crab imperial, the house specialty. There's no roast beef on the menu, as in most British pubs, but there are pasta dishes and New York strip steak.

Two dinner items turn up on the lengthy lunch menu. We tried both the English cottage pie, a piping-hot dish of ground beef, peas and tomatoes, layered with mashed potatoes and melted cheese, and a ploughman's delight. The latter was mostly vegetables and wimpy cheese and came with the wrong kind of bread, but did have some Branston pickle. The taco salad at the next table looked to be a better bet.

We were mighty impressed with the lineup of international beers. And a pint of Watney's (one of several on tap) went down just fine.

(302) 645-2373. Entrées, $11.95 to $19.95. Lunch daily, 11 to 5; dinner nightly, 5 to 9 or 10.

Diversions

The sense of history and the quiet waterside attractions are what lure most visitors to Lewes.

History. The historic section of Delaware's oldest town – usually missed by motorists rushing to or from the Cape May-Lewes Ferry – is compact and eminently walkable. Most of the historic sites are spread out along Front, Second and Third streets in a quarter-mile stretch between Savannah Road and Shipcarpenter Street. The Lewes walking tour brochure points out 40 sites of special interest in the area that was discovered by Henry Hudson and settled by the Dutch in 1631. They range from the 1730 **Fisher-Martin House,** a gambrel-roofed structure moved from nearby Coolspring in 1980 to become the information center for the Lewes Chamber of Commerce and Visitors Bureau, to the 1850's Greek Revival **Doctor's Office,** a medical and dental museum, one of six buildings in the Lewes Historical Society complex. Other attractions include the 1797 **Cannonball House,** the last remaining Lewes house bearing a cannon-ball scar from the War of 1812 and now occasionally open as a marine museum, and **St. Peter's Episcopal Church Cemetery,** an unusual sight so close to downtown. Like many walking tour brochures, it neglects to point out some of the more interesting buildings. You'll enjoy chancing upon the 1790 **Rodney House,** home of one of Lewes's first families and now the site of the Surf and Sands Florist sandwiched between stores on Second Street. It looks much older than the better-known 1665 **Ryves Holt House** at Second and Mulberry streets, believed to be the oldest house still standing in Delaware. Two little finds are at the far end of West Third Street: one of the few remaining Dutch-style homes from the 18th century at 320, its fence brightened in summer by morning glories, and across the street at 321, an 18th-century Sussex County saltbox restored in 1981 as a private home. The **Lewes Historical Society Complex** at Shipcarpenter and Third streets, next to Shipcarpenter Square, harbors six buildings ranging from a 17th-century plank house, a log cabin that's one of the oldest extant buildings in the area, to the **Thompson Country Store,** where you obtain tickets for a guided tour of the complex. Open mid-June through Labor Day, Tuesday-Friday 11 to 4, Saturday 10 to 12:30. Admission, $6.

Zwaanendael Museum, Savannah Road and Kings Highway.

Built in 1931 for the town's Tricentennial, this exotic Dutch Renaissance building could be straight out of Holland. It is an adaptation of the town hall at Hoorn. Now

a state museum, it devotes its main floor to the story of the H.M.S. DeBraak, a British warship with a Dutch name that sank in a storm off Cape Henlopen in 1798 after it had stopped in Lewes for supplies. Supposedly laden with gold, it had defied treasure-seekers for nearly 200 years until 1986. It was found beneath 30 feet of sand in water 80 feet deep. More than 25,000 objects – but no gold bounty – were recovered from the ship-wreck. A few hundred are shown in a dozen vignettes, of which many find the one reflecting the life of a seaman aboard the ship most interesting. Artifacts from religious medallions to clay pipes to galley pots and plates are on display. Some credit the widely publicized recovery of the DeBraak with having first put on the tourists' map this quiet town steeped in maritime history and riverboat pilot lore. The museum's second floor contains changing local history exhibits (at our visit, one on African-American education in Sussex County, including an intricate little dollhouse-like, one-room school). History buffs also will find such relics as a stemmed drinking glass given to local governor-to-be David Hall and other Revolutionary War leaders by George Washington, an 1897 Lewes School class ring and a Delaware woman's collection of glass (inexplicably from Sandwich, Mass.) Also available are materials surrounding the 1926 collapse of the famed Cape Henlopen lighthouse, erected

Zwaanendahl Museum is Lewes landmark.

in 1763 as the second lighthouse in the new world but no match for the shifting sand dunes here.

(302) 645-1148. Open Tuesday-Saturday 10 to 4:30, Sunday 1:30 to 4:30. Free.

Cape Henlopen State Park, Lewes.

A mile east of Lewes, just past the Cape May-Lewes Ferry Terminal, lies this 4,103-acre park at the mouth of the Delaware Bay. It offers four miles of beach on ocean and bay, as well as nature trails, a bird sanctuary, the famed "walking dunes" shifting across the pine forest, and the Great Dune, at 80 feet the highest between Cape Hatteras and Cape Cod. The Seaside Nature Center has aquariums, a touch tank containing two horseshoe crabs and other exhibits of particular interest to youngsters. The bathhouse is large and modern, and the ocean beaches relatively uncrowded. When the surf's up here, families tend to prefer the town beaches along the calmer bay. Worth the effort is a short climb up a 115-step spiral staircase to the top of the restored observation tower, one of several relics from the abandoned Ford Miles military installation. Here, where patrollers watched for German submarines as arms were stashed in bunkers and gun emplacements below during World War II, you can scan the sea and landscape from the high-rises of Rehoboth Beach across the bay to New Jersey's Cape May. The views of the sunsets here are spectacular.

(302) 645-6852. Park open 8 a.m. to sunset, year-round. Cars, $5 in summer.

Nassau Valley Vineyards, 33 Nassau Commons.

The story of this fledgling winery, Delaware's first, is really that of Peggy Raley. A drama graduate of American University, the breathless and blithe blonde spent a couple of years "globetrotting" for Friends of Wine magazine before coming home to her father Bob's burgeoning office and retail complex in the Nassau section of Lewes. He launched her with 5 percent seed money. She borrowed the rest to open the winery after writing and personally shepherding the enabling legislation through the state legislature. Until the local harvest is big enough, supplemental grapes and production facilities have been offered by friends at Chaddsford, Ingleside Plantation and Meredyth wineries. Jill-of-all-trades Peggy, who's partial to red wines, touts her limited edition cabernet sauvignon, graced by an Old Testament painting by local artist Tom Wilson, first of an artist series. Her wines also include chardonnay and rosé. Peggy pours samples in the tasting room after visitors take a self-guided tour alongside the production facility, an unusually showy and informative visual display that's almost like a museum on the history of winemaking. Peggy was talking of big things to exemplify the name of her winery, which she said is a play on the Napa Valley. Fifteen buildings that her father moved to the site "as a little restored Williamsburg" are to become shops.

(302) 645-9463. Open Tuesday-Saturday 11 to 5, Sunday noon to 5.

Shopping. For a small town, Lewes is blessed with unusually sophisticated shops and unusually friendly shopkeepers. Most are located along tree-shaded Second Street and a few along Front Street. Amanda Lucks, former owner of the Inn on Canal Square, started with a small gourmet and coffee shop, hence the name **Sugar & Spice.** It has grown like Topsy and now stretches back through a warren of rooms displaying local artworks, handpainted birdhouses and weathervanes into a huge Christmas shop. Some of the most interesting wares are stocked by Gavin and Lou Braithwaite, who own **Puzzles** (all kinds of puzzles), **The Stepping Stone,** where we coveted everything from carved egrets to great windsocks, and the adjacent **Union Jack** (all things British). We liked the umbrellas bearing cats and dogs, respectively, **at Nature's Touch of Lewes,** a boutique full of clothing, jewelry and gifts, many with an animal accent. A tall blue heron in the window lured us into **Thistles,** a wonderful trove of stained-glass lamps, hand-painted oyster Santas for Christmas tree decorations, silverware, children's clothing and a few items of women's apparel. Behind it is **Greenhorn,** featuring Southwestern jewelry, blankets and cookbooks along with enough vests, hats and mountain items to give it a distinctly Western flair. Underneath is **Auntie M's Emporium,** which the owners (one an antiquer and the other a writer) likened to "browsing in someone's basement." We were taken by all the old books and wrought-iron garden items here; the owners also have another store in the old firehouse and jail at 116 West Third.

Art, pottery and gifts with a statuary theme are featured at **The Saxon Swan,** where we liked a neat statue bearing bird feed in its outstretched hands. **The Gift Network** stocks handcrafts, quilts, wood crafts, dolls and miniatures. The **Dockside Gift Shop,** here since 1977 ("long before Lewes was discovered by tourists," says owner Mary Perez), looks like your standard nautical gift shop but has unique touches, from shirts and bags silk-screened by a local artist to lighthouse replicas, birds and scrimshaw. Women's apparel is featured at The Jetty, Figure Head and Twila Farrell. Antiques are everywhere, but nowhere in such quantity as with assorted dealers at the **Lewes Mercantile Antique Mall.** Garden accessories, period furniture and a complete line of Cat's Meow villages, including 23 Lewes pieces, are among the offerings at **The Swan's Nest.**

Take a break from your shopping rounds with ice cream from **King's Homemade Ice Cream Shop,** a Delaware institution to which many folks repair after dinner as well as all day long. Or stop at the **Oby Lee Coffee Roastery** for a pastry to accompany your morning espresso. **Cinnamon Falls** offers pastries and a few lunch items to accompany its gourmet coffees at stand-up tables facing the canal or at sit-down, wrought-iron tables out front. Another place for a snack to eat in or take out is **A Taste of Heaven.**

Extra-Special ⸻

Shipcarpenter Square. The developer of this novel residential complex eschewed the new construction prevalent elsewhere and moved 35 rundown or abandoned structures to the western edge of the Lewes historic district. Built between 1720 and 1880, they came from around the Delmarva Peninsula. Now these ramshackle buildings that most people wouldn't have paid a cent for are restored as private homes, upgraded with modern kitchens and bathrooms and surrounded by railed patios, fancy gardens and homey outbuildings. Some liken it to Colonial Williamsburg, but this close-together, close-in compound beats Williamsburg for livability, as attested by all the Mercedeses and Corvettes parked in the driveways. Particularly appealing are the looks of the 1795 timbered log house from Maryland and the dark red 19th-century schoolhouse from Milton, both now charming homes. You can walk or drive around the both the perimeter and the interior of the horseshoe-shaped community to see the unusual "telescope" house from Accomac, Va., or the colorful Victorian house from Wilmington College.

Court House that served as first state capitol is centerpiece of historic New Castle.

New Castle, Del.

The Smallest of Wonders

In the state that proclaims itself "Small Wonder," surely New Castle is the smallest wonder of all. And perhaps its most choice wonder.

This is the town where Peter Stuyvesant laid out the green in 1651, the town where William Penn set foot in the New World in 1682, the town that became the first state's first capital. But Wilmington and Dover eventually overshadowed its early importance. A plan to restore the old town into a second Colonial Williamsburg was aborted in the late 1940s. And so New Castle remains – the living example of a rare Dutch-English-American river town from the Colonial era. The population of this historic district roughly three blocks wide and five blocks deep numbers 1,500, about the same as in its heyday.

The old town is often bypassed, hidden just off Interstate 95 south of the towering Delaware Memorial Bridge. The past is everywhere apparent along the cobblestoned, tree-lined streets clustered beside the Delaware River. Like the better-known historic district of Charleston, New Castle has a Battery park. It also has The Strand and The Green. There's a wonderful sense of access to a waterfront sheltered from the industrial disarray on all sides. Here you walk around the waterfront park, down Packet Alley, up the pedestrian path beside the Presbyterian Church to the green and the gravestones beside Immanuel Episcopal Church, and peer into the handful of stores along Delaware Street.

Two centuries of architectural styles are displayed in more than 50 landmark structures. Five are open to the public as museums showing the Dutch and English Colonial periods. Others, where life continues today amid a patina of yesteryear, are revealed to the several thousand visitors who come here the third Saturday of every May for "A Day in Old New Castle," a local tradition since 1924.

Still, only about 30,000 tourists visit New Castle annually, many of them on bus tours. It is not a visitor-friendly town. There is no information center for

Armitage Inn faces the strand where William Penn set foot in America.

orientation purposes or brochures, and the fledgling New Castle Visitors Bureau operates impersonally through a post office box and a toll-free number, (800) 758-1550. Until the mid-1980s, there was only one guest house. Now there are five, but the lack of accommodations means that many visitors must head for motels along the Route 13 strip, the other New Castle more obvious to transients.

For New Castle really has two identities. One is the modern-day sprawl away from the river, not really New Castle but bearing its address since the New Castle post office serves a wider area, a situation that "gets everybody confused," according to one local historian. The other is the easily defined old town, separate and apart – a small National Landmark Historic Area of Colonial and Federal vintage, likened to that of Charleston and the French Quarter but considered unique in the country.

The old section of New Castle is one of those rare places where the hackneyed phrase "step back in time" truly means something.

Inn Spots

All but one of New Castle's guest houses have emerged in the last dozen years. A town ordinance limits most new B&Bs in New Castle to three rooms.

Armitage Inn, 2 The Strand, New Castle 19720.

A walk-in cooking fireplace in a kitchen dating to 1670 testifies to the age of this handsome brick house facing the strand where William Penn set foot in the New World. Transformed into an elegant B&B in 1995, it was occupied by a Revolutionary War patriot who served as the early town's chief magistrate and began a tradition of hospitality when he provided sustenance for weary post riders passing through with news of the war's progress.

Steve Marks, a 25-year area resident who tired of the printing business, and his wife Rina did a masterful job of readying the 1732 residence for contemporary guests. On either side of a front foyer facing Battery Park and the river are a formal parlor notable for lovely oriental rugs and a wall of good-luck symbols, and a huge rose-colored dining room outfitted with a table set for ten. Both rooms are full of collections from the couple's travels. The rear of the house includes a library and a porch overlooking a walled garden and a cottage.

The original wide-planked wood stairs ascend to a suite and four guest rooms, all with private baths, featherbeds, TVs and telephones, hair dryers and other amenities. Newest is the Angelica Suite, second-floor rear, with a hand-crocheted cover on the queensize canopy bed and a sitting room that was once a nursery. The prized White Rose Room has a king four-poster bed draped in white fabric, a bay window facing the river and a large bath with one of the inn's three whirlpool tubs. Queen beds are tucked beneath the sloping roof lines in the two third-floor rooms, one enhanced by floral stenciling.

Steve prepares and serves a gourmet breakfast to remember. Typical items are fresh fruit, homemade muffins and breads, apple-peach crisp and french toast. His maple-cream cheese pastries were featured in Bon Appétit magazine's Colonial Thanksgiving issue.

(302) 328-6618. Fax (302) 324-1163. Four rooms and one suite with private baths. Doubles, $110 to $185. Suite, $180. Two-night minimum at certain times. Children over 12. No smoking.

Fox Lodge, 123 West 7th St., New Castle 19720.

The Gothic Revival mansion known locally as "The Castle" is becoming a European-style country B&B with a hunt theme. Elaine and William Class moved from Southern California in 1995 for a change in occupation and lifestyle. Elaine, an interior decorator, was undaunted by the challenge of restoring a 33-room mansion that had seen better days. "I'm taking it one room at a time," she said, opening the first three bedrooms in 1996. Building regulations stymied her plans for six more bedrooms, all with private baths, on the second and third floors.

Built by a physician named Lesley, the main floor with its thirteen-foot-high ceilings retains vestiges of its use as a doctor's office. Elaine pointed out the small waiting room, which was converted by the Classes into their private family room, and the examining room, with its fireplace

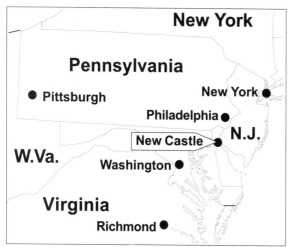

and pressed-tin walls. The physician obviously put more emphasis on his family living quarters than on his office. The original, eight-foot-high cast-bronze chandelier is a focal point of the manorial drawing room. Another is the two enormous neo-Gothic Revival wicker club chairs with tassels and ceramic legs. All but one of the nine fireplace mantels are made of marble, the exception being the one of carved walnut and Mercer tiles in the dining room. The wood shutters on the windows of the library are "so beautiful that we decided not to cover them up with velvet swags," Elaine said. In fact, this isn't what people expect of a Victorian B&B. She enhanced the Gothic colors and features with contemporary accents and California furnishings. "I'm not a slave to Bradbury and lace everywhere. The architecture here is so strong and masculine that I don't want the decor to detract."

Check out the trompe-l'oeil railing painted in the 1920s along the wall of the hand-carved, dark oak staircase. It's so real that many a guest reaches out to hold on.

On the second floor are three guest rooms with private baths, queensize beds, twelve-foot-high ceilings and décor that's unusual, to say the least. The master bedroom is named for Jane Lesley, the physician's wife, whose "ghost still visits us and goes to town on occasion," says Elaine (that's another story). She designed and built the bed's headboard of California yucca stems and a rope holding a mosquito net canopy. There are two wing chairs for seats, but only one bedside lamp other than lights on the ceiling fan for reading.

The Malvern Room, named for Elaine's mother, has a violet blue floor, tin ceiling and trim, a queensize wicker bed and a free-standing green washstand in the room. The Lisa Room, named for her daughter, is striking for the wrought-iron gates and antique porch posts that pass for the headboard of the queen bed. It opens into Zula, named for her daughter's Siberian husky, which may be rented as a rather spare living room with a sofabed, two twig chairs and no lamps to form a suite. Off it is an unfinished rooftop porch with a view of the Victorian and medieval gardens under restoration on the property.

A lodge-style, hunt breakfast adheres to the masculine theme of Gothic times. Juice and cereal precede such possibilities as fresh oatmeal soup (inspired by Jacques Pepin), kippers, cold sliced ham, a cottage cheese sundae, and grilled mushrooms and tomatoes. In the afternoon, guests are offered beer, wine, herbal teas and snacks in Piglets Tavern, a roving place that eventually will land in the former basement kitchen. Poetry readings, singing, music, séances and Gothic romance movies are scheduled periodically.

(302) 328-0768. www.foxlodge.com. Three rooms and suites with private baths. Doubles, $105 to $135, as suite $185. Children over 12. No smoking.

The Terry House, 130 Delaware St., New Castle 19720.

This Federal brick townhouse was built in the early 1860s by a banker for his family. It harbors comfortable lodgings and two lovely rear verandas, one above the other, with views across the Battery Park to the water.

The house contains three guest rooms with queensize canopy or poster beds, private baths, telephones and cable TV, plus a small single room. Those in front look onto Market Square and the Old Court House; two in the rear yield views of the park and river when the foliage is off the trees. Fresh flowers, dried-flower wreaths, bedside chocolates, scatter rugs on bare redwood floors and period antiques are the norm. Decorative touches include a shelf displaying a collection of cups and saucers in one room.

Guests enjoy a handsome parlor, quite elegant with ornate carved friezes, swagged draperies and a brass chandelier. The side verandas on two stories and the deep, shady rear lawn are also furnished for relaxation.

Breakfast is served at a table for eight in the formal dining room, full of mahogany pieces in the Queen Anne and Federal styles. The fare includes fresh fruit, cereal, muffins and breakfast casseroles, perhaps an egg dish or puff pancakes.

The Terry House was sold as this edition went to press. Buyers James and Lena Buckler, owners of the Flower Farm Inn in Kennett Square, Pa., planned to move here. James, a former photographer for the Smithsonian, said they would fill their new B&B with antiques "from wall to wall and from end to end."

(302) 322-2505. Fax (302) 328-1987. Three rooms with private baths. Doubles, $90 to $98. Children over 10. No smoking.

William Penn Guest House, 206 Delaware St., New Castle 19720.

The restored 1682 house in which William Penn slept was the first of New Castle's modern-day lodgings. Irma and Dick Burwell bought the residence in 1956. "When I asked what I should do with it," Irma recalls, "someone suggested a B&B. I said I could do the bed, but not the breakfast." That's because she already was involved in the Coffee House, a restaurant next door.

Now retired, the Burwells do serve breakfast – continental style, with fresh fruit and homemade muffins or croissants – to overnight guests who stay in four air-conditioned bedrooms. It's taken amidst fancy lace and sterling in the dining room behind a pleasant parlor in this townhouse that's one room wide, a couple of rooms deep and three stories high.

William Penn slept in one room, second floor rear, now outfitted with quilt-covered twin beds, an oriental rug and a little black and white TV. It shares a clawfoot-tub bathroom with a front double-bedded room, also with TV. Two more bedrooms on the third floor share a tiled bath.

(302) 328-7736. Four bedrooms with shared baths. Doubles, $65 to $95. No smoking.

Rodeway Inn, 111 South du Pont Hwy., New Castle 19720.

Too bad this little local prize long known as the Dutch Village Motor Inn had to take on national airs with a Rodeway affiliation. But still special is the configuration of little duplexes that look not unlike haciendas, strung along a winding driveway back from the highway and amazingly quiet (testimony in part to the building techniques of the early post-war era). Lawn chairs are scattered about the grounds.

Two rooms go off an enclosed foyer in each duplex. The larger rooms in which we've stayed contain two double beds, expansive wraparound cantilevered windows that open and big closets with coat hangers and luggage racks. There's room to spare in each for a TV on a dresser, a table and two cushioned chairs.

Continental breakfast is included in the rates.

The Rodeway connection coincided with the arrival of owners Pierre and Peggy Olivero, who formerly owned the Terry House B&B. They said that, despite high AAA and Mobil ratings and a toll-free number, a stand-alone motel with a local name was no longer viable. This remains a good spot to know about.

(302) 328-6246 or (800) 321-6246. Forty rooms with private baths. Doubles, $64 to $74.

Blue and gold dining room is dressed for dinner at The Arsenal at Old New Castle.

Dining Spots

The Arsenal at Old New Castle, 30 Market St., New Castle.
Built by the federal government as an arsenal in anticipation of the War of 1812, this handsome, cupola-topped building facing the green has served a variety of purposes, among them a school and a restaurant called the Newcastle Inn, nicely authentic and catering to bus tours and private parties.

The restaurant was abruptly closed in 1994 shortly after a fire at the David Phinney Inn and restaurant, leaving historic New Castle without its two key dining spots – a situation repeated again in the winter of 2000. The reopened David Phinney suddenly closed indefinitely, and the renamed Arsenal on the Green restaurant closed temporarily for renovations by new owners.

Tika and Dick Day, who operate Jessop's Tavern (see below), reopened the Arsenal with a military motif. The theme starts in the entry foyer, where diners encounter a cannon and framed uniforms of Confederate and Union soldiers on the walls. To the left is the Eagle & Cannon Tavern, sporting another cannon, a flag from an old Delaware battalion and a series of Civil War paintings loaned by local artist Philip Wikoff. To the right is the high-ceilinged 1812 Room, elegant in blue and gold with Schumacher wallpapers and fabrics, a faux fireplace and brass chandeliers. An upstairs ballroom, decorated in pale green with green damask curtains, is keyed to the Colonial era and the Revolutionary War.

Executive chef Tim Bell from Jessop's oversees a varied menu of traditional American fare with European influences. Dinner dishes vary from dijon-encrusted salmon, seafood norfolk in puff pastry, and shrimp and lobster fra diavolo to cornish game hen with apricot glaze, veal marsala and chateaubriand for two. Chicken breast topped with crab imperial and hollandaise sauce is a local favorite.

Listed as starters under "1812 Overtures" are cheese-topped crabmeat and artichokes with toasted garlic bread slices and a signature item called militia mozzarella, lightly breaded and sautéed with a tomato concasse. Pineapple slaw accompanies deviled oysters on the half shell. Changing desserts might be apple pie, chocolate mousse cake and raspberry cream cheese torte.

Lighter, less expensive items are offered all day in the tavern. *(302) 328-1290. Entrées, $14.95 to $22.95. Lunch, Tuesday-Saturday 11:30 to 3. Dinner, Tuesday-Saturday 5 to 10. Tavern, Tuesday-Saturday 11:30 to 10.*

Jessop's Tavern, 114 Delaware St., New Castle.
The former Green Frog tavern, a dark pub with mediocre food, gave way in 1996 to this cheerful pub and Colonial-style dining room. It's named for Abraham Jessop, a cooper who built the original structure in 1724.

Top-to-bottom renovations added a fireplace, a modern kitchen, wood plank floor and nautical oil paintings. The locals were quickly impressed with the large portions of substantial American food at prices out of the past. And there are accents from the English, Dutch and Swedish heritage of the region.

Proprietors Tika and Dick Day raise pub grub above the usual genre in classics like shepherd's pie and fish and chips, as well as hefty sandwiches and such appetizers as grilled English flat bread, Swedish crayfish and Dutch oysters Van Dyke. The chef shines at dinner, producing a variety from grilled trout stuffed with pineapple and grilled salmon topped with crab imperial to chicken fricassee, roast duck, lamb chops, porterhouse steak and prime rib with caramelized onions and brandy-glazed mushrooms.

Swedish apple pie with vanilla custard sauce, bread pudding, fruit cobbler and angel food cake topped with seasonal fruit and whipped cream are among the desserts.
(302) 322-6111. Entrées, $12.95 to $19.95. Lunch, Monday-Saturday 11 to 3. Dinner, Monday-Saturday 5 to 10.

Lynnhaven Inn, 154 North du Pont Hwy. (Route 13), New Castle.
Built years ago as a country inn/restaurant when this still was out in the country, the Lynnhaven remains a beacon of good food and serenity in the midst of the frantic commercial strip that developing New Castle has spawned. The colors of the handsome facade – beige with burgundy trim – are repeated inside the two main dining rooms, which contain well-spaced tables and booths for two and an early American decor. Horsey paintings grace the walls and plates; trays and decoys line shelves here and there. The pleasant brick and beamed lounge with its curving bar displays ship models and nautical antiques.

More decoys and wood-carved fish are shown in lighted display cases in the foyer. They're the work of Andrew Asimos, brother of owner-manager George Asimos, whose family has run the restaurant since 1957.

A team of four chefs, each with impressive credentials, prepares an extensive menu of basically American fare with an emphasis on local seafood. Shrimp aegean, Maryland crab cakes, seafood stir-fry over saffron rice, blackened chicken and shrimp, veal parmigiana, prime rib and steak diane are among the possibilities. House salads come with both the main courses and six pasta dishes. Start with escargots en croûte, clams casino or stuffed jalapeño peppers, or a cup of authentic snapper turtle soup. Finish with chocolate mousse, cheese cake or a changing selection of cakes and pies.

Some of the dinner dishes as well as selections listed under light fare turn up on the menu for lunch, which is popular with the business crowd.
(302) 328-2041. Entrées, $15.95 to $26.95. Lunch, Monday-Friday 11:30 to 3:30. Dinner, 3:30 to 10, Saturday 4 to 10, Sunday 1 to 9.

Air Transport Command, 143 North du Pont Hwy. (Route 13), New Castle.

Near the airport is this Disneyland of a theme-park restaurant, an incredible mélange that's most un-New Castle-like but immensely popular for the novelty of it all. Tanks and military craft are scattered about the outside of a building that's a cross between a castle and a military camp. Wend your way across a bridge and through a maze to the dining room – make that three, seating 200 amid a collection of World War II memorabilia. This is candlelit, white-tablecloth dining at tiered tables with views of the airport runways. Get yourselves ensconced in one of the intimate side-by-side booths for two and you can't get out – until the staff slides away the heavy table, which rolls on wheels.

At our visit, the "specialties maison" were as diverse as calves liver, chicken moutarde, shrimp stir-fry and lemon veal, but most people seemed to go for the seven kinds of steaks and prime rib. We went with the flow, choosing prime rib and a petite filet mignon. Neither proved as memorable as the surroundings.

(302) 328-3527. Entrées, $13.95 to $28.95. Lunch, Monday-Saturday 11 to 3. Dinner, 3 to 10 or 11. Sunday, brunch 9:30 to 3, dinner 3 to 10.

Cellar Gourmet, 208 Delaware St., New Castle.

When a chiropractor purchased the 1802 Janvier House in the early 1980s, he was determined to turn the basement into a badly needed healthful and informal family restaurant. With a dirt floor and low ceiling, the project was quite a challenge and the front wall fell in. Now shored up with a new wall, the interesting room has local scenes etched into tables and benches built into the rocks.

Under the ownership of Sue Ellis, the lunch menu offers salads, sandwiches, light bites and vegetarian items. Desserts range from a variety of ice creams to warm caramel-apple pie, and at one visit included a sticky bun à la mode. Sue also runs a coffee shop upstairs.

(302) 323-0999. Open Tuesday-Sunday, 9 to 4.

Diversions

Not a reconstruction of replicas, New Castle is a living museum of superb restorations virtually unchanged since the mid-1800s. "The spirit of the town is not that of an antiquarian society at all," says the definitive book *New Castle on the Delaware,* a federal WPA writers' project compiled in the 1930s and revised in the 1970s. "The dwellers are as preoccupied with their own affairs as are Americans elsewhere. They take the town as a matter of course, a part of the background of their business, and like it as it is....The distinction of New Castle today is due to the busy daily life that has gone on in it without break through the centuries, achieving a fairly congenial blending of old and new in activity and interests. This is something rather rare in our country, rarer than in parts of Europe where a town normally has not only length, breadth and height, but also an imposing time dimension accepted as one of the realities of the place."

New Castle Heritage Trail. Most of the structures in the long two square blocks in the center of old New Castle are detailed in a brochure available at the municipal office. Walking is the best way to see the sites. Join New Castilians as they walk or jog around **The Battery** park beside the Delaware. Poke along the undulating brick sidewalks of **The Strand,** pausing to look at the vestiges of the old store with an early Ivory Soap billboard painted three stories high on the side of a brick dwelling along **Packet Alley.** Cut through a garden walkway beside the historic 1707 **Presbyterian Church** to the shady Green. Prominent Delawareans are buried in the graveyard at **Immanuel Episcopal Church** (1703), which since 1924 has sponsored the famed A Day in Old New Castle the third Saturday in May on the Green. Other sights worth noting are the **Old Town Hall and Markethouses** with an unusual open archway connecting Delaware Street and the Market Place, the 1789 **Academy,** the 1809 **U.S. Arsenal,** the original **ticket office** for the old New Castle-Frenchtown Railroad, and the **Town Wharf,** where little remains to validate the claim that New Castle was once an important shipping and transportation center.

New Castle Court House, Delaware Street.

The largest structure in downtown New Castle, this is the oldest surviving courthouse in Delaware (1732) and also served as Delaware's first state capitol. The capital was moved to Dover and the county seat to Wilmington, and the scene of so much early history is now virtually still except for public tours offered by the Delaware State Museums. "We are interpreters, not docents," said the site supervisor. "We try to bring the building and the situations that occurred in it alive." The courtroom contains a judge's bench, witness stand and prisoner's dock.

(302) 323-4453 or (800) 441-8846. Open Tuesday-Saturday 10 to 3:30, Sunday 1:30 to 4:30. Free.

The Dutch House, 32 East Third St.

This improbably low-slung house with a door, two windows and overhang roof is New Castle's only complete surviving house built prior to 1700. It's also believed to be the oldest brick house in Delaware. Typical of Dutch Colonial architecture, it is furnished with early Dutch furniture and artifacts, including a Dutch Bible and a courting bench.

Another house museum run by the New Castle Historical Society is the **Amstel House,** Fourth and Delaware Streets. George Washington was a wedding guest in 1784 in this imposing Georgian house built a half century earlier. Later the home of Gov. Nicholas Van Dyke, it has antique furnishings and a complete Colonial kitchen on view.

(302) 322-2794. Open March-December, Tuesday-Saturday 11 to 4, Sunday 1 to 4; weekends in January and February. Adults, $2.25 each house; combination ticket, $4.

Old Library Museum, 40 East Third St.

Its fanciful hexagonal structure and three-level skylight make this an unusual site for a library. Philadelphia architect Frank Furness designed it in 1892 for the New Castle Library Company's collection of classics and law books. Today it is owned by the Trustees of the New Castle Common, which preserves 700 acres of early lands around the town in something of a civic coup for old New Castle. It's leased to the New Castle Historical Society for exhibits and a slide presentation on the town.

(302) 322-2794. Open Thursday-Saturday 11 to 4, Sunday 1 to 4. Free.

Shopping. Although this has always been a working town, most of the commerce has moved with suburbia up to Route 13. The Visitors Bureau guide to old New Castle cites sixteen places of interest, five lodgings and ten places to shop, one of them a realty office and others seeming to change every year or two. Biggest of the stores is **O'Donalds Variety & Souvenir Store,** one of the old school,

George Read II house is one of the more exceptional Georgian house museums anywhere.

with an ice cream parlor at the side. Antiques and collectibles are featured in the adjacent **Opera House Antiques Center.** English tea is served weekend afternoons in the **Victorian Tea Room** of the opera house in which Jenny Lind and Enrico Caruso once sang.

Specialty stores of interest are Bobbie Morrow's **Stitches That Count** needlepoint shop; **Lauren Lynch Antiques & Co.,** four Colonial rooms with furniture, linens, art and such, and **Gifts-n-Stuff Ltd.,** where the emphasis is on the latter. Two exceptional rare book stores are **Oak Knoll Books,** upstairs in the Opera House Antiques Center, and **James Goode & Co.,** which took over the Oak Knoll site and is a treasure trove of architecture and garden books collected by a retired Smithsonian curator.

Extra-Special

George Read II House and Garden, 42 The Strand, New Castle.

"The grandest mansion and oldest gardens in New Castle," says the sign outside. Actually one of the outstanding Georgian house museums anywhere, this was completed in 1804 by the prosperous lawyer-son of a signer of the Declaration of Independence. It's a huge house with an unimpeded view of the river, towering above its neighbors along The Strand. Now owned by the Historical Society of Delaware, it is a living museum of the decorative crafts from the Federal period. An iron balcony and palladian window surmount the handsome doorway, itself topped by a fanlight. Inside are incised marble window sills and lintels, a stunning Greek key trompe-l'oeil cornice decoration in the entry hall, and elaborately carved detailing in the woodwork, masonry and plastering. The house and its attached servants' wing are surrounded by formal gardens designed in the style of Andrew Jackson Downing, foremost landscape architect of the mid-19th century. The Colonial Revival taste of later owners is preserved in three rooms that contrast with the restored Read interiors. There is a small museum shop in the basement entry.

(302) 322-8411. Open March-December, Tuesday-Saturday 10 to 4, Sunday noon to 4; weekend hours in January and February. Adults, $4.

Chadds Ford, Pa.

Wyeth and du Pont Country

Although the Battle of the Brandywine stamped Chadds Ford's place in history, the Wyeth family has given it cachet.

This two-bit hamlet along the Brandywine is named for the farmer and tavern-keeper who ferried travelers across the river at "John Chad's fording place." Here is where George Washington made his stand in 1777 against British troops on the march from nearby Kennett Square to the new nation's capital at Philadelphia. Some of the British crossed here as expected; others outwitted Washington by outflanking him to the north. The biggest battle of the Revolution went to the Crown.

The bucolic landscape later inspired many an artist, among them Howard Pyle, father of modern American illustration. Most famous of his students in classes at Chadds Ford was N.C. Wyeth, who settled his family along the Brandywine early in the 20th century and launched three generations of artistic talent here. Andrew Wyeth was born in Chadds Ford and still is said to go out on foot daily to seek inspiration for his work. The works of America's foremost family of artists are the cornerstone of the famed Brandywine River Museum.

The Brandywine winds past forests, meadows and hillsides in a rural, almost Vermont-like strip through encroaching exurbia. Side by side with pastoral landscapes that are the backdrops of Wyeth paintings lie the du Pont estates, substantial tract houses, shopping areas and office parks of the Philadelphia-Wilmington corridor. Busy U.S. Route 1 traverses the area's midsection and crosses the Brandywine, as did the British, at Chadds Ford.

The hamlet's appeal derives partly from its scenic landscape, its trademark houses and barns of gray fieldstone and its abiding ruralness, utterly unexpected in the midst of so much development. Its winding, back roads are made for getting lost.

The appeal of the broader Brandywine Valley, which fans out on all sides from Chadds Ford, comes mainly from its uncommon concentration of sophisticated

Old stone wagon is on view outside stone barn housing Chadds Ford Historical Society museum.

museums. Most owe their existence to one branch or another of the du Pont family, a name as strongly identified with the region as that of the Wyeths.

Together they lend sophistication to one of America's most celebrated landscapes.

Inn Spots

Accommodations range from country hotels and chain motels to small inns and home-stay B&Bs. We concentrate here on a variety situated near Chadds Ford or reflective of its particular ambiance. The geography involves a narrow section along the Route 1 corridor from Lima to Kennett Square and along the north-south Route 52/100 corridor from Chadds Ford to Fairville and across the state line into Delaware.

The Inn at Montchanin Village, Route 100 at Kirk Road, Montchanin, Del. 19710.

An historic 19th-century workers' village, built by industrialist E.I. du Pont to house laborers who worked at the nearby du Pont gunpowder mills and factories along the Brandywine River, now houses and feeds guests in high style. With an uncanny knack for anticipating the needs of sophisticated travelers, local preservationists Missy and Daniel Lickle set about creating 33 bedrooms and suites plus a 55-seat restaurant in eleven buildings.

The twenty-acre site, a terraced enclave sloping toward the Brandywine, represents the core of the old village named in honor of du Pont family matriarch Anne Alexandrine de Montchanin, and has been in the family for five generations.

Guest accommodations and amenities were dictated by the idiosyncrasies of a row of turn-of-the-century duplexes, dependencies, a schoolhouse, a blacksmith shop, a stone barn and the du Pont railroad station.

Most of the accommodations are one- or two-bedroom suites with sitting areas and wet bars. Our quarters in Belin turned out to be fairly typical. It contained a cozy downstairs sitting room with plump sofa and chair covered in chintz, a TV atop a gas fireplace and a kitchenette area in the corner with wet bar, microwave and mini-refrigerator, complete with automatic icemaker and stocked with soft drinks and mineral water. Coffee and end tables were charmingly painted with flowers and rabbits. Everything was colorfully decorated in mix-and-match patterns that flow together. Up steep stairs was a skylit bedroom with a king bed dressed in Frette linens, about the most

Comfortable furnishings and fireplace typify rooms at The Inn at Montchanin Village.

comfortable we've had the pleasure of luxuriating in, and a stunning, huge, all-marble bathroom. The latter came with chandelier, a deep tub embedded in marble, a separate shower encased in thick clear glass and, if you turned on the right switch, heated towel racks. Wood-look venetian blinds covered the windows, padded hangers and ironing equipment were in the closet, and a country window had been painted whimsically on the wall beside a real window.

The inn's distinctive cowbird logo – a bird perched on the back of a leaping cow – was everywhere (monogrammed on the terry robes, embedded in the marble above the bath). The bed was turned down with chocolates and a copy of the weather forecast, and a thermos of ice water was placed beside.

Breakfast the next morning was served beside the front windows in Krazy Kat's, the inn's dramatic restaurant (see Dining Spots). Fresh orange juice and muffins were preliminaries to the main event, a choice including eggs benedict and an omelet with smoked bacon, brie and chives, tasty walnut-raisin toast, garlicky browned potatoes and garnishes of large blackberries.

Afterward, Missy Lickle led a tour of the six-acre site, a steeply sloping complex sandwiched between main road and train track. Golf carts are lined up to transport luggage from parking areas. All is artfully landscaped and full of surprises, from picket fences to gaslights to porches with wicker rockers.

Room sizes and configurations differ, but each appeals in its own right. The Jefferson offers wicker porches front and back and a bathroom walled in travertine marble up to the vaulted ceiling. Missy, who decorated with goods from her nearby gourmet emporium known as Everything But the Kitchen Sink, incorporated fine antiques and heirloom furniture, Staffordshire figurines, colorful animal print and floral fabrics, and a delightful sense of whimsy. Dan's penchant for architectural hardware shows up in antique Bennington doorknobs and iron door pulls and hinges commissioned from a local forger.

(302) 888-2133 or (800) 269-2473. Fax (302) 888-0389. Eleven rooms and 22 suites with private baths. Doubles, $160 to $180. Suites, $190 to $500. Two-night minimum weekends. No smoking.

Whitewing Farm, 370 Valley Road, West Chester, Pa. 19382.

One of the early occupants of a suite at this stylish B&B fashioned from the former estate of the treasurer of the du Pont Company was a Cabinet-level official from the Clinton administration. "We're calling it the Lincoln Room," quips Edward DeSeta, innkeeper with his wife Wanda. "Except you don't have to pay $50,000 or $100,000 a night."

In fact, the suite upstairs in the main house goes for $180 a night and represents good value, considering all the amenities at this lavish estate reflecting the good life in the heart of du Pont country. The DeSetas moved to their dream of a farm in 1992 with three children and no intention of running a B&B. An innkeeper/ friend who had overbooked called breathlessly one day to ask the DeSetas to put up her guests in their pool house. "All you have to do is serve them breakfast," Wanda recalls being told. "And I've been serving breakfast ever since."

The 43-acre property is perhaps less a traditional B&B than a small resort, what with a swimming pool with a newly built-in jacuzzi, a twelve-foot-deep fishing pond, ducks quacking around lily ponds and a waterfall, a ten-hole chip and putt golf course, a tennis court, a greenhouse and perennial gardens for the growing of flowers. But for the new suite, the other accommodations are not in the sprawling fieldstone and clapboard mansion dating to 1796, but rather in four outbuildings where guests are left pretty much on their own. And, after showing guests to their rooms, the members of the busy DeSeta family go their various ways, although they're up early for the breakfast hour that starts at 7:30.

The family lives upstairs in the mansion, but share the lovely downstairs with guests. A knockout country kitchen with french doors onto a terrace was created from five small rooms. From it come the cookies and pumpkin bars that greet arriving guests. Unfolding one after another are a paneled reading room with fireplace and TV, a living room full of substantial antiques and some of the couple's diverse collections, a huge beamed game room with fireplace, pool table, TV and even a small kitchen for refreshments, and a large sun porch overlooking the grounds.

Two comfortable guest rooms are in the converted stables, and three in the carriage house. Renovated for the purpose, each has a queensize bed (one is kingsize), modern bathroom (shower only) with marble floor, TV and a veritable library of books. They're decorated in a hunt theme with pale yellow walls, splashy fabrics and thick green carpeting.

Our quarters in the Gatehouse Suite included a skylit living room with a fireplace and sofabed, a book-lined den with one plush chair in front of the TV, a skylit bedroom with kingsize bed, a beauty of a bathroom done in marble with a bouquet of rosebuds (this in autumn) reflected in the mirror on the vanity, a modern kitchen and a terrace with a gas grill. We could understand why a Texas family considers it home during their annual six-week summer stay.

Two simpler rooms were fashioned from the former men's and women's

Main house and pool house look onto pond at Whitewing Farm.

changing facilities in the Pond House. The decor is garden style, the bed head-board is a picket fence and a patio with wrought-iron lounge chairs faces the idyllic pond, with its frogs croaking and its fountain lit at night. Recently upgraded, they now have built-in cabinets for the TV and marble floors for the bathrooms.

The DeSotas are not through. In 2000, they were adding two large fireplaced suites in another structure and an exercise facility, gathering/breakfast room and upstairs library in an old hay barn. Ed had just acquired a 1930 Ford Model A sedan and a 1938 Ford pickup truck in which to taxi guests. These joined two antique carriages and two sleighs they keep in a new barn they built across the street. Ed was crazy about his new horse named "A Little Bit Tipsy," a companion for the cow his wife bought him for his birthday.

A cook prepares and the DeSotas serve a breakfast worthy of the site. Orange juice, cream cheese and raspberry coffee cake and made-to-order omelets were the fare when we were there. Ed sometimes gets so involved in conversation he forgets to serve. "We have guests who come here and never leave the property," says he. After a stay here, we understand why.

(610) 388-2664. Fax (610) 388-3650. Seven rooms and two suites with private baths. Doubles, $125 to $169. Suites, $195 to $259.

Fairville Inn, Route 52 (Kennett Pike), Box 219, Mendenhall, Pa. 19357.

Fifteen of the Chadds Ford area's most comfortable and attractive accommo-dations are located in this welcoming complex of a country house, a carriage house and a converted barn at the edge of Fairville, the heart of Château Country. Tom and Eleanor Everitt, New Jersey natives who gave up the life of corporate nomads, took over a going establishment in 1999 and began to put their personal stamp on it.

The most choice accommodations are the ten out back in the Carriage House, built by an Amish family, and in a nearby barn named the Spring House. They were designed by the former owner's uncle, architect Rodney Williams, founder of Vermont's famed Inn at Sawmill Farm.

Each is the epitome of elegant comfort. Accented with barnwood, beams and occasional cathedral ceilings, eight rooms have gas fireplaces. All boast rear decks or balconies looking across three acres of fields toward a pond. Lamps with pierced shades cast pleasant shadows. All possess spacious full baths (ours had two vanities and a separate dressing area; the towels were thick and matched the decor), king or queen beds, oversize closets, unobtrusive TVs, phones, elegant country furnishings, crisp and colorful chintzes, and flowers from a prolific garden. Each of the two spacious suites has a balcony with wrought-iron furniture, a sitting room with a loveseat, and a bedroom with a kingsize canopy bed and two wing chairs by the fire.

A private residence until 1986, the original 1826 house contains a spacious living room with a stunning copper table bearing some of the magazines displayed throughout the inn, the breakfast area with pink and white linens and copper utensils hanging about, an office/reception area and four upstairs guest rooms. "We want to move toward more of an English country manor look for the public rooms," said Tom.

The Everitts' first move was the addition of a hot breakfast entrée every day. In addition to the traditional fresh orange juice, cereal, yogurt and pastries, they offer a farmer's omelet, vegetable frittata or, the day of our visit, pancakes with strawberry topping, garnished with blueberries and pineapple. With breakfasts like this, they envisioned the need for a larger breakfast room, which they planned to create by expanding into the front office and reception area. Their cook also bakes the tortes and scones for afternoon tea, which is a culinary treat as well.

(610) 388-5900 or (877) 285-7772. Fax (610) 388-5902. Thirteen rooms and two suites with private baths. Doubles, $150 to $185. Suites, $195 to $205. Two-night minimum most weekends.

Hedgerow Bed & Breakfast Suites, 268 Kennett Pike (Route 52), Chadds Ford 19317.

Massed plantings of impatiens brighten the facade of the handsome Victorian home that has been in owner John Haedrich's family since the 1950s, and lately has been showy enough that passersby along Kennett Pike paused for a closer look. When John and his wife Barbara took possession in 1988, friends asked why they didn't open it as a B&B. With a "house full of kids," John said, it was more practical to use their rear carriage house instead.

The Haedrichs started modestly by offering two guest rooms sharing a bath in the air-conditioned carriage house, set well back from the road beyond a spreading sycamore that shades much of the back yard. We barely recognized the place at our next visit, such was the transformation. Beautifully landscaped, the entire carriage house is now used and looks like a small house. Upstairs are two rambling suites. Downstairs are a deluxe suite and common facilities, including an inviting parlor and a stylish dining room open to a designer kitchen.

We'd happily settle into the spiffy Longwood Suite, the latest ground-floor addition with its own entrance and screened patio, hand-inlaid cherry parquet floors and antique Victorian furniture made in Chester County. The entry hall with a floor of slate from Brazil opens into an elegant living room with a sofabed, a corner fireplace, a wet bar with mini-refrigerator and microwave, and french doors onto the patio. To the side is a large bedroom, lovely in white and pale green, with

Potted flowers on front loggia welcome guests to Hamanassett manor house.

a kingsize iron and brass bed. At one end is an alcove with a writing desk and a marble-top bureau. At the other end is a smaller alcove with closet space and a vanity with wash basin. Beyond the living room is a two-part bathroom containing a whirlpool tub in one section and vanity in the other.

Upstairs, the original two bedrooms now form the Winterthur Suite with a sitting room, a queen four-poster in one bedroom and two twin beds in a sun porch. The Brandywine Suite has a sitting room, a queen canopy in the bedroom and an alcove with a twin bed.

All accommodations come with TV, phone and central air conditioning.

From her dream of a kitchen, Barbara has supplemented her original hearty continental breakfast with main dishes like bacon and eggs or baked french toast. The meal is served in the dining room looking onto a brick terrace and, beyond, a gazebo and fish pond.

(610) 388-6080. Fax (610) 388-0194. Three suites with private baths. Suites, $135 to $170 for two; $20 each additional. Two-night minimum stay. Children over 15. No smoking.

Hamanassett, 725 Darlington Road, Box 129, Lima 19037.

What a manse is this! What gardens and grounds! What a nice place to stay, thanks to the heritage of an uncommon manor house and the straightforward, no-nonsense charm of its owner, a retired school teacher who has lived here since her marriage in 1949.

The mistress of the manor is Evelene Dohan – "every other letter is an E – when I was born, my mother must have screeched, 'eeee,'" quips this eminently quotable woman who must have been a memorable teacher. Here, single-handedly except for a commercial cleaning and grounds service, she offers six comfortable guest rooms and a suite, all with private baths and TV/VCRs and most with oversize beds. Her literature conveys the grace of an heiress as well as the strictures of a school marm.

"I want people to feel at home when they're not at home," says Evelene. We'd gladly stay in any of the guest rooms on the second and third floors of this manor house in which she raised five children. All are quite spacious, nicely furnished in traditional, unshowy decor and outfitted with "an abundance of antiquities, many of which have been in the family for centuries." Rooms have sitting areas, full baths, big windows, well-worn oriental rugs and an air of lived-in comfort. Three rooms contain small refrigerators stocked with wine, beer and snacks. A two-bedroom suite comes with a formal living room. A two-room affair with two double beds and a living room would be a suite anywhere else, but because the rooms are "connected through an open archway, it is not a suite," the lodging literature insists. It's quite a pad, nevertheless, for $95.

Guests spread out around the large Federal-era fireplace in the main living room/library, its shelves stocked with more than 2,000 volumes; in a cozier Green Room parlor with another fireplace outlined in Delft tiles (except for three substitutes made by her late father-in-law, and she defies you to determine which); in a huge, brick-floored and plant-filled solarium to end all solariums, and on the majestic front loggia overlooking the gardens. Guests enjoy strolling through the formal English boxwood gardens with statues of Psyche and Aphrodite and inspecting the colorful flower gardens everywhere. "This is no Longwood," the owner apologized, but the plants are so prolific they keep the weeds at bay from July on.

Breakfast is taken at individual lace-covered tables in a chandeliered dining room open to the solarium. Evelene "studied at the Cordon Bleu, so cooking doesn't bother me." She prepares an extravagant buffet spread: juices, stewed fruit and melon, cereals, a couple of hot dishes such as tomato-mushroom omelets and pancakes with raspberries from the garden, Virginia ham, turkey sausage, Philadelphia scrapple, creamed mushrooms with basil sauce and assorted pastries from croissants to sticky buns.

You leave Hamanassett's 48 hilltop acres well-fed and restored, returning down the winding driveway past forests and gardens to Route 1, a half mile and another world away.

(610) 459-3000. Six rooms and one suite with private baths. Doubles, $100 to $125. Suite, $120 to $170. Two-night minimum required. Closed mid-July to mid-August. Children over 14. No smoking. No credit cards.

Scarlett House Bed & Breakfast, 503 West State St., Kennett Square, Pa. 19348.

Victoriana reigns in this stone house with rust-colored shutters astride a hill at the edge of Kennett Square. Samuel and Jane Snyder, who ran a small B&B for eight years in Long Island, wanted a bigger place in which to entertain and display collections from their travels. "We saw the woodwork and fell in love with the inside of this house," said ebullient Jane. They are only the third family to occupy the house built in 1910 for the Scarlett family.

Guests enter a wide foyer notable for chestnut woodwork, doors and stairs. Each of two window nooks on either side of the door contains facing benches that are replicas of originals in the old Quaker Meeting House in Kennett Square. Off the foyer are two fireplaced parlors. One is a ladies' parlor sporting a collection of music boxes and the other a less formal setting where Jane chats with guests.

Upstairs is another sitting area, this one beside sunny windows full of plants on the landing, plus a suite and three guest rooms, two of which share a hall bath. Each comes with prized antiques, ceiling fans, bathrobes, toiletries and a long-stemmed rose. The rear suite offers an ornate Jenny Lind walnut queensize bed with matching dresser and a side sitting room. The front Victorian Rose room has an Empire chest and lacy pillows on the high-back walnut queensize bed. One of the shared-bath rooms has a sitting area in what used to be a sleeping porch.

"I love china, silver, lace and flowers," Jane says, "so this a great outlet for me." She leads the way to two chandeliered dining rooms in the rear, where lace-covered tables bear lavish displays of roses and floral draperies dress the windows. The tables are set with Limoges service plates, and Jane has a different china pattern for every day of the week.

Both she and Sam love to cook. Their three-course breakfast begins with a fruit and cereal course, perhaps muesli with cantaloupe, honeydew and dried apricots. The main course could be "egg in the hole" garnished with crab, Kennett Square mushrooms, sour cream and caviar, accompanied by sweet-potato rounds spiced with cinnamon and nutmeg. Another day might yield a four-cheese and crab quiche, accompanied by cherry tomatoes stuffed with roasted garlic, basil and goat cheese. The dessert course could be a chocolate-macadamia coconut cake served with non-fat yogurt, bananas and star fruit.

In the afternoon, Jane offers complimentary refreshments in the second-floor sitting area. A hidden mini-refrigerator is stocked with cold beverages, and sherry, fruit and cookies are at the ready.

Outside are a broad, wraparound porch and English gardens. The Snyders have added a fish pond and a pergola in back.

(610) 444-9592 or (800) 820-9592. Fax (610) 925-0373. One room and one suite with private baths; two rooms with shared bath. Doubles, $85 to $105. Suite, $135. Two-night minimum weekends, April-December. No smoking.

Meadow Spring Farm, 201 East Street Road (Route 926), Kennett Square 19348.

Santas and dolls dressed in their Christmas best made this farmhouse-turned-B&B a highlight of the annual Candlelight Christmas tour in Chadds Ford. It's a bit of a Christmas fantasyland all year long. Innkeeper-collector Anne Hicks has turned her home into a gallery of whimsical animals in all guises, dolls and country antiques, from Noah's ark on the mantel to surplus dolls stored in the attic. We were charmed by the hundreds of cows of all varieties, many sent by guests.

The Hicks family has lived in the 1836 farmhouse for 50 years; daughter Sissy Hicks, chef-owner of the Dorset Inn in Vermont, grew up here. With her daughter Debbie and occasional help from one of eight grandchildren, Anne opens the farmhouse to guests in six air-conditioned rooms, each with TV and four with private baths. One queensize room has a fireplace and a sleigh bed and another, the Chippendale, has a crocheted canopy bed and a huge bathroom that was converted from a bedroom. Both beds are covered with Amish-made quilts. Antique wedding gowns hang on the wall in a twin bedroom featuring Laura Ashley linens and quilts. Two rooms over the garage are newer and furnished in more contemporary country style.

Guests enjoy the living room full of inanimate animals, a dining room with the long table centered by a carved cow and her calf, a lovely porch with garden furniture looking onto gardens and a swimming pool, and another enclosed porch with a hot tub. Fruit pancakes and mushroom omelets with scrapple or sausage are specialties at breakfast. It's served in the dining room or on the screened porch, where Anne offers tea or wine in the afternoons. She also puts up 200 jars of jam made with local fruit each year.

Guests are welcome to fish in the farm pond, feed the rabbits or play ping-pong or pool in the downstairs game room. Families particularly like the feel of a 200-acre working farm.

In 2000, Anne sold the property and the new owner planned some renovations. He asked her to continue to run the B&B indefinitely, which she agreed to do. "I love doing this," she said.

(610) 444-3903. Four rooms with private baths and two rooms with shared bath. Doubles, $85 to $95. Two-night minimum on weekends. Children welcome. No credit cards.

Dining Spots

The Gables at Chadds Ford, 162 Baltimore Pike, Chadds Ford.

The handsome, historic stone and frame barn that was once part of a dairy farm is now a stylish restaurant specializing in California cuisine with an Asian accent. Jack McFadden, area restaurateur for 30 years and known recently for successes at the nearby Marshalton Inn and at The Restaurant and The Bar in West Chester, invested more than $1 million into what he considers his best effort so far. "I call this my grown-up restaurant," he said. His loyal following agreed.

The place is named for the 23 gables added to the barn in an 1897 Victorian facelift. An interior design aficionado who did the architectural renderings himself, he scouted up three art deco bronze chandeliers and matching sconces for the bar area, where a grand piano greets arriving customers and the metal milking stools are cushioned with a deep red faux ostrich skin. Leaded glass windows separate the bar from the 120-seat dining room. Jack calls the decor "barn chic." The linens are white, the floors heart of pine, the walls white wood and brick and crackle painted with gold tint, and dining is by candlelight. A sparkling new upstairs room with a 2½-story ceiling handles functions and overflow.

The extensive menu is the kind upon which every item appeals. We'd happily make a dinner of such appetizers as ahi tuna with wasabi and soba noodle salad, sautéed escargots with mushroom ragoût, crab cakes with fried leeks and soy-coconut sauce, and a frisée salad with panko-encrusted chèvre, pinenuts and raspberry vinaigrette. The duo of dumplings – tuna and cilantro, vegetable and ginger – are as good as they get.

Or you could make a meal of pastas like creamy crab ravioli or linguini with shrimp and scallops. Main courses range from Thai marinated grouper with wilted greens and citrus-glazed salmon with ancho chile rice to sautéed duck breast with fig and black currant chutney, grilled pork tenderloin with port demi-glace and roasted lamb with red pepper cabernet butter.

Desserts include crème caramel, chocolate mousse and fresh fruit napoleon. Like the rest of the meal, they are presented on oversize white plates garnished and decorated to the hilt.

(610) 388-7700. Entrées, $17.95 to $23.95. Lunch, Tuesday-Saturday 11:30 to 2:30. Dinner, Tuesday-Saturday 5:30 to 10:30. Sunday, brunch 11 to 2:30, dinner 5 to 9.

Works of three generations of Wyeths hang on walls of Chadds Ford Inn dining room.

Chadds Ford Inn, Routes 1 and 100, Chadds Ford, Pa.

The house built by Francis Chadsey, the English Quaker who purchased 500 choice acres here from William Penn's commissioner of land grants in 1703, is now the Chadds Ford Inn. His eldest son, who lived nearby, ran the ferry that crossed the Brandywine. In 1736, John Chad turned the house into a tavern, a role it has upheld virtually ever since.

The place where Colonial officers were entertained during the Revolution now provides sustenance to Andrew and Betsy Wyeth, who live up the road, as well as to countless passing travelers. The low beamed ceilings and wainscoting enhance the works of three generations of Wyeths on the walls. The restaurant has two dining rooms on either side of the center entry hall downstairs and three more upstairs, plus an atmospheric tavern in back. Candles are lit at lunchtime, even though sunlight streams through the windows recessed in the thick stone walls.

The historic restaurant was acquired in 1998 by a group that also owns Buckley's Tavern and the Marshalton Inn nearby. The wide-ranging menu became New Americanized with the change in ownership.

The new menu is categorized under small bowls, big bowls, small plates and big plates, and reads like something from a new millennium bistro rather than the 265-year-old Brandywine Creek "tavern at Chad's fording place," as described on the back cover. Gone were the mustard-sauced Australian loin of lamb and the tender grilled venison steaks topped with port wine and plum sauce that we had enjoyed a few years earlier. In their place were braised lamb shanks, grilled duck breast with apricot glaze and herb-seared tuna steak served over orzo. The only holdovers from old seemed to be shepherd's pie and beef wellington. The locals weren't entirely happy. Tourists would not realize the difference.

(610) 388-7361. Entrées, $14.95 to $22.95. Lunch daily, 11:30 to 2. Dinner, 5:30 to 10 or 10:30, Sunday 4 to 8.

Krazy Kat's, Route 100 and Kirk Road, Montchanin, Del.

This polished restaurant occupies the former blacksmith shop in the restored Montchanin village that once housed workers at the du Pont powder mills. Owner Missy Lickle chose the unlikely name for an eccentric spinster who once lived there "and was crazy as a cat," in the words of her grandmother. The feline theme extends from the cat sculptures clad in Japanese robes in each of the front windows to the tables set with zebra-print cloths and china in the colorful jaguar jungle pattern. The tables in two rooms are large and well spaced, the walls radiate a warm salmon color, and a fire burns in one of the original forges up near the ceiling.

It's an enchanting setting for exceptional contemporary American fare overseen by executive chef Fred Kellerman, who came here from Philadelphia.

One of us started with the zesty bluepoint oyster gratin teamed with prosciutto, tri-color bell peppers, shallots and parmesan cheese. The other sampled the salad of field greens, a first-rate mixture dressed with toasted pinenuts, stilton cheese and a zippy roasted garlic vinaigrette. Main courses range from blackberry-braised cornish game hen with sweet white corn flan and green leek and shiitake ragoût to herb-grilled veal chop with roasted red pepper and rosemary oil vinaigrette, marinated asparagus soufflé and parsnip chips. The signature sautéed crab cakes were bound with a shrimp mousseline and served with honey-jalapeño tartar sauce and sweet potato fries. The sautéed Chesapeake rockfish was of the melt-in-the-mouth variety, sauced with bluepoint oysters in a tomato-fennel cream and accompanied by crisp haricots verts and flavorful dark wild rice. Our bottle of Sterling sauvignon blanc ($19, from a well chosen and affordable list honored by Wine Spectator), was poured in huge wine glasses, surpassed in size only by the balloon-size globes used here for red wines.

The dessert recitation included a walnut-praline tart and crème de cassis crème brûlée. We settled for the intense raspberry and mango sorbets, architecturally presented with enormous blackberries and an edible orchid in an almond tuile.

Although a place for serious dining and undeniably elegant, the feline motif and lack of pretension impart a refreshing light-heartedness. Both the meal and the setting were among the happiest of our travels.

(302) 888-2133. Entrées, $22 to $27. Lunch, Monday-Friday 11 to 2. Dinner nightly, 5:30 to 9:30. Jackets requested.

Maxwell Creed's, 503 Orchard Ave. at Route 1, Kennett Square, Pa.

This exciting new restaurant evolved from the Market Place deli hidden behind Phillips Place. Gone is the deli, its space having been supplanted partly by a bar. The old specialty-food section in front is now a reception area with bar seats, a handful of dining tables and wall shelves artfully stocked with chafing dishes, pans, vine wreaths, books and magazines. Beyond is a low-ceilinged dining room with barnwood walls accented by local art, an end wall bearing a colorful mural of a courtyard scene, and dark green-clothed tables seating about 40. A two-level brick patio out front accommodates another twenty in season.

Such is the stylish yet homespun setting for inspired fare offered by talented local chef Ray Maxwell, a graduate of the Restaurant School in Philadelphia, and restaurateur Ken Creed, former golf pro and bon vivant who oversees the front of the house. Chef Ray makes creative use of locally cultivated mushrooms, the house specialty. He's partial to such exotica as ostrich and buffalo, and flies in fresh moonfish every Thursday from Hawaii. Interestingly, Ken and the wait staff finish most dishes at tableside. The signature starter at both lunch and dinner is a complex mushroom soup, served in the shell of a roasted acorn squash and topped with jarlsberg cheese. Ours tasted more sweetish than savory, but was a worthy preliminary for a lunch that also included an assertive smoked wild mushroom and duck salad and a sensational crab and cheese sandwich. Everyone raves about the crab cakes topped with citrus hollandaise, available at both lunch and dinner. Ditto for the grilled vegetable napoleon layered with portobello mushrooms, fresh mozzarella and four kinds of vegetables.

For dinner, expect main courses like Chilean sea bass en papillote, chicken "gran champion" (an award-winning concoction stuffed with truffles and basil and served over a sherry-caramel sauce – the chef *is* partial to sweets), ostrich filet with bosc pears and madeira demi-glace, and free-range buffalo steak topped with smoked portobello and roasted red peppers.

Most diners finish, at least the first time, with the specialty dessert called strawberries Henry VIII. Plump berries are mixed with white and brown sugar and lemon juice, flamed with cognac and finished with ground pepper, then served over cinnamon ice cream. Other choices might be key lime tart, mixed berry crumble and triple chocolate terrine with chocolate shavings on top.

The select wine list is priced from the twenties up.

(610) 388-9450. Entrées, $15.95 to $25.95. Lunch, Tuesday-Saturday 11:30 to 2. Dinner, Tuesday-Sunday 5 to 9 or 10. Sunday brunch, 11 to 3.

Half Moon Restaurant & Saloon, 108 West State St., Kennett Square, Pa.

Exciting new American cuisine at remarkably reasonable prices is featured in this new hot spot built – literally – by young restaurateur Scott Hammond from an old candy kitchen. With a few helpers, he constructed the 35-seat mahogany bar and back bar in the front of the long, high-ceilinged downtown storefront, a popular watering spot for a young crowd. He also built the booths and tables in the rear, where diners both casual and serious gather away from the hubbub to enjoy the inspired fare of Tennessee chef John Stewart, once the private chef for Gov. Lamar Alexander.

Scott named the place for a favorite after-ski haunt in Montana with the intention of opening a microbrewery called Total Eclipse. The restaurant proved so successful that the brewpub plans were shelved in favor of a major expansion calling for a large new kitchen and an indoor-outdoor rooftop dining area.

From an appealing menu made for grazing, we enjoyed the spiced bluefish wrapped in a potato crust with a shrimp and crawfish court bouillon, julienned mixed vegetables and melt-in-the-mouth mashed potatoes, and cashew-encrusted chicken sautéed with chèvre, served with assertive curried vegetables and jasmine rice. With a bottle of Lost Horizon chardonnay, the dinner tab for two came to less than $40.

At least one-quarter of the changing menu is devoted to "grazers," many with a cajun or Southwest bent. Consider the stuffed portobello with crab and crawfish imperial, the gator and crawdads creole over cheese grits, and even the rattlesnake and rabbit rellenos (described on the menu as a poblano chile pepper "stuffed with R&R sausage, feta and jack cheeses, covered with a chipotle corn batter and baked"). Or sample escargots in exotic mushroom sauce over a saffron potato cake, a crispy ginger-fried lobster salad with watercress and plum dressing, a crab cake sandwich, grilled elk chop gremolata, chocolate-chip cheesecake or apple-cranberry tart. The tastes are great, and so are the values.

(610) 444-7232. Entrées, $11.95 to $19.95. Lunch, Monday-Friday 11:30 to 5:30. Dinner, Monday-Friday 5:30 to 10, Saturday 6 to 10.

Sovana Bistro & Pizza Kitchen, 696 Unionville Road, Kennett Square, Pa.

Young chefs Nick Farrell and Frank Delvescovo run this jaunty new establishment in the Willowdale Town Center shopping complex off Route 82 north. It's a soaring, stark space painted pale green. Exposed ducts shine beneath a skylight. A large wall mural conveys the local landscape, showing houses from the area.

The dinner menu is made for grazing. You might order a first course of sautéed calamari with roasted tomato chili sauce, shrimp and vegetable tempura or pan-seared tuna loin over asian greens with a wasabi mustard dressing. There's a choice of five salads, including one with lump crabmeat and avocado on organic greens with a dijon vinaigrette. Jumbo shrimp, roasted tomatoes and asparagus topped with melted mozzarella turn up on a featured pasta dish. Or how about a pizza of prosciutto, goat cheese, roasted peppers and arugula? The options seem endless.

Main courses tempt, perhaps grilled salmon over couscous topped with citrus-mango salsa, pan-seared tuna with a white port-ginger sauce, and roasted veal rib chop with prosciutto, sage and peas.

Expect similar treats for lunch, or settle as we did for the tasty broiled crab burger with dijon mustard sauce.

(610) 444-5600. Entrées, $15 to $23. Lunch daily, 11 to 2:30. Dinner nightly, 5 to 10. BYOB.

Buckley's Tavern, 5812 Kennett Pike (Route 52), Centreville, Del.

Built in the late 1700s, this consists of an intimate, noisy tavern in front, a pretty, white-linened interior dining room and an airy garden room at the back. There's also an open-air bar on two upper levels outside. Votive candles flicker on bare, rich wood tables flanked by comfortable, cushioned chairs in the garden room, our choice for dining on two occasions.

The former tavern and dinner menus have been combined into one short, interesting menu appealing to a variety of tastes and pocketbooks.

Burgers or hummus, barbecued pork sandwich or goat cheese bruschetta, chicken chili with black beans or Thai beef and noodle salad, farfalle with smoked salmon and roquefort or roasted Long Island duckling – here's the ultimate grazing menu. At one visit, we liked the crab cakes with a fresh coriander tartar sauce and the linguini with smoked chicken and red peppers. At another, the shrimp ravioli with tomatoes and rosemary and the shrimp and scallops with green peppercorns in puff pastry were winners.

The special cappuccino-pecan-praline ice cream was a hit among desserts, as was a fuzzy navel peach pie with a peach brandy custard sauce, which looked and tasted like a creamsicle.

The wine store located in the front of the building keeps the tavern's wine selection interesting and reasonably priced.

(302) 656-9776. Entrées, $11.95 to $19.95. Lunch, Monday-Friday 11:30 to 2:30, Saturday to 3. Dinner nightly, 5:30 to 9:30 or 10. Sunday brunch, 11 to 3.

Diversions

Brandywine River Museum, Route 1, Chadds Ford.
The Civil War-era grist mill converted into a modern museum is known for its incomparable collection of art by the Wyeth family as well as fine collections of American illustration, still life and landscape painting associated with the Brandywine heritage. Spectacular glass additions overlook the river as well as the adjoining wildflower gardens and nature trail developed by the Brandywine Conservancy, which marked its 30th anniversary in 1997 and preceded the museum by a few years. Andrew Wyeth's work, reflecting the valley and its people as well as the Maine coast, is shown in the special Andrew Wyeth Gallery, which constantly changes with additions loaned by the family. At our latest visit, a special exhibit told the story of the Wyeths' early relationship to Chadds Ford.
(610) 388-2700. Open daily, 9:30 to 4:30. Adults, $5.

Longwood Gardens, Route 1, Kennett Square.
One of the world's great horticultural displays is showy year-round, thanks to the gardens and conservatories that once were the 350-acre private preserve of Pierre S. du Pont. Spring begins in January and the spectacle changes monthly through Christmas in the twenty Crystal Palace-type conservatories, which we find even more colorful and exotic than the outdoor gardens. Illuminated fountain displays are choreographed to music on summer evenings.
(610) 388-1000 or (800) 737-5500. Open daily, 9 to 5 or later. Adults, $12 ($8 on Tuesdays).

Winterthur Museum, Garden and Library, Route 52, Winterthur, Del.
The world's premier collection of American decorative arts and antiques, assembled by Henry Francis du Pont, is displayed in 175 period room settings in the main house and in a new building with three exhibition galleries. Only some are on view at any one time, such is the scope of the collection and the size of the nine-story mansion. The interior can be seen on an assortment of guided tours, sometimes fully booked well ahead. The layman may be well enough served by Winterthur's new building dedicated to the art of looking at (and learning from) things. The Galleries at Winterthur shows 1,000 of the museum's pieces arranged in galleries on two floors. Trams take visitors on tours of the lavish gardens developed by "head gardener" du Pont on his 980-acre estate.
(302) 888-4600 or (800) 448-3883. Open Monday-Saturday 9 to 5, Sunday noon to 5. Adults, $8. Tours and Walks, $13 to $21.

Brandywine Battlefield Park, Route 1, Chadds Ford.
In the biggest battle of the Revolution, 18,000 British and 11,000 Americans met at Chadds Ford. This one went to the Brits. They outflanked George Washington, who was defending Chadds Ford, and encircled his troops from the north. Now a 50-acre state park, it has a visitor center that presents a thirteen-minute slide show on the battle. Washington's headquarters in the Benjamin Ring House and Lafayette's quarters in the Gideon Gilpin House are open periodically for tours. The actual battlefield is on unmarked lands, "two miles north as the crow flies and five roundabout miles by car," according to a park guide.
(610) 459-3342. Open Tuesday-Saturday 9 to 5, Sunday noon to 5. Grounds open to 9 in summer. Building tours, $3.50; battlefield, free.

The **Chadds Ford Historical Society** has a museum and visitor center in a barn across from its **John Chads House,** Route 100, a quarter mile north of Route 1. The 1725 house is furnished as it was when the ferryman and farmer for whom the village was named lived here – that is to say, sparely. The society also operates the **Barns-Brinton House,** a restored 18th-century tavern nearby. Houses open May-October, weekends noon to 5, rest of year by appointment. Adults, $2.

Chaddsford Winery, Route 1, Chadds Ford.
This boutique-style winery with lots going on has been producing good wines since 1981. Operating from a converted barn, it imports grapes from around the area to make "new American classics from the Brandywine Valley." These include the Proprietors Reserve White (rated a model for regional whites), classic European varietals and a first-class chardonnay. Proprietor Eric Miller comes from a winemaking family (his father owns Benmarl Vineyards and Winery in New York's Hudson Valley). His wife Lee has authored a book about wine. *(610) 388-6221. Open daily, noon to 6. Closed Mondays, January-March.*

Shopping. The area's most sophisticated shopping extends along Kennett Pike (Route 52) from Fairville, Pa., site of a cluster of antiques shops, through Centreville to Greenville, Del. We're particularly partial to Centreville, where old buildings along the wide street have been converted to house such favorites as **Troll of Scandinavia** (for interesting takeout food), the **Jolly Needlewoman, The Sporting Gentleman** and **Wild Thyme,** all neatly detailed in a new brochure touting it as "still the perfect rest stop, from 1750 until today." We're drawn to **Communiques,** a great paper, book, card and gift shop, where coffee's always on tap and poetry readings are among the special events.

The largest selection of Wyeth reproductions anywhere is featured at **Chadds Ford Gallery,** in a brick house in front of the **Chadds Ford Village and Barn Shops.** Antiques stores and malls abound along Route 1 in Chadds Ford. Dealers are grouped at **the Brandywine River Antiques Market** and the **Pennsbury-Chadds Ford Antique Mall.**

Extra-Special

Hagley Museum, Route 141, Wilmington, Del.
The original du Pont mills and powder works, estate and gardens offer 230 acres of Brandywine history. More than the other museums, this lives up to its slogan, "something for everyone." A shuttle bus takes visitors around the tranquil grounds along the Brandywine. The Henry Clay Mill exhibits trace America's industrial expansion. Water flowing through the mill races power the massive stone mills in the powder yard. Pause for lunch in the simple Belin House Coffee Shop atop Blacksmith Hill and visit the workers' housing area. Then see how the boss lived in Eleutherian Mills, the first du Pont family home built by E.I. du Pont in 1803. The Georgian-style residence is furnished to reflect the tastes of five generations of du Ponts who lived there. Espaliered fruit trees set off the beautiful yet functional French garden outside. The Hagley, we think, is most evocative of the Brandywine heritage. *(302) 658-2400. Open daily 9:30 to 4:30, mid-March through December; weekends only 9:30 to 4:30 and one tour weekdays at 1:30 in winter. Adults, $9.75.*

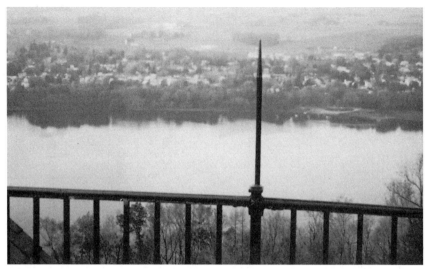

Village of Marietta is on view across Susquehanna River from overlook.

Western Lancaster County, Pa.

Beyond the Tourists

Much of the Lancaster County of Pennsylvania Dutch fame is a land of strange names and quaint places – a sea of smorgasbords, outlets, motels and commercial enterprises taking advantage of the Amish-Mennonite connection and, alas, undercutting the very notion of "The Plain People."

That applies to eastern Lancaster County, where tourists arrive by the busload, three million a year strong. Western Lancaster County is, for the most part, a place apart.

Here, the picturesque rolling farmlands of the east flatten as they approach the broad ridge cresting along the Susquehanna River. The Amish and Mennonites are far less conspicuous. So are the trappings of tourism. The western section wears an historic face, one unfettered by the commercialism of its eastern counterpart.

Mount Joy, Marietta and Columbia. These are the sleepy rural villages and river towns that dwell in the western county, surrounded by the ubiquitous farmlands that manage to survive in the face of creeping Lancaster suburbia.

Mount Joy, the biggest town, marks something of a dividing line between the frenzied quaintness of Pennsylvania Dutch country and the serenity beyond. Marietta is a long and narrow strip of a river town, as authentic as they come; nearly half the town is on the National Register. Columbia was a gateway to the west when it was Wright's Ferry, crossing point to the Susquehanna frontier. It was an important enough river site in the 1790s that it was one of the potential locations for the new nation's capital.

Congress ultimately chose a capital along the Potomac River, not the Susquehanna. The development of the area, which blossomed during the heady river and railroad days of the 19th century, was stunted in the 20th. Buildings now

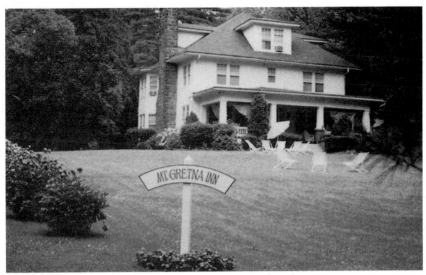

Overseeing broad lawn is Mount Gretna Inn, the biggest house in town.

considered historic were bypassed by the building boom. They stand as mute testimony to an earlier era.

Betty Groff, the guru of Pennsylvania Dutch cookery, and her Groff's Farm restaurant put Mount Joy on the national culinary map. The sophisticates who came to this side of the county were charmed by its lack of clutter and tourism. The Groffs opened a country inn nearby, more inns and B&Bs followed and lately, western Lancaster County is becoming a destination in search of an identity.

No one – not tourism directors, innkeepers nor restaurateurs – has come up with a name for the area other than western Lancaster County. But they all see it as different from the rest of Lancaster County, a place apart.

Inn Spots

Mount Gretna Inn, 16 West Kaufman Ave., Mount Gretna 17064.

Opened in 1988, this is the only B&B in the Cinderella town of Mount Gretna, a hilltop aerie of pine groves, Lake Conewago, religious campgrounds, arts and music. And it's some B&B.

It was built in 1921 in the American Arts and Crafts style by local entrepreneur Abraham Lincoln Kaufmann, who developed the 50-acre subdivision known as The Heights. His was (and remains) the biggest house in Mount Gretna.

Robin and Keith Volker from nearby Elizabethtown purchased a turnkey operation in 1994. They had spent many a summer vacation in Mount Gretna, Keith said, and "for fifteen years my wife had been trying to talk me into becoming an innkeeper, when this perfect place became available." Keith continued as a field engineer for his own computer company while Robin became full-time innkeeper.

The main floor is dramatic in lodge style with a fireplaced living room big enough for the occasional concert on the grand piano, two dining rooms set with china and crystal, and a great wide, deep front porch overlooking a manicured lawn.

Upstairs on the second and third floors are seven bedrooms of varying size. All have private baths and queensize beds, and six have gas fireplaces. Stickley Arts and Crafts furniture and original paintings by local artists are featured. Most in demand is the Chestnut Suite with a Victorian bed from the Louisiana plantation owned by the former owner's family and two sitting areas amid oriental rugs, side table, dresser and armoire. Also popular are the Weeping Pines with burl maple furniture and private porch and the rear Black Walnut Room with antique poster bed made of a solid piece of black walnut and a plush chaise with matching ottoman. The Volkers call two third-floor rooms with soft canopies over the beds their romantic hideaways. Another third-floor room, decorated in an equestrian theme, includes a microwave and refrigerator.

Candlelight breakfasts are gala here. One autumn morning began with baked peaches and sour cream pound cake. The main course was angel puff incorporating four low-fat cheeses and fresh basil. Pumpkin-chocolate chip muffins were offered to finish. Other main dishes could be sausage casserole, Scottish griddle scones and stuffed french toast. Afternoon tea is served with crudités on the porch. Complimentary soft drinks, bottled water and packaged snacks are in the rooms.

(717) 964-3234 or (800) 277-6602. Fax (717) 964-3641. Seven rooms with private baths. Doubles, $95 to $125. Children over 12. No smoking.

The Columbian, 360 Chestnut St., Columbia 17512.

A magnificent tiered staircase passes ornate stained-glass windows at the entry to this turn-of-the-century brick mansion with beige trim and a wraparound veranda. An outstanding example of Colonial Revival architecture, it was painstakingly restored in 1988 and converted into a B&B.

Young owners Chris and Becky Will offer six air-conditioned bedrooms, each with private bath, and two suites, one with its own balcony. All have queensize beds, comfortable sitting areas, TVs, and fresh flowers and fruit. Four have gas fireplaces. They are decorated in Victorian or English country style, accented by paintings, crafts, needlework and quilts. Our room, though smaller than some of the others, came with a dainty window seat outfitted with lots of pillows. The rear Bucher Suite offers a painted brass bed and large sitting area with sofa, plus a

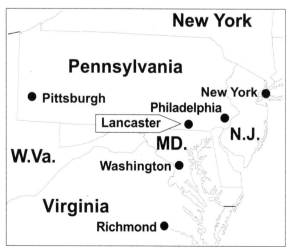

small adjoining room with a twin bed. On the third floor is the new Fendrich Suite with gas fireplace and clawfoot tub ("for those romantic baths – who needs a jacuzzi?" asks Becky).

Centerpiece of the foyer is an antique victrola. At our visit, Chris "couldn't wait" for Christmas when it was to get quite a workout from his collection of old records. Principal listeners other than guests were then-toddlers Katy and Zach, whom their parents describe as "our entertainment committee."

Becky serves a hearty country breakfast. A typical repast could start with half a grapefruit, banana-nut or applesauce-raisin bread and a hot fruit dish, perhaps blueberry kuchen, for which Becky has printed copies of the recipe. The main dish could be baked egg casserole, cinnamon pancakes, waffles, French toast strata, quiche or egg casserole. We were offered a choice of peach pancakes with peach sauce or a dish of hard-boiled eggs chopped in a cheese sauce on an English muffin with ham. Both were excellent.

Ever improving, the Wills added a large patio with an outdoor garden railroad layout with a model train running year-round.

Lately, they acquired a house up Chestnut Street and converted it into the **Clock Tower B&B.** It has three bedrooms, two with queensize and one with a double bed ($65 to $70). Guests have kitchen privileges and continental breakfast. It's designed especially for long-term visitors to the National Watch and Clock Museum.

(717) 684-5869 or (800) 422-5869. Six rooms and two suites with private baths. Doubles, $85 to $99 weekends, $75 to $89 midweek. Suites, $105 and $125 weekends, $95 and $115 midweek. No smoking.

The Olde Square Inn, 127 East Main St., Mount Joy 17552.

From the front porch, guests enter directly into the living room of this neoclassic residence built in 1917 by a local builder who apparently did not want a foyer.

Later a boarding house, it was opened in 1991 as a B&B by Fran and David Hand, York County residents who drove by, saw the house for sale and knew it was for them. After two years of work, they were ready with four guest rooms, all with private baths, TVs and VCRs.

The largest is the Royal Room, which "we bill as fit for a king and his queen," says Fran, and is decorated with castles and such. The deep red wallpaper bears large blue flowers, and the twin beds can be joined as a king. The TV is hidden in an armoire. The Charleston Room, which Fran named for her favorite city, holds a queensize iron bed and is decorated in vivid florals with hats as accents. Its bathroom has a double shower with two seats. The Ivy Room comes with ivy and roses on the wallpaper and handpainted on the queen bed, the armoire and chest of drawers.

On the main floor are two living rooms, one with a fireplace. Beyond is a dining room elegant in beige and teal. Fran serves guests a full breakfast of fresh fruit, juice, homemade muffins and breads, and a main dish like baked sausage casserole, pancakes and sausage, or a baked egg casserole.

Out back is her pride and joy, the Enchanted Cottage, converted in 1997 from a brick carriage house. It's a large space with a circular jacuzzi tub in one corner. A three-sided glass fireplace faces the jacuzzi as well as the queensize iron bed and a sitting area with a sofabed. All the lights operate on dimmer switches. A kitchenette comes with a microwave and refrigerator. Hand-painted vines, flowers and brickwork decorate the sponge-painted walls. Thick carpeting, a ceiling fan and built-in stereo system are other attributes. The three-section bathroom has a double vanity and a shower area big enough to accommodate a wheelchair. Outside is a brick patio up against the sidewalk.

See-through fireplace and circular jacuzzi are features in cottage at The Olde Square Inn.

Also outside is a new eight-person hot tub for inn guests. Fluffy robes are provided for guests to wear on their way to soak.

(717) 653-4525 or (800) 742-3533. Fax (717) 653-0976. www.oldesquareinn.com. Four rooms and one cottage with private baths. Doubles, $95 to $125. Cottage, $199. No smoking.

The River Inn, 258 West Front St., Marietta 17547.

They don't get much more historic than this 200-year-old house, lovingly tended by Joyce and Bob Heiserman and once featured in a Colonial Homes magazine cover story on Marietta.

The Heisermans live in half of the fourteen-room duplex house and turn over to guests the other half, including a parlor-library, tavern room and dining room. The entryway features magnificent crown molding and a painted checkered floor.

All three guest rooms have queensize beds and private baths. They are decorated simply to the Colonial and Federal periods with oriental rugs, plaster walls and painted woodwork.

The nicest room, across the back of the house, has a fireplace, a canopy bed and two wing chairs. The largest is in front, facing the railroad track and the Susquehanna River. It contains both a queen and a twin bed.

Guests spread out in the cozy fireplaced parlor-library, well stocked with books and a TV set, and a tavern room with a reproduction bar modeled after one in Williamsburg. Here they can store food in the refrigerator, mix drinks and imagine themselves back in the 18th century.

The adjacent Colonial dining room is notable for a large pierced-tin chandelier, handmade wall sconces, braided rugs and a fireplace. Here or on the long rear screened porch outfitted in wicker, the Heisermans serve a full breakfast, perhaps herbed omelets, pancakes or french toast with bacon or sausage.

The couple also have bicycles for guests to use, and Bob will take people fishing in his boat with advance notice.

The porch is a grand spot for taking in the 200-foot-deep back yard with its formal holly garden, Colonial herbs and flowers that turn up in colorful arrangements throughout the house.

(717) 426-2290. Fax (717) 426-2966.Three rooms with private baths. Doubles, $65 to $90. Children over 10. No smoking.

Country Gardens Farm Bed & Breakfast, 686 Rock Point Road, Mount Joy 17552.

The name here says it well, but let us embellish. The gardens are prolific, their bounty used to decorate the house and play a big role at breakfast. The 170-acre farm, primarily cattle and crops, includes a pen with four sheep, a goat and chickens. The bedrooms are homey and comfortable, and the breakfasts are something else.

Andrew and Dotty Hess, who have spent most of their lives working on the farm, raised seven youngsters in their house before turning it into a B&B in 1992. "We'd been doing B&B for 38 years," quips Dotty, "and figured it was time we were paid." They offer four bedrooms, two with private baths – one attached to the coveted Balcony Room, which comes with a queensize bed and an outside balcony for viewing the surrounding farmlands.

Quilted wall hangings are draped over the chairs and sofas in the extra-large living room. Made by an Amish woman, they're for sale, as are Dotty's floral wreaths and dried flower arrangements.

The living room also holds quite a conversation piece – a photograph of the Hess family reunion, showing three generations and 213 people (of a possible 239) descended from Andrew's parents (he was one of nine children, each of whom had up to nine children, who in turn have had up to seven children). Most live in Lancaster County, and it turns out that Dotty is a cousin of noted restaurateur Betty Groff (see Dining Spots). Both grew up close to each other in eastern Lancaster County, were married about the same time and "moved up here about the same distance apart as before."

Most guests congregate in the family room off the dining area and country kitchen at the side of the house. Here is where the Hesses serve a bountiful country breakfast. The meal includes bowls of fresh fruit from the garden, baked oatmeal and a succession of main dishes served family style: perhaps scrambled eggs with cheese or cheese strata and ricotta cheese pancakes or french toast, accompanied by vegetables of the season, from asparagus and snap peas to corn and tomatoes. "Some folks go out of here thinking they've just had dinner," Dotty concedes.

After breakfast, Dotty takes any children to the "hen house pen" out back to gather eggs and feed the sheep.

(717) 426-3316. Two rooms with private baths and two with shared bath. Doubles, $65 to $75, plus $10 each child. No smoking.

Cedar Hill Farm B&B, 305 Longenecker Road, Mount Joy 17552.

Stay in this handsome 1817 fieldstone-stucco farmhouse and you're really on a working farm, out in the country on a wooded hillside beside Little Chiques Creek. Gladys and Russel Swarr (he was born here and his family has owned the property since the 1870s) raise thousands of chickens as well as corn and soybeans on 51 acres.

The five air-conditioned bedrooms with private baths are more elegant than city slickers might expect at a farm. Each is nicely decorated with family heirlooms. One with a queensize, carved-oak bed (the bedroom suite was made by

Original kitchen at Cedar Hill Farm B&B includes a walk-in fireplace.

Russel's grandfather) overlooks the creek. Access to the front balcony belongs to the queensize honeymoon room, country pretty with a wicker sitting area. Its large bathroom contains a sit-down shower. A third room with a double bed is small and furnished in Victorian style. The largest room at the rear has two double beds, a full bath with a separate vanity under a skylight and a desk chair from the school Russel attended. The newest room has a kingsize brass bed and comes with a whirlpool tub.

Common facilities include a double parlor, a TV room with VCR and stereo, and a front porch furnished in wicker. Gladys serves breakfast in the original kitchen in front of a walk-in fireplace that's atmospheric as can be. She calls it continental-plus "because I don't serve eggs" – everything but, perhaps a fresh fruit and cheese platter, fruit cobbler, cereals, muffins and coffee cake. Baked oatmeal casserole is a recent guest favorite.

(717) 653-4655. Fax (717) 653-4655. www.800padutch.com/cedarhill.html. Five bedrooms with private baths. Doubles, $75 to $80. No smoking.

The Country Stay, 2285 Bull Moose Road, Route 1, Box 312, Mount Joy 17552.

Candles glow year-round in the windows of this beautiful 1880 brick Victorian farmhouse, and you may hear church bells chiming in the distance upon arrival. You also will no doubt be greeted by one of the barnyard cats, fifteen at last count.

Owners Darlene and Lester Landis, who have three children, raise beef and grain on their 98-acre farm. A Victorian suite in a separate section of the house has a private bath, while two other bedrooms share a bath. A hat is perched on one post of a carved Victorian headboard on the old rope bed in a room with thick brown carpeting, a bay window with frilly curtains and a window seat. Another bedroom contains braided rugs and a queen canopy bed covered with an Amish quilt. Homey touches, floral arrangements and country crafts abound in the bedrooms and in the small guest parlor adjacent to the breakfast room. "We try to make this feel like home for guests," says Darlene.

In the morning, she dons a period costume to serve a continental-plus breakfast of fresh fruit and homemade pastries, perhaps rhubarb bread, shoofly cake, blueberry buckle and coffee cake. She may add a more substantial dish like meat and potato quiche. Darlene makes the crafts she sells in her Country Craft Cupboard on the premises, and Lester may entertain guests on the player piano in the family room.

(717) 367-5167. Fax (717) 367-1843. One suite with private bath and two rooms with shared bath. Doubles, $65. Suite $110. Two-night minimum holiday weekends. Children over 10. No smoking.

West Ridge Guest House, 1285 West Ridge Road, Elizabethtown 17022.

Her children having left the nest, Alice Heisey decided to share with overnight guests the family home in an outlying residential section of West Donegal. That proved successful, so she and husband David turned the onetime chicken barn that had been headquarters for his contracting business into a guest house with five spacious bedrooms, a large living room with dining area and a carpeted room with a jacuzzi and exercise equipment.

This is not your typical B&B, even though it does everything a B&B should and more. The Heiseys cater more than others to corporate business and have outfitted their rooms accordingly. Each contains a queen or kingsize bed, modern bath, air-conditioning, TV and telephone. Some have private decks overlooking sections of the 23-acre farm, broad lawns, a gazebo, two fishponds and a swimming pool.

The modern rooms in the guest house are individually decorated in different styles.

The Williamsburg Room is the biggest, possessing a queen four-poster bed, cherry furniture, a blue and red color scheme, a sitting area with two stuffed chairs and a sofabed, and a whirlpool tub. The Wicker Room is in pale pinks, greens and whites – even the bed is wicker. Country curtains and spreads identify the Country Room, which has a queen and a double bed. Ornately carved chairs, fringed lamps and a crocheted bed cover mark the Victorian Room, a fantasy in teal and red. We liked our quarters in the Anniversary Room, where the whitest, laciest kingsize bed imaginable is reflected in the mirrored headboard. Black floral wallpaper strips break up the white of the walls, mauve wing chairs and carpeting provide color, and a gas fireplace adds romance. Candles in many guises are the theme here.

Four more rooms are available upstairs in the Heisey home next door. They range from a small room with an oval bed built into the wall to a two-bedroom executive suite with two TVs, gas fireplace and a whirlpool tub in one bedroom. The main floor of the Loft Suite is all bath with forest green tiles, mirrors, double jacuzzi tub and separate shower. The upstairs loft is a knockout in mauves and greens with a large sitting area, sofabed and fireplace and a queensize bed on the other side of the room.

Bowls of assorted candies are placed in the rooms, which have such unexpected flouncy touches as little wool puffs on the coat hangers and artificial flowers around the candle bases. A refrigerator in the hallway is stocked with sodas and snacks for sale. Alice serves a full breakfast in the dining alcove off the large

Main house and converted chicken barn face swimming pool at West Ridge Guest House.

living room. Guests write their choices on a checklist the night before. Eggs any style, french toast and cereal were the offerings at our visit.

(717) 367-7783 or (877) 367-7783. Fax (717) 367-8468. Seven rooms and two suites with private baths. Doubles, $60 to $110. Suites, $100 to $120. No smoking.

Dining Spots

Accomac Inn, South River Drive, Wrightsville.

Dating to 1775, this fieldstone inn overlooking the Susquehanna across from Marietta at what used to be the landing for Anderson's Ferry is known far beyond the region for fine dining.

The historic dining room is all white with dark brown trim and a white fireplace at one end. White tapered candles stand tall on each well-spaced table, set with fanned napkins, pewter service plates and fresh flowers in pewter vases. Fine paintings adorn the walls, and window tables catch a glimpse of the river across a screened porch (everyone gets a water view when the porch is used in summer).

It's an altogether lovely, authentic 18th-century setting for classic French fare at prices considered high for the area. One of us started with an excellent warm salmon and shrimp terrine with a pernod-spinach-cream sauce. The other chose a salad of belgian endive, toasted pinenuts, grapefruit sections and watercress with a raspberry dressing. A small loaf of French bread, surrounded by an army of sweet-butter curls, accompanied.

Entrées range from seared tuna with roasted garlic over a plum tomato couscous to steak diane and roast duck flambéed tableside with a cider-citrus glaze. Good choices were grilled duck au poivre, served with wild rice and julienned peppers, carrots and leeks, and an outstanding dish of sautéed venison with duck liver mousse in a port cream sauce. Portions were small but exquisite. Bananas foster made a worthy ending.

The teak wood bar in the small side lounge is the place for an after-dinner drink. We might have tarried had we not faced the roundabout way back to the highway – small signs mark the way in, but you're on your own going home.

(717) 252-1521. Entrées, $20.25 to $32.25. Dinner nightly, 5:30 to 9:30. Sunday, brunch 11 to 2:30, dinner 4 to 8:30.

Log cabin has been transformed into French restaurant called Josephine's.

Josephine's, 324 West Market St., Marietta.

The newest dining sensation in western Lancaster County – some call it world-class – is this charming restaurant in an 18th-century building that originated as a log cabin. The log walls, beamed and paneled ceiling, gleaming hardwood floors and freestanding candles convey an elegant, historic ambiance in three dining rooms. Copper pans hung around the fireplace mantel in the oldest room add a French accent. Owner Jean Luc Sandillion chose the area because it reminded him of the rolling countryside of his native Poitiers. He named the restaurant after his wife's mother.

His chefs are known for superb, contemporary French food. People rave about the seafood gratinée, the baked salmon with strawberry coulis, the veal with morels in cream sauce, the filet of beef bordelaise and the rack of lamb, either roasted dijonnaise or sautéed forestière.

Good starters are the specialty crab cake with salmon mousse baked in a cassoulet, frog's legs provençal and an unusual salad of sautéed duck livers with a honey-sweetened balsamic vinaigrette served over mixed greens. Favorite desserts include crème caramel, raspberry napoleon and apple tart.

The lunch fare is like that which you'd expect to find in the French countryside.

The choice, primarily French wine list is on the pricey side. A few local Nissleys make up most of the domestic offerings.

(717) 426-2003. Entrées, $15.95 to $22.95. Lunch, Tuesday-Friday 11:30 to 2. Dinner, Monday-Saturday 5 to 9.

Groff's Farm Restaurant, 650 Pinkerton Road, Mount Joy.

Betty Groff started serving weekend dinners in her home as a hobby more than 30 years ago for visitors who wanted to meet a farm family and taste the local cuisine. Betty, who grew up as a tenth-generation Mennonite on the other side of Lancaster County, had married Abe Groff and felt isolated without family and friends in Mount Joy, so this was her way of keeping in touch with people.

The rest, as they say, is history. They turned a 1756 fieldstone farmhouse into a thriving restaurant. They opened the high-style Cameron Estate Inn in 1981. A few years ago, they expanded their original restaurant with a glamorous sun porch and acquired a liquor license. Lately, they have converted their farmland into a championship golf course. Betty, the author of four cookbooks, is nationally known as the guru of Pennsylvania Dutch cookery.

Although housed on a farm, Groff's no longer is really a farm restaurant. Rather it is a fashionable, social place where the patrons ask after Betty and trade gossip with the waitresses. The food has taken on a sophisticated air, thanks to the lighter touch that Betty has given to the hearty dishes associated with the area as well as her son Charlie's additions of seafood and an à la carte menu to the traditional family-style menu. Charlie, a Culinary Institute of America grad, is the executive chef and manages the restaurant with his wife Cindy, although he's turned his attention to the golf venture lately.

Certain things never change, says Betty. All the coffee cups are turned up at each place setting, and the waitress asked "would you like coffee now?" as we were seated for lunch in the sun porch, pretty in peach and white. A platter of four relishes – corn, coleslaw, pickled celery and chow-chow – and apple butter for the bread arrived soon after. One of us had to try the house specialty, chicken stoltzfus, a luscious and filling dish of tender chicken smothered in cream sauce and served over flaky diamonds of buttered pastry – perfect for lunch. This came with thick stewed tomatoes and Southern-style green beans cooked in ham broth, served family style. Our other choice was a chicken and Canadian bacon melt, a bit dry and tough, garnished with chips and pickles. For dessert, we shared an excellent Amish vanilla pie embellished with butterscotch ice cream. The $13 tab wasn't bad for lunch in a country club setting.

The menu is considerably expanded at night. Most first-timers order off the family-style menu. Each person gets to choose an appetizer and dessert, but the whole table shares the main course – served family style, all you can eat. Main courses are chicken stoltzfus, hickory-smoked ham, prime rib and seafood, available singly or in various combinations. Prices ($16 to $26.50) include everything from soup to dessert. You may not want the latter, especially if you have sampled the moist chocolate cake and Betty's cracker pudding served as you are seated – "so you can enjoy these treats while you still have room for them," the menu advises.

If the entire table so decides, diners can order à la carte – much the same fare, plus broiled New York strip steak, baked stuffed flounder and broiled lobster tail.

After lunch, we perused copies of Betty's best-selling cookbooks, which are displayed in stacks here and there, and acquired some Groff's Farm relishes to take home.

(717) 653-2048. Entrées, $13.75 to $17. Lunch, Monday-Saturday 11:30 to 1:30. Dinner by reservation, Monday-Friday 5 to 7:30, Saturday seatings at 5 and 8. Sunday brunch, 10 to 2.

Alois's, 102 North Market St., Mount Joy.

The creative menu for six-course meals changes often in the old Central Hotel portion of Bube's Brewery. This is the nation's only microbrewery surviving intact from the 1800s and is now home to three separate restaurants under the ownership of young entrepreneur Sam Allen.

Named for Alois Bube, a German immigrant who built the brewery during Lancaster's heyday as the Munich of the New World, this section was the brewmaster's house. You think the hotel's brick exterior with its aqua and purple wood trim and shutters is colorful? Check out the flamboyant interior, four intimate dining rooms themed to their names (Canopy, Peacock, Dragonfly and Trophy), an upstairs banquet room with incredible handpainted walls and a Victorian bar to end all bars. Furnished like a Victorian parlor, it has an old gaming table with shelves underneath for drinks in one corner and, over the massive bar, a revolving silver ball like those from '40s and '50s dance floors, casting beams of light around the room.

Chef Ophelia Horn mixes cuisines and styles – Sam calls it all "interpretive international" for the leisurely dining experience that begins in the bar. Oil lamps flickered and New Age music played here as we had drinks and the hors d'oeuvre course, small portions of roast beef pâté with onion pastries, creole quiche and crabmeat nachos on white flour chips. We asked not to be seated in the Trophy Room, where patrons dine beneath the mounted heads of animals. Instead we were assigned to the Canopy Room, named for the ceiling shaped like a canopy. As in all the others, its walls were lavishly decorated with a mix of intricate handpainted and handstenciled art.

Our white-clothed table bore a candle, napkins and nothing else. Utensils came with each course, and salt only upon request.

The prix-fixe meal is presented course by course, with the only option being the main course (a choice of buttermilk chicken skewers or marinated shrimp skewers, one recent evening). Service was inordinately slow for a quiet night and a meal that was supposed to be paced. Gradually we got our soup course (cock-a-leekie), a mesclun salad with creamy pepper dressing and strawberry sorbet. Our main courses arrived on salad-size plates, the veal medallions with port and ginger accompanied by potatoes and the filet mignon by rice, carrots and zucchini. The blueberry cassis pie was chilled, intense and refreshing. Chocolate twigs came with the bill.

Although the meal is competently prepared and represents good value, be fore-warned: the bar bill for a couple of house drinks and a bottle of wine likely will approach the tab for food.

(717) 653-2057. Prix-fixe, $26. Dinner by reservation, Tuesday-Sunday 5:30 to 9 or 10, Sunday to 8.

The Catacombs, 102 North Market St., Mount Joy.

If Alois's is the height of Victoriana, the Catacombs is positively medieval. A serf in medieval garb greets diners and leads them on a tour of the brewery as they descend 43 feet into the stone-lined vaults that were the aging cellars of Bube's Brewery. Here are round-ceilinged rooms totally lit by candles; in fact, the stone wall at the end of one room is covered with candle drippings, the better to hold steady more candles. Owner Sam Allen and his father made the heavy pine tables, dressed in white linens and set with pewter tankards and plates.

This is the setting for medieval feasts staged most Sundays at 5 year-round. The $30 tab includes wine and ale, live music and entertainment, tax and tip. Everyone gasps as burly chefs carry in a whole roasted pig.

On other nights, a fairly versatile menu is offered. Entrées run the gamut from flounder stuffed with crabmeat to tournedos of beef with cracked peppercorns. Chicken satay, stuffed mushrooms and sausage en croûte are among the appetizers. Dessert could be chocolate-chip cheesecake or kahlua pie.

Upstairs in the brewery's original bottling plant is **The Bottling Works,** an atmospheric restaurant and tavern serving lunch and light fare. Interesting salads and sandwiches, gourmet burgers and bargain-priced entrées are featured. An adjacent outdoor **Biergarten** adds 80 seats to the 300 inside the brewery's three restaurants.

Bube's Brewery also offers The Cooper's Shed, a brewery store and cooperage museum. The store is in the original cooperage (barrel working shop). A large collection of antique cooper's tools is on display

(717) 653-2056. Entrées, $17.95 to $23.95, Dinner nightly, 5:30 to 9 or 10. Lunch in Bottling Works daily from 11, Sunday from noon; dinner nightly from 5:30, from 5 on weekends.

Prudhomme's Lost Cajun Kitchen, 519 Cherry St., Columbia.

Yes, you read the name right. David Prudhomme, nephew of *the* Paul Prudhomme, and his wife Sharon opened this restaurant and entertainment center in 1997 at, of all places, the edge of Pennsylvania Dutch country. "We took a wrong turn, got lost and decided to stay," David quipped as he explained the name.

Actually, he grew up in Acadian Louisiana, worked in his uncle's sausage plant and met his Yankee wife while working in the area as a stonemason. The couple gutted the main floor of the old Rising Sun Hotel, put in a new kitchen and hung a Preservation Hall sign over the bar. The decor in two dining areas seating 90 is thoroughly Cajun.

Besides renovating and hosting, the couple also do much of the cooking – "from scratch," David asserts. The recipes are their own, except for Enola's eggplant piroque, borrowed from Paul's older sister Enola, who attended their opening. Expect the usual suspects: gumbo, jambalaya, po'boys, crawfish étouffée, blackened catfish, and fried or sautéed alligator platter. Plus some surprises: Sharon's chicken toes ("our version of chicken fingers"), shrimp fais do do (done three ways) and blackened pork chops, topped with homemade pepper jelly that the couple bottle and sell here. David makes a mean pecan-banana layer cake, while Sharon's specialty is sweet potato pie.

Cajun entertainment – "not the real stuff, but as close as we can get in Pennsylvania" – is offered three nights a week. You just know that everyone has fun here.

(717) 684-1706. Entrées, $6.95 to $17.95. Lunch, Tuesday-Saturday 11 to 2:30. Dinner, Monday-Saturday 4:30 to 10.

Railroad House, West Front and South Perry Streets, Marietta.

This architecturally significant, four-story Federal hotel was in its heyday when the trains stopped next door. It fell on hard times and was derelict when Donna and Richard Chambers restored it into a restaurant and tavern and also fixed up the bedrooms.

Dining is in several venues. One is the Music Room, where handsome yellow and green swag curtains match the walls, oriental rugs cover the dark wood floors and a sheet of "America" is on the music stand next to a victrola. Another is the large Blue Room, stenciled and wainscoted. Beyond is the Country Room, where a collection of clocks is backlit on the mantel of the huge open fireplace that served the original kitchen. Light fare is available weekends in the downstairs **Arrivals Tavern,** where posters of the Orient Express and railroad memorabilia complement the beamed ceiling and the 30-foot-long copper bar. You also may dine on an appealing outdoor courtyard with black wrought-iron furniture overlooking flower and herb gardens. There are whimsical touches: a Victorian shoe on the wall here, two stuffed rabbits in an Adirondack twig loveseat there.

The same care extends to the kitchen, where Rick and his chef oversee a huge menu. A pasta dish called straw and hay – lobster, scallops and shrimp over spinach and egg fettuccine – is a favorite with customers. Rick also touts the broiled crab cakes, chicken moutarde, lamb chops and steak diane. Stuffed mushrooms, clams casino and caesar salad are among the starters. Desserts could be any number of flavored cheesecakes (oreo, mocha, amaretto and pumpkin-pecan), cappuccino torte and peanut butter pie. Strolling minstrels play on Saturday nights.

The establishment also offers twelve guest rooms, eight with private baths (doubles, $59 to $99).

(717) 426-4141. Entrées, $16.95 to $24.95. Lunch, Tuesday-Saturday 11 to 2. Dinner, Tuesday-Sunday 5 to 9 or 10. Sunday brunch, 11 to 4.

Loreto's Ristorante, 173 South Fourth St., Columbia.

Mama makes the pastas and sauces here and her sons run this Italian-American restaurant in a small corner restaurant with a brick facade. The owners advertise a beautiful hardwood Victorian bar, but it is the mother's pastas that draw most of the attention.

The menu is predictable. Favored appetizers are the antipasto salad and steamed clams. Pasta dishes are of the old school. Main courses run to broiled flounder, crab cakes, shrimp scampi, chicken marsala, veal parmesan, veal oscar and grilled sirloin Italiano. Tirami su, spumoni, amaretto cheesecake and cannoli are typical desserts. Espresso and cappuccino accompany.

(717) 684-4326. Entrées, $13.95 to $17.95. Lunch, Tuesday-Friday 11 to 2. Dinner, Tuesday-Saturday 4 to 9 or 10, Sunday to 8.

Diversions

All the attractions of Pennsylvania Dutch Country are at hand from a base in western Lancaster County. The tour buses head to Bird-in-Hand, Paradise, Intercourse and such; we prefer the more staid, picturesque towns of Ephrata and Lititz. Hershey and Gettysburg attractions are nearby.

A heritage tour and map, called **River Towns and Roadside Stops,** suggests a sightseeing route to some of this area's historical sites. The map is available at most inns and attractions. The recommended route provides an overview of western Lancaster County as well as a close-up look at specific points of interest.

The National Watch and Clock Museum, 514 Poplar St., Columbia.

Tick-tocking away the seconds in unison, the country's largest collection of precision watches and clocks draws visitors from across the country. Since opening in 1977, the museum has grown to more than 8,000 timepieces divided chronologically into galleries, from early pocket sundials to moonphase wristwatches. A turtle floating in oil in a silver bowl tells the time by swimming to the numbers on the side of the bowl of the tortoise clock. A mouse climbs along the numbers to show the time on the hickory dickory dock wall clock. A statue of a woman stands atop a pedestal and dangles the pendulum that drives a French clock. The masterpiece is the Engle Monumental Clock, whose creator called it the eighth wonder of the world, fourteen feet high with 48 moving figures illustrating Greek mythology and the twelve apostles. *(717) 684-8261. Open Tuesday-Saturday, 10 to 5; Sunday noon to 4. Adults, $6.*

Wright's Ferry Mansion, 38 South Second St., Columbia. This stone house was built in 1738 for a remarkable English Quaker, Susanna Wright, whose pursuits spanned a spectrum from writing to the raising of silkworms. It contains an outstanding collection of Pennsylvania furniture and accessories in the William and Mary and Queen Anne styles from the early 1700s. Textiles, English ceramics and glass also are displayed to good advantage. *(717) 684-4325. Open May-October, Tuesday-Wednesday and Friday-Saturday 10 to 3. Adults, $5.*

Veterans Memorial Bridge, Columbia. The multi-arched, reinforced concrete bridge stretches 6,657 feet across the broad, shallow Susquehanna to Wrightsville. When built about 1930, it was the longest of its type in the world. Ironically, the walls totally obscure any view of the river as you drive across. The bridge is closed one Saturday in October for the annual **Bridge Bust.** A double-decker bus shuttles back and forth the 20,000 area residents who turn out to enjoy arts and crafts, food and entertainment.

The First National Bank Museum, 170 Locust St., Columbia, (717) 684-8864. This is the only known bank still preserved in its original setting in the United States. Tours highlight the president's office and the massive vault.

Chickies Rock County Park, Route 441, Chickies. Good hiking trails lead to the edge of the cliffs and what one enthusiast advises are a couple of the best overlooks in the East, high above the Susquehanna. Named for a native tribe that once lived here, the park won the award for "best view" in a Lancaster County magazine poll.

Walking Tour of Marietta. Two and a half miles long and three blocks wide, this town of 2,700 grew up along the Susquehanna River. Basically unchanged from the 18th century, its eight-block center representing nearly half the town was placed on the National Register of Historic Places as a well-preserved example of a 19th-century industrial town. In 1997, the town received honorable mention for "exceptional aesthetic merit" in a Prettiest Painted Places in America contest. Two of the oldest-looking buildings we've seen, early log structures, stand out along East and West Market streets. A map with a detailed guide to 90 historic places is published by the Marietta Restoration Associates, which sponsors a popular candlelight house tour the first Sunday in December. There's also a walking path along the river.

Shopping. For real Pennsylvania Dutch flavor, you need head no farther than **The Country Store,** 906 Mount Joy-Manheim Road, Mount Joy. The Mennonites run – and also patronize – this place, where you'll find all kinds of bulk foods, cheeses, luncheon meats, pretzels, apple butter and Martin's handcooked potato chips, which we hear are the very best. Oh yes, you'll also find baseball cards and inspirational music tapes. Otherwise, western Lancaster County is not prime shopping territory, the eastern part of the county having cornered the market.

Mount Joy's strung-out downtown includes **Room with a View,** an interiors and gift shop, and **Elizabeth's,** an upscale women's apparel store. We liked all the handmade dolls and wreaths among the gifts and collectibles offered by Althea Johnson at her large **Country Haus Gift Shop,** located in her home at 558 East High St., Elizabethtown. In Columbia, **Hinkle's** combines a pharmacy, restaurant and gift shop of the old school. **C.A. Herr Family Hardware** is a three-story jumble where the basic hardware has been supplemented by household goods, work clothes and even a toy train display. It's been augmented by the **C.A. Herr Annex,** a co-op space that spreads antiques and collectibles through three buildings. The **Susquehanna Glass** outlet store also has a clearance center for extra savings; area innkeepers have had their B&B glasses engraved with their logo here. The **Poplar Street School for the Arts** includes an emerging crafts co-op and gallery.

Across the Susquehanna River in Wrightsville is the **John Wright Warehouse,** host to changing enterprises, among them the large **Country Store** and the **Riverside Foundry** restaurant, a casual place for breakfast or lunch on a canopied terrace beside the river.

Farmers' Markets. Shopping for local foods and crafts is usually best at farmers' markets, and Lancaster County markets are some of the best. Locals tout the **Columbia Market House** at Third and Locust Streets, built in 1869 and operating continuously since. Visitors can tour the dungeon underneath, originally storage space for farmers and the borough's lockup for drunks and felons during the Gay 90s. Also worth a look is the old opera house next door, newly restored as a municipal building. The market here operates Fridays from 7 to 4 and Saturdays from 7 to noon. Columbia's market was surprisingly empty the Friday morning we were there, and seemed to stress crafts more than food.

Extra-Special

Le Petit Museum of Musical Boxes, 255 West Market St., Marietta.

After David Thompson and George Haddad sold their gift shop and old country store in northern New Jersey and retired to Marietta, they found they missed their customers. Their trim green brick Federal townhouse also was overflowing with antique treasures they wanted to share. So in 1994 they opened a museum in their home. The name is a bit of a misnomer. The museum is not particularly petite and the 76 music boxes represent only the tip of the iceberg. Visitors will find such remarkable collections of New England art glass, clocks, Bennington pottery, baskets, toys, china and more tastefully displayed throughout the main floor that a special exhibit is mounted for each collection once a month. "Visitors are stunned – they're not ready for so much," says David. In the library he points out a rare American horse trough basket and a painting of Westminster Abbey that chimes. The largest Swiss 1896 disc musical box resides in the living room next to the museum's smallest music box, hidden in an album on a table. Lift the bread basket on the dining room table and it plays. Ditto for the seat on a child's chair and the statue of an inebriated man leaning against a lamppost, whistling "Show me the way to go home." The star of the collection is now a seven-foot-high Regina music box, the largest ever made in America. There's so much in this fascinating house museum that David guides up to eight people through on hourly tours, while George is at work downstairs producing their own antique music boxes for sale.

(717) 426-1154. Open March-December, Saturday and Monday 10 to 4, Sunday noon to 4. Adults, $3.

Monuments and cannons are everywhere in Gettysburg National Military Park.

Gettysburg, Pa.
Trappings and Treasures

There are two aspects to Gettysburg, the small town that embraces the decisive battlefield of the Civil War. One side is the tourist trappings that draw 2.5 million visitors annually and threaten to out-Niagara the Niagara Falls scene in the annals of tourism. The other is the rural tranquility and sense of history that prompted Dwight and Mamie Eisenhower to make a Gettysburg farm their first and only permanent home. The two aspects manage to co-exist quite nicely, thanks in part to a semi-rural location and to the tenure of the National Park Service.

Sure, there are incursions that should not demean such hallowed ground: the domineering National Tower, the Civil War Wax Museum, the countless ancillary attractions ranging from war stores to a family fun center to a General Lee's Family Restaurant. Even the commercialism of the National Park Service's electric map and cyclorama programs is jarring. Not a particularly distinguished-looking town, Gettysburg gets downright tacky in places.

Yet there also are the treasures: the 1,432 monuments and markers that dot the rolling hills of the vast battlefield and cause Civil War buffs to choke up. The site of Lincoln's Gettysburg Address. The Eisenhower Farm full of poignant memories. The stately brick Gettysburg College campus. The rural byways that lead to all kinds of pleasures and discoveries.

The composite makes Gettysburg a classic middle American tourist destination, just as the Eisenhowers were the classic middle American couple of the post-World War II era.

The epic movie and mini-series on "Gettysburg," adapted from the Michael Shaara novel *Killer Angels* and shown on Ted Turner's TV network, cast the town in the national spotlight and gave it even more banner years for tourism.

Despite all its history, the inns and B&Bs of the modern idiom came late to a Gettysburg where high-rise motels were the rule. The first B&B emerged only in 1984. Many have followed, in town and in the surrounding countryside, especially to the south and east – the part of the area that we feature here. They make a choice base for experiencing the best that Gettysburg has to offer.

Inn Spots

Antrim 1844, 30 Trevanion Road, Taneytown, Md. 21787.

The most upscale inn in the area – indeed, one of the more upscale anywhere – is this expanding paragon of elegance twelve miles southeast of Gettysburg in the Maryland border town of Taneytown (pronounced Tawneytown).

The Antrim dates to 1844, when a Pennsylvania farmer began building the seventeen-room manor house and outbuildings for a working plantation. During the Civil War, Union Gen. George Meade made this his headquarters and watched Confederate troops move toward Gettysburg from its widow's walk. The house had been boarded up for 60 years when Dorothy and Richard Mollett, Baltimore restorationists, acquired it in 1988 to fulfill their dream of running an inn. They started with four rooms and now have twenty-two, plus a restaurant of distinction (see Dining Spots), an enclosed wedding pavilion, a black-bottom marbleite swimming pool that looks like a reflecting pond, a gazebo, an Omni tournament tennis court, a croquet course and a putting green, all for people with means and leisure time.

Guests arrive to find their names calligraphed on cards with their room assignments at the entry. Fourteen-foot-high ceilings dignify the spacious common rooms on the main floor and four original bedrooms on the second. No expense has been spared to make everything perfect. Each guest room has a different personality but the same amenities – private marble baths, step-up canopy feather beds, oriental rugs, swagged valances. Crisp and pristine, they are cloaked in luxury. Men tend to favor the vast George Washington Clabaugh Room with a 19th-century half-tester bed from New Orleans. Women are partial to the Lamberton Room, pretty in white and floral prints. The footed, free-standing shower in the Meade

Room is like nothing we've seen. The posts on the 1820 Honduras mahogany canopy bed weigh 150 pounds each. We enjoyed the Boucher Suite, with a canopied kingsize feather bed, well-worn oriental rugs, a front morning porch and an evening garden porch from which we watched the sun set over the Catoctin Mountains.

What Dorothy calls four funkier rooms with

Handsome brick manor house is heart of plantation buildings at Antrim 1844.

canopies hanging from sloping ceilings and bathrooms with two-person jacuzzis grace the third floor.

Most prized are thirteen newer fireplaced suites with jacuzzis or two-person steam showers in plantation outbuildings. The private decks beside the stream that come with the deluxe Sleigh and Carriage suites in the small yellow Barn are perfectly idyllic. So is the Ice House Suite with queensize four-poster bed and chintz loveseat. Half-doors open onto the garden on one side and the pool on the other, and clouds are painted on the ceiling to complete the indoor-outdoor transition.

The Smith House, moved to the property from the center of Taneytown, contains three deluxe suites. Top of the line is the top-floor Taney, with a queen poster bed. Its bath comes with a double jacuzzi, two-person steam shower and working fireplace. Besides a sitting room with the inn's only TV/VCR, a sunroom faces the sunset and a balcony overlooks the gardens.

Six more suites emerged recently in a carriage house. The ultimate is the U.S. Grant on the lower level, with a kingsize poster feather bed, extra-large bath with two-person jacuzzi and separate shower with a bench, and a sitting room with a sofabed. A CD player, working fireplace and a courtyard are among its amenities.

The main house is an architectural and decorative masterpiece. All shows to great advantage in the dining room with cobalt-blue lacquered walls and a crystal chandelier above a table for fourteen and in the two formal rear drawing rooms opening one onto the other, brimming with fine antiques, marble fireplace mantels and a profusion of fresh flowers. A corner of the library harbors a nifty English mahogany telephone booth that Richard found on an antiquing expedition and was just the ticket for sophisticated privacy. The library is "where everyone hangs out," in Dorothy's words, on facing plush leather sofas. That is, when they're not enjoying the formal gardens or the views of the Catoctin Mountains from the large, enclosed veranda dressed in plush tropical wicker.

The Molletts and their friendly staff pamper guests with a complimentary bar containing wine and champagne, turndown service with chocolates, port and a rose, and a wakeup tray placed on a butler stand outside the door of each room an hour before breakfast. Don't over-indulge on its muffins and fruit, however. Ahead lies a leisurely feast of belgian waffles, scrapple, ham and hash browns, or perhaps eggs benedict, beautifully served amidst fresh flowers, gold-edged china, silver and crystal goblets. Dorothy decorates the plates with all kinds of garnishes, just one more example of an innkeeper who cares.

(410) 756-6812 or (800) 858-1844. Fax (410) 756-2744. Eight rooms and fourteen suites with private baths. Doubles, $200 to $225 weekends, $125 to $150 midweek. Suites, $275 to $375 weekends, $200 to $300 midweek. Two-night minimum weekends. No smoking.

Baladerry Inn, 40 Hospital Road, Gettysburg 17325.

Once a field hospital for the adjacent battlefield, this restored 1810 farmhouse is nicely located out in the countryside and outfitted with the creature comforts that are important to the ratings guidebooks and their inspectors.

It was opened by ex-New Yorker Caryl O'Gara, who wanted to provide the kind of accommodations she and her late husband Tom sought on their travels. She offers four bedrooms with private baths in the original main house and its addition, and four larger rooms (two with corner fireplaces) in a converted carriage house in back. All but one have queensize beds and come with tiled baths, light painted walls, plush carpeting and Pennsylvania House reproduction furniture.

The main inn's two-story, beamed great room is a manorial expanse with individual breakfast tables, sitting areas, wood stove and a decorative loft backed by a remarkable stained-glass window that is illuminated at night. Soft drinks are available in a help-yourself wet bar. Off the great room is a large, trellised brick patio, a good spot for relaxing and taking in the tranquil woodland scene. A common room and wicker-furnished sun porch in the new carriage house doubles as a conference center. The spacious grounds include gardens and a tennis court.

Breakfast in the great room or on the dining terrace consists of juice, a fruit plate, cereal and a main course such as french toast, griddle cakes or bacon and eggs.

(717) 337-1342. Eight rooms with private baths. Doubles, $105 to $135. Two-night minimum most weekends. Children over 14. No smoking.

The Gaslight Inn, 33 East Middle St., Gettysburg 17325.

The most upscale inn in Gettysburg emerged Cinderella-like in 1995 from a ramshackle downtown apartment house. Dennis and Roberta Sullivan put the finishing touches on what they planned as "a deluxe in-town oasis" with nine custom-decorated guest rooms. All have queen or king beds and private baths, four with two-seat steambath/showers and two with double jacuzzi tubs. Six have gas fireplaces. Telephones and TV sets are in each room.

The rooms are beauties. A Louis XIV bedstead and a rococo table lend a French provincial look to the romantic, third-floor Lily Room in front. Its see-through gas fireplace is open to the double jacuzzi in the bathroom and the queensize bed in the room, where the walls are rag-rolled in shades of taupe, shrimp and blue. The June Rose Room, incorporating roses on the comforter, is light and dainty. The Sweet William in the rear, rich in burgundy and cream, has a queensize brass

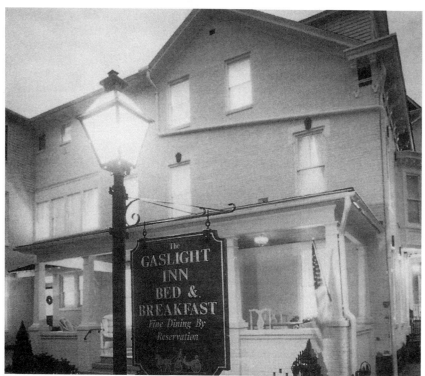

The Gaslight Inn has been beautifully transformed from a ramshackle apartment house.

bed with an antique Persian carpet for a bed cover, plus access to the third-floor balcony. That balcony is also available to occupants in the adjacent Aster Room, dressed in beige and blue with a kingsize featherbed, sofabed and chaise lounge. The handicapped-accessible Daisy Room at the rear of the ground floor opens onto a pleasant brick patio.

The rear of the second floor holds a small TV room with video library and a balcony for general guest use. Other common areas include a formal double parlor separated by pocket doors and decked out in oriental draperies that puddle on the floor, and an elegant dining room with a large cherry gateleg table and four stained-glass wall hangings backlit for accents.

Outside are a side porch and a gaslit brick patio beside lovely rear gardens and a fountain.

"Food is very much a feature here," according to Roberta, formerly a caterer in Montgomery County, Md. Breakfast can be a healthful, light continental affair or a full meal, always with an egg dish and perhaps crêpes with strawberries and champagne sauce. Coffee or cold beverages are served with a variety of baked goods in the afternoon.

Although she no longer offers dinner to guests, she has a professional kitchen and prepares dinner for groups by reservation.

(717) 337-9100. www.thegaslightinn.com. Nine rooms with private baths. April-November: doubles $110 to $150 weekends, $100 to $135 midweek. Rest of year: $100 to $135. Two-night minimum certain weekends. Children over 12. No smoking.

Mural of local structures encircles dining room at The Brafferton Inn.

The Brafferton Inn, 44-46 York St., Gettysburg 17325.

"Experience Gettysburg in the home where its history began," proclaims the advertising for this interesting inn. And history it has in spades. Built in 1786, the original fieldstone house was the first in Gettysburg's historic district. A ricocheting bullet fired during the Civil War battle left its mark on an upstairs fireplace mantel. Troops flanked the stairway as Catholics worshipped in a bedroom while their church became a hospital for the wounded. The dining room is encircled by a fascinating mural of eighteen local structures, painted by artist Virginia Jacobs McLaughlin, who lately was involved in the restoration of Mount Vernon.

All ten bedrooms have private baths and two are suites, their sitting areas equipped with pullout sofas and TVs. The sitting room of one suite on the main floor occupies what had been a small shop. A family suite on the third floor is a great space with beamed cathedral ceiling and a wall of stone and brick.

Six of the guest rooms are in a brick and clapboard house connected to the main structure by a glass-covered brick courtyard that the owners call an atrium. It opens onto the rear patio and a small garden, a pleasant refuge given that this is the heart of downtown Gettysburg. Some rooms in this house lack windows and are lit by skylights; they're small and somewhat stark in the Colonial style, with room for only one chair (for more comfortable seats, head to the atrium or the front parlor decorated in elegant early 19th-century style). The bedrooms have whitewashed walls with woodwork in Williamsburg colors, quilts, samplers and coverlets that match the remarkable stenciling. Benches and rockers, braided rugs, Civil War books, hats on racks and masks on the beds carry out the theme. A local potter made the salad bowls that form some of the sinks. We're partial to the quiet garden room in back with a carved four-poster queen bed. Upstairs in the main fieldstone house are the other four guest quarters with 200-year-old floors and walls. One of the three larger bedrooms here holds a queensize bed, as does the third-floor suite. Tables in the appealing dining room are set with white ironstone plates and assorted bowls. Breakfast, featuring a main course like peaches and cream french toast or strawberry pancakes, is served by new owners Bill and Maggie Ward.

(717) 337-3423. Eight rooms and two suites. Doubles, $90 to $120. Suites, $135 to $150. Two-night minimum weekends April-November. Children over 8. No smoking.

Battlefield Bed & Breakfast, 2264 Emmitsburg Road, Gettysburg 17325.

Costumed hosts, carriage rides, history programs and even artillery demonstrations come with your room at this B&B full of personality. It's located on 46 acres bordering the National Military Park and containing two small ponds, several streams and farmlands maintained as a wildlife preserve. The original 1809 section of the house "was in the midst of the Civil War battle," points out Florence Tarbox, owner with her husband Charles.

The rambling farmhouse, built of granite quarried on the property, has been expanded several times. Eight comfortable guest rooms in several sections are named for four Union and four Confederate units that fought on the South Cavalry Battlefield. They are tastefully decorated to the theme with Civil War historic art in décor ranging from Victorian lace to old country farmhouse.

Two guest quarters with fireplaces are in the original stone building with beamed ceilings and hooked rugs on the rustic chestnut floors. One on the ground floor comes with three old wooden chairs, one a potty seat. The upstairs suite has a step-up queen poster bed with comfortable chairs, a small sitting room and a large bathroom.

Upstairs in a 1971 addition is a large and airy room with vaulted ceiling and two double beds. It's dedicated to the 1st Texas Infantry, although a cabinet display of miscellaneous collections renders the Texas connection obscure until you note the artworks. A main-floor suite with a queensize bed in the main room and two twins adjacent is good for families.

You can sleep in a queen bed beneath portraits of Generals Jackson and Lee in the 7th Georgia Infantry Room upstairs in a 1993 addition. A wall mural sketches the pond outside the window. A sheer canopy queen bed and a stone wall enhance the Hart's Battery Room, while Rush's Lancers Room is light and airy with lace curtains and a matching decorative canopy.

The common areas are unusually spacious. There's a dark and historic living room with a walk-in fireplace and a TV in the original house. It opens off the main room, a huge one with a long table dressed for what looked to be a dinner party at our visit ("we set our breakfast table early," Florence advised). Around the perimeter are smaller tables, sitting areas and a quasi-office section with menus, brochures and the like.

The Tarboxes and their staff don Civil War-era costumes to serve breakfast. Fruit and pastries precede the main dish, which could be apricot cream french toast, heart-shaped pancakes or egg casserole with sautéed vegetables. Afternoon tea is available by appointment.

After breakfast, Charlie Tarbox, dressed as an artillery lieutenant, demonstrates the life of a soldier. He gives an artillery demonstration, may fire muskets or a cannon, and offers guests a ride in his horse-drawn courting buggy. Ghost story

Monuments frame The Doubleday Inn, only B&B located on the Gettysburg Battlefield.

tellers and Civil War historians entertain periodically. Comments in the inn's guest book testify to the uniqueness of the experience.

(717) 334-8804. Fax (717) 334-7330. Eight rooms with private baths. April-December: Weekends, doubles $155 to $175, suites $165 to $199; midweek, doubles $135 to $155, suites, $145 to $185. Rest of year: weekends, doubles, $149 to $169, suites, $159 to $199; midweek, doubles $129 to $149, suites $139 to $179. Children welcome. No smoking.

The Doubleday Inn, 104 Doubleday Ave., Gettysburg 17325.

The only B&B on the Gettysburg Battlefield, the Doubleday occupies a splendid location in a residential section atop Oak Ridge. On view are monuments and battle markers in front, the college campus and the town in back, and busloads of tourists going between.

Charles Wilcox, a Chicago area banker, and his wife Ruth Ann purchased the white clapboard house built in 1929 and have been redoing one room at a time. They offer nine guest rooms, five with private baths and two sharing at either end of the house. The Civil War is the theme and rooms are named after people involved, says Ruth Ann. "This was the site of the first day's battle and a lot of soldiers died on our grounds."

Rooms are rather small (one large enough only for a bed and a luggage rack) but sprightly, as the Wilcoxes have decorated for an English country look. Murals are painted on the walls of the Loft Room, everybody's favorite, with a double and twin bed up a staircase from the bathroom. The two largest are on the main floor, the dainty Bell Jefferson Room in pink and green and the more masculine Marse Robert, with a paneled library air and an open bathroom screened by a lace partition.

The Doubleday makes up for any shortcomings in lodging space with marvelous public areas. Besides an elegant parlor and dining room, there are a rear patio, a side porch with a hanging swing and another patio, and a second-floor balcony.

Civil War memorabilia is displayed throughout. Accessories reflect some of the owners' trips to England over the last few years. The Wilcoxes also offer English tea in the afternoon or evening.

A country breakfast is served by candlelight on fine linens and china or, in summer, on the side porch. The meal includes juice, fresh fruit and a main dish like cheese strata, rum-apple french toast or blueberry pancakes.

(717) 334-9119. Five rooms with private baths and four rooms with shared baths. Doubles, $94 to $114. Children over 8. No smoking.

The Herr Tavern & Publick House, 900 Chambersburg Road, Gettysburg 17325.

Located atop Herr's Ridge, around which the Battle of Gettysburg began, the old Herr Tavern survived the battle but lost a war, so to speak, when a severe windstorm blew out its west wall in 1987. Owner Steve Wolf quickly rebuilt the restaurant and added five B&B guest rooms with shared baths in the Colonial style overhead.

Old-fashioned rooms sharing baths didn't work, he found, so a few years later the "new" rooms were upgraded to appeal to what a fellow innkeeper called "the new money crowd." All were given private baths, fireplaces and television, and two have jacuzzis.

That niche apparently worked. In 1997, seven deluxe rooms with queen beds, gas fireplaces, TVs and double jacuzzis were added above a new banquet hall. The fireplaces in the sitting areas are angled to be visible from the jacuzzi tubs in the bathrooms. Each room is furnished a bit differently with period furnishings. A local craftsman built some of the beds.

In the main building, two large rooms facing the highway retain their Colonial feeling with creaky floors and period furnishings, stenciling and dried flowers. Three formerly small rooms that shared a bath have been converted into two rooms with private baths. One is small with a double bed; the other is big enough for a queensize canopy poster bed, VCR, a mirrored double jacuzzi with shower and twin vanities.

The crowning touch is the Garden Suite in the attic of the main house. Any semblance of Colonial style has been taken over by an oversize round bed, wicker furniture, gray carpeting, a mini-refrigerator, microwave and private deck, plus a day mattress covered with pillows on the floor beside the wood stove.

Guests have use of an upstairs sun porch with reading materials and card games. The downstairs sunroom is the setting for a full breakfast, perhaps eggs or crêpes, fruit and danish pastries.

(717) 334-4332 or (800) 362-9849. Fax (717) 334-3332. Eleven rooms and one suite with private baths. Doubles, $90 to $170 weekends, $65 to $145 midweek. Suite, $170 weekends, $145 midweek.

Dining Spots

Antrim 1844, 30 Trevanion Road, Taneytown, Md.

Knowing diners are drawn from far and wide to this wonderfully restored plantation complex a dozen miles southeast of Gettysburg. Innkeepers Richard and Dorothy Mollett have fashioned three elegant dining rooms seating 65 in their old smokehouse, summer kitchen and slave's kitchen – each a dramatic setting in brick, tartan plaid and hunter green – as well as an elegant dining room in which we first dined in the main inn. So successful have the Molletts been that they built an addition to the smokehouse with 60 more seats.

We enjoyed a fabulous, well-paced dinner here. The experience begins at 6:30 with cocktails and complimentary hors d'oeuvres in the bar, where two loveseats face each other beside the huge brick hearth, and in various common areas. Strolling waitresses pass the appetizers as classical music wafts through the inn. At 7:30, diners adjourn to the restaurant wing, where oil portraits of major Civil War generals watch over the proceedings and a pianist plays on weekends. Dinner is served in six courses, prix-fixe for $55 midweek and $62.50 on weekends. One recent meal started with oyster bisque or a goat cheese-stuffed tulip on a bed of spinach with beet aioli and a choice of salads. Sorbet cleared the palate for the main course, a choice of grilled swordfish with two tomato coulis sauces, pheasant breast stuffed with spinach and pinenuts, or filet of angus beef with sage jus.

Crème brûlée flavored with pumpkin and an apple strudel with crème fraîche completed what a Baltimore magazine reviewer called "a near-perfect dinner." A recent entry in the guest book touted "the best meal we've had west of Europe."

(410) 756-6812 or (800) 858-1844. Prix-fixe, $55 to $62.50. Dinner by reservation, nightly at 7:30.

Dobbin House Restaurant and Tavern, 89 Steinwehr Ave., Gettysburg.

Almost everybody's favorite restaurant locally is the 1776 Dobbin House, upstairs on two floors of the Alexander Dobbin dining rooms or in the basement in the stone-walled Springhouse Tavern that is most people's vision of what eating out in Gettysburg should be about.

The tavern is illuminated by candles even at noon. It was so dark we could barely read the menu, a lengthy affair with an historic theme. When finally we could see – and decide – one of us settled for an excellent baked French onion soup and a so-so spinach salad. The other was tempted by the tavern's special mile-high sandwich ($5.95), "meats and such piled almost as high as the stone walls of the Dobbin House but much straighter!" But with a choice of only two meats it seemed no bigger a deal than the No. 33 club sandwich, roast beef and swiss cheese, which also added bacon, for $5.25. There was no denying the atmosphere, although service was slow as molasses. And the roll that one of us requested to go with the salad turned out to be cold and stale and cost an extra 50 cents.

Afterward, we adjourned upstairs for a look at the main floor, a ramble of small rooms with bare tables and high-back or windsor chairs. Proceed to the second floor where you'll find more dining rooms, some with tables covered by glass. The largest called the Bedroom contains the startling sight of three tables for six under bed canopies, "wherein one can actually dine in bed," according to promotion materials.

For some, the gas-fired fireplaces diminish the otherwise authentic Colonial atmosphere. But most praise the food listed on a lengthy menu that rarely changes. Entrées cover the gamut from "drunken scallops drowned in chablis" and crab cakes to veal madeira, roast duck and prime rib.

Desserts run to cheesecake, pecan pie, black forest cake and warm gingerbread. The bound wine list contains affordable varieties, except for the special Chaddsford Gettysburg chardonnay at $42.

(717) 334-2100. Entrées, $16.75 to $21.95. Tavern open daily, 11:30 to 11. Dinner in Dobbin House, 5 to 9.

Upstairs dining room at Dobbin House.

Pedestal chairs in Herr Tavern dining room.

The Herr Tavern & Publick House, 900 Chambersburg Road, Gettysburg. Rebuilt in 1987, this establishment appears spanking new, in contrast with the creaky old of some of its compatriots. The biggest room is the contemporary-style tavern, light and airy with big windows and a long faux-marble bar.

The original tavern is known for a "salty past," according to old newspaper accounts. It's now the main dining room, pretty with green fanned napkins on white-over-salmon tablecloths, stenciled walls and a working fireplace. Most striking are the unusual wood and leather chairs on pedestals, which the hostess likened to those in church choir lofts. Altogether, 180 diners can be seated on the main floor and in the stone basement rooms.

The extensive menu covers all the bases and rarely changes except for specials. Dinner appetizers range from potato skins to escargots with prosciutto in puff pastry. Entrées include broiled rainbow trout, seafood creole, grilled swordfish, chicken kiev, veal marsala, blackened prime rib and filet mignon béarnaise. Four pastas also are offered. Complimentary cheese and crackers precede the meal. The dessert tray might yield fuzzy navel peach pie or french silk pie.

Sandwiches, omelets and a few entrées like scampi sauté and chicken salad in a pineapple boat comprise the bulk of the lunchtime fare, served in the tavern.

(717) 334-4332 or (800) 362-9849. Entrées, $13.50 to $26. Lunch, Monday-Friday 11 to 4, Saturday 11:30 to 2. Dinner nightly, 5 to 9.

Blue Parrot Bistro, 35 Chambersburg St., Gettysburg.

The chef trained at the Culinary Institute of America and gives cooking lessons, so the food is a cut above. The menu is not all that innovative, however. And the surroundings are downright funky: a bar in front with three booths and some parrot paraphernalia to live up to the name (from a previous incarnation), a rear dining room with another bar and a pool table, and at the end of it all the kitchen, quite a hike from the front. Tables are covered with paper mats over striped cloths over white linens. Assorted lamps or candles and dried flowers in marmalade pottery jars complete the picture.

From a large lunch menu we sampled a hot chicken salad, a grilled brochette on a bed of tossed greens that left one of us still hungry. The other was more than satisfied with a delicious, hearty corn chowder and a vegetarian pita pizza, whose leftovers helped fill up the salad-eater. Each meal was served on a different platter, and ice water came in oversize glasses. Oyster crackers for munching at the bar were a pleasant extra.

The nightly specials are supposed to be the best part of the dinner menu, upon which eggs benedict, of all things, once headed the list of entrées. More recent possibilities were categorized under grills, seafood and pasta. Choices ranged from fried brown rice with beans and veggies or fettuccine tossed with pesto and vegetables to pan-fried catfish with bistro slaw, breaded chicken on creamed white beans with tomato and sweet pepper salsa, and two versions of steak. Desserts could be crème caramel, mocha swirl cheesecake and fresh fruit with zabaglione.

(717) 337-3739. Entrées, $12 to $18. Open Tuesday-Saturday, 11:30 to 8:30 or 9:30.

Farnsworth House Inn, 401 Baltimore St., Gettysburg.

This nice-looking theme restaurant, part of a complex of Shultz family enterprises, is devoted to the Civil War period. Oil paintings of opposing generals Meade and Lee hang over the fireplaces and the walls bear Civil War photos, letters and even a carpetbag in a frame. Pewter tankards and plates top the bare wood tables, dimly lit by lalique-style oil lamps. Taped Civil War music plays in the background, and sometimes it can be a bit much.

The chef adapts the menu to the period as well. Goober peanut soup, game pie, "real Virginia ham – salty and dry," Yankee pot roast, pumpkin fritters and sweet potato pudding are specialties. Baked flounder and prime rib are available for the less adventurous. The price includes a relish tray, homemade spoon and Jennie Wade breads with local apple butter and choice of vegetables. Among homemade desserts are rum cream pie, black walnut ice cream and walnut-apple cake. Civil War period drinks are featured in the lounge.

(717) 334-8838. Entrées, $12.95 to $17.95. Dinner nightly, 5 to 9 or 9:30.

The Altland House, Route 30, Abbottstown.

Contemporary dining in an historic atmosphere is offered by the Haugh family in this landmark facing Abbottstown's Center Square.

The food and atmosphere are highly rated, drawing many from Gettysburg fifteen or so miles to the west. The extensive menu runs the gamut from meat loaf, shepherd's pie and creamed chicken with waffles to charbroiled tuna steak, shrimp scampi and filet mignon with béarnaise sauce. Oyster pie, jambalaya, chicken oscar and stuffed chicken Smithfield are among the specialties. A favorite starter is York County turtle soup served with sherry.

(717) 259-9535. Entrées, $8.95 to $27.95. Lunch, 11 to 5. Dinner, 5 to 10.

Diversions

The Civil War and the battlefields are the main attractions. All kinds of salient ventures, many of them commercial and/or hokey, capitalize on the theme.

Gettysburg National Military Park.

Gettysburg is virtually surrounded by 25 square miles of battlefields, where the Civil War's bloodiest battles were fought on the first three days of July 1863.

President Lincoln delivered his Gettysburg Address later that year when he dedicated the Gettysburg National Cemetery. More than 1,400 monuments and markers, countless cannons and stone walls, three observation towers and 31 miles of marked avenues comprise the park. To avoid being overwhelmed by it all, start at the park visitor center – forerunner of a planned but controversial new visitor center and museum.

The best way to experience the site is to hire one of 90 licensed guides at the park visitor center for a two-hour tour ($35) in your own car. Most retired history teachers and Civil War buffs, they are passionate about their subject as they point out the obvious and not so obvious. You also can tour the battlefield on a double-decker bus ($12.95), one with a guide and the other with earphones for listening to a taped narration, or you can rent tour tapes for $10 to $15. A map points out highlights along a 23-mile self-guided tour that takes two to three hours, varying with stops and traffic. Bicycling may well be the most rewarding way to go.

The Eternal Light Peace Memorial, the North Carolina and Pennsylvania memorials, Little Round Top and the optional Culp's Hill side tour are personal favorites.

The visitor center contains a theater with an electric map program that shows with colored lights various troop movements during the battle (the 30-minute show costs $3). Nearby is the Cyclorama Center, where an 1884 painting of Pickett's Charge is displayed with a sound and light program inside a circular, 26-foot-high auditorium (adults, $3).

(717) 334-1124. Park open daily, 6 a.m. to 10 p.m. Free.

Other Tours. An informative, self-guided **Civil War Walking Tour** of 35 downtown Gettysburg sites illustrates the impact the battle had on what was a small rural community in 1863. By reservation, **Ghosts of Gettysburg,** 271 Baltimore St., (717) 337-0445, offers 90-minute candlelight walking tours past downtown and campus sites of ghostly happenings and eerie sightings twice nightly in summer at 8 and 9:45. The guides proclaim Gettysburg to be, acre for acre, "the most haunted place in America."

Scenic Drives. The Gettysburg Convention & Visitors Bureau details a **Scenic Valley Tour** covering 36 miles through the rolling orchard country of the west and north sides of Adams County. It also details an **Historic Conewago Tour** of 40 miles to the east and northeast of Gettysburg. Make your own tour to the southeast to include Taneytown, Littlestown, the horses at Hanover Shoe Farms, the lakes of Codorus State Park and the Stone Mill shop at Brodbecks.

Antiquing in New Oxford. East of Gettysburg is New Oxford, a Victorian town with a beautiful circle in the heart of downtown. It's a mecca for antiquers; 36 dealers within a few blocks of the circle are designated in a brochure.

Shopping. Gettysburg is full of stores specializing in Civil War memorabilia (the best is **Fields of Glory**) and tacky souvenirs. Some of the town's better shops are gathered under the **Old Gettysburg Village** umbrella at Baltimore Pike and Steinwehr Avenue. In the downtown center, good art and crafts by local artisans draw visitors to one side of **Gallery 30**; the other side offers a choice selection of books. Handcrafted jewelry and home and garden accessories are featured at **Presents. Codori's Bavarian Gift Shop** is worth a look, as is the **English Rose Cottage** for dried flowers and pottery. South of town in Littlestown are three establishments linked in a country crafts shop tour, **The Quilt Patch, Koony's Barn** and **Smokehouse Crafts.**

For a break, stop for espresso at the **Gettysburg Coffee Company.** Healthful lunches and afternoon tea are offered at **Thistlefield's Tea Room.**

Our favorite shopping is a half-hour's drive away in Brodbecks at **Stone Mill Clay and Woodworks,** four levels with room after room of tasteful things. It's the gallery and shop of Inez and Jerry Fenster, she a potter and he a woodworker, who live upstairs in the old paper mill dating from the 1700s and whose studios and output flow through a most intriguing building. Her hand-thrown pottery and his inlaid tile tables and cupboards are showcased with the works of other artisans. Wooden spoons, Amish paintings, floral arrangements, quilts, linens, specialty foods, painted birdhouses, folk art, jewelry, decorative accessories – you name it, they've got it. The year's highlight is Stone Mill's annual Christmas show, when the shop is open Tuesday-Sunday. Otherwise, it's open Wednesday-Sunday, but closed in January.

Extra Special

Eisenhower National Historic Site, Gettysburg.

There's something altogether endearing about the Eisenhower Farm, a monument to the 1950s and the only home President Dwight D. Eisenhower and his wife Mamie ever owned. Fifty Norway spruce trees, birthday presents from each of the state Republican chairmen in 1955, line the long driveway into the 231-acre farm, which is reached by a five-minute ride on a shuttle bus leaving every fifteen minutes from the National Park Visitor Center. The rural site is very different from the Gettysburg that many tourists see; the bus driver pointed out two separate herds of deer as we arrived. The Eisenhowers bought a seven-room brick farmhouse in 1950 and added wings on either side for entertaining. The self-guided tour starts in the living room, where a guide notes that "the house was furnished in gifts" from friends and dignitaries. You learn that Ike considered this "the stuffiest room in the house," far preferring the long rear sun porch where the couple ate breakfast while watching the farm scene and had dinner in front of the TV. An easel bears a copy of the painting Ike was working on at his death. Among Mamie's collections are two gold plates from Tiffany & Co., juxtaposed with a plate she bought at Stuckey's and figurines of presidents and first ladies from cereal boxes. Ike's library contains favorite books plus U.S. Army Registers and volumes of Order of Battle Maps from operations in Italy. A glass door allows a peek into the linen closet, where most of the towels are pink, Mamie's favorite color, and monogrammed "MED" and "IKE." Past a funny little 1950s kitchen is Ike's paneled den, a favorite haunt. The self-guided tour ends outdoors with a look at Ike's brick barbecue, his putting green and a garage containing a Crosley runabout with a fringe on top, its front fender emblazoned with "Ike and Mamie" in stenciled script. Ike used the last to show guests like Winston Churchill and Charles DeGaulle around his farm. Visitors get to share part of the 1950s and the great middle American experience. Unfortunately, all the shades inside the house are drawn (or at least they were at our visit) so you can't see the views the Eisenhowers could.

(717) 338-9114 or (877) 438-9829. Hour-long tours, 9 to 4, daily April-October, Wednesday-Sunday rest of year. Adults, $5.25.

Photo by Bob Lambert

On football weekends, Penn State's Beaver Stadium is focal point of the Happy Valley.

State College, Pa.

The Happy Valley

They call it Happy Valley, this long and lush valley nestled beneath Mount Nittany – a contented, rather inaccessible enclave that retains something of a Brigadoon-like innocence amidst the mountains of central Pennsylvania.

The Pennsylvania State University transformed its hometown into a burgeoning metropolis from its early years as center of the most important ironmaking region in the country. Penn State and the surrounding town are inevitably linked. Think of State College and most think of football weekends and the Nittany Lions. The university's 40,000 students equal the population of all State College.

Although Penn State is the dominant presence in the valley, the valley is more than Penn State. The valley's lure is so strong that it calls many alumni to make it their home. "This is a pulse point of the world, like a vortex," suggests Cheryl Bohn, who was drawn from Pittsburgh to take over one of the area's many new B&Bs.

There's much to appeal to visitors as well as residents, especially at times other than football weekends. That's when upwards of 100,000 fans turn the valley into a happy (if the Lions win) homecoming circus –the biggest by far in the East.

To the north of State College is Bellefonte, the prosperous Centre County seat, founded on ironmaking and home to seven governors. The Victorian treasures in its National Register historic district prompt some to call it "The Cape May of the Mountains."

To the east is Boalsburg, an historic village that defines the word quaint in Pennsylvania terms. It's the birthplace of Memorial Day and home to a house museum with the nation's closest ties to discoverer Christopher Columbus.

All around are mountains, streams and lakes that make this a happy place for recreation. Spring Creek is a fly fisherman's paradise. America's only all-water cavern can be toured by motorboat. Stone Valley Recreation Area is the center of hiking and boating activity.

"The Happy Valley is a 1970s thing," says one local booster. "It sounds like something we should have recovered from, but haven't."

In 1990, Garth Brooks earned $4,000 when he pinch-hit for an entertainer at the Centre County Grange Fair. In 1997, he made millions at five sold-out concerts in Penn State's sparkling new Bryce Jordan Center.

Mae McQuade, dean of the area's innkeepers, cites the change as "a metaphor for our happy valley. We are a treasure waiting to be discovered."

Inn Spots

As a university town, accommodations are booked far in advance for football and special-event weekends and may go begging at slow periods. Most rooms carry higher charges and minimum stays for special events, which include football weekends, graduation and the Central Pennsylvania Festival of the Arts.

Carnegie House, 100 Cricklewood Drive, State College 16803.

Patterned on the great country-house hotels of the British Isles, this luxurious establishment is one of the more welcoming we've encountered. Resident innkeepers Peter and Helga Schmid personally greet guests, show them their rooms and maintain hands-on oversight throughout their stay.

The German-born couple has an obvious love affair with their inn. They played key roles in its creation with principal Phil Sieg and partners, including William Schreyer, chairman of Penn State's board of trustees and chairman emeritus of Merrill Lynch, and Joe Paterno, Penn State's well-known football coach. Peter, whose career in hotel management included stints locally at the Toftrees Resort and the Nittany Lion Inn, dreamed of a place of his own as a retirement project.

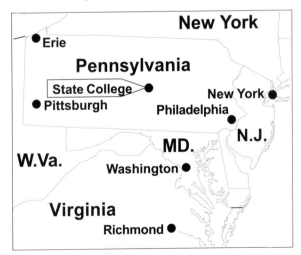

Phil Sieg owned the property, part of philanthropist Andrew Carnegie's farm, which inspired the name. He also had the vision for imparting the richness of Scottish country houses into a new architectural package that is indigenous to the Northeast, complete with dormers and cupolas.

The preliminary plans for an eight-room B&B blossomed into a full-scale inn that opened in

Carnegie House occupies tranquil location adjacent to Toftrees golf course.

1994 with 22 guest accommodations, a restaurant, elegant common rooms and a small gift shop.

The bedrooms are beauties, with an aura of spaciousness, comfort and luxury that belies their affordable price tag. Each different, most have kingsize poster beds, sitting areas, TVs hidden in armoires, large closets with removable coat hangers and huge bathrooms with soaking tubs and walk-in showers. Woolen throws and colorful pillows are a decorating trademark. A tray of plump strawberries and a bag of homemade cookies wrapped in a pink ribbon were welcome goodies at our summer visit.

More culinary prowess was evident in the dining room. Dinner begins with cocktails and complimentary hors d'oeuvres in the richly paneled library, which is big enough for several conversational groupings at once. Peter Schmid enters the adjacent Thistle Bar, "the smallest bar in town," to mix "the biggest drinks in town," among them a mean martini. You order from the nicely varied, five-course menu ($35 prix-fixe) before entering the handsome dining room, which overlooks the 17th green and fairways of the Toftrees golf course.

Appetizers at our visit were a stellar grilled shrimp with curry-yogurt dressing on a cucumber and melon salad and tasty slices of beef tenderloin on a potato and corn cake. Soups (the signature leek and a puree of broccoli) and a house salad followed. Among main courses, we enjoyed the medallions of lamb loin in a dijon and merlot demi-glace, paired with snow peas and a potato cake, and the grilled filet of beef with blue cheese and bourbon jus, served with roasted potatoes and grilled vegetables. Desserts were a lemon charlotte topped with wild blueberries and red currants and an assortment of Penn State Creamery ice creams and frozen yogurt.

Continental breakfast includes assorted fruits, juices, homemade granola and light pastries. The Schmids go all-out on a Scottish breakfast on Sunday mornings.

(814) 234-2424 or (800) 229-5033. Fax (814) 231-1299. Twenty rooms and two suites with private baths. Doubles, $150 and $195. Suites, $275. $25 surcharge on special weekends. No smoking. Dinner prix-fixe, $35. Lunch, Tuesday-Saturday 11:30 to 1:30. Dinner, Monday-Saturday 6 to 8:30.

The Fairmount is a gray limestone house in residential section near downtown.

The Fairmount, 234 West Fairmount Ave., State College 16801.

A handsome, substantial gray limestone house in a residential section just south of downtown State College is the base for four comfortable guest rooms with queensize beds and private baths and common facilities of distinction. The residence is the home of Bonnie and Peter Marshall and their three offspring. The B&B is the pre-retirement project of Peter, State College's city manager, and Bonnie, director of development for Penn State's College of Liberal Arts. Amazingly, the couple, who travel widely in their professional lives, do all the work themselves, from preparing gourmet breakfasts to cleaning the ten bathrooms on the property.

The Marshalls opened their B&B in 1995 in preparation for the time a few years hence when their last child goes off to college. At this stage, they offer two rooms upstairs in the main house and two in a rear carriage house, with more in the plans as they become empty nesters.

The Centre County Room on the second floor bears memorabilia from the home area. The Pittsburgh Room, devoted to Peter's hometown, has a rare iron bed.

Out back are two larger, more private quarters. The Williamsburg-inspired Garden Room has a wicker-style bedroom set. The Chester County Room, depicting Bonnie's background, is outfitted in burgundy and plaids and hunting pictures. Both have TVs and telephones. Bonnie furnished all the rooms with family pieces in a mix of styles.

Beautiful oriental rugs dot the dark stained floors in the main house, where guests gather in a double parlor decorated with hunting colors and a TV/VCR in front and a more formal parlor in back. Alongside is a long enclosed stone porch with another TV and some interesting tiles above the fireplace. A rubbing of the tiles has become the Fairmount's unusual logo.

Breakfast is served in a sunny room overlooking the rear slate terrace or in a formal dining room. The Marshalls take turns in the kitchen, preparing perhaps grand marnier french toast, puff pastry with scrambled eggs and smoked salmon, sour-cream belgian waffles or baked eggs with tarragon and leeks. Abundant fresh fruit and juices come first. On weekdays, when the couple faces workday chores, one or the other is on hand to serve a continental breakfast.

(814) 237-1101. Four rooms with private baths. Doubles, $95 to $115 weekends, $75 to $85 weekdays, $115 to $130 special events. No smoking. No credit cards.

Chatelaine at Split Pine Farmhouse, 347 West Pine Grove Road (Route 45), Box 326, Pine Grove Mills 16868.

Mae McQuade's beloved pre-Civil War home just southwest of town is filled with treasures, many collected during years of living around the U.S. and Europe with her late husband, an army officer. But cherished above all is the finely detailed corner cabinet in the dining room that he made for her. It holds her most precious pieces of china, from an astounding collection on display here and there around the house.

Years of entertaining military brass prompted this gracious hostess to open one of central Pennsylvania's first B&Bs in 1985 – the same year she graduated Phi Beta Kappa from Penn State after returning to college to finish her degree.

The Chatelaine has two bedrooms on the second floor with private baths, and two bedrooms on the third sharing, although they are usually rented as a suite or for one couple. "I started with a swan Christmas plate," says Mae of the Swan Room, which is the favorite. Now it is filled with swans, even to the fixtures in the bathroom and the shape of the soap. It has a kingsize bed.

In the Black Chintz room, the unusual walls are covered with shirred chintz fabric of flowers on a black background. The cannonball poster bed is queensize. A handsome chair that she got for ten cents, a stand that cost a quarter, and a Wells Fargo desk purchased in Kansas are accents. The room's hall bathroom has lavender art glass, lit from behind, in lieu of a window.

We slept in the third-floor Dawn Room, eclectic to say the least, with a king bed, TV and what Mae calls "happenstance decor." Some of the childhood clothes and toys of her four children are on display. Black and white bathrobes, to match the black and white wallpaper, are provided for the hall bath, a mini-museum under the eaves. Across the landing is the twin-bedded Twilight Room. A memorable piece here is the carved bear in two pieces. Mae's artistic daughter Amanda sketched the mural on the stairway leading to the third floor, an interpretation of childhood dreams. Another daughter, Delia, painted the wonderful fantasy birds in the downstairs hall. Guests relax in the comfortable living room, with its white sofas and many magazines, or at a table amid Mae's gardens on the wide front lawn. In the morning, juice and coffee or tea is delivered early outside the bedrooms. We savored our candlelit breakfast of cantaloupe with blackberries and incredibly rich meringue french toast (made with croissants) with orange sauce, served on a beautifully set table. Other dishes from Mae's extensive repertoire could be fresh fruit mélange with tamarind-ginger sauce, German plum cake, huevos verdes, Swiss omelet roll, Florentine crêpe cups and chocolate chip banana bread.

The trunk of the venerable white pine in front of the house is split, which accounts for part of the name. Mae considers herself the chatelaine, or "keeper of the keys." She turns the keys gladly, pampering guests in her charming house.

(814) 238-2028 or (800) 251-2028. www.virtualcities.com/pa/chatelaine.htm. Two rooms with private baths and two with shared baths. Doubles, $80 to $90; special events, $115 to $135. Two-night minimum for special events. Children over 12. No smoking.

The Reynolds Mansion, 101 West Linn St., Bellefonte 16823.

Charlotte and Joseph Heidt, both Penn State alumni (as are many innkeepers in this area) and now among the town's guiding spirits, bought the magnificent red sandstone Reynolds Mansion, built in 1885 by bachelor business tycoon William F. Reynolds, the town's first millionaire. They undertook several months of renovations and opened it as a B&B in 1994.

Guests have the run of the main floor with its marble vestibule, beautifully furnished parlor with a handcarved tiled fireplace, a large billiards room and a cozy snuggery filled with books and magazines that you can read in front of the fireplace. Stunning parquet floors, stained-glass windows, twelve-foot walnut ceilings and polished and intricate woodwork abound. But this is no fussy Victorian. Charlotte advises that they furnished with country Colonial pieces from their former home and Victorian pieces they have picked up in the area.

Three guest rooms are on the second floor. The choice Colonel's Green Room in which we stayed is almost a suite, with an entrance hall, a large bathroom with shower, and a huge jacuzzi tub in the corner of the bedroom. It has a kingsize bed and a working fireplace. Grace's Garden Room, light and airy with Laura Ashley fabrics, has a queen bed, loveseat, plants in the turret and a steam shower with a waterfall that pours cool water down one's back. Cherubs are painted on the ceiling of the mushroom white Louisa's Cherub Room, which has a delicate spread on the queen bed, fireplace, jacuzzi and separate shower.

Two large rooms with queen beds and gas fireplaces were added on the third floor in 1998. The jacuzzi in the Nittany Blue Room is in the turret, while the jacuzzi in the Woodlands looks out into the top of a huge sycamore tree. The newest Grand Tour, tucked in the eaves, has a queen bed, stove and jacuzzi. It is decorated with prints and books from Europe.

The spacious grounds include a rear carriage house that the Heidts were thinking of converting into an English country cottage.

Charlotte, one of the most calm and unflappable hostesses we have met, serves a pre-breakfast of mini-muffins and coffee on the upstairs landing. Joe makes the real breakfast for guests before he disappears into his office for his work day as a computer programmer. At the lace-covered table in the chandeliered dining room with walls of striped mahogany, a plate of eight kinds of fruit and a choice of four juices are standard. We feasted on french toast stuffed with apples and cream cheese, almost like a soufflé, with a side of sausage. Other main dishes could be zucchini frittata, quiche lorraine or a strata with asparagus and mushrooms. There is always dessert; heart-shaped sand tarts or perhaps cinnamon twists.

Decanters of bourbon and blackberry brandy await guests in the evening.

The Heidts do things up in style. For Christmas, they decorate their vestibule with an eighteen-foot-high tree so big it takes seven men to carry it in.

(814) 353-8407 or (800) 899-3929. Six rooms with private baths. Doubles, $125 to $160 weekends, $95 to $105 midweek; $125 to $150, special events. Two-night minimum for special events. Smoking restricted.

Earlystown Manor, Route 45, RR1, Box 181A, Centre Hall 16828.

Built as a B&B, this substantial brick house set well back from the road eight miles east of State College is the retirement project of Zane and Anne Smilowitz, both longtime Penn State employees. The vast grounds are being landscaped by Zane, whose avocation is gardening, and a farm pond was in the works at our visit.

Showy red sandstone Reynolds Mansion offers deluxe overnight accommodations.

The Smilowitzes offer five spacious bedrooms with private baths, queen beds and large closets. They are nicely appointed with traditional reproduction furnishings, and each offers a pleasant view of the surrounding countryside. A second-floor sitting area in the hall contains a guest refrigerator and snacks.

Besides family quarters, the main floor holds a living room and dining room. Zane cooks a full breakfast, his favorites being crêpes, a bread pudding casserole with apples that he likens to french toast, and an oven omelet with mushrooms, onions, green peppers and cheese. Fruit, cereal and pastries also are available. *(814) 466-6481 or (877) 466-6481. Fax (814) 466-6118. Five rooms with private baths. Doubles, $85 to $95; special events, $140 to $150. Two-night minimum for special events. Children over 12. No smoking.*

Springfield House Bed & Breakfast, 126 East Main St., Box 240, Boalsburg 16827.

Ensconced in the midst of quaint downtown Boalsburg is this 1847 structure, which derives its name from the era when the community was called Springfield because of numerous springs found in the area. A graceful porch wrapping around the Federal-Victorian house provides a vantage point for observing the passing scene.

Cheryl Bohn, a government worker from Pittsburgh, returned in 1996 to the Penn State area in which she had matriculated to fulfill her dream of operating a B&B. To a turnkey operation she added the frills, among them candies on the pillows, bathrobes and dainty décor. The five rooms are billed as suites because of their size. All have armoires, small TVs and private baths, three of which are side by side across the hall from the rooms. Three rooms occupy much of the second floor. The other two are in a rear carriage house; the one upstairs has one of the inn's two queen beds and an efficiency kitchen with wet bar.

The main floor of the house holds a casual gentlemen's sitting room in what had been a doctor's office and a more formal ladies' parlor in what once was a one-room cabin.

Breakfast is served in the dining room, on the porch or in the garden. The meal begins with fruit, breads and muffins, and a tray of cheeses, cold cuts and vegetables in the European tradition. The main course could be apple dumplings, omelets or crêpes. "I like to cook on a whim," says Cheryl.

(814) 466-6290 or (888) 782-9672. Five rooms with private baths. Doubles, $85; special events, $115. Children over 12, small pets accepted. No smoking.

Starry Night B&B, 1170 West Branch Road, State College 16801.

Handsome oriental rugs everywhere are a feature of this new B&B in a 1920s farmhouse presented to Chet Esber and his bride by his grandfather, a longtime rug dealer. The house was renovated to provide four guest rooms with private baths and a living room with a fireplace. A long side porch yields a view of a stream cutting across the secluded, 40-acre property, known for its fireflies, sunsets and starry nights.

The beamed, main-floor Uncle George's Room comes with an antique double sleigh bed, gas fireplace and a private screened porch. Upstairs, Webb's Room has a queen sleigh bed and a full bath. Mother Betse's Room offers a queen bed, chaise lounge and purple tiles in the bath. The furnishings throughout might be called contemporary farmhouse, although Chet refers to them as an eclectic mix of antiques.

Breakfast is deluxe continental or, as Chet calls it, healthy. Expect fruits, cereal, yogurt, croissants, sweet breads and bagels.

(814) 234-8111. Three rooms with private baths. Doubles, $75 to $90; special events, $135 to $150. No children. No smoking.

The Queen, A Victorian B&B, 176 East Linn St., Bellefonte 16823

The owner's museum-quality collections entice visitors to this restored, eighteen-room Queen Anne-style mansion in Bellefonte's historic district.

Nancy Noll, whose ornately furnished home could have qualified as a shop at our early visit, proudly displays items gathered from her great-grandfather's three general stores. In her kitchen are a huge shopping block, rolling pins, cans and lots of advertising art. She has plenty of room to exhibit her Victorian memorabilia, Santas, hunting and fishing items, and – her pride and joy – a collection of black Americana.

Besides collections, Nancy is into cooking, as evidenced by her typical Sunday breakfast of fresh fruit cup with apples, bananas and pecans in an amaretto cream sauce, followed by eggs benedict with her own secret hollandaise sauce that she calls "the governor's." Another day might yield her oven-baked french toast with apples, cinnamon and pecan sauce. Her partner, Curtis Miller, bakes the french bread, pastries, baklavas and muffins.

They offer guests a couple of spacious rooms with queensize beds. The romantic and feminine Anne's Room, the original master bedroom with a round tower and curved glass windows, has an appliqué-carved oak bed that belonged to Nancy's grandmother, a roll-top desk and a bathroom with a slipper tub. The Governor's Suite appears more masculine with its hunting and fishing collectibles. It has a fireplace and a separate sitting area in the turret.

Spring flowers outline grounds of The Queen, a Victorian B&B.

A collection of Santas surrounds the fireplace in the entry foyer. In the parlor are a working victrola, player piano, stereoscopic viewers and the Victorian wallpapers characteristic of the rest of the house. Breakfast is served amidst antique glassware and linens in the large dining room. Guests may use a hot tub in a spa room.

At our visit, Nancy had her eye on a couple of more rooms to be converted into guest quarters as restoration continues.

(814) 355-7946 or (888) 355-7999. Fax (814) 357-8068. One room and one suite with private baths. Memorial Day to New Year's and peak winter/spring weekends: double, $125; suite, $155. Rest of year: double, $90; suite, $125. Children accepted. No smoking.

Cooke Tavern Bed & Breakfast, Route 45, RD 2, Box 218-A, Spring Mills 16875.

"Welcome to Cooke Tavern, also known as the Money Pit," quip Greg and Mary Kay Williams of their handsome, red-brick Georgian property. The young couple have fulltime jobs as well as a hands-on renovation project that won the Centre County Historical Society's preservation award for 1995.

Theirs is a B&B with considerable charm, historic authenticity and a bathroom that must be seen to be believed.

Built in 1808 as a tavern, the house has a spectacular three-story open winding staircase, eleven-foot-high ceilings, seven fireplaces, original locks and hardware, and much hand-stenciling. The tavern room on the main floor retains its original yellow pine floor and now holds quite a collection of nutcrackers atop the piano. Mary Kay rag-rolled the walls of the elegant dining room in blue-green and gold and sponge-painted the walls of the parlor in the rear.

Two upstairs ballrooms have become bedrooms, one with a kingsize iron canopy bed and one with queensize bed, done in Williamsburg Colonial styles. They and the Peach Room with an antique brass and iron double bed share two baths.

But what baths! The principal one is a Roman bath, modeled on the ones they had experienced at the Baden-Baden spas in Germany. Complete with pillars and trailing vines, it has a corner jacuzzi with a fountain, a separate shower, a double vanity, and a small television set and refrigerator facing the toilet. Occupy this bath and it could well go unshared!

"The rest of the house was restored to the period, but there were no bathrooms here and no plumbing – only an outhouse – so we felt a Roman bath was fair game," explained Greg with a twinkle.

The dining room is the setting for a candlelight breakfast: fresh fruit, Sally Lunn bread and perhaps mushroom-cheese strata or baked french toast.

Mary Kay was thinking of converting a rear cabin into a shop.

(814) 422-8787. Three bedrooms share two baths. Doubles, $95 to $105; special events, $115 to $125. Two-night minimum for special events. Children over 12. No smoking.

The House on Top of the Hill, 606 Rosslyn Road, Huntridge Manor, Boalsburg 16827.

This large contemporary ranch house, built of stone in 1989 on eleven hilltop acres, takes guests in two bedrooms furnished in country style. Each has a private bath, queensize bed and remote-control TV. One on the main floor has access to a screened porch. The other on the lower level has a private entrance and a terrace overlooking the Tussey Mountain ski area and the Elks Country Club.

Sharon Au, owner with her husband Jim, serves a full breakfast of seasonal fruits, homemade muffins or pastries, and a main dish. Her Christmas morning egg bake is a favorite.

(814) 466-2070. Fax (814) 466-6622. Two rooms with private baths. Doubles, $70; special events, $125. Children accepted. No smoking.

Rest & Repast, Box 126, Pine Grove Mills 16868.

Linda Feltman represents 60 mostly part-time B&Bs that take in guests by reservation, mainly on peak weekends. Energetic Linda knows each property well and prospective guests find her booking service a good matchmaker.

(814) 238-1484. Fax (814) 234-9890. Doubles, $50 to $100.

Dining Spots

The Hummingbird Room, Route 45, Spring Mills.

Arguably the area's finest dining is offered by Eric and Claudia Sarnow in a National Register landmark manor home built in 1847. The couple left Philadelphia, where he was sous chef for six years at the renowned Le Bec Fin, to open a 22-seat Hummingbird Restaurant in the Woodward Inn in eastern Centre County in 1993. They purchased the Fisher House and moved the Hummingbird Room closer to State College two years later, retaining the name but expanding dinner service from three to five nights a week.

Dining is in a variety of small rooms on the first and second floors. Burgundy-linened tables are set with stunning Villeroy & Boch china. Dishes arrive under silver cloches and tablecloths are crumbed between courses.

The French menu is available à la carte or prix-fixe, $34 for three courses. The reputation of the lobster bisque, the house-smoked salmon with a lobster and artichoke salad, and the sautéed lobster with morels over homemade pasta preceded our visit. Good things also were said about the filet of beef rossini with

Landmark mill is site of Gamble Mill Tavern restaurant.

black truffle sauce and the loin of veal with smoked veal sausage, cognac sauce and truffled mashed potato.

We were smitten by the wild mushroom ravioli and the cold seafood pâté with lobster and salmon for starters. The roast duckling with raspberry sauce and the filet of pork tenderloin with dijon mustard-tomato-cornichon sauce and a goat cheese soufflé were superior main dishes. Claudia prepares the desserts, which include an excellent chocolate-hazelnut dacquoise, orange cheesecake with grand marnier, rhubarb cobbler and kiwi sorbet. Eric uncorked the Mount Nittany Vineyard & Winery champagne with a saber in the napoleonic style.

(814) 422-9025. Entrées, $18 to $25.50. Dinner, Wednesday-Sunday 5 to midnight.

The Gamble Mill Tavern, 160 Dunlap St., Bellefonte.

The first Bellefonte building to earn placement on the National Register, this three-story mill dates to 1785 as part of the earliest settlement in the Nittany Valley. Self-taught chef Courtney Confer and manager Jeanne Murphy started in 1986 with a soup and sandwich restaurant. Now the full-service facility heads most lists of favorite eating spots and includes a revolving art gallery.

Dining is on several levels in rooms of varying size. Tables are grouped in the cobblestone carriageway, where millstones are embedded on the floor. There are a tavern room of brick and wood, a loft-style dining area full of hanging plants, and a huge dining room for functions or overflow.

The mill is a sight to behold, both for its art and its history. The food measures up, as evidenced by our lunches of a chicken salad with honey-mustard dressing and a warm Polynesian chicken salad with avocado, melon and bell peppers in a fabulous orange-ginger dressing. Our tablemates liked their creole pasta, mesquite-grilled shrimp with black beans and roasted pepper salsa, and char-grilled vegetable pita. Cappuccino torte and an ice cream puff were tasty desserts.

At night, the setting is elegant for Courtney's specialty beef wellington, seafood strudel, grilled salmon caribe, crab cakes, chicken montrachet, mustard-crusted rack of lamb, and seared venison loin and sausage with raspberry sage sauce. The wine list is small but choice and affordable.

(814) 355-7764. Entrées, $14.95 to $24. Lunch, Monday-Saturday, 11:30 to 2:30. Dinner, Monday-Saturday, 5 to 8.

The Victorian Manor, 901 Pike St., Lemont.
The quaint hamlet of Lemont holds this handsome light green Victorian house with red and burnt yellow trim and a copper roof. Built in 1892, it has a variety of dining rooms, one with a different lamp on every white-clothed table, and a glassed-in, wraparound porch pretty in pink and cream. The service plates bear the restaurant's logo.

The extensive continental menu offers main courses like fillet of salmon with béarnaise sauce, dover sole meunière, chicken marsala, roast duckling with sweet and sour sauce and veal oscar. Chateaubriand and rack of lamb are prepared for two. About the only contemporary touches we noted were garden-herb ravioli with red pepper coulis and mesclun-stuffed swordfish marinated in ginger and lime juice.

The smoked seafood and hot appetizer samplers appeal for starters. The latter contains escargots, mushrooms stuffed with crabmeat, grape leaves stuffed with lamb and rice, and baked clams with crabmeat. The crab bisque is another favorite. Espresso trifle, baked alaska, bananas flambé and ice cream pie are among the desserts.

Lily's cocktail lounge on the lower level is open on weekends.

(814) 238-5534. Entrées, $14.50 to $26.50. Dinner, Tuesday-Sunday from 5.

Duffy's Boalsburg Tavern, 113 East Main St., Boalsburg.
Steaks and seafood are the specialties in this handsome stone building, a stage stop tavern dating to 1819. There's a good variety of menu choices, served in both formal and informal surroundings with appropriate Colonial atmosphere.

The extensive menu is heavy on snack food, from "porridge of the day" (home-made soup) to a "Colonial sampler" of Buffalo-style wings, potato skins, mozzarella sticks and fried zucchini. Eight kinds of burgers, twice as many sandwiches and croissants are on the all-day menu.

The tavern's specials include rainbow trout sautéed with a lemon-peppercorn sauce, grilled tuna steak with citrus butter, almond chicken and New York strip steak. The formal restaurant menu is more elaborate, with offerings from crab cakes served with saffron risotto to venison roulade with mushroom duxelles and bourbon whipped sweet potatoes.

The 22-inch-thick stone walls are as solid as the day they were erected, keeping the interior temperatures a cool 68 degrees even in summer. The terrace is a favorite for outdoor dining in season.

(814) 466-6241. Entrées, $13.95 to $19.95. Lunch, Monday-Saturday 11:30 to 2; dinner, 5 to 10, Sunday 4 to 9:30. No smoking.

The Tavern Restaurant, 220 East College St., State College.
This ramble of rooms along the historic walkway, beside the Centennial Pig sculpture and just below the Penn State campus, is dark and historic with wood

paneling, green and white tablecloths and all kinds of university memorabilia. It's of the genre that students and nostalgic alumni love, and has been a State College fixture since its founding in 1948.

The menu, printed daily, features good old American fare with cajun and Italian accents. It lists spaghetti with marinara sauce for $7.45 and the optional Italian meatballs cost 95 cents each. Typical starters are shrimp cocktail, hot garlic and potato soup, marinated herring and escargots. Main courses range widely from sautéed sea scallops primavera, crab cakes and marlin steak with lemon-tarragon butter to chicken cordon bleu, yankee pot roast with red wine, veal parmesan and New York strip steak. The price includes as many choices from the old-fashioned vegetable and salad menu as one wishes. The vegetable platter – also an all-you-can-eat, unlimited selection – goes for a bargain $5.95.

The Tavern's fans consistently vote it the area's best restaurant.

(814) 238-6116. Entrées, $8.95 to $15.95. Dinner nightly, 5 to 10 or 10:30, Sunday to 8:30.

The Allen Street Grill, 100 West College Ave., State College.

Located above the busy Corner Room Restaurant, another Penn State institution, is this large and more contemporary retreat with a second-floor porch overlooking "The Wall," a favorite campus gathering spot.

Where the Corner Room's ultra-extensive menu is rather basic, the upstairs gets upscale in the collegiate idiom with such main dishes as jambalaya, crab cakes rémoulade, chicken bordelaise and mixed grill. Pastas are interesting, as in tomato-vodka shrimp over orecchiette or fettuccine tossed with salmon and gorgonzola.

Starters include tomato-pesto bruschetta, black bean and cheese quesadilla and a nacho platter billed as downtown's biggest and best, enough for two or more to share. Carrot cake and chocolate mousse pie are the desserts of choice.

The Corner Room serves three meals a day. It began as Jack's Road House in 1855, the year the agricultural predecessor to Penn State was founded. Both restaurants are in the landmark Hotel State College, most of whose original 70 rooms have been converted to apartments or shops.

(814) 231-4745. Entrées, $9.95 to $14.95. Lunch daily from 11. Dinner, 4:30 to 10 or 11.

Baby's Burgers & Shakes, 131 South Garner St., State College.

For a different slice of American life head to Baby's, a 1950s-style diner with friendly young waitresses who are actresses, the requisite jukebox and an antique Coke machine. No normal diner, this. It's a big place with a big menu billed as "one you can pronounce." The original one-third pound-burger goes for $3.29, most sandwiches are $3.99 and a fried chicken dinner in a basket with fries and a roll goes for $4.99. Accompany with thick milk shakes, malts or a root beer float.

(814) 234-4776. Open Sunday-Thursday 7 a.m. to 10 p.m., weekends to midnight.

Diversions

Penn State is the focus for most visitors to the Happy Valley. The valley ranks high as one of the best places to live, with the state's highest education and lowest unemployment rates. Residents cite its metropolitan attractions amid small-town charm, with countryside and mountains nearby. Its middle-American status is highlighted by the fact that State College is home to the busiest Wal-Mart store in the nation, so busy that it now has two.

Pennsylvania State University drives the Centre County economy and brings the world into the isolated valley. Its Bryce Jordan Center, the 16,000-seat basketball arena, draws major entertainers and quickly became the top-grossing venue its size upon opening in 1996. Beaver Stadium always sells out its 93,000 seats for football games.

Founded in 1855 by local iron tycoons as the Farmers' High School, it became a land-grant agricultural college in 1862 and much of its 5,000-acre campus consists of farm fields.

The focal point of the campus is a small area around the **Nittany Lion Shrine,** a replica sculpted in limestone of the North American mountain lion that once roamed the University Park campus. Nearby is the world-famous **Penn State Creamery,** the first to offer collegiate classes in making ice cream. Ice cream gurus Ben & Jerry got their start from a correspondence course here. People line up to buy one of the eighteen flavors, including peachy paterno, named for head football coach Joe Paterno, a Penn State icon, community benefactor and friend of everyone hereabouts.

Almost next door to the Creamery, bronze lion paws mark the entrance to the **Palmer Museum of Art,** the largest between Philadelphia and Pittsburgh. The post-modern Renaissance palace addition in 1993 by architect Charles W. Moore was his last work before his death. Many of the museum's collections, from Asian ceramics to rare coins, have been donated by alumni.

Check out the stunning **Land Grant Frescoes** around the stairwell and mezzanine of the administration building called **Old Main.** They were painted in the 1940s by Henry Varnum Poor to depict the founding, aspirations and early endeavors of Penn State. One mural shows Abraham Lincoln with a student. The shaded lawns of **Main Mall** with its double row of old elms leads to downtown State College. Across the mall is the **Earth and Mineral Sciences Museum,** with the country's largest collection of mineral art.

State College itself is known as Tree City USA. Trees line the downtown streets along the southern edge of the Penn State campus. The downtown has interesting stores and hosts the annual Central Pennsylvania Festival of the Arts in mid-July. South of downtown is Fraternity Row and large fraternity houses amid substantial residences. With 60 fraternities and 26 sororities, Penn State claims to be the largest Greek campus in the country.

American Philatelic Society, 100 Oakwood Ave., State College, (814) 237-3803. Stamp collectors from around the world visit the research library and view changing displays at the society's national headquarters. A glass case contains the membership application of the society's most famous member, Franklin D. Roosevelt. Its first executive director happened to live in State College, advised Bill Welch, State College mayor and editor of the American Philatelist journal, as he led a tour. "He was the grain of sand around which this pearl was built." The building has its own post office branch, with an antique postal window from Bellefonte. Tours are offered upon request.

Centre Furnace Mansion, 1001 East College Ave., State College.
The mansion where Penn State got its start is the only remaining building from

Happy Valley provides backdrop for picnic in farm gazebo outside State College.

the iron-producing industry that prospered around the wilderness site in the mid-1800s. Still visible is the stack built in 1847 of the Centre Furnace Ironworks. The community that existed around the ironworks was the first town in the region of significant size. Its co-owners and ironmasters donated 200 acres of land for a school to educate farmers, the forerunner of Penn State. Bequeathed to the Centre County Historical Society, the mansion houses original furnishings and exhibits artifacts and documents relating to the iron industry. The house and grounds are undergoing restoration. *(814) 234-4779. Open Sunday, Monday, Wednesday and Friday, 1 to 4.*

Bellefonte. When French statesman Talleyrand, exiled from France during the revolution, came across the Big Spring here, he supposedly exclaimed "Quelle belle fonte." The hilly town of 6,300 has been called Bellefonte since. The underground spring, with a daily output of 11½ million gallons, is the source of Bellefonte's water supply. Now rather unspectacular, with no evidence of a fountain and surrounded by concrete walls next to the pumping station on Water Street, it looks like a large, clear pool. The adjacent Talleyrand Park at the foot of downtown is credited with the rebirth of Bellefonte. Townspeople turn out with box suppers for the Sunday evening band concerts here in summer.

Iron ore brought the town's founders here and contributed to its flourishing Victorian era. Penn State buildings bear names of Bellefonte benefactors who kept the fledgling college afloat. Its status as a county seat gave it political impact (seven governors, including one from Kansas and one from California, lived here). Several grand commercial buildings take up entire blocks of downtown, and impressive 19th-century mansions in a variety of styles line Linn and Curtin streets. The new **Bellefonte Museum for Children & Families** emphasizes local history and culture. Says energetic mayor Candace Dannaker: "We're excitement waiting to happen."

Fisherman's Paradise. One of the East's most famous catch-and-release fly fishing areas is along a picturesque stretch of Spring Creek called Fisherman's Paradise southwest of Bellefonte. Licensed fishermen can try their luck near the Bellefonte Fish Culture Station. The area is the home of the Richardson Chest Fly Box Co., producer of top custom-crafted models.

Boalsburg. Four miles east of State College is this quaint hamlet settled in 1808 by Scotch and Irish. The cemetery here was birthplace in 1864 of Memorial Day, when three young girls started placing flowers on the graves of relatives who died in the Civil War and ended up decorating the graves of all war victims. Decoration Day grew from there. The original streets and structures around the village "diamond" remain much as they were a century ago, housing shops, B&Bs and restaurants.

Boal Mansion Museum and Columbus Chapel, Old Boalsburg Road, Boalsburg.

The 1789 mansion has been home to nine generations of the Boal family who were among the founders of Boalsburg and Penn State. Furnishings and paintings throughout the main floor testify to this well connected family's connections with the likes of Queen Isabella and Napoleon. A hallway portrait shows a grandson of Christopher Columbus posing with a globe, and an 1860 rosewood reed organ is said to be one of six in the world. The ninth-generation man of the house still lives upstairs, but had just left to go swimming, our guide advised. The tour's highlight is the Columbus Chapel at the side of the property. It ended up in Pennsylvania when a fifth-generation Boal married the niece of a direct descendant of Columbus. Mathilde de Lagarde Boal inherited the chapel attached to a castle in Spain. She transported its contents, including woodwork, artwork, confessional and choir loft, and rebuilt it here in 1909. The fascinating collection features religious artifacts, furnishings and the explorer's personal possessions dating to the 1400s. Mass is still said here every Columbus Day and Christmas for family and friends.

(814) 466-6210. Open Tuesday-Sunday 1:30 to 5, May-October; 10 to 5, mid-June to mid-September. Adults, $5.

Mount Nittany Vineyards & Winery, Houser Road, Linden Hall.

Retired Penn Staters Joe and Betty Carroll, who grew up on Hoosier farms, are literally Mom and Pop operators of this small winery downhill from their home. They planted their first grapes in 1984 on the southern slopes of Mount Nittany and opened their chalet winery in 1990. They now produce sixteen varieties and 10,000 gallons a year. The Tailgate Red and Nittany Mountain white and blush are most popular. Visitors can sample wines in the showroom above the wine cellar or on a small deck overlooking a pond.

(814) 466-6373. Open Friday 1:30 to 5, Saturday 10 to 5, Sunday 12:30 to 4.

Shopping. Downtown State College is where most of it's at, and there's more than the predictable chain stores and others appealing to university types. Everything Penn State for the Penn Stater, even a baby bottle emblazoned "I'm a Nittany Lion," is available at **Lion's Pride.** We never saw so many varieties of stuffed animals as at **The Animal Kingdom;** there's even a room with a collection representing endangered species. Look for gifts, accessories and handpainted birdhouses at **Beppa's** and handcrafts from many countries, some a little retro, at **Sunshine Imports.** Cute furniture for children, nice totes and aprons and engraved glassware impressed at **Initially Yours by BJ.** Check out the award-winning display windows at **Gift Adventures. Tadpole Crossing** is one of the better nature stores we've seen. **Bostonian Ltd.** has offered preppy men's and women's clothing since 1957, when it opened as a men's shoe store. **Mr. Charles** goes back 56 years with ladies' apparel, though most of the stock now is quite mod. **The Artisan Connection** represents 140 artisans, most from Pennsylvania. **Appalachian Ski and Outdoors** is a great store for the sportsman. One of the most colorful shops is **Kitchen Kaboodle,** where we eyed Portuguese china, fused glass pieces (some with intricate lilacs), gadgets like a bacon press, cappuccino cups, pasta dishes and cookbooks.

In Bellefonte, **Adam & Art** is a spacious gallery, featuring distinctive art and sculptures from "Bellefonte's Creative Spirits," 23 talented local artists. **The Black Cat** shows gifts from another group of local crafters. **Ruffles & Treasures** offers homemade crafts and gifts. An art teacher makes a lot of his jewelry at **Creekside Rocks & Gems.** Poetry readings and entertainment are among the draws at the interesting **Cool Beans Coffee & Tea Shop.** So are its Governor's Blend espresso, the book *Free Refill* (a collection of poetry, art and musings from customers in their original handwriting), and its eco-friendly Grow Joe food for potted plants, which recycles the shop's leftover coffee grounds.

In Boalsburg, **The Federal House** offers wonderful gifts and garden accents, along with Christmas items, jewelry and boxes for the tooth fairy. Collectibles and gifts are featured at **Lindsay's on the Diamond. The Henley House** displays classic women's wear and accessories. Cookware and gourmet foods are among the wares at **The Country Sampler** and **A Basket Full Country Store & Gift Shop.**

Extra-Special

Penn's Cave, Route 192, Centre Hall.

A cave is a cave is a cave. Except when it's America's only all-water cavern, plus a wildlife sanctuary. Former Gov. Andrew Curtin from Bellefonte called the cave "Pennsylvania's greatest natural wonder" around the time of the Civil War. Visitors board flat-bottom motorboats for an hour-long guided tour through the half-mile-long cavern of limestone and shale carved by an underground stream. Boats go out through the underground cavern to Lake Nitanee for a glimpse of wildlife and then back through the cavern. Lit by the boat's spotlight or in color by hidden cavern lights, glittering stalactites and stalagmites appear in wild profusion. Some are clustered in formations given names like the Statue of Liberty, Garden of the Gods and the Strait of Gibraltar. Others are shaped like a buddha, an Arizona cactus, the Nittany Lion and a Chinese dragon chasing a tortoise. It sounds hokey, but isn't. It's quite a show. Bring a jacket, for the cavern temperature is a cool 52 degrees all year. Less compelling for adults but of interest to children is the 90-minute tour of the 800-acre Penn's Cave Farms and Wildlife Sanctuary. We saw Texas longhorn steers, baby bears, tiny white-tailed fawn, two timber wolves and four gray wolves. The resident elk and mountain lions didn't show up that day.

(814) 364-1664. Tours every half hour, daily 9 to 5, mid-February through November and December weekends, 9 to 7 in summer. Cavern tour, $10; wildlife tour, $12.

Canadensis, Pa.

Heart of the Poconos

For all its glitz and glitter, its honeymooners and heart-shaped tubs and honky-tonk, the Pocono Mountain area suffers a bum rap. There's a section of the Poconos where the glitz image does not apply – a quieter, more old-fashioned and more rural refuge, less sullied by all that mars much of the region.

That refuge is the area around Canadensis, a dot on the map and a traffic light at a crossroads. Add its neighbors in the tight little stretch from Cresco and Mountainhome to Skytop and South Sterling. Country inns, restaurants, antiques stores, hiking trails, mountains and waterfalls are mixed in just the right blend for "unhurried leisure," as one innkeeper bills it.

Elsewhere in the four-season vacationland known as the Poconos, tourism has taken on immense proportions. Resorts, whirlpool tubs, golf courses, ski areas, souvenir shops, outlet stores, theme parks – you name it, they've got it, almost too much. Some studies showed that by 2000, the four-county region would host eighteen million visitors a year.

People come here from the cities for the outdoors – "the near country," the Pocono Mountains Vacation Bureau hypes it. But the onslaught threatens to blight the natural assets that are sought. Some of the Poconos are becoming rather like what visitors are escaping from.

Canadensis is a rural area that many outsiders have never heard of. Its name is taken from the botanical name for the hemlock tree that furnished the bark for the leather tanning industry, which was the lifeblood of this region before tourism took hold. The area has managed to retain the natural attractions that originally beckoned Pocono-goers. It's a mountainous, forested retreat surrounded by three state parks, the home of the venerable Pocono Playhouse and the focus for a cluster of old country inns and new B&Bs.

Here, away from the fray, is the heart of the Poconos, the way they used to be.

Inn Spots

The French Manor, Huckleberry Road, Box 39, South Sterling 18460.

The crème de la crème of lodging spots in the Poconos is headquartered in the fieldstone château built in 1932 atop Huckleberry Mountain for Joseph Hirschorn, the mining tycoon whose art collection is now housed in the Smithsonian. He modeled this house after his manor in the south of France. Later sold to Samuel

Fieldstone château built in 1932 for Joseph Hirschorn is now The French Manor.

Kress of department store fame, it was transformed in 1986 into a small country inn of distinction and was acquired a few years later by Ron and Mary Kay Logan, who had taken over the nearby Sterling Inn in 1982.

Despite its attributes, this is a low-profile establishment that's little known in the area and relatively unknown outside. Beneath its imported Spanish slate roof and beyond the Romanesque arched entry are a manorial restaurant (see Dining Spots) and four guest rooms and a suite, plus a downstairs lounge that looks like what it was: a huge, dark-paneled basement recreation room with a TV set in the corner.

Often kept open (perhaps to entice curious diners into a future stay?) is the Monte Carlo Room near the entry foyer. It is on the majestic side, its walls and ceiling paneled in cedar. A fancy headboard dresses the kingsize bed, two bright blue armchairs await nearby and there's a full bathroom. Go upstairs to the Florence Room with its canopied four-poster, massive dresser and elaborate bath-shower curtain and on to the spacious Venice Room. Here you'll find another ornate headboard and two armchairs, one on either side of the room.

The pièce de résistance is the Turret Suite, whose living room has a TV in the armoire and windows on three sides to take in the mountaintop view. Even that pales beside its bedroom, one floor above and again with windows on three sides. A colorful Southwest-looking quilt tops the kingsize bed, and baskets in recessed shelves provide decorative accents.

The woods throughout the house are cedar and pecky cypress. Leaded glass doors and windows, stone fireplaces, paintings, sculptures and antiques attest to the care lavished by Hirschorn and the 165 craftsmen and artisans he imported from Europe to build and furnish the structure, a task that took five years.

There's much more. The main floor of the Carriage House is home to the lavish Genevieve Suite, with a canopied kingsize mahogany bed facing a gas fireplace and a sitting area with loveseat and TV. A corner of the room holds a double

Brookview Manor occupies hilltop property facing Brodhead Creek.

whirlpool tub on a platform and the bathroom contains a shower. Upstairs, the Brigitte Suite offers two more bedrooms, a living room, fireplace and jacuzzi.

Now top of the line are six fireplace and jacuzzi suites, all with private balconies, in a new building called La Maisonneuve adjacent to the manor.

The grounds contain trails for hiking and cross-country skiing. Guests also may use the recreational facilities of the Sterling Inn less than two miles away. A full breakfast is included in the rates.

(570) 676-3244 or (800) 523-8200. Six rooms and nine suites with private baths. Doubles, $160 to $210 weekends, $135 to $175 midweek. Suites, $250 to $275 weekends, $190 to $210 midweek. No children.

Brookview Manor, Route 447, RR 1, Box 365, Canadensis 18325.

Built in 1911 as a summer vacation home for a prominent Scranton family on four hilly acres across from Brodhead Creek, this was renovated into a B&B in the mid-1980s and has had five owners since. The latest, Roman Perepelkin, is originally from Russia. He took over a going concern that had been upgraded into one of northeastern Pennsylvania's more stylish B&Bs.

The entire first floor is given over to guests: a living room, a music corner with a grand piano in the turret next to three bowed windows with remarkable curved glass and window sills, a den and TV room, a game room, a wraparound porch containing rockers and what could be the biggest swing in the county, and a lineup of three adjoining rooms in which breakfast is served – a fireplace room, a sun porch and a picture-window room with striking stained glass.

That breakfast includes fresh fruit, muffins and perhaps french toast made with Italian bread or a soufflé of ham and eggs or sausage and tomato. Afternoon refreshments are served on the porch or in front of one of four fireplaces.

Upstairs in the main house are seven accommodations, all with private baths and outfitted with country furnishings and antiques. A favorite is a side suite with a carved queensize bed, a sun porch outfitted in wicker and a spacious bath. On the third floor are two nicely renovated rooms, one with queen poster bed and corner fireplace and the other light and airy with floral fabrics and a step-up jacuzzi. The rear carriage house has been reconfigured into three guest rooms, all with private baths and two with jacuzzi tubs. They're now among the most in demand. The main house, attractive in yellow with dark red and green shutters, is shaded by giant hemlocks. Behind the Brookview property are an additional hundred acres that guests can explore. Almost everyone takes the 30-minute hike to a hidden waterfall.

(570) 595-2451 or (800) 585-7974. Fax (570) 595-0177. Eight rooms and two suites with private baths. Doubles, $100 to $150 weekends, $90 to $135 weekdays. Children over 12. Smoking restricted.

Crescent Lodge, Routes 940 and 191, Cresco 18326.

This refurbished, contemporary lodge in the Paradise Valley section offers a restaurant, fourteen upstairs guest rooms and twelve outlying cottages, some with kitchens, fireplaces, oversize jacuzzi tubs and private sundecks or patios. Run by the Dunlop family and upgraded lately, it has some of the facilities and feeling of a small resort.

The upstairs rooms, most with queen beds but a few with doubles, are lavishly furnished in the country inn style. The ones we viewed had vivid wallpapers, canopy four-poster beds with thick comforters, wicker chairs and antiques. All come with TVs, telephones and thick carpeting.

The colonial theme gives way to contemporary in seven individual and five duplex cottages, which come in nine configurations. These vary from deluxe rooms with two double beds to a deluxe cottage with queensize canopy bed, TV/VCR, fireplace, sunken jacuzzi and full country kitchen. One we saw was fancily decorated with matching wallpaper borders, swagged canopies and curtains around the in-room jacuzzi tub. A "jacuzzi villa" was done in Southwestern decor, with kingsize bed, ceiling fan, sunken jacuzzi tub and see-through corner fireplace.

The ultimate is the secluded mountain hideaway, a stone cottage up a pathway along a mountain. It has a queensize canopy bed, fireplace, sunken jacuzzi, country kitchen, balcony and sundeck.

Breakfast is available in the inn's elegant main-floor restaurant (see Dining Spots). The complex includes a gift shop, a cocktail lounge, large pool, "fitness trails," tennis court and shuffleboard court.

(570) 595-7486 or (800) 392-9400. Fax (570) 595-3452. Fourteen rooms and seventeen cottage units with private baths. Rates EP: Weekends in summer and winter: doubles $115 to $175, cottages $180 to $330. Weekends in spring and fall, doubles $105 to $150, cottages $165 to $330. Midweek in summer and winter: doubles $90 to $135, cottages $140 to $330. Midweek in spring and fall, doubles, $85 to $130; cottages, $135 to $330. Two-night minimum advance reservation required most of year.

The Sterling Inn, Route 191, South Sterling 18460.

This is the most with-it of the area's old country inns, and the recreational facilities on the 103-acre property give it a bit of a resort flavor. The place is as old as some of the buildings dating to the mid-19th century on its park-like campus and as new as the ten cottage suites with fireplaces and jacuzzis erected in 1997. Big draws are cross-country skiing, tobogganing, ice-skating, horse-drawn sleigh rides and an indoor pool and spa in winter and a small private lake for swimming and boating, the Wallenpaupack Creek, tennis, a nine-hole putting course and a 90-minute, self-guided nature trail in other seasons. Perhaps folks who hike the nature trails make use of all the walking sticks stowed in a milk pail beside the inn's front door.

Nearly half the 66 lodging units are in the sprawling main inn, where a large living room separates the reception area and restaurant (see Dining Spots) from the new indoor pool and bar area. Most rooms here are rather small and pleasantly old-fashioned, one with twin beds and two armchairs, others with king or queensize beds and perhaps a daybed.

Definitely worth the extra tab are the inn's four deluxe suites and the eight Victorian fireplace suites in converted buildings out back by the creek.

Our corner suite on the inn's second floor was a nice surprise with two large rooms, two closets, television and lots of space to spread out. A mix of fancy French provincial off-white furniture

Rockers line veranda of The Sterling Inn.

blended with modern tweedy sofa and chairs, and two more chairs were available in a reading area with windows on three sides beside the kingsize bed in the bedroom.

The road noise that was the only disturbance here is not a problem in the eight fireplace suites in the Nearbrook and Wayside buildings out back. You'd never guess these deluxe, carpeted rooms with franklin stoves, queensize four-posters and decks or balconies onto the babbling brook started as garages.

The ultimate quarters are the ten new fireplaced suites in five duplex buildings, each with queen bed, sofabed, jacuzzi, kitchenette and outside deck. The rest of the accommodations include a new suite with fireplace and jacuzzi and standard rooms in an old lodge and guest house and four cottages of one or two bedrooms.

Three meals a day are served in the dining room. The day's breakfast choices are recited by the waitress and yield such dishes as eggs any style with local ham or sausage, pancakes and corned-beef hash.

(570) 676-3311 or (800) 523-8200. Fax (570) 676-9786. Thirty-eight rooms and 27 suites/cottages with private baths. Rates, MAP. Doubles, $180 weekends, $158 midweek. Cottage/suites, $220 to $280 weekends, $190 to $240 midweek. Deduct $50 for B&B.

The Pine Knob Inn, Route 447, Canadensis 18325.

New owners are at the helm of this 1847 inn that occasionally shows its age. Cheryl and John Garman from Harrisburg have redecorated a few rooms, added a wedding gazebo and installed in a corner of the dining room an unusual "dynamic wine rack" – so named because it's always changing.

The L-shaped common room in this homey inn is a real common room. It's full

Fresh snow provides mantle of white around main house at The Pine Knob Inn.

of Victorian and traditional sitting areas, with a Christmas village of ceramic houses on the fireplace mantel lighted year-round. People asked the owners not to take them down, so the holiday decorations remained up – slightly camouflaged by flowers interspersed in summer. Walls here and in other common areas are hung with artworks painted by participants in the annual art workshops the inn sponsors.

There are seventeen guest rooms (nine in the main inn and eight in the North and South guest houses out back), plus a two-room "honeymoon bungalow" for two. All have private baths, and most have brass, cherry high back or oak beds covered with cheery quilts. The Garmans have added queen and king beds to twelve rooms. The rest are twins or doubles. Carpeting covers the floors, and rooms have accents of little wreaths, a stenciled stool here and poof curtains there. Furnishings include collectibles and pieces from of antique glass. Bathroom amenities amount to clean towels and a little bar of Ivory soap, plus the occasional quilted shower curtain. The clientele approves. "People they feel like they're in Grandma's house, it's so comfortable," reports John.

White Adirondack chairs are scattered about the lawn. The property includes a tennis court, volleyball court, a 60-by-40-foot swimming pool and a pagoda between the pool and Brodhead Creek, a mecca for fly-fishermen.

(570) 595-2532 or (800) 426-1460. Fax (570) 595-6429. Seventeen rooms and a cottage with private baths. Doubles, $168 to $190. Cottage, $200. Two-night minimum on peak weekends.

Farmhouse Bed & Breakfast, Grange Road, HCR 1, Box 6B, Mount Pocono 18344.

An antiques collector and professional chef runs this restored 1850 homestead that's not like any farmhouse we've seen. Jack and Donna Asure turned the home of his parents, who formerly owned Memorytown across the street, into a B&B of character and comfort. Part of a complex of family residences on six treed, landscaped acres, this has five suites, all with private baths, remote-control television, telephones, small refrigerators and air-conditioning.

The enormous, wood-paneled living room-dining area is a showcase for the Asures' antiques and collections. "We collect everything," says Jack. That ranges from an authentic cigar-shop Indian in the entry to Stangl pottery to depression ware to shot glasses. A large TV is ensconced in the old bake oven. Guests take breakfast at a long table in a sunny corner of this wondrous room. "Donna bakes," perhaps carrot and pineapple muffins or blueberry croissants, says Jack. "I'm just the cook and bottle washer". He offers a choice of eggs, from benedict to broccoli and cheese omelet, or rum-raisin french toast, potato pancakes and belgian waffles.

The other side of the main floor contains the wood-paneled Parlour Suite with a queensize bedroom, a pretty quilt in peach and green, and a library-like living room with a stone fireplace. Upstairs is the Master Suite with a freestanding cast-iron fireplace in the living room and a queen bedroom. Outside, the farm's original icehouse is now a cottage. You enter into a cozy living room, where a fireplace has been built into the now-whitewashed stone walls. Stairs lead to a balcony and a bedroom.

In 1994, the Asures divided a ranch house on the property into two suites. The Sundown offers a large living room with fireplace, a bedroom with queensize four-poster and a bath with a sunken garden tub. The Sunup lacks a fireplace but adds a full kitchen, a queensize bedroom and a combination tub-shower.

(570) 839-0796. Fax (570) 839-0795. Four suites and one cottage with private baths. Doubles, $100 to $120 weekends, $90 to $110 midweek. Two-night minimum weekends. No children. No smoking.

Skytop Lodge, Route 390, Skytop 18357.

Off by itself just north of Canadensis is this grand mountaintop resort built in 1928, commanding 5,500 acres of private woodlands, lakes and hills and a devoted repeat clientele. It's a favorite for conferences (one of us attended a corporate newspaper seminar here a decade ago and found it perfect for the purpose, but not the kind of place to which we'd return for a tête-à-tête).

Skytop has all the sports facilities you could want, from a golf course by the lake to its own ski slope, a toboggan run, indoor and outdoor pools and a fitness center. Three meals a day, served in formal dining rooms, are included in the rates.

The tiered, angled fieldstone hotel contains 130 rooms and mini-suites. There also are 40 guest bedrooms in ten cottages – four bedrooms each with porches, refrigerators and laundry facilities. Half the cottage rooms have queen beds and the rest are twins. Thirty-one of the hotel rooms contain twin beds; 39 rooms have queen beds and 31, kingsize. Twenty mini-suites have king or queen beds and sitting areas, while two VIP suites come with a separate bedroom and parlor.

The newest addition is the **Inn at Skytop,** a $5.7 million "golf resort within a resort" located a short distance from the main lodge. It has twenty suites with king beds, gas fireplaces, mini-refrigerators, TV/VCRs and private balconies. Two of the most deluxe add jacuzzi tubs. Other facilities include a public restaurant and cocktail lounge.

(570) 595-7401 or (800) 617-2389. Fax (570) 595-9618. One hundred five rooms, 44 suites and 40 cottage units with private baths. Rates AP: May-October: doubles and cottages, $420 weekends, $375 midweek; suites, $515 to $600 weekends, $450 to $520 midweek. Rest of year: doubles and cottages, $410 weekends, $305 midweek; suites, $470 to $550 weekends, $360 to $475 midweek. Two-night minimum on weekends.

Artworks and hanging plants adorn rear dining room at The Homestead Inn.

Home in the Mountain, Monomonock Road, Mountainhome.

A block off Route 101 in Mountainhome is this home that Ruth and Leon Robinson purchased to run with their family as a B&B. Built about 1963 and turned over totally to guests, it offers a large living room with big-screen TV, a large dining room, a sitting room and a kitchen on the first floor. Upstairs are five bedrooms, furnished in traditional style. The Rose and the Butterfly rooms have private baths. The Willow, Blue Moon and Sandlewood share a full bath and a half-bath.

The pride of the property is the large, angular swimming pool and deck in the back yard, where guests are welcome to hang out.

In the mornings, Ruth, who lives elsewhere, and her daughter Becky come in to prepare a breakfast of the guest's choice. Eggs, pancakes and french toast are the usual options. Daughter-in-law Wendy Robinson helps out with administrative duties.

(570) 595-9540. Fax (570) 894-2582. (Mailing address: RR2, Box 14, Cresco 18326). Two rooms with private baths and three rooms with shared bath. Doubles, $55 to $75. No smoking.

Dining Spots

The Homestead Inn, Sandspring Drive, Cresco.

Consistently good food in pleasant surroundings is the hallmark of the Homestead, lovingly run by Susan and Drew Price.

Susan , though schooled as a business major, enjoyed cooking as an avocation. As newlyweds in Philadelphia, the Prices operated a catering business in addition to holding full-time jobs. They moved to the Poconos in 1980 to convert the large barn-like structure into an attractive restaurant that's country casual. Its transformation is depicted in some of the original paintings displayed on the walls.

Three dining rooms in prevailing brown and white seat nearly 100 amid barnwood or redwood walls, an occasional aquarium, starched green floral linens, votive candles and Wyeth prints.

The Homestead gained a measure of fame when TV producer Woody Fraser, a Poconos vacationer and fan of the Homestead, featured the owners on ABC's Home show.

Susan oversees the kitchen, from which emanate such entrées as herb-encrusted Norwegian salmon with lemon-lime dill sauce, crabmeat-stuffed brook trout en croûte, scallops chardonnay, sautéed chicken wrapped with prosciutto, grilled pork tenderloin with tarragon-mustard sauce, filet mignon au poivre and grilled veal chop with honey barbecue sauce. Hot biscuits and breads, tossed salad and fresh vegetables accompany.

Among starters are snapper soup, escargots in puff pastry, seafood crêpe and smoked mozzarella with tomatoes and basil. Raspberry cheesecake, chocolate-peanut butter pie, rum cake and white chocolate mousse with raspberry sauce are favorite desserts. The well-chosen wine list is priced from the teens to the $40s.

(570) 595-3171. Entrées, $15.95 to $22.95. Dinner, Monday-Saturday 5 to 9, Sunday 4 to 9. Closed Monday, September-May.

Pump House Inn, Sky Top Road, Canadensis.

The red pump in the original well outside the entrance to this 1842 former stagecoach inn provides the name for this elegant bastion of special-occasion dining. The imposing foyer inside is like a library, where proprietor John Keeney takes telephone reservations at an old desk and greets patrons upon arrival. He leads them to the Pub Bar, dark and intimate and atmospheric as can be, or to a couple of small, dark dining rooms brightened with pink linens, the front porch whose four tables are highly prized or the far grotto room with its waterfall wall and all kinds of nooks and alcoves. Trenton oyster crackers, flickering oil lamps and place settings of three forks and three spoons each are on the tables.

It's a sumptuous backdrop for French-American fare that has been pleasing a well-heeled clientele since the early 1960s. The short menu is supplemented by daily blackboard specials. For starters, you might try the sensational baked pecan brie over warm spinach, beer-batter shrimp with pungent fruit sauce or poached shrimp and scallops on a bed of grilled eggplant and tomatoes with a ginger-lime sauce.

Main courses range from chicken breast topped with grilled tomatoes, smoked mozzarella and tomato-basil sauce to rack of lamb. The poached salmon could be stuffed with grilled scallops and crabmeat, the basil shrimp served with garlic on a bed of pasta and the veal sautéed with shrimp and a mustard-marsala sauce. There's no wine list; instead the wines are displayed on racks between dining rooms. Patrons view the array, affordably priced from the mid-teens and up, and pick their choice.

To finish with a flourish, how about chocolate mousse, raspberry crème brûlée or white chocolate cheesecake?

The Pump House also offers three basic guest rooms above the restaurant, as well as four more modern rooms with queen beds and reproduction furniture in the rear Carriage House. A guest cottage with living room, sun porch and terrace accommodates two to four people. Continental breakfast is included in the rates.

(570) 595-7501. Entrées, $13.95 to $25.95. Dinner, Tuesday-Saturday 5 to 9, Sunday 2:30 to 8. Closed Monday-Wednesday, December-April. Doubles, $65 to $85.

The French Manor, Huckleberry Road, South Sterling.

The dining room in what was the great room in Joseph Hirschorn's manor home has 40-foot-high peaked and beamed ceilings and massive fireplaces at either end, each with a gigantic grape wreath above. The setting reminded us of a certain lovely pousada at which we once dined in Portugal.

A plush beige carpet with borders of burgundy and green covers the floor, the linens are pink and green, and a bouquet of carnations and baby's breath was on each table at our visit. From picture windows on one side of the room, you can see the slate terrace and mountains beyond. Oriental screens and lamps and a mix of chairs from ladderback to French provincial complete a look that's rather sophisticated for the area. Classical music adds to the splendid setting,

A pianist plays at night, when the haute French menu lists such appetizers as a terrine of house-smoked salmon layered with caviar and wrapped in leeks, pan-seared duck foie gras with a melange of preserved stone fruit, and escargots bourguignonne. A mixed green salad

Majestic dining room at French Manor.

garnished with kumquats and roasted hazelnuts and a lemon sorbet intermezzo are included in the price of the entrées. Among recent choices were grilled tuna with preserved ginger and leeks, breast of pheasant in a sauce of quail eggs scrambled with champagne and chanterelles, medallions of veal with roquefort and foie gras, and rack of lamb encrusted in cured olives, Moroccan lemon and goat cheese. The execution seems to live up to the pretensions of its prose, at least at our extravagant lunch (since discontinued). Desserts could be raspberry linzer torte, chocolate mousse, apple custard torte and cannoli. The wine list is short and expensive.

(570) 676-3244 or (800) 523-8200. Entrées, $19.95 to $34. Dinner nightly except Monday, 6 to 9; Also closed Tuesday-Wednesday, November-April. Jackets required. No smoking.

Crescent Lodge, Routes 940 and 191, Cresco.

Here's a glamorous setting for dining in two large rooms with heavy leather and wood armchairs at well-spaced tables and artworks hung in gilt frames. A pianist plays on weekends, the service is polished and the ambiance is perfect for a special occasion, the kind where you would appreciate châteaubriand bouquetière presented with a flourish tableside for two.

Chef Wayne Dunlop, representing the third generation of Dunlops at the family-owned lodge, oversees an ambitious continental menu. Here you'll find almost anything from broiled brook trout and Long Island duckling with orange sauce to bouillabaisse, veal oscar and beef wellington.

A complimentary bowl of marinated vegetables starts the meal. Appetizers include clams casino, lobster ravioli, veal cannelloni and batter-dipped alligator strips with a chilled curry dipping sauce. Strawberry ice cream pie, coupe romanoff and peach melba are signature desserts. The wine list is better than the area's norm.

(570) 595-7486 or (800) 392-9400. Entrées, $16.95 to $24.95. Dinner nightly, 5:30 to 9 or 10. Closed Monday and Tuesday, November-April.

The Sterling Inn, Route 191, South Sterling.

A stone fireplace helps divide into two intimate sections the long dining room at this inn hidden behind towering rhododendron bushes. It's pretty in pink and white, but rather too brightly lit for intimate dining and with tables rather too close for comfort on busy nights.

The changing menu is printed daily. Among appetizers, we tried the chicken liver pâté with crackers and mussels on the half shell with tarragon and tomatoes. The tossed salad was mostly iceberg lettuce, but this lapse was redeemed by the savoyard potatoes and the excellent mix of sautéed snow peas and yellow squash that accompanied our prime rib with dijon cream sauce and broiled loin lamb chops with a homemade tomato chutney. A $19 Mirassou cabernet was one of the cheaper selections from the short wine list. Other entrée choices might include pan-seared Jamaican-rubbed swordfish with a tomato and mandarin-orange relish, brown-sugar cured chicken breast with maple syrup-walnut sauce and osso buco that innkeeper Ron Logan calls "awesome buco." A perfect key lime pie was an excellent choice from desserts that covered the gamut from tapioca pudding and rainbow sherbet to walnut pie and honey cheesecake with raspberry topping.

Although there's quite a range in prices on the menu given the public, all items on the same but unpriced menu are available to house guests on the MAP plan without surcharges – a rare policy that we find refreshing. Innkeepers Ron and Mary Kay Logan know how to keep their guests happy.

(570) 676-3311 or (800) 523-8200. Entrées, $15.75 to $22. Lunch daily, noon to 1:30. Dinner, 6 to 8:30 or 9. No smoking.

The Pine Knob Inn, Route 447, Canadensis.

The menu arrives in an old book in this inn's 65-seat dining room, sprightly in pink with white floral overcloths, rose napkins and lalique-style candleholders. It makes for some interesting reading to embellish the menu proper, which is short yet varied.

Main courses cover the bases from coconut-crusted jumbo shrimp sautéed with basil-papaya dressing and poached dill-encrusted salmon with asparagus crème anglaise to pan-seared duck breast with peach coulis served on a portobello mushroom, and filet mignon béarnaise. Surf and turf is the priciest item.

Start with clams casino, teriyaki shrimp or wild mushroom tart. Finish with a seasonal pie or one of the specialty liqueured coffees.

New owner John Garman's "dynamic wine rack" has improved the wine situation here.

(570) 595-2532 or (800) 426-1460. Entrées, $14.95 to $29.95. Dinner nightly, 6 to 9; fewer days in off-season; Friday-Sunday in winter.

The Cook's Touch, Route 390, Mountainhome.

Dave and Cindy Cook lend youthful energy and considerable cooking talents to this newcomer, warmly received for American fare at affordable prices. They took over a large space that had been home to a succession of restaurants and "started from scratch," in Dave's words. He preps and does the cooking, while his wife oversees the 90-seat dining area with timbered walls and decor in beige and brown.

Dave hand-butchers his meats, obtains the freshest of seafood and cooks everything to order – no mean task, given the scope of the menu and the size of the dining room. Although featuring American cuisine, his chicken dishes vary from cajun to française to florentine. The veal comes marsala, parmesan, italiano or with pesto in lemon wine sauce, "our own creation." Baked stuffed flounder, hickory barbecued pork chops, lamb chops, teriyaki tenderloin and delmonico steak indicate the range. Soup or salad come with each dish.

Stuffed mushrooms, smoked trout and mussels marinara are among appetizers. Desserts include chocolate mousse, a cordial parfait, hot fudge sundae and a birch beer float.

(570) 595-3599. Entrées, $9.95 to $15.95. Dinner, Tuesday-Saturday 5 to 10 or 11, Sunday noon to 8. Also open Monday in July and August.

Diversions

From golf courses to ski areas, fishing lakes to mountain trails, the Poconos are a four-season recreation destination. The specifics are outlined in countless brochures and periodicals, including "This Week in the Poconos" and "News of the Poconos."

Promised Land State Park, ten miles north of Canadensis, is the most popular of three state parks in the vicinity. The area along Route 390 into Promised Land is as notable for the profusion of rhododendron and mountain laurel, a majestic sight in the late spring, as it is for the funny little cabins that line the highway year-round. The 3,000-acre state park at an elevation of 1,700 feet is surrounded by 8,000 forested acres. Good fishing and swimming are available in a tranquil setting – power craft are banned from the lake, though you can rent rowboats, sailboats, pedal boats and canoes. For more exciting boating, head a few miles north to **Lake Wallenpaupack,** Pennsylvania's largest. **Gouldsboro** and **Tobyhanna** state parks also offer good swimming, boating and picnicking.

Waterfalls. Bushkill Falls is billed as the Niagara of Pennsylvania and is quite commercial. **Buck Hill Falls** is reached by a well-groomed trail from a parking lot near the old Buck Hill Falls resort. The falls tumble 200 feet in three major drops along a mile of picturesque glen. It's not as spectacular as Bushkill, but most people like it better. Innkeepers at area lodging establishments can steer visitors to their own favorites.

Pocono Playhouse, Mountainhome, (570) 595-7456. One of the nation's longest-running summer playhouses has brought Broadway to the Poconos since 1946. A recent season opened with "La Cage aux Folles" and closed with "Big River." Shows are staged Wednesday-Sunday nights, plus Wednesday, Thursday and Sunday matinees.

Shopping. Antiquing and the new Tannersville outlet stores have their devotees, but the main intersection of Canadensis tells something of its priorities. It has a service station, an Indian Trading Post, the Sunrise Foodmart, the Calico Kitchen, a Methodist church and that's about all, except for **The Kitchen Garden,** which features everything for the herb garden and herb enthusiast, plus herbal teas and tea gifts. The better shopping is along Route 390 in Mountainhome and Cresco.

Holley Ross Pottery at La Anna is widely advertised for "distinguished china and threefold entertainment" – demonstrations, woodland park and large factory showroom. Bus tours descend here, and you might find a nice bean pot, a mixing bowl or a coffee mug at a good price. As for the rest of it, take it, puh-leeze. In Mountainhome, **Christmas Memories** claims to display the Poconos' largest line of collectibles. More collectibles, dolls, teddybears and gifts are on display at **Wonderful Things.** The relocated and expanded **Cooks Tour,** in something of a hardware store setting in Mountainhome, is a kitchen shop without peer, especially in terms of cookware, gadgets and utensils you can't find elsewhere.

Theo. B. Price Inc. at Cresco must be seen to be believed. It's part lumber company and part country store, with a mysterious jumble of things from oyster crackers to light bulbs, dried flower arrangements to carved decoys and Santas, all mixed in together. The **Ella C. Ehrhardt General Store** in Newfoundland is like a time capsule, purveying some of the same kinds of items it did when it opened in 1860. Also near Newfoundland is **Reece Pottery,** where Thomas Reece crafts interesting functional and sculptural stoneware.

Extra-Special

Callie's Candy Kitchen and Pretzel Factory, Route 390, Mountainhome and Cresco.

We never thought we'd see so much candy until we – and a few tour buses – met up with Callie's Candy Kitchen, founded in 1952 in Mountainhome and now a three-generation family enterprise that opened a pretzel factory in Cresco in 1985. The family patriarch still gives occasional candy-making demonstrations, which attract young and old, and there are plenty of free samples. We defy anyone to get through the huge store showroom without succumbing to one of the tempting fudge flavors from macadamia nut to piña colada. Or the chocolate-covered potato chips with the texture of chips and the taste of chocolate. Or the Pocono Mountain Crunch, a mix of butterscotch, crispied rice and ground cashews that is the best-seller. What next? Pretzels, that's what – plain or chocolate-covered, filled with peanut butter, available in bite-size chunks, sticks and rings, plus pretzel dogs and pretzel pizzas. The pretzel factory just down the road in Cresco also makes gourmet popcorn in 60 flavors, from hot jalapeño to apple pie. The pretzel factory is all glassed-in so viewers can watch the goings-on.

(570) 595-2280. Candy kitchen open daily 10 to 5, summer to 8; weekends only in January.
(570) 595-3257. Pretzel factory open daily 10 to 5, weekends only January-March.

The Inn at Philips Mill, as depicted by artist Raymond E. Halacy.

Bucks County, Pa.

Romance Along River Road

What could be more special than the River Road section of Bucks County, sixteen miles of pristine paradise along the Delaware River? William Penn called it "the most beautiful of landscapes," even more beautiful than England's Buckingham, the shire in which he was born and after which this was named. We call it romantic, even magical, any time of year.

River Road, the winding state Route 32, hugs the river and its adjacent canal as it wends north from New Hope to Upper Black Eddy, linking hamlets that have changed little since the Revolution. The river remains largely untouched by development; its flow varies from rushing to gentle, depending on location and season. Beside it is the Delaware Canal, which flourished for a century as mules plied the towpath, drawing barges behind. The canal's quaint wooden bridges, moss-covered locks and stone aqueducts attest to times past.

There are treasures: Phillips Mill, the cradle of the Bucks County Art Colony. Centre Bridge, an area of substantial edifices in keeping with its English name. Lumberville, a string of houses, stores and inns up against the river. Point Pleasant, the area's population center, if a few hundred souls can be called that. Erwinna, where large historic landmarks are spread across a river plain.

Hillsides awash with mountain laurel and rhododendron descend to the flatland strip along the river. Sturdy stone houses punctuate the countryside, looking for all the world like those of Britain's Cotswolds. Authentic country inns provide lodging and sustenance for travelers, as in the past.

This is Bucks County at its best, away from the hustle and bustle of touristy New Hope and the encroaching suburbia from Philadelphia and Doylestown. It's a place tailor-made for a rural retreat, for canoeing, walking the towpath, browsing the few shops, eating well and rejuvenating one's spirits at a country inn or B&B. Ramble along the river and succumb to its romance.

Inn Spots

The inns here, as well as the restaurants that follow, are in geographical order from south to north.

The Inn at Phillips Mill, North River Road, New Hope 18938.

Hanging pots overflowing with fuchsias, wooden casks filled with all colors of mums, wreaths of Christmas greenery or a profusion of spring bulbs – depending on the season, these mark the entrance to this small and adorable yet sophisticated inn. When you see its facade of local gray stone, smack up against an S-turn bend in the River Road, with its copper pig hanging over the entrance, you would almost swear you were in Great Britain.

That impression is heightened as you register at the reception desk and observe the low-ceilinged dining rooms (see Dining Spots). Upstairs are four charming guest rooms and a suite; cheerily decorated by innkeeper Joyce Kaufman, whose architect husband Brooks did the restoration of the 1750 barn. One has its own sitting room. Honeymooners request the third-floor hideaway suite, where fabric covers the ceiling. Most beds are four-posters or brass and iron and are topped with quilts. Antiques, handpainted trays, dried-flower arrangements and embroidered cloths on the nightstands abound. They don't advertise it, but sometimes the Kaufmans rent a cottage in back of the inn. A small swimming pool also may be used by guests.

A continental breakfast (juice, flaky croissants and coffee) is delivered to your room, wrapped in a blue and white checked tablecloth in a basket.

(215) 862-2984. Four rooms, one suite and one cottage with private baths. Doubles, $80. Suite, $90. Cottage, $135. No credit cards.

Centre Bridge Inn, 2998 North River Road, New Hope 18938.

This striking white structure with red shutters built in Colonial Williamsburg style has a large restaurant-tavern, guest accommodations and an advantageous location beside the Delaware River across the bridge from Stockton, N.J. Fires destroyed inns that had occupied the site since 1705, so this reconstruction is of early 1960s vintage.

Overnight guests enter an enormous formal vestibule, with a fireplaced parlor on the river side. Ahead are the three most desirable quarters. Room 9 has a queensize four-poster bed, TV, two plush chairs on thick carpeting, cedar-lined bath and private river-view terrace – "our nicest room," according to our guide. A "contemporary suite" in tropical motif offers a kingsize bed, TV, sitting and dressing areas and a river view. A two-room suite in front has a queen brass bed and sitting room with sofa, loveseat and TV.

Fountain is centerpiece of courtyard beside canal and river at Centre Bridge Inn.

Upstairs are seven more rooms, five with four-poster canopy beds (one with two canopied doubles) and all outfitted lately with TV. All are air-conditioned, have private baths and are notable for antiques and colorful Schumacher wall coverings, though some appear a bit dated.

A continental breakfast is served in the suites, the parlor or outside on a deck off the main floor, which has one of the nicest views of the river anywhere.

The downstairs tavern-dining room with beamed ceilings, stucco walls and huge open fireplaces could not be more attractive, nor the glass-enclosed porch overlooking the river more inviting. The food can be very good, but the dining room also has a reputation for inconsistency. The updated continental menu ranges from grilled yellowfin tuna with cilantro pesto to grilled lamb steak with rosemary-mint butter. We recall a happy evening sipping after-dinner drinks at the bar as a pianist entertained.

(215) 862-2048. Fax (215) 862-3244. Eight rooms and two suites with private baths. Doubles, $100 to $125 weekends, $80 to $105 midweek. Suites, $145 and $150 weekends, $125 and $130 midweek. Two-night minimum weekends.

Entrées, $21.95 to $29.95. Dinner nightly, 5:30 to 9:30 or 10, Sunday brunch.

1740 House, River Road, Lumberville 18933.

For serenity, motel-style privacy and a quiet location in a quaint hamlet beside the Delaware, this appeals to repeat visitors who book the same rooms year after year. The 1740 House was opened in 1967 by well-traveled New Yorker Harry Nessler and his wife. They built it to look old; each room in two wings opening from a front corridor and extending to patios or balconies perched out back at canal's edge.

Individually decorated, the 24 spacious rooms and a suite on two floors have king or twin beds, large bathrooms (some with showers only), comfortable chairs with reading lights, nightly turndown service, detachable wooden coat hangers, and pleasant outdoor seating areas overlooking the river. There are no televisions or phones to intrude.

1740 House at Lumberville.

Instead, enjoy the peace and quiet of the river from your balcony or porch, catch some sun around the small pool, read in a couple of small parlors, and meander up River Road to the center of Lumberville to walk the canal towpath or cross the footbridge to an island park in New Jersey.

A buffet-style breakfast is served in the cheery garden dining room, where you're likely to end up sitting family-style with other guests. Help yourself to juice, cereal, croissants and a hot dish like scrambled eggs or creamed chipped beef, and toast your own homemade bread or English muffins.

Since the death of Harry Nessler at 92 (he manned the front desk at the inn until the end), the 1740 House has been run by his grandson, Robert John Vris. He continued the tradition, although he did stop serving dinner for houseguests. He has opened up the rear grounds to the river with a new landscaped terrace.

(215) 297-5661. Twenty-four rooms with private baths. Doubles, $125 weekends, $80 midweek. Two-night minimum weekends. No credit cards.

Tattersall Inn, River and Cafferty Road, Box 569, Point Pleasant 18950.

This manor home of pale aubergine plastered fieldstone with wood trim of cream and dark green is set amid holly trees and rhododendrons. It was once the home of Ralph Stover, the best-known member of the ubiquitous Bucks County clan of mill owners.

The B&B originally was opened in 1983 by the owners of the Inn at Phillips Mill to accommodate their overflow. Donna and Bob Trevorrow from nearby Centre Bridge took over Tattersall in 1998. She quit her job to take up innkeeping full-time.

They offer six bedrooms, all with private baths and queensize beds and two with gas fireplaces. The Highland Room is done in Black Watch tartan. The Royal Lavender Room has lavender moiré covering the walls and a lace canopy over the bed, plus a chaise lounge and a gas-log fireplace. The Wintergreen Suite adds a sitting room. The main-floor Squires Room also has a hand-crocheted canopy for the queen bed as well as a sofabed.

Cider and cheese are served in the afternoon in the beamed rear tavern room, now a common room with a wonderful big fireplace, old wood floors, hunting prints and comfy sofas.

Donna serves a full country breakfast – perhaps baked eggs, pancakes or french toast – in the dining room or on the veranda. Or you can have continental breakfast in your room.

(215) 297-8233 or (800) 297-4988. Fax (215) 297-5093. Six rooms with private baths. Doubles, $90 to $140 weekends, $75 to $125 midweek. Two-night minimum weekends. No smoking.

EverMay-on-the-Delaware, 889 River Road, Erwinna 18920.

Dating to the 1700s and enlarged in 1871, this three-story gold and tan Victorian mansion has the patina required for a listing on the National Register of Historic Places. It's set back from the road on a broad lawn facing the river, the perfect setting for the air of calm and quiet that the innkeepers try to project – though we were a bit startled to find chickens pecking away on the side lawn at one of our visits.

EverMay is the bed-and-breakfast and gourmet-dinner venture of William and Danielle Moffly, antiques dealers who acquired the inn in 1996 and live on the premises.

Guest rooms are located upstairs in the manor house as well as in a nearby carriage house and cottage. All with private baths and telephones, they are furnished with collectibles and antiques from the Victorian era. We found ours in the Carriage House a bit austere, despite the presence of fresh flowers and a large bowl of fresh fruit. Some inn rooms retain the original fireplaces. Walnut beds, oriental rugs, marble-topped dressers, fancy quilts and lacy pillows are among the furnishings.

A fire often burns in the fireplace and decanters of sherry are at the ready downstairs in the double front parlor, where afternoon tea with cucumber or watercress sandwiches and cookies is served at 4. At bedtime in your room you may find fruit and candy and a liqueur in a little glass with a doily on top.

Although continental, breakfast in the rear conservatory room is quite special. Ours yielded orange juice, incredibly flaky croissants and pastries, one with cream cheese in the center, and the pièce de résistance at our visit: a compote of fresh strawberries, red seedless grapes, bananas and honeydew melon, garnished with a sprig of mint and dusted with confectioners' sugar – colorful and pretty.

(610) 294-9100. Fax (610) 294-8249. www.evermay.com. Eighteen rooms and suites with private baths. Doubles, $135 to $350; two-bedroom suite, $340. Two-night minimum weekends.

Isaac Stover House, 845 River Road, Erwinna, Pa. 18920.

A showplace. That's the way to describe this 1837 Federal-Victorian mansion on twelve acres facing the Delaware River. Two British-born New Yorkers purchased the property in 1999 from Sally Jessy Raphael. The radio-TV personality had opened it first as a frilly Victorian B&B, representative of the later third-floor added to the original Federal structure. She eventually closed the place, only to reopen it in 1995 after redoing the entire house to showcase the Federal period. Then she closed it permanently in 1997.

Along came Sooze Plunkett-Green and Jane Brinton, who had tired of their careers in the entertainment industry. "We figured if we were going to be on stage, we might as well come down and make breakfast," said Sooze with her droll British sense of humor.

The house was virtually empty, and the partners spent nearly six months

Delaware River is on view from second-floor balcony for guests at Bridgeton House.

furnishing and redecorating. "We have finished the parlors and added our touches," said Sooze. "It's eclectic English decor, with a touch of whimsy – more like the English country home that we would live in." She was thrilled that among the first guests were "two fashion guys who said it was like staying in someone's home and not a stuffy inn."

The women offer six guest rooms. Four on the second floor have private baths, one across the hall. Two on the third floor share a bath. The rooms were in transition from the times we had seen them, but they have queen beds, down comforters and decorative accents of ivy in one, birds in another.

The main floor remains a designer's dream, from the deep formal parlor to the rear porch outfitted in wicker, from the taproom paneled in pecan wood for lively happy hours and convivial breakfasts to the showplace kitchen with custom-designed "critter" tiles and a huge fireplace. From said kitchen, the innkeepers dispense a pot of tea or a glass of sherry in the afternoon and breakfast in the morning, taken at small round marble tables in the taproom. The sideboard holds "a spa breakfast" of juices, granola and smoked salmon. To that is added the choice of a full English breakfast, with eggs, sausages or bacon, mushrooms, potatoes and fried green tomatoes.

(610) 294-8044. Fax (610) 294-8132. Four rooms with private baths and two rooms with shared baths. Doubles, $125 to $195 weekends, $125 to $150 midweek.

Bridgeton House, 1525 River Road, Box 167, Upper Black Eddy 18972.

With sweat and TLC, restorationists Charles and Bea Briggs have transformed this onetime wreck of an apartment house built in 1836 into a comfortable B&B with a great location beside the river. Although smack up against the road, the inn has been opened to the rear for a water orientation.

A rear parlor and upstairs balconies look onto a landscaped courtyard beside the canal.

Lovely stenciling, fresh or dried flowers, a decanter of sherry and bowls of potpourri grace the dining room, where breakfast is served. Following a fruit course (perhaps baked pears in cream or a fresh fruit plate) comes a main dish: waffles with strawberry butter, eggs Roxanne, or mushroom and cheese omelets. Fresh lemon breads, muffins, and apple cake likely accompany.

Most of the guest accommodations overlook the water. Each was exceptionally fashioned by Charles, a master carpenter and renovator, and interestingly decorated by Bea. Some contain four-posters and chaise lounges; all have private baths, country antiques, colorful sheets, fresh flowers and intriguing touches. Our main-floor room came with lovely stenciling and a private porch. Two small suites have gas fireplaces.

Bea calls the dramatic penthouse suite Bucks County's ultimate. It has a twelve-foot cathedral ceiling, a kingsize bed, black and white marble fireplace, marble bathtub, backgammon table, black leather chairs, a stereo-TV center and a full-length deck looking onto the river.

(610) 982-5856 or (888) 982-2007. Fax (610) 982-5080. Six rooms and four suites with private baths. Peak season: doubles, $169 weekends, $129 midweek; suites, $189 weekends, $169 midweek; Penthouse, $279 weekends, $249 midweek. Rest of year: doubles $119 weekends, $99 midweek; suites, $169 weekends, $149 midweek; Penthouse, $249 weekends, $225 midweek. Children over 8. No smoking.

Dining Spots

Hotel du Village, River Road at Phillips Mill Road, New Hope.

The food is country French, but the chef-owner is Algerian and his hostelry is Tudor English in an early boarding-school setting. The main dining room in the former Lower Campus building of Solebury School looks like one in an English manor house, with a glowing fire at each end, a beamed ceiling, small-paned windows and a fine Persian carpet on the floor.

Chef Omar Arbani arrived in Bucks County from Algeria by way of culinary endeavors in France, Denmark, London and Washington, D.C. His aim is "the kind of home-style country cuisine you'd find in the restaurants of Bordeaux or Burgundy on a Sunday afternoon," according to his wife Barbara, a former New Jersey teacher who manages the dining room, bar and a new banquet facility.

The menu and prices rarely change. We found the crusty, piping-hot French bread excellent, particularly when spread with the house pâté. Our tournedos with artichoke heart and béarnaise sauce were heavenly. So were the sweetbreads with green olives, mushrooms and madeira sauce. Potatoes sautéed with lots of rosemary, crisp beans and grilled tomato with a crumb topping accompanied. Moist black forest cake, crammed with cherries, and cafe royale were sweet endings to a rich, romantic meal.

Dining here takes precedence over the accommodations. Nineteen rather spare rooms with private baths in a converted stable reflect their boarding-school heritage. Continental breakfast and access to a pool and two tennis courts on the ten-acre estate are included in the rates (doubles, $90 to $110).

(215) 862-9911. Fax (215) 862-9788. Entrées, $15.95 to $20.95. Dinner, Wednesday-Saturday from 5:30, Sunday 3 to 9. Restaurant closed mid-January to mid-February.

The Inn at Phillips Mill, 2998 North River Road, New Hope.

Looking as if it had been transported from the British Cotswolds, the quaint gray stone building right at the S-turn bend in the River Road has a copper pig above the entrance – a symbol of the stone barn's origin as a gristmill that stood next to the village piggery. Architect Brooks Kaufman and his innkeeper wife Joyce transformed it into a country French restaurant.

The dining setting is romantic as can be. Candles augment light from the fireplace in low-ceilinged rooms with dark beams and pewter service plates and water goblets. The menu, written in French with English translations, is executed by chefs whose names are listed at the bottom. The terrine of veal, pork and foie gras and the escargots with garlic-walnut demi-glace are favored appetizers. We enjoyed a springtime special, Maryland crabmeat in half an avocado, which was really special. We've never tasted such a tender filet mignon with such a delectable béarnaise sauce or such perfect sweetbreads in a light brown sauce as on our first visit. On another occasion, we liked the sautéed calves liver in a cider vinegar and the veal medallions with roasted shallots in cognac sauce.

Pastry chef Roz Schwartz's desserts are triumphs, among them a lemon ice-cream meringue pie, about six inches high and wonderfully refreshing, and a vanilla mousse with big chips of chocolate and chocolate fudge sauce.

(215) 862-9919. Entrées, $16 to $26. Dinner nightly, 5:30 to 9:30 or 10. BYOB. No credit cards.

Black Bass Hotel, Route 32, Lumberville.

For rustic charm, you can't beat this 1740 establishment straight out of England and so loyal to the Crown that, when George Washington crossed the Delaware just below here, the hotel supposedly wouldn't let him in. Wander around the dark, beamed dining rooms and look at all the British memorabilia collected by veteran innkeeper Herbert Ward, as well as the pewter bar that came from Maxim's in Paris.

Though we recall a memorable dinner from some years ago, we like the Black Bass best for lunch, when you can feast on the riverside scenery outside the long rear dining porch, or up close on a new ground-level dining terrace. Many favor the Charleston Meeting Street crab, a fixture on both the lunch and dinner menus. We enjoyed the New Orleans onion soup, thick with onions and cheese, which came in a proper crock. The crisp greens in the house salad were laden with home-made croutons and a nifty dressing of homemade mayonnaise, horseradish, dijon mustard and spices. Hungry after a lengthy hike along the towpath, one of us devoured seven of the nut and date mini-muffins that came in a basket.

The dinner menu ranges from seared salmon with leek compote and savoy cabbage to seared beef napoleon layered with potato crisp, walnuts and gorgonzola. Desserts here are exceptional: perhaps walnut cheesecake with sour cherry sauce and crème fraîche, or fresh fruit cobbler with wild turkey whiskey sauce.

Upstairs are seven bedrooms sharing two baths ($80) and three suites ($150 to $175).

(215) 297-5770. Entrées, $21.95 to $26.95. Lunch, Monday-Saturday 11:30 to 3. Dinner, 5:30 to 9:30. Sunday, brunch 11 to 2:30, dinner 4:30 to 8:30.

Golden Pheasant Inn, 763 River Road, Erwinna.

The glamorous plant-filled solarium in this 1857 fieldstone inn was the setting

Set back from the river on broad lawns is EverMay on the Delaware, known for fine dining.

for one of our more memorable meals, so we're glad that the rest of the restaurant has been fixed up as well.

French chef-owner Michel Faure, who was well regarded at the nearby Carversville Inn and Philadelphia's Le Bec Fin, and his wife Barbara have restored the two dark inner Victorian dining rooms to an elegant country French look of the 1850s, showcasing an extensive Quimper collection from Brittany.

We'd still choose the solarium, where you can see the canal and the trees illuminated at night, to enjoy some of Michel's dinner creations. Start perhaps with his renowned lobster bisque, pheasant pâté or smoked trout. Continue with such main dishes as crab croquette in the Brittany style, shrimp provençal, grilled duck, filet mignon béarnaise or rack of lamb with a rosemary-garlic-mint demi-glace. Worthy endings include cappuccino cheesecake, crème caramel, homemade sorbets and, a specialty, Belgian white chocolate mousse with a raspberry coulis.

The Faures, who live on the premises, offer five guest rooms and two suites with private baths, the total seeming to vary with the number of their offspring in residence (doubles, $95 to $175).

(610) 294-9595. Entrées, $18.95 to $26.95. Dinner, Tuesday-Saturday 5:30 to 9. Sunday, brunch 11 to 3, dinner 3 to 8.

EverMay on the Delaware, River Road, Erwinna.

The culinary tradition at this charming country inn continues under the ownership of antiques dealers William and Danielle Moffly, who live on the premises. They and chef William Finnegan have maintained the inn's reputation for stellar contemporary American fare.

The six-course meal is prix-fixe, with little choice except between two entrées – grilled swordfish with papaya-mango salsa and rack of lamb with rosemary jus, at a recent visit. It's served at a single 7:30 seating, usually booked far in advance.

The meal is taken in a main dining room where the draperies match the upholstered chairs, in a rear garden room or at tables for two in an intimate porch/conservatory pretty in white and light brown, with windows onto the back lawn. Our meal here was one of the best we've had, nicely presented and paced. Hors d'oeuvres of smoked trout salad, sundried tomato crostini and country pâté with green peppercorns were served first. Next, in order, came a suave chicken and leek soup, sautéed chanterelles on a saffron crouton, and a salad of boston and mache lettuces, garnished with violets and toasted walnuts and dressed with a sherry vinaigrette.

These were mere preliminaries to the entrées: Norwegian salmon poached in white wine, served with hollandaise sauce and garnished with shrimp, and tender lamb noisettes wrapped in bacon and topped with a green peppercorn butter. These came with thin, crisp asparagus from Chile, rice pilaf and a sprig of watercress.

A cheese course of perhaps St. André, montrachet and gorgonzola precedes dessert. Ours was a perfect poached pear, set atop vanilla ice cream, butterscotch sauce, golden raisins and pecans.

(610) 294-9100. Prix-fixe, $62. Dinner by reservation, Friday and Saturday at 7:30, Sunday at 6:30. Jackets requested.

Bucks Bounty, 991 River Road, Upper Black Eddy.

The Adirondacks meet the Southwest in this restaurant and pub put together by Dutch chef Johan Van der Linden. It's notable for the unique vaulted ceiling, extravagantly colorful in yellow, red, turquoise and black – the design taken from an Alaskan Indian blanket. Long, narrow mirrors atop the wood wainscoting that doubles as the back for banquettes are bordered by Adirondack scenes. Sturdy Adirondack chairs are at green-clothed tables topped by glass.

It's a trendy, unexpected setting for food that Johan calls American/ continental with German influences and Italian specialties. He's at his best at dinner, when the affordable menu ranges from simple pastas to sautéed sweetbreads and filet mignon. Crispy roasted Long Island duck with his own Chinese barbecue sauce and chicken dijonnaise are signature dishes. Start

Adirondack motif prevails at Bucks Bounty.

with smoked trout, onion soup au gratin or wilted red leaf salad with feta cheese and sesame seeds. Favorite endings are peach cobbler, crème brûlée and shoofly pie.

The lunch menu is not as interesting, although the food is good. One of us had an excellent tuna salad sandwich, while the other got the soup and half-sandwich special. The onion soup was tasty and the half liverwurst sandwich with a big slice of raw onion more than substantial.

Ever-improving, Johan converted the old section with a takeout window into a cozy pub. He created a shady garden courtyard for outdoor dining on the side.

(610) 294-8106. Entrées, $13.95 to $19.95. Lunch, Tuesday-Friday 11:30 to 3:30. Dinner, Tuesday-Sunday 5:30 to 10. Weekend brunch, 9 to 3:30.

Chef Tell's Manor House, 1800 River Road, Upper Black Eddy.

Chef Tell Erhardt of Philadelphia television fame has taken over the former

Upper Black Eddy Inn along the Delaware River and is doing a land-office business. The 1830 Federal-style manor is quite a sight, what with a long sun porch facing the river across the road and an elegant inner dining room with blue and white fabric upholstered chairs.

Chef Tell's German specialties – among them, sauerbraten and wiener schnitzel – are featured. The rest of the lengthy dinner menu takes on international overtones: baked shrimp in a ring of mousseline potatoes, sautéed Swedish-style pork loin, grilled chicken Bangkok, roast duck "my way" (crispy with red cabbage and spaetzle) and filet mignon béarnaise. Ditto for the specials, perhaps seared Chilean sea bass with ginger-hoisin sauce or rum and molasses-glazed salmon with banana salsa.

Sunday brunch is an all-you-can-eat buffet, with pastries, entrée choice (from pain perdu to lobster soufflé) and free-flowing champagne for $19.95.

The Pastry Shop offers sticky buns, muffin and such, along with exotic coffees, teas and German beer. Open Wednesday-Sunday 9 to 6.

(610) 982-0212 or (800) 424-3385. Entrées, $12.95 to $20.95. Lunch, Saturday 11:30 to 2:30. Dinner, Wednesday-Saturday 5:30 to 8:30 or 9. Sunday, brunch 10:30 to 2:30, dinner 4 to 8. Pastry Shop, Wednesday-Sunday 9 to 6.

Diversions

The Delaware River and the adjacent Delaware Canal provide diversion enough for most. For action, New Hope and its galleries, shops and nightlife are just down River Road – but all that is a different world.

Walk the Towpath. The best way to experience both river and canal and their surroundings is to walk the towpath, which also is used by joggers and the occasional bicyclist. Start in Lumberville at the footbridge to Bull's Island, a New Jersey state park. The gardens, back yards and architecture of English-type manor houses intrigue. A footbridge leads to the Cuttalossa Inn, where the outdoor terrace begs one to pause for lunch or a drink. For the makings of a picnic, cross the highway bridge at Centre Bridge to Stockton, N.J., to pick up food to go at Errico's Market and a bottle of wine at the well-stocked Phillips wine store. Not far downriver is Phillips Mill, an ever-so-British looking cluster of stone houses hugging the River Road. The old miller's house and surroundings were taken over by artists around 1900, thus launching New Hope's reputation as an art colony. The 1756 grist mill has been preserved by the Phillips Mill Community Association as a landmark, cultural center and site for its highly regarded annual fall art exhibition. Not far beyond is Lenteboden, the business and residence of Charles Mueller, the bulb specialist whose gardens – lavish with daffodils, tulips and hyacinths – herald the arrival of spring. Like almost everything else along the towpath, they're free and open for the exploring.

River Pursuits. Canoeing, rafting and tubing are so popular here that the Bucks County River Country enterprise in Point Pleasant has become the East's largest water recreation facility. Tubing is its biggest operation; with up to 3,500 people a day renting inner tubes for floats of three to six miles. Canoeists are transported up to Tinicum, Upper Black Eddy or Riegelsville for trips downriver of six to twelve miles. The New Hope Mule Barge Co. hauls tourists on mule-drawn barges along the old Delaware Canal past Colonial homes, artists' workshops, gardens and countryside from downtown New Hope north to the Route 202 bridge and back.

Parks. The entire River Road area is so utterly unspoiled that it seems like one big park. And so some of it is. The aforementioned towpath is part of the **Delaware Canal State Park,** a 60-mile strip following the canal along Bucks County's riverfront. **Tinicum Park** offers picnicking, boating, hiking and more on its 126 acres beside the river in Tinicum, just north of Erwinna; here also are the historic **Erwin-Stover House** and the **Stover's Mill Gallery,** open to visitors on weekends. **Ralph Stover State Park,** just north of Point Pleasant, has 37 hilly acres for fishing, hiking and swimming along Tohickon Creek. It adjoins **Tohickon Valley County Park,** one of the largest of Bucks County's parks.

Shopping. A complex of buildings centered by a picturesque red wood and fieldstone barn built in 1749 is part of **River Road Farms** in Erwinna. The barn houses **Chachka,** one of our favorite stores. An interesting gift shop, it also accents some unusual food items, including Thai and Indonesian. "People say they have to go to many different stores in New York to find what we have here," says proprietor Dick deGroot, who makes the wild and wonderful Gentleman Farmer preserves and relishes at his home next door. Chachka also hosts outdoor festivals with seasonal food and entertainment on certain weekends. The **Lumberville Store** is an institution in Lumberville, a country store with a post office, book section, sundries, antiques and a deli (great sandwiches). Point Pleasant is notable for **Kinsman Co.,** garden tools and gifts, and **Poor Richard's,** an in-your-face hodgepodge, indoors and out, of wicker, brass and copper antiques. Smaller antiques shops are scattered here and there along the River Road. If you want still more shopping, just cross the river to the New Jersey side (Milford, Frenchtown, Stockton and Lambertville) or head down river to New Hope.

Sand Castle Winery, 755 River Road, Erwinna, (800) 722-9463. Two brothers from Czechoslovakia moved to a 72-acre estate above the Golden Pheasant Inn to grow vinifera grapes – the "noble vines of Europe," they call them – in the old-world tradition. Paul and Joe Maxian offer wine tastings beneath a tent canopy and in a reception trailer on a hilltop overlooking the countryside. They lead tours through their underground wine cellar and show pictures of their planned winery building patterned after a 10th-century Czech castle. The winery started production of riesling and chardonnay before adding expensive barrel-aged cabernet sauvignon and pinot noir, priced at $18 and $19 respectively.

Extra-Special

Bucks County Covered Bridges.
Nostalgia and romance are triggered by covered bridges that preserve a vanishing piece of Americana. Bucks County still has eleven of its original 36 covered bridges, all excellent examples of the lattice-truss construction patented in 1820 by Ithiel Town, a Connecticut architect. The oldest bridge was built in 1832. Five of the bridges are in the River Road area between Point Pleasant and Frenchtown. One at Uhlerstown spans the Delaware Canal; the shortest, at Erwinna, crosses Lodi Creek. Another was relocated for preservation purposes but burned in 1991. A Bucks County Tourist Commission brochure touts the virtues of covered bridges and provides a detailed map for a day's tour. Make a wish as you enter a wishing bridge or steal a kiss on one of the kissing bridges.

Sign tells story of the swallows of Lambertville at Delaware River entrance to town.

Lambertville, N.J.

On the Verge of Chic

Some time ago, the New York Times referred to a village of our acquaintance as "on the verge of chic." The same could be said today for Lambertville.

This sleepy New Jersey river town, a product of the Industrial Revolution and the 19th century, languished until lately. It was at the edge of chic, overshadowed by New Hope, Pa., its better-known neighbor across the Delaware River. History, artists and an enduring quaintness gave New Hope the best of everything. But Lambertville? This was the town through which New Yorkers had to pass to get to New Hope. Even that need was obviated after the new Route 202 toll bridge bypassed Lambertville.

Time was on Lambertville's side, however. The three A's – arts, authors and antiques – strained New Hope's limits and spilled into Lambertville. They found a receptive host, one untouched by the 20th-century building boom and urban redevelopment.

The first restaurant of note opened in 1980; the first B&B in 1983. Next a group of investors turned the old train station into a restaurant and built an adjacent luxury inn-hotel. Suddenly, Lambertville was "in." Now its main streets are chock-a-block antiques stores and art galleries. It has a wider variety of quality restaurants than does New Hope. Visitors are discovering the advantages of staying in Lambertville – close to New Hope, but without the crowds and hassle.

Lambertville has its own identity, that of an emerging town of 3,900 on the way to becoming the little city it calls itself. Since 1994, its Chamber of Commerce has produced annually a helpful brochure to guide tourists. Just up river is Stockton, itself a class act, centered by the old inn with the wishing well immortalized in the song, "There's a Small Hotel." Beyond is Rosemont, a crossroads hamlet where an old chicken farm is now a complex of business enterprises, one of them advertising the largest selection of handcrafted furniture in the country. Most of the area's riverfront with its parallel Delaware & Raritan Canal has been turned into the longest and narrowest strip of state parkland in the nation.

Although Lambertville is on the verge of chic, its surroundings are about as rural as they get in the nation's most densely populated state.

Inn Spots

Lambertville House, 32 Bridge St., Box 349, Lambertville 08530.

Lambertville's landmark hotel, which had been closed for eleven years, was grandly restored in 1997. New Hope developer George Michael bought the four-story structure dating to 1812 and added contemporary amenities as he returned it to its original luster. His son, Brad, became the innkeeper and set about attracting the high-end market.

The restored facade is a knockout with a two-story veranda along the stone front and stucco walls above painted beige with green and burgundy trim.

An elevator serves the 24 guest rooms and suites on the top three floors, each with marble bath and jetted tub (six are double jacuzzis). Twenty-one have gas fireplaces; eight offer balconies and six are suites. Beds are queen or kingsize. The formal furnishings are period antiques and reproductions. Rooms come with a writing desk and one wing chair. Touch-pad telephones with data ports, remote-control TV hidden in armoires or in cupboards over the fireplaces, waffle-weave robes, Gilbert & Soames toiletries, make-up mirrors, hair dryers and bottles of mineral water are among the amenities. Instead of a do-not-disturb sign, a stuffed pussycat hangs on the inside door handle with a little note to "put the cat out" to avoid being disturbed.

The six courtyard suites, two on each floor, are larger and have balconies overlooking the rear courtyard. The one we saw had a queen poster bed with an elegant quilt and a see-through fireplace serving bedroom and bath area. It contained a large jetted tub for two and a wicker chair, and opened onto a balcony as well as a bathroom with a glass shower.

Two more courtyard suites, retail shops and conference facilities are offered in a couple of buildings across the courtyard.

A continental-plus breakfast, included in the rates, is offered in a quaint basement breakfast room designed to look like a French kitchen with tiled floor, tiled fireplace, original rafters and wall sconces. Quiches are added on weekends.

The inn's main floor contains a reception foyer beside a stone wall, an elegant cocktail lounge called Left Bank Libations and a couple of up-scale retail shops, including the Greene & Greene Gallery.

Fieldstone fireplace enhances luxury guest room at Lambertville House.

(609) 397-0200 or (888) 867-8859. Fax (609) 397-0511. Twenty rooms and six suites with private baths. Weekends: doubles $189 to $249, suites $272 to $299. Midweek: doubles $162 to $222, suites $232 to $272. No smoking.

The Inn at Lambertville Station, 11 Bridge St., Lambertville 08530.

A group of investors spent more than $3 million in the 1980s to build this architecturally impressive, luxury hotel/inn on abandoned land that had been an eyesore along the Delaware River.

Check-in is at a counter resembling the ticket office of an old train station, but you'll probably be awed more by the soaring, three-story lobby, which is higher than it is wide. Each of the 45 guest rooms and suites is named for a major city and decorated accordingly by an antiques dealer who spared no expense.

Ours was the New York Suite, high in the trees above a rushing waterfall that lulled us to sleep. There were chocolates at bedside, the bathroom had a whirlpool tub and a basket of good toiletries, and around the L-shaped room were heavy mahogany furniture, leather chairs facing the fireplace and TV, handsome draperies, ornate mirrors and fine art. Afternoon tea or drinks from an honor bar are available in the lobby or on the adjacent creekside deck, a shady refuge in the trees. A small continental breakfast with carrot-nut muffins arrived at our door with the New York Times the next morning.

The large Riverside Room, facing the river with windows on three sides, is used for Sunday brunch ($18.95 for quite a spread).

(609) 397-4400 or (800) 524-1091. Fax (609) 397-9744. Thirty-seven rooms and eight suites with private baths. Doubles, $135 to $185 weekends, $95 to $105 midweek. Suites, $170 to $235 weekends, $135 midweek.

Chimney Hill Farm Estate and Old Barn Inn, 207 Goat Hill Road, Lambertville 08530.

Three deer were grazing in the back yard the day we revisited this pastoral retreat. "There are lots more," said Terry Ann Anderson, owner and innkeeper with her husband Rich. "They ate every chrysanthemum and daisy off our porch this fall. We also have a brood of wild turkeys, rabbits and big fat groundhogs."

The animals are appropriate at this opulent manor house, sequestered atop a wooded hill beyond a high-rent residential area on the southeast edge of Lambertville. It was once a working farm, and the restored gardens put in by former owner Edgar W. Hunt, an internationally known attorney, are spectacular in season.

The inside of the house borders on the spectacular as well, as you'd expect from a site that was a designer show house when it opened as a B&B. The Andersons, who moved here from northern New Jersey, have enhanced eight original guest rooms and added four luxury suites in a restored barn. In the main house, all but one have king or queensize beds and plump seating, and four have fireplaces. Each is awash in splashy fabrics, all Schumacher or Colfax & Fowler. The smallest room has space enough only for a double bed and one chair. The rear Terrace Room is bigger with tapestry fabrics, kingsize bed, a large bath with clawfoot tub and its own balcony. We liked the looks of the Hunt Room master suite, where the covers and canopy on the step-up queen bed match the gently swagged curtains, and the sofa and the oriental carpet pick up the theme.

Guests relax in the wonderful sunken main-floor sun porch, with windows on three sides and floors, fireplace and walls of fieldstone. Warmth and color come from ficus trees and the floral chintz that covers four wicker loveseats angled around a huge glass cocktail table. The splashy sun porch makes the attractive living room pale in comparison.

Breakfast is served by candlelight at six tables for two in the 1820 dining room that was the original room in the house (the wings were added by attorney Hunt in 1927). Terry offers fresh fruit, cereals and plenty of homemade pastries, from muffins with farm-made raspberry jam to croissants filled with fruit or cream cheese. Baked french toast is one of the additional treats on Sunday mornings. In the afternoon, port and cream sherry await in the butler's pantry, where tea, cider and snacks also are available. In each guest room is a "gift snack pack" with candy, goldfish and peanuts.

In 1999, the Andersons completed their long-planned expansion, joining a carriage house connected by a courtyard to a restored 1800 barn. The carriage house contains a party facility designed for weddings. Much larger is the barn, with a conference/board room and four luxury suites, each more showy than the last. Two on the main floor have queen beds, sitting areas with loveseats, TVs in armoires, corner gas fireplaces, guest convenience areas with refrigerator and microwave, and baths with jetted tubs and body showers. French doors open onto small patios. Upstairs are two larger, two-level suites. One, named in French for Magic Night, has a see-through fireplace facing both a living room with TV and a bath area with a large whirlpool tub beneath a brass chandelier in the corner, a bathroom with two-person shower and a spiral staircase to a loft with a Shaker queensize poster bed and another TV in a cabinet. The crowning glory is Suite 4, otherwise known as "the Steam Room," with the same features but with mood lights in the jacuzzi and something called a stereo steam room in the shower. The surround-sound stereo or CD music lulls guests as they steam and bake.

Manor house at Chimney Hill Farm is part of what once was a working farm.

On the grounds, the Andersons planned to add some alpacas, llama-like animals from Peru, to "enhance the farm aspect."

(609) 397-1516 or (800) 211-4667. Fax (609) 397-9353. www.chimneyhillinn.com. Eight rooms and four suites with private baths. Weekends: doubles, $145 to $195; suites, $235 to $295. Midweek: doubles, $125 to $189; suites, $157 to $195.

The Woolverton Inn, 6 Woolverton Road, Stockton 08559.

Built in 1792 as a manor house by pioneer industrialist John Prall Jr., whose mill is nearby, this is an engaging B&B on ten bucolic acres – where curious black-faced sheep check out guests from a field next to the parking area. Its location off a country road, atop a hill away from the river, assures a quiet night.

Three energetic new owners from Chicago have infused the inn with personality and pampering touches, both of which had been somewhat lacking in the past. They also set about upgrading some of the existing accommodations and added five new luxury rooms and suites.

"We want this to be welcoming and to capitalize on our rural, farm setting," said Mark Smith, co-owner with two friends, Carolyn McGavin and Matthew Lovette. "We hope guests find less of a business feeling and more a sense of visiting friends."

The friendly trio immediately added featherbeds and Egyptian cotton sheets to the eight bedrooms in the main house, all now with private baths – the lack thereof had been a shortcoming when we stayed here a decade earlier. They also were adding more comfortable sitting areas in the rooms. Plush towels, monogrammed terrycloth robes, fresh flowers and bedside chocolates already were the norm. Letitia's Repose, made from two rooms that shared a bath, offers a jacuzzi tub, a king fishnet-canopy bed and fireplace. Two other rooms on the second floor are quite spacious and come with kingsize featherbeds. Eventually, the new owners plan to reconfigure five small rooms on the third floor into four larger rooms.

At our latest visit, two guest rooms in the Carriage House, where the owners also live, were being converted into a luxury suite with kingsize bed, sitting area with a sofabed beside the fireplace, whirlpool tub and a separate shower for two. It also has its own private garden, a showcase for Mark's green-thumb talents.

Ready for spring 2000 were two rear "cottages" – actually built to look more like rustic barns, a re-creation of the historic farm outbuildings on the property. Each contains two guest suites with fireplaces, telephones and whirlpool tubs. In the planning stage were additional rooms in an existing 18th-century barn.

Guests have the run of the grounds, a pastoral retreat far from road noise and protected from suburban encroachment. A large and elegant living room is where snacks are offered. The trio hoped eventually to host afternoon tea here.

The dining room is the scene of elaborate breakfasts, served from 9 to 10. "We all cook and take turns in the kitchen," says Carolyn. A quiche of onions, apples, Canadian bacon and gruyère cheese was featured the day of our visit, along with homemade muffins and "pineapple upside up" cake. Matthew's fruit dish of apple-blueberry streusel baked in parchment paper is a favorite starter.

As you depart, the inn's two amiable sheep, Betty and Pâté, will likely mosey up to the fence to bid farewell.

(609) 397-0802 or (888) 264-6648. Fax (609) 397-4936. www.woolvertoninn.com. Twelve rooms and one suite with private baths. Weekends: doubles, $115 to $275, suite, $250. Midweek: doubles, $105 to $190, suite, $180.

Ma Maison Bed & Breakfast, 44 Coryell St., Lambertville 08530.

A culinary theme pervades this transformed Victorian architectural gem, thanks to a self-styled "passionate amateur chef." After studying at Le Cordon Bleu in Paris and elsewhere in France, Judith Donohue, took over the former Coryell Bed & Breakfast in 1999 and gave it a new name and a decidedly French accent.

Her purchase was no turnkey operation. "I didn't buy the business – just the phone number," said Judith, who had been in real estate in Bucks County and Philadelphia's Main Line for 25 years, loved old homes and liked the small-town Lambertville scene. She knocked down walls to improve the flow of a New Orleans-style townhouse, added bathrooms and bedrooms, and installed french doors out to the brick terrace and gardens. One of her additions was a 500-pound marble patisserie counter obtained from a bakery in Provence. "It fit here exactly as my kitchen island," she said, "so I knew this was meant to be."

She imparted a light and airy, country French look to four guest rooms, furnished with French and American antiques from a lifetime of collecting. The Brittany Room on the main floor retains the long, narrow bath at the side but has a new entry, a queensize tester bed flanked by Victorian side tables and a sitting area with sofa and coffee table. Upstairs over the living room is the Burgundy Room, with a bay window, wrought-iron queen bed and prized red and white antique toile hangings. French linens and an Amish Lone Star quilt enhance the curly maple queensize bed in the Provence Room. The third-floor attic was opened up to produce the Normandy Room, which has twin Edwardian sleigh beds that can be joined as a king.

Guests enjoy a large living room with fireplace and sunny bay window. The dining room is the scene of gala breakfasts and cooking-school dinners at an eight-foot French farm table made for lingering. Specimen plantings and brick paths enhance the side and rear gardens.

Judith offers cooking classes for house guests – her first in 2000 was a Provençal dinner. Participants spent the afternoon cooking and bonding and then sat down to

Jeffrey Totaro Photo

Judith Donohue serves guests in Provence style at Ma Maison Bed & Breakfast.

a dinner of mussels with persillade, provençal chicken stuffed with spinach and ricotta cheese, a light green salad with cheese, and fruit tarts.

The morning repast typically involves a warm fruit compote, hot or cold cereal, fresh bread or muffins and a cheese soufflé or an egg specialty of the day. Tea is offered in the afternoon. For special occasions, Judith will cook a three-course dinner to remember for $75 a couple.

(609) 397-8292. Fax (609) 397-3600. Doubles, $135 to $160 weekends, $100 to $125 midweek. Two-night minimum on weekends.

York Street House, 42 York St., Lambertville 08530.

This large Georgian brick home was opened as Lambertville's first B&B in 1983 after it had been glamorized as a designers' show house. It wasn't the first time it had received wide publicity – the Massey Mansion was featured in 1911 in House and Garden magazine shortly after a local coal merchant had built it as a 25th wedding anniversary gift for his wife.

Today's visitors are greeted by an imposing brick mansion set back from the street with pillared verandas on the front and side, nicely restored by new owners Beth Wetterskog, full-time innkeeper, and partner Nancy Ferguson, an emergency room physician at a Trenton hospital. They bought the house unfurnished and have been gradually renovating the rooms and furnishing them as they go along. Amazingly, they did the plumbing and carpentry themselves.

Mercer tiles compliment the working fireplaces in the main-floor common rooms and an original Waterford chandelier glitters over down-stuffed furniture in the living room, where there's an unusual chaise for two that's so comfy that "once you get on you don't get off," Nancy advised. Besides the living room, guests spread out on the side porch furnished in wicker overlooking the largest yard on the block, which was decked out in welcoming tiny white lights at our latest October visit.

Crystal knobs open the walnut doors to five large guest quarters. Three on the second floor have remodeled baths. Three on the third floor that shared two baths were converted into two rooms, each with private bath.

All with queen or kingsize beds, they are outfitted with TVs and telephones. Still the favorite is the second-floor front room with a lace canopy step-up queen bed, two wing chairs in the corner, an extra sink in another corner and – a startling sight in the bathroom – a freestanding toilet in the front bay window of what once was a dressing room. The partners were redoing in Victorian gingerbread a side bedroom with a wicker bed, window seat and a clawfoot tub in the bathroom beneath original stained-glass windows.

Signs in each room warn of a $150 fine for violation of the B&B's no smoking policy.

A full breakfast is served in the fireplaced dining room. Fresh-ground coffee accompanied croissant french toast the morning of our visit.

(609) 397-3007 or (888) 398-3199. Fax (609) 397-9677. www.yorkstreethouse.com. Five rooms with private baths. Doubles, $130 to $189 weekends, $95 to $125 midweek. No young children. No smoking.

The Bridgestreet House, 75 Bridge St., Lambertville 08530.

A pair of pre-Victorian structures started in the 1980s as a restaurant with a B&B adjunct. The restaurant eventually failed, and young owner Jeremy Weitz from New York now offers six guest rooms in the three-story B&B house. He occupies the former main-floor garden room and adds an innkeeper presence. Guests retain access to the rear garden and courtyard.

Three bedrooms have private baths and three share. Each is air-conditioned and has thick carpeting and remote-control TV. Upon taking over in 1999, Jeremy upgraded four beds to queensize and added amenities such as robes, slippers, hair dryers and English soaps. Victorian antiques embellish the rooms, but "with comfort and ease" in mind. A couple of rooms have beamed ceilings, and floral comforters and draperies brighten one room. Elaborate stenciling decorates the doorways off the corridors

Chocolate mints and a decanter of brandy await guests in each room, and wine and cheese are offered on weekends. In the morning, Jeremy sets out a continental breakfast buffet in the refurbished parlor. It consists of juice, seasonal fruit, yogurt and homemade breads and muffins.

(609) 397-2503 or (800) 897-2503. Fax (609) 397-4993. Three rooms with private baths and three rooms with shared baths. Doubles, $110 to $140 weekends, $75 to $95 midweek. Two-night minimum weekends in season. Children over 12. No smoking.

Dining Spots

Anton's at the Swan, 43 South Main St., Lambertville.

Shortly after it opened in 1990 in the Swan Hotel, this was picked by the New York Times as one of the year's ten best restaurants in New Jersey. It's still going strong, thanks to the inspiration of talented chef Anton Dodel, who leases the space from Swan owner James Bulger.

Anton is, in his words, spontaneous and eclectic. He's also versatile; at one

Wall of mirrors and paneling are backdrop for dining at Anton's at the Swan.

visit, he was sprawled on the floor preparing to rehang curtains an hour before a special wine-tasting dinner. His short menu changes monthly. We'd gladly have tried any of his six October entrées, but particularly the roast cod on ginger-pumpkin sauce, the sautéed lobster and apples over chive biscuits, and the grilled venison on persimmon and chile sauce. Starters included curried shrimp and pumpkin soup, garlic flan on warm black bean sauce, and grilled green tomatoes on herb bruschetta.

Desserts always include something chocolate and always a flan, but you might find a poached pear in caramel sauce or a cornbread pudding.

The backdrop for these culinary triumphs is a subdued room with paneled wainscoting, a wall of mirrors, step-down windsor chairs and white-linened tables topped with candles in hurricane chimneys. Anton rebuilt the hotel's kitchen in order to produce a sophisticated menu and style, "one like a well-established restaurant in France." He cooks more casual fare for the hotel's bar.

If you want to try a sampling of Anton's high-end fare, consider his special prix-fixe menu, $38 for appetizer, entrée, dessert and coffee.

(609) 397-1960. Entrées, $23 to $30. Dinner, Tuesday-Saturday 6 to 10, Sunday 4:30 to 8.

Hamilton's Grill Room, 8 Coryell St., Lambertville, N.J..

Former Broadway set designer Jim Hamilton and his daughter Melissa opened this gem, hidden at the end of an alley in the Porkyard complex beside the canal and towpath. Jim, an architect who designs restaurants, installed an open grill beside the entrance and built the wood-fired adobe pizza oven himself. Chef Melissa has turned over the Mediterranean grill concept to executive chef Mark Miller, and Jim says the food has never been better.

Hamilton's created the option of grazing portions to let weekday diners try "a little of everything." Nearly half the entrées are available in standard and smaller portions (at about half the price). You might start with a fennel and roasted tomato soup, an arugula salad with apples, saga cheese and hazelnut vinaigrette or pan-seared scallops with sweet pepper pesto. Or graze with half portions ($10 to $15) of entrées like grilled tuna with capers and golden raisins, grilled salmon with a leek and seaweed salad and garlic-crusted rack of lamb.

The menu is similar but pricier on weekends, when the open grill yields treats like a mixed grill of lobster, sea scallops and fish of the day, and seared salmon on a bed of coarse salt with ginger, red pepper and leek marmalade.

Our meal began with a menu standby, grilled shrimp with anchovy butter, and a crab cake on wilted greens and sweet red pepper sauce. Main courses were an exceptional grilled duck on bitter greens with pancetta and honey glaze and grilled ribeye steak au poivre with leek aioli. The oversize plates were filled with fanned razor-thin sliced potatoes and grilled zucchini and green and red peppers. The signature grappa torta and the grand-marnier cheesecake were fine desserts.

Patrons dine at a lineup of faux-marble tables in the mirrored grill room, beneath angels and clouds surrounding a huge gilt mirror on the ceiling of the Bishop's Room, around a changing decorative focal point in the dining gallery and, in season, outdoors around the fountain in the courtyard.

(609) 397-4343. Entrées, $17.75 to $28. Dinner nightly, 6 to 10, Sunday 5 to 9. BYOB.

Manon, 19 North Union St., Lambertville.

An air of whimsy reigns here, from the colorful exterior of burnt orange and blue-green with gingerbread trim to the ceiling painted like Van Gogh's starry night. With a relocated and expanded kitchen, there's more room for young chef-owner Jean-Michel Dumas, who grew up in Provence, to work his culinary wizardry. There's also an extra table for patrons in the intimate, 36-seat dining room in front. The chef and his American wife Susan have added a garden terrace with a few tables in back.

Gutsy food is served in robust portions. The French menu often starts with his trademark anchovy relish and an assortment of raw vegetables, the house pâté, escargots in pernod and salads like warm goat cheese or watercress with pear, endive, walnuts and roquefort. Soup of the day could be garlicky mussel or pistou.

Among the eight entrées are a classic bouillabaisse, grilled salmon on a bed of cabbage with lobster mushroom sauce, breast of chicken with garlic sauce, calves liver with a shallot-wine sauce, and rack of lamb with herbs de provence. Desserts include crème caramel, tarte tatin, chocolate mousse, marjolaine and nougat ice cream with raspberry sauce.

(609) 397-2596. Entrées, $18.50 to $25. Dinner, Wednesday-Sunday 5:30 to 9 or 10. Sunday brunch, 11 to 2:30. No credit cards. BYOB.

The Fish House, 2 Canal St., Lambertville.

Restaurant/theater designer Jim Hamilton's latest marquee attraction in his hometown is this one-of-a-kind food emporium transformed in late 1999 from an old factory beside the canal in downtown Lambertville.

The simple name is deceptive yet quite descriptive. It's a happening mix of seafood restaurant, raw bar, diner, gourmet food market, chef's table and sideshow on two floors around a central open kitchen. From the wraparound mezzanine, diners can watch the cooks at work as they feast on the likes of sautéed soft-shell crabs, slow-roasted salmon, oyster pan roast and whole fish of the day. That is, if they can take their eyes off the fanciful 50-foot-long mural depicting an underwater wedding on one wall or the waterfall cascading down another wall.

"We saw a niche market for fish in this area," said Jim. He produced a casual dining space with wooden tables and a diner-style counter on the main floor and a more formal, tableclothed setting upstairs. Other attributes are an open kitchen, an extensive raw bar and glass display cases where "all our larder" from crab cakes and packaged meals to olive oils and condiments is for sale. The retail area includes items from breads to flowers. A garden terrace offers outdoor dining.

Executive chef Paul Ripley originally worked with Melissa Hamilton at Hamilton's Grill Room. His early dinner menu was short but sweet. Starters were mussel-scallion soup, pan roast of the day, a raw bar selection and house-smoked salmon and corn blinis with crème fraîche. Main dishes included grilled Scottish salmon with stewed white beans, seared tuna with cod cake and tomato broth, whole fish with aged sherry vinaigrette and lobster "any way." Herb-roasted chicken and T-bone steak also were available. Desserts were a fruit tart, bread pudding with vanilla caramel sauce and chocolate truffle cake.

(609) 397-6477. Entrées, $14 to $24. Lunch and dinner daily, 11:30 to 10. Retail shop open from 10.

Church Street Bistro, 11½ Church St., Lambertville..

This space hidden behind Mitchell's bar has proved a launching pad for restaurateurs who moved on to bigger and better things. The latest is Patrick Given, who started here as sous chef under Europe-trained chef David Kiser, an instructor at the French Culinary Institute in Manhattan. Patrick took command later and, local consensus had it, the "new bistro cuisine" became even better.

Two areas separated by a divider sport a country bistro look with white-clothed tables, spaced nicely apart, and accents of copper pots. The setting is serene and the feeling authentic French. There's an outdoor courtyard for dining in summer.

The short dinner menu changes seasonally and offers some of the area's more interesting dishes, with an emphasis on low-fat preparation. Patrick employs organic produce, farmed seafood and hormone-free veal, poultry and beef for what he calls "cuisine du marché." Starters might include herb-crusted calamari over baby field greens with a lemon-balsamic vinaigrette and sundried tomato-basil pesto, grilled portobello mushrooms with gorgonzola cheese in a roasted garlic cream sauce, and a bouchée of duck confit with caramelized onion, kalamata olives and goat cheese.

Main courses range from grilled tilapia with fire-scorched red peppers, braised celery, kalamata olives and capers to grilled Australian sirloin of lamb with a roasted shallot lamb jus. Typical are grilled Atlantic salmon with tomato-coriander sauce, black pepper-crusted Chilean sea bass with shiitake mushrooms in a ginger-soy-mirin glaze and a cassoulet of red beans and stewed tomato with wild boar sausage, duck confit and garlic sausage.

Desserts might be warm apple tart with homemade vanilla ice cream, pumpkin cheesecake and ginger crème brûlée. The well-chosen wine list is affordably priced.

(609) 397-4383. Entrées, $17 to $25. Lunch, Friday and Saturday noon to 3. Dinner, Wednesday-Saturday 5 to 9 or 10. Sunday, brunch noon to 3, dinner 3 to 9.

Lambertville Station, 11 Bridge St., Lambertville.

Once abandoned, Lambertville's 2½-story train station took on new life as a stylish Victorian restaurant and lounge. Diners on several levels of the glass-enclosed Platform Room watch geese glide by and lights reflect off the waters of the Delaware & Raritan Canal. The food is so good and fairly priced that we've returned more than once – an unusual occurrence given our normal wanderlust.

The first time, our party of four sampled the unusual appetizer of alligator strips, which we dipped into a mustard and green peppercorn sauce. The carpaccio of buffalo also was very good. (Lately the pair have been combined on skewers and served with pineapple-mango chutney.)

Among entrées, the jambalaya was spicy, the boneless roast duck was properly crispy and came with a raspberry sauce and polenta, the medallions of buffalo sautéed with mushrooms and brandy cream sauce were more than ample and the veal medallions with jumbo shrimp in garlic butter were excellent. A superior honey-mustard dressing enhanced the house spinach salad. Lime-almond cheesecake and key lime mousse pie were fine desserts.

(609) 397-8300. Entrées, $13.95 to $22.95. Lunch, Monday-Saturday 11:30 to 3. Dinner nightly, 4 to 10 or 11. Sunday brunch, 10:30 to 3.

Rick's, 19 South Main St., Lambertville.

The decor of this storefront restaurant is negligible (pine paneling, a linoleum floor and tables topped by red and white checked oilcloths). And there's no menu – the night's fare is scrawled on a couple of blackboards. But the place is packed with people who appreciate good, true food at fair prices.

A couple of the town's best chefs tipped us off to what was going on at Rick Buscavage's place. Tired of his role as a partner in a large Japanese restaurant on Philadelphia's waterfront, he bought this hole-in-the-wall restaurant of 35 years, moved with his wife Kathy into space upstairs, and started serving up his favorite Italian "comfort" foods.

The blackboard descriptions are deceptively straightforward, but the delivery is worthy of a highfalutin' northern Italian trattoria charging twice the price. A dish of chopped tomatoes with arugula and herbed olive oil arrived with Italian peasant bread as our bottle of wine was uncorked and we studied our options. There were a ravioli sampler, an arugula salad with aged provolone, caesar salad, pastas like tortellini alfredo, penne arrabbiata, potato gnocchis with gorgonzola sauce, and spaghetti with mushrooms and leeks, and heavier dishes like veal parmesan on pasta or chicken bolognese on spinach fettuccine.

We sampled Kathy's antipasti, a substantial array of Italian meats and cheeses, most of which we took to our cooler to make excellent sandwiches the next day, followed by a salad of baby field greens tossed with goat cheese, hazelnuts and roasted red pepper dressing. Then we shared pencil points (penne) with prosciutto, roasted garlic, asparagus and mushrooms, a heaping portion for $10.95. The dinner bill for two totaled $25, not counting the sensational tiramisu that Rick had just made and insisted we try, over our faint protests.

Rick's is that kind of place, totally unpretentious but with class. The crowd is young and convivial, the owner tablehops between or after cooking stints and everyone seems to know each other, or does by the end of the evening.

(609) 397-0051. Entrées, $10 to $14. Lunch, Wednesday-Friday 11:30 to 2. Dinner, Wednesday-Saturday from 5:30, Sunday 4 to 8. BYOB. No credit cards.

De Anna's, 18 South Main St., Lambertville.

Here's another small, convivial place in which De Anna Menzel continues the culinary magic launched by her predecessor, Paul Blasenheim. She took over the former Chef Paul's in 1990 upon his retirement. The only physical change involved partitioning off the open kitchen from which Paul liked to converse with customers. De Anna confesses to being too shy to be part of the dining scene; her statement is her food, which is robust Italian.

The menu lists a dozen homemade pasta entrées, from basic with marinara sauce to extravagant with calamari fra diavolo. We were smitten by two flavorful pastas, one with prosciutto and peas and the other with sundried tomato and pinenut cream sauce, which came with zesty salads and a couple of robust breads. The portions were ample and the leftovers made a great lunch the next day.

Desserts, for those who leave room to indulge, include blackberry jam tart, belgian chocolate-espresso cake, ricotta cheesecake and Italian ice.

The place couldn't be smaller – six tables seating twenty. Illumination is entirely by candles that flicker in hurricane lamps, reflecting on the glass tabletops. Big pillows and cushions rest on the wall benches.

(609) 397-8957. Entrées, $11.50 to $14.75. Dinner, Tuesday-Saturday 5 to 9:30 or 10, Sunday 4 to 8. BYOB. No credit cards. No smoking.

The Stockton Inn, 1 Main St., Stockton.

Remember the Rodgers and Hart Broadway show song, "There's a Small Hotel?" This is that small hotel, the lyrics were written here and guests still make wishes at *the* wishing well.

Band leader Paul Whiteman used to sign off his national radio shows from Trenton with the announcement that he was going to the Stockton Inn for dinner (one of the fascinating murals in the dining room pictures Whiteman fallen from his horse on his way home to nearby Rosemont after imbibing too much). In 1935, the inn gained national fame as the press head-quarters during the Lindbergh kidnapping trial.

The food rises and falls with the chefs in the kitchen. Our dinner began with a trio of salmon (vodka-cured gravlax, hot smoked salmon from the inn's smoker and salmon rillettes). It was a sensational presentation, thanks to an assortment of sauces, capers, red onions and delicious baguette toasts. We also liked the special salad, an arrangement of arugula, goat cheese, roasted red peppers and sundried tomatoes with a complex, smoky taste.

Murals enhance Stockton Inn dining room.

Among entrées, the boned and rolled chicken stuffed with mushroom duxelles and flanked by an array of green beans, carrots, braised red cabbage and layered potatoes was excellent. So was the veal sauté with sundried tomatoes and roasted garlic. Rain forest crunch ice cream with fresh raspberries was a refreshing ending.

The setting is comfortable and romantic in six historic dining rooms seating a total of 175. On chilly evenings, we particularly enjoy the intimate front rooms with fireplaces, crisp white tablecloths and candles, and subtly illuminated local murals on every wall. Painted by artists during the Depression in exchange for room and board, they are quite remarkable. In season, there's dining on five outside terraces amidst two waterfalls and a pond stocked with golden trout, near the wishing well made famous by the Rodgers and Hart song. The Old World Garden Bar on the upper terrace has a dance floor. The main inn has a glamorous bar and a cozy pub in front.

(609) 397-1250. Entrées, $17.95 to $26.95. Lunch, Monday-Saturday 11:30 to 2:30. Dinner, Monday-Thursday 4:30 to 9:30, weekends 5 to 10. Sunday, brunch 11 to 2:30, dinner 3:30 to 9.

Atrio Cafe, 515 Bridge St., Stockton, N.J.

Chef-owner Ricky Franco, a native of Brazil who cooked in New York at the Plaza and the Waldorf-Astoria hotels, is one of the trio that opened this cafe named for their partnership, "a trio." The decor in hunter green and burgundy is simple. The eclectic cuisine with a Brazilian "flare," as they advertise, is quite sophisticated.

Appealing main courses range from pan-seared salmon with peppercorn sauce on a chickpea cake to roasted rack of lamb topped with a cannellini bean, mushroom and wine demi-glace. The ravioli might be topped with a shrimp, tasso ham and chickpea sauce. The monkfish could be sprinkled with black pepper, splashed with mustard-curry sauce and served over watercress with a roasted shallot dressing.

Start with lump crab cakes with a sweet onion salsa or a salad of pepper-crusted scallops and grilled portobellos with watercress and shaved parmesan. Finish with key lime pie or a tart of poached pear with ginger-mascarpone cream.

(609) 397-0042. Entrées, $16.95 to $19.95. Lunch, Thursday-Saturday 11:30 to 3. Dinner, Tuesday-Saturday from 5. Sunday, brunch 10:30 to 3, dinner 4 to 8. BYOB.

Meil's Restaurant, Bridge and Main Streets, Stockton.

Creative American comfort food with an old-fashioned slant is the theme on the extensive menu at this Lambertville transplant, a cramped little bakery and restaurant fashioned from an old gasoline station. On a warm winter's day, we eyed the picnic tables on the blacktop parking lot in front before deciding to sit inside. The decor is simple but jaunty: colorful balloon curtains over the windows, quilts on the walls (one wall has a montage of black muffin pans) and tables covered with mint-colored oilcloths.

All kinds of interesting salads, sandwiches and egg dishes are featured at lunch. We sampled a classic salad niçoise and a not-so-classic huevos rancheros, with an unexpected and unwanted ton of chili between the eggs and the tortilla, and the accompanying salsa lacking fresh coriander.

Night brings some of the daytime fare as well as hefty pastas and main courses from meatloaf and mashed potatoes to peanut shrimp and rosemary-rubbed rack of lamb with pineapple-mint cream sauce.

You also can get almost anything from buttermilk biscuits and blueberry muffins to beef stew and chicken pot pie to go. Exotic omelets are available at breakfast, served with seasoned red-skin potatoes and French bread.

(609) 397-8033. Entrées, $12.95 to $21.95. Breakfast 9 to 3, weekends 8 to 3. Lunch, 11 to 3. Dinner, 4:30 to 9 or 10. Closed Wednesday. BYOB. No credit cards.

Diversions

A Lambertville phenomenon that's rather diverting is that of wine bars and pubs. **The Boat House** at 8 Coryell St. in the Porkyard is an elegant bar, where wines are featured by the glass and where the walls are paneled with old twelve-foot-high doors. Hamilton's Grill and the Boat House team up to provide food and drinks at the adjacent **Wine Bar.** Another good place for a drink and maybe a snack is **The Swan Hotel,** where the public rooms are filled with art and antiques. The main bar has comfortable leather chairs to sink into and a greenhouse wall looking out onto a small garden with a fountain, which is spotlit at night. A pianist plays show tunes on weekends. **The Inn of the Hawke,** 74 South Union St., is a neighborhood pub with a long horseshoe-shaped bar in the center room and a dining room looking onto a pleasant outdoor courtyard. Two young sisters have upgraded both the dining operation and the seven upstairs guest rooms, but this remains essentially a drinking establishment.

Walking Tour. The Lambertville Area Chamber of Commerce has published a walking tour for historic buildings and points of interest. The self-guided tour takes about 45 minutes. The map details 22 buildings, the oldest being the landmark Lambertville House, built in 1812, now nicely restored. Other buildings on the tour date to the late 19th century, and one (the Massey Mansion, now the York Street House B&B) is as recent as 1909. For more ancient history, visitors have only to walk across the bridge to New Hope, where 18th-century structures are much in evidence.

Delaware & Raritan Canal State Park. For nearly a century, the old D&R Canal was one of America's busiest. A 22-mile-long navigable feeder canal stretching from above Stockton at Raven Rock south through Lambertville to Trenton brought water from the Delaware River to the main canal, which ran from Bordentown to New Brunswick. The canal and its adjacent towpath by the Delaware River are now part of New Jersey's longest park. The towpath is a favorite of joggers and hikers.

The Prallsville Mills, Route 29, Stockton. Once a thriving little commercial center, the 18th-century mills were abandoned until 1973, when they were included on the National Register of Historic Places and became part of the D&R Canal State Park. Local citizens formed the Delaware River Mill Society to restore and interpret the mill site, which includes a four-story gristmill now used for periodic arts and crafts exhibits, lectures and concerts. Original mill machinery is on display.

Shopping. Antiques stores and art galleries are proliferating lately along Bridge and North Union streets, where the shopping seems to get better every year. Two of the nicest and newest are the avant-garde **A Mano Gallery** of contemporary crafts, an offshoot of one across the river in New Hope, and **Greene & Greene Gallery**, a specialist in contemporary crafts and the furniture designs of Jeffrey Greene, which moved here from New Hope. Bucks County artists are shown at **Artfull Eye.** Lots of flowery and garden theme things are featured at **Joanna Hearts,** whose stock runs from cards and teacups to fabrics and aromatic home accessories. Not to be missed is the **Porkyard,** a former sausage factory complex now given over to a restaurant and a wine bar, plus **Blue Raccoon** for great home and garden antiques and accessories, **Porkyard Antiques** and **Coryell Gallery.** A rear terrace overlooks the Delaware River behind **Rivergate Books;** pick up a good book and start it outside. We like the cappuccino bar at **Lambertville Trading Co.** on Bridge Street, where you can quaff single or double espresso, cappuccino or mochaccino and the aromas are luscious. Pumpkin truffles, Bavarian espresso cake, black currant scones, oils and vinegars, cheeses and many varieties of coffee beans are available. Also on Bridge Street, **Dresswell's** has some interesting casual clothes for men and women, including sportswear from Jackeroos. **The Sojourner** is a treasure trove of apparel and gift items from around the world; a huge selection of dangling and colorful fish earrings was $10 a pair. **The 5 & Dime** on North Union Street specializes in collectible toys, comic watches, plastic, paper, advertising and the like from 1900 to the '70s.

South of town is the **Laceworks,** a mill complex with a changing array of outlet stores. **Riverrun Gallery** here features contemporary art and was having a show of original artworks and crafts, all priced for under $300. **Prestige Antiques** operates out of a warehouse of a place. Antiquers in the know head for the **Lambertville Antique Market,** a mile and a half south of town along Route 29 and rated by the New York Times as one of the nation's ten best. This is where many local shopkeepers and innkeepers find their prizes, and dealers come from across the country to buy and sell authentic pieces. The market and its companion **Golden Nugget Antique Flea Market** operate weekends year-round.

If you need a bottle of wine for one of those BYOB restaurants, you'll find exceptional selections at **Welsh's** in Lambertville and **Phillips'** in Stockton.

Extra-Special

Cane Farm, Route 519, Rosemont.

Three generations of Canes have transformed a 94-acre farm once home to half a million chickens into a furniture-making center and a complex of crafts workshops and retail showrooms in old chicken coops. The idea was that of Charles Cane, who gave up one of New Jersey's largest poultry operations for more versatile pursuits upon his retirement in 1965. The implementation was left to son Phil Cane, a woodworker at heart. Lately joined by his two sons, Phil and staff make much of the handcrafted furniture on display in a 580-foot-long showroom called **Cane Farm Furniture.** You'd never know these were once chicken houses and hatcheries, so complete is the transformation with windows along one side, carpeted or brick floors, and classical music playing. One old coop after another stretches nearly the length of two football fields, showing what Phil calls the largest collection of country furniture in America. The stock ranges from reproductions of antique tables, Shaker cupboards and windsor chairs to decoys, pewter, brass light fixtures, hunting prints and, lately, aviation art. Talented Phil, who restores old cars and builds racing boats, says he's also "a collector and an accumulator." He needs little persuasion to show his antique guns, Indian relics, historic documents, old postmarks and what-not in an area marked "Ephemeral and Miscellaneous."

(609) 397-0606. Hours vary. Showrooms generally open Friday and Saturday 10 to 5, Sunday 1 to 5.

Victoriana and verandas reign in Cape May scene looking toward turreted Inn at 22 Jackson.

Cape May, N.J.

Grande Dame of Victoriana

Bed and breakfast as an American phenomenon got its start in Cape May. It also has been elevated here to its highest form.

Tom and Sue Carroll are credited with launching the phenomenon in the early 1970s when they turned the Windward House on Jackson Street into a Victorian B&B in this most Victorian of towns. The registered National Historic Landmark community has since spawned about 100 more B&Bs. And entrepreneurs in what they call the B&B capital of the United States host seminars for prospective innkeepers from across the country. The phenomenon locally was raised to high art through formal teas, exotic breakfasts and even B&B house tours. Lately, some of the inns' brochures have become state-of-the-art and as showy as the rest of the B&B experience here.

In the 19th century, America's first seaside resort was the playground for no fewer than five presidents, and Benjamin Harrison made Cape May his summer White House. Less than a century later, it was down at the heels when citizens banded together to save the landmark Emlen Physick House from demolition. Thus was born the Mid-Atlantic Center for the Arts (MAC), a community dynamo that not only promotes the arts but also restores structures, stages tours and sponsors events.

Thanks to MAC, Cape May seems to be a series of festivals all year long, from Crafts in the Winter to a Christmas Candlelight House Tour. Cape May's celebrated Victorian Week is now an annual ten-day extravaganza in October.

The year-round population of 4,800 swells many-fold in the summer in this town at the southern end of a peninsula, a point actually below the Mason-Dixon Line, where the Atlantic Ocean meets the Delaware Bay. Visitors come to ogle the largest collection of authentic Victorian structures in the country, to relax on the beaches and enjoy the wildlife, including some of the East's best bird-watching. At the heart of it all are the inns and B&Bs, an integral part of the Cape May experience.

Inn Spots

Almost every house in Cape May's historic district seems to be turning into a B&B. In a whimsical turn, a sign in front of the 1882 Christopher Gallagher House notes its distinction from all its Jackson Street neighbors: "a private residence." The Cape May custom is for the innkeepers to serve – and often sit with – guests at breakfast, and later to help with dinner plans as they review the menus during afternoon tea or beverages.

The Mainstay Inn, 635 Columbia Ave., Cape May 08204.

Preservationists Tom and Sue Carroll launched the B&B movement in Cape May at the Windward House, now under different ownership, and purchased the Mainstay in 1975. The 1872 Italianate villa was built by two gamblers as a gaming and entertainment club for gentlemen. It is one of the town's few Victorian structures that have gone through more than a century with no transitions. The fourteen-foot-high public rooms are lavishly furnished in Victoriana, right down to the sheet music on the piano. Especially notable is the ceiling of the entrance hall, where a stunning combination of seventeen wallpapers makes a beautiful pattern.

The twelve accommodations in the inn and in the pleasant 1870 Cottage next door are named for famous visitors to Cape May. Lace curtains, stenciling, brass and iron bedsteads, armoires and rockers comprise the museum-quality decor. The Henry Ford room has its own small porch and the Bret Harte room (with many of his books in a case) opens onto the entire second-floor veranda. Climb a steep ladder with a wavering rope for a railing to the tower on the third floor, where, with cushions on two sides and windows on all four, you get a good view of the town. The inn and the cottage, both with wide verandas and green rocking chairs, are separated by a brick walk and a handsome trickling fountain. The front gardens are brilliant with flowers.

Four modern, two-bedroom suites with queensize beds are located in the

Mainstay's newer annex, the Officers' Quarters, a restored naval officers' building across the street. It's an appropriate addition, since Tom is a Naval Reserve officer. Each suite contains a spacious living room with a dining area, a loveseat facing the gas fireplace and the TV in a corner cupboard, a kitchenette with a mini-refrigerator, and a marble bathroom with whirlpool tub and shower. They are decorated in country style, giving "a totally different

Pacesetting Mainstay Inn is headquartered in landmark 1872 Italian villa.

experience than at the main inn –contemporary elegance rather than Victorian splendor," says Sue. The stairway railing came from the old Lafayette Hotel here, thanks to a former mayor who had saved it in storage. The Mainstay's trademark green wooden chairs also appear on the front porches of each suite. Guests who stay here have tea at the main inn; continental breakfast is delivered to their quarters.

Sue's recipes for her breakfast and tea goodies are so sought after that she has published six editions of a small cookbook called "Breakfast at Nine, Tea at Four." In summer, breakfast at the main inn is continental-plus, served buffet-style on the veranda; other seasons it is formal and sit-down at two seatings at 8:30 and 9:30 at a table for twelve in the dining room. Chicken-pecan quiche, ham and apple pie, hash browns quiche, western oven omelet, California egg puff, cheese strata and stuffed french toast with strawberry sauce are among the specialties.

The Carrolls are still hands-on innkeepers, here daily for breakfast and after-noon tea, despite their tenure as the nation's longest-running innkeepers – 30 years in 2000. "We don't know anybody who has done this longer," says Tom, who also heads the board of MAC, the ubiquitous Mid-Atlantic Center of the Arts.

Tours of the museum-quality inn are offered, lately daily from 11 to 1:30 (self-guided, $3 to benefit MAC) and sometimes more elaborately, four days a week at 4 ($7.50, when visitors join guests for tea). Except in summer, when iced tea is served on the veranda, teatime is inside and formal. The tea is served from a copper container and accompanied by cucumber sandwiches, cheese straw daisies, toffee squares, spiced shortbread, chocolate-chip meringues and the like.

"Young children generally find us tiresome," the inn's brochure advises sensibly. Except for the spiffy Officers' Quarters, the Mainstay is, as Tom Carroll says, "a total Victorian experience."

(609) 884-8690. www.mainstayinn.com. Twelve rooms and four suites with private baths. Doubles, $170 to $275, mid-May to mid-October and all weekends; $95 to $185, midweek rest of year. Officers' Quarters: $245 to $310, peak season and all weekends, $145 to $235 midweek mid-October to mid-May. Three-night minimum in season and most weekends. Officers' Quarters open year-round; inn closed January to mid-March. No smoking.

The Queen Victoria, 102 Ocean St., Cape May 08204.

Toned-down Victoriana and creature comforts are offered by Dane and Joan Wells in Cape May's largest B&B operation, the only one open every day of the year. The Wellses, who along with Tom and Sue Carroll are considered icons by their fellow innkeepers, started with twelve rooms and eight private baths in their original 1881 corner property. In 1989, they turned the Victorian house and carriage house next door into eleven luxury rooms and suites. Here they offer the niceties that many of today's travelers want: queensize brass or iron canopy beds, bedside clocks and reading lights, sitting areas or rooms, mini-refrigerators, whirlpool baths, television, fireplaces and air-conditioning.

In 1994, they took over the former Heirloom 1876 House across the street and renovated it for reopening in 1995 as **Queen's Hotel,** an elegant historic hotel. It has eleven rooms with private baths featuring whirlpool tubs or glass-enclosed marble showers, TVs, telephones, in-room coffee-makers, affordable prices and more privacy. "Twenty percent of our guests have been looking for this kind of thing," said Dane, which he likened to a hotel's concierge floor. "It's for the person who wants historic surroundings without all the B&B trappings."

Back in the main facility, furnishings in both guest and public rooms are not so high Victorian as in other Cape May inns. They are authentic in the post-Victorian Arts and Crafts style. Each house has a parlor, one in the original building with a piano and a fireplace and the newer one with TV, games and jigsaw puzzles. Pantry areas are stocked with the makings for popcorn, tea, sherry and such. The library in the original inn contains volumes on architecture, art and history collected by Joan when she was executive director of the Victorian Society in America.

Breakfast at a recent visit included choice of juice, homemade granola, blueberry-cinnamon muffins and three kinds of homemade breads, a main course of hash-brown potato bake with ham slices, plus a basket of toasting breads. Baked eggs, cheese strata, spinach or corn casserole and stuffed baked french toast with warm strawberry sauce are other possibilities. The hearty meal is offered in the splendor of two Victorian dining rooms.

(609) 884-8702. www.queenvictoria.com. Fifteen rooms and six suites with private baths. Doubles, $95 to $230; suites, $140 to $290. Lower midweek, November-March. Three-night minimum in season and peak weekends.

The Virginia Hotel, 25 Jackson St., Cape May 08204.

Built in 1879 as Cape May's first hotel, the Virginia has been grandly restored as what general manager Curtis Bashaw, co-owner with his father, calls a deluxe "boutique" hotel. Tiny white lights frame the exterior year-round, newspapers hang from a rack outside the dining room and appear at your door in the morning,

Don Pearse Photo

Evening lighting enhances gingerbread trim of verandas around Virginia Hotel.

and a pianist plays in the pleasant front library during the dinner hour in the acclaimed Ebbitt Room (see Dining Spots).

On your way upstairs check the stained-glass window in the landing; a local craftsman spent a year looking for old glass with which to restore it. The second and third floors contain 24 modern, comfortable guest rooms that vary widely in size and shape. Like the public rooms, they are furnished in a simple yet sophisticated manner. Bedrooms are equipped with private baths with new fixtures, telephones and remote-control TVs and VCRs hidden in built-in cabinets. Room service is available, terrycloth robes are provided and the hotel's guest services packet is one of the more informative we've seen.

The decor is mostly soft peaches and grays, for a restful look. There are eleven standard-size rooms, eleven premium and two extra-premium at the front of the second floor with private balconies. Five have a sofa and two upholstered chairs each, though one premium room with a kingsize bed has room for only one chair. The wraparound balcony on the second floor gave our already expansive room extra space and was particularly pleasant the next morning for a continental breakfast, delivered to the room at the time specified, of fresh orange juice, fruit, danish pastries and croissants.

Curt sees this as the prototype for other small luxury hotels that he and his father want to develop along the East Coast. A fine prototype it is.

(609) 884-5700 or (800) 732-4236. Fax (609) 884-1236. www.virginiahotel.com. Twenty-four rooms with private baths. Doubles, $190 to $325 in July and August and weekends Memorial Day to mid-October. Rest of year, $135 to $275 weekends, $90 to $260 midweek. Three-night minimum weekends in season, two-night minimum midweek in summer and weekends rest of year.

Manor House, 612 Hughes St., Cape May 08204.

Amid Cape May's haute Victoriana and large inns with owners usually around only at breakfast or teatime, the Manor House is a refreshing change. The impressive, gambrel-roofed house with warm oak and chestnut foyer and striking furnishings seems almost contemporary in contrast.

Innkeepers Nancy and Tom McDonald from Philadelphia, who had stayed as guests here many times, considered the B&B a model when they bought it in 1995. They've maintained the tradition of good food, and added a secluded lower-level room with kingsize bed, full bath and private entrance.

Upstairs are nine guest rooms and a suite with private baths. They are nicely furnished in antiques, with brass and wood king or queensize beds, handmade quilts and light Victorian print wallpapers. A third-floor suite stretches across the front of the house with a kingsize bed, a sitting area and a whirlpool tub by the window in the bathroom. There are handmade "napping" signs for each door knob. Nancy plays "cookie fairy" at night, stocking the cookie jar with treats, including her favorite chocolate chip pecan hearts.

The McDonalds serve sumptuous breakfasts, employing many of the former innkeepers' recipes. Among favorites are "asparageggs" (poached eggs and asparagus on homemade English muffins with mornay sauce), a corn and egg pie with jalapeño cheese and tomato relish, vanilla whole-wheat waffles, a french toast sandwich made with raisin bread stuffed with cream cheese, apple crêpes and corn quiche. Juice, fresh fruit and sticky buns, a house signature, round out the meal.

Afternoon tea time brings cheese spreads, bean dip, salsa, coconut-macadamia bars and chocolate streusel bars. Guests partake in a front room with a striking stained-glass-front player piano or a library with two plush loveseats in front of a fireplace.

(609) 884-4710. Fax (609) 898-0471. Nine rooms and one suite with private baths. Doubles, $135 to $190, suite $220. Off-season, doubles $90 to $115, suite $150. Closed in January. Three-night minimum in July and August. Children over 12. No smoking. Closed in January.

The Inn on Ocean, 25 Ocean St., Cape May 08204.

A billiards table greets guests as they enter this B&B, which is furnished in light-hearted Victorian style. It's part of a billiards room just off the front entry, where owner Jack Davis's model Pontiac racing cars line the fireplace mantel and two of his seven sets of golf clubs are stashed in the corner. The room has a distinctly masculine air, an aspect that sets it apart from most B&B rooms in Cape May. Also unusual is this inn's theme of accommodations: five suites with private baths, oversize beds, TVs, wet bars, microwave ovens and thick carpeting.

Jack, who retired from General Motors, and his wife Katha opened their B&B in 1993 after a total overhaul of a three-story apartment house that was "barely fit for human habitation," in Katha's words. The walls are colorfully painted in sage green, pale yellow or pink, with coordinated fabrics and comforters. The bath in the Veranda Room was designed around an elaborate pedestal sink. A working clawfoot tub occupies a rear corner of the Promenade Room, while the shower is located in the bathroom. Besides sitting areas and the aforementioned amenities, Katha's lilting decor includes straw hats and accents like a pin cushion here and an old shaving brush and bowl there. A third-floor suite has a bedroom with a kingsize bed and a clawfoot tub, a glass-enclosed shower in the bathroom and a sitting room with fireplace and TV.

Guests enjoy a wicker-filled front porch, an open porch on the second floor

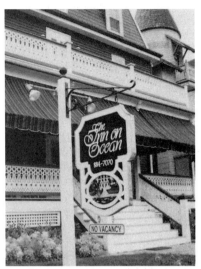

with a good view of the ocean at the end of the street, a parlor with a fireplace and a pleasant pink dining room, where the table can extend to seat twenty. This is the setting at 9 o'clock for some memorable breakfasts, employing different table settings every day. An apple baked in chardonnay, an omelet supreme with salsa and cornbread, and cinnamon coffeecake were the treats at our visit. French toast with fruit was the main event the next day. The professional nurse in her spurs Katha to "try to mitigate our sins with a lot of fresh fruit." She also offers heart-healthy breakfasts. Afternoon tea time brings sherry in front of the fireplace, lemonade and brownies on the front porch, and tea or wine and cheese.

Wide front porch at The Inn on Ocean.

Jack, who says his innkeeping wife is the toughest boss he ever had, gets in his licks as a golf instructor and as a basketball coach for local youth leagues. He also may tempt you into a game of billiards.

The Davises also rent a four-bedroom cottage a block from the ocean in Cape May Point for $2,000 a week in summer.

(609) 884-7070 or (800) 304-4477. Fax (609) 884-1384. www.theinnonocean.com. Five suites with private baths. June-September: doubles, $159 to $199; third-floor suite, $249 to $279. Off-season: doubles, $129 to $189; suite, $249 to $299. Three to four-night minimum summer weekends. No smoking. Closed January-March.

Inn at 22 Jackson, 22 Jackson St., Cape May 08204.

Presiding over the front parlor at this B&B is Minerva, a lady (?) ensconced at the edge of the sofa with her shoulders wrapped in mink, a wine bottle in the pocket of her apron and a wine glass in hand. "Minerva was our resident housekeeper," says innkeeper Barbara Masemore. "But guests kept sending her expensive gifts and she's too prissy now to clean house. So she minds Eliza, my mother's doll."

The presence of Minerva sets a whimsical tone for this B&B run by Barbara, an interior designer from Gettysburg, Pa., and her husband Chip, a contractor. They won a 1992 county beautification award for their restoration of this former apartment house, whose facade is strikingly vivid in navy blue and bright purple with white trim. Five suites come with king or queen beds, TVs, wet bars, microwave ovens and such. "We wanted to serve a different niche in Cape May," Barbara explained. "We tried to determine what Chip didn't like about B&Bs. He missed having TV, a gin and tonic at 5 o'clock and not being able to reheat his doggy bag from dinner for lunch the next day. So we offer modern conveniences, yet retain the charm of Victoriana."

Victoriana there is aplenty, from the unusual curved armoire in the Holly Suite to the clawfoot tub in the bathroom of the Windward Suite. And there are collections everywhere: Barbara's are dolls and majolica; Chip's are toys, games and depictions of bawdy women from days of yore – "the higher up in the house you go," says Barbara, "the bawdier they get." A mounted boar's head and a life-size cardboard cutout labeled Betty Boop oversee the sitting room of the Jackson Suite, whose porch faces Jackson Street. The two-bedroom Turret Suite on the third floor comes with a deck and a bathroom yielding an ocean view and a secret balcony for two overlooking Jackson Street. In back of the house is a two-story apartment annex that the innkeepers advertise as a cottage. It has a living room with gas fireplace and a kitchen on the main floor and two bedrooms with bath on the second floor, where a balcony affords an ocean view.

A full breakfast is served in the stunning dining room with bleached solid oak furniture, deep red painted walls and a ceiling trimmed with several showy Victorian wallpapers. The fare could be blueberry buckle and baked omelet with Canadian bacon, or baked apples with raisin-bread french toast and sausage. If you're so inclined, there's "fresh cereal right off the truck," a reference to the cereal boxes stashed in a truck on a shelf displaying toy vehicles and dolls. Afternoon tea also follows the alternating sweet and savory themes: chocolate-chip cake one day, baked crab spread the next.

(609) 884-2226 or (800) 452-8177. Fax (609) 884-0055. Five suites with private baths. One-bedroom suites, $95 to $250. Turret Suite and cottage, $135 to $300 for two, $180 to $400 for four. Two-night minimum stay weekends and in summer. Children over 12, younger in cottage. No smoking.

Leith Hall, 22 Ocean St., Cape May 08204.

In their colorful Victorian B&B (moss green with accents of deep peach and mustard), preservationists Elan and Susan Zingman-Leith are working miracles with wallpaper and paint. "We're trying to create an 'aesthetic movement' house," says Susan. Since Japanese things were the rage at that time, the parlor, with its Bradbury & Bradbury wallpaper dotted with swallows, plum blossoms and the rising sun has an anglo-Japanese look.

Eight guest accommodations, all with private baths, reflect the fun the couple has had with the painting techniques popular at the time. The Iris Room off the parlor has rag-rolled walls and a dragonfly and butterfly pattern on the ceiling. The floors are stenciled with lily pads. New in 1998 was the two-bedroom Audubon Suite "with everything anyone has ever asked for," in Elan's words: a queen brass bed in one room and two twins in the other, a gas fireplace, whirlpool tub and color TV, not to mention a paneled Bradbury & Bradbury frieze of birds and flowers plus other bird-related accessories.

Bedrooms on the second and third floors have views of the ocean (especially good on the third floor) and beds have been positioned so you can lie in bed and see the water. There are exotic touches, such as the white net draped from a ring over the bed in the checkerboard-stenciled Empire Room and silver and gold stars painted all over the ceiling in the Turkish Suite. The latter has an Arabian Nights feel, a queensize bed and a new whirlpool tub. Bathrooms sport nifty reproductions of ads from magazines of the era.

Breakfast is served in the small parlor (and the even smaller library off it) at two seatings, 8:30 and 9:30. Elan, the cook, loves to serve big breakfasts of perhaps scrambled eggs with cream cheese and dill, mixed berry pancakes or apple and cheese crêpes. There are always granola and fresh fruit as well. At teatime you might find scones and crumpets, brownies or even chocolate mousse cake. In summer it's served outside on the big wraparound porch.

Let us not overlook the sub-theme of Scotland. There are engravings of the town of Leith. The Highland Room on the second floor has wonderful murals from the highlands, stenciled thistles and now handpainted Scottish angels looking down from the sky on the ceiling. And in December Susan wraps balls for the Christmas tree in tartan. After only a few years of decorating, she says, "already my tastes are getting more complicated." We can't wait to see what she and Elan come up with next.

Meanwhile, they've co-authored a beautiful, insightful coffee-table photographic book called *The Secret Life of Victorian Houses*. Their own house shares many of the secrets.

(609) 884-1934. Five rooms and three suites with private baths. July-August and weekends June-October: doubles $130 to $175, suites $210 to $220. Fall to spring: doubles $85 to $125, suites $135 to $160. Three-night minimum weekends in season; two-night minimum weekends rest of year. Children over 12. No smoking.

The John F. Craig House, 609 Columbia Ave., Cape May 08204.

Some of the best breakfasts in town are served in this attractive carpenter gothic summer cottage dating to 1866. Frank Felicetti, formerly a lawyer in Wilmington, Del., and his wife Connie live in the house, so are more involved than was former owner David Clemans, who sold to open the Cucina Rosa restaurant here. About the only changes fnoted by longtime guests are hands-on innkeeping and evening turndown service, accompanied by homemade fudge or cookies – "whatever we've baked that day," say the enthusiastic cooks.

The house, which comes in two sections, contains seven air-conditioned guest rooms and a two-room suite. They are done in typical Cape May style, with lots of wicker and oriental rugs, marble-top tables and elaborate period wallpapers. Victorian linens and laces grace every window and turn up on tables and dresser tops as well as in antique crocheted bedspreads. All beds but one are queen or kingsize. Eastlake and Renaissance Revival antiques and original gasoliers prevail.

Blended coffees and teas are put out for early risers at 7:30. Breakfast is served at 8:30 and 9:45 seatings in the pretty dining room with its lace tablecloth and scallop-shell wallpaper. There are always seasonal fruits on the table as well as homemade muffins. The entrée, which comes out on a piping-hot plate garnished with fruit, could be anything from lemon french toast spiked with rum to a bacon and gruyère cheese casserole to eggs with cream cheese and scallions in a ramekin, accompanied by rosemary-flavored new potatoes. Blueberry-cornbread pancakes with grand marnier sauce are a house favorite. Herbed popovers, homemade sourdough or dark molasses breads, biscuits and coffeecake might accompany. Frank does the cooking, while Connie serves.

She also bakes the pastries and the goodies that accompany afternoon tea, put out on the sideboard in the dining room. Ginger cake, lemon-poppyseed bread, French pineapple upside-down cake, mushroom pâté with swiss cheese, hot artichoke dip and guacamole are among her specialties.

(609) 884-0100 or (877) 544-0314. Fax (609) 898-1307. Seven rooms and one suite with private baths. Doubles, $85 to $165. Suite, $125 to $190. Closed January and February.

Rhythm of the Sea, 1123 Beach Ave., Cape May 08204.

The name of this B&B derives, of course, from the ocean surf across the street. It also reflected the spring and fall concert series presented by visiting musicians in its huge living room centered by a concert grand piano under its former owners. New owners Wolfgang and Robyn Wendt have changed the theme in favor of a decided culinary emphasis.

The 1915 summer house is unusual here in that it is furnished simply in the Arts and Crafts style with Stickley furniture and Mission-style lanterns, wooden blinds and table linens. Almost everything is handmade in the Craftsman style. "Many guests say they're tired of Victorian clutter and frills," says Robyn. "They find this to be more masculine, more open and spacious."

Seven large bedrooms come with queensize beds and private baths, and the painted walls are done in the rose, pumpkin and olive palettes of the period. The look is spare and pure. The Wendts equipped the rooms with TV/VCRs, but in an era of cellular phones decided to forgo telephones in the room "to offer the getaway you deserve," according to Robyn, The new Library guest room, hidden behind bookshelves off the second-floor hallway, comes with a wicker settee and an ocean view from the bed. The Wendts, who moved into the rear carriage house, converted the former owners' quarters in the main house into a two-bedroom suite with a sitting room.

The couple relocated here in 1997 from Rock Hall, Md., where they had run a restaurant and managed the Inn at Osprey. Avid sportsmen who love to sail, they had met at a ski lodge in Colorado. Robyn, a well-traveled New Zealander, is into hospitality. Her German-born husband, a European-trained pastry chef, shows off his baking talents during afternoon tea and cooks four-course dinners for inn guests by reservation, $65 per person. He also teaches cooking classes.

"Guests have commented we should open a restaurant," Robyn reports. "We may take them up on that in the near future."

A full breakfast is offered from 8:30 to 9:30 at four tables in the huge dining room. Fresh juices and fruit precede the main course, a favorite being eggs oscar. Wolfgang bakes his own brioche with a cinnamon swirl, tops it with seasonal berries and accompanies it with peppered bacon.

(609) 884-7788 or (800) 498-6888. Seven rooms and a three-room suite with private baths. Mid-May through October: doubles $175 to $255, suite $355 for four. Rest of year: doubles $89 to $215, suite $295. Three-night minimum in summer and peak weekends.

The Southern Mansion, 720 Washington St., Cape May 08204.

For several years, all Cape May has been agog over the goings-on at the historic George Allen Estate, the town's largest and most elaborate mansion. Barbara and Rick Wilde, newly wed and barely turned 30, poured sweat equity and millions of dollars into restoring the 100-room Italianate villa into an elegant boutique hotel – claiming to be "the biggest and best in town."

Occupying much of a two-acre square block in the heart of Cape May, the house has ten fireplaces, shiny Honduran mahogany floors, twelve-foot-high molded ceilings, cast-bronze chandeliers, 23 gold mirrors and 5,000 square feet of verandas and solariums. Amazingly, the original furnishings, chandeliers and artworks were intact, many stored in the basement and ready to outfit ten more guest rooms added in a new wing.

Gilt and gold fabrics brighten Blue Master Bedroom at The Southern Mansion.

Financing the restoration with house tours (daily at 1, for $10 and much in demand) and the backing of her father, a Philadelphia physician, the couple opened in 1995 with the first of fifteen ample guest rooms on three floors of the main house. They vary widely but come with an assortment of ornate, step-up king and queen beds, televisions cosseted in armoires, gilt-edged mirrors and chairs, gold damask bedspreads and draperies, velvet recliners and settees, writing desks and telephones with modems. Some of the bathrooms are small with clawfoot tubs; others have huge walk-in tiled showers with seats.

The larger, more deluxe rooms in a new wing are the ultimate with kingsize beds, some with fireplaces, porches and double jacuzzis. One we saw has a poster bed of honduran mahogany matching the floor, fabric draperies puddling to the rich wood floor, oriental rugs, a Victorian settee and a TV hidden in a carved teak armoire. The bathroom has a two-person shower with tiled fish designs and a marble seat. Most deluxe is a bi-level suite with its own solarium.

Beside the wing is an Italianate pool with columns and a waterfall.

The main floor has a catering kitchen, an enlarged solarium restaurant seating 160 for sit-down dinners, and a ballroom with six gold mirrors that "looks like Versailles," as Barbara envisioned it. The bright aqua and butter-yellow ballroom of the main house is now a parlor with sofas, tables bearing vases of long-stemmed roses and end walls of 23-carat gold-leaf mirrors reflecting into infinity. Beyond is a sunken solarium where a full breakfast is offered for house guests. Typical entrées are eggs Chesapeake with hollandaise sauce, strawberry-yogurt pancakes and grand marnier french toast with raspberry compote. When we were there, it was set for a mouth-watering buffet lunch of crab cakes and salads for one of the corporate retreats to which the inn caters. Afternoon tea and wine and cheese with crudités are served in the parlor later in the day.

In 2000, Barbara planned a gradual move into a full-service restaurant for house guests in the enlarged solarium. Already, chef Brian Parker was preparing prix-fixe dinners on Saturday nights ($65 for four courses). The fare included lobster bisque or coconut shrimp with mango salsa, caesar salad, and perhaps lobster alfredo, jerked red snapper, filet of beef or grilled lamb stuffed with smoked mushroom mousseline.

"We offer the amenities of a hotel but retain the antiques and charm of a B&B," said Barbara, now a mother of two and relieved of day-to-day operations by a general manager. Then, with a sweep of her arm as she surveyed the nearly completed scene, she added: "We did it. I mean, we really did it."

(609) 884-7171 or (800) 381-3888. Fax (609) 898-0492. Twenty-four rooms and one suite with private baths. Summer and weekends off-season: doubles, $200 to $305, suite $325 to $360. Off-season: doubles, $190 to $285 weekends, $140 to $275 midweek. Suite, $300 to $325 weekends, $265 to $290 midweek. Two-night minimum midweek and three nights on weekends in July and August. Two-night minimum weekends rest of year.

Dining Spots

Daniel's on Broadway, 416 South Broadway, West Cape May.

Meals here have been likened to dining in a private home, but with a difference. The owner is a fabulous cook, and the house is a beauty. Harry and Kristin Gleason opened it as a restaurant that captivated Cape May with its style, charm and food.

Harry said he "wanted a change" after running his family's restaurant outside Valley Forge, Pa. He built an addition onto the previous kitchen in the oldest rear portion of the handsome yellow Victorian/Colonial house, which dates to the 18th century. Five diminutive dining areas on two floors seat a total of 95 amidst swagged windows, antique chandeliers, ornate six-foot mirrors, and splashy floral arrangements. Well-spaced tables are set with cream cloths, large stemware and shaded oil lamps.

Chef Harry offers contemporary American fare, artfully composed and presented. For appetizers, he might sear peppered ahi tuna with sesame aioli, scallion-infused oil and wasabi and accompany with vegetable confetti, or glaze coconut beer-battered shrimp with Jamaican rum and serve with grilled mango. The Tuscan salad is a tomato tower layered with mozzarella, prosciutto and basil, drizzled with balsamic vinegar and extra-virgin olive oil.

Signature entrées are grouper Charleston, sautéed with lobster, corn, leeks and plum tomatoes in a lobster-sherry sauce, duet of duck (caramelized breast and confit of duck strudel with a red currant and port wine reduction) and filet mignon stuffed with stilton cheese, sauced with shiitake mushrooms in red wine and served with herb mashed potatoes and fried spinach.

Chocolate lava cake in a ramekin, frozen grand-marnier soufflé and triple berry napoleon are winning desserts.

(609) 898-8770. Entrées, $23 to $27. Dinner nightly, from 5. Sunday brunch 11:15 to 1:30. Closed in January. BYOB.

The Ebbitt Room, The Virginia Hotel, 25 Jackson St., Cape May.

Named for the original owners of Cape May's first hotel, the small, candlelit

Elegant Ebbitt Room provides fine dining at Virginia Hotel.

dining room in the restored Virginia Hotel is an exceptionally pleasant setting for some of the best food in Cape May. In a town where restaurants get noisy and hectic, this remains an oasis of calm and professionalism, one worthy of owner Curtis Bashaw's aspirations for a small boutique hotel. Elegant in peach and gray, the high-ceilinged room has swagged draperies, crisply linened tables, delicate wine glasses, art deco wall sconces and birds of paradise standing tall in vases on dividers.

New 30-year-old executive chef Michael Merlo, who trained at leading Philadelphia restaurants, continues the tradition of fine American cuisine. His main dishes range from pepper-crusted salmon with mustard-chive sauce and cumin-crusted scallops with red pepper vinaigrette to pan-roasted New Zealand rack of lamb with red wine sauce.

Excellent hot rolls with a crisp crust preceded our appetizers, one an eggplant and gorgonzola crostini served with red onion pesto and the other a very zesty caesar salad, both served on black octagonal plates. The roast cornish game hen was heavily herbed and rested on a bed of caramelized vegetables on a parsley-flecked plate, and the filet mignon was served with a grilled three-onion salad and roasted potatoes. On another occasion we liked the shrimp margarita, flamed in tequila and served with avocado cream sauce and roasted tomato salsa, and the pan-roasted quail with grapes and green peppercorns. These came with a medley of zucchini and carrots, and potatoes shaped like mushrooms.

For dessert, we enjoyed an upside-down fig cake and pecan-praline cheesecake. Service by young waitresses is graceful and competent. And the live piano music emanating from the lobby lends a glamorous air to this fine addition to the Cape May dining scene.

(609) 884-5700 or (800) 732-4236. Entrées, $22 to $30. Dinner nightly, from 5:30.

Water's Edge, Beach Drive and Pittsburgh Avenue, Cape May.
Chef-owner Neil Elsohn and his wife Karen, who is hostess, offer some of the most inspired dishes in town in this sleek, hotel-style dining room in front of La

Mer Motor Inn. The well-tailored expanse of banquettes and booths is dressed in white cloths topped with rose-colored runners and flickering votive candles.

On one occasion, we enjoyed an appetizer of strudel with escargots, pinenuts and an ethereal garlic cream sauce before digging into poached fillet of Norwegian salmon with lime and salmon caviar, and sautéed sea scallops with tomatillos, cilantro and grilled jicama. On our second visit, we grazed happily through appetizers and salads. These included scallop chowder, spicy pork and scallion empanadas with pineapple-ginger chutney, fusilli with grilled tuna, oriental vegetables and szechuan vinaigrette, and grilled chicken salad with toasted pecans, grilled red onions, mixed greens and citrus vinaigrette.

Main courses include such standouts as blackened tuna steak with mango-lime hollandaise, seared shrimp with creole mustard sauce, and grilled pork tenderloin with spicy black bean sauce and crispy sweet plantains. Desserts could be raspberry cheesecake with citrus anglaise, banana-bread pudding with hot chocolate sauce and bittersweet chocolate-walnut pâté with espresso and vanilla sauces.

In summer, a lounge menu is served in the spacious bar. Salads and appetizers are available there anytime. The brunch menu contains some exotic items; the meal is quite salubrious when taken on the outdoor deck with ocean beyond.

(609) 884-1717. Entrées, $23 to $32. Dinner nightly from 5, mid-June to Columbus Day; Wednesday-Sunday in off-season and weekends in winter. Closed January to Valentine's Day.

410 Bank Street, 410 Bank St., Cape May.

This restaurant's enclosed outdoor courtyard, enveloped in plants and tiny white lights, is a lovely setting for dinner. Owners Steve and Janet Miller, who also run an Italian restaurant called Frescos next door, are theater set designers and their background shows.

A Chinese chef presents a gumbo of New Orleans, French and Caribbean dishes, many grilled over mesquite wood and most with cajun-creole overtones. We loved the special seviche and butterflied quail on warmed greens for appetizers, which also included Bahamian yellowfin tuna beignets and fresh Jersey asparagus amandine in a puff-pastry cornet.

Among entrées are shellfish filé gumbo, blackened prime rib and baby rack of lamb with foie gras. Our choices of blackened red snapper with pecan sauce and yellowfin tuna in Barbadian black bean sauce, served with crisp vegetables and rice pilaf, were too much to finish. After all, we had to save room for the highly rated key lime pie, which was the real thing. So is everything else, from crawfish bisque to possibly the best bread pudding with hot bourbon sauce you'll ever taste. There's even a French-style roast – a special meat, fowl or game dish offered nightly.

If you can't eat on the courtyard, settle for one of the screened porches or the small, intimate dining rooms adorned with New Orleans posters inside the restored 1840 house.

(609) 884-2127. Entrées, $23.50 to $30.95. Dinner nightly, 5 to 11, May to mid-October. BYOB.

Union Park Dining Room, 727 Beach Drive, Cape May.

The restaurant in the 85-year-old Hotel Macomber has been infused with new spirit and style by Crystal and Charles Czworkowski, she a hotel general manager and he an attorney in Boston. They moved to the town where she had summered with her parents to buy and operate the 34-room beachfront hotel in 1996.

Crystal oversees the interior dining room, a high-ceilinged, summery space appointed mostly in white and evocative of the Cape May of the 1930s. The chef's contemporary fare and presentation earn good reviews.

We liked the sound of everything on the menu, which ranges widely from pan-roasted Alaskan halibut with an olivada broth to a signature roasted rack of Wyoming lamb with dijon herb crust, often presented wigwam style with asparagus spears perched over garlic-mashed potatoes.

Favorite starters are caramelized diver scallops with a coconut-cucumber salad, grilled portobello mushroom stuffed with lump crabmeat and cheese, and a layered parfait of Scottish smoked salmon and

Setting is summery at Union Park.

lump crabmeat with crème fraîche and bermuda onions, two chives rising like antenna with a dollop of black caviar between.

Amid the complexities are three signature dishes named for the owners' young children. One is Daughter Cezanne's apple cloud, crisp phyllo triangles holding sautéed apples, flanked by a scoop of vanilla ice cream and a pool of hot caramel sauce. The triple chocolate terrine comes with a tangy raspberry-cranberry coulis.

(609) 884-8811. Entrées, $24 to $28. Dinner nightly, from 5, Mother's Day to October. Closed weekdays in off-season and mid-December to mid-March. BYOB.

The Washington Inn, 801 Washington St., Cape May.

Surrounded by shade trees and colorful banks of impatiens, this historic white building run by brothers David and Michael Craig is considered far and away the best of the larger restaurants in town. Originally a plantation house built in 1840, it contains four elegant dining rooms, including a Victorian garden room and a pretty wicker-filled front veranda done up in pink.

And although it offers no lodging, the glamorous and atmospheric establishment has the feeling of an inn. Check out the upstairs ladies' room, which an innkeeper termed the nicest in the entire state. Beautifully decorated in florals, it has a window seat and fresh flowers on the vanity. Personal touches abound, not the least of which is the beautiful mahogany bar that founder Arthur Craig crafted for the lounge.

Executive chef Mimi Wood's American/continental menu blends the traditional with the more creative. Start with her signature sea scallops wrapped in bacon, or perhaps garlicky escargots with tomato and fennel tapenade or a crab cake with a creamy roasted pepper sauce. At a recent visit, we liked the sound of her specials, creamy mustard scallop bisque, shrimp louis and grilled portobello mushroom stuffed with shiitakes, crabmeat and smoked gouda.

For main courses, she might stuff flounder with crab imperial and top it with a brandy lobster cream sauce, and pan sear sesame-crusted salmon with ginger-mirin beurre blanc and a dollop of wasabi. A sauté of shrimp and scallops tossed with tomatoes and garlic, served over pepper-speckled linguini, is called Jewel of Provence. The grilled Kansas sirloin might be flavored with cambozola, roasted vidalia onions, cracked pepper and red wine reduction. The rack of lamb, rubbed with olive oil and herbs, is served with a pineapple-mint essence.

The menu ends with "romantic international coffees." Desserts could be frozen key lime pie, crème brûlée, strawberry napoleons and lemon-glazed cheesecake with raspberry sauce.

The 10,000-bottle wine cellar earns the Wine Spectator Grand Award.

More than 300 recipes are published in the fine *Washington Inn Cooks for Friends* cookbook.

(609) 884-5697. Entrées, $18.95 to $31.95. Dinner nightly, 5 to 10, May-October; Wednesday-Sunday 5 to 9, rest of year.

Peaches at Sunset, 1 Sunset Blvd., West Cape May.

Cape May's prettiest restaurant may be this establishment with an offbeat name, derived from chef-owner George Pechin's nickname and its location at the head of Sunset Boulevard.

A nicely restored Victorian house, vivid in peach with aqua trim, holds two small dining rooms divided by a walnut-trimmed aquarium full of tropical fish. Overhead are a stained-glass panel and a wild tropical design on the ceiling. Dining is al fresco on a raised rear deck leading to a gazebo with a few pint-size tables.

The contemporary dinner menu might offer eight entrées, among them Caribbean-style shrimp with rum and mint sauce, Cuban chicken stuffed with prosciutto and plantains, grilled duck breast with peach sauce and tournedos of beef with twin tapenades of artichokes and olives.

Start with the creamy clam chowder that we once savored during lunch at the owner's former Peaches Cafe, the signature roasted garlic served with mascarpone cheese and grilled sourdough bread or Thai crab served in endive leaves. Finish with bourbon-pecan pie or crème caramel.

(609) 898-0100. Entrées, $18.95 to $25.95. Dinner nightly from 4:30, May-October; weekends rest of year. BYOB.

Cucina Rosa, 301 Washington St. Mall, Cape May.

David Clemans, who has a reputation as one of the best cooks in town, opened this authentic and popular Italian restaurant after selling the John F. Craig House, his B&B of many years.

"We take relatively standard southern Italian dishes and make them very carefully," says David. Everything is done from scratch, from the marinara and meat sauces to semolina bread.

Main dishes run from basic pastas to lobster oreganata. Widely acclaimed is the chicken portofino, stuffed with mozzarella and Italian sausage specially made for the restaurant, rolled and baked with tomato sauce and served with pasta. Other treats include grilled swordfish and lamb chops, each marinated in olive oil and Italian spices and served with fried potatoes sautéed with peppers and onions or pasta with a choice of sauce.

Desserts are David's forte. He makes fruit pies that change daily, lemon cheesecake and a rich chocolate cake. He also offers ice creams and sherbets.

The 64-seat restaurant in rose and green is at a corner location along the mall. It spills outside with sixteen tables on a sidewalk patio in season.

(609) 898-9800. Entrées, $12.95 to $18.95. Dinner nightly, 5 to 10, Sunday 4:30 to 9:30. Closed January to mid-February. BYOB.

The Mansion House, 311 Mansion St.

"Sorry we missed the last 143 years," said the sign hailing the arrival in spring 2000 of an upscale seafood restaurant. Perry and Susan Collier were transforming a Civil War-era summer cottage built after the original Mansion House, a huge Cape May hotel, burned in 1857. They own the popular Collier's Liquor Store at the other end of the edge-of-downtown block.

The Colliers added a dining porch and a modern kitchen to the small two-story house that now seats about 50 for fine dining. Keeping it in the family, son Aaron is the restaurant manager.

The menu was being finalized by chef Joe Lotozo, whose food we loved when he was at the old Bayberry Inn in a corner of the Congress Hall hotel. Later the first chef at the Ebbitt Room in the Virginia Hotel, he planned to feature "eclectic seafood" here in the traditional and contemporary American style.

(609) 884-0200. Entrées, $18 to $28. Dinner nightly, from 5. Closed January and February.

Diversions

Victorian Cape May. The nation's largest concentration of Victorian gingerbread structures – some 670, ranging from cottages to sprawling hotels – is on display in the historic district. The best way to see them is on foot or bicycle or, better, through a variety of tours offered by the Mid-Atlantic Center for the Arts, (800) 275-4278. MAC offers two distinct **guided trolley tours:** the East End (the best if you only have time for one) and the West End. Each takes about half an hour and costs $5.50. MAC guides also lead several **walking tours,** each 90 minutes and $5. MAC sponsors boat cruises, moonlight trolley rides, gourmet brunch walks, kitchen tours, an Inns and Outs of Cape May tour and Cape May INNteriors Tours and Teas. Individual inns are opened for tours under their own auspices as well as through Mansions by Gaslight, Victorian Sampler and Christmas Inns tours.

Emlen Physick House and Estate, 1048 Washington St., (609) 884-5404. The eighteen-room house designed by Victorian architect Frank Furness was the first to be saved by MAC and the property serves as its headquarters. Many of the original furnishings have been returned to the house for display purposes. Tour highlights include an upstairs library with Japanese wallpaper, even on the ceiling, the owner's bachelor bedroom and the fan collection in his mother's bedroom. Cape May's only Victorian house museum has restored the Carriage House Gallery for changing exhibitions. It also offers **The Twinings Tearoom,** where tea luncheons and afternoon tea are offered daily inside amidst old horse stables and outside on a canopied patio. Forty-five-minute house tours cost $7.

Cape May Point Lighthouse, Cape May Point State Park. MAC continues to restore this 1859 landmark, which has been reopened for tours. The hardy climb the 199 tower stairs to the Watch Room Gallery just below the lantern for a panoramic view (adults, $4). A visitor center in the restored Oil House on the lighthouse grounds contains a photo mural showing the lighthouse view, a twelve-minute video detailing the structure and a museum shop.

Performing Arts. MAC sponsors a spring series of chamber music concerts known as the **Cape May Music Festival.** The East Lynne Company, an equity group in residence here in summer, presents a **Victorian Theater Festival** July through September. **Cape May Stage** mounts a number of summer shows at the Welcome Center, while the **Chalfonte Cabaret** is staged weekends at the Chalfonte Hotel. Live performances are part of three-day **Victorian Holmes Mystery Weekends** in March and November.

Birding and Wildlife. Cape May lies on the heavily populated Atlantic Flyway and more than 400 species of birds head north and south through Cape May Point. Good areas for nature-watching include South Cape May Meadow, Cape May Point State Park, Higbee's Beach Wildlife Management Area and the Cape May Bird Observatory.

Swimming is fine along Cape May's beach (the required beach passes may be purchased, and often are complimentary to inn guests), and at Higbee's and Sunset beaches and Cape May Point State Park.

Shopping. Despite its Victorian charm and influx of tourists, Cape May's forte is not shopping, although the situation has improved lately. The Washington Street Mall is where most of the action is. Our favorite here is **The Whale's Tale,** a ramble of rooms containing everything from shell magnets to an extraordinary collection of cards. Another good gift shop is **McDowell's Gallery of Gifts. For the Birds** carries excellent things for nature lovers and **Swede Things** speaks for itself. Check out the wallpaper borders and elegant fixtures at **Fralinger's** original saltwater taffy emporium, even if you're not into taffy. **Love the Cook,** a gourmet kitchen shop chock full of goodies, is run by Rhona Craig of the Washington Inn. The **Cape May Linen Outlet** offers good bargains, especially in placemats.

Extra-Special _____

Cape May Diamonds, Cape May Point.

A lot of fuss is made over the quartz pebbles found only locally and known as Cape May Diamonds. The semi-precious stones of diverse colors vary from the size of little peas to marbles and walnuts. They're bright and clear when found in the wet sand, but, alas, they become dull as they dry. When cut and polished, they can be set in gold or silver to make attractive jewelry such as rings, bracelets and necklaces. One of the best places to find Cape May diamonds is at Sunset Beach in Cape May Point, where you'll also see the shell of the USS Atlantis, a World War I concrete ship that ran aground in a storm and has been trapped here ever since. We burrowed into the sand here looking for "diamonds" and finally latched onto someone who seemed to know what he was doing. He demonstrated how to separate the good stones from the bad, or we'd never have known.

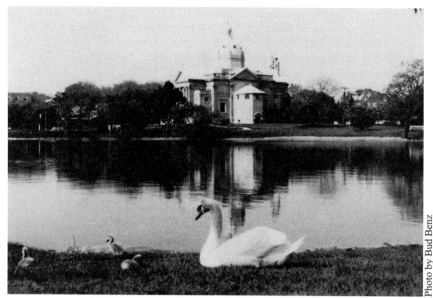

Photo by Bud Benz

Landmark St. Catharine's Church faces parkland across Spring Lake.

Spring Lake, N.J.

Jewel of the Jersey Shore

Among the seaside towns strung out along the Jersey shore is one that stands apart. No boardwalk bric-a-brac. No honky-tonk. No video arcades. No hangouts for young singles.

Spring Lake planned it that way. A century of tight zoning regulations and community resolve has produced a genteel enclave of substantial homes, manicured lawns, a tree-lined shopping district, a pristine boardwalk and not one but three lakes a stone's throw from the sea. All this within a long hour's drive of New York City or Philadelphia.

Enterprising developers launched Spring Lake in the late 19th century. They planned four neighboring towns, each having its own railroad station and a lavish hotel catering to a wealthy clientele from Philadelphia, northern New Jersey and New York. Additional hotels, large guest houses and elegant estates followed. The four communities united to become Spring Lake, which celebrated its centennial in 1992.

The town retains the elegance of its past. The Warren Hotel clings to its summer social season. The stately Spring Lake Community House accommodates a library and theater groups in manorial surroundings. The recreation commission sponsors summer concerts at the park gazebo and model-boat regattas on Spring Lake. The 1992 Centennial Clock, with benches and colorful flowers at its base, would be at home in a European town square.

This is an eminently livable community for those who can afford houses starting at $300,000 and oceanfront properties of $1 million or more. The two-mile shoreline is pristine, its boardwalk uncluttered by anything more than a few covered benches and pavilions containing swimming pools at either end. Weeping willows frame and wooden footbridges cross Spring Lake, the meandering, natural spring lake in the center of town. It and two other lakes at either end of town yield a landscape rare for a seaside community.

No chain motels are among the 26 lodging establishments, ranging from old hotels to B&Bs, and no more can be licensed. The number of rooms has declined recently from 1,000 to 500, so the population of 5,000 year-round increases only to about 6,000 in summer. "The town consciously chose to stay a community rather than become a resort," says Michael Robertson, innkeeper at the Normandy Inn and former executive director of the Chamber of Commerce. "For a quiet, romantic getaway, this is the place – only an hour away from everything, but an island of tranquility."

Inn Spots

Hollycroft, 506 North Blvd., Box 448, Spring Lake 07762.

Hidden behind a curtain of holly in a wooded residential area, this 1908 mountain-style hunting lodge is unique in the area. You'd expect to find it in the Adirondacks, perhaps, but not at the Jersey Shore. When you're sitting in the living room, you can look out across Lake Como and see the Atlantic beyond. In summer it's like being in the country with an ocean view; in the winter, when the towering ironstone fireplace is ablaze, it's like a ski lodge with an ocean view. That's the way the original owners planned it – one partner wanted a shore house and the other a mountain house, so this oversize log cabin in the Arts and Crafts style was their compromise.

"We bought it in 1985 as a private home, tore it apart and have been putting it back together ever since," said Mark Fessler, an architect and innkeeper with his wife Linda. Their handiwork has produced one of the more inviting and charming B&Bs we've seen. The public areas on the sprawling first floor include a large and welcoming living room paneled in knotty pine, a log-beamed dining room and a brick-floored sun porch with fireplace beside the flagstone terrace, all taking advantage of the lake/ocean view. Stylishly and with great taste, the house displays portions of Linda's multitude of collectibles, from miniature English cottages to a Sicilian donkey cart chair.

The Fesslers have decorated in eclectic country style eight comfortable guest quarters with private baths. All but two have king or queen beds and four have fireplaces. Each room comes with bottles of Perrier and the Hollycroft's own soaps. Unusual touches abound: a custom-made iron bed with a twig bird cage atop the canopy

Formal dining room is set for breakfast at Sea Crest by the Sea.

and lace curtains around the headboard in the Grasmere room, a twig accessory hanging from the rafters and on the wall behind the queen bed in the Somerset. The Ambleside has an English scrub pine canopy bed shipped back from one of the couple's many trips to England, a clawfoot tub and a private porch with a hanging swing seat. A favorite room is the spacious Cotswold Cottage at the far end of the main floor. It has a king bed, ivy painted on one wall, a wicker sofa, a window seat, Cotswold cottages pictured on the wallpaper border and in prints on the walls, and floral fabrics on the bedspread, curtains and table skirts. Another favorite is the Windsor mini-suite with queen bed and fireplace, sitting room with TV/VCR and a soaking tub for two.

The most deluxe is a cathedral-ceilinged suite, aptly named Lords of the Manor. It offers a queensize French iron canopy bed beneath hand-painted clouds and sky on the ceiling, a chaise and two leather chairs facing a massive stone fireplace, a small sitting room, TV and wet bar, and a wicker-furnished screened balcony facing the lake. The bathroom has a separate shower and a soaking tub for two beside an arched window looking onto the water.

Talented Linda decorates lavishly for the seasons and makes all the handicrafts, which are for sale in her little Hollycroft Country Store off the entry.

The Fesslers put out a substantial buffet breakfast on a sideboard and table in the dining room. It's likely to include juices, fresh fruit, black-raspberry crumbles, Irish soda bread, raspberry-chocolate chip muffins and creamy scrambled eggs or ham and cheese egg strata. Sherry awaits in the living room in the afternoons.

(732) 681-2254 or (800) 679-2554. Fax (732) 280-8145. Five rooms and two suites with private baths. Mid-May through September: doubles, $145 to $165; suites, $235 to $295. Rest of year: doubles, $125 to $145; suites, $215 to $275. Two-night minimum weekends in summer. Smoking restricted

Sea Crest by the Sea, 19 Tuttle Ave., Spring Lake 07762.

New owners Fred and Barbara Vogel have purchased this old-timer on a residential street half a block from the ocean. In a town where Victoriana reigns only slightly less preciously than in Cape May, their twelve-bedroom inn finds its own niche. "We're more eclectic," said the innkeeper. "We cater to adult fantasy and romance."

That translates to a Christmas wonderland in the Sleigh Ride Room, the Velveteen Rabbit Room for a favorite childhood tale, a stars and stripes ribbon around the portrait in the G. Washington Room, a cocoon of butterflies in the Papillon and a beaded curtain through which you enter the Casablanca Room. A favorite is the third-floor Yankee Clipper, where windows yield a view of the ocean to the east and south. A card lists the furniture in each room and guest diaries reveal the thoughts of previous occupants.

The former library on the main floor has become the Queen Victoria Suite, with canopy feather bed, sitting room with fireplace and small refrigerator, and a bath with separate shower and jacuzzi for two. A soaking tub for two occupies space at the side of the sitting room in the similarly appointed Teddy Roosevelt Suite, which also has a private balcony.

All rooms possess queensize beds, private baths with Caswell-Massey toiletries and TV/VCRs. Eight rooms have fireplaces and several have feather beds. The beds are dressed in linens of Egyptian cotton, French damask and Belgian lace and have six pillows on top. Equally fetching are the common areas, from a graceful living room to a luxurious wraparound veranda to a dining room with a majestic French oak table and sideboard. The dining room has been expanded lately into what was once the original kitchen with a wood stove, so that when the inn is full, all 24 guests can be served at once.

The Vogels serve a bountiful gourmet breakfast starting, as their brochure puts it, at the civilized hour of 9 o'clock. Fresh fruit, homemade granola, muffins and scones are accompanied by a Scandinavian blend of coffee reduced in caffeine. The main event could be frittata, featherbed eggs or french toast. Afternoon tea is served beside the player piano.

(732) 449-9031 or (800) 803-9031. Fax (732) 974-0403. Ten rooms and two suites with private baths. Mid-May through September: doubles, $165 to $235; suites, $275. Rest of year: doubles, $155 to $169; suites, $255. Two-night minimum June-September (three nights on weekends). Two-night minimum weekends rest of year. No children. No smoking.

Normandy Inn, 21 Tuttle Ave., Spring Lake 07762.

Haute Victoriana reigns inside this five-tone olive green and gold Italianate villa with Queen Anne accents – the only Spring Lake B&B to be listed on the National Register. Innkeepers Michael and Susan Ingino note that only two pieces of furniture remain from the inn they purchased in 1982. They have renovated and replaced with authenticity and prized antiques.

The mood is set in a pair of fancy pink and red common rooms containing a rococo damask parlor set, an antique English tall case clock and marble sculptures. A Chickering grand piano occupies center stage in the huge, pillared dining room, where there's an extensive breakfast menu as well as daily specials for house guests. Complimentary wine is available all day on the side sun porch, where there's a television set, baskets hang from the ceiling and wicker furniture makes a comfy retreat.

Upstairs on the second and third floors are fifteen air-conditioned guest rooms and a suite with crocheted bedspreads and lace curtains. Two large second-floor front corner rooms are most prized. One has a tester bed whose posts are at least

Guests are accommodated in high style in Normandy Inn.

ten feet high, two upholstered chairs beside a table and a private porch. The other has a queen bed with a nine-foot burled wood headboard. Among the treasures are an 1860 signed Herter bed, a woven Brussels carpet and a reproduction of the bedroom wallpaper from the home of Robert Todd Lincoln. Victorian lamps, old portraits and antique furnishings dignify the rooms. Some on the third floor are rather small, although two at the rear have been turned into the Audenreid Suite with a sitting area, a gas fireplace, a kingsize bedroom and a soaking tub.

Two new rooms on the rear of the main floor have been fashioned from the owners' quarters. The result is a large room with fireplace and an impressive bathroom with peacock wallpaper, a marble jacuzzi, separate shower and a chocolate-brown w.c.

Telephones and televisions lately have been incorporated into all bedrooms. Michael and Jeri Robertson have joined the Normandy as resident innkeepers.

(732) 449-7172 or (800) 449-1888. Fax (732) 449-1070. www.normandyinn.com. Seventeen guest rooms and one suite with private baths. June-September: doubles, $147 to $215, suites $297. Rest of year: doubles, $116 to $169; suites, $250. Two-night minimum in July and August (three nights on weekends); two-night minimum weekends rest of year except in winter. Well-behaved children accepted.

La Maison, 404 Jersey Ave., Spring Lake 07762.

Spring Lake's oldest guest facility is now a spiffy, French-style B&B, owned and operated by Julianne Corrigan. Taking over from a francophile in 1999, she claimed at age 32 to be the youngest innkeeper in New Jersey, but experienced from her work as a property manager in New York.

La Maison offers five rooms and two suites, all with private baths, TVs, telephones, queensize French-style sleigh beds, country French reproduction furniture, all-white duvets and down comforters, balloon curtains on the windows, Monet prints or original artworks on the walls and cozy sitting areas. The two-room Monet Suite, one of three guest quarters on the third floor, is enhanced by beautiful French wallpaper in blue and yellow. The Louis XVI Room on the first floor has a new double jacuzzi, teak accessories and flooring, and a TV/VCR.

Out back is a small efficiency cottage called La Petite Maison. It has a wicker and leather sitting room with a sofabed and TV, a queen sleigh bed in an alcove, a clawfoot tub in the skylit bathroom, a New York-style kitchen and a couple of porches, plus a barbecue grill for occupants.

The French theme continues during breakfast each morning. Creative fruit dishes, perhaps poached pears in an orange-raspberry sauce, precede a main dish of belgian waffles, goat cheese omelets, quiche lorraine or crème brûlée french toast. Julie garnishes each with fresh herbs picked from her garden. Tartes tatin, baguettes, breakfast pastries, granola and cappuccino or espresso accompany. The meal is taken in a chandeliered dining room or on the wraparound front porch. In the afternoon, brie and other cheeses, breads and fruit are offered.

Besides hospitality, La Maison is known for fine art. The walls of its entry and living room are hung with paintings, some collected by Julie's brother and others by watercolor artist Paula Jordan, who lives across the street. The works of the local artists are for sale.

The library features more artworks collected by Julie's brother as well as leather-bound editions of literary classics.

(732) 449-0969 or (800) 276-2088. Fax (732) 449-4860. www.lamaisoninn.com. Five rooms, two suites and one cottage with private bath. Mid-May to mid-September: doubles, $185 to $255; suites, $235 to $250; cottage, $325. Rest of year: doubles, $125 to $195; suites, $150 to $185; cottage, $220 to $255. Midweek: deduct $25. Children under 16 in cottage. Three-night minimum in July, August and holiday weekends, two-night minimum rest of year. No smoking.

Victoria House, 214 Monmouth Ave., Spring Lake 07762.

Masses of impatiens and a giant hydrangea bush brighten the exterior of this gray-green, Queen Anne-style residence with white gingerbread trim and an extra-large wraparound veranda furnished in wicker. Built in 1882 and a guest house for some years, it was revived in 1993 by owners Robert and Louise Goodall. "We've hung 250 double rolls of wallpaper and refinished all the floors," said Louise, who was busy performing both functions at our first midweek visit to get the house ready for Spring Lake's annual Christmas tour.

What do-it-yourself elbow grease, modest carpentry talents and a terrific eye for design can do is manifest throughout the Goodalls' house, but most particularly in their six guest rooms and two suites. Two of the most popular make the most of their corner turrets. "There seems to be something about being in a turret that guests like." The newest quarters with a turret stretches across the front of the house. It's the Manor Suite with kingsize mahogany bed and a decor of Ralph Lauren fabrics. A double arched entrance leads into a sitting room with antique fireplace, TV/VCR, CD player and refrigerator. The other turret room is the Rose Rendezvous with a kingsize bed, sitting area and a fireplace.

An armoire made from a gun cabinet enhances the Garden Bouquet Room, and a colorful quilt tops the kingsize bed in Cottage. The antique armoire gives the rich blue and burgundy Eastlake Room its name, while its sitting area with a fireplace adds warmth. The Delft & Wicker Room lives up to its title with a blue and white decorative scheme and lots of wicker. Two rear rooms that shared a bath have been turned into the Victorian Hideaway suite with raised ceiling and a spiffy sitting area, plus a two-person whirlpool tub.

Lavish landscaping and wraparound veranda greet guests at Victoria House.

The common areas are equally compelling. There's a TV in the turreted parlor, and four original stained-glass windows brighten the stairway landing. A rare hand carved, Circassian walnut sideboard matches the chairs flanking individual lace-covered tables in the dining room. A full breakfast is served here or on the side porch, overlooking the showplace small garden created by Robert, a landscape architect. Typical fare involves juice, fruit, granola and a main dish, perhaps cheese strata, quiche or french toast. One guest wrote in the hall diary that the waffles with peach sauce were out of this world.

Louise, who did the decorating, is a fulltime mother as well as a hands-on innkeeper. Her husband helps nights and weekends.

(732) 974-1882 or (888) 249-6252. Fax (732) 974-9702. Six rooms and two suites with private baths. Mid-May through September: doubles: $155 to $215; suites, $250 to $325. Rest of year: doubles, $115 to $175; suites, $195 to $275. Two-night minimum stay in July and August and weekends in season. Children over 12. No smoking.

The Chateau, Fifth and Warren Avenues, Spring Lake 07762.

Billing itself as the Tiffany of Spring Lake's small hotels, this is gradually becoming less hotel-like and more like a large B&B. The evolution involves a conscious decision of owner Scott Smith to offer elegant accommodations, personal service and, given the size of rooms and their amenities, good value for Spring Lake. The main lobby has been expanded to include a showy breakfast area, full of chintz floral armchairs at pink-linened tables. Continental breakfast is offered here – free midweek in the winter and $4.99 the rest of the time.

The hotel, dating to 1888 and in Scott's family for 49 years, is located at the end of Spring Lake and overlooks two parks and the town gazebo. Thirty-nine guest rooms and suites are in three buildings characterized by lots of public spaces, from decks to porches to a second-floor gazebo. Ceiling fans, wicker furniture and Waverly fabrics are the common denominator in each room. All also have TV/VCRs, refrigerators, wet bars, marble bathrooms and two phones with data ports. The ultimate are ten luxury suites with wood-burning fireplaces and jacuzzis or soaking tubs for two. We were happy to be ensconced in a large "classic parlor" with a sitting area, wet bar and two double beds in the Villa. A former residence facing the town gazebo, it contains six rooms that had been the Chateau's best until they were surpassed by the addition built in 1989 to house luxury suites, some with private balconies or porches.

(732) 974-2000. Fax (732) 974-0007. Thirty-nine guest rooms and suites with private baths. Mid-June to early September: doubles, $159 to $239; suites, $219 to $269. Spring and fall: doubles, $99 to $169; suites, $129 to $179. Winter: doubles, $69 to $125; suites, $99 to $139. Three-night minimum weekends in summer; two nights in spring and fall.

White Lilac Inn, 414 Central Ave., Spring Lake 07762.

Built around 1881 with a Southern look, this onetime seasonal guest house has triple-tiered porches accented with beautiful iron work in the New Orleans style. "The house looks like it belongs in the South," says innkeeper Mari Slocum. She undertook extensive renovations in 1995 to turn it into an eclectic Victorian B&B full of lace, lilacs, art and collections.

"I'm a pack rat at heart," says Mari, a former school art teacher. Her pale pink Victorian parlor offers evidence: a breakfront full of antique china and glassware, a two-tiered table holding carousel animals, a rare dual-view stereo opticon from 1857. The front library/TV room, notable for an elaborate ceiling she wallpapered herself, holds an album of progress pictures she calls her renovation book. Photos of family members are found in most of the common areas and nine guest rooms, along with lilac accents and lots of lace.

Stuffed animals holding welcome cards on the beds greet guests in the rooms, all but two with private baths and all but one with queensize beds. Five have TV sets. Gilbert & Soames toiletries and Poland Spring water are in every room.

The newest Great Gatsby room, designed to be Art Deco at its best, comes with a fireplace and a whirlpool tub. Lilacs grace the comforter and pillows on the white iron bed in the second-floor White Lilac Suite, which offers a corner fireplace, wicker chairs, TV, a clawfoot tub in the room, a shower in the bathroom and french doors onto the wraparound porch.

The best view comes a floor above in the fireplaced hideaway called Room at the Top, where a private balcony yields a view of Wreck Pond and, when the leaves are off the trees, the ocean four blocks away. Most rooms follow a lacy Victorian cottage theme, but the Vermont Cabin is quite an exception. The last room to be refurbished, Mari wanted something different so it reflects family ties to Vermont. Two third-floor rooms are her family-oriented Three Sisters and the patriotic Hail to the Troops.

A full breakfast is served at nine tables for two in the lacy white Garden Room, which is warmed by a gas fireplace in cool weather. Fresh fruit and pastries precede the main dish, perhaps Mari's signature cinnamon-raisin french toast, a ham and cheese omelet or asparagus quiche.

(732) 449-0211. Eight rooms and one suite with private baths. July through Labor Day: doubles, $125 to $220. Late spring and early fall: doubles, $115 to $200. November-April: doubles, $100 to $175. Children over 14. No smoking. Closed in January.

Gazebo-shaped solarium at Ashling Cottage contains hundreds of window panes.

Ashling Cottage, 106 Sussex Ave., Spring Lake 07762.

Every morning a sumptuous breakfast is served by new owners Joanie and Bill Mahon in the gazebo-shaped solarium at the front of this engaging Victorian cottage. The fare includes fresh fruit compote, cereal, banana-nut bread and perhaps waffles or a crêpe dish. Their first guests raved about the individual omelets, which featured choice of ham, cheese, onions, scallions, mushrooms – "or all of the above," as Bill described it.

Hundreds of windows in the solarium, containing the original glass dating to 1877, yield views onto Spring Lake across the street and a glimpse of the ocean beyond. "You couldn't face a better way to start the day," says Bill, who had just finished washing all of them two months after they acquired the inn in 2000.

Joanie and Bill returned to the Jersey Shore, where he grew up, from Westport, Conn. "I'd been on a Christmas tour here and saw this house," said Joanie. "It was so different and charming. Little did I know I'd end up living here."

The Mahons undertook two months of renovations and refurbishing to appeal to overnight guests. They refinished the original floors and lightened up the decor in what Bill calls "fresh beach style." His wife's theme, he said, was "less is more – and lots of flowers everywhere."

All ten guest rooms hold queensize beds except for one with two twins. Eight have private baths. Two on the third floor with in-room wash basins share a hall bath and often are rented as a suite. No. 4 on the third floor, up in the treetops surrounded by century-old sentinel sycamores, is a favorite. Most in demand in summer is a rear first-floor room with a private porch.

Among the upgrades was a new kitchen. A newly refurbished one-bedroom cottage with kitchen is also available.

(732) 449-3553 or (888) 274-5464. Fax (732) 974-0831. www.ashlingcottage.com. Eight rooms with private baths and two rooms with shared bath. Mid-May through September: doubles, $179 to $260; cottage, $325. Rest of year: doubles, $79 to $160. Cottage, $225 to $250. Two-night minimum weekends. Children over 14. No smoking.

Seasonal hotel has been refurbished into the stylish Spring Lake Inn.

Spring Lake Inn, 104 Salem Ave., Spring Lake 07762.

"It didn't look like this when we bought it," Pat Gatens says in an understatement. She and husband Jim, New Yorkers both, took over the old seasonal Spring Lake Hotel in 1995 and refurbished it into a classy B&B.

The 80-foot-long Victorian porch lined with rockers and the large lobby full of rich wood harken back to the 1888 hotel's past. So does the vast square dining room alongside, a beauty with a twelve-foot-high ceiling and a handful of tables spaced well apart for breakfast. The handsome rear parlor with wainscoting is furnished with a mix of traditional and contemporary seating, oriental rugs and "a wee drop of Irish," says Pat.

Eight guest rooms off the wide second-floor hallway are quite different. All are stylish and comfortable with interesting wallpaper treatments, private baths and queensize beds. The Victoria Rose has a cannonball four-poster bed and, surprise, a floor lamp for reading in the w.c. alcove in the bathroom. The bathroom in Serenity is as large as the bedroom. The Canopy Room contains a step-up bed. The Corner Room has not one but two bathrooms for some reason. Pat points out the rooms in which priests and nuns have stayed (they seem to run in the family) as she gives a tour; "that's the nuns' room," she says of what otherwise is called Nostalgia.

A ninth guest room at one end of the third floor is so large it has a double bed in each corner and, again, two bathrooms. Six additional B&B rooms are located in the newly refurbished third floor. The two-room Tower View is the gem, colorful in mauve with a sitting room and, beneath a chandelier, a queensize sleigh bed literally surrounded by windows with views of the ocean.

Breakfast is continental in the summer, full in the off-season. Cinnamon french toast, blueberry pancakes and scrambled eggs inside a baked potato are favorite dishes.

Ebullient Pat, quite a character, sent us on our way with a loaf of her Irish sodabread and the distinct impression that the Spring Lake Inn would not long remain "the town's best kept secret."

(732) 449-2010. Fifteen rooms with private baths. May to mid-October: doubles, $165 to $225 weekends, $125 to $175 midweek. Rest of year: $90 to $190. Two-night minimum weekends in season. No smoking.

Dining Spots

Spring Lake's restaurant choices are limited by zoning regulations and a lack of liquor licenses. But there are plenty of options nearby.

Whispers, 200 Monmouth Ave., Spring Lake.
New owners have upgraded the highly regarded dining room in the Hewitt-Wellington hotel. The cream and pink room is a picture of elegance with a marble floor, upholstered chairs, and four crystal chandeliers that coordinate with the long-stemmed crystal vases and wine glasses on the tables.

Chef-partner Mark Mikolajczyk, who offers excellent contemporary fare, has turned this restaurant into the local place to go. Main courses could be grilled mahi-mahi Caribbean style, horseradish-crusted roasted red snapper, grilled veal chop or filet mignon with port wine sauce. Butternut squash served in its natural shell and tuna carpaccio with wasabi sauce were among the starters at our latest visit.

(732) 449-3330. Entrées, $17 to $26. Dinner, Wednesday-Sunday 5 to 9. Closed in January and February. BYOB.

Old Mill Inn, Old Mill Road, Spring Lake Heights.
Overlooking a tranquil mill pond with an eight-foot water wheel just west of town is this impressive establishment that's almost everybody's favorite for fine food and surroundings. If it no longer looks much like the grist mill it once was, that's because the restaurant established here in 1938 has burned five times, the latest in 1985. From the ashes emerged a behemoth with two main-floor dining rooms seating a total of 240, a lobby bigger than most restaurants and an upstairs function room that caters 100-plus weddings a year.

A remarkable stained-glass rendering of the New York skyline takes up most of one wall in **Joe's Place for Steak,** a serious steakhouse that's dark and plush in rich wood and hunter green. The larger main Green Room, frilly and feminine, offers water views and was obviously popular for Saturday lunch when we were there. Best of all at midday is a window table in the bar, away from the hubbub and seemingly perched over the water beside a flotilla of ducks. The taped piano music was so pure we thought it was live. We enjoyed a spicy Manhattan clam chowder, an abundant spinach and avocado salad, and two crab cakes on a pool of herbed cream sauce, nicely presented with a side of yellow and green squash, cauliflower and green peppers. A bread basket with good, crusty rolls and a blueberry and a bran muffin came with. The french fries were made by hand with the skins left on, and the excellent salad accompanying the crab cake was tossed with a zesty raspberry vinaigrette. It was obvious that the kitchen cares and maintains interest and quality along with quantity.

For dinner, owner Joe Amiel recommends any of the seafood dishes ("we have wonderful lobster, crab and fresh fish"), the extra-crispy roast duck with raspberry-

Window tables in Green Room overlook pond outside Old Mill Inn.

port wine sauce and the prime rib with horseradish sauce. The steakhouse fare can be ordered in either venue. Start with lobster bisque, carpaccio or oysters rockefeller. Finish with cheesecake, Swiss chocolate pie or ice cream. Honored by Wine Spectator, the wine list offers a good mix between high end and low end, with lots in between.

(732) 449-1800. Entrées, $18.95 to $27.90. Lunch daily, 11:30 to 3. Dinner nightly, 3 to 10 or 11. Sunday, brunch 11 to 3, dinner noon to 10. Closed Monday in off-season.

Sisters Café, 1321 Third Ave., Spring Lake.
Four sisters who grew up in Spring Lake are involved in this small restaurant with innovative contemporary fare, incongruously served amid vestiges of its former status as a luncheonette.

"We used to come in here when we were kids," said Culinary Institute of America-trained chef Marianne O'Hearne, spokeswoman for the four. She and Kris Dier, who had cooked in the area for years, staff the kitchen, while Suzanne O'Hearne handles the front of the house and an out-of-town sibling oversees the business end.

Opening in 1997 and gaining a receptive following, the O'Hearne sisters inexplicably retained the prominent lunch counter but upgraded the rest of the place with tables on two levels. White linens, oil lamps and fresh flowers are the norm at close-together tables, some in the rear along a side banquette. Family pictures and memorabilia are displayed in a handsome built-in bookcase running the length of the side wall in front.

The short dinner menu changes weekly. Typical starters are a crispy risotto cake with rock shrimp, herbs and roasted mushrooms and Maryland crab cakes with chipotle aioli.

Entrées could be spiced mahi-mahi with tropical fruit sauce, roast chicken breast stuffed with spinach and provolone, and New York strip steak with green peppercorn sauce.

Desserts include carrot cake with maple cream cheese icing, mocha fudge torte with white chocolate sauce, and apple-blueberry crisp with vanilla bean sauce.

Lunch selections intrigue as well, among them a grilled chicken, bacon and avocado salad with lemon-yogurt dressing, an open-face blue cheese sandwich with pears and walnuts, and a sweet potato, apple and cheddar turnover over greens.

(732) 449-1909. Entrées, $15 to $18. Lunch, Tuesday-Saturday 11 to 3. Dinner, Tuesday-Sunday 5:30 to 9 or 10. Saturday breakfast, 8 to 11. Sunday brunch, 8 to 2. BYOB.

Bella Luna, 703 Belmar Plaza, Ninth Avenue and Main Street, Belmar.

With a chef from the famed Bouley in New York City, this stylish restaurant and espresso bar was an instant hit upon opening in 1997 in a shopping plaza. Owners Florence and Patrick Shalloo, both with hotel and hospitality backgrounds, fashioned a spare, high-ceilinged space with lemon yellow walls and white-clothed tables spaced well apart.

It proved a pleasant setting for an inspired meal on a slow autumn weeknight (usually, we understand, the place is jammed). A basket of peasant bread came with a zesty apple-rosemary olive oil and herbed shallot butter as we placed our order. The zuppa di vongole with clams, sausage and cannellini beans was almost a meal in itself, particularly when paired with the assertive salad of baby spinach with roasted red peppers, portobello mushrooms and goat cheese, and an appetizer of smooth lobster ravioli with marscarpone cream on a sweet red pepper coulis. Also a standout was the rigatoni with smoked salmon and pancetta, followed by a refreshing lemon torte with a raspberry coulis and fresh berries. With a bottle of BYOB wine, the tab came to about $40 for two for a memorable dinner.

Those with hearty appetites choose among the likes of grilled salmon with truffled vinaigrette, seared tuna with a mango-chile salsa, an acclaimed fisherman's stew, chile-rubbed pork chop with spiced apple chutney, and polenta-crusted rack of lamb with whole grain mustard and port wine.

(732) 280-7501. Entrées, $13.50 to $18.75. Dinner nightly except Tuesday from 5. BYOB.

Armadillo Crossing, 1605 Main St., South Belmar.

The ice water comes with lemon wedges in mason jars, a muddy cowboy boot rests on a shelf and a stuffed beaver stands near the restrooms in this interesting little Southwest haunt just north of Spring Lake in South Belmar. The blackboard menu reads like Tex-Mex with a cajun accent, although young chef-owner Brian Mahoney demurs. "Up-and-coming Southwest food," the Spring Lake native calls it. "No tacos or burritos or anything like that."

The complimentary plate of white bean dip with tortilla chips, cucumber and zucchini slices and black olives nearly made redundant our dinner appetizers of roasted garlic with feta cheese and red peppers (sensational) and a salad of exotic mushrooms on assorted baby lettuces (sublime). The waitress who explained the ins and outs of the menu employed a lot of "very hot" qualifiers, which turned out to be particularly true in the jerked chicken with kiwi salsa, accompanied by interesting sweet potato fries and a zesty corn salad. Slightly milder, as it was supposed to be, was the grilled Arizona chicken with avocado and kiwi sauce and Mexican rice. Both main dishes were excellent and arrived in such abundance that part left in doggy bags for lunch the next day. Desserts included an acclaimed key lime pie, strawberry-amaretto cake and cappuccino-hazelnut cake, but alas no icy refreshments to cool such assertive fare. The peppermint candies that came with the bill had to suffice.

The place is tiny, the music soft and the barn-red walls glow at night when the lights are dimmed and the oil candles lit. You don't even notice that the tablecloths are mismatched and that the decor is of the tag-sale variety.

(732) 280-1880. Entrées, $13.95 to $16.95. Dinner, Tuesday-Sunday 5 to 10. BYOB.

The Avon Pavilion, Ocean Avenue, Avon-by-the-Sea.

They dole out hot dogs and hamburgers by day at this snow-white pavilion right over the beach. Come evening, they dress up the summery interior with tablecloths and candlelight and offer a menu featuring gourmet, low-sodium and low-fat entrée specials denoted by heart symbols.

The lapping waves are the backdrop for interesting pastas and main dishes like broiled salmon with citron verte sauce, grilled yellowfin tuna with spicy creole sauce, stir-fried shrimp and vegetables on steamed rice, chicken française and grilled strip steak smothered with mushrooms, sweet vidalia onions and garlic. Instead of salad, the place serves a tomato concoction with olives and onions in which to dip your bread; regulars say it's to die for.

The "New Joisey" clam chowder with a Jersey Shore zip is a favorite starter. Otherwise, begin with bay and booze shrimp (steamed in beer and Old Bay spice) or caesar salad with a unique chardonnay caesar dressing. Finish with key lime mousse or toll house pie à la mode.

(732) 775-1043. Entrées, $14.95 to $18.95. Dinner nightly from 6, summer only. BYOB.

Rod's Old Irish Tavern, 507 Washington Blvd., Sea Girt.

Favorite among a number of Irish pubs in an area only lately shedding its moniker as the Irish Riviera is this large green house with white trim and a canopied entrance at the edge of downtown Sea Girt, an attractive residential town on Spring Lake's southern border. Green and white is the color scheme inside as well, from the checkered tablecloths in the enormous pub to the curtains separating leather booths and tables in the dining room. There's a garden cafe beyond.

The same menu spanning the spectrum from a jumbo hot dog to blackened sirloin steak is served throughout the establishment. This means you can enjoy grilled swordfish or one of the famous chicken pot pies while watching one of the dozen or so big-screen TVs around the central bar, or a burger, sandwich or barbecued ribs in the dining room, and vice-versa. Mix and match shrimp scampi, fettuccine primavera, a nacho platter, chef's salad, oysters on the half shell and such. Portions are huge and prices affordable.

(732) 449-2020. Entrées, $12.95 to $17.95. Lunch daily, 11:30 to 2:30. Dinner nightly, 5 to 11.

Tara Lynn's Unique Cuisine, 217 Jersey Ave., Spring Lake.

The name is a bit of a mystery at this pint-size establishment opened in 1997 by chef Tara Bartz and partner Lynda Milligan in the former Victorian Bean Café. The tea room/coffee house/café offers a continental-style menu during the day and blackboard specials at night.

What's unique? "Look at the menu," we were advised. It offered a panoply of sandwiches and salads in the $5.95 to $7.95 range. The former bear names like thon, poulet, jambon and "oeuf" (the last for roasted eggplant – the name at least is unique – with roasted red peppers and garlic, red onion and herbed goat cheese).

Salades are of the de mozzarella, de épinard and de hummus variety. Tara Lynn's "unique shakes" are called butter rum, tirami su, chocolate espresso and the like.

The dinner menu is posted daily in the window and recited by a waitress who kindly gave us her notes. Cajun mako shark, baked chicken with dijon tarragon sauce and london broil with mushrooms and onions were among the main dishes that night. Three kinds of pies and a port wine pear tarte were the dessert choices.

The place seats up to 28 people at intimate tables or at a rear counter/bar.

(732) 449-3299. Entrées, $11.95 to $14.95. Open daily, 9 to 9, to 7 Tuesday-Thursday in off-season. BYOB.

Diversions

A New York Times article claimed that "it's not so much what there is to do, it is what there is not to do that makes Spring Lake special." The prime attractions, of course, are the quiet boardwalk and pristine beach, plus the parklands surrounding the town's namesake lake. One could spend hours walking the streets and admiring the gardens and manicured lawns of Spring Lake, where commercial lawn services must rank as the town's single most prosperous business niche. Check out the manicured masterpiece surrounding the residence at 301 West Lake Drive. The lawn is clipped to one-fourth inch high and maintained daily like a putting green.

Within easy striking distance are Atlantic City, New York, Philadelphia, gambling, racing, arcades and what have you. From these you can return quickly to the refuge of Spring Lake.

The Beach. Two miles of wide beach (continually restocked with fresh sand) and New Jersey's longest non-commercial boardwalk separate the Atlantic Ocean beach from sand dunes and Ocean Avenue. Spring Lake's boardwalk contains only a few pavilions with benches and two larger pavilions harboring saltwater pools, rest rooms and food stands at either end. Beach passes are sold here, although most inn guests are loaned passes by their hosts. Even on chilliest days, lots of people stroll or jog on the boardwalk.

Theater. The Spring Lake Theatre Company has expanded its repertoire and schedule to stage eight shows year-round in the Spring Lake Community House. The English Tudor building built in 1923 by a former mayor and state senator includes a library and a 360-seat theater. Tickets are in the $15 range and sell out early; call 449-4530.

Gazebo Concerts. The town recreation commission sponsors outdoor concerts in Potter Park on varying nights roughly every other week in summer. Jazz bands, the Atlantic Wind Ensemble, the Ocean Grove Band, the Happy Days String Band, a folksinger and an Irish balladeer were among recent performers. Townspeople and visitors bring chairs or blankets and pretty well fill the park.

St. Catharine's Church, Third and Essex Avenue. Built beside the lake between 1901 and 1907 by a wealthy resident as a memorial to his daughter, this striking edifice resembles the Romanesque St. Peter's Basilica in miniature and is well worth a visit. Two 800-year-old bronze standards from Rome line the entrance to the church. The high altar is made of the same Carrara marble used by Michelangelo and the stained-glass windows were made in Bavaria. A professor from Rome painted the interior frescos. The church is one of two in the same parish in Spring

Lake, a heavily Roman Catholic community. The total enrollment of Spring Lake's single public elementary school is less than that of the parochial school.

Shopping. Four blocks of tree-lined Third Avenue are home to small stores run by committed owners and an unusually high number of real-estate offices. Perhaps the biggest drawing card is the **Irish Centre,** which features all kinds of Irish imports reflecting the resort's heritage. Another is the old-fashioned **Spring Lake Variety Store** filled to the brim with all kinds of things, including beach chairs hanging from the ceiling. Clothing and accessories are more sedate specialties of **The Camel's Eye, Village Tweeds** and **Courts & Greens,** whose names indicate their priorities. Adorable bears clad in little smock dresses are in the windows of **Teddy Bears by the Seashore,** where two former Macy's buyers offer discounted clothing for children and their parents. We admired the cute clothes at **Samantha's. Spring Lace** is a mercantile confection full of lace and Victoriana (much of the Victorian lace on windows and tables at local inns was obtained here). Some of the most sophisticated cards, stationery, books and desk accessories we've seen anywhere are stocked at **Noteworthy By-the-Sea,** now in an expanded location next to its original store.

New stores and galleries seem to pop up at every visit. We know innkeepers who covet every single item at **Kate & Company,** where country pine furniture and home accessories are imaginatively displayed. We admired an intricate cathedral bird-cage show table for $995. Fine American crafts are among the "irresistibles," some made by the owners, at **The Moon & Sixpence.** Art enthusiasts admire the offerings of the **Spring Lake Gallery, Evergreen Gallery, ArtEffects** and **Thistledown Gallery.**

Sweets lovers get their fill at the **Third Avenue Chocolate Shoppe** and **Jean-Louise Homemade Candies,** where the day's special at one visit was chocolate-covered grapes. Snacks are available to eat in or take out next door at **Freedman's Bakery.** Gourmet pizzas and sophisticated entrée specials are offered at the **Spring Lake Gourmet Pizzeria,** a sleek place that lives up to its claim of being "not just another pizzeria." The **Spring Lake Bottle Shop** is the place to pick up a good bottle of wine for restaurants where you bring your own.

Extra-Special

Historic Allaire Village, Allaire State Park, off Route 524, Allaire.

Part of a 3,000-acre state park, this outdoor living-history museum re-creates the days of New Jersey's early iron industry. Interpreters dressed in the work clothes of the 1830s portray the daily life and times of early iron workers and their families at the historic Howell Works, an industrial community established between 1822 and 1850 when bog ore was smelted. They demonstrate early crafts and open-hearth cooking in some of the twelve houses and buildings in a restored village. Other buildings include a snack bar and a general store/museum shop. The Pine Creek Railroad displays six antique trains, two of which offer ten-minute rides. Listed on the National Register, this mini-Sturbridge is part of 3,000-acre Allaire State Park just west of Spring Lake.

(732) 938-2253. Grounds open year-round. Visitor center open Wednesday-Sunday 10 to 5, Memorial Day to Labor Day, Saturday-Sunday 10 to 4 in September and October. Buildings open Saturday-Sunday 10 to 4, May-October. Parking, $3 weekends.

East Hampton, N.Y.

Village Beautiful

East Hampton, let it be said up front, is too-too. Too posh, too trendy, too social, too expensive, too precious, too much.

At the same time, let it be said that it is also beautiful. Classy. And, at other than peak visiting periods, rather serene. Almost perfect. Not too-too perfect.

For New Yorkers, there is no better-known summer place than the Hamptons,

some 110 miles east near the tip of Long Island's South Fork. The Hamptons collectively embrace, from west to east: Westhampton and Hampton Bays, which for most are quite skippable. Southampton, perhaps the best known of the Hamptons, the Palm Beach of the North. Bridgehampton, which is consciously understated. And East Hampton, more subdued than flashy Southampton.

It's not hard to understand why this was called "America's Most Beautiful Village" in the early 1960s by a national magazine. Town officials differ over whether it was the Saturday Evening Post or National Geographic; their indecision suggests that to East Hampton it doesn't matter.

The wide main street of the historic village passes a long green with a pond and a graveyard, a windmill, English-style edifices and substantial old homes before

Old Hook Windmill frames Mill House Inn.

it reaches shady, suave downtown East Hampton. Take Ocean Avenue down to the beach, arguably the nation's cleanest and one of its most beautiful. Meander along side streets in the estate area, where thick privet hedges screen the manicured estates of the rich and famous. Some of the more illustrious – and less flamboyant – make up the Blue Book of the Hamptons, which is discreetly stacked for sale on the counter at the local bookstore. Pause for a look at Home Sweet Home, the Mulford House, Clinton Academy, Miss Amelia's Cottage, Guild Hall, the Tudoresque library and the Old Hook Mill, one among the nation's largest collections of windmills. This is the East Hampton that the transient visitor sees.

The East Hampton that the New Yorkers take over in the summer is the one where the scene is seeing and being seen: in chi-chi restaurants charging Manhattan prices, at inns demanding minimum stays of three to five nights, in boutiques catering to the celebrity and carriage trade, in the slick newspapers and magazines touting the Hamptons' social scene, in all the fitness centers and beauty salons and cosmetic makeover clinics that show where priorities lie.

Some New Yorkers would kill for a share in a house in the Hamptons each summer – or even for an invitation for a weekend. Others would be advised to visit at off-peak times to enjoy East Hampton's many charms, without its hassles.

Inn Spots

Accommodations vary from old inns to small, home-stay B&Bs taking in guests on summer weekends. Weekends, when minimum stays of three nights are the rule, are booked far ahead. Many inns require four-night stays on holiday weekends and two-night stays on spring and fall weekends. Lately, many have added in-room telephones with voice mail and modems, presumably for high-powered business and social types who can't stand to be out of touch.

The J. Harper Poor Cottage, 181 Main St., East Hampton 11937.

If you want to stay in an East Hampton mansion, how about this, one of the more stately in town? Gary and Rita Reiswig, former owners of the nearby Maidstone Arms, acquired the stuccoed Elizabethan manor facing the village green in 1996. Six months of renovations produced five guest rooms with private baths and the most elegant common rooms in town.

The Reiswigs had had their eye on the house for years. It became available following the deaths of Sid and Mim Perle, who had run it as a low-key, three-room B&B in conjunction with the 1770 House inn and restaurant they owned down the street.

The core of the house, named for former owner James Harper Poor, was built in 1650 as a tavern. It was expanded with servants' and master wings on each side in 1885. The sheer size, the mullioned windows, the skylit Colonial Revival staircase, the Arts and Crafts architectural embellishments and the carved lintel angels framing the front entrance lend irony to the name.

With great taste, the Reiswigs have done extensive refurbishing, favoring the simpler English Arts and Crafts style to the excesses of the earlier Victorian era. The sunken living room is a beauty with a grouping in the center of four arm chairs upholstered in fabrics matching the frieze of William Morris floral wallpaper atop the paneling, an oversize grand piano from the 1860s at one end and window seats overlooking the rear sculpture gardens at the other. The fireplace inglenook is decorated with a checkerboard of English Victorian art tile in blue and white. The beamed breakfast room with a huge fireplace also doubles as a tavern, its original purpose, where guests can enjoy their favorite beverage with snacks ranging from chips and salsa to handmade pizzas. In front is a fireplaced library/ reception room with more decorative tiling and light wood paneling.

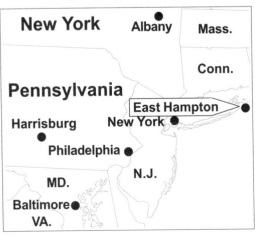

Upstairs are five regal guest rooms, all with private baths, queen or king beds, sitting areas, telephones and TV/ VCRs. Four have working fireplaces. Understated décor follows a garden theme with William Morris wallpapers and plush fabrics. Room 13 in the 1650 section retains the

Sculptures accent back lawn and gardens at The J. Harper Poor Cottage.

original beams, a paneled door hung on hand-wrought hinges, a huge fireplace, a clawfoot tub and separate shower, plus a front veranda that's a tight squeeze for two.

Out back are a spacious lawn and formal sculpture garden surrounded by twenty-foot-high arborvitae. Among the several lounging areas is an intimate breakfast nook hidden beneath a 200-year-old climbing wisteria.

That and the nearby patio are idyllic spots in which to linger over a hearty breakfast. Guests help themselves to fresh fruit, juice, cereal and baked goods before being served a main course, perhaps eggs, tarte tatin or lemon pancakes. The garden conveys such a European feeling that guests may forget they are in the heart of the Hamptons.

(631) 324-4081. Fax (631) 329-5931. Five rooms with private baths. June 23 to Sept. 10: doubles $395 to $495 weekends, $250 to $395 midweek. Late spring and early fall: $295 to $395 weekends, $225 to $295 midweek. November to mid-May: $195 to $295 weekends, $170 to $250 midweek. Three-night minimum on summer weekends.

Centennial House, 13 Woods Lane, East Hampton 11937.

This shingled Victorian hugging the main road at the edge of the estate district was built in 1876, the date having been inscribed in plaster in the Bay bedroom by one of the village's celebrated builders. It was owned by only two families before it was acquired in 1987 by David Oxford, a lawyer who had his office in the rear barn until he retired, and Harry Chancey, a PBS television executive in New York. In the midst of restoration, they turned their home into a B&B when the owners of the 1770 House inn followed up a casual suggestion by calling one night with a problem, the need for overnight lodging for a desperate couple. Their friends obliged, and one thing led to another.

Now the partners offer five elegant bedrooms with private baths and a three-bedroom cottage. Each is decorated to the Victorian hilt with antiques garnered mainly from estate and yard sales. Fancy fabrics, down comforters, white embroidered waffle weave robes and Neutrogena toiletries are in each room. So are sherry and port, chocolate truffles, TVs and bedside telephones, and a small refrigerator at the top of the stairs is stocked with drinks and snacks.

The Bay Room with the builder's initials inscribed in the wall beside the bookcase is most in demand. Its queensize four-poster is topped by a comforter and chintz floral pillows that match the balloon curtains in the bay window, from which it derives its name. The bathroom has a clawfoot tub and a sink ensconced in a 19th-century pulpit hand-carved from pine. The Bay Room has one of two new gas fireplaces in the house. The other is in the Rose Room, where the spiral-turned four-poster bed is wrapped in Waverly chintz that matches the window treatments and the clawfoot tub is draped with heavy tapestry. The Lincoln Room is so named for its Lincoln bed, designed the year he became president. The sunny rear Master Bedroom comes with Laura Ashley ticking and garlands, a kingsize bed and a day bed, and windows overlooking the garden.

The rear cottage, fully winterized, boasts a full kitchen, breakfast area, living room with a TV and stereo, gas fireplace, two baths and a front porch. It has a small twin bedroom and a queen bedroom downstairs, and a room upstairs with a king bed, TV and one antique rocker. The cottage, rented by the week in season, is available for two-night stays in the off-season.

The interior of the main house is done in the high Victorian style. Twin Czecho-slovakian crystal chandeliers illuminate the double parlor, where prized doggies Edwinna and Max are apt to preside in front of the Italian marble fireplace.

Outfitted in Williamsburg fabrics (the chair seats are coordinated with the wallpaper), the formal Georgian dining room is set as formally as if for dinner with cut-linen napkins and Rosenthal china. Breakfast is served here at a lace-covered table for eight and a smaller round table in a corner beside the book-shelves. Guests rave about the buttermilk pancakes, french toast or omelets prepared by David.

Out back are a small fitness room in a barn and a secluded pool behind the rose and herb gardens, where you feel as if you're a guest at someone's summer home. The guestbook is effusive with praise: "Relaxing, quiet, romantic, lovely, friendly" are recurring adjectives. "Your hospitality is unbeatable," summed up one happy guest.

These days, David holds the fort at Centennial House while for most of the year Harry oversees their deluxe new Kingsbrae Arms in St. Andrews, N.B., Canada's first five-star inn.

(631) 324-9414. Fax (631) 324-2681. www.centhouse.com. Five rooms with private baths and a three-bedroom cottage. Doubles, $375 to $425, Memorial Day through September; $250 to $295, rest of year. Cottage, $4,500 by the week only, Memorial Day

The Pink House, 26 James Lane, East Hampton 11937.

Despite an abundance of established inns here, architect/builder Ron Steinhilber felt there was a market for an upscale B&B. "People will pay a little extra for something really luxurious, that goes the extra mile," he said. So he took over a National Register-listed house, built by a local whaling captain across from the village green and pond in the mid-1800s, and imbued it with taste and personality – except for the pretty pale pink exterior, which he inherited and cannot be changed. The interior is not the locally prevailing Victorian look but country light.

Ron and a friend renovated the house themselves in 1990 and his architectural genius shows. So do his collections, from a platform light from Brooklyn's Myrtle

Pine pencil-post bed is draped in lace in Blue Room at The Pink House.

Avenue subway line in a corner of the living room to his grandfather's watercolors, and Salari bells from New Mexico. A row of lights illuminates the entry hall and focuses on collections in two shelves at the top of the stairs.

All five guest rooms come with private baths, telephones and TV. The Blue Room has a cushioned window seat, queensize pine pencil-post bed, and a huge marble shower and sink bearing the inn's own toiletries. Another favorite is the Elk Room, with Southwest decor, a jacuzzi and TV. The Twin Room, where the beds with pretty pink and green sheets can be joined as a king, contains a wall of iron artifacts. The Green Room has an Adirondack chair and a wicker queensize bed.

On the main floor is the Garden Room with a four-poster bed, a private entrance and its own flower-filled patio, where "guests feel like they're in a cottage at the Beverly Hills Hotel," says Ron. Calla lilies adorn the bathroom sink to carry out the garden feeling.

Recessed ceiling lights spotlight selected art in the living room with two facing loveseats and in the dining room, both of which have fireplaces. The front porch is furnished in wicker. Guests help themselves to soft drinks and ice from a refrigerator, and chocolates are on the beds at night.

Breakfast in the dining room or on the screened rear porch includes fresh fruit and juices, homemade granola and European roast coffee. The crowning glory might be banana-walnut pancakes, sourdough french toast with sautéed pears, heart-shaped waffles topped with raspberries or a cream cheese and chive omelet.

Outside is a lovely back yard, where guests enjoy a hedge-screened swimming pool. "Although our aim is to be elegant and deluxe," says Ron, "we're also rustic and homey. People feel at home here."

(631) 324-3400. Fax (631) 324-5254. Five rooms with private baths. Doubles, $295 to $395 in summer, $165 to $265 in spring and fall, $145 to $185 in winter. Three to four-night minimum on summer weekends, four to six nights on holiday weekends. Children over 5. No smoking.

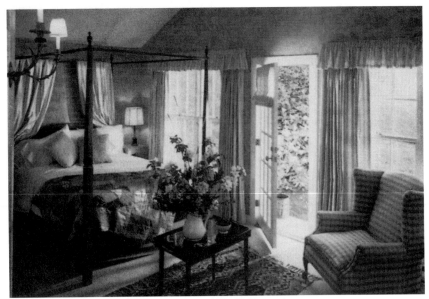

Waverly wallpaper and fabrics enhance cottage at The Maidstone Arms.

The Maidstone Arms, 207 Main St., East Hampton 11937.

Nicely situated across from the town pond and the gravestone-lined village green, this white clapboard structure looks the way a summery country hotel should look.

It was converted from a private home in the 1870s, and upgraded from a seasonal inn into a year-round hotel in 1992. A porch with white rockers faces the tranquil green. Inside two three-story buildings connected by a sun porch is a ramble of rooms, from restaurant and dining porches to sixteen bedrooms with private baths, TVs, phones and air-conditioning. Out back are three garden cottages that represent the crème de la crème.

Owner Coke Anne Saunders, a New York architect whose late father was Texan Clint Murchison, poured big bucks into a cosmetic renovation and refurbishing of the old inn. A major rehab was precluded by zoning restrictions, but visitors today find modernized bathrooms, new furniture and beds, new wallpapers and draperies, and what chef and general manager William Valentine calls "a brighter, more cheery feeling."

Accommodations vary in decor and size. Two small rooms we saw in the main inn – both with double beds – retain a snug, understated look even with the upgrades. More impressive are the garden cottages, each large and airy. We liked the one with vaulted ceiling, queensize poster bed, angled fireplace, sitting area with sofabed and armchair, and Waverly wallpaper and fabrics. Another cheerful bedroom, its wallpaper patterned with seashells and paired with tartan lampshades, won an honorable mention in Waverly's Country Inn Room of the Year contest. Besides the usual toiletries, a little sampler bag of local fragrances from Antonia's Flowers is in each room.

Guests share the wicker-filled front sun porch that doubles as a sitting room and breakfast room. It opens into a plant-filled room leading to gardens out back. The Water Room Lounge with a woodburning stove is a gathering place for games, drinks, light meals and cigar smoking. A continental breakfast of scones, English muffins and such is included in the rates. Breakfast also may be ordered à la carte.

The kitchen has been renovated to enhance the restaurant operation (see Dining Spots).

(631) 324-5006. Fax (631) 324-5037. Sixteen rooms and three cottages with private baths. weekends. Summer: doubles, $325 to $465; cottages, $565; three or four-night minimum required. Off-season: doubles, $148 to $275; cottages, $335; two-night minimum weekends. Children welcome. Smoking restricted.

Mill House Inn, 33 North Main St., East Hampton 11937.

Facing the parkland and gravestones surrounding the Old Hook Windmill, this is a country charmer of a B&B with eight guest rooms, all with private baths. The original 1790 colonial saltbox was turned into a Dutch Colonial during expansion a century later.

The beamed living room and dining room are properly historic and nicely decorated, the latter with yellow and blue wallpaper bearing a stunning teapot pattern. When we first stayed here, the guest rooms on three floors could best be described as homey. Now six rooms have gas fireplaces, six have queen beds and four have whirlpool tubs. All come with telephones and TV/VCR.

New owners Sylvia and Gary Muller added feather beds and down pillows and comforters in all the bedrooms when they took over in 1999. "It's so hard to get out of bed when you're floating in clouds of down," notes Sylvia. The history and character of the area are stressed through an equestrian theme in the main-floor Hampton Classic Room (its queen bed and day bed make it good for families), a floral theme in the Garden Room, an afternoon at sea in Sail-Away and mill memorabilia in the Dominy Mill Room. Top of the line are two third-floor hideaways, the Hampton Holiday with a cherry wood bed and a plush settee, and the Hampton Breezes with a pine bed, wicker loveseat and chair, and one of three antique armoires upon which an artist painted remarkable designs from a wallpaper sample.

There's room to spread out on a long enclosed front porch and in a spacious back yard. French doors in the dining room open onto a rear patio. Afternoon snacks are served by the living-room fireplace in the off-season.

The Mullers serve a continental breakfast buffet starting at 7:30. A full breakfast is offered from 9 to 11.

(631) 324-9766. Fax (631) 324-9793. Eight rooms with private baths. May-October: doubles, $295 to $425 weekends, $275 to $405 midweek. November-April: doubles, $245 to $385 weekends, $185 to $255 midweek. Three-night minimum weekends in summer, two- night minimum weekends rest of year. Children welcome. No smoking.

The House on Newtown, 172 Newtown Lane, East Hampton 11937.

This modest 1912 house built by a sea captain doesn't look like much, at least by East Hampton standards. Owners Mike and Marianne Kaufman ran it as a low-key B&B for eight years, filling by word of mouth and then branching out to lease seven other houses they own around town to summer renters. Their house-rental service, the first in town, made a difference.

In 1994, they received "a modicum of fame," as Mike tells it. First, the White House travel office called for accommodations for "some very important people" in connection with a fund-raising visit by Vice President Al Gore. Although their houses were already booked, the calls continued daily for possible cancellations.

In the midst of all this, upon the recommendation of the Maidstone Arms, ABC News asked if it could use the Kaufmans' Victorian living room as a backdrop for an interview with White House counsel Lloyd Cutler on "This Week with David Brinkley." The next morning the TV crews arrived, as did Cutler from his nearby home on Georgica Pond. All the goings-on at The House on Newtown made the front page of The East Hampton Star in a story headlined simply "Certainly Never in Kansas" – a reference to Mike's quote that if they had a B&B in Kansas, they wouldn't have the same stories to tell. "East Hampton is so exciting. We're at the epicenter of everything here."

The Kaufmans are fonts of lore regarding the epicenter, Mike having been a seventh-grade teacher here for more than twenty years. Like its owners, the B&B is welcoming and down-to-earth. All four bedrooms have private baths. Three have queensize beds (one has twins that can be joined as a king). They're full of sturdy oak furnishings and a lived-in look. Over the bed in one is a nifty painting of sandpipers by an artist who had once lived in the house. In the hallway a display case overflows with son Eric's wrestling trophies, and these turn out to be just the beginning.

A continental breakfast buffet of bagels, croissants, muffins, cereals, yogurt and fresh fruit is taken at round tables for two on the front sun porch. Guests enjoy privacy in a small sitting room outfitted in wicker, with a shelf lined with antique telephones overhead. People are more apt to gather with the innkeepers in the larger Victorian living room. The latter has a shelf lined with tea kettles, Victorian side tables, three sofas and two chairs.

(631) 324-1858 or 329-0672. Four bedrooms with private baths. Doubles, $250 to $270 in summer; early spring and late fall, $150 to $240. Closed November-April.

1770 House, 143 Main St., East Hampton 11937.

Seven guest rooms with private baths and a culinary accent are available in this white clapboard house beside the old Clinton Academy, New York State's first accredited high school.

The culinary tradition started with Mim Perle, a cooking instructor and caterer, who with her husband Sid bought the structure, which had seen many lives, in 1977. Planning this as a semi-retirement project, the Perles found it quickly became a hands-on, family operation. It is now run by their daughter Wendy Van Deusen, who shared cooking duties with Mim, and son Adam, who presided over the bar in the Colonial taproom with its old hickory beams and open dutch hearth.

The historic dining room had been closed for four years, but was scheduled to reopen in 2000 as **Cerulean.** Wendy's husband, Burt Van Deusen, said they found "a perfect match" in Cybele Cuzon, who owns a seasonal restaurant of the same name in Anguilla. She'd been looking for a summer venture, leased the space here and was doing modest redecorating to add a Caribbean accent. She planned to offer dinner here May through October, Wednesday-Sunday from 5.

Among the guest rooms, we like Room 10, a junior suite that has a queen bed in an alcove, a floral print on the walls and some of the period clocks and antique furnishings that abound throughout. It comes with a little sitting room with a desk and one of the inn's two working fireplaces, as well as a small dressing room and a private entrance. Three other rooms have queen canopy beds, two have double canopy beds, and one has twins that can be joined as a king. A suite in the carriage house with a queen canopy bed, a loft with twin beds, a cathedral-ceilinged living

Lodging and dining are offered by 1770 House in center of historic district.

room and a 2,000-volume library is the only place in town, we're told, where Yoko Ono will stay.

Guests gather in the beamed taproom or in a paneled library with a fireplace. Breakfast consists of fresh fruit, cereal and perhaps french toast made out of challah bread, belgian waffles or fresh herb omelets with scones.

(631) 324-1770. Fax (631) 324-3504. Seven rooms and one suite with private baths. May-October: doubles, $165 to $350. November-April: $120 to $250 weekends, $85 to $150 midweek. Three-night minimum weekends in summer, two-night minimum weekends rest of year.

Lysander House, 132 Main St., East Hampton 11937.

Their travels to Mexico and Japan are much in evidence at this welcoming and colorful B&B in a cozy Victorian farmhouse not far from downtown. "He worked and I shopped," Leslie Tell Hillel says of all the exotic pieces she and her husband Larry acquired while he was posted with Citibank in foreign lands.

Dramatic masks are lined up along the top of the walls in the front parlor. A wall of Japanese prints is the focal point of the side living room and dining area. Therapeutic duxiana mattresses from Sweden top the beds in three upstairs guest rooms with private baths.

All the folk art and eclectic furnishings are notable, as are the colors painted on the walls. One side bedroom with a double bed is a summery blue. The front master bedroom with a king bed is a cheerful pale yellow. And the rear suite is lavender in the queen bedroom and lavender-pink in the adjacent sitting room with sofabed. The walls of the hall and stairway are painted two colors: yellow for the sun on one side and blue for the sea on the other.

The hostess is into cooking as much as she is into art and color. For breakfast, she might jazz up the pancakes with mangos and the french toast with oranges and pecans. Another favorite is cheese frittata.

Chatty Leslie offers afternoon beverages and sends guests home with a bag of biscotti.

(631) 329-9025. Two rooms and a suite with private baths. May-October: doubles, $240 to $370 weekends, $200 to $320 midweek. November-April: $200 to $270. Children over 14. No smoking.

The Huntting Inn, 94 Main St., East Hampton 11937.

The closest inn to the center of town, this is within walking distance of stores and yet back from the street beside a shady English country garden, of which innkeeper Linda Calder is rightly proud. The only problem is that inn guests have to walk outside and halfway around the building to get to the garden retreat. The owners hope eventually to put in french doors allowing access from the sun porch to the garden, but in strictly regulated East Hampton such things take time.

Resembling a New England country inn, this white clapboard structure with green shutters is really ancient and protected (some would say prevented) from changes that would bring it into the 21st century. It was built as a home in 1699 by the Church of England for the Rev. Nathaniel Huntting; his widow turned it into a public house in 1751, a status it has maintained since. The front porch and main floor are given over to The Palm, one of two New Yorkish restaurant operations run here by co-owners Wally Ganzi and Bruce Bozzi. The other is at the associated Hedges Inn.

Upstairs, a narrow maze of corridors leads to eighteen air-conditioned guest rooms on two floors. Rooms vary widely in size and style. One of the largest harbors a beamed ceiling, kingsize four-poster bed and a velvet sofa. The bathroom has pine wainscoting stained to look like oak and a double jacuzzi and separate shower. Another is small with an old-fashioned tub.

Most rooms are decorated with vivid floral prints and dark carpeting. One charming room, sprightly with yellow paint and yellow floral duvet that matches the draperies, was awarded an honorable mention in Waverly's Country Inn Room of the Year contest. Our room was part of a two-room suite with a small bath in the middle. It had the floral wallpaper typical of the inn, tied-back lace curtains, a kingsize bed, a TV hidden in a corner armoire, new carpeting and a dark sitting room in which only one of the three lights worked. Ice was delivered with a complimentary bottle of S. Pellegrino water and one of the bureaus displayed a basket of toiletries, a little bag of local Antonia's Flowers fragrances and lotions, and two Lindor truffles.

A good continental breakfast buffet is spread out atop the Palm bar or, at peak periods, in the restaurant. Those who get there first may eat on the front sun porch so coveted by diners at night.

(631) 324-0410. Fax (631) 324-8751. Eighteen rooms with private baths. April through mid-October: doubles, $250 to $350. Rest of year: $195 to $275.

The Hedges' Inn, 74 James Lane, East Hampton 11937.

Beautiful flowers line the brick walk leading to this yellow clapboard inn dating to 1774. It stands at the entry to the village at the west end of the town pond – where the road makes a turn from the city to country life, according to one writeup. The secluded setting is residential, although much of the main floor gets busy at

Sleek, summery look prevails in side dining room at Nick and Toni's.

night as the James Lane Cafe, formerly the Palm Restaurant. Like the Huntting Inn, it's owned by Wally Ganzi and Bruce Bozzi of the Palm restaurants.

Some of the eleven guest rooms on the second and third floors here seem brighter and more up to date than those at the Huntting. Room 1, for instance, is light and airy with a queensize bed, a small fireplace, a dark red velvet loveseat, baskets of fruit and flowers, and a modern bathroom with a double black marble vanity. Room 6 offers a king bed against sky-blue wallpaper. A small upstairs corner room has a double bed with a wicker headboard, but has no chairs. Each room has a private bath and air-conditioning.

Fruit, cereal, bagels, muffins and croissants are put out in a cheery breakfast room. Wicker furniture on the front porch faces the pond.

(631) 324-7100. Fax (631) 324-5816. Eleven rooms with private baths. April through mid-October: doubles, $250 to $350. Rest of year: $195 to $275.

Dining Spots

East Hampton is a place for eating and eating well, often at prices approaching those in Manhattan. Many restaurants require gratuities in cash rather than on credit cards. Reservations often are hard to come by.

Nick and Toni's, 136 North Main St., East Hampton.

Nice and tony, this is one of East Hampton's "in" places, and not simply because of its wood-burning oven. We could tell the moment we arrived and were led through the entire place to a rear table, which was fine with us. We became aware of the Hampton glance – all eyes on new arrivals to see who they are and with whom. Even the deuces are angled with backs to the wall so each diner can watch the passing parade. And why not, when the restaurant's backer was Steve Ross, the late Time-Warner mogul who had a home in East Hampton, the place is run by his daughter and son-in-law, Toni Ross and Jeff Salaway, and the inspired cooks in the kitchen have a devoted following?

There's a variety of summery rooms with big windows and no curtains. Seating is on sleek, cushioned European contemporary chairs at tables set with crisp white cloths. The look is unadulterated: no candles, no flowers and fairly bright overhead lighting.

Dinner begins with dense Tuscan bread served with olive oil for dipping. For starters, we tried the night's soup, grilled tomato with a very smoky flavor and a sensational wilted dandelion salad with a bacon and mustard vinaigrette. Among main courses, we fell for the loin of pork with nectarines and swiss chard and the fettuccine with rabbit, lemon and rosemary. The house wine we had with appetizers was poured from an Italian pitcher, and meals came on various pottery serving pieces. With our meal we chose a sauvignon blanc from the nearby Hargrave winery among a number of good, affordable choices. Dessert was the day's special blueberry-peach buckle from a selection that included tirami su, "serious" chocolate cake and homemade ice cream.

The changing menu involves about eight appetizers, four pastas, side vegetables and six main courses, ranging from pan-roasted striped bass with truffled potato puree to ribeye steak with chilled lobster. From the wood-burning oven might come free-range chicken with garlic and rosemary and whole roasted fish with deep-fried radicchio and endive. Also available are pizzas like littleneck clams with garlic and goat cheese with wilted greens and spicy harissa.

Although the clientele is haute, this did not strike us as a haughty place, as many in the area are. But the reservation system is complex (those with unknown names may not get in), and the prices have risen lately.

(631) 324-3550. Entrées, $23 to $34. Dinner nightly, 6 to 10 or 11. Sunday, brunch 11:30 to 2:30, dinner 5 to 10. Closed Tuesday and Wednesday, September-May.

Della Femina, 99 North Main St., East Hampton.

In East Hampton, don't be surprised by the improbable. Here in 1992 was Jerry Della Femina, arguably the world's most famous ad man and full of Brooklyn bravado, opening a restaurant – named after himself – across the street from Nick & Toni's. Nine months later, he took over another restaurant on the waterfront, East Hampton Point. Soon followed an Italian food market and deli to go, also bearing his name. And a couple of years later he acquired a propitiously located lumber yard for, at the time, who-knew-what-purpose – not, wife-TV newscaster Judy Licht hoped, another restaurant. As New York magazine put it in an article headlined "The Adman Who Ate East Hampton," Jerry Della Femina has a way of making his presence known.

His first restaurant is understated, except perhaps for the prices and the flurry of reservations that are taken ten days ahead and sell out in a few hours at peak periods (there's a "power list" for VIPs). The 80-seat dining room is stark white except for beige cane chairs at well-spaced tables, a wood-paneled ceiling, tall straw wall sconces that look like sheaves of wheat and, near the far corner, a decorative fireplace with colorful jugs on the mantel. Boxes of fruits and vegetables add color in an opening between the dining room and the skylit bar, its walls plastered ever-so-suavely with framed caricatures of restaurant patrons. Trying to make a spot on that wall quickly became part of the restaurant's cachet.

The menu changes monthly. Look for starters like green gazpacho, grilled Hudson

Valley foie gras and carpaccio of ahi tuna with lemon-soy dressing, parmesan cheese and baby greens. Fettuccine with lobster, asparagus and sundried tomatoes is one of the stellar pastas. Main courses could be roasted Mediterranean daurade (a seldom seen fish) with tomato-thyme sauce, roasted organic California quail, and wood-grilled New Zealand venison chop with black pepper sauce. A six-course tasting menu, selected by the chef, is available for the entire table.

Summer desserts are refreshingly cooling, among them Italian plum and blackberry cobbler with blueberry ice cream, banana tarte tatin with ice cream and root beer float with chocolate ice cream. Other seasons yield treats like warm valhrona chocolate cake with passionfruit ice cream and a trio of chocolate sauces and raspberry brioche bread pudding with chambord cream sauce and raspberries.

Dining room at Della Femina.

(631) 329-6666. Entrées, $20 to $33. Dinner nightly, 6 to 11, fewer nights in winter.

The Maidstone Arms, 207 Main St., East Hampton.

New ownership has enhanced the grande dame of East Hampton restaurants. A spectacular floral arrangement in the entry hall is the only showy accouterment in the low-key refurbishment.

Known as the Boat Room, the front dining room with corner service bar is traditional and masculine with dark wood floors, a fireplace and ship's models and seascapes on the walls. The larger rear dining room is carpeted, light and airy. It's notable for Clarence House wallpaper imprinted with trompe-l'oeil shelves and panels of plates that match the real china displayed along the front wall.

Such is the setting for meals that measure up to the expectations of resident East Hamptonites, young and old, celebrating special occasions. Executive chef/general manager William Valentine returned to his native Long Island and the Maidstone Arms after a stint in Los Angeles. California and Pacific Rim influences show up in his masterful roast lacquered duck, everybody's favorite hereabouts. Flavored with five spices and coffee-mandarin glaze, its crisp mahogany skin and tender meat are perched atop scallion pancakes or soba noodles tossed with julienned vegetables. Other choices vary from potato-wrapped local monkfish on broccoli rabe with smoked tomato nage to roasted rack of Colorado lamb with chickpea fritter and tomato confit.

The rum-smoked salmon tartare "martini" is a signature appetizer. Desserts could be blueberry-almond layer cake with lemon mascarpone, chocolate chunk crème brûlée and a trio of homemade ice creams and sorbets.

(631) 324-5006. Entrées, $21.50 to $29.50. Lunch, Monday-Friday noon to 2:30. Saturday and Sunday brunch, noon to 3. Dinner nightly, 6 to 9:30, to 11 on weekends.

East Hampton Point, 295 Three Mile Harbor Road, East Hampton.
Formerly Wings Point, this used to be the place that everyone locally recommended for cocktails on an outdoor terrace beside the water. They didn't seem to eat here, which is why we were able to get an 8 o'clock reservation for a window table on a weekday evening when other restaurants were full.

Enter adman Jerry Della Femina, who whitewashed the dining room and removed walls so that every seat on two levels looks onto boats bobbing to and fro in the marina and the sunset across Three Mile Harbor – or into mirrors reflecting same. Now its tables are coveted as much for dining as for the view. The place looked appealing for a summer lunch, except that we (and other latecomers) were thoroughly ignored, we felt underdressed amid all the fashion and media peacocks, and we didn't care to spend $15 for a chicken BLT sandwich or a tuna niçoise salad. View carries only so far.

For dinner, the kitchen delivers such standouts as grilled Moroccan glazed salmon, grilled yellowfin tuna with wasabi crème fraîche and a perennial favorite, barbecued braised lamb shank over red onion and corn risotto. Start with Maine salmon and crab cakes with avocado tartar sauce or chilled port-roasted Hudson Valley foie gras roulade with rhubarb compote and toasted brioche.

Some of the kicky desserts bring back childhood memories: root beer float with chocolate-chip cookies, and toasted marshmallow and chocolate s'mores with tahitian vanilla bean ice cream, at un-childhood prices in the $7 range.

(631) 329-2800. Entrées, $22 to $35. Lunch daily in season, noon to 3. Dinner nightly, 5:30 to 10 or 11. Sunday brunch, noon to 3. Closed January-March and weekdays April to Memorial Day.

Bostwick's Seafood Grill, 39 Gann Road, East Hampton.
This spacious seafood grill commands the same water view as its higher-profile neighbor, East Hampton Point, but without the prices and pretensions. It's named for young chef-partner Chris Eggert's favorite fishing area in Gardiner's Bay, which shows where his priorities lie.

The seasonal place seats 140, most on a covered outdoor deck that can be enclosed in plastic and heated for use on chilly evenings.

Tiny white ribbed lights on the canopy barely gave off enough light to read the menu as we staved off hunger with a basket of lavasch and hot rolls.

The lobster ravioli was the meal's highlight, a superior appetizer with a divine basil and garlic cream sauce. The caesar salad also was good, and we liked the looks of the thin-crust, brick-oven pizza topped with spinach, bacon, garlic, tomato and more delivered to the next table

For main courses, one of us settled on a special of grilled yellowfin tuna, nicely charred and served on an oversize white plate bearing three swirls of mashed potatoes and a bed of sliced carrots and haricots verts. The other sampled the stuffed yellowtail flounder, a less successful dish with more of the same accompaniments. A Buena Vista sauvignon blanc was a satisfying choice from the affordable wine list

Desserts included Mississippi mud pie, chocolate mousse cake, key lime pie and raspberry sorbet.

(631) 324-1111. Entrées, $14.95 to $19.95. Lunch, Saturday and Sunday noon to 3 in summer. Dinner nightly, 5:30 to 10 or 11, Thursday-Sunday in off-season. Closed late September to May.

Santa Fe Junction, 8 Fresno Place, East Hampton.
Tucked away on a back street (and rather hard to find) is this trendy year-round venture, opened by Chris Eggert and Kevin Boles, who earned their spurs at Bostwick's. They undertook a substantial renovation, adding brick and rough-hewn cedar and french doors in place of windows.

The menu features Southwest fare – "not Tex-Mex," chef Chris pointed out. Dinner entrées include assorted fajitas, hickory-smoked ribs, crab cakes, local seafood, blackened tuna tacos, barbecued chicken enchiladas and mesquite-grilled ribeye steaks. Start with quesadillas, tamales, black bean raviolis or cornmeal-fried oysters. Finish with sopaipillas, chocolate-pecan pie or pumpkin cheesecake.

Although Chris oversees the food in both restaurants, his summer priority remains Bostwick's, because he's a water person at heart.

(631) 324-8700. Entrées, $14.95 to $17.50. Dinner nightly, from 5:30. Closed Wednesday in winter.

The Farmhouse Restaurant, 341 Pantigo Road, East Hampton.
Situated on four beautiful acres and framed by masses of zinnias, the historic Spring Close House has new owners, new decor and a creative kitchen featuring American bistro cooking with a Southern and a French influence. In the late 1600s, this dining room was the center of a 55-acre working farm. Today it specializes in farm-fresh food, and grows its own herbs and vegetables. From a wood-burning oven come chicken, local fish and gourmet pizzas.

The short menu starts with items like local mussels with smoked tomato sauce, roasted eggplant caviar and olive tapenade with wood-fired focaccia crisps, and crab cake with saffron-garlic mayonnaise. Main courses could be grilled Atlantic salmon with sweet corn and tomato ragoût, oven-roasted organic chicken with white cheddar polenta and grilled Australian rack of lamb.

Save room for dessert, perhaps pear cobbler, banana tart with vanilla ice cream and caramel sauce, the brûlée du jour or assorted homemade sorbets.

Canning jars and cans hold fresh flowers on each table in various dining rooms, outfitted in beige with dark green accents. Owners Fred and Susan Lieberman designed the country casual decor, augmented with antique toys from his collection and a delightful mix of whimsy, barnyard nostalgia and sophistication.

A large screened porch with flagstone floor has a billowing white canopy and Japanese lamps for outdoor dining in season.

(631) 324-8585. Entrées, $19 to $32. Dinner nightly, 6 to 10 or 11.

The Laundry, 31 Race Lane, East Hampton.
Only in a place like the self-assured Hamptons could a restaurant converted from a commercial laundry call itself that. This really was a laundry, and you still can see the big extractor outside. Inside all is dark and glamorous, with seating on two levels, a long bar against the outside wall, and seating in green leather-like booths or on red chairs and banquettes. A spectacular flower arrangement at the entrance is a trademark.

Chef Rob Rawleigh's menu changes daily and is very with-it. You might start with carpaccio of local tuna with mustard sauce, cornmeal-fried oysters with lemongrass mayonnaise and tomato salsa or a choice of two tapas for $11. The soup could be Tuscan tomato or chilled cantaloupe.

Entrées range widely from sautéed calves liver to grilled New York sirloin strip steak "dry aged 14 days." Pan-seared Nova Scotia halibut with spicy Asian stir fry, Japanese-style crab cakes with wasabi mayonnaise and grilled mahi-mahi with avocado salsa were among seafood possibilities when we were there.

Desserts run to macadamia-nut taco with coconut cream and tropical fruit, strawberry sour cream brûlée, warm strawberry-rhubarb crisp and banana bread with chocolate crème anglaise and pistachio ice cream.

Locals consider this a good late-hour dining spot. It's also popular with singles. *(631) 324-3199. Entrées. $18 to $28. Dinner nightly, 5:30 to 11 or midnight.*

The Palm Restaurant, 94 Main St., East Hampton.

Everybody raves about the Palm Restaurant at the Huntting Inn, one of a chain extending from Manhattan to ritzy points south and west. They love the huge steaks and chops and lobsters. They warn about being talked into ordering more potatoes and vegetables than you need (the menu says they're served family style for two or more but they can feed an entire family). And they love the scene, dark and clubby and masculine, with lots of booths and caricatures framed on the walls. And, of course, they love it for the celebrities. "Billy Joel would go there, not here," we were advised by an insider at the Hedges' Inn, whose former Palm Restaurant recently was converted into the James Lane Cafe.

This is a typical Manhattan steakhouse, transported to the summery Hamptons by the Huntting owner, whose grandfather was the founder of the Palm. We can't imagine why New Yorkers would come out here to pay more than $30 for a steak or prime rib, add $7 for hash browns or fried onions or string beans ($7.50 for creamed spinach that we hear is great), and $35 or more for a cabernet sauvignon. But thousands do, even lobster-lovers who always come at least once a summer to order lobsters weighing four or more pounds. Who's to question why?

(631) 324-0411. Entrées, $18 to $35. Dinner nightly, 5 to 11. Closed Monday and Tuesday in off-season.

Rowdy Hall, 10 Main St., East Hampton.

For what is called "French Bistro-English Pub" fare, drop into this convivial enterprise, named after a boarding house for artists and writers early in the century. It's owned by the folks from Nick and Toni's, so you know the prices are not exactly English pub style. But it's a popular place to hang out, as they say.

So nosh on a rowdy burger for $9.50, a croque monsieur for $10.50 (egads) or fish and chips for $14.50. A curly endive salad will set you back $7.50, and if you want a comforting pub dish like shepherd's pie, get out $17.50. Sides go for $4.50 each. The dinner menu ranges from pan-roasted salmon to grilled ribeye steak, and one of the favorite salads is arugula with goat cheese.

Bread pudding with bourbon sauce and apple crisp with vanilla ice cream are among desserts.

(631) 324-8555. Entrées, $14.50 to $24. Lunch daily, noon to 3:30. Dinner nightly, 5 to 10 or 11.

Diversions

Many people come to "America's most beautiful village" for the beaches, which have been ranked among the nation's cleanest. But there is much more to see and do.

Beaches. Parking at any village or town beach along Long Island's south shore is limited to fifteen minutes or requires a parking sticker indicating residency. All parking is banned from 10 a.m. to 4 p.m. on the residential streets lined with great estates near the beaches. For those without stickers, parking is available at Main Beach and Atlantic Avenue Beach for $15 on weekdays. Many inns have beach passes for guests.

Walking Tour. Walk Main Street in the heart of East Hampton's historic district from Montauk Highway to Newtown Lane. The **Town Pond** is a tranquil spot at the end of the village green, between Main Street and James Lane. Tombstones date back to the 17th century in the adjacent **South End Cemetery,** where many gravestones are so worn they are no longer legible. **Home Sweet Home,** the 1680 saltbox that was the boyhood home of poet John Howard Payne, who wrote the song of the same name, is open for guided tours and features fine furniture collected over three centuries. Nearby is an early windmill. The **Mulford Farmstead,** long the center of a working farm, also is open for tours in summer. **Guild Hall,** given to the town in 1931, is an art museum with three galleries and the John Drew Theater, the oldest playhouse on Long Island, the site for plays, musicals and concerts. Across the street is the charming brick and stucco, English-looking **East Hampton Library.** There's not a computer terminal in sight, but stacks of newspapers and two old typewriters can be seen through the front office windows of the **East Hampton Star,** the thick and newsy local weekly. Beside it is the **Wild Flower Garden of Long Island,** a shady oasis of native plants, the gift of the Garden Club of East Hampton. **Clinton Academy,** built in 1784, is marked as the oldest "academical" institution in New York State. It's used for Historical Society exhibits of period furniture, artifacts, decoys and dolls. School desks, handwriting lessons and quill pens are on view next door in the shingled **Town House,** a former school and town hall built in 1731. The 1735 **Osborne-Jackson House** is the headquarters of the East Hampton Historical Society. In the triangle between North Main and Pantigo Lane is the **Hook Mill,** a still-operable windmill open to the public for tours in summer.

Driving Tours. Residential streets in the estate area between Main Beach and Georgica Pond are worth a look-see. Tall trees, privet hedges and deep lawns screen some estates from view, but others are visible from the road and most show signs of big money and good taste. Another pleasant drive is along the dunes on Further Lane to Bluff Road in Amagansett.

Shopping. East Hampton's tree-shaded shopping district along Main Street and Newtown Lane is quite villagey and low-key, as opposed, say, to Southampton. Garden benches provide welcome seating every thirty feet or so. Two stores that everybody seems to like are the ultra decorated **Polo Country Store,** the second of summer resident Ralph Lauren's country stores, and the **Coach Factory Store,** where the handsome and expensive bags are sold at a slight discount (we got a discontinued model for half price, however). There are so many designer clothing shops that you wonder if visiting New Yorkers are simply too busy to shop in Manhattan; ditto for antiques and interiors stores. The options vary from **Cashmere Hampton, Bonne Nuit** (lacy lingerie and children's outfits), **Whitewash** (almost all white clothing) to **Victory Garden** ("antiques, etc." for garden and home) and **Long Island Sound** (music store). We coveted the incredible carved wood sculptures and acrylics (one of Noah's Ark and all the passengers for $2,400) at **Anne Kolb Gallery.** More to our price range were the handful of upscale outlet stores, spread out around sculptures and benches flanking the large lawn at

Amagansett Square. The trendoids pick up their gourmet foods at **Jerry and David's Red Horse Market,** owned by Jerry Della Femina and a partner from Dean & DeLuca, at 74 Montauk Hwy. One of the more exotic salad bars is located across the plaza at Red Horse to Go. Other good lunchy spots with salads, focaccia sandwiches, gourmet foods and such are **JL Bean** and **Barefoot Contessa,** both along Newtown Lane.

Farm Stands. Long known for potatoes and ducks, eastern Long Island has become a center for fresh produce. **Round Swamp Farm** at 184 Three Mile Harbor Road was featured in the New York Times as one of summer resident Craig Claiborne's favorite markets. It sells everything from fruits and exotic vegetables to preserves, fish, cheese, baked goods and more, and we picked up a couple of jars of their good salsas. We thought Round Swamp couldn't be topped, but it was – at least in terms of size and crowds – by the **Amagansett Farmers Market** on the Montauk Highway in Amagansett, a privately owned "stand" bigger than any we've seen. Here, at what is obviously a local gathering spot, everyone was buying cut flowers for the weekend, picking up oyster mushrooms and baby pattypan squash, and sifting through every salsa, mustard, oil and vinegar ever made. An incredible bakery produces the best sticky buns, and folks sit out front with croissants and cappuccino from the espresso bar. There also are a section of prepared foods and a great meat market.

Extra-Special

Wolffer Estate/Sagpond Vineyards, 139 Sagg Road, Sagaponack.

Long Island has become known for fine wines, since the Hargrave Vineyard pioneered on the North Fork in the 1970s. Lately, the South Fork is diverting attention from North Fork vintners. Here, a stunning, state-of-the-art winery opened atop a hill above the Atlantic Ocean in 1997. It looks like something straight out of Tuscany with its blue shutters on a sand-colored façade, imposing gates, colorful gardens and a fountain at the entry. Windows in the cathedral-ceilinged tasting room look onto the tanks in the fermentation room. Christian Wolffer, German-born international venture capitalist, bought the property on the north side of the Montauk Highway to raise horses, and his Sagpond Farm is considered the top stable on the South Fork. He then planted 50 acres of grapes in 1987. Winemaker Roman Roth from Germany produces award-winning chardonnays, merlots and pinot noirs in the European style. Bone dry rosé, champagne and dessert wines are newer releases among Sagpond's production of 10,000 cases a year. Prices range from the rosé for $12.99 to a 1995 pinot noir for $34.99. It claims to be the only New York State winery whose offerings are carried in all five of Manhattan's highest ranked restaurants.

A new addition is the **Wolffer Estate Farm,** on the southern edge of Sagpond Vineyards at 3312 Montauk Hwy. Along with wines, it offers fresh produce, potted plants, gourmet coffee, breads and Sagpond Farmstead Cheese.

(631) 537-5106. Showroom daily, 11 to 6. Tours by appointment.

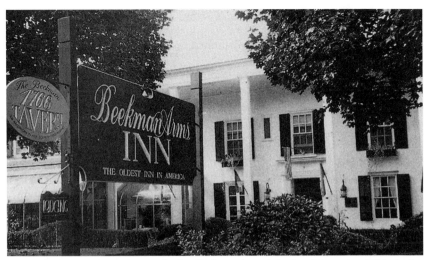

America's oldest continuously operating inn, Beekman Arms, is landmark in center of Rhinebeck.

Rhinebeck, N.Y.

Jewel Along the Hudson

Among New York State towns, few are so old – and noticeably so – as Rhinebeck.

Located in the northern Hudson Valley a couple of miles inland from the river, the village was settled in 1686 by the Dutch as Kipsbergen. German immigrants who moved there around 1713 named it for their native Rhine river and "beck" meaning cliffs. The Livingstons, the Astors, the Vanderbilts, the Roosevelts and others of America's landed gentry followed.

Rhinebeck claims eight miles of the Hudson Valley's Sixteen Mile Historic District, whose great riverfront estates from the Gilded Age are well known. Less known is the fact that Rhinebeck – with 437 sites listed on the National Register, most out of the public eye on side streets – embraces one of the nation's largest historic districts.

The Beekman Arms, America's oldest continuously operated inn, occupies a prime corner at the village's main intersection. Across the street is an old-fashioned cigar store and newsstand, which still advertises cigars on its façade and displays pipes and tobacco inside and, sign of the times, a walk-in cigar humidor. On another corner, the old-line Rhinebeck Department Store with updated apparel claims to "continue tradition." Fanning out from the main intersection are a variety of stores, some with a New Age bent, and restaurants old and new. Most reflect a simpler past or pace rather than a gentrified, hectic present.

Farther from the center are other attractions. The Dutchess County Fairgrounds is home of New York State's second largest agricultural fair, plus periodic crafts and antiques shows of considerable renown. Antique airplanes perform stunts at the Old Rhinebeck Aerodrome. The heritage of the grand estates lives on at the Wilderstein Restoration, the Mills Mansion, Montgomery Place and Clermont. The Omega Institute links people with self fulfillment and the New Age.

Tiny Rhinecliff, where the train still stops, slumbers alongside the Hudson. Away from the villages, the rural landscape that attracted the Hudson River School painters remains pastoral – remarkably so, given its proximity to the nation's largest metropolitan area.

What the New York Daily News headlined "the renaissance of Rhinebeck" has vaulted the village lately into a destination for tourists.

"When people think of Rhinebeck, they think of the Beekman Arms," notes Nikola Rebraca, a New York restaurateur who recently restored the Belvedere Mansion into an inn and restaurant. "It's like the anchor store. They have history behind them. Everybody else plays second fiddle."

That may be changing. At least four restaurants give the Beekman dining operation a run for its money among knowing diners. Other inns and B&Bs have emerged, most in the last few years. Some on the fringe tend to come and go.

"Rhinebeck is rapidly becoming the focal point of everything in the Hudson Valley," notes architectural historian Ward Stanley, who moved from Philadelphia to open the Veranda House B&B in a mansion listed on the National Register.

Yet this is no slick, cutesy, movie-set town. Rhinebeck goes its own way. Visitors so inclined may come along.

Inn Spots

Beekman Arms, 4 Mill St. (Route 9), Rhinebeck 12572.

America's oldest continuously operating inn ages gracefully. It dates to 1766, and nowhere more noticeably than in the dark and beamed, low-ceilinged Tap Room, where candles are lit even at noon. In the newer rooms in the separate Delamater Courtyard area, the accommodations are up-to-date, some even verging on the luxurious. The food in the Beekman 1776 Tavern is often at the cutting edge.

The Beekman (or the Beek, as it's called locally) claims history, obviously, among its many facets. The feeling of antiquity is tangible in sections of the main building, which doesn't look all that old, what with its restored Georgian pillared facade and a contemporary solarium dining room facing the front lawn where George Washington and his troops drilled during the Revolutionary War. But the

requisite wide-plank floors, overhead beams and stone hearth greet guests in the lobby, often the busiest place in town. A guest log from 1887 is embedded in a coffee table in the far parlor, where we marveled over the glass-enclosed, tabletop replica of an old tavern. Everything is in miniature, down to the most intricate tiny liquor bottles and bar stools.

Upstairs in the main building, the thirteen guest rooms on the second and third floors were remodeled and redecorated with fresh Colonial décor and folk art accents in 1995. We were shown a couple of rooms that were described as typical. Each has twin beds, plump matching chairs, a TV hidden in a chest, a washbowl inlaid in a wooden cabinet in the bathroom and a wooden butler with a tray holding a few amenities. All contain English pants presses, telephones and a decanter of sherry. Most remain dark and historic, as you'd expect from their heritage.

Behind the main inn are six motel-style rooms with in-room refrigerators. Restaurant owner Larry Forgione's American Spoon Foods are featured in the Beekman Country Store at the side of the inn. An Antique Market and Art Gallery occupies a barn in back.

The most comfortable accommodations are the 40 of later vintage in the Delamater complex a block up the street from the main inn. The gingerbread-trimmed Delamater House was built in 1844 in the rare American Gothic style for the founder of the local bank. The original marble fireplace warms its guest parlor. The spacious front-corner bedroom opposite offers one of the inn's few kingsize beds and a plush wicker sitting area. Television sets are hidden in the armoires of it and the five upstairs guest rooms. Sherry awaits in decanters, a rear kitchen is available for guests, and front and rear porches are great for relaxing.

Behind the house are top-of-the-line rooms in the cathedral-ceilinged Carriage House and five other guest houses scattered around the perimeter of the Delamater Courtyard. All have beige facades with brown trim and colorful red roofs. Each holds four to eight rooms. The Germond House, which was moved to the site, contains a conference center as well. Rooms we toured in the carriage house have two Shaker-style double beds or a king bed on a level slightly raised above the sitting area, with sofabed, TV, antique chests and writing desks. Crossbeams accent the ceilings. The bathrooms are modern and outfitted with the amenities one expects. Twenty-three rooms contain working fireplaces.

Guests here take continental breakfast in a side building with a gift shop and tables overlooking the interior courtyard lawn.

Charles LaForge Jr., owner since 1958, is the longest lasting of the Beekman's fourteen landlords listed on a plaque at the entry. He oversees the main inn. Innkeeper Doris Masteen handles the Delamater complex, which seems to go its own way with a separate telephone number and reception area.

(914) 876-7077 or (800) 361-6517. Delamater House (914) 876-7080. Fifty-seven rooms and two suites with private baths. Inn and motel: doubles, $80 to $120. Delamater complex: $85 to $150. Children accepted.

Belvedere Mansion, 10 Old Route 9, Box 785, Rhinebeck 12572.

There are nine mansions in the mid-Hudson Valley that you can visit but only one in which you can stay, say Nikola and Patricia Rebraca, who claim the distinction. Longtime New York City restaurateurs, they took over the hilltop mansion overlooking the Hudson in 1993 to turn it into a restaurant and inn.

Erected in 1900 after fire destroyed the original home built in 1760, the pillared, Greek Revival mansion is named for its beautiful view. The interior is a fantasy reflecting the Gilded Age, lavishly decorated with 18th-century French antiques, trompe l'oeil and a cloud-painted ceiling. Sumptuous silk and damask fabrics adorn the walls and vintage fixtures light the rooms.

Upstairs are five guest rooms of mansion proportions. The rear Roosevelt Room with an English Tudor canopy bed is masculine in chocolate brown with gold trim. "There are a lot of pictures to get crooked around here," Patricia noted as she straightened a couple while showing us around. All rooms have private baths with abundant marble, ceiling fans and matching French Empire beds (most queensize) and mirrored armoires. The Astor and Lafayette in front offer fireplaces and river views. Art deco lighting fixtures and a gilded clawfoot slipper tub grace the Vanderbilt Room. Two twin beds are joined as a king in the Livingston Room, where a writing desk occupies a private nook beside an oval window and the walls of the fanciful bathroom are painted blue to look like the sea.

Behind and to the side of the mansion is a motel-like lineup of accommodations with separate entrances in the former carriage house. Euphemistically called cottages, they're decorated differently with as much pizzazz as their simplicity and space would allow (a handpainted bureau here, a wicker chair there). The most popular is the River Queen, devoted to the riverboat era and boasting a handmade canopy kingsize bridal bed. Six have king beds. Four "cozies" each have a double bed tucked away in an alcove, a bathroom and not much more. They're perfectly serviceable, but not exactly the kind of place where you'd want to hang out and, at any rate, most have no places to sit.

More accommodations emerged in 1999 in a renovated lodge in the Adirondack style beyond the carriage house. Ten rooms here are dressed in Ralph Lauren and Laura Ashley country style. All have bathrooms with slate floors and walls (even the showers), and some have whirlpool tubs. Lighting is low, the chairs cane and the feeling rather Oriental – Nikola calls it "very Zen like." Rooms open off a wraparound cedar porch shared by guests.

A country breakfast is served in the dining room or on the terrace. It generally includes a choice of omelets with Coach Farm goat cheese and oven-dried tomatoes, walnut-crusted french toast or Hudson Valley pear pancakes.

The ten-acre property includes a rear pool with cabanas, a tennis court and a pond with a gazebo. At a recent visit, an elaborate French garden was being planted and a trellised glass conservatory furnished with lounges was ready beside. Next on the agenda was a paneled library/common room off the bar.

(914) 889-8000. Fax (914) 889-8811. Twenty-five rooms with private baths. Doubles, $225 to $275 in mansion, $175 in lodge, $95 to $150 in cottages. Two-night minimum on weekends.

The Mansakenning Carriage House, 29 Ackert Hook Road, Rhinebeck 12572.

The Manhattan celebrities and CEOs drawn to this luxury hideaway in the country view it as a place for escape and romance. They don't want to chat idly with other guests or eat breakfast at a big communal table, says owner Michelle Dremann. "They cherish their privacy and independence, so they have everything they need in their rooms."

Michelle started in 1990 with two rooms and a suite in the main 1895 Colonial house that actually was the carriage house for a larger estate listed on the National Register and hidden in the woods some distance away. She now has four more suites, a husband and a child, and two fulltime innkeepers to assist.

The seven romantic hideaways here range from a small bedroom with a hall bath in the twelve-room main house to a sumptuous suite fashioned from four horse stalls in the former Stable. Five suites have fireplaces, three have jacuzzi tubs and four have private balconies or decks.

Mansakenning Carriage House is ready for overnight guests.

A Philadelphia artist painted the remarkable stencil designs, and Michelle decorated the bedrooms to the hilt. The queen or kingsize beds are dressed with Ralph Lauren linens and down comforters. TV/VCRs, telephones, Caswell-Massey toiletries, terry robes and a basket of extra towels are the norm. A coffeemaker, a decanter of sherry and a refrigerator stocked with complimentary beverages are in each room.

Michelle says Joan Rivers prefers the original Manaskenning Suite, light and airy with a kingsize bed beneath a beamed cathedral ceiling and eleven windows on three sides. An oriental rug accents the polished wide-board floor and two casual chairs face the fireplace. French doors open onto a narrow wraparound balcony.

Others like the largest Country Covert Suite on the main floor of the Stable. The corner fireplace is positioned to face the kingsize bed, and the jacuzzi is enclosed in wainscoting that matches the bedroom ceiling. A bird's nest is handpainted under a sheer half canopy above the Victorian trundle bed in a sitting room in one of the former horse stalls. The bedroom desk is next to a built-in ladder and a grain feeder from the original hayloft.

A wall in the Stable's upstairs hallway is a garden delight of handpainted flowers, birds, butterflies, a squirrel on a wheelbarrow and even a ladybug tucked in a blossom. Guests in the Huntsman's Hideaway find trompe l'oeil books painted on the fireplace mantle and incredible handpainted walls that look like wallpaper in the bathroom. At the other end of the hayloft is the sunny Fox Den with kingsize canopy bed, fireplace, jacuzzi and private deck.

Breakfast is delivered in a hefty basket with the local newspaper to the guest rooms at the decadent hour of 9:30. Guests, most still in their robes, take it at a table in their room or on a balcony. The fresh orange juice is in a chilled glass flask and the homemade croissants, scones, mini-bagels and rugelach are in a heated cookie tin. The exotic fruit is a work of art surrounding the main dish, in our case diminutive slices of french toast stuffed with pecans and cream cheese,

Veranda House occupies 1845 Federal residence that was once a church parsonage.

garnished with edible flowers and so good alone we passed on the side of peach-apricot sauce. The menu, printed daily, might yield cheese blintzes or buckwheat crêpes filled with smoked salmon. Their recipes have been included in a couple of inn cookbooks.

Guests rarely venture forth from their quarters into the huge living room with game tables that go begging most of the time in the main house, where the family occupies the first and third floors. They may walk around the five acres of wooded grounds, relax on Adirondack chairs or play croquet or badminton.

(914) 876-3500. Fax (914) 876-6179. www.mchrhinebeck.com. Two rooms and five suites with private baths. Doubles, $150 and $295 weekends. Suites, $295 to $375 weekends, $195 to $250 midweek. Main house reserved for family Sunday-Thursday. By reservation only. Two-night minimum on weekends. Children over 17. No smoking.

Veranda House, 82 Montgomery St., Rhinebeck 12572.

Once an Episcopal church parsonage, this attractive 1845 Federal house listed in the National Register took on a new role in 1993. Ward and Linda Stanley of Philadelphia bought the residence at the north end of the village's historic district to run as a B&B, and a charmer it is indeed.

They offer five air-conditioned guest rooms with telephones and private baths. One contains an original marble sink like one at the nearby Clermont mansion, a guest told Ward. Four have a variety of queensize beds, from four-poster Shaker with lacy canopy to antique brass. A side room that gets both morning and afternoon sun has old-fashioned wood twin beds convertible to king. Two bedrooms, one downstairs in what had been a dining room and the other above, are architecturally notable for their bay windows attached to a five-sided bay.

The Stanleys have outfitted the common areas with rather modern furniture from their Philadelphia home. The fireplaced living room opens onto a breakfast room as well as a cozy TV room/library with books specializing in art and architecture. The original parquet floors and pretty glassware are on display throughout. Ward, who recently retired from a university job teaching architectural history, hosts lively wine and cheese hours for weekend guests on the wicker-filled front veranda or on a new terrace off the dining room.

Linda serves a full breakfast, starting with juice, a fruit plate and a homemade pastry, perhaps fresh scallion and gruyère muffins or sour-cream coffee cake. Orange-yogurt pancakes, zucchini and feta cheese crêpes or eggs Veranda (her own version of eggs benedict with portobello mushrooms) could be the main course. Apple or pecan strudel might follow. Ward's special coffee from New Harmony Coffee Co. of Philadelphia is freshly ground each morning.

Breakfasting on the terrace, a couple from South Africa said they felt right at home. The response was prompted by the mythical rhinoceros sculpted by the Stanleys' daughter and lurking under the trees in the side yard.

(914) 876-4133. www.verandahouse.com. Five rooms with private baths. Doubles, $130 to $150 weekends, $120 to $140 midweek, including tax. Two-night minimum most weekends. No smoking.

Olde Rhinebeck Inn, 37 Wurtemburg Road, Rhinebeck 12572.

This rambling, low-slung house began in 1738 as one room. Fittingly it's the dining area, where Jonna Paolella – proud to have been designated at age 28 as the youngest owner-innkeeper in America – serves up fruit smoothies and lavish breakfasts as up-to-date as today.

Open to her kitchen, it's the heart of the house and the place where she begins tours of a structure that oozes history in almost every inch between wide-plank floors and hand-hewn beamed ceilings. "I'd never even been in an historic house this old," said Jonna, before she saw it in 1998 as the fulfillment of a dream by the daughter of an innkeeper in Brooklyn's Park Slope section. "Why, here you can sleep in a place built before Mozart was born."

The dining room focuses on a long trestle table this born-to-be-an-innkeeper crafted of stained white oak salvaged from Jimmy Cagney's barn in nearby Stannardsville. The chair seats were upholstered in fabric from an old church. An old pig barn on the property furnished the wood for the kitchen cabinets, and the counter tops are made of wood from a carriage barn across the street. The stone floor of a sunken TV/family room off the kitchen came from a nearby gristmill. The woodwork in the living room is patched and weathered and shows its age (1745) and National Register status.

Her guests sleep in three-going-on-five bedrooms that convey creature comforts amidst antiquity and are named for inns that inspired her. The floors creak in the Ryefield Suite as you step out of the rare queensize bed, from which six inches had to be cut from the legs for the elaborate carved-wood canopy to fit beneath the hand-hewn chestnut ceiling beams. Beyond is a dressing/sitting room with a day bed. The queen bed angled in the corner of the light and airy Spirited Dove Room wouldn't fit going up the steep, narrow stairway. "So we blew open the side wall – hence the balcony," says Jonna, referring to the appealing hideaway overlooking a stocked fishpond on the pastoral property.

Each bedroom comes with satellite TV, CD player, terry robes, stocked guest refrigerator and fresh flowers. The Spirited Dove adds a jacuzzi tub, while the Deer Hill has a separate sitting area and a private covered porch.

Each also is equipped with a table for breakfast, but most guests prefer to eat communally in the dining room. The meal starts with juices or fruit smoothies and an elaborate fruit platter. The main event could be baked french pear pancakes with sides of potatoes and eggs and a maple-pumpkin-walnut mini-loaf. Other options include fluffy German pancakes and sweet-potato frittatas.

Welcome amenities might be fruit, fudge made with goat's milk, cookies and assorted pastries. Entertainment is provided out back by Jonna's two pygmy and pygora goats. Feedings take place twice a day, and the goats respond with the makings for goat cheese.

(914) 871-1745. Fax (914) 876-8809. Two rooms and one suite with private baths. Doubles, $275 to $295 weekends, $225 midweek; $175 to $195 midweek, off-season.

Whistle Wood Farm, 11 Pells Road, Rhinebeck 12572.

Tucked away in the wooded section of a rural horse farm is a rambling ranch house full of character, not the least of which reflects the owner. Maggie Myer opened her house as a B&B in 1983, offering rooms with shared baths and cupcakes for breakfast. She's come a long way. Her accommodations now have private baths (three of them jacuzzis), queensize four-poster beds and ceiling fans. And her hearty buffet breakfasts, pictured in magazines, even entail desserts.

"How about a piece of apple pie or lemon-poppyseed cake?" Maggie asked as we arrived at mid-morning, pointing to treats left on the buffet table from the breakfast spread just finished. Her guests had demolished her mixed fruit platter and french toast with bacon before leaving for a day at the Omega Institute nearby.

The homey, much-lived-in farmhouse holds a front sunroom, a barnwood living room with a big stone fireplace and a dining area with a striking horse mural. The country pine table here seems to play second fiddle as a breakfast venue to the front sunroom and the front or rear decks. Baskets, pans and lanterns hang from beams in the country kitchen that's the heart of the house.

Three guest rooms in one wing range from the small Tumbleweed Room with a pastel quilt, ruffled curtains and a hall bath to the rear Juniper Room with quilts on the walls, an extra day bed and its own deck onto a berry patch. The other end of the house harbors the spacious Wyoming Room named for Maggie's western accessories, including an antique quilt, Indian blankets and a stained-glass rocking horse. A canoe rests on the rafters above the sturdy pine bed, and a twin bed is around the corner in an alcove. The spacious bath has a jacuzzi for two. Sliding glass double doors open to the front and side gardens complete with fountain.

The newest and most deluxe accommodations are nearby in a renovated barn with a common living room and outdoor patios. Both the Morningside and Northwind rooms have queen beds, pine-paneled walls, stone fireplaces, skylit cathedral ceilings and jacuzzi tubs. The mix of Adirondack and antique furnishings is enhanced by oriental and Indian rugs.

Maggie also puts up guests a few miles away in the two-bedroom Lake Cliff Cottage at Beaver Point on a small lake, where turtles, beavers and a mute swan named Harold hang out.

Here, guests share the property with up to twenty horses, three dogs and a donkey. "One guest called me Martha Stewart with spurs," volunteered Maggie. She likens herself to Johnny Appleseed: "I'm always planting flowers everywhere."

(914) 876-6838. Fax (914) 876-5513. Six rooms and one cottage with private baths. Doubles, $135 to $325 weekends, $95 to $225 midweek. Cottage, $325 weekends, $225 midweek. Two-night minimum on weekends. No smoking.

The Mulberry Street Guest House, 25 Mulberry St., Rhinebeck 12572.

Local antiques dealer Kristine Stein and her husband Ray share their lovely, antiques-filled home with overnight guests.

The 1880 Victorian house, located in the historic district, is furnished to the period. Upstairs are two air-conditioned guest rooms with private baths. The Bay Room features a rice-carved queen canopy poster bed and a loveseat in the handsome side bay window. A carved mirrored armoire is a prized possession here. Two twin beds can be joined as a kingsize in the Charleston Room, which has two chairs upholstered in floral and Victorian floral decor throughout.

A full breakfast is served in the large, formal dining room with a side bay window and French toile wallpaper. Fruit and muffins precede a hot main course.

Guests relax in the elegant, formal parlor or a small, more casual library with a TV and an upright piano.

(914) 876-5478. Two rooms with private baths. Doubles, $120 to $130. Two-night minimum in season. No smoking. No credit cards.

Dining Spots

Cripple Creek Restaurant, 18 Garden St., Rhinebeck.

Artistry of the performing as well as the culinary kind embellish this restaurant that took center stage under new ownership in 1999. The food is flavorful, seasonal and mostly indigenous, with an emphasis on organically raised meats, grains and produce from area farms. CIA-trained chef David Bruno calls the fare "regional American with Asian and French influences." Co-owner Bing Yang is responsible for the Asian influence, while partner Dennis Giauque, accompanist for two of the Three Tenors and assistant conductor of the Metropolitan Opera, reflects a musical heritage. Manager Patrick Hayes, a former concert pianist, has a master's degree from the Juilliard School of Music.

The new team took over the failing Cripple Creek Café when their planned new Rhinebeck restaurant – Bing's, advertised as a New York supper club – burned to the ground three days before it was to open. They enhanced the L-shaped room with taupe walls, gray carpeting, white over black linens, black chairs and accents of faux marble. White fabric billows beneath the ceiling, and a corner built-in bookshelf displays books, vases, a small picture of Dennis with Luciano Pavarotti.

Classical music plays in the background, but that is about the only musical accent as the owners bide their time for opening the planned supper club. Patrick said that even then, they would continue to operate Cripple Creek.

The food was terrific but the service languid during a mid-week lunch. The day's roasted garlic and potato purée soup was teamed with half a grilled vegetable and mozzarella sandwich. Homemade potato crisps and a small salad of rice and cranberry beans accompanied this and the other sandwich, an extra-assertive grilled spice-rubbed pork loin with apricot mustard on peasant bread. The delicate and ever-so-flavorful pear tarte tatin with hazelnut ice cream was worth the wait.

Dinner fare is creative and portions substantial. Expect main dishes like pan-seared sea scallops with French green lentils and baby bok choy, sautéed arctic char on jonah crab potatoes with braised fennel, and rosemary-marinated roast lamb on soft polenta with vegetable marmalade. Starters could be cranberry bean and smoked bacon soup with crème fraîche or house-cured duck confit on a ragoût of white beans, garlic and escarole. Finish with a chocolate grand marnier terrine, the house selection of berry ices or ice cream in a honey crisp, or a sampler plate of most of the day's desserts.

(914) 876-4355. Entrées, $15 to $25. Open daily except Tuesday, noon to 9.

Hilltop Belvedere Mansion is named for its beautiful view of the Hudson River.

Belvedere Mansion, 10 Old Route 9, Rhinebeck.

New York restaurateurs Nikola and Patricia Rebraca, who had run Panarella's restaurant on Manhattan's West Side since 1979, now operate this fancy new restaurant. Patricia is executive chef, teaming with chef Patricia Panarella to provide contemporary regional cuisine.

The hilltop mansion seats 60 diners in three high Victorian dining rooms of the chandelier, fireplace and gilt-framed painting variety. Forty-five more can be accommodated at tables beneath green umbrellas on a spacious side deck in season. There's also a romantic table for two or four in a little tearoom at the head of the stairway landing.

It's an elegant, formal setting for contemporary regional food. The dinner menu is straightforward and quite affordable. Appetizers vary from a napoleon of salmon carpaccio with corn and scallion pancakes to ravioli of Coach Farm goat cheese and duck confit with saffron cream. Entrées could be sesame-encrusted yellowfin tuna with baby bok choy with ginger mirin, grilled pork medallions on creamy mascarpone polenta and New Zealand rack of lamb with a crimini mushroom and potato lasagna. Expect surprises like pan-seared Alaskan cod served over ratatouille or sautéed ocean perch over a purple peruvian potato with fennel and blood orange reduction.

Homemade desserts include chocolate truffle cake with mango crème anglaise, raspberry swirl cheesecake with berry coulis and a trio of sorbets.

(914) 889-8000. Entrées, $18 to $26. Dinner, Wednesday-Sunday 5:30 to 9:30.

Le Petit Bistro, 8 East Market St., Rhinebeck.

Chef-owner Jean-Paul Croizer has retired, but this long-running establishment didn't miss a beat. Two of his waiters bought the place in 1997. Head waiter Brendan Callan moved into the kitchen and partner Dan Bleen manages the front. Brendan has quietly updated the fare, although he insists the menu remains the same. And Yvonne Crozier stayed on, so regulars still get a hug and a kiss upon arrival.

Pine walls and floors give the 40-seat dining room and half-circle bar at the side a country-French look. Except for globe lamps inside wooden frames, the decor is simple and the atmosphere convivial and intimate.

The French menu starts with classics like onion soup, pâté maison, smoked trout and escargots. Dover sole meunière is a house specialty. Sea scallops with crushed black peppercorns and cream sauce, duck with orange sauce, veal piccata, frog's legs, rack of lamb provençal and steak au poivre are among the choices. Grilled tuna niçoise, poulet marengo and rainbow trout with crabmeat and grenobloise sauce were specials at our latest visit.

Desserts include crème caramel, mocha mousse, raspberry frappe and peach melba.

(914) 876-7400. Entrées, $17.75 to $23.95. Dinner, Thursday-Monday 5 to 10, Sunday 4 to 9.

Calico Restaurant & Patisserie, 9 Mill St. (Route 9), Rhinebeck.

A perfect five-star rating from the Poughkeepsie restaurant reviewer followed the opening of this intimate little charmer in a twenty-seat storefront across from the Beekman Arms. The stars were for the food offered by Culinary Institute of America grad Tony Balassone and the baked goods of his wife Leslie.

The patisserie in front opens at 7 a.m. for croissants and brioche from a display case stocked with delectable treats. Come lunch time, the kitchen offers a handful of interesting choices, perhaps seafood chili with cornbread, house-smoked salmon fillet served on a mixture of greens and roasted porcini mushrooms, pizza of the day and sliced flank steak on a toasted baguette. The gratinéed vidalia onion soup laced with Anchor Steam ale makes a good starter. So does the roasted garlic soup with crème fraîche and herbed brioche croutons.

At night, Tony prepares such treats as sautéed flounder served atop a spinach, shrimp and portobello mushroom hash; a classic bouillabaisse, breast of free-range chicken stuffed with spinach and goat cheese, and rack of New Zealand lamb with mint-infused eggplant and vegetable stew.

Start with a whole roasted garlic head served with gratinéed Coach Farms goat cheese, pesto sauce and croutons. Finish with one of the more than twenty exceptional desserts from the pastry case.

Artifacts and calico items adorn a shelf above the pale blue wainscoting of this pure and simple place beloved by the locals. It has a full liquor license. The wine list features boutique vineyards and good values.

(914) 876-2749. Entrées, $16.95 to $19.95. Lunch, Wednesday-Sunday 11 to 3:30. Dinner, Wednesday-Sunday 5:30 to 9:30 or 10:30.

The Beekman 1776 Tavern, Route 9, Rhinebeck.

The restaurant at the Beekman Arms reopened to unprecedented fanfare after it was leased in 1991 to celebrity chef Larry Forgione, owner of An American Place in Manhattan. Forgione, who since has opened a third restaurant in Miami Beach and seldom is in the kitchen here, regularly updates a menu that incorporates American classics and regional ingredients. A chef from Argentina, Tony Nogales, executes his commands.

The classic Tap Room and Colonial dining rooms glow with the patina of age. Quite in contrast is the large, plant-filled solarium dining room overlooking the main street.

The American-to-the-max menu lists such appetizers as marinated forest mushrooms with Coach Farm goat cheese polenta, crispy fried squid with tarragon mayonnaise and local camembert crisp with field greens and gooseberry chutney.

Typical main courses are cedar-planked Atlantic salmon atop a creamy corn pudding, Eastern yellowfin tuna garnished with bok choy and steamed sticky rice, honey-glazed Adirondack duck on a stone-ground corn cake, and Colorado leg of lamb with mint pesto. Those with more traditional palates can try glazed country-style meatloaf, Pennsylvania Dutch free-range turkey pot pie, pizza of the day or a burger on a fresh sesame bun.

Desserts include old-fashioned double-chocolate pudding, fruit crisp, homemade ice cream and sorbet of the day.

Obviously, the menu implies excitement, many of the accompaniments are interesting and unusual, and the prices are far lower than they would be in Manhattan. But the food critics' raves seem to fall on deaf ears locally.

(914) 871-1766. Entrées, $15.95 to $23.95. Lunch daily, 11:30 to 3. Dinner, 5:30 to 9 or 9:30. Sunday, brunch 10 to 2, dinner 3:30 to 9.

Diversions

The area's history and rural environment are the main drawing cards for visitors.

Rhinebeck Walking Tour. Copies of a walking tour developed in 1980, just after Rhinebeck was listed on the National Register as "among the most cohesive and best preserved historic environments," are still distributed by the Rhinebeck Historical Society at the Chamber of Commerce visitor center. The tour points out prime examples among the more than 400 Colonial and Victorian structures listed on the National Register, especially along residential Montgomery, Livingston, Chestnut and Mulberry streets. Rhinebeck claims half of an area known as the Sixteen Mile Historic District, composed of 30 contiguous riverfront estates associated with the landed gentry of the 18th, 19th and early 20th centuries.

Wilderstein Preservation, Morton Road, Rhinebeck.

This towering, 35-room Queen Anne Victorian on a 40-acre riverfront site was owned and occupied until 1991 by the Suckley family, descendants of the early Livingston and Beekman families. Its opulent interiors were decorated by J.B. Tiffany and its grounds landscaped by Calvert Vaux, Frederick Law Olmsted's partner in the design of New York's Central Park. The estate's intricate network of paths, rustic gazebos and sheltered garden seats offer walkers scenic adventures and contemplation. Interior visitors are intrigued by the legacies of its last occupant, Margaret Lynch Suckley, a distant cousin of Franklin Delano Roosevelt. She worked with the president as archivist at the Presidential Library in nearby Hyde Park and often kept him company in Washington and on train trips. FDR called her Daisy and she gave him his famous little dog, Fala. After her death in her 100th year in 1991 at Wilderstein, friends cleaning her cluttered bedroom found a battered suitcase beneath the bed. Inside were Daisy's diaries and the letters the pair exchanged. The resulting book, *Closest Companion,* details their intimate friendship.

(914) 876-4818. Open Thursday-Sunday noon to 4, May-October. Adults, $5.

Mills Mansion, Old Post Road, Staatsburg.

A few miles downriver from Wilderstein, this Beaux Arts mansion of 65 rooms was the country estate of Ruth Livingston Mills and her husband, financier Ogden Mills. Built in 1832 and expanded in 1895 by architect Stanford White, it contains gilded ceilings, marble fireplaces, ornate furniture and art objects from around the world. The grounds sweep down to the river, offering some of the best views along the Hudson. A paved path leads to an old boathouse.

(914) 889-8851. Open Wednesday-Saturday 10 to 5, Sunday noon to 5, May to Labor Day, Wednesday-Sunday noon to 5 through October. Adults, $5.

Montgomery Place, Annandale-on-Hudson.

This 23-room Federal mansion dating to 1805 is furnished with 200 years of Livingston family possessions. The 434-acre riverfront property contains working pear and peach orchards, towering black locust trees, ornamental rose and herb gardens. Woodland carriage and walking trails wind through the property and down to the river.

(914) 758-5461. Open daily except Tuesday, 10 to 5, April-October, also Saturday-Sunday 10 to 5 in November and December. Guided house tour, $6; self-guided tour of grounds, $3.

Other Mansions. The foregoing landmarks are the closest to Rhinebeck, but more are nearby. Just to the north lie **Clermont,** oldest of all the Hudson River estates and occupied by seven generations of Livingstons from 1730 to 1962, and **Olana,** the Persian-style hilltop home designed by and for Frederic Edwin Church, one of the foremost Hudson River School artists. To the south are the opulent **Vanderbilt Mansion,** the **Home of Franklin D. Roosevelt National Historic Site** and the companion **Val-Kill,** Eleanor Roosevelt's retreat.

Ferncliff Forest Preserve, River Road and Mount Rutsen Road, Rhinebeck, (914) 8765-3196. This 192-acre sanctuary was part of a vast estate owned by John Jacob Astor. Extensive trails lead to a pond, a lookout tower and foundation stones from the original 59 farms that made up Astor's 2,800 acres. Picnic tables make it a good stop for hikers and bicyclists.

The Old Rhinebeck Aerodrome & Museum, 44 Stone Church Road, Rhinebeck.

Endearingly indigenous to old-fashioned Rhinebeck is this collection of hangars, bleachers, booths, signs and antique "aeroplanes" that looks on busy days like an old county fair, when pilots in biplanes barnstormed the countryside. When our children were young, we joined the multitudes for one of the weekend air shows and found it a lot of laughs. The oldtime melodrama revs up the skies, as World War 1-vintage planes perform daredevil stunts in a flying circus that culminates in a climactic dogfight. Fifteen-minute barnstorming flights in a 1929 open-cockpit biplane are available before and after the shows for $30 a person. The Aerodrome's new museum building and hangars are full of old airplanes, engines, vintage cars, motorcycles and memorabilia.

(914) 758-8610. Open daily 10 to 5, mid-May through October; adults, $5. Air shows weekends at 2:30, mid-June to mid-October; adults, $10.

Entertainment. In its 200-seat tent out Route 308 east of town, **The Center for Performing Arts at Rhinebeck** stages upwards of 50 performances, from musicals to magic shows, in July and August. A permanent year-round structure was in the works. From fall through spring, the **Rhinebeck Chamber Music Society** presents Saturday night concerts monthly at various locations.

Shopping. The **Antiques Market & Art Gallery** behind the Beekman Arms displays the wares of 30 dealers on two floors. An old wooden sign inside the front door at our visit advertised the Beekman Arms: "modest rates, dinner $1."

Forty more dealers show at the **Rhinebeck Antique Center,** 7 West Market St., and serious antiquers will find plenty of other haunts.

Shopping is best along East Market Street. The **Rhinebeck Department Store** "continues the tradition" of the former Hudson Valley Department Store. You'll find a Rhinebeck T-shirt among its wares, which seem to be mostly clothing. A new addition to the **Book Corner** is **Country Touch,** where James and Kelli Ellithorpe offer homemade fudge and candies as well as related gifts. **Identities** offers women's apparel and sportswear. Offbeat designer apparel is shown at **Haldora** and **The Elegant Villager.** Side-by-side stores are **Summer Moon** ("a natural place for home and body") and **Winter Sun** with handworks and clothing from around the world. The **Omega Bookstore** sells texts of particular interest to those who attend the workshops in personal growth and development at the lakeside campus of the Omega Institute for Holistic Studies, 260 Lake Drive. **Earth's Rewards** offers New Age gifts, crystals, incense and a group meditation room. **Bread Alone,** an offshoot of a bakery based across the Hudson in Boiceville, is a retail store and café with a Tuscan country look. The organic breads, pastries, soups, sandwiches and coffees are highly rated. **Kitchen & Home** has two floors of an old house crammed to the ceilings with high-tech kitchen ware, gadgets, cookbooks, oils and vinegars, ceramics, birdhouses and much more.

Around the corner on Mill Street, beyond the corner **United Smoke Shop,** are the **Heritage Art Gallery** and **Habitu** for home/life/gifts. "There's a lot to see," the shopkeeper advised, as we eyed everything from cards to picture frames to handpainted birdcages. Hidden down Garden Street are **The Hamlet of Fine Craft and Art,** featuring Hudson Valley works; **Galeriá Borikén,** showing Puerto Rican and Latin arts and crafts, and **Kiddlydivy,** a children's boutique.

Extra-Special _____

The Rhinebeck Post Office, 14 Mill St., Rhinebeck.

Who'd expect a post office to be a special place? Adjacent to the oldest inn in America, this was erected in 1939 as a replica of the first home in Rhinebeck, built in the late 17th century by Dutchman Henrick Kip. Open the old wood door of the stone building and you're in a most un-post-office-like fantasyland of paneled walls and brass chandeliers. Antique airplanes are suspended from the beamed ceiling, lintel stone is displayed in a glass cabinet, and historic photos and documents are framed on the walls. All around the perimeter of the upper walls are what everyone locally calls "the murals." They were painted by artist Olin Dows and depict – somewhat obscurely for the uninitiated – the story of the people, landmarks and development of Rhinebeck. The thirteen panels show such sights as the Kip brothers buying Rhinebeck from the Indians and John Jacob Astor's first car being towed uphill by a team of farm animals. The panel of "contemporary Rhinebeck" (1939) includes a group listening to radio news. The post office was dedicated by none other than Rhinebeck neighbor Franklin D. Roosevelt in the company of the Crown Prince of Denmark, Cabinet Secretary Henry Morgenthau Jr. and Postmaster General James A. Farley. The foreword to the Rhinebeck Historical Society's little picture book about the murals called it "without doubt the most thoroughly dedicated small-town post office in the western hemisphere."

(914) 876-4073. Open Monday-Friday 8 to 5, Saturday 8 to 3.

Georgian Revival brick buildings present attractive vista in Saratoga Spa State Park.

Saratoga Springs, N.Y.

The City in the Country

Ever since George Washington came here following the decisive battle of the Revolutionary War nearby and tried – unsuccessfully – to buy one of the Saratoga springs, the high and the mighty have been drawn to Saratoga.

They come for the restorative powers of its mineral-water springs, the only carbonated waters east of the Rockies. They come to watch the horses at America's oldest and most scenic thoroughbred racetrack. They come for the amenities of the meticulous Saratoga Spa State Park, a complex of columned brick Greek Revival buildings and archways harboring a resort hotel, a theater, swimming-pool pavilions and baths, all set among lawns and towering pines sheltering a golf course, a skating pond and more. They come for the concerts at the Saratoga Performing Arts Center, summer home of the New York City Ballet, the Philadelphia Orchestra and many a visiting pop-rock performer. They come to eat and drink, to bet and be merry, to see and be seen.

Saratoga, recently promoted as "the city in the country," is many things to many people. It's too many to be totally encompassed unless you come – as the Vanderbilts and Whitneys, the Paynes and the Phippses do – for the season. The season here is August, the traditional thoroughbred racing period (lately extended to five weeks and five days and opening in late July). With Saratoga's increasing emphasis on the arts, however, a secondary season is all summer long.

Many a superlative applies to Saratoga. A Fortune magazine cover article in 1935 said the convergence of society and big money in Saratoga each August creates "America's dizziest season in America's daftest town." From the Gay Nineties on, more than 20,000 visitors could be housed in one of the world's great concentrations of grand hotels (all but two long since torn down). The rich and famous built "cottages" of 30 to 40 rooms along North Broadway and Union Avenue.

Some of those Victorian mansions are still occupied by the moneyed regulars who come each summer. Others are rented out by Saratogans who flee the August frenzy. Still others have been turned into lodging establishments.

Lately, Saratoga "has become a haven for B&Bs," according to Kate Benton, a native who returned with her husband to open her own. Indeed, B&Bs are opening "faster than we can keep track of them," adds Linda Toohey, executive vice president of the Saratoga County Chamber of Commerce. The Chamber has adopted guidelines that new B&Bs must have innkeepers living on the premises, must serve breakfast and must operate at least six months a year.

Saratoga bills itself as "the August place to be." But that's Saratoga at its most frenetic and most expensive. Go to Saratoga in August if you're into the racing scene. If not, go at less crowded, less pricey times to better savor the splendors of this urbane small city in the country.

Inn Spots

Accommodations are at a premium during the racing season, now the last week of July and all of August, and for major Skidmore College weekends. Reservations should be made far in advance for those dates, and prices may double or triple. Almost as quickly as the crowds descend, however, they leave. Accommodations tend to go begging from after foliage season until the next June.

Batcheller Mansion Inn, 20 Circular St., Saratoga Springs 12866.

The outside of this drop-dead B&B is a sight to behold, as befits what historians variously call Saratoga's most spectacular, conspicuous and architecturally fanciful residential landmark. Park on the side lawn where your special grass-covered parking space is posted with a sign bearing your name. Open the arched mahogany doors and prepare to be overwhelmed. The living room with its gilt-edged mirrors and enormous crystal chandelier is extravagant. The mahogany-paneled library with its plump red velvet sofas beside the fireplace and towering ficus trees by the tall windows in the bay is dramatic. The impressive dining room holds a long table set for twelve and four side tables for two. Just when you think you've seen everything, you enter a kitchen to end all kitchens. It's a breathtaking space, long and narrow and 26 feet high – contemporary and stark white except for three soaring, twenty-foot-tall arched windows that bring the outside in. Oh to have a kitchen like that, except surely the cook must feel on

Saratoga's most conspicuous residential landmark is now The Batcheller Mansion Inn.

stage as passersby along Whitney Place stop to gawk. After all this, the nine guest bedrooms may be a bit of a letdown, even though they are decorated to the utmost and one is so large it holds a billiards table in the middle.

The house was built in 1873 in what has variously been called flamboyant French Renaissance and High Victorian Gothic styles with Moorish minarets and turrets. Original owner George S. Batcheller was a lawyer, judge and ambassador, who eventually spent most of his life abroad but retained the 28-room castle as his pied-à-terre. It had been condemned and abandoned as a rooming house when a bachelor attorney bought it for $25,000 in 1972. He started a restoration that culminated in 1994 in two whirlwind months of conversion from a sometime residence into one of the grandest B&Bs of all.

The current owner, local developer Bruce J. Levinsky, had failed in efforts to sell the mansion as a residence and ultimately decided a B&B would be more feasible.

The nine bedrooms on the second and third floors come with private baths, queen or kingsize beds, fancy wallpapers and coordinated fabrics, oriental rugs atop thick carpeting, writing desks, television sets, telephones, mini-refrigerators, monogrammed bathrobes, thick towels and Haversham & Holt toiletries.

They vary widely in size from two small front rooms with hall baths to the third-floor Diamond Jim Brady Room, outfitted with a billiards table, kingsize iron canopy bed, a sitting area and a huge bathroom with an oversize jacuzzi, large stall shower and mirrored wall (two other rooms have smaller jacuzzis). Some rooms, with their TV sets and phones prominent atop their large working desks, would be at home in a business hotel. The Lillian Russell Room has two queensize beds and only a single settee for seating, while the Katrina Trask Room comes with a circular porch – reached by ducking through a window. The Rip Van Dam Room with its horsey theme and maple furniture is the only non-Victorian room.

An elaborate continental breakfast is served during the week, with a full breakfast on weekends. Resident innkeeper Sue McCabe offers a choice of french toast or eggs any style to accompany fresh fruit and pastries.

(518) 584-7012 or (800) 616-7012. Fax (518) 581-7746. Nine rooms with private baths. April-October: doubles, $170 to $275 weekends, $135 to $230 midweek. Racing, $250 to $395. Rest of year:$140 to $225 weekends, $120 to $200 midweek. Two-night minimum most weekends, four nights racing weekends.

The Westchester House, 102 Lincoln Ave., Box 944, Saratoga Springs 12866.

One of Saratoga's oldest guest houses, this Queen Anne Victorian structure has been accommodating guests for more than 100 years. But it has been greatly enhanced since its purchase by Bob and Stephanie Melvin of Washington, D.C. They had traveled extensively and stayed at B&Bs before they opened their own, and Stephanie said they approached the endeavor differently than others in town. "Comfort was paramount to us," she advised. "So while we have very fine things, we encourage people to feel at home. We want the rooms to be restful and our guests to feel special." The hallmarks here are hospitality, plus attention to detail, amidst a residential garden setting.

Hospitality comes easily to Stephanie, an opera singer who performs occasionally in Saratoga. She has arranged antiques, "old" art and contemporary artworks to co-exist in a welcoming environment. Brass and copper chandeliers, oriental paper-cuttings on the walls, high ceilings and gleaming wood floors topped with oriental rugs dignify the common rooms. Rich woodwork, oak newel posts on the staircase banister, blue tiles, two elaborate fireplaces and distinctive wainscoting are all original.

All seven upstairs guest rooms have handsome private tiled baths and all but one have king or queensize beds, except for one with two three-quarter beds. We were comfortable in the Jefferson Room, where the new kingsize iron bed is dressed in fine linens. Air-conditioning, ceiling fans, fresh flowers and chocolates embossed with the Westchester House logo are among amenities in all the rooms.

Guests relax in six distinct sitting areas amid terraces and Victorian gardens on the extra-large side lawn bordered by a thick hedge of spirea – a real in-town oasis in summer. Or they gather on the wraparound porch overlooking the Melvins' colorful, old-fashioned perennial borders for tea and cookies or wine and cheese. They relax at other times in either of the two main-floor parlors, where decanters of sherry are at the ready.

A continental breakfast is served stylishly and with lively conversation amid pink linens, china, crystal mugs and stemmed glasses in the dining room or on the porch. Juice, fresh fruits, fresh breads and muffins and sometimes cheese are the fare. After breakfast, Bob snaps photos of guests, which he and Stephanie forward with a thank-you note to remind them of their stay. Happy customers, they know, are repeat customers.

(518) 587-7613 or (800) 581-7613. www.westchesterhousebandb.com. Seven rooms with private baths. Doubles, $95 to $175. Racing, $200 to $290. Off-season, $85 to $150. Closed December and January. Two-night minimum weekends. Children over 10. No smoking.

Saratoga Arms, 495-497 Broadway, Saratoga Springs 12866.

The owners of the Saratoga Bed and Breakfast have restored a hotel built in 1873 by Gideon Putnam's grandson into a small downtown concierge hotel. Noel and Kathleen Smith acquired the four-story building that had been used lately for transient housing. "It was horribly neglected but never abused," said Kathleen. "We found the original chandeliers, fireplaces and woodwork beneath layers of subsequent renovations."

Kathleen spent months at auctions to furnish sixteen guest rooms in high Victorian style. Her aim was for a "clean-cut Victorian look," on the order of her deluxe 1850 Brick House at the Saratoga B&B.

The Smiths, who moved from the B&B into quarters in the hotel, keep the front entrance locked to ensure privacy for guests. A wraparound front porch outfitted in wicker overlooks the Broadway scene.

The main floor holds a formal sitting room with a prized black floral carpet and not one but two dining rooms. "We have a lot of guests to feed for breakfast," Kathy points out.

A modern elevator takes guests to fourteen rooms on the second and third floors. All have tiled baths (some with whirlpool tubs, others with clawfoot tubs); telephones and TVs. Six have restored gas fireplaces. Beds are king, queen or twin-size. Each room has at least one fine piece – an armoire here, a full mirror there – along with antique and reproduction furnishings and the splashy decor that is Kathy's trademark.

Quarters differ in style and size. A third-floor room with kingsize poster bed is decorated in black and white French toile, from wallpaper and draperies to bed coverings and shower curtain. Another with two queen beds is colorful in moss green and lavender florals and adds a small sitting room just big enough for two chairs. A colorful wooden piece serves as a headboard above the king bed in another room. Light from tall windows lends a bright and airy look to each high-ceilinged room. Expect to find coordinated fabrics, hand-painted dressers, and custom-made Kleenex boxes and wastebaskets handpainted by a local artist.

Two premier rooms are situated on the walkout lower level, opening onto a sunken front terrace. Each with a fireplace and cool ceramic tile floors, they come with two-person jacuzzi tubs and separate showers. One has a small kitchenette and, with a separate outside entrance, is like a maisonette apartment.

Aforementioned artist has inscribed a local quote or factoid onto a tile at eye-level in each shower bath. The inscriptions make for good icebreakers as guests swap secrets at the breakfast table in the morning.

Breakfast is a hearty affair. Noel handles the cooking while Kathy converses with guests. The fare was vegetable or cream cheese and herbed omelets the day of our visit. Irish scones often accompany.

(518) 584-1775. Fax (518) 581-4064. www.broadwaysaratoga.com. Sixteen rooms with private baths. Doubles, $150 to $250, May-October; $275 to $450, racing; $125 to $225, rest of year.

Saratoga Bed and Breakfast, 434 Church St., Saratoga Springs 12866.

Some of Saratoga's most luxurious B&B accommodations are offered by Noel and Kathleen Smith and eldest daughter Amy in their 1850 House. The four sumptuous suites there are a far cry from the simpler 1860 farmhouse in which they got their start as Saratoga's first B&B across the street, or their basic motel that gives them an unusually broad range of accommodations and prices. Not to mention The Saratoga Arms, the small downtown concierge hotel they opened in 1998. As Noel proudly describes it, "we've now got all the bases covered."

When the Smiths started, four of the Saratoga B&B's five rooms shared baths. The original farmhouse now has four lodgings, all with private baths. They vary from a couple of small rooms with double beds and maple and oak furniture to two larger rooms with fireplaces, wicker furniture and queensize beds topped by colorful quilts made by a local church guild.

The 1850 Brick House across the street has four suites, three with kingsize beds. All have splashy coordinated fabrics, antique walnut and mahogany furniture, glistening hardwood floors, TVs, telephones and bottles of Saratoga water. The most lavish is the rear Irish Cottage Suite, quiet and private with two queensize beds and two curved loveseats facing the TV and fireplace. The Waverly violet fabrics match the curtains and wallpaper; even the clawfoot tub is painted violet. One man who stayed here claimed it was like "waking up in a Bonwit Teller shopping bag," Kathleen reports.

The sun porch here is the summertime setting for a full breakfast for guests in both houses. Amy might prepare french toast with sausage one day and a cream-cheese omelet with bacon the next. Juice, fresh fruit and corn muffins or toast round out the fare.

The Smiths recently added a water garden and lots of Adirondack chairs to their grounds.

(518) 584-0920 or (800) 584-0920. www.saratogabandb.com. Four rooms and four suites with private baths. May-October: doubles, $65 to $95; suites, $120 to $145. Racing: doubles, $85 to $145; suites, $160 to $225. Rest of year: doubles, $65 to $95; suites, $110 to $135. Two-night or three night minimum stays on summer weekends. Children over 10. No smoking.

The May West Inn, 142 Lake Ave., Saratoga Springs 12866.

Mae West is featured in this fantasyland of a B&B. Eloise and Bruce Palmisano, transplanted New Jerseyites, didn't want a horse theme for the substantial 1913 residence they converted into a B&B in 1998. They also didn't like the idea of people "sitting around on the couch sipping tea – a Saratoga B&B should be more lively than that." So the Palmisanos put a billiards table in the W.C. Fields Room front and center, beside the richly paneled entry hall and adjacent to the side parlor full of plush velvet furniture and ornate carved burl woodwork. The butler's pantry off the dining room holds a cappuccino machine that gets a workout day and night. And the side lawn has a swimming pool with a curving slide, statuary and a hot tub.

Eloise went through 12,000 yards of fabric as she decorated five upstairs guest rooms to the hilt. All the bed covers, shams and window treatments are hand-done and double layered.

The opulent Diamond Lil, also known as the purple room for its deep purple satin draperies puddled to the purple-carpeted floor, comes with a kingsize bed and a balcony overlooking the pool. The Fightn' Jack Room is masculine in showy purple, gold and green. It has a wrought-iron bed with a long wooden bench at its foot, and a bathroom with a stained-glass window and one of the B&B's two whirlpool tubs. Twinkling lights are draped around the lavender and lace canopy of the kingsize bed in the light and airy Peaches Room. The rear Angels Room contains a kingsize poster bed plus two twin beds for traveling families. The Tillie Room, richly dressed in eggplant colors against a white backdrop, holds a fainting couch from Bruce's childhood home.

Sticklers for Mae West detail, the Palmisanos embossed the insignia from Mae West's mink coat on all the guest towels. There are Mae West robes and essential oils for aromatherapy in every room, plus Saratoga water of lemon-lime essence. Also standard are TVs, phones and mini-refrigerators. Chocolates are placed on the pillows at turndown.

The chandeliered dining room is the setting for a sumptuous breakfast of fresh orange juice, fruits and the local Oscar's smoked meats. The main course might be eggs benedict, praline pancakes or grand-marnier french toast.

During racing season, there's a complimentary open bar for guests. Bruce mixes a mean martini to accompany his wife's artichoke and crab dip.

(518) 583-2990 or (800) 959-6722. Five rooms with private baths. Doubles, $250 in summer, $325 in racing, $89 in off-season.

The Mansion, 801 Route 29, Box 77, Rock City Falls 12863.

When Gary Collins televised ABC's Home show live from The Mansion a few years back, the innkeepers put on an outdoor buffet breakfast for the TV entourage

of 40 under the lights at 4 o'clock in the morning. The overnight guests got the usual breakfast spread a little later that day, after the excitement was over.

The incident tells two things about this establishment seven miles west of town. One is that of all the possible Saratoga settings, this was the one chosen for a national telecast from Saratoga. The other is that breakfast here is quite an event, TV crews or not.

The setting is the 23-room Venetian villa built in 1866 as a summer home by self-made industrialist George West, known as "The Paper Bag King" for his invention of the folded paper bag. The mansion is full of striking details, like the six marble fireplaces with massive carved mantelpieces soaring to the fourteen-foot-high ceilings, brass and copper chandeliers with etched Waterford globes,

Double parlor at The Mansion.

etched-glass doors and parquet floors of three woods.

The house, which had been converted into a Victorian B&B with four guest rooms and a suite, was acquired in 1999 by Louise Brown and Lori Dutcher, a practicing attorney. They share their house with guests who luxuriate in grand parlors, four bedrooms and a suite amid priceless Victoriana, and enjoy a swimming pool and four acres of landscaped grounds across from the mills. Off the central hall with its deep green rug and an unsigned Tiffany chandelier is a double parlor with recessed pocket doors and an old hand pump organ. One parlor is furnished in Empire furniture and the other in Eastlake.

Upstairs is a small, plant-filled alcove, where you can sit on bentwood rockers and admire the river and falls across the road. Four spacious guest rooms come with queen beds, private baths and the original inside shutters. Armoires, wing chairs and puffy comforters are among the furnishings. A selection of hard candies is in each room, as are fresh flowers and plants that attest to Louise's green thumb and eye for arranging. The main-floor guest suite in which we happily spread out has a queen bedroom and a sitting room with a Victorian couch from Saratoga's old Grand Union Hotel, parquet floors and marble fireplaces.

Classical music from Louise's extensive collection of tapes plays in the front library, a fascinating room so full of coffee-table books and magazines that one of us could hardly be pried away for breakfast.

The weekend's gourmet feast quickly tempered any reluctance. A bowl of exotic fruits centered by an alstroemeria blossom was followed by fresh orange or grapefruit juice. Next came a platter with a variety of delectable breads, including lemon-poppyseed and banana-nut. The main course was a vegetable omelet with a slice of ham, although yours might be a strata or baked french toast with blueberry topping. Chocolate-almond coffee was poured throughout at a long, linen-covered table topped with votive candles and fresh pastel roses from a florist. A flame flickered from an Aladdin's lamp in front of the mirror on the fireplace mantel.

Breakfast is continental-plus on weekdays. In season, it may be offered on a side porch with outdoor bistro furniture or in a gazebo on the side yard. Afternoons bring homemade cookies and pastries, offered with Saratoga spring water.

(518) 885-1607. Fax (518) 885-6753. www.thesaratogamansion.com. Four rooms and one suite with private baths. Doubles, $95; suite $120. Racing: doubles, $165 to $185; suite $210. Children over 14. No smoking.

Union Gables, 55 Union Ave., Saratoga Springs 12866.

Locally known as the Furness House, this three-story mansion with a corner turret was converted in 1992 into a ten-room B&B, Saratoga's largest and one of its more laid-back and comfortable. Jody Witkop Roohan and her four children make the restored house their home.

Union Gables offers ten bedrooms with private baths in the circa 1901 Queen Anne Victorian with a corner turret and wraparound veranda, and out back in a renovated carriage house. The rooms – spacious, airy and uncluttered – have been professionally decorated with partial-canopy beds and colorful fabrics. Each is named for a sibling. Annie, a front-corner turret room, has a painted sideboard, interesting periwinkle glaze painted walls and a white floor painted with ribbons, a kingsize bed and a single wicker chair. Edward also has a king canopy bed and two armchairs. Bill offers a king bed, seating area and a small porch overlooking Union Avenue. Kate's room is dark and horsy; a horse's collar is wrapped around the mirror in the bath, and a great wreath hangs above the queensize bed.

All rooms come with king or queen beds, TV/HBO and telephones, air-conditioning, mini-refrigerators stocked with a sampling of Saratoga's sparkling waters and a Victorian country – as opposed to haute – decor. "We want to provide the best of both worlds," Jody said, referring to the contemporary amenities in a Victorian masterpiece. There's an exercise room, and outside are a tennis court and a hot tub.

Rich paneling abounds throughout the house, especially in the large foyer and the huge living room/dining area, where you may be left to rattle around on your

Corner turret and wraparound veranda identifies Union Gables.

own. The continental breakfast spread includes fresh fruits, yogurt, cereals and pastries from the Bread Basket in the morning. It can be taken at a table for eight or outside on the great veranda with 80 feet of frontage on storied Union Avenue.

The house, designed by noted Saratoga architect R. Newton Brezee for a local manufacturer, blends Richardson and shingle styles. The variety of exterior surfaces (limestone, sandstone, pressed brick, wood shingles and slate) and their diverse planes produce an ever-changing play of lighting effects enhanced by the deep red, beige and dark green color scheme.

(518) 584-1558 or (800) 398-1558. Fax (518) 583-0649. www.uniongables.com. Ten rooms with private baths. Late May-October: doubles, $135 to $155. Racing, $240 to $265. Rest of year: $110 to $145. Children and pets accepted. No smoking.

Longfellows Inn and Restaurant, 500 Union Ave., Saratoga Springs 12866.

Perched on a knoll east of town is this pair of elaborate tan dairy barns with bright red roofs built in 1915 as part of a 1,000-acre dairy farm. One barn has long been a restaurant. In 1998, the second – previously used for storage for the restaurant – was converted by owners Steve and Yvonne Sullivan into a stylish eighteen-room inn with a Saratoga theme and creature comforts.

Each room comes with a kingsize or two queen beds, TV, telephone and a modern bath with jetted tub and separate glass-enclosed shower. Bath amenities include Caswell-Massey toiletries, hair dryers and antique mirrors. The decorative theme is country Shaker with hints of Victorian Saratoga, as in the tasseled window shades. Vivid hunter green and beige wallpaper borders run atop the wainscoting beneath walls accented with Saratoga photos, each room reflecting a different variation on a local horse theme. Windows in all rooms yield views of the distant Adirondacks.

Original beams are used to good advantage beneath the vaulted ceilings of the eight second-floor loft suites. These have sitting areas with sofa and chair, wet bars and TV here as well as upstairs in the kingsize loft bedroom, which have skylights over the beds.

Interesting local photos from George S. Bolster Collection, benefiting the Historical Society of Saratoga County, enhance the inn's corridors and are for sale.

Guests are welcomed with baskets containing a pair of the locally ubiquitous blue bottles of Saratoga water and a box of Saratoga Sweets chocolates. Turndown service and room service from the restaurant are available.

A deluxe continental breakfast – with pastries baked by the restaurant's pastry chef – is put out with fruits and cereals in the Rose Room of the restaurant.

(518) 587-0108. Fax (518) 587-6649. Seventeen rooms and one two-bedroom suite with private baths. May-October: doubles $115 to $145, suite $295; racing: doubles $245 to $275, suite $495; rest of year, doubles $95 to $115, suite $295.

The Lombardi Farm Bed & Breakfast, 41 Locust Grove Road, Saratoga Springs 12866.

A solarium with a hot tub/jacuzzi, gourmet breakfasts and Nubian and French Alpine goats in the barn are diverse attractions at the B&B that Kathleen and Vincent Lombardi run on the outskirts of town. The focal point is the large solarium that joins two houses, one old and one new. Kathleen serves her leisurely breakfasts here at four lace-covered tables overlooking a jungle of plants and a jacuzzi.

Off one side of the solarium, in the new house to the rear, is a guest living room with a TV and a piano. Off another side, again in the new wing, is a large main-floor bedroom with a canopy queensize bed, a wicker sitting area and a private bath outfitted with all kinds of lotions and colognes. This room has doors to an outside deck "so private that guests can sit out in their pajamas and enjoy their first cup of coffee," says Kathleen. Upstairs in the rear wing are two guest rooms with private baths. One decorated in a native American motif has a kingsize bed. The other has a double and a twin bed with hand-carved headboards.

Off the front of the solarium is the new country kitchen, the heart of the old house (circa 1840). Guests gather here around the wood-burning stove for hot mulled cider and home-baked goodies.

Upstairs is a master bedroom with kingsize canopy bed and private bath. Vince built an ingenious partial canopy decorated with silk roses above a queen bed tucked between the chimney and an outside wall in another bedroom. The bed in a nearby room has a lace canopy hand-crocheted by Kathleen's great-grandmother. An attic suite comes with a kingsize bed, a sitting room and a Niagara massage chair. Although they have a choice of seven accommodations, zoning regulations allow the couple to offer only four at a time.

Kathleen's "heart-smart" breakfasts start with an individual fruit platter, presented like a picture. Then might come coeur à la crème featuring the goat cheese made on the farm or toffee toast that is like candied bread – made with thick slices of french bread dipped in an egg batter and baked with a toffee syrup. Corned-beef hash with poached eggs, chocolate crêpes, ham soufflé with raspberry meringues and peach strudel, crème caramel and orange-oat waffles are among her imaginative dishes. There are always four or five courses.

(518) 587-2074. Four rooms with private baths. Doubles, $110. Racing, $150. Children welcome except in racing season.

Two acres of grounds make for plenty of party and activity space for guests at The Eddy House.

The Eddy House, Nelson and Crescent Avenues, Saratoga Springs 12866.

"Welcome home...to your private Saratoga estate," begins the brochure for Saratoga's first B&B, a winner of a place operated by Barbara and Tom Bertino. "Staying home should be this good!" it concludes.

We agree, but don't let their "home away from home" theme mislead. This is a sophisticated house where a continuing house-party atmosphere draws a repeat clientele partial to horses and the nearby tracks.

The Bertinos – he a retired athletic director and she a former interior designer on Long Island – used to summer in Saratoga so their children could be exposed to the ballet, arts and horses. When the children left the nest, Barbara recalls, they urged their parents to move to Saratoga "and do what you like best – to cook and entertain." That was in 1984, and they've been cooking and entertaining since in a house and property that are suited to the role.

Guests may use every downstairs room in the 1847 Federal house. They include a summery parlor, pretty in pale yellow and blue with a collection of rare flow blue china on the wall, another living room in pink and teal, a cozy wormwood-paneled library with TV and a winterized rear porch. The formal dining room is a sight to behold, what with a large oak parquet table, the original white brick fireplace, an unused corner staircase upon which figurines and pictures are displayed and a table with every imaginable cordial to which guests may help themselves. Between the pre-dinner setups and vegetable dips and the after-dinner nightcaps, the house-party atmosphere is understandable.

Upstairs in the rear are three rooms sharing a bath. They're named Lavender, Yellow and Teddybear for their decor. The Lavender is particularly striking for its floral-print wallpaper on walls and ceilings, nicely color-coordinated with a rainbow of towels. In the front of the house sharing a bath are two larger corner bedrooms. One has a queensize bed and an antique fainting couch that opens to a double bed. It's a fantasy in black and burgundy against pink walls. The other is in navy and white with a kingsize bed and white wicker.

Barbara's buffet breakfasts are such a hit that friends of guests often show up for the meal. Fresh berries and fruits from the Bertinos' organic gardens in back get things off to a good start and turn up in her homemade preserves that get lathered on the bran muffins and breads. The main course might be Swedish pancakes with lingonberry sauce, frittatas, oat waffles or orange french toast. Smoked pork chops or ham steaks cooked on the outdoor grill might accompany.

The party continues outside with volleyball, badminton, bocce and even a golf ball net, plus a game room in the garage. A twelve-foot-high hedge surrounds the nicely landscaped, two-acre property.

(518) 587-2340. Five rooms with shared baths. Doubles, $90 to $100. Racing, $140 to $170. Two-night minimum stay. Smoking restricted. No credit cards.

Brunswick Bed & Breakfast, 143 Union Ave., Saratoga Springs 12866

Their simple brochure notes "B&Bs are not for everyone. We have no television, private phones, room service or a swimming pool. We do have much warmth and concern."

Alinda and Kirk Nichols, who managed this former guest house for eleven years, bought the deteriorating 1886 Victorian Gothic structure in 1995 and began a gradual upgrading. They carefully renovated and redecorated all rooms to the period, updated the bathrooms and eliminated the shared-bath situation.

They now offer ten rooms, all with queen beds and private baths. A couple of rooms open onto porches, one has a gas fireplace and two have whirlpool tubs. Three bedrooms on the first floor have mini-refrigerators. Guests also can use a guest kitchen with full refrigerator, stove and microwave.

The decor is simple but sprightly. Talented Linda handpainted the walls in two rooms with stripes that look like wallpaper. She sponge-painted walls in another room in multiple colors coordinated with the wainscoting.

There's a small rear sitting room for guests. The Nicholses offer a continental breakfast of fruit, cereals and homemade muffins, drop biscuits and coffeecake.

(518) 584-6751 or (800) 585-6751. Ten rooms with private baths. Doubles, $99 to $119 weekends, $79 to $99 midweek. Racing: $179 to $249. Winter: $59 to $99.

Adelphi Hotel, 365 Broadway, Saratoga Springs 12866.

One of only two of the great old Saratoga hotels still standing, this is the place to stay if you want to relive Saratoga's glory days. The four-story beauty with the columned veranda in the heart of downtown was built in 1877. The Adelphi had been closed for four years when Gregg Siefker and Sheila Parkert of Nebraska bought it in 1978 and started its ongoing restoration into a fantasy of Victoriana.

"It was a complete wreck, but we were lucky because it was never modernized," said Sheila, who made the curtains, sought out the antiques and now arranges the spectacular towering floral arrangements that grace the lobby.

We've seldom seen so much lace or so many crazy quilts in the 34 air-conditioned guest rooms and suites, each with private bath, telephone and television. All are spacious and feature lofty ceilings, ornate woodwork, antiques and lavish doses of Victoriana. For a change of pace, check out the Adirondack Mission Room with its twig furniture, a sitting room in Stickley Arts and Crafts style, and a bathroom paneled in dark wood slats. Across the hall is a suite furnished in French country style.

A complimentary continental breakfast of fresh fruit and coffee cake is served

Flanked by pergola and flagstone terrace, Adelphi Hotel's pool is sylvan oasis.

in bed, on the second floor in the High Victorian Parlor or outside on the Grand Piazza, the geranium-bedecked porch overlooking Broadway.

The elaborate Victorian lobby, bar and upstairs parlor have been overhauled recently. The sight-to-behold lobby is an extravaganza of palms, crystal chandeliers and plush sofas and chairs. The walls and ceiling have been newly hand-stenciled in an exotic, over-the-top Neoclassic style by a stencil master from California.

Cocktails, tea, supper, dessert and coffee are served seasonally in the **Cafe Adelphi,** a Victorian bar incorporated into the rear of the lobby and extending beyond to a back porch and a charming courtyard garden. The latest addition here is a swimming pool surrounded by an elaborate pergola and flagstone terrace, a sylvan oasis in the heart of Saratoga.

(518) 587-4688. Fax (518) 587-0851. Thirty-four rooms and suites with private baths. Doubles, $105 to $165; racing, $175 to $260. Suites, $140 to $215; racing, $260 to $380. Three-night minimum on race weekends. Closed late October to mid-May.

Dining Spots

Saratoga offers more restaurants per capita than any town in upstate New York. We offer here a selection of favorites. Serving days and meal hours vary widely, especially off-season. To avoid disappointment, check ahead.

43 Phila Bistro, 43 Phila St., Saratoga Springs.

Culinary excitement issues from this suave American cafe-bistro that's considered the best in town. Michael Lenza, an ex-South Jersey chef, cooked locally at Sperry's before launching his own venture. His wife Patricia oversees the 50-seat dining room, which is lovely in peach and terra cotta. The bar and banquettes are custom-made of bird's-eye and tiger's-eye maple. Caricatures of local businessmen brighten one wall.

Arriving almost as we were seated for dinner was a dish of assorted spicy olives marinated in olive oil, the oil useful for dipping the accompanying bread from Rock Hill Bakery, an area institution. Among starters were a smooth chicken-liver pâté served with crostini and cornichons, a terrific trio of smoked seafood (with capers in a little carrot floret and roasted red-pepper crème fraîche) and an enormous pizzetta, a meal in itself.

Had we eaten more than a sliver of the pizzetta we never would have made it through the main courses, a choice of four pastas and risottos and eight entrées. The Tuscan chicken pasta with roasted peppers, olives and white beans was a lusty autumn dish. The fillet of sole in parchment on a bed of julienned vegetables and rice, a signature item, turned out a bit bland. Other possibilities might be sesame-crusted yellowfin tuna with a wasabi-miso vinaigrette, veal rib chop milanese with crabmeat and saffron risotto, and grilled filet mignon served on focaccia toasts with gorgonzola butter.

The pastry chef is known for distinctive desserts, including a 43 Phila chocolate cake soaked in kahlua, a white chocolate raspberry tart, and a peanut butter mousse in a chocolate ganache shell with mocha crème anglaise. We settled for a dish of plum-port sorbet, a refreshing ending to an uncommonly good meal.

In season, chef John Winnek offers some mighty superior crab dishes, from soft-shell crabs with Thai curry sauce to Maryland crab cakes with rémoulade, corn piccalilli and hush puppies. He also bottles for sale the 43 Ketchup that accompanies his black angus steaks.

(518) 584-2720. Entrées, $21 to $36. Lunch daily, 11:30 to 3. Dinner nightly, from 5. Sunday brunch in off-season, 11 to 3.

Chianti, Il Ristorante, 208 South Broadway, Saratoga Springs.

David Zecchini from Rome, whose grandparents run a restaurant there, and his wife Maria run this hot new restaurant transformed from a fast-food eatery.

"I built this restaurant piece by piece," said David. He made the handsome table-tops with Italian tiles, hand-painted the ceiling a burnt sienna color, and installed an open kitchen with a shiny copper effect at the rear. He also created the prototype for the colorful new service plates custom-made for the restaurant. Close-together tables seat 70 inside and an additional 40 on the front patio.

David's labor of love includes a passion for food. His is creative, robust and considered good value. Among antipasti are bruschetta topped with garlic and tomato, carpaccio marinated in truffle oil and topped with gorgonzola, fried calamari with spicy marinara sauce, and grilled scampi tossed with wild greens. Can't decide? Consider the chef's-choice antipasto sampler, $13.95 for two.

Two risottos, one with porcini mushrooms and the other with crab and scampi, come highly recommended. So do pastas like tagliatelle in a light porcini mushroom-cognac sauce and capellini with scampi in a lobster grappa sauce.

Favorite main courses are scampi marinated with mint in a balsamic-lemon sauce, chicken with artichokes in a lemon-wine sauce, braised pork loin in a port wine sauce, veal saltimbocca, and filet mignon with a wild mushroom sauce.

Desserts range from lemon or orange sorbet to profiteroles, tirami su and a light lemon torte finished with pinenuts and powdered sugar.

David is apt to break into song as he works in the kitchen. It's the friendly, neighborhood kind of a place where the patrons join in.

(518) 580-0025. Entrées, $14.95 to $19.95. Dinner nightly, from 5:30. Closed Monday in off-season.

Chez Sophie Bistro, 2853 Route 9, Malta Ridge.

Long considered the Saratoga area's finest restaurant, Chez Sophie is back on track after a decade's absence. Sophie and Joseph Parker turned up south of town in a sleek stainless steel diner that once housed Sam's Place, and her coterie of fans could not have been happier.

Flawless French fare and a seasonal schedule had been Sophie's trademarks over the years, starting in 1969 in the rural restaurant that was an addition to their home north of town in Hadley, then in an elegant Saratoga townhouse and eventually back at the Hadley retreat. That ultimately closed, and Sophie took a break for a few years as she sought a more urban, year-round venue.

The Parkers bought the diner in 1995, did some renovation and rechristened it a bistro. It has black booths and banquettes, white tablecloths and lacy cafe curtains on the windows, through which the setting sun casts colorful streaks of light. The bar holds some of Joseph's fantastic wire sculptures, produced in his Hadley gallery. His sketches serve as menu covers.

Sophie has discarded her traditional prix-fixe format in favor of à la carte. Expect appetizers like mussels billi-bi, house-cured smoked salmon and goat cheese in puff pastry. Main courses vary from fillet of sole in lobster sauce to a trio of grilled quail to roasted veal loin chop to steak au poivre. Dessert could be a light crème caramel, rich chocolate mousse, fresh lemon cheese pie or our old favorite, vacherin, a meringue filled with vanilla ice cream and served with raspberry purée and chocolate sauce.

While his wife is in the kitchen, Joseph makes sure folks in the front of the house are well looked after. Son Paul oversees the all-French wine list.

(518) 583-3538. Entrées, $19 to $29. Dinner, Tuesday-Sunday from 5:30, nightly in August. Closed January to mid-February.

Sperry's, 30½ Caroline St., Saratoga Springs.

Once owned by Charles "Chubby" Sperry, a thoroughbred owner and trainer, this unlikely-looking establishment attracts a racetrack crowd in summer and locals the rest of the year. It looks like a gin mill, and only those in the know would venture inside. The decor is quite forgettable: a long bar, a black and white tile floor and, at either end of the room, dark old booths and tables covered with blue and white checked cloths. Beyond is a large covered patio for additional seating in season.

Chef-owner Eldridge Qua is known for consistently good food at reasonable prices. The menu rarely changes, but the preparations and specials do.

For lunch, one of us enjoyed a great grilled duck breast salad with citrus vinaigrette and the other a cup of potato-leek soup with an enormous open-face dill-havarti-tomato sandwich, served with a side salad. Unfortunately, service was so laid-back as to be slow and disinterested. We had to go to the bar to ask for – and then to pay – the bill.

The dinner menu ranges from jambalaya to steak au poivre. Grilled Atlantic salmon with Thai sauce and wasabi, cajun-spiced catfish with southwestern salsa and guacamole, and grilled chicken with roasted peppers, ham and aged provolone were specials at a recent visit. Desserts include seasonal fruit tarts, cheesecakes, crème caramel and chocolate-cointreau mousse.

(518) 584-9618. Entrées, $14.95 to $21.95. Lunch, Monday-Saturday 11:30 to 3. Dinner, 5 to 10, Sunday to 9.

Longfellows Inn and Restaurant, 500 Union Ave., Saratoga Springs.

The owners of the historic Olde Bryan Inn have taken over the famed Caunterbury restaurant complex. They gave the old horse and dairy barns a facelift and toned down the former Disneyesque theme to create a pleasing Federal-style steakhouse and grill before adding bedrooms for an inn.

It's still quite an eyeful, this grand barn of a space with an amazing variety of venues for dining. There are dining rooms on several levels behind the façades of "village houses" set around what had been an interior lagoon. One room has a wooden footbridge crossing a pond full of goldfish. Other rooms are smaller and more standard. The tavern and wine cellar with a fireplace is favored in winter. All told, the place seats 425 – if there's a wait, check out the enormous upstairs cocktail lounge with its lighted ficus tree.

A mesquite grill produces a variety of steaks and other items, perhaps swordfish steak with melon-lime salsa, bourbon-glazed salmon fillet, walnut-encrusted breast of chicken with a dried cranberry and honey-balsamic glaze, and twin pork chops with an Asian plum and ginger sauce. Slow-roasted prime rib is a specialty.

The menu also offers appetizers from a lobster and asparagus tart to mesquite-grilled Southwestern chicken strudel. Cheesecake, triple chocolate terrine, apple-walnut pie and crème brûlée might be on tap for dessert.

(518) 587-0108. Entrées, $14.95 to $21.95. Dinner, 4 to 11, Sunday 2 to 10.

The Wine Bar, 417 Broadway, Saratoga Springs.

A shared interest in wine and travel prompted Judith Evans and her daughter Melissa to open this wine and tapas bar in 1999. They gutted a former hair salon to produce one of Broadway's most beautiful buildings, inside and out. The contemporary interior in grays and mauves is elegant and stylish – a cross between New York and San Francisco, in Melissa's words. Tables flank a long granite bar, and a glass-enclosed room with a humidor serves as a smoking lounge.

More than 50 wines by the glass are offered. They may be upstaged by the food, as prepared by Susan Fairgrieve, a chef from northern California. Her opening menu offered three exotic cheeses, a cheese sampler and a terrine of chicken-liver pâté, plus tapas and desserts.

You could make a satisfying meal of "small plates" like a salad of local greens, Bartlett pears, blue cheese and pinenuts; a wild mushroom croustade, seared sea scallops wrapped in smoked salmon with chive nage, and pepper-crusted beef carpaccio. Herb-roasted prawns with spaghettini and vermouth cream and beef tenderloin with truffled potatoes and cognac reduction serve heartier appetites.

Desserts might be warm blueberry cobbler with vanilla ice cream, tarte tatin with lavender crème anglaise and vanilla bean rice pudding with zinfandel poached pear and cinnamon caramel sauce.

(518) 584-8777. Small plates, $6 to $14. Open Wednesday-Sunday, 5 to midnight.

Diversions

There are so many things to do and see here that we cannot possibly do them all justice. And visitors who tried to do them all in one trip would wear themselves out. Here is a selection:

The Horses. Drive around the east and south sides of Saratoga and you'll be amazed at the number of stables, racetracks, horses, horse people and hangers-on, especially in August. Louisville has its Kentucky Derby and Baltimore the Preakness, but the real high rollers come to Saratoga for six weeks of racing and allied activities. Socialite Marylou Whitney's annual gala at the Canfield Casino to benefit the National Museum of Dance launches a whirlwind of balls and fund-raisers all through August. The **Saratoga Race Course** off Union Avenue, oldest thoroughbred flat track in the country (1863), attracts the highest average daily attendance of any track (about 28,000) for its recently extended season from late July through August. As many as 50,000 show up for its major Travers Stakes race. Because so many winners of Triple Crown events have lost at Saratoga, the track has become known as "the graveyard of favorites." The place is massive: 17,000 seats, hundreds of stables, five restaurants and an infield with a pond upon which floats an Indian canoe, painted the colors of the owner of the last Travers winner. Breakfast at the track – watching the morning workouts and mixing with the trainers – is a tradition.

Open from mid-January to late November is the **Saratoga Equine Sports Center,** near Crescent and Nelson avenues. Considered by some the world's most beautiful half-mile track, the standardbred harness track opened on a former Whitney estate in 1941. Races are staged Tuesday-Sunday in July and August. Tours are available, and the **Saratoga Harness Hall of Fame** has exhibits in an old horseman's building. World-class polo also is offered at the **Whitney Polo Field** here in summer

National Museum of Racing and Hall of Fame, Union Avenue and Ludlow Street.

Enter not through a turnstile but a set of starting gates next to a life-size fiber-glass horse and jockey frozen at the moment of a race's start. The sounds of horses loading, jockeys yelling and stalls flying open propel you into an arena that does for horse racing what Cooperstown's Hall of Fame does for baseball. It relates the past, present and future of thoroughbred racing through the latest in you-are-there museum gadgetry. An impressive, fifteen-minute film called "Race America," a montage of racing from coast to coast, is shown in the Hall of Fame auditorium. Famous jockeys and trainers explain their techniques through videos in a simulated racetrack area.

(518) 584-0400. Open daily in racing season, 9 to 5; rest of year, 10 to 4:30, Sunday noon to 4:30. Adults, $5.

The Canfield Casino, Congress Park.

John Morrissey, the U.S. Congressman who was principal sponsor of the thoroughbred racetrack, opened the gambling casino in 1870 in what is now a downtown park and sculpture garden separating Broadway from Union Avenue, the main corridor to the racetrack. In the casino-turned-Canfield Museum, the Historical Society of Saratoga Springs traces the town's growth from a frontier village into a flamboyant international resort in two museums and an art gallery.

(518) 584-6920. Open June-September, Monday-Saturday 10 to 4 and Sunday 1 to 4. Closed Monday and Tuesday rest of year. Adults, $3.

National Museum of Dance, 99 South Broadway.

The nation's only museum devoted exclusively to professional dance occupies the former Washington Baths, now beautifully restored through the beneficence of the Cornelius Vanderbilt Whitneys. Since its opening in 1986, three exhibitions relating to the history of dance have been mounted each year. The focal point is the Mr. and Mrs. C.V. Whitney Hall of Fame, honoring the principals of American dance.

(518) 584-2225. Open Memorial Day to mid-December, Tuesday-Sunday 10 to 5. Adults, $3.50.

Saratoga Spa State Park, off Route 9 South.

Perhaps the grandest park of its kind, this is a 2,000-acre island of serenity at the edge of the Saratoga hubbub. Enter through the soaring Avenue of the Pines past one of two golf courses. All the Georgian Revival brick pavilions, arched promenades, domed ceilings and marble arcades are flanked by pools, fountains and deep, pine-shaded lawns. Of special interest are the Hall of Springs, the Spa Little Theater, the classical Victoria Pool and the larger, Olympic-size Peerless Pool. Besides swimming, there are places for walking, running, cross-country skiing and ice-skating. The park was created to protect the springs, which at the turn of the century were in danger of being commercialized into oblivion. Most of the construction took place in the mid-1930s as a WPA project. "The park is unique in the state and maybe the world," said the manager. "You couldn't build this today."

(518) 584-2535. Open daily, 8 a.m. to dusk. Parking $4, Memorial Day to Labor Day.

Saratoga Performing Arts Center, Saratoga Spa State Park.

An amphitheater at the edge of the state park has seats for 5,100, and up to 25,000 more crowd the lawns for performances here. The New York City Opera is in residence in June, July brings the New York City Ballet and August the Philadelphia Orchestra. The Saratoga Jazz Festival and the Saratoga Chamber Music Festival also take place here. Special-event superstars range from Bonnie Raitt to James Taylor, Linda Ronstadt to Steve Winwood.

(518) 587-3330. Prices vary, generally $13 on the lawn and $17.50 to $82.50 for reserved seats.

The Springs. Long before racing took hold here, Saratoga was renowned for its carbonated mineral springs. What made Saratoga different from other watering spas, however, was the racing and the high rollers it attracted. The fizzy waters, often smelling like eggs gone bad, can be sampled at more than 50 springs around town. A pavilion recently was built around the original Congress Spring in Congress Park, the downtown layout designed by Frederick Law Olmsted. Nearby are the domed Columbian Spring pavilion and the Hathorn Spring on Spring Street. North of downtown near Excelsior and High Rock avenues are the High Rock Spring and Red Spring, named for the color of its water. The heaviest concentration is in Saratoga Spa State Park. You can drink the waters, if you like, or soak in them.

The Lincoln Mineral Baths, Saratoga Spa State Park.

The Lincoln Bathhouse – built in 1930 as the largest of its kind in the world – is a good place in which to relax after over-indulging in Saratoga's good life. Stress and pain float away as you sink into a deep tub of hot, bubbly, beige mineral water in a private room, $16 for twenty minutes, followed by a half-hour's nap while wrapped in hot sheets. For $30 more, a massage therapist will massage you from head to toe. Other wrap, facial and spa treatments are available by appointment.

(518) 583-2880. July and August: daily 9 to 4, Saturday to 4:30. June and September: Wednesday-Monday 9 to 4. Rest of year: Wednesday-Sunday 9 to 4. Mineral baths are offered without appointments.

Yaddo Gardens, Union Avenue.

A private estate turned into a working arts community, the 55-room mansion just east of the flat track has played host since 1926 to 200 artists, writers and composers each year in an environment free of distractions. Some get their inspiration from the atmospheric rose and sculpture gardens, which are open to the public and well worth seeing. Modeled after formal turn-of-the-century Italian gardens, they have a colonnaded, rose-covered pergola as the dominant feature. On the terrace below are four oblong beds of red and white roses joined by a central Florentine fountain. Tucked among pine trees above the pergola is a rock garden of Japanese design.

(518) 584-0746. Grounds open daily, 8 a.m. to dusk. Free.

Shopping. Most of the good stores in this real, working downtown are stretched along wide, tree-lined Broadway with its massed plantings of colorful impatiens and a couple of side streets, Phila and Caroline.

Until the arrival of **Starbucks, Eddie Bauer** and **Borders Books & Music,** about the only "chain" store was a branch of the **House of Walsh,** the classic clothing store based in Williamstown, Mass. Nearby on lower Broadway is **Symmetry,** where we ogled some of the most beautiful works in glass we have seen. It's really more like a glass art gallery. **Nostalgia** is a good place to pick up a gift, perhaps a scented candle, a wreath, a picture frame or a mohair throw. **Celtic Treasures** speaks for itself. **Designers Studio** shows fine contemporary American crafts. The best hats for the track, many made on premises, are available amidst the "vintage ladies' finery" at **Saratoga Trunk.** Gifts for the horse lover are featured at **Impressions of Saratoga;** many convey an animal or a local theme. A scaled-down version of **Mabou,** a mini-Bloomingdales here back in the 1970s and '80s, has returned to Saratoga with trendy gifts, antiques, fashions and home accessories. Stop for a coffee, latte or pastry at **Uncommon Grounds.** Check out the relocated **Putnam Market** at 433 Broadway. Sisters Cathy Hamilton and Gloria Griskowitz offer a juice bar, delectable sandwiches, salads and prepared entrées to go, baked goods, imported chocolates, a butcher shop, gift baskets and even an "olive tasting bar."

Extra Special

Caffé Lena, 47 Phila St., Saratoga Springs.

The oldest continuously operated coffeehouse in the country, this was run from 1960 until her death in 1989 by Lena Spencer, called "the Mother Teresa of folk music." Her friends and patrons have banded together to continue the tradition since. "It's been a struggle, but we've endured," said one. Her legacy remains in the small upstairs room full of atmosphere as patrons enjoy the music along with good coffees, teas and homemade pastries (no smoking and no alcohol). Many are the name folksingers and cabaret singers who have entertained at Lena's. Bob Dylan and Don McLean first found an audience here; Arlo Guthrie sang here long before the rest of the world heard his music. The tradition, as they say, continues.

(518) 583-0022. Open Thursday-Sunday from 6 or 7.

Westport/Essex, N.Y.

Where the Adirondacks Meet Lake Champlain

Is there a less likely place than a corner of the nation's second most populous state to find quaint 19th-century villages relatively unscathed by time? This is the region where the Lake Georges, the Lake Placids and the Old Forges have been marked by wanton commercialism on the edges of the East's largest forever-wild area. So it is an agreeable surprise to leave the Adirondack Northway and head east through unspoiled countryside to the area where the Adirondack Mountains meet Lake Champlain.

Here is Westport, a hillside village where a library, rather than a town hall or a church, dominates the village center and the green is called the Library Lawn. A tradition of local beneficence began with the gift of both library and lawn in the early 1800s. It continued in 1991, when the land across the street was given for a village park leading down to the Northwest Bay of Lake Champlain and a sandy swimming beach open to one and all.

Here is Essex, an old-fashioned place with one of the most intact ensembles of pre-Civil War village architecture in America. The entire village is on the National Register of Historic Places and persists as a living history museum. One cannot be unimpressed by the beauty of its lakeside setting as well as by its architecture.

Both Westport and Essex occupy particularly scenic sites beside Lake Champlain. Looming behind are the Adirondack High Peaks. Across the lake are the Green Mountains of Vermont.

History gave this section of Lake Champlain pivotal roles in the American Revolution and the War of 1812. The lake became the primary route for travel and commerce between Canada and the new republic. By 1850, Westport and

Essex were among the largest and busiest communities on the lake, each with populations of 2,300. The coming of the railroad brought summer visitors, who filled the area's hotels and inns. "Social Notes from The Westport Inn" was a feature in the New York Times and the Boston newspapers. Prestigious Camp Dudley prospered here as America's oldest summer camp for boys.

The reduction of train service and the rise of the interstate highways freeze-dried the area's development in the 1950s. One finds here not mere vestiges but rather the essence of the look and the lifestyle of half a century or a century ago.

Picket fences and flowers surround All Tucked Inn.

Contrary to trends elsewhere, most of Westport's old inns have been converted into private residences. The railroad depot is now an equity summer theater. The yacht club is a public restaurant. The country club is open to the public. Boats are launched from public launching sites and busy marinas. The Lake Champlain ferry arrives in Essex every half hour in summer from Charlotte, Vt. Tourists find excellent brochures for walking tours of Westport and Essex and their historic sites.

What these villages don't have is traffic lights, chain stores or fast-food outlets. Such things weren't needed in days of yore, nor are they needed here today. Westport and Essex offer other virtues. They are two of the more appealing lakefront towns we know of, far from the hordes. Touches of sophistication are interspersed amid the charms of yesteryear.

Inn Spots

All Tucked Inn, 53 South Main St., Box 324, Westport 12993.

The new name was "the first thing that dawned on me," Tom Haley said of his 1993 purchase of the former Gables adjunct to the Inn on the Library Lawn a few doors away. He entered it in a national contest and, lo and behold, the name won fourth place.

The cutesy name perhaps does not do justice to this rather stylish, full-service inn with a guest dining room and nine bedrooms, all with private baths. Or perhaps it does. Energetic Tom, a former lobbyist for the state Civil Service Employees Association in Albany, shelters guests in rooms with sitting areas, caters to their every whim and plies them with afternoon refreshments, home-cooked dinners and ample breakfasts. "Eating here is not a low-cholesterol event," he says.

He'll prepare anything from a back-yard cookout – perhaps chicken and ribs, or filet mignon –to a candlelight dinner with soup, salad, entrée and dessert, $20 for four courses. The day we were there he was serving black bean soup, tossed salad, chicken with stilton and sundried tomatoes in a port wine sauce, and three-berry cobbler. He might make peasant soup (sausage with white beans and leftover veggies) or clam chowder ("which people tell me is the best they've ever had"). Dessert is likely to be an ice-cream sundae. "Sweets are my weakness," he explains, "and I make what I like." Dinner is optional and BYOB, served by reservation around 7.

Breakfast is not optional. Tom prepares fruit, homemade raspberry or apple muffins, sausage and bacon, and offers a choice of three main courses: eggs (from omelets to eggs benedict), pancakes or french toast.

Bedrooms are scattered about the summery, country-style house and reached by different stairways. Most have queen or king beds and sitting areas with wing chairs, and three have fireplaces. A main-floor suite comes with a private porch. They're cheerfully decorated down to their coordinated sheets, quilts and bed covers. Horse prints and memorabilia reflect the owners' love for the Saratoga racing season.

Tom runs the inn on weekdays while his wife, Claudia Ryan, a lawyer, is in Albany. Claudia sheds her lawyer's mantle on weekends and becomes a waitress, serving Tom's meals to receptive guests.

(518) 962-4400 or (888) 255-8825. www.alltuckedinn.com. Nine bedrooms with private baths. May-October: doubles, $65 to $110. Rest of year: $55 to $110.

The Inn on the Library Lawn, 1 Washington St., Box 390, Westport 12993.

This is the largest inn in a village that once had many, including the storied Westport Inn across the street. The Westport was torn down in 1966, and its abandoned site was given to the village as a public park with a swimming beach beside the lake in 1991. The site of the old inn's foundation has been a public ice-skating rink for years.

Actually, this inn occupies what used to be annexes of the Westport Inn. The inn, whose entry is on the side across from the Library Lawn, wears its age well. Susan and Don Thompson have reinvigorated the place, gradually upgrading the rooms and reinstating lunch service on weekends. They also offer four-course gourmet dinners for guests by advance notice.

All ten air-conditioned bedrooms have private baths and seven have television sets. Decor is simple but fresh. Susan has stenciled some of the floors and added accent pieces like wallpaper borders and straw hats. Rooms have high ceilings (some twelve feet), period furnishings and braided rugs, and five yield views of the lake. The largest is now a suite with a wicker loveseat and chair, a queen brass and iron bed, and a sitting room with a sofabed. Rates vary according to size, type of bed (twins, double and queen) and view.

Guests share an old-fashioned common sitting area full of books and magazines in the upstairs hall. The main room on the front of the ground floor, long the site of the inn's restaurant, is now a fireplaced lounge area where complimentary beverages are served, as well as a dining room open to the public for lunch on weekends. The fare is salads and sandwiches in the $5 to $7 range, plus blackboard specials. The meal also may be taken outdoors on a pleasant side deck overlooking the lake.

In the morning, the dining room and deck are the setting for a full breakfast. Typically, juice, fruit and breads precede choices like eggs with salsa, ham quiche,

Three architectural styles are combined in The Victorian Lady.

apple french toast and blueberry pancakes. Don cooks the main courses and Susan handles the fruit course and the baking.

(518) 962-8666 or (888) 577-7748. Ten rooms with private baths. Mid-May to mid-October: doubles, $69 to $95; suite $115. Rest of year: doubles, $59 to $85; suite, $105. No smoking. Lunch in season, Friday-Sunday 11:30 to 2:30.

The Victorian Lady, 57 South Main St., Box 88, Westport 12993.

Colorful in shades of pale yellow with light blue and brick red trim, this charmer dating to 1856 combines three architectural styles. The original 1856 home is Greek Revival, the front facade with mansard roof and three-story tower is Second Empire, and the full veranda added in the 1880s is of the Eastlake style. Wayne and Doris Deswert, who winter in Florida, took over the former Doll House B&B and spent a year refurbishing before reopening in 1994.

The main floor contains a formal, high Victorian parlor furnished with antiques, plus an informal living room outfitted with TV and modern wicker. The parlor is notable for its English embossed wall coverings. Rich paneling and woodwork are evident throughout.

Upstairs are three bedrooms with private baths. A front room offers a queensize brass bed and a day bed, while a second room opens onto a wicker-furnished porch. Grammy's Room in the back comes with twin poster beds, a few dolls and stuffed animals. It has an old dresser converted into a lavatory sink and a long closet for a bathroom. It may be rented with the adjacent Garden Room to form a two-bedroom family suite. The premier accommodation is a suite on the top floor of a recently constructed rear carriage house, designed and built to replicate the main house. It holds a kingsize bed and a sitting area with TV.

Continental breakfast is offered upon request in an upstairs sitting room. Most guests wait for the three-course breakfast served by candlelight in the formal dining room, however. Fresh fruit, orange juice and homemade muffins precede the main event, perhaps quiche or blueberry waffles.

Tea is served in the afternoon. It's often taken on the 1,200-square-foot front veranda that catches a glimpse through the trees of Lake Champlain. The veranda contains a swing and a hammock, just like at Grandma's house – to which many guests liken The Victorian Lady.

(518) 962-2345 or (877) 829-7128. www.victorianladybb.com. Three bedrooms and two suites with private baths. Doubles, $110 to $125. Suites, $125 and $150. Two-night minimum, Memorial Day to Labor Day. Closed mid-October to Memorial Day. No smoking.

The Gray Goose, 42 North Main St., Box N, Westport 12993.

Shades of gray and geese are the decorative themes for this little Victorian B&B and gift shop lovingly run by Elizabeth Kroeplin, a New Jersey transplant who had spent summers here. She offers three guest rooms with private baths, one with a double bed and the others with twins. Two on the first floor on either side of the shop open onto a front porch, with a view of Lake Champlain beyond buildings across the road. Each has its own private entrance and is decorated with period furniture, white frilly curtains and gray, geese-covered bedspreads that match the shower curtains. A third bedroom on the second floor has antique maple beds, a wicker loveseat and a clothing hook in the form of a wooden goose. The atmosphere is simple and homey.

Guests may use Elizabeth's skylit sunroom, cozy with a wood stove, as well as the front porch. She offers an optional continental breakfast for $3, including juice and homemade muffins, served at a table set with cloth placemats in her shop or on the front porch.

The shop is a family affair. She and her sister and an aunt make most of the handicrafts for sale. Grapevine wreaths are Elizabeth's specialty.

(518) 962-4562. Three rooms with private baths. Doubles, $70 to $75. Closed mid-November to mid-May.

Champlain Vistas, 183 Lake Shore Road (Route 22), Willsboro 12996.

You want vistas? From this hilltop B&B two miles north of Essex, Lake Champlain and Vermont's Green Mountains are the front yard, so to speak, and the High Peaks of the Adirondacks are the back yard. The views were what prompted Barbara Hatch to move here upon her retirement as business manager of the computer center at Rensselaer Polytechnic Institute in Troy.

She had sailed on Lake Champlain for years, so was quite keen to buy part of the historic Owens Farm on the western shore, renovate its mid-18th-century farmhouse (listed on the National Register of Historic Places) and make it her year-round home and B&B. She offers five guest rooms, three with private baths and the others sharing. The rooms are named for their views. The main-floor Champlain room has a queen bed and a private bath, as does the Green Mountain Room with its original wallpaper of yellow jonquils on the second floor. Closets hold bathrobes for the occupants of the Mount Mansfield and Adirondack rooms, with a double or twin beds.

A striking mahogany table made by Barbara's father-in-law graces the formal dining room. A delightful sun porch adjoins. Guests also enjoy the square, beamed living room that is both stylish and homey. Quite spacious, it has a spinning wheel

Side lawn is the place for relaxing and taking in views at Champlain Vistas.

in one corner and a fireplace made from fieldstones gathered on the 300-acre property.

The property also houses a large barn with an attached shed and a peaked-roof grainery, which Barbara recently converted into a small art gallery with a smattering of antiques. Behind her house is a prolific grape arbor furnishing the makings for preserves and wines, and behind that a storage shed that has been transformed into a small exercise and fitness center. "It faces the most wonderful pastoral setting," she says, "so you can work away and not feel miserable."

Barbara serves a full country breakfast of fruit, juice, cereals, homemade muffins and a main course of perhaps bacon and eggs, french toast or waffles. In the evening, guests sit on the side lawn and watch the moon shimmering across the waters of Lake Champlain.

(518) 963-8029. Three rooms with private baths and two rooms with shared bath. Doubles, $85 to $105. Children welcome. No smoking.

The Stonehouse, Church and Elm Streets, Essex 12936.

This restored 1926 Georgian stone house looks as if it's been transplanted from the British countryside. Which is why it attracted Sylvia Hobbs, who lives in England and spends the summer and holidays here.

She shares her gracious home full of antique furnishings with overnight guests in four bedrooms, with a variety of bed sizes. On the second floor, we liked the looks of the master bedroom with its coffered ceiling, crown canopy bed, full bath and more chairs and sofas than two people could possibly occupy. Some might prefer to escape to the attic hideaway with a queen bed and sofa and a bath with clawfoot tub, shared with a double-bedded room adjacent.

On the main floor are a large and elegant living room, a formal dining room and a small room for TV, "which we don't encourage," advises Sylvia. Wine is offered at the end of the day on the candlelit porch, and sherry is poured on chilly evenings in front of the fireplace.

Breakfast is a treat at individual tables on the sunny garden terrace. Sylvia calls it "superior continental," which translates to a fresh fruit platter, juices, cereals, homemade breads and muffins, and bagels obtained from Montreal.

(518) 963-7713. Two rooms with private bath and two with shared baths. Doubles, $75 to $135. Open Memorial Day to Columbus Day and some holidays. No credit cards.

The Essex Inn, 16 Main St., Box 324, Essex 12936.

Its pillars and verandas on the first and second floors running the length of the house, this 1810 Federal structure with a Greek Revival colonnade lends quite a presence to Essex's little main street.

For some years, the inside was a presence as well under the ownership of a Burlington artist and restaurateur. A more mainstream presence was instilled by new owners John and Trish Walker from downstate New York. They toned down the eccentricity, upgraded the guest rooms, revived the restaurant operation (see Dining Spots) and instilled a much-needed personal touch.

"We're trying to turn it back into an old inn again," says Trish. Gone are the kitchenettes and the huge stuffed alligator that formerly surprised guests on a built-in bed. Antique beds, quilts, period pieces and traditional artworks are the décor now. The Benjamin Franklin Room contains matching antique twin beds. The Fitzgerald has an antique double bed. The

Pillars dignify facade of The Essex Inn.

e.e. cummings suite offers a kingsize bed as well as an alcove with a twin trundle bed leading onto the veranda.

The Walkers were adding a handicapped-accessible guest room with its own entrance on the first floor. The common room was converted into another dining room for the expanding restaurant operation. A new common room was in quarters vacated by the small **Essex Inn Book Shop** that was relocated to another section of the inn.

A full breakfast, served on the veranda in season, is complimentary for overnight guests. Specialties include blueberry or raspberry pancakes and french toast with brandied fruit sauce.

(518) 963-8821. Five rooms with private baths and two rooms with shared baths. May-October: doubles, $80 to $120. Rest of year: $70 to $95. Children and pets welcome. No smoking.

Dining Spots

Le Bistro at the Westport Yacht Club, Old Arsenal Road, Westport.

Long a focus of Westport social life with its dances and regattas, the old yacht club was sold in the 1940s as Westport experienced a decline in tourism and was converted into a private home. After a disastrous fire in 1982, the place was rebuilt as a public restaurant.

Perched like a yacht club along the shores of Northwest Bay, it enjoys a panoramic water view up and down the lake. A front cocktail platform, a side deck, a lovely canopied porch and a serene inner dining room take full advantage. That the decor is so sophisticated and the food so good is a bonus.

Chef-owner Bernard Perillat, co-owner of the popular Chez Henri at Sugarbush in Warren, Vt., moved here in 1996 when his lease for Le Bistro du Lac in Essex expired. Here he offers a similar bistro-ish menu, which is quite like the Sugarbush model and changes periodically.

We lunched on his house pâté with a side salad and a salade niçoise, tasty but different with cauliflower substituting for the usual potatoes and bits of bacon, anchovy and warm tuna. A signature dessert – frozen sorbet cake ($5), layers of passion fruit, raspberry and black currant topped with frozen kiwi and served on a raspberry coulis with lady fingers – was a sensational ending.

Dinner entrées range from changing preparations of chicken and pasta to rack of lamb with rosemary herb sauce. Duck with fruit or pepper sauce, salmon with beurre blanc and filet of beef au poivre are standards. They're supplemented by such nightly specials as blackened tuna with mustard sauce, grilled mahi-mahi with salsa, pork tenderloin charcuterie and ragoût of sweetbreads and shiitake mushrooms. The classic onion soup gratinée, country pâté, escargots in puff pastry and endive salad are popular starters. Desserts run to mousses, crème caramel, ice cream and sorbet.

(518) 962-8777. Entrées, $13.95 to $23. Lunch daily in summer, 11:30 to 3. Dinner, 5 to 9 or 9:30. Open mid-June to mid-September.

The Westport Hotel, 114 Pleasant St. (Route 9N), Westport.

If its unprepossessing exterior in a commercial area prompts you to pass on, don't. Hidden behind the evergreens is an elongated restaurant of great appeal, particularly the rear porch screened by trellises and evergreens and looking like something you might find in California – or in an old Adirondack lodge. Hanging bushel baskets contain the lamps. Brightly painted wooden tulips are on the tables and shelves, and there's quite an assortment of mismatched chairs. All the wooden posts and beams and greenery provide lots of atmosphere. There's additional outdoor dining on the front and side porches. The interior dining rooms are more traditional, with white-clothed tables, beamed ceilings and walls enhanced with paintings by local artists. A pot of impatiens decorates each table, inside and out. A huge picture of a dog team and sled dominates the bar.

Chef-owner Ralph Warren used to own the College Inn Restaurant and Lounge in South Hadley, Mass. Here he's gone more upscale with a fairly extensive, changing dinner menu featuring healthful, low-fat choices. Entrées run from vegetarian dishes and raspberry chicken to Montreal peppered sirloin steak and New Zealand rack of lamb with honey, garlic and thyme. Clams casino, marinated herring and chilled shrimp and salsa are among the appetizers.

Upstairs off a long central corridor are ten guest rooms, clean but spartan ($45 to $85). Six have private baths.

(518) 962-4501. Entrées, $12.95 to $18.95. Breakfast daily, 8 to 2. Lunch, 11:30 to 2. Dinner, 5 to 9.

The Essex Inn, 16 Main St., Essex.

The expanding restaurant taking up the front veranda, three main-floor rooms and a little bar has been upgraded by new chef-owner John Walker, a Culinary Institute of America graduate. The food has improved, too, and three meals a day are served on a more consistent basis than under previous ownership.

Antiques and period art enhance the candlelit dining rooms, which Trish Walker, the chef's wife and hostess, has tried to make "relaxed and early American."

The short dinner menu features main dishes like sautéed shrimp with sundried tomatoes and mushrooms over angel-hair pasta, boneless pork loin with cider sauce and filet mignon with béarnaise sauce. House salads come with. Starters vary from shrimp cocktail to escargots, grilled portobello mushrooms over greens and bruschetta with mozzarella. Trish prepares the desserts, her signature being warm apple crisp with vanilla ice cream. Chocolate tarts, cheesecakes and fruit pies are others.

(518) 963-8821. Entrées, $12.75 to $16.95. Open daily except Tuesday in summer: Breakfast 7:30 to 10. Lunch, 11:30 to 2. Dinner, 5:30 to 9. Off-season: Breakfast Saturday and Sunday, lunch Friday and Saturday, dinner Thursday-Sunday.

Upper Deck at Willsboro Bay Marina, 68 Klein Drive, Willsboro.

This stunning, summery waterside restaurant is the inspiration of sailors James Arvay, a Plattsburgh architect, and Denise Mavor, who has a restaurant background. They combined talents in 1997 to produce a contemporary main dining room on two levels. Six garage doors open to the outside, complimenting a canopied deck on one end and an open deck on the other. The boats in the marina and the Adirondacks across the bay provide all the décor one needs, and the sunsets across the water are spectacular.

Even dreary weather that forced us inside failed to mar a summer lunch. One of us enjoyed a mandarin chicken salad, while the other was happy with a mozzarella flatbread pizza that came with a tasty rice salad.

The highly acclaimed fare is called "casual contemporary," as in dinner dishes of cioppino, tandoori salmon, rotisserie chicken and mixed grill kabobs with Thai peanut marinade over couscous. Starters vary from shrimp rémoulade to escargots bourguignonne. Desserts at our visit were limited to Minnesota cheesecake, tiramisu and vanilla ice cream.

(518) 963-8271. Entrées, $12.95 to $18.95. Lunch and dinner daily in summer, Friday-Sunday through mid-October.

The Galley, Westport Marina, 1 Washington St., Westport.

What owners Dee and Bob Carroll call Lake Champlain's most active marina includes a busy restaurant operation in the old sea plane hangar, whose arched roof gives it something of a boathouse feeling. It's a cavernous place, made more cozy with such personal touches as a gallery of Westport waterfront scenes along one wall, newspapers and games in the restored desk from the old freight office on the dock, and a free paperback book exchange in the pigeon-hole pass-throughs once used for selling tickets to steamboat passengers.

The Carrolls keep the place jumping with activities like weekly lakeside barbecues with visiting entertainers on summer Saturday nights.

The extensive, all-day menu is affordably priced. Among specialties are tortilla salad, chicken-chutney-curry salad and teriyaki sirloin sticks from an old family recipe. Complete dinner platters include pan-seared salmon, shrimp and scallop kabobs, fishermen's platter and ribeye steak with Montreal pepper sauce.

All this is taken on redwood picnic tables inside or outside under umbrellas beside the boats.

(518) 962-4899. Entrées, $9.50 to $14.25. Breakfast daily, 8 to 11, Sunday to noon. Lunch and dinner, 11 to 8 or 9. Open mid-June through Labor Day.

Diversions

Westport's prime location on one of Lake Champlain's largest bays has always offered a protected port for boats of all kinds. The old steamboat Ticonderoga – now on display across the lake at the Shelburne Museum – berthed here nightly early in the century. Visitors today have considerable access to the lake from the new Ballard Park, the public boat-launching site, the Westport Marina and the Westport Yacht Club.

Westport Walking Tour. An exceptional guide to the town was prepared by the Westport Historical Society and the Westport Chamber of Commerce. A 36-page booklet with photos, descriptions and maps outlines the tour, which totals five miles and can be covered in two to three hours. The starting point is the landmark **Westport Library,** a restored beauty whose all-wood interior with cathedral ceiling resembles an Adirondack lodge. The library is as much the dominant force as it is the dominant structure in town. The Library Lawn is the setting for concerts each summer. You'll likely be struck by the number of buildings that at one time served as inns. Today, most are private homes.

The Depot Theatre, Pleasant Street, Westport, (518) 962-4449. Westport's refurbished Delaware & Hudson railroad station now serves as a town museum and as the summer home of the professional Depot Theatre (the Amtrak train also stops here daily in each direction on its run between New York and Montreal). Founded in 1979, the equity theater presents four shows a season, one of them sometimes a new American musical, in the old freight room. There are also special mid-week shows and art shows in the depot. Shows generally run for two weeks over long weekends. Tickets, $15 to $20.

Meadowmount School of Music, Lewis-Wadhams Road, Westport, (518) 873-2063. Students ranging in age from 8 to 30 converge each summer on this summer school for accomplished young violinists, violists and cellists training for professional careers. You might hear a budding Itzhak Perlman or Yo-Yo Ma, both alumni, at free concerts given in the Memorial Concert Hall Wednesday and Sunday evenings at 7:30.

Boat Tour. A 1948 Chesapeake fishing boat, the **Philomena D,** was converted into a 46-passenger yacht that gives two-hour narrated historical tours around the lake from the Westport Marina. Tours, Friday-Monday in summer, 1 to 3. Adults, $10.

Essex Tour. This is one interesting village, from the sunburst of mustard and maroon splashed across the facade of the 1800 firehouse greeting visitors at the main intersection in town to the 1790 Wright's Inn now serving as a town office across the street. Twenty-eight village landmarks are detailed in "Essex: An Architectural Guide;" 24 more also are shown in the outlying town. The descriptions and accompanying maps make your travels more informed. The entire village is on the National Register and claims one of the more prized collections of Federal, Georgian Revival and Greek Revival architecture in the country.

Sunburst Tea Garden, South Main Street, Essex, (518) 963-7482. The Sorley family serve English cream teas at tables beside a garden with a fountain on their back lawn overlooking the lake in summer, Wednesday-Sunday 2 to 5, weather permitting. Homemade scones with jam and fresh whipped cream, cakes and a variety of teas are featured. They also offer a modest room for overnight guests in their 1813 Cape Cod house.

Shopping. There's not a lot, but the situation is improving – particularly in Essex – and you will find a few places in which to spend your shekels. In Westport, we liked **The Westport Trading Co.** at 2 Pleasant St., where Kip Trienens makes gorgeous stained-glass hangings and lamps. Pottery, baskets, twig furniture, windchimes and birdhouses abound here. **The Bessboro Shop** at 26 Main is a small department store with classic clothing and gifts. Everything for boats and cottages and those who reside in them is available at the **Ship's Store** at the Westport Marina.

If you need a pick-me-up after shopping or walking tours, stop at **McQueen's Food & Fountain** in Westport, a restaurant and ice-cream parlor from yesteryear. Order a fried egg sandwich for $2 or an old-fashioned banana split for $3.50.

Essex, which as recently as the early 1990s had only a couple of stores of note, is experiencing a mini-burst in retailing. **The Store in Essex** on Main Street has changed from an old-fashioned emporium into an upscale center of eclectic folk art, featuring works of New York and Vermont artisans. At **Natural Goods & Finery,** Sharon Boisen stocks wonderful candles, Vermont honey lights, herbal items, vintage jewelry and clothing with flair. Sophisticated country woodsy merchandise, collectibles and crafts are offered at **Adirondack Spirit.** Hand-dipped candles and accessories are featured at **Adirondack Chandler.** Look for antiques, paintings, garden items and more at **Neighborhood Nest.** Furniture, clocks, linens, china and collectibles are among the offerings at **Margaret Sayward Antiques.** The little wood cats with the sign "Better to feed one cat than many mice" intrigued at **Wade's Woods and Crafts.** Jim and Mary Wade also design wooden replicas of Essex's Main Street.

Extra-Special ───────────────────

Camp Dudley, Camp Dudley Road, Westport. (518) 962-4720.

The historic marker near the entrance designates this as the oldest boys' camp in continuous service in the United States (1885). It's extra-special to one of us, who was a happy camper back in the late 1940s when half the fun was getting there on the special Camp Dudley train from Albany, New York, Syracuse and points beyond. Today's campers fly in from Sri Lanka and St. Louis or drive in with their parents, who boost occupancy rates at local inns and B&Bs. To an old alum, the sprawling complex looks the same except for a new-fangled curving slide at Swim Point and an indoor gymnasium with two basketball courts and, sign of the times, a weight-lifting room. Still the same are all the eight-bunk fireplaced cabins spread along the lakeshore and around the perimeter of the 250-acre campus, the cavernous Dining Hall, the nightly shows at Witherbee Hall, the activity at Avery Boathouse and enough sports facilities to accommodate 480 campers whose parents spend a small fortune for the month or two-month stay. Casual visitors can introduce themselves at the main office and ask for a look around.

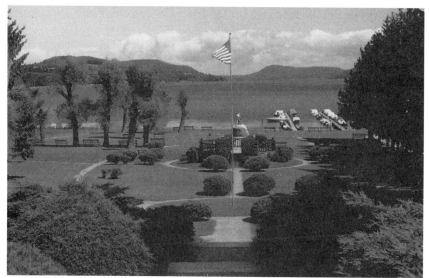

Cooperstown shows its patriotism and serenity in Lakefront Park.

Cooperstown, N.Y.
The All-American Village

Few places its size (population, 2,200) are so embedded in the American consciousness as the upstate New York village of Cooperstown.

Native son novelist James Fenimore Cooper gave it and Otsego Lake, his "Glimmerglass," a romantic place in the history of literature through his *Leatherstocking Tales*. Abner Doubleday supposedly invented the game of baseball here, and the Baseball Hall of Fame stands as the shrine to America's national pastime. The Farmers' Museum captures the spirit of New York State's rural life of the 19th century.

Although Cooper and Doubleday get most of the credit, the impetus for the Cooperstown we know today stemmed from latter-day native sons, the Clark family of Singer sewing machine fame. The house that Edward S. Clark built in 1932 on the Cooper property beside Otsego Lake is now the Fenimore Art Museum, a showcase for the New York State Historical Association's masterful collections of folk and decorative art. Stephen C. Clark Sr. paid $5 for an early baseball that led to the formation in 1939 of the National Baseball Hall of Fame. He founded the Farmers' Museum in 1943, the third prong in his visionary effort to develop for Cooperstown a clean industry, tourism. Another prong has emerged with the evolution of the Glimmerglass Opera, thanks to more local benefactors, the Busches of beer fame.

The three museums – celebrating baseball, art and rural life – reflect the essence of small-town America and inspire for Cooperstown the logical moniker, "The Village of Museums." But Cooperstown is no mere display-case relic. It's the living Norman Rockwell town where flower baskets hang from the downtown lampposts, flags fly in front of homes large and small along its tree-shaded streets, there's only one traffic light and, but for a new CVS pharmacy, no outside chain store or motel has been allowed to sully its all-American purity.

"Time has stood still here and people fight tooth and nail to keep it that way," says Laura Zucotti, the ex-New York restaurateur who now operates the J.P. Sill House here as a B&B. And well they should. Cooperstown is a neat and tidy-looking community with an air of obvious prosperity. The Bassett Hospital, affiliated with Columbia University, is the village's biggest employer and a training site for doctors. The impressive Clark Sports Center is a multi-purpose counterpoint to baseball's historic Doubleday Field. Main Street is dominated by the institutional presence of the Hall of Fame and the lakeshore by the stately Otesaga resort.

The Otesaga, a few old inns and small up-the-lake motels monopolized visitor accommodations until 1984, when the first B&Bs emerged. That year, four pages in the 36-page Cooperstown Area Guide were devoted to accommodations. A decade later, the guide had swelled to 72 pages, 32 of them for lodgings – by 2000, 37 of the 88 pages were so dedicated. Many were opened by former metropolitan New Yorkers who found nirvana here away from the mainstream.

Cooperstown, enveloped in hills, is not really on the way to anywhere else and therefore access is difficult. That helps explain its singularity, but scarcely prepares unsuspecting visitors for what they find – a picturesque lakeside village that's far more than a baseball shrine. Here is a Brigadoon dreamland suspended in time.

Inn Spots

Thistlebrook, 316 County Road 28, RD 1, Box 26, Cooperstown 13326.

Except for a few Gothic-patterned windows, nothing about the facade of this big red barn prepares one for the treasures found inside. Paula and Jim Bugonian, corporate types from the Kingston area, crossed the mountains to visit her parents in Cooperstown, found the 1866 barn, bought it the same day and started creating one of the more dramatic, stylish and all-around comfortable B&Bs anywhere.

"We don't have children," says Paula, "so everything we've done – all the gifts we've given – have been for our home. And we love to share it."

The shared home is also a work in progress. The Bugonians opened with two guest rooms, had five at our last visit, and were finally readying their own quarters in the rear of the barn. In the process, they've thought about, and provided, just about everything a guest could want.

The interior spaces, formerly occupied by working artists who used them as galleries,

Pillared living room of Thistlebrook is an unexpected sight inside an old barn.

soar to ceilings sixteen feet high in the living room. French doors and tall windows open onto an expansive deck, overlooking gardens, trickling water fountains and, beyond, a meadow, stream and hillside alluring to deer, ducks and red-winged blackbirds.

The large living room is elegantly outfitted like the rest of the place in a mix of European and American furnishings and antiques. The dining room holds an antique table big enough to seat twenty, an intricate Queen Anne bar cabinet from which sherry or port are dispensed in the evening, and a 200-year-old Chinese china cabinet that is Paula's pride and joy. The library alcove on the stairway landing harbors an array of books and upscale magazines to occupy guests "since we don't have TV," Paula notes. Sit there beside the window, take a batch to your room, the common areas or the sunken sun room with exercise equipment and a jacuzzi – you'll find the perfect nook or cranny since, as the hostess says, "I love little groupings of seats where people can sit and read or chat."

Such groupings are evident in the spacious guest rooms, all sited on different levels for utmost privacy. Two at the side are light and airy, with windows onto the meadow, white walls and floral prints. One, Paula's favorite, comes with a queen bed set between French kidney-shaped night tables, a comfy chaise and wing chair, a little French armoire and a unique writing desk hidden inside a chest of drawers. Upstairs in the darker front of the house is the master suite, where a kingsize bed resides on a raised platform beneath a nicely angled, vaulted ceiling. It's flanked by plush chairs and faces a wall of books and a sitting area with sofa and an overstuffed chair and ottoman big enough for two. Gothic-style doors lead into a sight-to-behold bathroom with tub, separate shower, bidet and a long double vanity in front of mirrors implanted in a Gothic window frame. Downstairs in front is another bedroom with a kingsize bed and a sitting area. The newest is the former owners' quarters in the upstairs Loft Suite at the far end of the barn. A far cry from its onetime status as a hayloft, this is a substantial, cathedral-ceilinged space

Opera performers Gwen and Fred Ermlich entertain at Creekside Bed & Breakfast.

with a kingsize mahogany bed (raised to take advantage of the view through wide rear windows). Paula has decorated it in rust and soft green for a country gentleman look. The sitting area contains two sofas, an armchair and a wicker settee.

The Bugonians' brand of hospitality matches their luxurious accommodations. They put out coffee and fruit at 7:30 in the morning, prior to serving a full breakfast with fresh fruit cup, banana or corn bread and a main dish like french toast with ham and browned cinnamon apples, blueberry-orange pancakes, vegetable omelets or lemon-dill scrambled eggs with mini bagels or croissants. Afternoon libations are offered, followed by sherry, chocolates and cookies in the evening.

(607) 547-6093 or (800) 596-9305. www.thistlebrook.com. Two rooms and three suites with private baths. Doubles, $120 to $145. Closed November-April. Two-night minimum weekends. Children over 12. No smoking.

Creekside Bed & Breakfast, 138 Fork Shop Road, Cooperstown 13326.

The hosts at this elegant B&B on the delightfully named Fork Shop Road beside the delightfully named Fly Creek are among the most interesting people around. Fred and Gwen Ermlich – he a former priest and she a onetime Playboy centerfold – helped found and have performed with Glimmerglass Opera. And their B&B digs are a bit theatrical in two rooms, two suites and a cottage, all with private baths, queen or kingsize beds and TV/HBO.

"This is my Saints and Sinners gallery," Gwen said as she led us up the stairs lined with photos from her shows and modeling career, including one as a centerfold (clothed) in the Japanese edition of Playboy magazine in 1970. We were to be ensconced in the Penthouse Suite, an open, third-floor hideaway complete with sitting room and dining area. That was more spacious for a rainy evening than the one we'd booked, the Bridal Chamber, a mostly white cocoon of lace and frills, plus a canopied queen brass bed, a skylight and a beautiful curved armoire. This room has since been enlarged into a suite with an 18-by-22-foot living room harboring a year-round Christmas bridal tree decorated in wedding memorabilia, a parquet floor, tapestries, bisque lamps and a grouping of leather chairs and sofa beneath a crystal chandelier – not to mention a Romeo and Juliet balcony. Less extravagant but functional is the three-room cottage out back, where there's lots of room to spread out on peach-colored sofas in the living room with wet bar beneath a dramatic twenty-arm brass chandelier. The bedroom has a canopied bed, and the dining room and a spacious side deck overlook lawn and creek. The Garden Room comes with an antique kingsize bed and a fifteen-foot expanse of picture windows overlooking the garden.

The Ermlichs share with guests the rest of their home, including an atrium entry and a wraparound deck off the beamed and paneled rear family room – an expansive space that's perfect for the opera parties the Ermlichs frequently host. "This house is so happy when it's filled with people," Gwen says.

The actress in her demands that she serve her husband's lavish breakfast on a dining-room table set with lace cloth, dainty china, elaborate silver, lit tapers in the candelabra and a showy centerpiece of dried flowers. Tiny white lights twinkle here and there to add to the charm, and she changes the place settings daily so that "the meal becomes as dramatic as an opera." At our visit, orange juice, fresh fruit cocktail and coffee cake preceded Fred's dilled scrambled eggs, bacon, baked apple slices and English muffins, on which we tried Gwen's three sensational liqueur-flavored butters (peach, raspberry and strawberry).

(607) 547-8203. Three rooms, two suites and a cottage with private baths. Doubles, $89 to $106. Suites, $110 and $149. Cottage, $149. Two-night minimum on peak weekends. No smoking.

Angelholm, 14 Elm St., Box 705, Cooperstown 13326.

Painted mint green with dark green trim, this 1805 house on a residential street backs up to Doubleday Field, and guests can frequently hear – if not see – baseball games being played. Fred and Jan Reynolds retired here from Ridgefield, Conn., in 1992 after having stayed frequently with the original owners over five years. "This was almost like moving into our own house," says Jan. They changed the decor from Victorian to Federal, built a small addition to expand the rear side veranda and two rear bedrooms, and added two baths.

They now offer five air-conditioned bedrooms with private baths, good swivel reading lights over the beds, countless oriental rugs and runners, and collections of dolls here and there. Most in demand are three large corner rooms, two with queensize beds and one with antique twins joined as a king. The Reynoldses have added queen beds and reconfigured the two smaller center bedrooms so that their former hall baths now open en suite. The rear Doubleday Room with antique iron bed and a day bed comes with plush carpeting made out of recycled pop bottles. "We use only recycled stuff in this house," Jan points out.

The hosts share the main floor with guests. The fireplaced living room with fine oriental rugs opens into a snug little library with TV and another fireplace. The library opens onto the rear side veranda, where formal tea or iced tea and lemonade are served in the afternoons and the guests help themselves to Jan's "never-empty cookie jar."

Breakfasts are an occasion. A former caterer who loves good food, Jan offers juices, a fruit course like blueberries with lemon-yogurt sauce or peaches with honey-cinnamon glaze, braided coffee bread with pecans and cinnamon, sausage or bacon and a main dish like blintzes filled with sour cream and topped with toasted coconut or country egg scramble incorporating red potatoes, leeks, and red and green peppers. Fred, the raconteur, holds forth in the dining room.

(607) 547-2483. Fax (607) 547-2309. Five rooms with private baths. Doubles, $105 to $120, June-October; $80 to $90, rest of year. Children over 10. Closed mid-February to April. No smoking

Duke's Oak Bed & Breakfast, Route 80, Box 406, Springfield Center 13468.

On a hillside eight miles north of Cooperstown, this large tan house with beige trim is almost within hearing distance of Glimmerglass Opera House. Which is why Don and Mary Ellen Fenner bought it in 1986 and gradually rescued it, she said, "from wrack and ruin." Glimmerglass boosters (he's treasurer of the Opera Guild), they put up opera crews in their house for years until their daughter and son-in-law, Cynthia and David Staley, returned in 1997 to operate it as a B&B.

Running the turn-of-the-century house was a godsend for Cynthia, who studied hotel and restaurant management at the University of Denver. All the renovations and decorating were completed, and there was room on the third floor for both families. The Staleys operate the B&B, although Mary Ellen says she irons the sheets and plays the breakfast music. The last means she plays the grand piano or the harpsichord in the music room while guests eat breakfast across the hall in the dining room.

The music room is the heart of the house, and it's the room that guests enter through a new rear entrance. Shelves near ceiling level both here and in the front foyer are home to eye-catching collections of bottles, plates and what-not. "Dad's a collector," explains Cynthia. "We have at least three of everything, and that's in the house. There's more of everything stored in the barn." Cynthia was eyeing the barn for another role: a couple of future guest rooms or suites.

On the second floor of the house are three bedrooms with private baths, one with an adjoining queen-bedded room that's rented as a suite. There's a TV and telephone in each room, and each is tastefully outfitted with antique furniture and a secretary desk. The smallest has a double bed. The largest is the master bedroom with queen bed and spacious bath with double vanity.

Out back is the barn-red Acorn Cottage, hidden in the woods up the hill and overlooking a stream in a ravine. Fresh and light, it has a living room and kitchen, bedroom and sleeping loft with double-bedded accommodations for six.

Cynthia cooks pumpkin waffles, blueberry pancakes, omelets or quiches for breakfast. Fresh fruit, homemade granola and muffins accompany.

. The two-bedroom suite is named for its last owner, Thomas Goodyear, "patron saint of Duke's Oak" and donor of the turkey farm property that is now the Glimmerglass site. The Duke's Oak property was home to the late Duke's Oak Theater, which took its name from an obscure quote in Shakespeare's "A Midsummer Night's Dream."

(607) 547-2179. Three rooms and a cottage with private bath. Doubles, $85 to $110, June-August, $75 to $90 rest of year. Cottage, $155, June-August; $120, rest of year. Two-night minimum summer weekends. Children over 10. No smoking.

The J.P. Sill House, 63 Chestnut St., Cooperstown 13326.

The architectural magnificence of this yellow brick Italianate Victorian built in 1864 by Cooperstown bank president Jedediah P. Sill has landed it on both the state and national historic registers. Add its remarkably lavish handprinted

Ex-banker's Italianate Victorian home is now The J.P. Sill House.

Victorian wallcoverings, prized antiques and an aura of status cultivated by the innkeeper, former owner of New York's famed El Morocco restaurant. The accommodations are fit for royalty, though it's hard to imagine royalty sharing bathrooms, as do people in three of the six guest quarters here.

Laura and her late husband Angelo Zuccotti literally stumbled upon Cooperstown shortly after they closed El Morocco in 1988 because of a decline in their carriage trade. "I'd always wanted a B&B," she said. "We found this house and thought, wouldn't it be nice to fix it up?" The sale was closed in three weeks and they started restorations designed to make the carriage trade take note.

The most striking aspects of the decor are the reproductions of Victorian wallpaper designs created by William Morris and others. The front parlor sports seven different papers on the walls and even the ceiling; the dining room has eight. The parlor is awash in oriental rugs, Victorian furnishings, bookcases reproduced by a preservationist and a replica of the house holding a TV inside. Decanters of port and cream sherry await guests here, as well as complimentary drinks from the bar.

Japanese-Italianate paper adorns the dining room, where El Morocco's first menu from 56 years ago hangs framed near the kitchen door. Here is offered a bountiful buffet breakfast: perhaps strawberries and cream, fresh juice, homemade granola and a savory entrée, maybe a puff pastry, salmon en croûte or ham and cheese. Laura, who studied at the Cordon Bleu, is known for her lemon and coconut breads. On Sundays she likes to serve a smoked salmon platter and cream cheese along with the New York Times. The repast is taken around the formal table, set with tapestry mats atop a lace cloth, or on the wicker-filled side porch off the dining room.

A front corner of the main floor is given over to a suite that's arguably the most extravagant in town. It's the only guest accommodation with a private bath in the main house. And what a bathroom – a huge space with a whirlpool tub and a vibrator for one's back, a wicker rocker and chair, floral wallpaper and windows onto the side lawn. The suite, decorated by Laura Ashley's son, is papered with eight different patterns to represent the Iris and the Dragonfly. A Laura Ashley duvet covers the ornate queensize brass bed angled in a corner and an armoire hides the TV/VCR and stereo system facing an armchair and two wicker chairs.

Upstairs are three more guest rooms, all with queensize beds and more showy wallpapers. One has a wicker sitting area. Another has a fireplace, a signed Eastlake armoire and a powder room with Laura Ashley appointments. The rooms share two bathrooms, one containing the original pewter tub and a new shower and the other with shower only.

Constantly upgrading, Laura has acquired Frette bedspreads from Italy for summer, to stand in for the Laura Ashley quilts and goose down comforters she favors in winter. She also furnishes linen bathrobes for summer; Ashley robes for winter. All bathrooms are outfitted with hair dryers, shaving mirrors and a complete line of Perlière toiletries.

At the side of the house is a carriage house recently converted from apartments into a pair of two-bedroom suites designed for families. Each has sitting room, dining area, kitchen and bedrooms with queen and double beds. They're furnished with antiques and wicker in what Laura calls "Laura Ashley Welch cottage style in the palest primrose colors." Telephones and TV/VCRs are among the extras.

Following her husband's death, Laura continued to operate but had the house up for sale in 2000.

(607) 547-2633 or (877) 547-2677. Fax (607) 547-2632. Three rooms with shared baths and two suites with private baths. Doubles, $100. Suite, $150. Two-bedroom suites $175, $225 for four. No smoking. Closed Columbus Day to Memorial Day.

Landmark Inn Bed & Breakfast, 64 Chestnut St., Cooperstown 13326.

A johnny-come-lately as Cooperstown B&Bs go, this actually predates the J.P. Sill House across the street. Bank president Jedediah P. Sill built this 21-room mansion for his family in 1856, and a counterpart – almost a reverse of this house – for his daughter in 1864. Co-owner Linda Schuermann likes to stand in the front doorway and point out to visitors that her front walk lines up perfectly with the front door of the daughter's house it faces.

She and her husband Bob, who moved to Cooperstown in 1980 from northern New Jersey, spotted the house for sale and bought it in partnership with fellow B&B innkeepers Marjorie and Ed Landers of The White House Inn (see below). "I'd always wanted to do a B&B," said Bob, "and this house was perfect for it."

The Schuermanns moved into the house in 1999 to become resident innkeepers and began renovations of what had been eight apartments. They offer nine guest rooms with king or queensize beds and private baths. Each has a different decor and layout. A ground-floor bedroom is a beauty with a queen bed angled from the corner beneath an 11½-foot high ceiling. A TV, armoire and mini-refrigerator are among accoutrements here as in all the rooms. Upstairs in front are two suites, one with an extra room with twin beds and the other an extra room with a double bed. The latter has a long, narrow bath with a clawfoot tub oddly positioned so as to partly block the traffic flow, but "guests love it," says Linda. In the rear is a room with a queensize bed and a large bath. A nearby bath has a double vanity incorporated inside an antique dresser. Linda painted the table legs red, white and blue for the President's Room. All rooms are brightened by colorful quilts and furnished with antiques and prints depicting local history.

The main-floor common areas retain many of their original features: parquet floors, columns and leaded-glass windows. In front is a double parlor, the rear

Rockers on circular porch are great for enjoying view of lake at The Otesaga Hotel.

portion of which is used as a dining room. Beyond that is another dining room with its original yellow-tiled fireplace. The Schuermanns serve a full breakfast of fresh fruit, muffins and perhaps a baked egg dish or baked french toast at lace-clothed tables in each dining room.

(607) 547-7225. Fax (607) 547-7240. Nine rooms with private baths. Doubles, $125 to $150, May-October; rest of year, $85 to $110. Two-night minimum weekends in season. No smoking.

The Otesaga Hotel, 60 Lake St., Cooperstown 13326.

Here is one of New York's grand resort hotels, opened in 1909 and still owned by the Clark family. A doorman beneath a columned portico and a palatial lobby in green and red chintz greet arriving visitors; a pianist plays in the lobby during afternoon tea and in the dining rooms for dinner. A sweeping rear veranda looks across the swimming pool, a luncheon terrace and the broad lawns to Otsego Lake, with an eighteen-hole golf course beside.

The four-story brick hotel offers 136 rooms and suites. During a $20-million renovation in 1999, rooms were gutted for the installation of new plumbing and electrical work and every window was replaced. Cheerfully decorated in country florals, the rooms we saw were fresh in pale blue with twin beds, two armchairs, yellow floral spreads and curtains, lamp stands painted with flowers, television sets with HBO and large, modern baths with pedestal sinks. Irons, hair dryers and fluffy Egyptian-cotton towels are among the amenities.

A sumptuous breakfast buffet and prix-fixe dinners are served in two beautiful, connecting dining rooms, while a lunch buffet is available on the Lakeside Patio. Lunch and dinner also are served in the casual Hawkeye Bar & Grill (see Dining Spots), a favorite of locals. There's live music with dancing nightly in the Templeton Lounge. Jackets are required for the evening meal in the dining room.

(607) 547-9931 or (800) 348-6222. Fax (607) 547-1271. One hundred twenty-six rooms and ten suites with private baths. Rates MAP: Memorial Day to Labor Day, doubles $310 to $340, suites $435 to $470. Off-season: doubles $290 to $320, suites $415 to $450. Open mid-April through October.

The Cooper Inn, Main Street, Box 311, Cooperstown 13326.

On broad lawns in the center of town, this distinguished brick mansion dating to 1812 is owned by the famed Otesaga resort hotel. It's quite inn-like, with a graceful double parlor and with an honor bar off the entry foyer, and a cozy breakfast room in which donuts and danish are served at five tables.

The facility's ten rooms and five suites are all different, furnished in period hotel style with double or twin beds, desks, TV sets, telephones, walk-in closets and non-working fireplaces. Hair dryers and steam irons are among the amenities. The wing hidden behind dense trees contains five two-bedroom suites. Guests here have access to all the facilities of the Otesaga, a short drive away.

In 1998, all public and guest rooms were redecorated, with spiffy new fabrics and window treatments and original oil paintings on the walls.

(607) 547-2567 or (800) 348-6222. Ten rooms and five suites with private baths. Memorial Day to Labor Day: doubles, $175; two-bedroom suites, $255 for four. Rest of year: doubles, $145; suites, $200. No smoking.

The Inn at Cooperstown, 16 Chestnut St., Cooperstown 13326.

Built in 1874 in Second Empire French style as the annex to the old Fenimore Hotel across the street, this is the baby of Michael Jerome, a Cornell Hotel School grad and preservationist from Elmira, who occupies an apartment on the property with his wife. He acquired the hotel in 1985 and quickly received a state historic preservation award for a painstaking restoration that is ongoing.

The exterior is strikingly handsome. Inside, the eighteen rooms with private baths on two upper floors vary. One rear room with a queensize bed was barely big enough for a chair and a dresser. Rooms are advertised as having twins or queensize beds, although a couple we saw were set up differently: one with two twins and a matching day bed, and another with a kingsize bed that we were told was available only for walk-ins.

Frilly sheer curtains, country decor and basic furniture are the rule, although Michael points out that he is continually adding furnishings. Half have renovated bathrooms with hair dryers and toiletries, and more baths are being redone each year. Some have unusual tiled corner showers with new terrazzo bases that, except for the wraparound curtain, are open to the rest of the bathroom.

A newly renovated suite includes a sitting room and a bedroom with queensize bed and full bath. It comes with a wet bar, refrigerator and a private telephone.

The main floor offers two pleasant sitting rooms in a double parlor, where a television set and telephone are available. Coffee, juice and homemade breads and muffins are served in a couple of small breakfast rooms. Rocking chairs on the wide front veranda offer relaxation and a view of the passing scene.

(607) 547-5756. Fax (607) 547-5756. Seventeen rooms and one suite with private baths. Doubles, $155 in summer, $120 to $155 in spring and fall, $90 to $98 in winter. Suite, $140 to $230. Smoking restricted.

Strawberry Hill Farm, Greenough Road, RD 3, Box 245, Cooperstown 13326.

"Peace and quiet" are what Jocelyn Rauscher and her husband Andrew, a physician at Bassett Hospital, like most about their 120-acre farm. They offer two grand rooms with private baths and television, as well as abundant common space and gardens. With their children off to college, the Rauschers have plenty more room options, although Jocelyn says she quite likes her sitting room and

Strawberry Hill Farm faces field of wildflowers and backs up to English gardens.

her husband likes his, so further guest rooms in the rambling three-story Federal farmhouse with seven working fireplaces are in limbo.

Meantime, guests enjoy their own handsome rear living room with fireplace and a formal dining room and frequently spill into the enormous country kitchen, which opens onto the hosts' family room. A front main-floor bedroom has a lace canopy queensize bed and a small bathroom with a stunning European sink handpainted with flowers. Upstairs is a secluded bedroom with queen wicker bed, ivy stenciling and dark green carpeting, and Gilbert & Soames toiletries in the full bath. A connecting bedroom with twin beds is available for families.

The British-born Rauschers' floral interests are manifest in the delightful English gardens they have created in back. Water trickles in fountains, morning glories climb a trellis and a rope hammock beckons. If you don't become immobilized here, you can amble along the walking path they have blazed through the eight-acre field of wildflowers across the road.

Jocelyn prepares a continental breakfast with fresh fruit salad, croissants, and homemade zucchini bread or muffins.

(607) 547-8619. Two rooms with private baths. Doubles, $75 ($85 in August). No smoking. Closed November to April.

Overlook Bed & Breakfast, 8 Pine Blvd., Cooperstown 13326.

Another family home, this one along a stately boulevard near the heart of town, the Overlook has been taking guests since 1989 when six of Jack and Gayle Smith's seven children had left the nest. The main section of a manse that required five servants in its heyday dates to 1888.

A harmonium in the foyer and an extensive collection of music boxes hints at this family's musical interests. A spacious, fireplaced living room has lots of seating and oriental rugs. A corner TV room contains a leather sofa and a wall of family pictures. Guests help themselves to an extended continental breakfast on the sideboard in the fireplaced dining room; they can eat there at a table for six or head outside to one of the commodious porches.

Upstairs are three light and spacious guest rooms and a suite, created when the Smiths vacated the master suite and "moved up to the servants' quarters – which was quite fitting," Gayle quips. That opened up a huge room with queensize poster bed, a sitting area with a beige leather sofa that converts to a bed in front of a console TV, a large bath and walk-in closet. A room in the front corner has a double four-poster bed; it shares a hall bath with a larger turret room, pretty in blue and pink with twin poster beds, a floral sofa and a wall of decorative plates from the musical "Annie." A rear room with a double poster bed enjoys a private bath and small sitting area.

(607) 547-2019. Fax (607) 547-7052. One room and one suite with private baths; two rooms with shared bath. Summer: doubles, $85 to $99; suite, $125. Rest of year: doubles, $75 to $85; suite, $99. Two-night minimum weekends most of year. Children accepted.

The White House Inn, 46 Chestnut St., Cooperstown 13326.

A large back-yard swimming pool, screened from neighbors by tall hedges, is a draw at this new B&B in an 1835 Greek Revival house listed in the national historic registry. So are the fancy breakfasts offered by Marjorie and Edward Landers, who took over the former dentist's office and residence in 1996.

Gregarious Ed refers to four "areas" rather than guest rooms as he leads a tour of the rambling, 21-room structure, which is deceptively small on the outside and strikes some as a hodgepodge inside. One area is a family apartment above the former dental office with a living room, kitchen and two bedrooms, one with twin day beds and the other with a queen bed and a crib. Another area is on the main floor of a wing off the Greek Revival structure. Here are a more traditional configuration: a front bedroom with queen bed, chocolate brown walls, antique furnishings and private bath, and a mini-suite with a small library/TV room, bath and a bedroom with a queensize bed that Marjorie draped with a curtain-like canopy to cover up an unused door. Upstairs in this wing are the third and fourth areas, actually a family suite with a room with twin beds, a hall bath and a sitting room with futon and TV. Beyond, available separately or jointly, is another bedroom with queen bed and private bath.

Marge, an artist, has decorated with her paintings and creations made with artificial flowers. Her artistry takes another dimension at breakfast, served formally on Rosenthal china in the smallest dining room you ever saw, a windowless affair sandwiched in the middle of the house between a front parlor, the mini-suite and a large, fireplaced gathering room at the rear. Typical fare includes juice, homemade muffins, a pineapple boat filled with fruit and a main dish, such as scrambled eggs with cream cheese and chives or baked french toast with a caramel bottom.

Marge was about to turn her artistry to a stairwell when Hall of Fame inductee Phil Niekro stayed here. He and other athletes left their signatures for posterity on the bare wall, prompting Ed to start a Wall of Fame.

(607) 547-5054. Fax (607) 547-1100. Three rooms and two family suites with private baths. Doubles, $95 and $100. Family suite and apartment, $165 for four. No smoking.

Dining Spots

Hoffman Lane Bistro, 2 Hoffman Lane, Cooperstown.

Formerly the Terrace Cafe, this was reopened in 1999 by two young chefs with top credentials. David Neil, a Culinary Institute of America grad who opened

Gabriella's on the Square here, was about to return to Philadelphia when he met up with Mark Loewenguth, a New York Restaurant School alumnus. Mark was finishing a two-year assignment to launch the Fenimore Café and The Herder's Cottage restaurants at the state museums. "It was serendipitous," Mark said. "We both wanted to do our own restaurant and this building was available." Their aim was to create an affordable, neighborhood-style restaurant – "the place where the locals go," he said. A year-round following testifies to their success.

Milo Stewart Jr. Photo

The pair did most of the renovations themselves, painting three dining areas on three levels a soothing taupe with white trim and hanging the walls with the local photos of father-son photographers Milo Stewart Sr. and Jr. Striking colored glass bottles, obtained at a New York

Mid-level dining area at Hoffman Lane Bistro.

flea market, hold olive oil and serve as centerpieces on each table. White butcher paper atop the white tablecloths provides doodling areas for the crayons stashed at each table.

Regulars return again and again for the meatloaf, the chicken potpie and the spaghetti with meatballs and marinara sauce. But there's far more than comfort food here. The pan-fried crab and crawfish cake with wilted spinach and creole mustard beurre blanc is a signature appetizer. Another starter is maple-glazed lamb tenderloin on a skewer grilled with grapes and served over arugula with red pepper and blue cheese. Main courses range from tuna steak au poivre to boneless duck breast with ginger-orange glaze to coffee-encrusted ribeye steak finished with pepperwood pinot noir sauce. Dessert could be a classic crème brûlée, chocolate mousse cake or black raspberry cheesecake.

Similar inspiration mixes with the traditional on a lunch menu priced from yesteryear.

In season, customers spill from the main-floor bar area out onto a 50-seat dining terrace enclosed in a fence bearing grapevines hand-painted by a local artist.

(607) 547-7055. Entrées, $12.95 to $17.95. Lunch daily in summer, 11:30 to 2:30. Dinner nightly, 5 to 9. Closed Sunday and Monday in off-season.

The Blue Mingo Grill, West Lake Road (Route 80), Cooperstown.
Among the area's hottest seasonal dining tickets is this seasonal lakeside establishment with the odd name (taken, co-owner Michael Moffat says, from the local Indian tribe of Blue Mingo who appeared in the works of James Fenimore Cooper).

Now featuring the creative grill cuisine of a chef from New York's famed Arcadia Restaurant, this started simply in 1987 as a hot-dog stand called Dot's Landing behind Sam Smith's Boatyard, about two miles north of Cooperstown. The hot-dog stand's founders, Sam Smith's daughter Cory and husband Michael, now run the restaurant and boatyard (plus several retail ventures) in partnership with another daughter, Robin, and her husband Jaime Butchard.

Here, two Adirondack-style dining porches open off the marina store. The Moffats polyurethaned the tables with local memorabilia, hung watery artifacts on the walls and dress the place with linens and flowers at night. Diners look across the lake to Kingfisher Tower as they sample such starters as Indian griddled corn cakes with smoked salmon and sour cream, oven-roasted quail with grilled sweet potato and port, and wild mushroom and goat cheese napoleon.

The blackboard menu of contemporary/fusion fare changes nightly, but expect main courses like grilled salmon with red pepper marmalade, grilled lobster with roast corn butter, roast duck with chipotle sauce, and coriander-crusted New York strip steak with oven-roasted tomatoes. House salads, grilled mixed vegetable skewers and roast garlic mashed potatoes or house rice accompany.

The lunch menu ranges equally widely, from baba ghanoush to Asian grilled chicken with Thai peanut-ginger sauce on vermicelli to the boatyard dog, the hot dog that made Dot's Landing famous.

(607) 547-7496. Entrées, $18.95 to $26.95. Lunch daily, 11:30 to 2:30. Dinner, 5 to 10. Closed Labor Day to Mother's Day.

Gabriella's On the Square, 161 Main St., Cooperstown.

Albany waitress Donna Marquardt found she liked the restaurant business so much that she and husband Bob opened their own in 1997. They gutted a former restaurant facing a main downtown intersection and redesigned it with what Donna called a country French provincial look. They offer contemporary continental cuisine with an Italian accent.

Heavy white linens and cut-glass shaded oil lamps on the tables, swagged lace curtains on the windows, pale yellow walls and gas fireplaces convey a warm, elegant look in two dining rooms seating about 80. The seasonal menu offers main courses like mixed seafood over linguini with lobster cream sauce, pan-seared salmon with a sambuca cream sauce, grilled pork loin with caramel bourbon glaze, confit of pheasant with cider-raspberry sauce and herb-crusted rack of New Zealand lamb, each with its own distinctive accompaniments.

Among starters are a pan-fried lump crab and crawfish cake that one partaker said was to die for, and steamed mussels topped with toasted garlic crostini and olive tapenade. The signature dessert is tirami su. Others include a chocolate terrine, granitas and lemon soufflé.

An appealing bistro menu offers such treats as beef stew served in a Danish bread bowl and grilled flank steak with herb-crisped potatoes and seared spinach.

(607) 547-8000. Entrées. $16.95 to $22.95. Bistro, $7.95 to $14.95. Dinner, 5 to 9 or 10, Sunday 1 to 7:30. Closed Tuesday in off-season.

The Hawkeye Bar & Grill, 60 Lake St., Cooperstown.

The casual American grill on the lower level of the Otesaga resort has leapt into the forefront of local dining favorites lately.

As compared with the fancy upstairs Dining Room and Lakeside Patio, which are considered special-occasion places and rather stodgy, the grill fare is more contemporary and the decor casual. It's immensely popular with people who like the Otesaga cachet, the lakeside setting and the reasonable prices. They speak highly of such dinner entrées as Eastern salmon fillet with dill cream sauce, grilled sea scallops with spinach-butter sauce, roast half duck with sundried cherry sauce or lamb chops with juniper berry-merlot sauce. You can settle for a burger, a sandwich, a caesar salad or a risotto, or graze on appetizers like an onion blossom, a trilogy of smoked seafood, or oriental pork dumplings. Sandwiches, salads and some of the dinner appetizers are available for lunch.

Like most resorts of its ilk, the Otesaga's upstairs is a local favorite for a summer lunch or Sunday brunch on the outdoor terrace or in the beautiful, chandeliered dining room all in pristine white with red accents. We headed here for lunch, until we found they weren't serving outside on a mild September day and the lunch buffet in the dining room cost $14 for an array that looked like a glorified salad bar with seafood newburg, rice and green beans at the end.

The fancy setting lends itself less to a quick weekday lunch than to a leisurely Sunday brunch. The extra tab for brunch ($19) yields omelets, salad and meat platters, and steamship round, and the venue is usually on the outside terrace overlooking the lake.

The printed dinner menu (prix-fixe, $32) changes daily. Au courant choices are mixed in with traditional fare. They range from fresh fruit cup with cointreau to jonah crab au gratin, chicken consommé to chilled midori melon soup, prime rib with horseradish popover to grilled swordfish with three-mustard sauce.

(607) 547-9931. Hawkeye Bar & Grill, entrées, $12.75 to $22; lunch, 11:30 to 3; dinner, 6 to 9:30. Dining Room, lunch or brunch on Lakeside Patio, depending on weather, noon to 2; dinner nightly, 6 to 8:30; jackets required.

The 1819 House, County Route 11 at Greenough Road, Cooperstown.

Local consensus anointed the old Terrace Café as best in town during its heyday. Now relocated to a larger, more historic structure several miles south on a former hops farm, this enterprise seems to be a case of out of sight, out of mind. People mention it when prompted, but seldom volunteer it in their list of dining favorites.

Owner Robert Paul and Baltimore-trained chef Lynn Hathaway have maintained the Terrace's culinary tradition in a trio of nicely restored upstairs dining rooms and a downstairs tavern with a stone fireplace. "We try to do things nobody else around here does," says Lynn, citing particularly his seafood and veal dishes, including veal london broil with mustard sauce, a specialty.

If not exactly cutting-edge, Manhattan style, the fare has its moments, as in the tangy goat-cheese lasagna, layered with prosciutto and marinara sauce, a dish we found surprisingly refined, and the veal scaloppine sautéed with zucchini, tomatoes and pernod. The crab cakes and grilled andouille sausage with creole mustard are favorite starters. The specialty dessert, bread pudding with a delicious whiskey sauce, is so rich that a little goes a long way.

A tavern menu offers lighter fare.

(607) 547-1819. Entrées, $12.95 to $17.95. Dinner, Tuesday-Sunday 5 to 9 or 10.

Clete Boyer's Hamburger Hall of Fame, 4874 State Hwy. 28 South, Cooperstown.

Although you probably won't see the eponymous major-league ball player, this roadside haunt is full of New York Yankees memorabilia and has a menu to match. It offers twelve versions of burgers named – with little obvious rhyme or reason – for

Yankee stars, three types of hotdogs, hot sandwiches and a short menu ranging from chicken parmesan to ribeye steak. Desserts are of the pie, rice pudding and Jell-O ilk. Breakfast is served all day.

(607) 544-1112. Open daily in summer, 6 a.m. to 11 p.m.; winter, 7 a.m. to 8 p.m.

Diversions

In baseball land, you'd expect to find a baseball theme, from the Short Stop restaurant and Third Base ("the last stop before home") to the Cooperstown Bat Co. But there's much more to this appealing village, some of which we concentrate upon here.

National Baseball Hall of Fame and Museum, Main Street, Cooperstown. Enshrined here in 1939 on the apparently erroneous theory that Abner Doubleday invented the game in Cooperstown a century earlier, the four floors dedicated to America's national pastime are what draw most visitors to Cooperstown. This is a museum in which hordes of men and boys stand mesmerized for hours – in front of an old uniform, a signed baseball, a recital of statistics, or the bat Mark McGwire used to stroke his 500th home run. Since a major addition in 1979, it has been transformed from a primitive museum with tabletop glass cases and encyclopedic sweep into a scattershot, state-of-the-art story of the game. The zoom-in, flashback approach is tailor-made for today's attention spans and the increasing enormity of the subject matter. Ever expanding, the museum opened a new National Baseball Library & Archive complex with exhibits on "Scribes and Mikemen," and in 1999 opened the Barry Halper Gallery for changing exhibits. Everyone has his favorites (ours include the section on baseball parks and the lifelike statues of Babe Ruth and Ted Williams carved from single pieces of laminated basswood); others prefer the awesome cathedral dedicated to the more than 200 Hall of Famers or the statistics spewed out by IBM computers. Who can fail to appreciate the magic of the thirteen-minute multi-media presentation in the Grandstand Theater? The audience sits in grandstand seats, shouts of "play ball" and "get your popcorn here" punctuate the ever-so-realistic crowd noise, the organ pumps up the fans and, well, it's almost like being in the old ballpark. Little wonder that everyone joins in the rousing "Take Me Out to the Ballgame" finale. Visitors exit through the ultimate baseball gift shop.

(607) 547-9988 or (888) 425-5633. Open daily, May-September 9 to 9; rest of year 9 to 5, to 8 on weekends except January-March. Adults, $9.50.

The Farmers' Museum, Lake Road, Cooperstown. This, not the Hall of Fame, was the primary destination for our seventh-grade class trip back in upstate New York in the late 1940s. The museum, only five years old at the time, was already known among educators and made a worthwhile outing for a day's immersion in early New York State history. The main barn displays agricultural artifacts and early crafts. Nearby is the relocated resting spot of the memorable Cardiff Giant, originally foisted on an unsuspecting public as a petrified prehistoric man and looking mighty big to seventh-graders. Beyond is the 1845 Village, nearly twenty historic buildings assembled from within 100 miles of Cooperstown, nestled against the hillside with cows grazing and chickens wandering about nearby. Buildings are furnished and staffed for the period. The Toddsville Store has a cast-iron stove, a printing office issues leaflets and the old

Bump Tavern offers occasional 19th-century dinners with period music. The Herder's Cottage restaurant, which has picnic tables out front, offers a variety of country-style fare. On a gorgeous autumn day, strolling the grounds, admiring the old buildings and looking across the stone walls to the golf course, Otsego Lake and the flaming hillsides, we felt this was close to paradise.

(607) 547-1450 or (888) 547-1450. Open daily, June-September 10 to 5; rest of year, Tuesday-Sunday 10 to 4. Closed January-March. Adults $9.

Fenimore Art Museum, Lake Road, Cooperstown.

Magnificent, yet somehow personal and homey, is the lakeside mansion built in 1932 on the site of novelist James Fenimore Cooper's farm. It's been the home of the New York State Historical Association since 1945. The stately portico leads to room after room of fine and decorative arts. A twelve-minute slide show provides a good orientation, and the descriptions throughout the galleries are unusually informative. The paintings in the ballroom include many from the Hudson River School. Thomas Cole's landscape scene from Cooper's *Last of the Mohicans* is especially appropriate in a gallery holding works associated with the novelist. Changing portions of the association's unsurpassed collection of folk art are displayed. The American Indian Wing exhibits the definitive Eugene and Clare Thaw Collection of more than 500 works of American Indian art. A recent renovation reorganized the galleries of the original building to allow the museum to display more of its extensive collections. The museum's **Fenimore Cafe** offers a light continental menu, with seating indoors and outside on a lakeview terrace.

(607) 547-1400 or (888) 547-1450. Open daily, June-September 10 to 5; rest of year, Tuesday-Sunday 10 to 4. Closed January-March. Adults $9.

Brewery Ommergang, 656 River Road (County Hwy. 33), Cooperstown.

During the 1900s, most of the hops in America were grown within 40 miles of Cooperstown. This stunning new structure on a 136-acre former hop farm along the Susquehanna River is the first farmstead microbrewery to be built in America in more than a century. Opened by beer importers Don Feinberg and Wendy Littlefield in partnership with several Belgian brewers, it is the only domestic brewery devoted solely to producing Belgian beers, which are considered some of the world's best. Guided tours show how this authentic, Belgian-style brewery open-ferments its beer and then bottle-conditions it in a warm cellar. Visitors smell the rare Styrian and Saaz hops and savory spices used in making ales and get a taste of the specialty Belgian malts. A gift shop is stocked with Belgian treats.

(607) 547-8184 or (800) 656-1212. Open Monday-Friday noon to 7 and weekends 11 to 7, Memorial Day through Labor Day. Rest of year, daily noon to 5.

Sightseeing. Catch the **Cooperstown Trolley** for a scenic ride between three free outlying parking lots and the village's major attractions. The trolley runs daily from 8:30 a.m. to 9 p.m. in summer and 8:30 to 6 on weekends in late spring and early fall. An all-day pass costs $2. This may be the best way to get around on busy days, when visitors outnumber the resident population. The Lake and Valley Garden Club publishes a brochure outlining a walking tour of 44 local sights. The restored **Cooperstown & Charlotte Valley Railroad** offers scenic diesel-powered train rides between Cooperstown and Milford four times daily except Monday in summer. The sixteen-mile trip takes about 90 minutes. **Classic Boat Tours** offers daily hour-long excursions on Otsego Lake aboard an all-wooden boat that cruised the lake at the turn of the century for the Clark and Busch families.

Shopping. Baseball cards and paraphernalia are on sale everywhere, of course, from the **National Pastime** to **Mickey's Place** (for Mickey Mantle memorabilia) to **Cap City,** which sprung up to capitalize on the baseball cap craze. Even the venerable **Church & Scott Pharmacy** sells baseball bats. Check out the suave, decorated Christmas tree with a baseball orientation in the window at **A Cooperstown Christmas.** A long garden path leads to the hidden courtyard outside **Moon Dreams,** an inspirational music, book, crafts and jewelry store; it offers a pleasant tearoom and café with pastries, international lunches and light suppers. The prime place for deli items, cheeses, artisan breads and baked goods from an open-hearth bakery, gourmet coffees and specialty foods is the upscale **Danny's Main Street Market,** where we picked up a stuffed focaccia sandwich. **Tin Bin Alley** offers gourmet jellybeans and bins of candies along with gifts. Other good shops include **Global Traders, Muskrat Hill** for gifts and specialty foods, **Willis Monie** for used and rare books, **Homescapes** for decorating, and **Metro Fashion** and **The Purple Star** for women's clothing. The works of 50 artisans are shown at **Riverwood. Lake Classic Designs** stocks select gifts and apparel at the Sam Smith's Boatyard marina.

Just north of town in Fly Creek are two worthy side-by-side destinations. **Fly Creek Cider Mill** is a complex of weathered buildings dispensing a variety of ciders, plus apple bread, apple butter, apple pies, candied apples, specialty food items and much more. You can watch cider being made from a vantage point upstairs off the gift shop, where the owner sells pretty dried arrangements from flowers and weeds she collects and air dries. Exotic ducks frequent the pond out back. At the nearby **Christmas Barn** you'll also find really special Christmas things. Dozens of trees, all with different themes, display hundreds of ornaments. Just about everything else for Christmas decorating is here as well.

Extra-Special

Glimmerglass Opera Festival, Route 80, Cooperstown.

The high retractable walls roll down as the lights dim in the 900-seat Alice Busch Opera Theater on Thomas Goodyear's former turkey farm above the lake that James Fenimore Cooper called Glimmerglass. The sense of drama heightens as another performance by one of the nation's best regional companies begins. Founded in 1975, this has become a major attraction. The $5 million, semi-open-air theater funded in 1987 by the Busch family represents the first major opera house built from scratch in America in several decades. And a sophisticated place it is for so rural a setting. The gilded ceiling is staggered in a quilt pattern for acoustical purposes, lamps adorn the balconies and the European-opera-house look is elegant and intimate, remarkable for a building designed to resemble a hops barn. Catered picnics may be ordered ahead and consumed beside a reflecting pond or on the hillside across the road, overlooking Otsego Lake. "Opera previews," free 35-minute programs, are scheduled one hour before performances. For the 25th anniversary season in 2000, 43 performances of four operas were scheduled. They ranged from Puccini's *La Bohème,* the world's most popular opera, to John Philip Sousa's *The Glass Blowers,* which had not been staged in 85 years.

(607) 547-2255. Box 191, Cooperstown. Matinees, Sunday, Monday and occasionally Tuesday and Saturday at 2; evenings, Thursday-Saturday at 8. Tickets, $22 to $90.

Village parks and downtown buildings back up to northern end of Skaneateles Lake.

Skaneateles, N.Y.

'Stress-Free' Village by the Lake

This storybook village is stunningly situated at the head of pristine Skaneateles Lake, a sixteen-mile-long lake so blue and pure that it serves as the water supply for the city of Syracuse.

The Iroquois word for "long lake," it is pronounced Skanny-AT-las, although visitors quickly find themselves slipping into the local vernacular, "SKINNY-at-las."

The lake has long been a low-key summer playground for the moneyed. As early as the 1840s, visitors eager to "take the waters" were attracted to a health spa founded by a local physician. By the turn of the century, Skaneateles was attracting worldly summer residents including cousins of Teddy Roosevelt, whose Roosevelt Hall was one of the grandest of the mansions built around the village end of the lake. Presidents Theodore and Franklin Roosevelt visited here.

So perhaps it should have come as no surprise when another First Family, Bill and Hillary Clinton, chose Skaneateles for their summer vacation in 1999 at the home of a local developer. For Mrs. Clinton's candidacy for the U.S. Senate from New York, it was better than Martha's Vineyard or the Hamptons.

The village of 2,800, which until then was unfamiliar to most beyond upstate New York, took the presidential visit in stride. The media coverage put Skaneateles on the map, although many townspeople in this strongly Republican enclave tried to ignore their five days of instant celebrity. Still, they kept bumping into the Clintons all over town. "It was surreal," said one local promoter. "It takes a village," added an innkeeper. "She came up with that. This is a good place for it."

The charms of Skaneateles have been a given for generations of summer-home owners and, increasingly, year-round resident who commute to Syracuse or work in the locally owned Welch Allyn Inc., a growing medical diagnostic instruments company. It was only in 1995 that, in an effort to boost tourism, the mayor proclaimed the village "a stress-free zone."

Except for the Sherwood Inn, which dates to 1807, inns and B&Bs only came into being in the 1990s. The same goes for most restaurants, except for The Krebs, a landmark that has been feeding travelers since 1899.

Instead, Skaneateles is known as the place where people sing along with the community band at Friday evening concerts around the lakeside gazebo. Where the mail is still delivered to summer cottagers by boat. Where the stores occupy historic homes or a picturesque block of three-story commercial buildings along East Genesee Street. Where church bells toll the hours. And where the golf and polo clubs are private but the lake is accessible to everyone from parks on either side of downtown.

Visitors and local folks alike go for soup and burgers at Johnny Angel's Heavenly Hamburgers. They line up to get into Doug's Fish Fry or to sample ice cream from Blue Water Chill. Crowds are drawn to the annual antique and classic boat show in July, the Skaneateles Festival chamber music series in August, and the Dickens' Christmas in Skaneateles events in December.

This is tranquil, small-town stuff of the kind that locals call "life in the past lane." And, unless you're trying to find a downtown parking spot on a summer weekend, it's blessedly stress-free.

Inn Spots

Sherwood Inn, 26 Genesee St., Skaneateles 13152.

Occupying the prime lakefront position in the center of town, this venerable inn serves as the hub of village activity by virtue of its location as well as its age. It was built by Isaac Sherwood as a stagecoach tavern, and has served as a tavern or inn almost continuously for nearly 200 years.

Local entrepreneur William Eberhardt, owner since 1974, took over a faltering venture and has upgraded it over time. The main floor has

Flags fly in front of main entrance of lakefront Sherwood Inn.

been refurbished and expanded, and about half the guest rooms have been renovated. "So there's a mix of old and new," according to our guide.

Guests enter from a front entrance across the street from a park facing Skaneateles Lake or through a newly renovated main entrance on the side. The lobby welcomes with its fireplace, Stickley furniture, landscape paintings and the oriental carpets and runners that typify the public spaces and corridors throughout. With its reception desk, a small gift shop, a staircase to guest rooms and entries to the main dining room, the dining porch and tavern, the lobby conveys a community focus as well as a sense of place.

Upstairs on the second and third floors are an unusually wide variety of rooms and suites, each tastefully decorated in a different style. There are a couple of small and basic rooms, quite serviceable, as well as larger and more lavish quarters that would command considerably higher prices elsewhere. We were assigned to Room 31, "one of our nicest" – a corner lakefront affair with a fireplace, queensize bed and the only full-fledged jacuzzi tub in the establishment. Decorated in reds and mauves in high Victorian style, it came with four gilt-framed paintings of nudes on the walls, an antique loveseat, a TV visible only from the bed, an overhead chandelier and two gas-style bedside lamps with 40-watt bulbs. It seems this was the honeymoon suite, and no previous occupants had ever asked for a stronger lamp with which to read by.

A tour the next day turned up a number of large and appealing rooms and suites with comfortable sitting areas (and reading lamps). Some have canopy beds and Colonial furnishings; others are traditional. One has a steam shower and another an enclosed porch. Most in demand are the renovated rooms, which generally face the lake. All have telephones, televisions and interesting fabrics and window treatments. Six come with fireplaces and whirlpool baths.

Continental breakfast is complimentary on the enclosed front porch.. It's a beauty

Twin stone gates at entrance identify Hobbit Hollow Farm.

of a space in summery cream colors. Big windows open onto the park and lake. Cut-up fruit, packaged cereals, English muffins for toasting and pastries from the Patisserie behind the inn are featured.

(315) 685-3405 or (800) 374-3796. Fax (315) 685-8983. Fourteen rooms and six suites with private baths. May to Columbus Day and all weekends: doubles, $85 to $145; suites, $110 to $225. Midweek, rest of year: doubles, $75 to 125; suites, $95 to $225.

Hobbit Hollow Farm, 3061 West Lake Road, Skaneateles 13152.

Some of the grandest new accommodations in the Finger Lakes region are offered at this substantial, century-old Colonial Revival on a 320-acre hillside horse farm overlooking Skaneateles Lake. Here you get the feeling for the good life, as lived by prosperous residents along the lake's posh west shore.

Michael and Noreen Falcone, who live lakeside across the street, bought the property to save it from development. They totally rebuilt the original farmhouse and spared no expense in furnishing it in the style of an elegant country house. Forty horses are boarded and roam the pastures.

Guests enter the side door of what looks to be two complete houses joined by a hallway wing in the middle. In the reception foyer is a stunning mural of the house and its setting. On one side of the foyer are a cozy library with TV and a lemon-yellow dining room where breakfast is served at a table for eight. On the other side are two sumptuous living rooms, each open to the other. At the far end of the house is a nifty porch facing the lake.

Upstairs, widely separated from each other because of the layout of the house, are five guest rooms of varying size. Standard are triple-sheeted beds with high-thread-count Italian linens, heavy draperies puddled to the floor, MacKenzie-Childs accessories, telephones, terry robes and hair dryers. The smallest room, basically for overflow, is barely big enough for a double bed tucked in its bay window and has a bath across the hall. Another, with an 18th-century Italian queen bed, has a bath with shower and soaking tub.

The remaining rooms are substantially larger. The Chanticleer, done in French country style, offers a queensize pencil-post bed and a huge bath with a large soaking tub. The front-corner Lake View room is aptly named. It comes with a carved oak queen poster bed, a double armoire, gas fireplace, thick oriental rugs, a marble-encased double whirlpool tub and a glass-enclosed, walk-in shower. The Master bedroom occupies the other front corner and is even grander, with a majestic kingsize poster bed facing a gas fireplace, two plump silk-covered chairs, a double whirlpool tub, and a large screened porch furnished in wicker.

Innkeeper Richard Flynn offers wine and cheese every evening around 6.

Breakfast is served amidst sterling, Waterford and Wedgwood. The main course could be a puffed ham and cheese omelet, blueberry pancakes, belgian waffles or cinnamon-roll french toast stuffed with seasonal fruit.

(315) 685-2791. Fax (315) 685-3426. Five rooms with private baths. Doubles, $120 to $270, May-December; $100 to $250, rest of year.

The Arbor House, 41 Fennell St., Skaneateles 13152.

It's not all that prepossessing from the outside, this odd-looking brick building billed as having been built in richly detailed Federal style in the mid-1800s. But looks can deceive. The interior is thoroughly up-to-date and laden with creature comforts. The decor is stylish, and there are ingenious touches.

Tom and Nancy Shaver, described as local property owners and entrepreneurs, purchased the property near others they owned with no idea for its use. When a niece got married, they found a lack of visitor accommodations in town. So they decided to open it as a B&B.

The Shavers ripped up linoleum to restore hardwood floors and found original exterior brick walls hidden by sheet rock after becoming interior walls in later additions. They added bathrooms, installed stained glass, and shopped auctions and antiques shops for furnishings. Thanks to Tom's background in a carpentry business, they did most of the renovations themselves. They opened in 1999 with five comfortable guest rooms and plans for more.

The theme is grapes, and an arbor in front arches over a sign bearing the name. Rooms are named after grapes native to the region.

The largest is the Concord master suite on the main floor. It comes with a kingsize bed open to a sitting room with a daybed, a gas fireplace, and a pristine, brick-walled bath painted white, with a double jacuzzi and separate shower.

Upstairs is the Glendora, also with a double jacuzzi and a gas-stove fireplace. Like the other second-floor rooms, it has a queensize poster bed and designer bed coverings that match the window treatments. Subdued pastel-painted walls, telephones and a single chair are the norm. Two other rooms have jacuzzi tubs. Each tub is ingeniously enclosed in an archway that echoes the arbor theme.

More ingenuity shows up in the dining room, the original part of the house. What once had been a window is now a recessed china cupboard displaying plates decorated in different grape designs. The original exterior brick wall behind it now enhances the spacious kitchen.

Innkeeper Renee Valentine puts that kitchen to the test, preparing breakfasts to order for guests. She'll do omelets, french toast, pancakes, home fries, "the works." It's taken at a table for six in the dining room or on the side sun porch. Oriental rugs and local artworks grace the pleasant front common room.

For the future, the Shavers envisioned more rooms in a barn behind a renovated office structure they own nearby.

(315) 685-8966 or (888) 234-4558. Fax: 315-685-6104. Four rooms and one suite with private baths. May-October and all weekends: doubles, $125 to $140; suite, $170. Midweek rest of year: doubles, $110 to $125; suite, $145.

Mirbeau Inn & Spa, 851 West Genesee St., Skaneateles 13152.

Newly opened in May 2000, this $7-million luxury resort is patterned after a French country estate and notable, in the words of a Syracuse newspaper headline, for "Monet and Money."

Three local residents set out to create a soothing establishment combining the amenities of a boutique country inn and world-class spa facilities with the residential feeling of a cloistered French château. It's designed to look as if it has been transported from the area around French impressionist painter Claude Monet's gardens, a concept after which Mirbeau patterns itself.

Set behind a stone wall off U.S. Route 20, Mirbeau occupies a wooded hillside on the western edge of the village, away from the lake and on the site of a former motel. Most of the twelve-acre complex consists of a cathedral spruce grove behind the inn and spa. Guests can walk a meditation trail through the spruce forest to a meditation garden.

Skaneateles architect Andrew Ramsgard, one of the three partners, created buildings that take advantage of the wooded, sloping lot and the water that flows through the center of the property. Rather than the simple gray stone aspect of Monet's house at Giverny, however, these take on turreted, castle-like proportions, are built of concrete and stucco, and are colored in the earth tones of Provence.

Eighteen guest quarters, a restaurant and the spa occupy the soaring main lodge, which is quite a sight for upstate New York. Behind and to the side of the lodge are four villa-style cottages of similar French provincial design, each with four guest rooms. All curve around a serene, central landscaped area of tiered lily ponds and gardens with, yes, a replica of the famed bridge in Monet's garden.

Each of 34 guest rooms comes with a kingsize or two queen beds, fireplace, sitting area and large bathroom with soaking tub, walk-in shower and double vanity. Some rooms open onto hospitality areas and may be joined as suites.

The main lodge, where an artist was hand-painting designs above a fireplace in the lobby at our pre-opening visit, is oriented toward the rear, where tall windows overlook ponds and gardens. Near the lobby is one of the waterfalls that trickles through the property and adds to the calming influence of the spa. The rear wing of the lodge holds nine spa treatment rooms, steam and sauna rooms, a weight room and motion studio. Outside are hot and cold plunge pools. Spa treatments vary from $65 for a pedicure to $350 for four-and-one-half hours of treatments, relaxation periods and a spa lunch.

Across the lobby from the spa area is the **Mirbeau Dining Room,** with beamed ceiling, French and American impressionist paintings on the walls, French antiques and a terrace for outdoor dining. Executive chef Edward Moro cooked at the Little Nell Hotel in Aspen, Colo., and at the historic Hotel Hershey in his Pennsylvania hometown. Here he offers what is touted as "French country estate cuisine," available to the public as well as spa guests.

Main lodge of Mirbeau Inn & Spa resembles French château on hillside west of village.

The dinner menu changes daily. The meal is prix-fixe, $65 for five courses, plus canapés to start and les mignardises to finish. Among typical offerings is an appetizer of New York State fois gras with caramelized pears, spiced brioche and huckleberries. Main courses could be Nova Scotia salmon with littleneck clam chowder and roesti potato cake, charred beef tenderloin with foraged mushrooms and truffle mashed potatoes, a roast of the day carved tableside and "the year's first lamb chop" with white beans and lamb cassoulet. Desserts range from warm chocolate cake with caramelized banana, bourbon ice cream and toasted walnuts to sorbet and fruit "so fresh I don't know what it is," in the chef's words.

In Provence collecting furnishings for their establishment at our visit were the three principals, lawyer and ex-Pyramid mall developer Gary L. Dower, Linda F. Dal Pos and architect Ramsgard. They view Mirbeau as the prototype for a series of non-urban resort spas across the northern United States.

(315) 685-5006 or (877) 647-2328. Fax (315) 685-5150. Thirty-four rooms with private baths. Doubles, $295 to $385.

Prix-fixe, $65. Lunch daily, 11:30 to 2:30. High tea at 4. Dinner nightly, 6 to 10.

Lady of the Lake, 2 West Lake St., Skaneateles 13152.

Beige with chocolate trim, this Queen Anne Victorian built around the turn of the century is aptly designated. It's owned and run by Sandra Rademacher, who named its guest rooms after ladies who owned the house in the past and embellished their contents with lots of feminine froufrou. And it occupies a prime corner position facing Shotwell Memorial Park at the head of the lake.

Sandra shares her home with guests in three upstairs bedrooms. The largest is the Stella, named after the home's builder. It has a white iron kingsize bed covered, like beds in the rest of the house, with a white duvet comforter. Sandra points out antiques such as the cherry Empire dresser, a canvas-covered steamer trunk and decorative windows, but others may notice first the lady mannikin clad in white.

Across the hall and away from the street is the sunny DeEtta, named after DeEtta Smith, who with her physician husband raised three daughters and practiced medicine here. Boasting a glimpse of the lake, it has a double brass bed, lace-skirted dressing table and a pumpkin pine bachelor's chest. Again, however, you may notice first the framed wall hanging of undergarments that belonged to the owner's grandmother. Dolls are grouped around the hallway leading to the rear Mary, named for the woman who bought the house from Stella in 1920. It comes with a queensize bed and a full bath across the hall.

The main floor is a Victorian beauty, starting from its beveled glass front doors leading into the entry hall. Along the side of the house are two double parlors and a rear dining room, each open to the other. The front parlor is more formal with a piano, while the middle parlor is a library with fireplace and TV. Oriental rugs grace the hardwood floors, and Victorian wallpapers are employed with abandon.

The dining-room table is set for six. Breakfast is continental midweek and gourmet on weekends, as in "egg blossom," German pancakes or "breakfast in a loaf."

The wraparound porch is furnished in wicker. The welcome mat at the door advises: "I golf therefore I'm not here." Sandra's answering-machine message indicated she's a poet as well.

(315) 685-7997 or (888) 685-7997. Three rooms with private baths. Doubles, $85 to $115 weekends, $75 to $105 midweek. Children by arrangement. No smoking.

The Gray House, 47 Jordan St., Skaneateles 13152.

The owners' name is Gray, which matches the color of the building's exterior. And the location is next to the Gray Funeral Home. So visitors have little trouble finding this establishment, where a sign designates a "rooming house" but Valerie and Bob Gray have been offering it as a B&B since 1990.

The family live above their funeral home, and rent out part out of the Gray House next door as an apartment. One side of the main floor off double parlors holds two guest rooms. The Milford, named for a judge who built the turn-of-the-century house, has a queen wrought-iron bed. Adjacent is the Brice Room, with a double and a single bed, both made of mahogany. Upstairs in the rear is the Bishop Suite. It offers a queensize cherry four-poster bed with a fishnet canopy, angled from the corner, a small sitting room with a daybed and TV, and a small kitchen. Furnishings and decor are purposely Victorian of the dark and frilly school.

Valerie comes over in the morning to set out a continental breakfast spread of fruit, cereals, danish and English muffins. Guests can use the kitchen, and avail themselves of a small rear sun porch overlooking the backyard swimming pool. Who knows? If the Grays are swimming, guests may be invited to join in.

(315) 685-0131 or 685-5224. Two rooms and one suite with private baths. Doubles, $89 to $110. Suite, $115 to $130. Two-night minimum summer weekends and holidays.

Dining Spots

Rosalie's Cucina, 841 West Genesee St., Skaneateles.

A plaque on the wall in the rear foyer says this superior restaurant was "built with great love for my sister" and, after listing the architectural credits, adds "with way too much money." Both the love and the money are manifest in the chic

Impressive downstairs wine cellar is set for diners at Rosalie's Cucina.

Tuscan-style trattoria, wine cellar and bakery – a testament to the late Rosalie Romano from Phil Romano, the restaurant impresario who started the Fuddruckers, Eatzi's and Romano's Macaroni Grill chains.

It seems that Phil, who grew up in nearby Auburn and lives in Texas, still summers on Skaneateles Lake and "wanted a nice place to eat," in the words of Gary Robinson, co-owner with Eddie Colella, Rosalie's cousin. "He'd been all over Italy, so he built this the way he wanted it for himself."

His $1.5 million investment includes a stylish 125-seat restaurant backing up to an open kitchen, a downstairs wine cellar and an upstairs Romano Room for family reunions and private parties, a bakery, an outdoor bocce court, a small vineyard for show, and an elaborate herb layout and vegetable garden for real.

The delightful Mediterranean-style courtyard is a holding area for the waiting crowds, who are given bread sticks, olives and cheese to stave off hunger.

Inside the salmon-colored building is a dark and spacious dining area understated in white and black. Black chairs flank well-spaced tables covered with white butcher paper over white cloths. A few columns break up the expanse. The white walls are enlivened with thousands of splashy autographs of customers, who pay $25 each to charity to enshrine their name and the date for posterity. A prime column in the middle was signed by President and Mrs. Clinton and daughter Chelsea, who enjoyed dinner here on the second night of their 1999 vacation.

Six chefs, most of whom had been executive chefs elsewhere, team up with early head chef Greg Rhoad to vary the menu daily. The specialty is prime meats, as in aged New York strip steak and grilled veal loin chop. The grilled lobster tails with orzo and spinach and the lamb loin with white wine and garlic are done according to family recipes. So are the scampi alla Rosalie (with artichokes and garlic butter) and the veal piccata. Portions are huge, as we found out sampling the signature farfalle con pollo (chicken with pancetta, asiago cream, red onions and peas). That and one of the enormous salads were plenty for two to share. Even so, part of the pasta dish went home in a foil wrap shaped like a swan, along with several loaves of the dynamite bread that begins the meal (extras are freely given and accepted at the end of the evening).

Antipasti include carpaccio, pizza margherita, manicotti, steamed mussels and grilled portobello mushrooms. Of the insalatas, the one with arugula, prosciutto, reggiano and lemon is special.

The homemade desserts change daily. The pastries and breads come from **Crustellini's,** the bakery at the rear of the establishment, where several varieties of sensational "hand-made breads" are for sale Wednesday-Sunday from 9 a.m.

A strolling mandolin player serenades tables and adds a touch of Italian charm. The staff continues Rosemary's legacy in her cucina that love built.

(315) 685-2200. Entrées, $18 to $29. Dinner nightly, 5 to 9 or 10.

Blue Water Grill, 11 West Genesee St., Skaneateles.

The closest-to-the-waterfront dining in town is offered by this jaunty newcomer, a high-ceilinged space with big windows and all painted in blue-green (to match the color of the lake). The colors change with the reflections from the lake and are constantly evolving, according to Dan Riordan, son of an Auburn restaurateur and co-owner with Bill Eberhardt of the Sherwood Inn.

The long, narrow, L-shaped restaurant wraps around an open kitchen and a bar. The seasonal venue of choice is a canopied outdoor deck that was so crowded on a summer Saturday we were lucky to snag a table for lunch. We could only get glimpses of the lake, inasmuch as the head-on view is blocked by a pre-existing boathouse structure. But you can feel the lake breeze, and there's no better place for an ample lunch of – our choice – a bistro burger with jalapeño potatoes and a Cuban wrap with pork, chicken and coleslaw.

The interesting, all-day menu starts with seafood gumbo, three varieties of nachos, steamed mussels in garlic pesto cream and a pizza margherita. Entrée-size salads include fajita with grilled chicken or portobello mushrooms, caesar and Mediterranean.

Among dinner specialties are shrimp scampi over linguini, baked scrod, Maryland lump crab cakes, St. Louis spare ribs and grilled filet mignon with bordelaise sauce. Steak santorini is New York strip with red peppers, garlic and feta cheese, served with smashed potatoes.

Out front is **Blue Water Chill,** a takeout place for cold beverages and ice cream. New for 2000 was the Blue Water's latest venture, **Cravings,** facing the lake across the street. It offers cappuccino, baked goods and high-end ice cream.

(315) 685-6600. Entrées, $9.95 to $17.95. Open daily, 11:30 to 10.

The Krebs, 53 West Genesee St., Skaneateles.

For more than 100 years, this home-style family operation has been synonymous with dining in Skaneateles. The formula hasn't changed in the four decades we've been following it: good food and lots of it – not gourmet, but fancy middle American fare like prime rib and lobster newburg.

But for a black and yellow neon sign and the street lined with parked cars, this white wood house ringed with red impatiens could be your grandmother's. Indeed, the restaurant occupies the home in which Cora and Fred Krebs started serving meals to neighbors in 1899. It has been expanded over the years to the point where the family's upstairs living quarters became a cocktail lounge in 1946 and the low-ceilinged dining rooms seat more than 150.

The furnishings are antique, the windows have sheer lace curtains and the tables are covered with white cloths, floral china and fresh flowers from the garden in

The Krebs has been a culinary landmark since 1899.

back. "Every effort has been made to keep the restaurant as you would have found it in the early 1900s," says Jan Loveless, owner since 1970 with her husband Larry.

There are no menus. Instead, what Jan calls "a moving buffet" is brought to the table and served family style. The multi-course meal is priced by theme: $32 for English sliced prime rib and pan-fried half broiler of chicken, $33 for shrimp cocktail and lobster newburg, and $39 for a seven-course "traditional" meal, including all of the above.

With every meal you get appetizers: tomato juice, fruit cup or "melon in season" and clear broth, cream soup or choice of salad. Relishes and homemade breads accompany. With the entrée come white potato, candied sweet potato, vegetable, beef gravy, creamed mushrooms and toast points, sweet rolls and creamed horseradish.

Finally, a platter of brownies and angel food cake accompany each dessert. The choice includes pies, pastries, ice cream or sherbet. Back in the '60s, our celebratory party of six could barely finish.

An à la carte tavern menu of sandwiches, salads and smaller portions of the dinner entrées is offered in the upstairs cocktail lounge.

The Krebs's original Sunday brunch – an assortment of breakfast items plus creamed chicken with biscuits and roast beef hash – remains an institution.

The more things change around it, the more The Krebs stays the same.

(315) 685-5714. Prix-fixe, $32 to $39; tavern entrées, $10.95 to $15.95. Dinner nightly, 6 to 9 or 10. Sunday, brunch 10:30 to 2, dinner 4 to 9. Closed late October to early May.

Sherwood Inn, 26 West Genesee St., Skaneateles.

As the hub of village activity, this was the first port of call for President Clinton's party the night they arrived in town to start their five-day vacation in 1999.

Spectators and media stood outside the inn awaiting the First Family's arrival in town and, just when they thought the motorcade had retired for the evening, Bill, Hillary and Chelsea Clinton arrived with the Secret Service for a late supper.

Although the inn had only an hour's notice when a White House staffer reserved under a different name, the staff rose to the occasion. The Clintons shunned a private dining area and shook hands with inn guests and diners. Accompanied by two White House aides, they ordered off the menu. The President chose the signature scrod Christopher with lemon beurre blanc. The First Lady had grilled salmon with pommery mustard sauce, and Chelsea ordered the portobello mushroom wellington, chef Chris Kuhn's version of beef wellington. He also offers touches of the trendy, as in yellowfin tuna au poivre and herb-crusted rack of lamb with rosemary jus.

The interior dining room is serene in rich cream colors, from table linens to walls and ceiling. The tables of choice are on the long and glamorous front porch, recently renovated and enclosed for year-round dining. Also popular is the historic-looking, dark paneled tavern, with wraparound windows onto the lake and village scene. Its extensive menu offers a range from sandwiches and salads to a scallop and shrimp brochette and petite filet mignon.

(315) 685-3405 or (800) 374-3796. Entrées, $17.95 to $22.95; Tavern, $10.95 to $13.95. Open daily for lunch and dinner, 11:30 to 9 or 10.

Doug's Fish Fry, 8 Jordan St., Skaneateles.

This is one of those places that you have to see to believe. Doug Clark, who looks like a bearded sea captain of yore, opened a fish house in 1982 and quickly became a local icon. The clippings and photos attached to the walls of the original building testify to his success.

Lines form outside, especially Friday evenings in season and in Lent. You enter, place your order at a counter and find a seat here or out back in a back Dining Building. The latter was restored for the purpose with communal picnic tables on two floors (one-way stairs up and the other way down to improve traffic flow). Across the alley is an outdoor picnic area bordered by flower gardens carefully tended by the owner himself. (He also drives an old red fire truck dubbed the "Dougy buggy" to shuttle diners upon occasion.) When your first name is called, you pick up your order and dig into what fans say is some of the best fried fish ever. "We fry in pure peanut oil and filter it twice every day," says Doug.

The no-nonsense menu is short and basic: fish sandwich, fish dinner with fries or onion rings and slaw, a frank or coney, shrimp cocktail, and four special dinners – chicken, shrimp, scallops and lobster – again with fries or rings and slaw. That's it, except for steamed clams, a frog's leg appetizer on Monday, Tuesday and Wednesday, and hard or soft ice cream cones.

The place advertises: "Three things some great restaurants do – accept credit cards, serve good coffee and take reservations. Doug's Fish Fry does none of these." It doesn't need to. Doug's is a true place, with something of the feeling of Boston's Durgin-Park in miniature.

(315) 685-3288. Entrées, $6.10 to $14.54. Open daily, 11 to 8, to 10 in summer. Closed first two weeks of January.

Johnny Angel's Heavenly Hamburgers, 22 Jordan St., Skaneateles.

This slick establishment is the carnivore's answer to Doug's Fish Fry. It's lovingly run by John Angyal, an ex-state trooper turned judge and town supervisor. For his third "and last career" he opened a burger restaurant in partnership with boyhood friend Phil Romano, the Texas restaurateur who designed it at the same time as he did Rosalie's Cucina. This has an open kitchen, communal tables covered with red and white checked cloths, a jukebox and a self-serve soft ice-cream machine amidst a vaguely high-tech look with exposed ducts, stainless steel and mirrors. There's a salad bar of condiments, plus beer on ice. The place-your-order-at-the-counter menu ranges from Texas chili to shrimp cobb salad to aged strip steak with fries and onion rings.

John, who took up cooking when he was sidelined from police work after back surgery, comes in every morning to make three kinds of soup, fifteen to twenty gallons of each. He and his staff smoke pork ribs and grind choice angus beef for half-pound burgers cooked to order on a cast-iron grill. The rest of the day, John kibitzes with customers. Another local icon who knows everyone in town, he's part of the show, telling tall tales and expounding on town doings and politics. For the Clintons' visit, he renamed his signature sandwich the "Hillary Special – Full of Baloney." Formerly the politician's special, it's a hamburger roll stuffed with grilled bologna topped with melted cheese. John went through 700 pounds during the Clinton visit. Mrs. Clinton heard about it, but did not come in. So he sent her a case of his bottled heavenly water named in her honor, "Skinny at Last." You never know what John might come up with next. At our visit, he was planning to take over a shop next door and open a wine and tapas bar.

Oh yes, the half-pound burger – a knife-and-fork affair – was mighty good, and John's cream of asparagus soup was first-rate. The ice cream reminded us of Dairy Queen days. Next time we'll come for breakfast and try his Angel sandwich with egg and cheese or his all-you-can-eat New Hope Mills pancakes.

(315) 685-0100. Entrées, $2.40 to 11.95. Open daily, 7 a.m. to 9 p.m.

Diversions

Skaneateles Lake was described as "the most beautiful body of water in the world" more than a century ago by New York governor William Seward of nearby Auburn. More recently, Rochester journalist-author Arch Merrill wrote of Skaneateles: "I know of no more attractive community in Upstate New York than this distinctive and immaculate old village. Few village main streets have such a setting."

No less than the Times of London declared it in 1910 a "real" summer resort, "composed for the most part of splendidly healthy young men and maidens who find their chief delight in physical exercises, with the additional stimulus of flirtation. The older members of the company play bridge or golf, fish, ride or drive, or watch their strenuous families."

Community band concerts, swimming and boating, Sunday afternoon polo games, golf at the Skaneateles Country Club and two public eighteen-hole courses, chamber music concerts at the Skaneateles Festival – these are the activities that divert Skaneateles residents and visitors today.

Happily, the lake is fully accessible to the public in the village center. Visitors enjoy a gazebo, a swimming area and a pier at Clift Park and a sunken terrace with monuments to veterans in the adjacent Shotwell Memorial Park. At the east end of downtown is Thayer Park, another quiet place to enjoy the lake view.

Boat Tours. The **Mid-Lakes Navigation Co. Ltd.,** run by several generations of the Wiles family, offers a number of Skaneateles Lake cruises. Fifty-minute sightseeing cruises are scheduled daily in summer. There are lunch and champagne dinner cruises aboard the double-decker Judge Ben Wiles. One of the most fun is the morning mailboat excursion on the classic wooden cruiser, the Barbara S. Wiles. Passengers take part in the 100-year tradition of mail delivery by boat to cottages around the 32-mile shoreline. The company also offers Erie Canal cruises and, lately, winter cruises around Florida's Lake Okeechobee. Its headquarters at 11 Jordan St. serves as the village's unofficial visitor information center.

(315) 685-8500 or (800) 545-4318. Lake cruises daily, May to September.

Skaneateles Festival, 28 Hannum St., Skaneateles.

During August, the village takes on a mini-Tanglewood air, thanks to the Skaneateles Festival, now entering its third decade. The festival quickly outgrew its start in the village Library Hall, evolving into a month-long chamber music series featuring guest artists and top orchestra musicians from across the country. Concerts are presented Thursday and Friday evenings in St. James Episcopal Church, where at intermission the audience can stroll through the adjacent lakeside park and purchase lemonade and cookies from children's sidewalk stands. On Saturday evenings, concert-goers tote picnics and spread blankets on the lawn as the festival orchestra performs from the porch at Brook Farm, a grand estate owned by festival founders two miles down the lake.

Skaneateles High School is the venue for a couple of special festival events. In addition, there are free daytime open rehearsals and a KidsFest! concert series for children.

(315) 685-7418. Concerts in August, Thursday-Saturday at 8. Tickets, $10 to $25.

Local Traditions. The village gazebo in lakeside Clift Park is the setting for outdoor **band concerts** every Friday evening in July and August. People sing and children dance to the music of the community band. Boaters pull up to watch from the lake. More than 60 boats race and parade during the annual **Antique and Classic Boat Show** the last weekend in July. On weekends from Thanksgiving to Christmas, the downtown area is the focus for the **Dickens' Christmas in Skaneateles,** a Victorian celebration. Costumed actors stroll the streets, interacting with shoppers and performing street theater. There are carolers, brass bands, a piper, horse-drawn carriage rides and roasted chestnuts. A number of stores offer refreshments and other treats.

Skaneateles Historical Society, 28 Hannum St.

History is well cared for in Skaneateles, with this society founded in 1961 in the vanguard. It publishes village histories, leads walking tours and shows its collections in the restored Skaneateles Creamery. Visitors find a cream separator and milk bottles, as well as teasels (from Skaneateles's teasel-drying days), an ornate gate from the grounds of Roosevelt Hall, a canoe from the old Skaneateles boat & Canoe Co. ("builder of boats that will last"), historic photos, boat models and changing exhibits, all of which convey a sense of place. A century-old poster advertising Sunday excursions on Skaneateles Lake aboard the steamer City of Syracuse proclaims, "as a summer resort, Skaneateles Lake has few equals."

(315) 685-1360. Open in summer, Thursday-Saturday 1 to 4; rest of year, Friday 1 to 4 and by appointment.

Shopping. Few villages take such advantage of their lakefront as Skaneateles. The lake is not only visible but also accessible from either end of the long downtown commercial block. Most shops are situated in restored houses designated in the historic registry or in a colorful block of three-story commercial facades that look much as they did in pictorial histories more than a century ago. The former Skaneateles Savings Bank's 1895 clock tower oversees the charming streetscape.

Start in the bank exhibit in the vault of the former national bank. The bank now houses **First National Gifts** as well as a satellite shop of Syracuse's Everson Museum of Art. Highlights in the commercial block are **The Bookie** for toys and books, **Gallop on Saddlery**, the **Vermont Green Mountain Specialty Co.** for chocolates and coffee, and the **Aristocats & Dogs Pet Boutique.** Across the street are **Chestnut Cottage,** a Christmas and Americana shop; **Pomodoro,** a house full of gifts and collectibles; **Rhubarb,** a small but superb kitchen and garden store, and the **Kinder Garden** for children's clothing. Around the corner on Jordan Street, look for the small but choice **Gallery Luna,** the **Elegant Needles** yarn shop and John Francis McCarthy's **Finger Lakes Photography/ Gallery.** Next to the Sherwood Inn, **Complements** features contemporary women's clothing and accessories in a handsome house at 32 West Genesee St.

Follow your nose to **Patisserie,** a sparkling new venture in a carriage house behind the Sherwood Inn. Here, Hawaiian baker Chris Uyehara and his wife Kelly create fabulous sweets and artisan breads in a retail shop that also supplies owner Bill Eberhardt's varied operations. The delectable pastries – blueberry turnovers, cranberry scones, marzipans, fancy cakes – are to die for. We departed with a loaf of sundried tomato ciabatta, described as "the Italian slipper bread" and looking the part.

Extra-Special _____

John D. Barrow Gallery, 49 East Genesee St., Skaneateles.

Nineteenth-century landscape painter John D. Barrow wrote: "Forgive me if I tell once more, the glory of our summer shore...'tis no vain boast to say, Earth has no fairer spot today." This two-room gallery celebrates the area he loved and painted so well. He returned to his adopted hometown in 1875 after twenty years of painting in New York, where he was part of the famed Hudson River School. He donated funds for a skylit gallery, to be built behind the Skaneateles Library, with the understanding that only his paintings would grace its walls. The gallery is home for more than 300 of his original paintings – many of them landscapes focusing on Skaneateles Lake. Some of the bigger paintings are framed in gilt. Others are mounted on wood wainscoting around the lower reaches of walls in both rooms. For its 100th anniversary in 2000, the gallery re-created the original Barrow exhibit.

(315) 685-5135. Open in summer, Monday-Saturday 2 to 4; rest of year, Thursday and Saturday 2 to 4.

Ithaca, N.Y.
The Little Apple

"Ithaca Is Gorges," say the ubiquitous bumper stickers hereabouts. The play on words is apt. Gorges slice through and around the biggest city in the Finger Lakes region, creating waterfalls that cascade almost into downtown. And the scenery is gorgeous, thanks to all the gorges, the surrounding hills and Cayuga Lake. The Cornell University campus, which straddles some of the most gorgeous of the gorges, is to our minds the most scenic in America.

Hills rise sharply all around this city cradled at the southern end of Cayuga Lake. Only the downtown and west side are flat. Everything else in Ithaca is on hillsides, some as steep as any in San Francisco. The views from parts of the Cornell campus and the posh Cayuga Heights residential section are as dramatic as those in Berkeley.

Ithaca is also called "The Little Apple," a reference to its big-city status as a cultural and arts center. Ithaca is home to both Cornell (an Ivy Leaguer with 12,500 undergrads and 5,600 graduate students) and Ithaca College (the largest private residential college in New York State with 6,400 students). The ivied Cornell and the modern Ithaca campuses sprawl across hilltops on opposite sides of town, though Cornell is much the larger presence. Together their student bodies nearly equal the year-round population of the city (29,500). The students and their top-notch faculties make for a lively academic and arts community.

Ithaca remains a small town at heart, however. One of our visits coincided with a flying trip by then Vice President Dan

Cornell landmarks overlook Cayuga Lake.

Quayle to visit his son at a summer soccer camp and to take in the panoramic view of Ithaca, as everyone does, from the fifth-floor gallery of the Herbert F. Johnson Museum of Art. The Ithaca Journal ho-hummed the story the next day under a one-column inside headline, "Quayle Drops In."

Where there is such scenery and sophistication, good restaurants, shops and inns are sure to follow. Ithaca harbors more than its share. One block of North Aurora Street in downtown has five restaurants in a row for starters. Downtown, with its former main street turned into a pleasant pedestrian mall, bustles at all hours, thanks to good shops, galleries and eateries. The area has the only four-diamond,

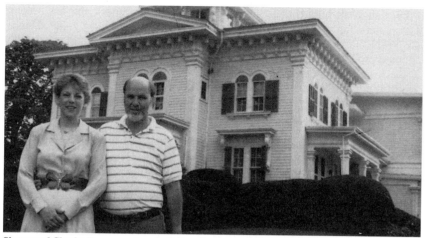

Sherry and Charles Rosemann have built Rose Inn into a highly rated inn and restaurant.

four-star country inn in New York State as well as more than 30 bed and breakfasts. Ithaca has the largest farmers' market on the East Coast for a city its size. It also has a winery inside the city limits, and is the starting point of the Cayuga Wine Trail. Three large state parks with waterfalls and gorges have Ithaca addresses, as do the Cornell Plantations gardens and the Sapsucker Woods wildlife sanctuary.

All these assets add up to a quality of life that ranked Ithaca first in the East in a book, *Rating Guide to Life in America's Small Cities.* Little wonder that the Ithaca area is one of the fastest growing in New York State.

Inn Spots

The Rose Inn, 813 Auburn Road (Route 34), Box 6576, Ithaca 14851.

In less than a decade, the old "House with a Circular Staircase" was transformed into New York State's first four-star, four-diamond country inn, as rated by Mobil

and AAA. That comes as no surprise to those who know Charles Rosemann, who moved to Ithaca to manage the Cornell University hotel school's Statler Inn, and his dynamic wife Sherry. The large and classic Italianate mansion they bought in 1983 had such potential that Charles left his Statler job to devote full time to the inn that Sherry seemingly had started somewhat as a lark.

Located in the hilly countryside twelve miles north of Ithaca, this has become a destination for travelers. Starting with five guest rooms and mostly shared baths, the Rosemanns have worked constantly to improve the guest quarters. A 1999 addition produced the newest suites, plus a large gathering room and a new entry in the front foyer so guests no longer have to arrive through the kitchen. Also available for guests' enjoyment are fine dining, a jazz club and more casual restaurant in the carriage house, outdoor terraces, a rose garden and formal gardens focusing on an open-air chapel – the last designed by their son for his wedding.

The inn's guest rooms are individually decorated by Sherry. Those in newer two-story additions capture the classic flavor of the rest of the house. They are luxurious, from their lace curtains, ceiling fans and fresh flowers to their luggage racks, terry robes, Vitabath and other amenities. In two, the bathroom fixtures (including a stretch-out tub) are from the Eastman House in Rochester. Folk art and antiques abound. Our rear suite contained a sunken jacuzzi in a garden-like space filled with plants, a majestic kingsize bed and antique furnishings in the bedroom, a large closet and a modern bathroom. At nightly turndown, a candle is apt to be lit beside the bed, the towels replenished, your toiletries neatly lined up on the bath vanity and your clothing hung in the closet. A thank-you note bids "Sweet Dreams."

Breakfast is an event worthy of the rest of the Rose Inn experience. Rose mats are on the polished wood tables, as are white baskets full of seasonal flowers. The juice glasses sport the Rosemann crest. Because fifteen varieties of apples are picked from their orchard, homemade cider is often poured. Also on the table are Sherry's jams and preserves – maybe spiced blueberry or strawberry-rhubarb. Local fruit is served in summer (we loved the raspberries); often with the Rosemanns' own crème fraîche. The main dish could be an omelet with smoked salmon and croissants, or perhaps cream cheese, bagels and lox. Charles's specialty is his puffy Black Forest apple pancake with raspberry syrup, which we found absolutely yummy. The coffee is his own blend of beans, including Kona from Hawaii.

The Rose Inn sets an elegant dinner table as well. The traditional prix-fixe meals in the main house gave way in 2000 to dinner served in the hunt-themed Carriage House restaurant at the side of the property. It's open to the public as well as inn guests.

New chef Robert Gedman, British-born and European-trained, came to the inn from the Four Seasons Hotel in Houston, Tex. The à la carte menu offers eight entrées from grilled ostrich loin to brandy flambéed lobster tail. Live music is played weekends from 7:30 to 11:30.

Whether it be for lodging or food or both, the Rose Inn is a class act.

(607) 533-7905. Fax (607) 533-7908. www.roseinn.com. Twelve rooms and ten suites with private baths. August, October and weekends Easter through Thanksgiving: doubles, $145 to $200; suites, $260 to $320. Rest of year: doubles, $115 to $175; suites, $230 to $290. Two-night minimum most weekends. No smoking.

Entrées $21.95 to $29.95. Dinner by reservation, Tuesday-Saturday 6 to 9:30, Valentine's Day to Thanksgiving.

Hanshaw House B&B, 15 Sapsucker Woods Road, Ithaca 14850.

She loves country inns, decorating and entertaining, so the wife of an Ithaca College dean put it all together in this sumptuous country B&B. Helen Scoones,

Hanshaw House B&B occupies restored 1830 farmhouse with a second-story addition.

who used to work for a decorator, did the decorating herself in this restored 1830 farmhouse with a second-story addition and a rear wing added for the couple's living quarters.

Hanshaw House has four air-conditioned guest rooms, all with private baths and two with sitting areas. Each is furnished with great panache and an eye to the comforts of home. We lucked into a large second-floor room with sitting area, queensize feather bed, down comforter and pillows, English country antique furnishings, a modern bath and plenty of space to spread out. We didn't need so much space, for we had the run of the house – a stylish living room outfitted in chintz and wicker with dhurrie rugs all over, a side TV room with gardens on view on both sides, and Adirondack chairs in a pleasant yard backing up to a small pond and woods full of deer, woodchucks and other wildlife.

In the new wing is Helen's "pièce de résistance," a formal dining room with a crystal chandelier, oriental rugs on pegged floors and french doors opening onto the rear patio and gardens. It's the setting for a gourmet breakfast served on blue and white china. Ours included fresh orange juice, an orange-banana yogurt frappe and Swedish pancakes puffed in the oven with peaches and crème fraîche. Other main courses could be quiche, frittata with homemade popovers, baked french toast with caramel sauce, baked eggs and heart-shaped waffles.

Early-risers are pampered with a choice of exotic coffees. In the afternoon, Helen greets guests with iced lemon tea or mulled cider and cookies in the living room.

Always upgrading her rooms, at a recent visit she showed the newly tiled bathroom, the floral sheets and the new curtains in a main-floor bedroom that she decorated in "MacKenzie-esque style," a reference to her favorite pottery from the nearby MacKenzie-Childs studio.

(607) 257-1437 or (800) 257-1437. Fax (607) 266-8866. www.wordpro.com/ hanshawhouse/ Four rooms with private baths. April-December: doubles, $95 to $145 weekends, $85 to $125 midweek. Rest of year, $85 to $105 weekends, $77 to $95 midweek. Two-night minimum weekends in season. No smoking.

The William Henry Miller Inn, 303 North Aurora St., Ithaca 14850.

This majestic mansion, part of the city's East Hill Historic District, offers nine of the more comfortable guest rooms in Ithaca.

How it became a B&B was serendipitous. "It's a long story," said Lynnette Scofield, innkeeper with her husband Ken. The house was built as a private home in 1880 by Cornell University's first student of architecture. Lynnette had always dreamed of the innkeeping life and was interested when an Ithaca native called and said the house was available. "She was afraid it would be chopped up for student housing and asked if we could save it to run a B&B." Lynnette quickly sold her small business. Friends helped them furnish the house with prized antiques and they opened after four months of renovations in 1999. "It's the best thing I ever did," says Lynnette.

Stately brick mansion is now William Henry Miller Inn.

The Scofields, who live upstairs in the carriage house behind the inn, offer seven guest rooms in a house full of American chestnut woodwork, stained-glass windows and working fireplaces. Off a grand hallway are a parlor with a coffered ceiling, piano and organ; a music and reading room with another piano, and a dining room. All have fireplaces.

Upstairs are six bedrooms with queen beds. Dane's Room, a large affair with shuttered windows, has a kingsize bed and a whirlpool tub. The Sanctuary, a corner room overlooking church steeples and rooftops, comes with a whirlpool tub and separate shower. The Library has a corner fireplace, spacious sitting area and built-in bookshelves. Each room has a telephone and a discreetly located TV.

The main floor of the carriage house in back has a two-room suite with a jacuzzi tub, plus a handicapped-accessible room.

Rather than afternoon tea, the Scofields serve dessert and coffee or tea in the evening. The treats might include sour cream apple pie, triple chocolate cake or spiced yogurt pound cake. A full breakfast is offered in the dining room, the parlor or in guest bedrooms. Fresh juice and a fruit course (perhaps a baked pear with raspberries and cream) accompany home-baked breads right out of the oven. The main course is usually a choice of sweet and savory: perhaps scrambled eggs with smoked salmon and cream cheese, or pecan waffles with warm syrup, each accompanied by bacon or ham.

Ken, a Cornellian who never left Ithaca after graduation, helps with breakfast before leaving for work. Lynnette tends to her "storybook inn" day and night.

(607) 256-4553 or (877) 256-4553. Fax (607) 256-4553. May-October: doubles, $110 to $155, November-April, $95 to $135.

Buttermilk Falls B&B, 110 East Buttermilk Falls Road, Ithaca 14850.

Guests leave this very personal B&B with full stomachs and hugs from innkeeper Margie Rumsey. You'd expect no less, for breakfast is quite a riot with guests in the dining room bartering and exchanging jams, seconds and whatnot with those on the porch, and Margie encouraging it all as she cooks up a storm on her AGA cast-iron cooker in the kitchen in the midst of all the fun.

First you help yourself to juices, including local grape and apple cider. Then you build your own "cereal sundae" with a hot whole grain (rye, at our visit), several kinds of fruits, local honey, yogurt sauce and four kinds of milk from skim to heavy cream. A big loaf of French or Italian bread is placed on each table, where people break off chunks and lather them with butter and one of Margie's homemade jams, perhaps gooseberry or apricot with ginger (here starts the bartering). There follow sticky rolls (as if anyone needs them), bacon and scrambled eggs jazzed up with herbs Margie manages to pick from the garden between courses. All the while she keeps up a steady chatter with guests on all sides.

Such is the start of a typical day – if there's any such thing as typical here – at this attractive white brick 1825 house, the closest private building to the foot of Buttermilk Falls. Energetic Margie, a one-woman dynamo, came to the home of her late husband's grandfather as a bride in 1948. When her youngest son graduated from Cornell in 1983, she opened it as Ithaca's first B&B and has been improving it ever since.

Now all guest rooms have private baths, though some are down the hall. Some retain a homey look (including built-in cupboards like those one of us grew up with). Good art of Finger Lakes scenes, oriental rugs and early American antiques grace each room. We enjoyed the large and luxurious downstairs bedroom with a woodburning fireplace and a double jacuzzi surrounded by plants in the corner, from which Buttermilk Falls can be glimpsed through a hedge. Recently, Margie painted pink the mahogany walls of an upstairs room with a little kitchen and out came the fancy Rose Room. She also redid the living room in a Colonial English tavern look, with Queen Anne loveseats facing each other in front of the fireplace. A rear carriage house contains a two-room cottage good for families.

Classical music plays throughout the public rooms. They include the plant-filled dining room notable for a long cherry table flanked by twelve different styles of windsor chairs made by her son Ed, the aforementioned eat-in kitchen and an attractive screened porch where we had breakfast, facing a garden in one corner.

(607) 272-6767. Fax (607) 273-3947. Six rooms with private baths. Doubles, $85 to $145. Jacuzzi room, $150 to $250. Children accepted. No smoking.

The Hound & Hare, 1031 Hanshaw Road, Ithaca 14850.

Lace, antiques and family heirlooms abound in this stately white brick house in a residential area, surrounded by tall trees and manicured lawns and gardens. Innkeeper Zetta Sprole's ancestors built the house in 1829 on property given them by George Washington for service in the Revolutionary War.

She opened her home in the late 1980s after her seven children had finished college. She named the bedrooms after her five daughters and quips, "the boys were quite relieved when I ran out of bedrooms."

The configuration of guest rooms and rates get confusing because each of the three main rooms joins an adjacent room for possible use as a suite.

The new Valerie room in the east wing of the house has a queen bed and a private bath with jacuzzi tub and golden candelabra. A spiral staircase leads to a planned new bedroom with a jacuzzi tub and private entrance below. The queen-bedded Victoria room uses the original hall bath, and can link up as a suite with the Carolina room with a double bed and its own bath. Facing the rear gardens is the Vanessa with a high brass queen bed. It adjoins the porch-like Christina room with antique step-up twin beds, so its occupants have a choice of sleeping accommodations or they can use it as a sitting room.

Zetta bills as "a Victorian fantasy" her well-dressed living room and a cozy library with TV and stereo. She offers afternoon tea and crumpets, and directs guests out to the back yard to enjoy herb gardens, rose beds and an old-fashioned lily pond and fountain.

Morning brings a candlelight breakfast served with fine china, silver and crystal in the dining room or on the porch. Apple pancakes or quiche could be the main course, supplemented by turkey sausages and fruit compote.

(607) 257-2821 or (800) 652-2821. Fax (607) 257-3121. Three rooms with private baths. Doubles, $85 to $125 in summer, $150 in spring and fall, $110 in winter. Two-night minimum fall weekends. No children. No smoking.

Columbia Bed & Breakfast, 228 Columbia St., Ithaca 14850.

Pair a young architect and a chef and you get this sparkling new B&B in a residential neighborhood. Kenn Young, a Cornell architecture graduate, and his wife Madeline, who cooked in Chicago restaurants, offer guest quarters in three buildings notable for custom-designed furniture, fireplaces, whirlpool tubs, skylights and decks.

Kenn, a Renaissance handyman if ever there was one, first restored and renovated the main house. Built in the 1830s in the Greek Revival style, it was in disrepair when the couple bought it in 1994. Now enhanced with vaulted ceilings and skylights, it holds their quarters as well as a living/dining area, plus an upstairs guest room with kingsize bed and private bath.

In 1998 Kenn designed and built a carriage house specifically as a B&B. It echoes the architectural style of the main house, to which it is connected by a wood deck. Its guest quarters come with fireplace, TV/VCR, full kitchen and whirlpool tub.

That proved so successful he followed up with the Gazebo, which Madeline considers her favorite. The eight-sided glass structure is a flight of fantasy, with its exotic interior beneath a periwinkle blue ceiling, white curtains, kingsize bed, marble bathroom, oversized whirlpool and shower, fireplace, TV and stereo. Guests liken it to sleeping in the clouds.

Given Madeline's cooking background, expect a sumptuous breakfast. Blended fruit juice, strawberries with grand marnier and cream, and assorted muffins and breads might accompany an exotic main dish, perhaps crème brûlée french toast. Afternoon tea and dinner are available on request.

Their property completed, the Youngs were looking to take on a larger inn. "We're enjoying this so much we want to go on to the next level," Madeline advised.

(607) 272-0204. Three rooms with private baths. Doubles, $125 to $195; $95 to $175 in off-season.

Side porch at The Federal House overlooks park-like setting.

The Federal House, 175 Ludlowville Road, Lansing 14882.

Antiques collector Diane Carroll closed her former Decker Pond Inn south of Ithaca and reopened north of town in the historic mill hamlet of Ludlowville. Here, instead of a pond, Diane has Salmon Creek Falls within earshot, plus a park-like setting. She has fashioned a great side yard, complete with prolific flower gardens, a gazebo, a trellis and an old bench. There's an expansive wicker-filled side porch for taking it all in.

Diane stripped the interior of the gracious 1815 house to its original woodwork and floors before decorating it elegantly in the Federal style. The fireplace mantels are believed to have been hand-carved by Brigham Young, who worked as an apprentice carpenter in the area in the early 1800s. Candles flicker by day in the handsome living room and at breakfast in the formal dining room.

From her enormous country kitchen that stretches across the back of the house, Diane prepares lavish breakfasts for guests. One day it might involve fresh orange juice, an apple-banana crisp with sour cream sauce, banana bran muffins and orange french toast with cinnamon-peach sauce. Another day could bring cantaloupe with lime-yogurt sauce and fresh mint, a zucchini frittata, bacon and blueberry muffins. Individual vegetable soufflés are served with steamed asparagus and broiled tomatoes on the side.

Upstairs in the rear of the house is the Seward Suite, named for William Seward of nearby Auburn, secretary of state under Abraham Lincoln. He courted his future wife in this, her uncle's summer house. It has a large and high-ceilinged bedroom with a queensize wicker bed and spiffy green and white decor, plus a sitting room with gas fireplace, day bed and TV. Also with air-conditioning and private baths are two more bedrooms, one with queen bed and one with king/twins, reached by a steep rear staircase. Each is decorated with flair and appointed with antiques. The front Lincoln Suite has a queensize canopy bed, gas fireplace and TV.

A collector with great taste, Diane sells antiques and gifts in her little Blueberry Muffin Gift Corner at the side entrance.

(607) 533-7362 or (800) 533-7362. Fax (607) 533-7899. Two rooms and two suites with private baths. Doubles: $90 to $95 weekends, $75 to $85 midweek. Suites, $125 to $150 weekends, $100 to $115 midweek. Two-night minimum weekends in season. No smoking.

La Tourelle, 1150 Danby Road (Route 96B), Ithaca 14850.

A French-style country inn or a glorified motel? We've heard plenty of references to both, though this white stucco building trimmed with brown certainly looks more like the former than the latter. The points of interest on a walking map of the grounds given to guests are listed in French, and what could be more French country inn-like than that?

La Tourelle was built in 1986 by Walter Wiggins, a partner in the well-known L'Auberge du Cochon Rouge restaurant next door (which was damaged by fire in 1994 and reopened as the John Thomas Steakhouse). The building is set back from the road on a 75-acre property descending to Buttermilk Falls State Park.

The plant-filled lobby is notable for colorful tiled floors. Three comfy sofas are in front of a stone fireplace, blazing in winter. Thirty-three spacious rooms and two suites are handsomely appointed in elegant country French style. Each has king or queen beds, good art, color TVs, VCRs (movies are available at the front desk), and tiled and marble bathrooms. A decanter of Spanish sherry awaits in each room.

The most memorable are the two round "romantic tower suites," which must be seen to be believed. Each has a sunken circular waterbed, a double jacuzzi just behind it, a TV mounted over the door and a mirrored ceiling. One has a fireplace.

An optional continental breakfast will be delivered to the room for $5.95 per person. Meals from the restaurant are available through room service.

(607) 273-2734 or (800) 765-1492. Thirty-three rooms and two suites with private baths. Doubles, $89 to $129. Suites, $125 to $225.

Thomas Farm, 136 Thomas Road, Ithaca 14850.

Electric candles glow in the windows year-round at this trim white farmhouse along a rural road southeast of Ithaca. Glenn Schneider and his wife Edie, whose family has owned the house since it was built about 1850, offer four bedrooms and a main-floor suite with a fireplace in the bedroom, hand stenciling on the ceiling, a kitchenette, and a private entrance onto a side patio.

Two rooms upstairs have new baths with jacuzzi tubs, and one is a two-room suite with an extra twin bed. All are handsomely appointed with antique wallpaper, quilts and brass beds, four of them queensize and one kingsize.

Edie Schneider greets guests with lemonade or tea and cookies on the side porch or on a patio on the other side of the house. In the morning, she prepares a hearty breakfast. Typical fare includes juice, fresh fruit, homemade muffins and a main course, perhaps an omelet, french toast or scrambled eggs with hash browns.

Guests enjoy sitting on the porches or relaxing beside the pond. The wooded, 120-acre farm property is laced with walking trails. Behind the house there's even a one-hole golf course, which is "a good uphill swing," according to Edie.

(607) 539-7477 or (877) 599-7477. Five rooms with private baths. Doubles, $95 to $125. No smoking.

The Statler Hotel, Cornell University, Ithaca 14853.

It's obviously not an inn, but no lodging guide for Ithaca would be complete without mention of the old Statler Inn. Like a phoenix reborn after an infusion of untold millions from the hotel industry, the three-story inn was transformed in 1989 into a nine-story monument to the Statler dream, quite appropriate for the operation that is part of Cornell's renowned School of Hotel Administration.

All is state of the art, from the richly paneled lobby with bowls of dried flowers grown at Cornell Plantations to the 150 guest rooms and suites. Computerized TV sets hidden in armoires allow you to order room service and settle your bill before checkout. Lord & Mayfair toiletries, Saratoga water, minibars stocked with New York wines and local art enhance the rooms, the rear half of which afford incredible views over Cornell landmarks toward Cayuga Lake.

The hotel's **Banfi's East Avenue Grill** offers a Sunday brunch that is a Cornell tradition, and dinners with Cornell specialties and northern Italian overtones. The room is serene and pleasant with damask linens on well-spaced tables, black lacquered chairs and banquettes, and full-length windows with a view of the campus. Half the staff are students.

(607) 257-2500 or (800) 541-2501. Fax (607) 257-6432. One hundred thirty-two rooms and eighteen suites with private baths. Doubles, $150 to $170. Suites, $225 to $375.

Peregrine House Victorian Inn, 140 College Ave., Ithaca 14850.

This 1874 brick Victorian located three blocks from the Cornell campus has been a B&B since 1986. At a recent visit, the cozy parlor with its two wing chairs beside the fireplace was decorated with vases of black-eyed susans and Queen Anne's lace, and fresh fruit and candy were set around for guests.

Each of the eight bedrooms on the second and third floors (four with private baths, four with w.c. and sink and sharing showers) are different. Most have a fresh Laura Ashley look. All are air-conditioned, and all have TVs and clock radios. Pretty linens, thick towels, soaps and shampoos (and even Woolite) are nice touches. Room 203, the largest, has tulips on the comforter and cabbage roses on the shower curtain.

Innkeeper Susan Vance took over the business lately from her mother, the founder. She offers "a plethora of choices" for breakfast, including juices, fresh fruit and eggs, french toast and blueberry pancakes. Specialty items on weekends could be belgian waffles or a tomato, cheese and bacon omelet. In the afternoon, tea or lemonade and gingersnaps are served on the front or side porches or in the parlor.

(607) 272-0919. Four rooms with private baths and four rooms with shared baths. Doubles, $89 to $109.

The Station Restaurant & Sleeping Cars, 806 West Buffalo St., Ithaca 14850.

Here's a switch. You can sleep in a restored railroad car at this offbeat "B&B" behind the Station Restaurant.

Terry and Barbara Ciaschi have converted two former dining cars into three private rooms. Each has a full bath (one with whirlpool tub), a gas-log stove/fireplace, TV and all the comforts of home. Wine and cheese are offered in the evening. Complimentary breakfast is offered the next morning nearby at Kelly's Dockside restaurant..

Paintings by chef-owner's wife enhance walls at Daño's on Cayuga.

Overnight guests may eat dinner in the owners' nearby restaurant, part of the former Lehigh Valley railroad station.

(607) 272-2609. Three rooms with private baths. Doubles, $129 weekends, $109 midweek.

Dining Spots

Daño's On Cayuga, 113 South Cayuga St., Ithaca.

Nearly everyone in Ithaca agrees that Daño's is tops on the city's dining list – for food, value and atmosphere. It's a remarkable accomplishment for a former European ballet dancer who took over a downtown storefront dive in 1990.

Daño (pronounced Dan-yo) Hutnik was born in the Ukraine, grew up in Czechoslovakia and was a ballet dancer for fifteen years in Vienna before entering the restaurant business in New York and San Francisco. A classified ad in the New York Times led him to Ithaca and this old space that he and his wife, artist Karen Gilman, transformed into a French-style bistro in peach and blue-gray. There's seating for 44 at white-linened tables topped with white paper against a backdrop of her striking artworks on the walls. Desserts are displayed in a nook at the side, and Edith Piaf music plays in the background. Daño table-hops at meal's end and proves to be quite the talker and philosopher.

The short menu of Central European, French and northern Italian fare is handwritten daily. Those in the know go for such specialties as oxtail stew with black and green olives and grilled brine-cured pork chop with spaetzle and braised red cabbage. We shared an appetizer of melted raclette with boiled potatoes, cornichons and pearl onions, the classic version and plenty for two.

Main courses range from veal sausage to filet mignon in a five-spice sauce with eggplant potato strudel and savoy cabbage slaw. We found superlative both the sautéed chicken breast with artichokes and sundried tomatoes and served with mouth-watering polenta sticks, and the linguini with shrimp, peas and scallions. We also liked the Hermann J. Weimer dry riesling, the only Finger Lakes choice on a fine wine list specializing in imported wines and rarely seen Californias. Crème brûlée and a bittersweet chocolate gâteau with raspberry sauce were fantastic endings to one of our more enjoyable meals in a long time.

Daño, ever looking to keep busy, in 1999 opened **Daño's on Seneca,** a Viennese-style pub called a heuriger. It operates weekends in season at Standing Stone Vineyards in Valois.

(607) 277-8942. Entrées, $13.95 to $21.95. Dinner, Tuesday-Saturday 5:30 to 9:30 or 10.

Madeline's, 215 The Commons, corner North Aurora and East State Streets, Ithaca.

The main floor of the old Rothschild's department store is unrecognizable in its latest transformation. The manager of the family-owned Thai Cuisine restaurant, Sunit ("call me Lex") Chutintaranond, started with a patisserie named for a favorite character from French children's literature. The establishment has since expanded into the city's handsomest restaurant. Slick and urbane, it would appear to be more at home in Manhattan than in upstate Ithaca. The look is modern-minimalist Asian, colorful and vaguely art deco, with a bar and tables spaced well apart on several levels.

Gregarious Lex, the head chef, oversees Pacific Rim fusion fare that dazzles in flavor and execution. Changing the menu every couple of months, he might pair French and Japanese or Italian and Asian. For dinner, he could serve shrimp in a roasted chile and coconut milk sauce over green tea rice or sear sea bass with a black bean sauce and Korean chile butter. He might roast his pork shank with a black tea citrus crust, and finish the New York sirloin with a port and three-peppercorn sauce. Accompaniments could be Asian soybeans, steamed baby bok choy, garlic-sesame bean sprouts, spinach ohitashi and chilled steamed napa cabbage.

Starters are as simple as chilled Asian soybeans in the pod and as complex as poke, the Hawaiian seafood preparation, served sashimi-style and seasoned with seaweed, chiles, onions and such. Asian shrimp cakes are offered with pickled cucumber and ground roasted peanuts. The house-baked focaccia with caramelized onions and kalamata olives is to die for. Ditto for the desserts, which fill sixteen feet of display cases in the restaurant. Pastry chef Gail Brisson prepares up to twenty patisserie-style treats a night from a repertoire of more than 50. We've heard their praises sung across the city.

The lunch menu is as interesting as the dinner. The bar features more than 80 single-malt scotches as well as rare cognacs, grappas and small-batch bourbons.

(607) 277-2253. Entrées. $12.95 to $16.95. Lunch, Monday-Saturday 11:30 to 3. Dinner nightly, 5 to 10 or 11.

Renée's, 202 East Falls St., Ithaca.

Within earshot of Ithaca Falls, the highest of the city's many waterfalls, lies this pristine bistro. It's run by Renée Senne, who cooked in a couple of local restaurants upon her return from studying at La Varenne in France and teaching at the New York Cooking School.

Candles flicker and classical music plays in her airy dining room, where hanging plants and ficus trees thrive, and in a small bar area beyond. We sampled Renée's work at a fine spring lunch (since discontinued). The cream of onion soup, a slice of French bread topped with fresh mozzarella, sundried tomatoes and basil, and a special of fettuccine with grilled shrimp and garlic cream sauce hinted at the treats in store at night.

Bar area at Renée's Bistro.

The possibilities for dinner range from herb-roasted game hen to beef tenderloin with sautéed mushrooms, bacon and gorgonzola. Innovative seafood preparations are highlighted: broiled salmon with yellow pepper coulis, grilled swordfish served with shrimp-filled ravioli, and grilled halibut with beurre blanc on steamed spinach.

Starters could be smoked salmon quesadilla, shrimp cakes with roasted pepper sauce, and a salad of warm new potatoes with chèvre on baby greens.

Renée's background as a pastry chef is reflected in such treats as mille-feuille, peach shortcake, apricot genoise with puree, and profiteroles with vanilla ice cream and dark chocolate sauce.

(607) 272-0656. Entrées, $16 to $23.50. Dinner, Monday-Saturday 5:30 to 10.

John Thomas Steakhouse, 1152 Danby Road (Route 96B), Ithaca.

A kitchen fire closed L'Auberge du Cochon Rouge, a French restaurant of renown, in 1994. When owner Walter Wiggins rebuilt, he surprised almost everyone by turning the hilltop farmhouse overlooking the Cayuga Lake valley into a New York-style steakhouse. He also surprised local skeptics, some of whom were persuaded that this was even better than its predecessor.

The restaurant's traditionally masculine decor lent itself to the steakhouse concept. L'Auberge sous chef William Peterson stayed on as chef, presenting a predictable menu ranging from roasted half chicken with mashed potatoes to T-bone steak. Prime beef is featured and the house specialty is porterhouse steak, $47 for two. There are grilled or blackened tuna, broiled swordfish, broiled salmon, shrimp scampi, a vegetarian platter and a couple of chicken dishes for non-beef eaters. Although all entrées come with a fresh vegetable, the usual salads and side orders cost extra.

Appetizers include smoked trout, baked deviled crab, shrimp cocktail and clams casino. Desserts range from old-fashioned bread pudding and assorted ice creams to triple berry strudel.

(607) 273-3464. Entrées, $16.95 to $27.95. Dinner nightly, 5:30 to 10 or 11.

Pangea, 120 Third St., Ithaca.

Talented young chef Paul Andrews took over the striking Italian trattoria known as Tre Stelle in 1998, did some refurbishing and changed the theme to modern

American. The sleek dining room, with a mix of art and artifacts on the walls, is light and airy. Colorful mismatched vinyl covers accent the white-clothed tables. A wraparound terrace provides sylvan courtyard dining beside vine-covered walls on three sides.

The seasonal menu favors local products and is categorized under small, medium, large, side and sweet plates. The bold-flavored dishes begin with starters like grilled squid with roasted chiles and togarashi-dusted scallops with grapefruit and greens. Medium plates might be grilled shrimp with avocado and papaya, grilled onion and watercress salad with feta and chickpeas, and grilled quail with warm sweet potato salad, stir-fried scallions, honey and soy glaze. Among large plates, consider pan-seared cod with paprika butter, grilled salmon with ginger-braised lentils, wilted spinach and saffron beurre blanc, and crispy duck breast with tamarind glaze.

Formerly for pizzas, the wood oven is now used for roasting rack of lamb with rosemary-coriander sauce. It also produces a chocolate lava cake that is Pangea's signature dessert. Other sweets include coconut brûlée and lemon cream napoleon.

(607) 273-8515. Entrées, $15.75 to $18.50. Dinner, Wednesday-Sunday 5:30 to 10 or 11.

The Heights Cafe & Grill, 903 Hanshaw Road, Ithaca.

Plainer than plain is this popular storefront operation in the Community Corners shopping plaza in tony Cayuga Heights, but the food is creative and sophisticated. Black upholstered chairs are at mottled gray tables, each topped with a votive candle in a little flowerpot. A few paintings and wall sconces complete the decor.

Diners pack the place for the American-Mediterranean fare of chef-owners James and Heidi Larounis, who brought in a new, Culinary Institute of America-trained chef in 2000.

Typical dinner entrées now are cedar-planked halibut fillet with roasted lobster vinaigrette, caramelized salmon fillet with a European-Thai cucumber salad, roasted lacquered duckling with a sundried currant balsamic glaze, and herbed veal chop with roasted shallot zinfandel sauce. Also available are brick-oven pizzas and assertive pastas like grilled chicken pesto "ala" Greque, Mediterranean seafood stew and ziti California style. Everything comes with choice of Greek or caesar salad.

Starters could be tomato-basil bruschetta, taramasalata (a caviar dip) with baked pita chips, and carpaccio of portobello mushroom with a grilled octopus salad. Desserts range from baklava to crème brûlée.

The short wine list, mainly from the Finger Lakes and California, is affordably priced.

(607) 257-4144. Entrées, $15.95 to $26. Lunch, Monday-Saturday 11 to 3. Dinner, Monday-Saturday 5 to 9 or 10.

Tower Club at Ithaca College, East Tower, Ithaca College campus. Route 96B, Ithaca.

The views of city and lake are awesome from this restaurant on the 14th floor of the East Tower at Ithaca College, high astride a hill south of town. Long a member-only club for the Ithaca College community, the establishment was opened to the public in 1999 and quickly became a winner, especially with the young professional crowd.

The food may be upstaged by the live music and dancing on weekends, but no one can fault the setting. The extensive dinner menu is typical upstate New York continental/Italian, from shrimp fra diavolo to veal saltimbocca. There are hefty sandwiches and an all-you-can-eat buffet for $8.95 at lunchtime.

(607) 274-3393. Entrées, $15.95 to $24. Lunch, Monday-Friday 11:30 to 1:30. Dinner, Thursday-Saturday 5 to 9.

Just a Taste, 116 North Aurora St., Ithaca.

This is billed as Central New York's largest wine and tapas bar. Originally opened by Lex Chutintaranond of Thai Cuisine, it has since been sold it to one of the cooks, Jennifer Irwin, and Stan Walton. They have made it better than ever with a carousel of treats that change daily, sometimes twice a day.

Sleek in gray, black and white with black lacquered chairs, the downtown establishment also has a small outdoor courtyard in the rear.

More than 50 wines are offered by the glass – in two sizes – or by the flight. Assorted beers are available from a beer bar.

We know folks who like to order a couple of flights and a selection of international tapas and while the night away here. We had to settle for a quick lunch, sharing a spicy breaded oyster served on a bed of spinach, a chicken teriyaki kabob with an array of vegetables, and a pizza of smoked salmon and brie (the most expensive item at $5.95). The last was great; the other two were marred by the missing house sauce (so spicy when we finally got it that one of us wished we hadn't) and no semblance of an "array" of vegetables. Cappuccino and a terrific pineapple cheesecake made up for the lapses.

The dinner hour brings tapas in appetizer and larger sizes, as well as several pastas and entrées. Expect tapas like flatbread with roasted squash and goat cheese, portobello and fennel pie over baby greens, and salmon gravlax tostada with cannellini hummus, cucumber-citrus relish and tobiko caviar. You can order treats like crispy fried quail legs with Chinese sausage in oyster sauce and spicy Mexican chicken on basmati rice in either tapa or larger sizes. Or try the penne with wild mushrooms, onions and romano or the grilled ribeye with fried russet potatoes, blue castello cheese and demi-glace.

For dessert, regulars demand more than "just a taste" of Jennifer's signature chocolate soufflé.

(607) 277-9463. Tapas, $3.50 to $7.25. Entrées, $8 to 14. Lunch/brunch daily, 11:30 to 3:30; dinner, 5:30 to 10 or 11.

Moosewood Restaurant, 215 North Cayuga St., Ithaca.

Once small and plain, this establishment on the lower level of the quirky Dewitt shopping mall is known to vegetarians around the country because of the *Moosewood Cookbook,* written by a former owner of the co-op operation, which had nineteen owners last we knew. Now there are six cookbooks associated with the enterprise. All are for sale along with other Moosewood memorabilia in the new Moosewood Bar and Cafe, which opens off the entry and features juices, coffees and a full bar.

Expansion and remodeling have produced a lighter look in blond pine, with yellow-sponged walls and wooden banquettes all around. The covered sidewalk cafe out front is pleasant and obviously popular in season.

Tofu burgers, pasta primavera and Hungarian vegetable soup are frequent choices

– the menu changes with each meal to take advantage of what's fresh. Pitas, frittatas, Caribbean stew, a mushroom-cheese strudel, a plate of Middle Eastern salads, cauliflower-pea curry and flounder rollatini are regulars. The blackboard menu lists an imaginative selection of casseroles, curries, ragoûts, salads and luscious homemade desserts like strawberry cream pie, lemon-glazed gingerbread, peach trifle and a pear poached in wine with whipped cream. We liked the sound of tagine, a Moroccan vegetable stew simmered with lemon and saffron on couscous, at one visit. Also tempting was a Chesapeake platter – baked catfish with old Bay seasoning, salt potatoes and stewed corn and tomatoes. The pasta al calvofiore with cauliflower and Italian cheeses and the Japanese braised eggplant appealed to others. The food varies, depending on which of the rotating chefs is in the kitchen.

The fish dishes are offered Thursday through Sunday, and Sunday nights are devoted to varying ethnic or regional cuisines.

(607) 273-9610. Entrées, $10 to $11.50. Lunch, Monday-Saturday 11:30 to 2; light cafe menu, 2 to 4. Dinner nightly, 5:30 to 8:30 or 9, summer 6 to 9 or 9:30.

Diversions

The beautiful Cornell University campus and its gorges and Beebe Lake are not to be missed. Pick up a city or a campus map to avoid getting hopelessly lost.

The Gorges. Cascadilla, Fall and Six Mile creeks slice through the city, and Ithaca Falls plummets 150 feet near the Ithaca High School campus. At the edge of town is **Buttermilk Falls State Park.** Buttermilk Creek drops more than 500 feet through dramatic rock formations in a series of cascades and rapids into a swimming hole at the foot of the falls. Nearby, trails in **Robert H. Treman State Park** wind through Enfield Glen for three miles, passing twelve cascades, sink holes and 115-foot-high Lucifer Falls. Just up Cayuga Lake is **Taughannock Falls State Park,** where the 215-foot-high falls are higher than Niagara. All have swimming, picnic areas and hiking trails.

Sapsucker Woods Sanctuary, 159 Sapsucker Woods Road, Ithaca. Home of the famed Cornell Laboratory of Ornithology, the sanctuary has 200 acres and more than four miles of trails through woodlands and over swamps and ponds. Huge picture windows in the Lyman K. Stuart Observatory look onto a garden filled with bird feeders and a ten-acre pond abounding with wildlife. Chairs and telescopes are provided. Original works by renowned artist Louis Agassiz Fuertes are hung in the hallways, and the Crow's Nest Birding Shop has a large selection of bird-related items.

(607) 254-2473. Observatory open Monday-Thursday 8 to 5, Friday to 4, weekends 1 to 4.

Ithaca Farmers' Market, Steamboat Landing, Ithaca. Ithacans are justly proud of one of the more flourishing farmers' markets in the East. All items for sale are grown, baked or produced by vendors within a 30-mile radius. We've been particularly impressed with the juried crafts and the ethnic foods. Entertainers perform and a festival atmosphere prevails. The market off Route 13 north of downtown operates Saturdays from 9 to 1, April-December.

Cayuga Wine Trail. The only Northeastern city we know of with a vineyard inside its limits is Ithaca. **Six Mile Creek Vineyard,** one of the region's newest, is nestled on the slope of a valley at 1551 Slaterville Road (Route 79). Picnic tables look across the vineyards and hills, a European-style setting for the sampling of chardonnays, rieslings, seyvals and such. Other wineries on the west side of Cayuga Lake, including **Knapp, Hosmer, Swedish Hill and Cayuga Ridge,** form the Cayuga Wine Trail. A special attraction for lunch and dinner is the fine **Knapp Vineyards Restaurant.** A welcome newcomer is the **Sheldrake Point Vineyard & Cafe** near the lake at Sheldrake Point.

Museums and Galleries. Housed in a stunning eleven-story building designed by I.M. Pei, the **Herbert F. Johnson Museum of Art** at Cornell University is one of the country's leading university art museums. The late Johnson Wax Co. chairman gave the building, best known for its Rockwell Galleries of Asian Art, nicely displayed on the fifth floor where wraparound windows offer awesome views in all directions and visitors can lose sight of the art for the scenery. Other notable collections are those of American art and decorative arts, including 200 pieces of Tiffany glass. Special exhibitions show its diversity and quality; we found one on "American Clothing: Identity in Mass Culture" to be of great interest. Other galleries are scattered about town and downtown. We were particularly impressed by the **Gallery at 15 Steps** and the **State of the Art Gallery.**

Shopping. The Downtown Ithaca Commons, formed by closing a section of State Street to vehicular traffic, is a downtown pedestrian marketplace that works. Trees, landscaping, benches and sidewalk cafes provide a pleasant people place, and plenty of people seem to be around at all hours. The Thursday night Concerts on the Commons are popular in summer. Most of Ithaca's better stores are not in the suburban malls but here. Among our favorites is **People's Pottery,** particularly strong on jewelry. We loved the special cat show at **Handwork,** Ithaca's co-op crafts store – crafted cats in all forms from tea cozies to enamel pins to stained glass to a scare cat for the garden. The expanded **Now You're Cooking** offers hard-to-find gadgets, classic cookware and unusual accessories. All kinds of outdoor equipment and clothing are available at **Wildware.** Check out the unusual women's fashions at **Angelheart Designs** and the men's apparel at **Benjamin Peters. The Plantation** offers tropical plants, home accessories and collectibles along with fine dinnerware and crystal. **Alphabet Soup** is a good children's store.

Extra-Special _____

Cornell Plantations, One Plantations Road, Ithaca.

The arboretum, botanical garden and natural areas of Cornell University arecollectively known as the Plantations. They total nearly 3,000 acres of woodlands, gorges, gardens and lakeside trails bordering the campus. We were quite unprepared for their size or their scope. The Robison York State herb garden, for instance, has sixteen theme beds and 400 species surrounded by antique and shrub roses. Nature lovers could spend hours here. A driving tour past sculptures, ponds, test gardens and tree collections (many of them marked as Cornell class gifts) gives a quick overview, but all the cyclists and walkers have the right idea. If time is short, at least take the self-guided walking tour around Beebe Lake. The Garden Gift Shop in the headquarters building offers all kinds of things from pressed-flower notepaper and magnets to floral glass window hangings.

(607) 255-3020. Gardens open daily, dawn to dusk. Free.

Sonnenberg Gardens and Mansion are a major drawing card for visitors to Canandaigua.

Canandaigua/Bristol Hills, N.Y.
The Chosen Place

The Seneca Indians were on the mark when they named this area Kanandagua, "The Chosen Place."

The settlement at the northern end of Canandaigua Lake became the capital of the western frontier. It was the seat of the vast Phelps-Gorham land purchase, the shire town of Ontario, mother of all counties west of Seneca Lake. In 1789 the first office was established here for the sale of land directly to settlers. Leaders of the young nation, four cabinet members among them, lived in stately mansions that still line the broad main street 200 years later.

The westernmost of New York's major Finger Lakes lies cradled between hills. They are particularly majestic at its southern end, an area that has been called "The Switzerland of America." The village there was renamed Naples after a French dignitary said during a visit two centuries ago that the only area of comparable beauty was Naples, Italy. New York's wine industry was born in Naples, and the town paints its fire hydrants purple for the annual Grape Festival in September.

Canandaigua, the western gateway to the Finger Lakes, is a busy summer resort town. Its location beside a lake at the edge of the Rochester metropolitan area makes it the fastest-growing city in upstate New York State (approaching 15,000). The workaday world and the world of summer cottages co-exist side by side. The redevelopment of Lakeshore Drive and Kershaw Park in 1997 improved a once tacky lakefront. The renewal of waterfront activity contrasts with the sound of outdoor music at the Finger Lakes Performing Arts Center and the unexpected show of opulence at Sonnenberg Gardens and Mansion.

Just minutes away is the rural tranquility of the Bristol Hills, rising sharply to the south and west of Canandaigua Lake. Here are hidden towns, country shops, the highest ski area between the Adirondacks and the Rockies, and a couple of the wineries that help make the Finger Lakes famous. The area holds a fond place in our hearts from our frequent visits when we lived nearby in Geneva and Rochester.

Poke along Canandaigua Lake's west shore and the hills and byways above. You'll know, as we do, why the Senecas called this their chosen place.

Inn Spots

Morgan-Samuels Inn, 2920 Smith Road, Canandaigua 14424.

Actor/farmer Judson Morgan, not J.P. Morgan as was originally thought, built this lovely English-style stone house in 1810. A brick wing was added in the early 1900s, and eventually it became the home of Howard Samuels, the plastic-bag inventor and manufacturer who ran unsuccessfully for governor of New York State. Julie and John Sullivan left jobs in Geneseo to buy the house in 1989 and convert it into a masterpiece of a B&B. "We had just visited another B&B," said bubbly Julie, "and knew we were meant to run one." They named it the J.P. Morgan House, only to discover they were in error and, honest to a fault, they renamed it the Morgan-Samuels in 1993.

At the end of a quarter-mile drive lined by maple trees, the house sits like a plantation on a rise with 46 acres of hay fields all around. The scene is truly bucolic. Ducks, turkeys and chickens roam around, and a heifer calf named Kimberly punctuated the tranquility with her mooing as we sat in the slate-floored garden room.

The serenely lovely garden room, a well-furnished living room, a cozy library with TV, a stone-walled and glass-enclosed tearoom with potbelly stove, a tennis court and no fewer than four landscaped patios (one with a trickling fountain and another with a lily pond and waterfall) are available for guests.

The house contains five guest rooms and the Morgan Suite, a beauty with early 18th-century French furniture, kingsize bed, an extra-long loveseat in front of the TV and a double jacuzzi in a corner of the bathroom. The Antique Rose Room has a fireplace, a new jacuzzi tub and one of the first kingsize beds ever made. The sunken Garden Room, where the eight Samuels children used to play, has been transformed into a house favorite with a queensize four-poster, a handmade rug

from Romania, a cut-lace bedspread from China and a parlor stove in the angled fireplace. The Victorian Room on the third floor, all in burgundies and greens with a tapestry look, has another fireplace, a wonderful bathroom with old stone walls, a kingsize canopy bed, a jacuzzi and lots of Italian marble, not to mention french doors onto a balcony.

Porch-like garden room at Morgan-Samuels Inn looks onto lawns and rural vistas.

A fountain sounds like a babbling brook beneath Evy's Chamber, which Julie recently transformed into a Victorian fantasy and named for her mother. It has a rosewood queensize bed, a corner closet ingeniously fashioned from the sideboard of a bed, and a bathroom with raised shower and ceiling in a former closet. Our room on the third floor, small but exquisitely done, featured a pretty Gothic window beneath a cathedral ceiling. The king bed, awash with fourteen pillows, nearly filled the room. It was neatly tucked into a niche between built-in shelves. The black floral rug matched the wallpaper border. All rooms are air-conditioned, have private baths and are equipped with reproduction radios and tape cassettes.

Breakfast is served in the beamed dining room, in a small breakfast room, in the garden room or on the patio. If the inn is full, all these spaces may be called into use. John is in charge of cooking – he and son Jonathan make an early-morning run to the supermarket to pick out the perfect fruit for the fruit platter, which usually contains two dozen varieties, depending on the season. We counted 26 (and Julie promptly added, "he forgot the blueberries") on the exquisitely put-together silver platter, including local Irondequoit melon, mango, two kinds of grapes, papaya, persimmon, figs, kiwis and prunes sautéed in lemon sauce. With that come fresh orange juice served in delicate etched glasses, a baked apple, muffins (the carrot muffins were huge and delicious) and sticky buns.

The main event involves a choice of fluffy buckwheat pancakes with blackberries, blueberries or pecans (or all three), scrambled eggs with herbs, french toast or a six-cheese omelet. We've tried them all but are partial to the omelet, one of the best breakfast treats we've ever had – it looked like a pizza with slices of tomato, scallions, red peppers, onions, jalapeño peppers, mushrooms and lots of herbs and parsley. Monterey jack, mozzarella, parmesan and blue cheeses were on top, and spicy sausage patties and sunflower seed toast (from bread made by Trappist monks) accompanied, as did hazelnut coffee.

Tea (iced or hot) is served in the afternoon, and John will do dinners Thursday-Sunday by reservation for eight or more guests ($55 each). The birds were chirping, the fountains trickling and classical music playing as we enjoyed dinner by candlelight with fine silver and china in the garden room. Our meal, which John said was typical, produced a procession of whitefish with horseradish sauce, pasta shells in a hot Bahamian sauce, garlic bread, a fabulous chilled peach soup and a mixed salad bearing everything from strawberries and apples to beets, snow peas and artichoke hearts, dressed with raspberry vinaigrette studded with bacon and capers. The main course was filet mignon with a sherry-herb sauce, sided with green beans, mushrooms, cauliflower, potatoes, and broccoli and cheese. Dutch apple pie with ice cream ended a spectacular meal. "I cook the way I like to cook," says John, who has no formal training. He certainly cooks the way we like to eat, although we would have had to be super-human to finish it all.

Music, mostly classical but perhaps New Age in the morning and haunting Gregorian chants at breakfast, is piped throughout the house and across the grounds. The Sullivans display quite a collection of oil paintings, and the bathrooms at their extra-special inn win a prize for the most amenities ever, including toothbrushes. Enchantment, it seems, is in the details.

(716) 394-9232. Fax (716) 394-8044. www.morgansamuelsinn.com. Five rooms and one suite with private baths. Mid-May through mid-September: doubles $129 to $199, suite $225. Foliage: doubles, $149 to $219, suite $245. Rest of year: doubles, $109 to $179, suite $195. Two-night minimum weekends and mid-May to mid-November.

Sutherland House, 3179 State Route 21 South (Bristol Street Extension), Canandaigua 14424.

Diane and Cor Van Der Woude realized a lifelong dream when they opened this B&B in 1994. Diane, who had been an executive in gourmet food sales with the Wegman's supermarket chain, and her Dutch husband, a carpenter, purchased the deteriorated 1885 Victorian-Gothic summer house, one of five built by Sutherland brothers along rural outer Bristol Street in Canandaigua. They undertook a painstaking renovation, knowing exactly what they wanted every step of the way (extra insulation between walls, for instance) and rebuilding accordingly.

The result is five guest accommodations, all with new bathrooms and TV/VCRs. The largest is a suite with a kingsize four-poster bed, a fireplace, a sitting room with baskets hung on the wall, a trundle couch, dressing table and a double whirlpool tub, and a bathroom with shower.

The rear Lillian's Lodge, a cathedral-ceilinged loft recently vacated by the couple's son, also has a king bed, Vermont Castings gas stove, rich arbor wallpaper and an unusual chair bed with an ottoman that opens into a twin bed. Another double whirlpool tub is a feature of the Dutch Treat room with queen poster bed, sitting area and gas stove. Two smaller rooms with queen beds and telephones also feature Diane's stenciling and the country and romantic touches evident throughout the house. One has a two-person shower.

Afternoon refreshments are served in the front parlor, notable for four Victorian sofas. Guests also help themselves to the contents of two stocked refrigerators, and enjoy the porches and grounds in summer.

As you might expect, Diane serves an elaborate breakfast at a large table in the dining room. Expect a choice of juices, fresh fruit and a fancy casserole, french toast or Canadian bacon and eggs. A fresh fruit medley with orange yogurt and blueberry-banana muffins were prefaces to a sausage hash-brown frittata at our summer visit.

Diane, whose recent business experience had been in human resources, took

Sutherland House occupies renovated Victorian-Gothic structure west of town.

readily to innkeeping. "I feel like I open a new novel each night as I meet and greet," she reports. "People want to talk and I like to listen."

(716) 396-0375 or (800) 396-0375. Fax (716) 396-9281. www.sutherlandhouse.com. Four rooms and one suite with private baths. Weekends: doubles, $100 to $175, suite $175. Midweek: doubles, $90 to $155, suite $155. No smoking.

The Acorn Inn, 4508 Route 64 South, Box 334, Canandaigua 14424.

Pink impatiens, geraniums and petunias accent the greenery around this handsome, dark brown shingled Federal stagecoach inn built in 1795 in the hamlet of Bristol Center. It is the home of Louis and Joan Clark, he a retired Canandaigua investment broker and she a retired medical office manager. Both are collectors of antiques and decorative arts.

The grounds include brick walks, a rear terrace, and perennial and rock gardens on several levels, enclosed by stone walls built by Joan. A jacuzzi spa is a focal spot in the gardens, and there are comfortable chairs and a hammock for relaxing.

The centrally air-conditioned interior is strikingly appointed in 18th- and early 19th-century English and American antiques and reproductions. The Clarks offer four elegant guest rooms, each with a canopied queensize bed and two with fireplaces. All have reading lamps within the canopy draperies for those who enjoy reading in bed, as well as reading lamps for the side chairs, large closets and thick insulation to muffle noise. TV/VCRs, thick terry robes and slippers for trips to the spa are standard in each room. The largest is the Bristol (the former ballroom) with a sitting area with TV/VCR and a spacious, well-appointed bath with a soaking tub and separate shower. The Hotchkiss Room comes with floor-to-ceiling windows overlooking a private brick terrace and the gardens, a sitting area with TV/VCR and a whirlpool tub.

Part of a research library of 5,000 books on art, antiques and architecture enhances the gathering room, where guests relax in front of the Rumford fireplace.

Oliver Phelps Country Inn is in restored Federal house along Canandaigua's wide main street.

The attractive dining room and the garden terrace are where the Clarks serve a full breakfast on antique china and heirloom silver. It might be fresh orange juice, melon garnished with raspberries, french toast and sausages. Pancakes and herbed omelets are other entrée possibilities.

Sherry is available in the evening, and a guest refrigerator is stocked with complimentary beverages and snacks. Chocolate acorns and a carafe of ice water accompany nightly turndown service. They typify the amenities that reflect the Acorn's four-diamond AAA rating.

(716) 229-2834. Fax (716) 229-5046. www.acorninnbb.com. Four rooms with private baths. Doubles, May-October: $135 to $205 weekends, $120 to $190 midweek. Rest of year: $135 to $195 weekends, $110 to $175 midweek. Two-night minimum peak weekends. No young children.

The Oliver Phelps Country Inn, 252 North Main St., Canandaigua 14424.

This 19th-century Federal beauty was "the worst-looking house on Main Street" when Joanne and John Sciarratta bought it in 1987. You'd never know it today, such is the transformation the energetic couple have given it. John painted and stenciled every room, his wife decorated with taste, and now it stands out as one of the best-looking houses among many lining the broad main street. The gazebo John built on the wooded side lawn is strategically placed for the view. The latest addition for guests is a hot tub on the back porch, overlooking the back yard.

The house was once owned by Judge Oliver Phelps, grandson of Oliver Phelps, a Revolutionary War leader who was responsible for the Phelps-Gorham land purchase of 1788. A Tiffany-style lamp with 1,200 pieces of colored glass hangs over the dining-room table. Here Joanne serves a full breakfast of fresh fruit and perhaps a soufflé, omclet, frittata or french toast. Blueberry pancakes and sausages were the fare the morning we visited.

Beyond is an enormous parlor, having been enlarged when a wall was removed during the era when this was a Christian Science church. A group of dolls and teddy bears is ensconced beside one of the sitting areas. Unusual clocks from the couple's collection are located throughout the house.

Upstairs are four air-conditioned guest rooms with private baths. Each bears John's intricate stenciling. Oliver's Suite has a sitting area with a working fireplace, a kingsize four-poster bed, a three-quarter brass bed and, for good measure, a cradle. There's a stenciled bench in a bathroom that is as big as many a bedroom, plus stenciling on doors of closets. Geese are the stenciling motif in the Country Duck Room, which has a queensize poster bed and a single bed. Floral stenciling and an Amish painting enhance the Tulip Room. A fourth room with a sloping ceiling has a white brass queen bed, stenciling in pinks and blues, and one of two in-room TVs.

(716) 396-1650. Four rooms with private baths. Doubles, $85 to $115. Suite, $145. Children over 6. No smoking.

The Vagabond Inn, 3300 Sliter Road, Naples 14512.
So you "vant to be alone," as Greta Garbo used to say. Here's the place, high on a remote mountaintop in the hills northeast of Naples. Just you and your significant other and up to four more similarly inclined couples cosseted in a luxurious, contemporary house designed for romance. With your own jacuzzi and a TV/VCR with a 400-movie library, and perhaps a fireplace to warm the night air. And a swimming pool, secluded patios and exotic landscaping just outside.

Celeste Stanhope-Wiley started in 1987 with a three-bedroom ranch house in an unconventional location, "alone on a

Terrace with moonlight view at The Vagabond Inn.

mountain" with a sharp 1,000-foot drop to the Italy Valley below. Now she shares 7,000 square feet with guests on two floors. You enter a 60-foot-long "great room" rich in natural woods with a seating area facing a stone fireplace at one end. At the other end is a dining-room table set for ten beside full-length windows onto a deck with a glorious view beyond. Although it's daytime, the room is dimly lit and little lights simulating candles flicker here and there.

The hostess shows you the well-equipped guest kitchen, employed by many guests for dinner since the nearest civilization is ten miles away by roundabout rural roads. Then she directs you to your room, perhaps the pine-paneled Lodge on the lower level, where the tulips handpainted on the headboard of the kingsize bed match the patterns on the pillows and bedspread. Two plush wing chairs flank the fireplace and a terrace awaits outside. Also in the room is a dining table for four – she had a lot of space to fill, Celeste explains. In the corner alcove beyond the bed is a whirlpool spa, right in the room, beside a bar, mini-fridge and microwave. Once ensconced in the Lodge, you may not be seen again until it's time to leave.

"Everybody needs to run away overnight," says Celeste. She knows. She relates that she was "thrown out of a convent in Greenwich," Conn., as a teenager and ran away from home in nearby Darien. She "went back to my roots" in the Caribbean, settling in Haiti and eventually turning up on her mountaintop. Vagabond, she calls it.

For those of a mind, the finest magazines vie with VCR movies for attention. A collection of recent Bon Appetit issues is in the queen-bedded Shannon (one of two bedrooms named for her grown daughters), blessed with a 27-inch TV set, garden patio, fireplace and a bathroom of cedar and mirrors with dimmer lights, hot tub and separate shower. National Geographic Travelers are in the Mahogany Room, where a stuffed gorilla peeks over the double four-poster bed. Architectural Digests grace the Bristol Suite, a grand main-floor space with a kingsize canopy bed, ironwood twig-style furniture on the screened porch, a private deck and an enormous bathroom containing a palm-bedecked jacuzzi for two, a fourteen-foot mirrored dressing area with twin vanities, and a separate shower.

Coffee and tea are available around the clock, as much to satisfy Celeste's needs as those of her guests. She serves "a very full breakfast" between 8 and 11 a.m.; "your arteries start hardening as you sit down." Fresh orange juice and fruits precede such baked goods as homemade muffins and "piña colada sweets," served with winery jams. Next comes the main course, perhaps crab and vegetable omelet or a 24-egg pie. By then it may be time for a nap.

Next time, Celeste may rent you her new garage suite called Heaven's Gate, into which she had moved, with privacy screens onto the pool area, walk-in closets and a mirrored bathroom to end all bathrooms, complete with a customized jacuzzi good for all the aches that ail you.

Lately, Celeste has turned portions of her great room and two adjacent rooms into a showcase for the sale of fine international crafts and jewelry.

(716) 554-6271. Two rooms and three suites with private baths. Doubles, $115. Suites, $195 to $225. No children. No smoking.

The Maxfield Inn, 105 North Main St., Box 39, Naples 14512.

Only six families have owned this pillared 1841 mansion in the center of Naples. The latest are Russell and Alice Cochran, retirees from the Rochester area who "wanted a big dining room for all our kids and grandchildren." They bought it as their home, and inherited a recently renovated B&B vacated by local school teachers who had their hands full with three young children. The former innkeepers "said we'd love running a B&B, and we do," Alice advised. "The guests are the best part of it."

The Cochrans have seven air-conditioned guest rooms, three with private baths and four sharing two, one of the latter sporting a jacuzzi. Rooms are outfitted with period pieces in pine, cherry or mahogany and have new wallpaper and carpeting or oriental rugs. A two-bedroom suite with a bathroom between is good for families.

Alice is so fascinated by the heritage of the inn she was writing a book about its original owner, Hiram Maxfield. He owned the area's first winery and had a 2,000-bottle cellar in the basement. He also ran the first bank in town, and its original door leads into the kitchen. The barn was part of the underground railroad.

The high-ceilinged front parlor and library, both light and airy, are full of the Cochrans' diverse collections of glass. Guests relax on the columned front porch or at an umbrella-covered table on the side lawn.

Maxfield Inn has been converted from residence of a former banker and winemaker.

The Cochrans have removed the carpet and restored the original oak and chestnut floors in the dining room, an unusual pattern of squares that look like tiles. Here they serve a breakfast that starts with fresh fruit – a bowl of blueberries and strawberries with whipped cream (red, white and blue) for the July Fourth holiday when we were there. Next came french toast with sausage. Scrambled eggs, hot breads and popovers are other favorites.

(716) 374-2510. Three rooms with private baths and four rooms sharing two baths. Doubles, $75 to $105. Children welcome. No smoking.

Dining Spots

Lincoln Hill Inn, 3365 East Lake Road, Canandaigua.

Everybody's favorite restaurant hereabouts is Lincoln Hill, and with good reason. It has a grand setting on a hillside overlooking Canandaigua Lake within earshot of the outdoor Finger Lakes Performing Arts Center shell. It has tables inside and out. It has an extensive menu. And the food is consistently good.

Cheryl and Bill Ward, who were teaching at Monroe Community College in Rochester, bought the 1804 brick homestead and converted it into a large restaurant, opening fortuitously in 1983 on the same day as the arts center shell. Inside are several small, cozy dining rooms with pastel linens, antique lace curtains and soft lighting. One room is strung with little white lights. A lounge contains remarkable modern American primitive paintings of the lake and the area as it was in the latter part of the 19th century by Adelaide Cook Kent, who was influenced by Rufus Porter.

But it was the open front porch with its white over floral clothed tables, citronella candles and fresh field flowers to which we were attracted on a summer's evening. It, plus an enclosed side porch and a back patio called the Garden Room, seat 120 outdoors, half again more than the number inside. For dinner, you can order light:

Porch with view of Canandaigua Lake is favored by diners at Lincoln Hill Inn.

an appetizer and a salad, an open-face prime rib sandwich or perhaps the ultimate appetizer platter, a sampling of seven. Or you can order roasted citrus salmon, coquilles st. jacques, pan-seared duck breast and confit, herb-crusted rack of lamb, and three versions of prime steak.

Dinners come with salad, including an excellent one with greens, mandarin oranges, walnuts and a honey-poppyseed dressing, and a garden salad with dijon vinaigrette. We liked the tender calves liver, grilled with onions and bacon, and the prime rib, a thick slab with horseradish sauce. The ample plates, garnished with edible nasturtiums from the gardens out back, yielded potatoes or rice, garlic cloves and zucchini stuffed with vegetables and cheese. French chocolate decadence is one of the good desserts.

(716) 394-8254. Entrées, $16 to $30. Dinner nightly in July and August, from 5; Tuesday-Sunday from 5 rest of year. Also closed Sundays in winter.

Koozinas, 699 South Main St., Canandaigua.

A fish is sculpted out of the wall at the entry and waves ripple across the walls of this ultra-colorful restaurant with a mod nautical look. It takes its name from the Greek word for kitchen, according to chef George Stamatis. He and his wife Christine opened their contemporary Italian-Mediterranean restaurant in the old Wegman's supermarket space in 1997.

There's a lot to look at in the large, high-ceilinged space: faux columns, colorful angles, a tiled kitchen and hanging fisherman lamps from Greece.

"We tried to give it flair," says George, whose food follows suit. He, a chef and six cooks man the open grill, producing a wide variety of wood-fired pizzas, pastas, panini, salatas and the like. The choices are staggering. You might start with bruschetta, polenta portobello, spanakopita or calamari salad. A cup of soup and half a panini sandwich makes a light supper. So does one of the thin-crust pizzas, or any of the dozen pastas, from pignoli with banana peppers and ziti to scallops sautéed with spinach, diced tomatoes, black olives, feta cheese and fusilli.

Main courses are fewer in number, but cover the bases: grilled shrimp with vegetables, wood-fired chicken topped with mozzarella, twin veal chops and Grecian T-bone steak topped with kalamata olives, plum tomatoes and scallions.

George makes most of the desserts, among them baklava, kahlua torte, berry tart and tirami su.

(716) 396-0360. Entrées, $11.50 to $14.75. Open Monday-Saturday, 11:30 to 11 or midnight. Sunday, noon to 10.

Nicole's Dining Room, Canandaigua Inn on the Lake, 770 South Main St., Canandaigua.

Taken over by the owners of Canandaigua Wine Co., the old Sheraton Inn was renamed the Canandaigua Inn on the Lake. They redid some guest rooms, but concentrated their efforts on the dining operation. An innovative chef elevated the fare, and the elegant dining room with upholstered armchairs, shaded candles and fanned napkins atop service plates is quite stylish. Big windows look onto the lake.

For dinner, expect such entrées as grilled salmon with ginger-black bean vinaigrette, roulade of chicken with tasso ham and roasted garlic sauce, and grilled center-cut pork chops with braised red cabbage and sweet potato casserole. Starters could be roasted red peppers with grilled bread, kalamata olives and New York State goat cheese and grilled vegetable napoleon with roasted red pepper sauce.

Locals love the restaurant's Sand Bar lakeside terrace for a summer lunch. The lounge is Baco's wine bar.

(716) 394-7800 or (800) 228-2801. Entrées, $15 to $30. Lunch, 11 to 4. Dinner, 5 to 10, to 9 in winter.

Casa de Pasta, 125 Bemis St., Canandaigua.

People come from miles around for the pasta in this red brick townhouse at the edge of downtown, we were advised. And the restaurant received the highest rating from a newspaper reviewer.

Owner Bruce Warren's menu is surprisingly bland, however. The pastas include five kinds of spaghettini or ziti with meatballs or mushrooms and such, linguini with garlic and parmesan cheese, lasagna, tortellini alfredo and ricotta stuffed shells. The specials are really special, said the reviewer: pasta puttanesca, gnocchi gorgonzola and veal madeira with pasta the night we were there.

Entrées run from whitefish marinara to shrimp scampi and filet mignon. Veal parmesan, braciole and chicken parmesan are menu fixtures. An Italian platter for two brings antipasto, garlic bread and a platter of lasagna, stuffed shells, meatballs and homemade Italian sausage. Pizzas are available except on weekends.

Diners enter through a bar presided over by the convivial owner-host. Beyond are two intimate, noisy dining rooms with pine wainscoting and red and white oilcloths and curtains – a spirited place for regulars who relish homemade Italian cuisine.

(716) 394-3710. Entrées, $11.95 to $19.95. Dinner nightly, 5 to 9:30 or 10.

The Holloway House, Routes 5 & 20, East Bloomfield.

As it has for years, the green neon sign still glows outside this historic tavern and restaurant dating to 1808 and facing the green in a charming hilltop town. Owners Fred and Doreen Wayne haven't changed the menu much since we found it somewhat dated in the 1960s. But folks love it, particularly the old-timers who dress up for lunch and make it their dinner.

There's a ramble of Colonial rooms with ladderback chairs at bare wood tables and frilly sheer curtains on the windows in this landmark on the National Register of Historic Places. The dinner menu starts with roast turkey (our informant said she'd had the best turkey dinner ever here the week before) and fried half chicken with biscuit to surf and turf and twin lobster tails. Specialties include broiled sea scallops with tartar sauce, baked stuffed flounder, seafood newburg en casserole and, on Saturdays, prime rib – ladies' cut or regular cut. Complete dinners (add $2.50) start with tomato juice, soup du jour or fruit shrub. They come with au gratin or mashed potatoes, two vegetables that are passed, tossed or fruit salad with French, Russian, Italian or blue cheese dressings, Sally Lunn bread and homemade orange rolls, and desserts like pies, angel food cake, strawberry shortcake and hot fudge sundae.

A Friday night summer buffet packs the crowds, with more than 25 items to choose from. The lunch menu features chicken fricassee, turkey à la king, and chicken livers and bacon. Who says the '60s are out of style?

(716) 657-7120. Entrées, $11.45 to $16.45. Lunch, Tuesday-Saturday 11:30 to 2. Dinner, Tuesday-Saturday 5:30 to 8:30, Sunday noon to 7:30. Closed December-March.

Bob's and Ruth's, Route 21 at Route 245, Naples.

A legend in the area, this started in 1950 as a diner and takeout stand, made its name with grape pie, and grew like topsy. The diner and takeout counter remain in front, where you can get a basic American sandwich (starting at $1.95 for egg salad) or a meal of roast chicken or prime rib, $5.95 to $14.95. Eat at the counter or one of the booths or outside at a picnic table in the adjacent Old Town Square Park.

In the rear and reached by a separate entrance is the Vineyard Lounge on one side and on the other, the **Vineyard Room** with two walls of windows looking onto a sea of grapevines and a great new outdoor dining deck. Decor is solid, green and brown, to match a solid menu. Most diners opt for the complete dinner, which includes a locally famous salad bar (homemade preserves, pickled fruits and vegetables, garden vegetables and more). The offerings run from turkey dinner to prime rib, which the menu used to tout as "the traditional celebrant dinner of this area." Now it's simply "a local favorite." Other possibilities include broiled rainbow trout, shrimp scampi, baby back ribs ("a Canadian treat"), broiled ham steak with pineapple and fruited sherry sauce, roast duckling flambéed tableside, veal parmigiana and filet mignon. Grape pie, famous all over the region, is the obligatory dessert in season.

(716) 374-5122. Entrées, $9.95 to $19.95. Bob's & Ruth's, open daily from 6 a.m. The Vineyard, lunch 11:30 to 3:30; dinner from 5, Sunday from noon.

Diversions

Finger Lakes Performing Arts Center, Lincoln Hill Road, Canandaigua, (716) 325-7760. Since 1983, the outdoor shell on the Finger Lakes Community College campus has drawn thousands for summertime concerts by the Rochester Philharmonic Orchestra and visiting entertainers. The RPO presents Saturday evening concerts, seating 2,600 in the shell and another 10,000 on the lawn,

Hills slope down to Canandaigua Lake, viewed here from the southern end.

although financial shortfalls curtailed the orchestra season lately. Guest entertainers over the years have ranged from Huey Lewis, Sting and John Denver to Steve Lawrence and Eydie Gorme, and Peter, Paul and Mary.

Sonnenberg Gardens and Mansion, 151 Charlotte St., Canandaigua.

What a treasure is this – and so unexpected in busy Canandaigua. Restored in 1973 after 40 years of neglect, the Victorian gardens are recognized by the Smithsonian as some of the most magnificent ever created in America. The 50-acre garden estate around their 40-room summer home was planned at the turn of the century by Mary Clark Thompson, a Canandaigua native who married Frederick F. Thompson, a New Yorker whose family started Chase Manhattan and Citibank. Widowed at 67, she traveled the world to create nine formal gardens, an arboretum, a greenhouse complex and more as a memorial to her husband (who, we were told, rather preferred his fishing cottage down Canandaigua Lake to Sonnenberg, German for "Sunny Hill").

Some 75,000 visitors a year admire the Japanese hill garden and tea house, the vast Italian garden with four sunken fleur de lis parterres and the Rose Garden launched with 4,000 bushes from the former Jackson and Perkins Rose Gardens in nearby Newark. Other attractions are Mrs. Thompson's favorite Blue & White Garden, a Pansy Garden in which even the bird bath is shaped like a pansy, and a rock garden entered through a canyon of puddingstone and including 5,500 feet of streams, waterfalls and pools fed by geysers and springs. In the middle of one particularly dry summer, we found the flowers a bit lackluster (not surprising, since a staff of only seven plus volunteers maintain what 75 full-time gardeners did for their founder). Still we marveled at the accompaniments: belvederes, statues, gazebos, arbors, a temple of Diana, a sitting Buddha, a fountain with a statue of Hercules and even a Roman bath. The vast South Lawn with its rare specimen trees is remarkable: Mrs. Thompson liked to give house parties and asked guests to bring trees to plant, each guest trying to outdo the other. A walking map guides visitors, but more informative are the guided tours of up to two hours in length, offered daily at 10 and 2.

The mansion, a testament to the extravagances of the Gilded Age, has its own delights, among them the Lavender and Old Lace gift shop. **The Festival of Lights,** in which the mansion is decorated and the gardens are gloriously illuminated with lights and themed figures, extends the season from Thanksgiving to New Year's.

(716) 394-4922. Gardens open daily, 9:30 to 5:30, mid-May to mid-October; also nightly in holiday season, 4:30 to 9:30. Adults, $8.

Granger Homestead and Carriage Museum, 295 North Main St., Canandaigua.

Gideon Granger, who was postmaster general for Thomas Jefferson, moved here in 1813 and resolved to build a homestead that would be "unrivaled in all the nation." This pale yellow Federal mansion is the result and its period rooms with original furnishings are on display. More than 40 horse-drawn vehicles, from coaches and sleighs to an undertaker's hearse, are shown in the Carriage Museum.

(716) 394-1472. Open Tuesday-Friday 1 to 4, mid-May to mid-October; also Saturday and Sunday 1 to 4, June-August. Adults, $4.

Boat Tours. Canandaigua is known as a summer resort and the best way to experience it is by boat. Town native Gray Hoffman gives enlightening narrated tours five times daily in summer under the auspices of **Captain Gray's Boat Tours,** from the dock at Inn on the Lake. He gives the history of the lake and tells who lives in which cottage on an hour-long tour that even natives find informative. The **Canandaigua Lady,** 169 Lake Shore Drive, the only authentic replica of a paddlewheeler in the Finger Lakes, offers lunch, dinner and sightseeing tours daily in summer. It is based at the new **Steamboat Landing Restaurant & Resort,** scheduled to open in fall 2000.

Shopping. A big stuffed pig wearing sunglasses sits outside on a wicker chair at **Renaissance – the Goodie II Shoppe** at 56 South Main St. Here are all the socially correct gifts, from jewelry to porcelain dolls, bath things, Port Merion china and lovely Christmas ornaments. Teddybears, cookbooks (we picked up Linda McCarthy's for a vegetarian son) and nifty paper plates and napkins abound. **The Country Ewe, Ltd.** specializes in handknit sweaters from around the world among its outstanding array of sportswear, outerware, accessories and gifts. From handloomed blankets to golf wear, this expanding store has something for anyone of style. North of town at 1901 Route 332 is **The Five Seasons,** two floors of a log building housing a gift shop to end all gift shops. Owner Sue Ellsworth is known for her handpainted crockery.

A fun shop to explore on the west side of Canandaigua is **Cat's in the Kitchen** at 367 West Ave. Here Laurel Wemett has collected, from tag sales and auctions, all the things our mothers and grandmothers used in the kitchen. She specializes in the Depression era to the 1960s, and it's fun to check the old canisters, cookie jars, china, pots and pans and the corner full of old cookbooks.

Farther afield is **Cheshire,** billed as "a little bit of New England awaiting discovery." **The Cheshire Union,** 4244 Route 21, is a renovated schoolhouse where Biff and Rusty Brundage run a gift shop, antiques center, the Schoolhouse Deli and the Company Store. Thousands turn out for its annual folk fair and antique show. "Everything Grape and More" is the theme of **Arbor Hill Grapery,** a delightful place at 6461 Route 64 in Bristol Springs. John and Katie Brahm, he a former Widmer's Wine Cellars executive, are proof that wines aren't the only good use for grapes. They sell grape-filled cookies, hot grape sundaes, grape pies, wine-motif wallpaper, vinegars, gewürztraminer wine jelly and their Arbor Hill Winery wines.

Tiny Naples is the home of some interesting shops around **Old Town Square.** The Village Corner complex is the home of **Classics,** an exceptional gift store. Owner Anne Schneider stocks its several rooms with an assortment of sophisticated wares, from linens, pottery and jewelry to cookbooks, candles and

Christmas ornaments. Naples offers a Saturday afternoon summer concert series at the Old Town Square park. The year's highlight is the annual **Naples Grape Festival** in late September with arts, crafts, entertainment, food and, of course, those sugary-sweet grape pies.

Widmer's Wine Cellars, 1 Lake Niagara Lane, Naples.

Swiss immigrant John Jacob Widmer, whose home is still on view, launched this hillside winery in 1888. We remember it fondly from its days under the aegis of the R.T. French Co. Lately sold to Canandaigua Wine Co., Widmer's is now part of the nation's third largest wine-producing firm. Its winery tour, one of the best in the East, starts with a twelve-minute video shown through the end of a wine barrel. The half-hour guided tour takes you through ancient subterranean passageways where wine is aged in oak barrels, past the famous rooftop sherry barrels and into the fascinating bottling and labeling room. The publicity notes "there are a number of stairs to traverse." The visitor may choose instead to relax in the air-conditioned Widmer's Wine/Food Center for an extensive wine-tasting and sales of wines, juices, jellies and Finger Lakes items. In the adjacent **Manischewitz** cellars, which moved in 1986 from Brooklyn, two rabbis are employed fulltime to oversee the making of kosher wines. Tours are offered Monday-Thursday except Jewish holidays.

(716) 374-6311 or (800) 836-5253. Open Monday-Saturday 10 to 4, Sunday 11:30 to 4:30. May-October; rest of year, daily 1 to 4.

Extra-Special

The Wizard of Clay Pottery, 7851 Route 20A, Bloomfield.

Out in the middle of nowhere in the Bristol Hills are seven geodesic domes that are home to ex-Rochester teacher Jim Kozlowski's pottery empire. Visitors

come from across the world – they mark their home-towns with pins on a map in his workshop – to see "the workshop where the wizard works wonders." The Wednesday we visited was his afternoon for golf, according to an assistant who called herself a wizette. So we had to be satisfied reading lists of the 29 steps to making a Bristoleaf pot and the twenty most often asked questions and their answers, both garnished with a sense of humor. Jim makes each piece individually, but a staff helps with the decoration. His trademark Bristoleaf pottery is decorated with delicate imprints from all kinds of leaves picked in the surrounding hills. He's most proud of his signed and numbered limited editions, particularly those decorated with leaves handpainted in gold and selling for up to $225 a bowl. Two domes house more than 1,000 pottery lamps with shades; another, bakeware and planters; still another, a zoo craft gallery of arts and crafts reflecting the animal kingdom. There are even a gazebo and a nature trail. It sounds hokey, but isn't really.

(716) 229-2980. Open daily, 9 to 5.

Index

T

U

Also by the Authors

Inn Spots & Special Places in New England. The first in the series, this book by Nancy and Richard Woodworth tells you where to go, stay, eat and enjoy in New England's choicest areas. Focusing on 35 special places, it details the best inns and B&Bs, restaurants, sights to see and things to do. First published in 1986; expanded fifth edition in 1998. 524 pages of timely ideas. $16.95.

Inn Spots & Special Places in the Southeast. The newest volume in the series, this book by Nancy and Richard Woodworth covers 26 special areas from North Carolina to Florida. With its emphasis on fine inns and good restaurants, the series now covers the entire East Coast, from Eastport, Me., to Key West, Fla. Published in 1999. 376 pages of new ideas. $16.95

Getaways for Gourmets in the Northeast. The first book by Nancy and Richard Woodworth appeals to the gourmet in all of us. It guides you to the best dining, lodging, specialty food shops and culinary attractions in 24 areas from the Brandywine Valley to Montreal, Cape May to Bar Harbor, the Finger Lakes to Nantucket. First published in 1984; fully updated and expanded sixth edition in 2000. 602 pages to read and savor. $18.95.

Waterside Escapes in the Northeast. This guide by Betsy Wittemann and Nancy Woodworth relates the best lodging, dining, attractions and activities in 36 great waterside vacation spots from Chesapeake Bay to Cape Breton Island, from the Thousand Islands to Martha's Vineyard. Everything you need to know for a day trip, a weekend or a week near the water is told the way you want to know it. First published in 1987; revised and expanded third edition in 1996. 474 pages to discover and enjoy. $15.95.

Weekending in New England. The best-selling travel guide by Betsy Wittemann and Nancy Woodworth details everything you need to know about 24 of New England's most interesting vacation spots: more than 1,000 things to do, sights to see and places to stay, eat and shop year-round. First published in 1980; fully revised and expanded fifth edition in 1997. 448 pages of facts and fun. $16.95.

These books may be ordered from your bookstore or direct from the publisher, pre-paid, plus $2 shipping for each book. Connecticut residents add sales tax.

Wood Pond Press
365 Ridgewood Road
West Hartford, Conn. 06107
Tel: (860) 521-0389
Fax: (860) 313-0185
E-Mail: woodpond@ntplx.net
Web Site: www.getawayguides.com

ON LINE: Excerpts from these books are found at www.getawayguides.com Check out this web site for updates on some of our favorite inns, B&Bs and restaurants in destination areas around the East.